GLOBAL HUMANITIES READER

UNIVERSITY OF NORTH CAROLINA ASHEVILLE HUMANITIES PROGRAM

The Humanities Program at the University of North Carolina Asheville explores what it means to be human. We examine the experiences of our shared humanity by looking at the oral, literary, and material expressions of our orientations and convictions, values and passions, and struggles and strategies for survival and thriving. In engaging with a wide and diverse set of perspectives, we consider both their original contexts and their ongoing influence on our times. These inquiries are strengthened through an interdisciplinary approach to the humanities that draws together faculty and subject matter across disciplines currently including: Africana studies, anthropology, arts, Asian studies, biology, chemistry, classics, economics, history, Indigenous studies, languages, literature, mathematics, philosophy, physics, political science, psychology, religious studies, sociology, and women, gender, and sexuality studies. Humanities helps us to make educated and ethical decisions as we strive to understand multiple perspectives on human experience, engage in culturally appropriate and community-centered problem solving, and thrive as global and local citizens of our own communities.

The *Global Humanities Reader* is a three-volume work edited by a team of faculty from UNC Asheville. The three volumes are *Volume 1—Engaging Ancient Worlds and Perspectives, Volume 2—Engaging Premodern Worlds and Perspectives*, and *Volume 3—Engaging Modern Worlds and Perspectives*.

Katherine C. Zubko and Keya Maitra, General Editors

Brian S. Hook, Sophie Mills, and Katherine C. Zubko, *Engaging Ancient Worlds and Perspectives*, Editors

Renuka Gusain and Keya Maitra, *Engaging Premodern Worlds and Perspectives*, Editors

Alvis Dunn and James Perkins, *Engaging Modern Worlds and Perspectives*, Editors

Cameron Barlow, Timeline and Source Preparation Editor

Global Humanities Reader

VOLUME III
Engaging Modern Worlds and Perspectives

VOLUME EDITORS:
James Perkins, Alvis Dunn, Katherine C. Zubko, and Keya Maitra

Copyright © 2022 UNC Asheville Humanities Program
All Rights Reserved

ISBN 978-1-4696-6638-9 (paperback: alk. paper)
ISBN 978-1-4696-6639-6 (ebook)

Published by the University of North Carolina Asheville Humanities Program

Distributed by the University of North Carolina Press
www.uncpress.org

Cover design and photo by Cameron Barlow, used by permission of the photographer.

CONTENTS

Contents by Chronology   xi

Acknowledgments   xv

General Editors' Welcome, Katherine C. Zubko and Keya Maitra   xix

   Getting to Know the Elephant   xix

   How to Use this Book   xxiv

Modern Worlds: An Historical Cross-Cultural Introduction, Tracey Rizzo   1

Comprehensive Timeline   32

RE/ORIENTING

   from *Books That Have Influenced Me*
   by Chandrasekhara Venkata Raman   37

   from *Ḥatata*
   by Zera Yacob   44

   from "Letter to the Grand Duchess Christina"
   by Galileo Galilei   54

   "The Negro Digs Up His Past"
   by Arturo (Arthur) Schomburg   62

   "The Painter" and from *Negro Sculpture*
   by Hannah Höch and Carl Einstein   70

   "Response to Ernest Renan's Criticism of Islam"
   by Jamal al-Din Al-Afghani   84

   from "Response to the Very Illustrious 'Sor Philotea'"
   by Sor Juana Inés de la Cruz   92

Selections from the Writings of Albert Einstein: 99
   "Internationalism of Science"
   "What I Believe"
   "Religion and Science"
   "Letter to Sigmund Freud"
   "Conversation with Rabindranath Tagore"

from "Self-Portrait of K'ang-hsi (The Emperor)"
by K'ang-hsi   115

"Teaching and Telling Stories" ("Contar")
by Gabriela Mistral   122

from *A Voice from the South*
by Anna Julia Cooper   129

NARRATING

from *Annihilation of Caste*
by Bhimrao Ramji Ambedkar   142

"A'n't I a Woman" and "Address to the First Annual Meeting of the American Equal Rights Association"
by Sojourner Truth   152

from *The Berlin Stories*
by Christopher Isherwood   159

Cherokee Sources during the Removal Period: 175
   1785 Treaty of Hopewell (US Government Document)
   Petitions of the Cherokee Women's Councils, 1817, 1818, led by Nanye'hi (Nancy Ward)
   "Memorial of the Cherokee Indians" (Cherokee Nation)
   "Address of the Committee and Council of the Cherokee Nation, in General Council Convened, to the People of the United States"
   by Lewis Ross et al.

"I, Too"
by Langston Hughes   196

from *The Interesting Narrative of the Life of Olaudah Equiano or Gustavus Vassa, the African*
by Olaudah Equiano   200

"Letter from Benjamin Banneker and Thomas Jefferson's Response"
by Benjamin Banneker and Thomas Jefferson   208

from *Narrative of the Life of Frederick Douglass, an American Slave* and
from "What to the Slave is the Fourth of July?"
by Frederick Douglass   216

from *Nisei Daughter*
by Monica Sone   226

from "Speaking Out Against Lynching"
by Ida B. Wells   232

from *Still Alive: A Holocaust Girlhood Remembered*
by Ruth Klüger   238

from "Strivings of the Negro People"
by W. E. B. Du Bois   247

"White Things"
by Anne Bethel Spencer   254

JUSTICE

"Declaration of Independence of the Democratic Republic of Vietnam"
by Ho Chi Minh   258

"Declaration of Rights of Woman and Citizen"
by Olympe de Gouges   263

"Declaration of Sentiments"
by Elizabeth Cady Stanton   271

from "The Emancipation of Women: Argentina 1876"
by María Eugenia Echenique and Josefina Pelliza de Sagasta   278

"The History of the Chinese Revolution" (Written January 29, 1923)
by Sun Yat-sen   287

"Letter to the United States President Andrew Jackson, 1831"
by Tuskeneah   294

from "Message to the Congress of Angostura"
by Simón Bolívar   300

from "A New Guatemala"
by Juan José Arévalo   307

from "The Rights of Women"
by Sayyid Ahmad Khan   314

from *A Vindication of the Rights of Woman*
by Mary Wollstonecraft   320

"What I Believe" and "Speech Against Conscription and War"
by Emma Goldman   336

REPOSITIONING

from *Ariel*
by José Enrique Rodó   353

"Correspondences between Gandhi and Tagore"
by Mohandas Karamchand Gandhi and Rabindranath Tagore   359

from *Democracy in America*
by Alexis de Tocqueville   373

"An Exhortation to Progress"
by Mustafa Kemal (Atatürk)   384

from "Our América"
by José Martí   389

from "Reminiscences of the Drafting of the New Constitution"
by Itō Hirobumi   403

from *The Soul of the Indian*
by Ohiyesa   412

from "Transferring the New Civilization to the Islamic Peoples"
by Şemseddin Sami Frashëri   420

from *Turkey Faces West*
by Halidé Edib   426

from "Why I Am a Pagan"
by Zitkala-Ša   434

WORKING

"Address at the World's Fair in Atlanta"
by Booker T. Washington   440

from *Black Bolshevik*
by Harry Haywood   447

"Grinding Song" (Tigrayan)   453

from *Manifesto of the Communist Party*
by Karl Marx   458

"The Principles of Anarchism"
by Lucy Parsons   479

Selections from the Writings of Marcus Garvey: 489
  "Negro Progress Postulates Negro Government"
  "The World as It Is: Insulting Negro Womanhood"
  "The World as It Is: The Internal Prejudices of Negroes"
  "Let the Negro Accumulate Wealth: It Will Bring Him Power"

from "The Structure of Class and Caste"
by Jorge Juan and Antonio de Ulloa   496

from *The War and Its Effect upon Women*
by Helena Marie Swanwick   500

from "The Worker's Union"
by Flora Tristán   506

POWER

from *Imperialism: The Highest Stage of Capitalism*
by Vladimir Lenin   512

from *Mein Kampf*
by Adolf Hitler   518

from *The Origins of Totalitarianism*
by Hannah Arendt   527

from *The Political and Social Doctrine of Fascism*
by Benito Mussolini   533

"The Revolution and the Negro"
by Cyril Lionel Robert (C. L. R.) James   541

from *The Second Sex*
by Simone de Beauvoir   554

Sultana's Dream
by Rokeya Sakhawat Hossain   560

from *The Well of Loneliness*
by Radclyffe Hall   573

from *The Wretched of the Earth*
by Frantz Fanon   579

Sources and Permissions   597

Tag Glossary   605

Index   615

CONTENTS BY CHRONOLOGY

1. from "Letter to the Grand Duchess Christina" by Galileo Galilei (1615) 54
2. from "Self-Portrait of K'ang-hsi (The Emperor)" by K'ang-hsi (1660) 115
3. from *Hatata* by Zera Yacob (1667) 44
4. from "Response to the Very Illustrious 'Sor Philotea'" by Sor Juana Inés de la Cruz (1690) 92
5. from "The Structure of Class and Caste" by Jorge Juan and Antonio de Ulloa (1743) 496
6. Selected Cherokee Sources During the Removal Period: 175

    Treaty of Hopewell (US Government Document) (1785)

    Petitions of the Cherokee Women's Councils, 1817, 1818, led by Nanye'hi (Nancy Ward) (1817–1818)

    "Memorial of the Cherokee Indians" (Cherokee Nation) (1829)

    "Address of the Committee and Council of the Cherokee Nation, in General Council Convened, to the People of the United States" by Lewis Ross et al. (1830)

7. from *The Interesting Narrative of the Life of Olaudah Equiano or Gustavus Vassa, the African*, by Olaudah Equiano (1789) 200
8. "Letter from Benjamin Banneker and Thomas Jefferson's Response" by Benjamin Banneker and Thomas Jefferson (1791) 208
9. "Declaration of Rights of Woman and Citizen" by Olympe de Gouges (1791) 293
10. from *A Vindication of the Rights of Woman* by Mary Wollstonecraft (1792) 320
11. "Grinding Song" (Tigrayan) (19th century) 453
12. "Message to the Congress of Angostura" by Simón Bolívar (1819) 300
13. "Letter to the United States President Andrew Jackson, 1831" by Tuskeneah (1831) 294

14. from *Democracy in America* by Alexis de Tocqueville (1835)   373
15. from "The Worker's Union" by Flora Tristán (1843)   506
16. from *Narrative of the Life of Frederick Douglass, an American Slave* and from "What to the Slave is the Fourth of July?" by Frederick Douglass (1845/1852)   216
17. from *Manifesto of the Communist Party*, by Karl Marx (1848)   458
18. "Declaration of Sentiments" by Elizabeth Cady Stanton (1848)   271
19. "A'n't I a Woman" and "Address to the First Annual Meeting of the American Equal Rights Association" by Sojourner Truth (1851/1867)   152
20. from "The Rights of Women" by Sayyid Ahmad Khan (1866)   314
21. from "The Emancipation of Women: Argentina 1876" by María Eugenia Echenique and Josefina Pelliza de Sagasta (1876)   278
22. from "Transferring the New Civilization to the Islamic Peoples" by Şemseddin Sami Frashëri (1883)   420
23. "Response to Ernest Renan's Criticism of Islam" by Jamal al-Din Al-Afghani (1883)   84
24. from "Speaking Out Against Lynching" by Ida B. Wells (1890)   232
25. from "Our América" by José Martí (1891)   389
26. from *A Voice from the South* by Anna Julia Cooper (1892)   129
27. "Address at the World's Fair in Atlanta" by Booker T. Washington (1895)   440
28. from "Strivings of the Negro People" by W. E. B. Du Bois (1897)   247
29. from *Ariel* by José Enrique Rodó (1898)   353
30. from "Reminiscences of the Drafting of the New Constitution" by Itō Hirobumi (1899)   403
31. from "Why I Am a Pagan" by Zitkala-Ša (1902)   434
32. *Sultana's Dream* by Rokeya Sakhawat Hossain (1905)   560
33. "The Principles of Anarchism" by Lucy Parsons (1905)   479
34. "What I Believe" and "Speech Against Conscription and War" by Emma Goldman (1908/1917)   336
35. from *The Soul of the Indian* by Ohiyesa (1911)   412
36. from *The War and Its Effect upon Women* by Helena Marie Swanwick (1916)   500
37. from *Imperialism: The Highest Stage of Capitalism* by Vladimir Lenin (1916)   512

38. "The Painter" by Hannah Höch and from *Negro Sculpture* by Carl Einstein (1920/1915)   70

39. "Correspondences between Gandhi and Tagore" by Mohandas Karamchand Gandhi and Rabindranath Tagore (1921)   359

40. Selections from the Writings of Albert Einstein: 99

    "Internationalism of Science" (1922)

    "What I Believe" (1930)

    "Religion and Science" (1930)

    "Letter to Sigmund Freud" (1932)

    "Conversation with Rabindranath Tagore" (1930)

41. "White Things" by Anne Bethel Spencer (1923)   254

42. "The History of the Chinese Revolution" (Written January 29, 1923) by Sun Yat-sen (1923)   287

43. "The Negro Digs Up His Past" by Arturo (Arthur) Shomburg (1925)   62

44. from *Mein Kampf* by Adolf Hitler (1925)   518

45. "I, Too" by Langston Hughes (1926)   196

46. from *The Well of Loneliness* by Radclyffe Hall (1928)   573

47. "Teaching and Telling Stories" ("Contar") by Gabriela Mistral (1929)   122

48. Selections from the Writings of Marcus Garvey: 489

    "Negro Progress Postulates Negro Government" (1929)

    "The World as It Is. Insulting Negro Womanhood" (1930)

    "The World as It Is: The Internal Prejudices of Negroes" (1930)

    "Let the Negro Accumulate Wealth: It Will Bring Him Power" (1935)

49. "An Exhortation to Progress" by Mustafa Kemal (Atatürk) (1930)   384

50. from *Turkey Faces West* by Halidé Edib (1930)   426

51. from *The Political and Social Doctrine of Fascism* by Benito Mussolini (1932)   533

52. from *Annihilation of Caste* by Bhimrao Ramji Ambedkar (1936)   142

53. "The Revolution and the Negro" by Cyril Lionel Robert (C. L. R.) James (1939)   541

54. "A New Guatemala" by Juan José Arévalo (1945)   307

55. "Declaration of Independence of the Democratic Republic of Vietnam" by Ho Chi Minh (1945)   258

56. from *The Berlin Stories* by Christopher Isherwood (1945)   159

57. from *Books That Have Influenced Me* by Chandrasekhara Venkata Raman (1947) 37
58. from *The Second Sex* by Simone de Beauvoir (1949) 554
59. from *The Origins of Totalitarianism* by Hannah Arendt (1951) 527
60. from *Nisei Daughter* by Monica Sone (1953) 226
61. from *The Wretched of the Earth* by Frantz Fanon (1961) 579
62. from *Black Bolshevik* by Harry Haywood (1978) 447
63. from *Still Alive: A Holocaust Girlhood Remembered* by Ruth Klüger (2001) 238

ACKNOWLEDGMENTS

As we sit down to compose these acknowledgments we are almost in disbelief that we have arrived at this point. We did not have a definitive roadmap when we started in 2017. Now a global pandemic later, we are at the finish line. Our student-centered approach served as our North Star. Working with many stakeholders we determined the steps of the process that brought us here. There were more than sixty people inside and outside of UNC Asheville who helped us with this project. Unfortunately we can't name every single one of them, but to them, using the South African expression, we say *ubuntu*! "*I am because you are; we are because you are.*" This project is because you are!

This *Global Humanities Reader: Engaging Modern Worlds and Perspectives* would not be possible without the support of the following individuals and funding sources.

This project benefited from an amazing **Reader Support Team**. Jessica Park was the hub facilitating all connections and communications, keeping the project organized every step of the way. She often helped us reimagine what the project could be with her timely interventions and keen eye for detail. Jon Morris handled the copyright issues with such competence and precision that we never had to deal with the countless emails and loose ends with multiple publishers. Cameron Barlow, our student partner, actualized *all* the graphic timelines and envisioned and created the comprehensive timelines from the ground up, in addition to his detail-oriented primary source preparation. It is no easy feat transferring pdfs of ancient sources into a Word format, undoing diacritical marks, weird spacing, and nineteenth- and twentieth-century publishing styles—ALL CAPS! The success of this project is due to their ability and willingness to routinely go beyond the call of duty exhibiting constant and tireless enthusiasm, unparalleled professionalism, and a collaborative spirit that found solutions for every problem.

Our colleagues from the UNC Asheville Career Center, David Earnhardt and Chelsey Augustyniak, became a part of this project early on and read many of the primary sources in the process of their creative collaboration on the Beyond the Classroom feature. Tracey Rizzo agreed to compose the unique cross-cultural historical introductions for each volume, a task made even more difficult since we wanted her to tell a story that not only offered integrated contexts for our primary sources but also would inspire the reader to expand their engagement. Tracey not only delivered on our request but worked indefatigably on multiple drafts. One of our amazing art historians, Eva Hericks-Bares, curated the images for the introductions that Tracey wrote and located usable high-resolution images with the appropriate licensing requirements. Her detailed captions bring these images into clear focus in relation to the overview of history. Amanda Bell provided tremendous research support by creating surveys and analyzing faculty and student data to support the shape of the primary guiding priorities and pedagogical features in the project. Our colleague Lyndi Hewitt and her students offered support in designing the student survey instrument. We are grateful to Heather Hardy, a member of our Asheville community, for diligently fact checking all the timeline information. Finally, we are thankful to John McLeod from the UNC Press Office of Scholarly Publishing Services and his colleagues, including Lisa Stallings and her team at Longleaf Services, for helping us navigate this complex process.

We thank our various **funding sources**. The generous support from the Mellon grant allowed us to first conceive and then execute this audacious project. We thank our colleague Brian S. Hook for his crucial leadership in securing the grant and getting the project started as its first general editor. We also thank then-provost of UNC Asheville, Joseph R. Urgo, for his unwavering support for the project at its early stages. A Thomas W. Ross Fund Publishing Grant from UNC Press provided critical support that made the various design aspects possible. Finally, we thank Katherine C. Zubko, who offered unfailing and constant support through her NEH Distinguished Professor in the Humanities funds whenever a supplementary need arose.

A number of other individuals offered unhesitating support for this project at various moments and we thank them for their steadfast encouragement: our colleagues Ameena Batada, Dee James and Melissa Himelein for providing important feedback on the General Editors' Welcome; Joevell Lee; Charlotte Smith; Steve Birkhofer; Wendy Mullis; Leah Dunn; Natalia Zubko; and peer reviewers for the cross-cultural introductions: UNCA History department colleagues, Saheed Aderinto (Western Carolina University), Steven Gerontakis (University of Florida), and Shawna Herzog (Washington State University).

Finally, we thank our **contributors**, who wrote source introductions and pedagogical features for all of the sources within this volume: Trey Adcock, Elena Adell, Mildred Barya, Kelly Biers, Kirk Boyle, Melissa Burchard, Bruce Cahoon, Reid Chapman, Regine Criser, Duane Davis, Alvis Dunn, Ann Dunn, Mark Gibney, Amanda Glenn-Bradley, Grant Hardy, Eva Hericks-Bares, Ali Heston, Sarah Judson, Keya Maitra, Rodger Payne, Ellen Pearson, James Perkins, Giovanny Pleites-Hernandez, Tracey Rizzo, Eric Roubinek, Samer Traboulsi, Greta Trautmann, Darin Waters, and Jeremias Zunguze. We also thank anonymous Humanities Program faculty whose introductions written for the previous Modern World volume we have gratefully repurposed with slight edits for this new volume.

In asking our contributors to craft the learning support items for each source, we asked them to do far more than simply writing a supporting introduction. Our contributors not only rose to the occasion but also revised their entries in response to the editorial feedback. Many of the contributors wrote multiple entries. Our colleague Grant Hardy modeled for us his devotion and excitement about student-centered pedagogy and thereby offered us crucial confidence to stay the course at various stages. And last, but not least, we thank our families who teased us for having too many tabs open on our computers and were patient and only mildly irritated on our behalf at times as this project took over countless hours spilling over into many nights and weekends.

GENERAL EDITORS' WELCOME

Katherine C. Zubko and Keya Maitra

PART I: GETTING TO KNOW THE ELEPHANT

Welcome to the University of North Carolina Asheville's *Global Humanities Reader: Engaging Modern Worlds and Perspectives*. Let us begin by sharing a story about the elephant and the blind men from South Asia:

> Several blind men are brought before a king and asked to describe an elephant. An elephant is brought to them and they proceed to feel it with their hands. One, who grasps the elephant's trunk, claims that an elephant is like a snake. Another, grasping a leg, claims it is like a tree. Yet another grasps the tail and says it is like a rope; and another, feeling the elephant's side, claims it is like a wall. The blind men then argue amongst themselves about the true nature of the elephant. Who is correct?[1]

You might be familiar with a different version of this narrative. What is instructive is that not only does the setting of the story shift based on who is engaging it, including Hindus, Buddhists, and Jains, but that the lesson of the narrative changes as well. Thus, while the Buddha takes it to reflect how the men "cling" to their individual "finding," the Jain view uses it as an example of their epistemological perspectivalism (*anekantavada*) or many-sidedness.

This version of the story is instructive also in what it does not emphasize; for example, it doesn't draw our attention to the ground where the elephant stands. Engaging with this narrative, especially in the context of the United States, the land can no longer be ignored or taken for granted but is central to one's becoming aware of our erased and fractured histories and our uncomfortable collective self-understanding.

---

1. Anand Jayprakash Vaidya, "Making the Case for Jaina Contributions to Critical Thinking Education," *Journal of World Philosophies* 3 (2018): 61–62.

We want to acknowledge and honor that UNC Asheville is on *Anikituwag*i (Cherokee) ancestral land and that we continue to build mutual, respectful relationships with the Eastern Band of Cherokee (EBCI) who are ongoing stewards of this area, and from whom we continue to learn. Acknowledgment is not enough, however, and it is our hope that these Readers help us put our commitment to this relationship into action.

We want to use the elephant story to remind us of insights that emanate from our understanding of UNC Asheville's Humanities Program:

- Exploration of truth and meaning is a collaborative affair involving perspectives from various cultures and occupants of different viewpoints within a single culture.
- No one discipline might have the final exclusive claim on truth, especially when it comes to enduring questions.
- The inquiry model, where asking questions is centered, is the most effective approach for fostering informed, engaged, and compassionate global citizens given its commitment to active, authentic, and open-minded learning.
- Finally, critical thinking has to be conceived in its global purview in order to open us to a wide spectrum of methodologies and epistemologies.

This welcome is primarily aimed at students so that the context for these Readers and the choices we have made may become more transparent.

Who We Are: The Humanities Program at UNC Asheville

On behalf of the editorial team—Brian S. Hook, Sophie Mills, Renuka Gusain, James Perkins, and Alvis Dunn—we are delighted to introduce three humanities primary source anthologies that have been created as the culmination of a multiyear faculty-led curricular revision process at the University of North Carolina Asheville. Our public liberal arts university's more than fifty-year-old Humanities Program consists of a four-course sequence taken by all of our students.[2] The Humanities Program serves as the hub of the wheel of our liberal arts mission. The different spokes of this mission are critical thinking, interdisciplinarity, cross-cultural commitments to diverse perspectives, and inquiry-focused learning. They are held together by an integrative and open-minded sensibility embodied in its curriculum design, delivery, and student learning outcomes.

Early on in the history of this program, faculty saw the need to create their own anthologies of diverse primary sources, as no other available anthology was suitable to meet their goals. These anthologies, published as the Asheville Readers, have periodi-

---

2. Margaret Downes, "The Humanities Program at University of North Carolina at Asheville," in *Alive at the Core: Exemplary Approaches to General Education in the Humanities*, edited by Michael Nelson et al. (San Francisco: Jossey Banks, 2000), 203–24.

cally been revised over these past decades, as faculty continually engage in curricular revision. The main audience for these Readers has always been our own university students who participate in our homegrown, interdisciplinary program.

Thanks to the generosity of a Mellon grant awarded in 2017, this new iteration of the Asheville Readers—renamed *Global Humanities Readers*—are able to evolve in ways that better support the needs of our students at UNC Asheville and beyond who find themselves in a complex, interconnected, and rapidly changing world. For the first time, the Readers will be available online free of cost not only to our students but also to high school, community college, and university students across North Carolina public educational online communities. These developments very much align with our own public liberal arts mission and that of the Humanities Program out of which these Readers have emerged.

Values That Guide Our Readers:
Diverse Cross-Cultural Perspectives and Inquiry Focus

Informed by surveys and discussions with faculty and students, the editorial team identified two main principles that have guided the shaping of these new Readers. The first is a commitment to placing materials from multiple, diverse perspectives in conversation with one another. Second is a focus on providing ways to cultivate our ability to ask questions—to inquire—while deepening our cross-cultural and cross-disciplinary engagements with the materials. We believe both values help you to see your own points of view as emerging from particular contexts, assumptions, and experiences, and that your own is only one of many co-existing views.

Furthermore, we are interested in promoting an openness to *your* encounters with materials. At times we have intentionally encouraged new insights by offering competing perspectives or challenging traditional viewpoints. In some ways, we want to foment intellectual chaos, uncertainty, and struggle by challenging the obvious or the given. Our goal is to enable the potential for growth and help you develop skillful facility in holding multiple perspectives. This is not to encourage a form of relativism but rather to foster a deeper understanding of context and position—whether disciplinary, cultural, and/or intersectional—that permeate your inquiry.

The Jain concept of *anekantavada* mentioned earlier speaks to these multiple co-existing perspectives, each limited to one's position and experience as exemplified in the parable of the elephant. But this story also speaks to the power of self-awareness of each perspective that in combination allows a different communal truth to emerge in contrast to a privileged preexistent ideal Truth (Elephant).

In order to acknowledge that the nature of truth is both communal and multi-faceted, students must engage in this study and effort as deeply as possible. Engaging deeply permits us to penetrate typical surface comparisons and unfounded generalizations. Better still, we are not trapped in judgments that perpetuate one dominant view of the world as the highest or only way to perceive it. To accomplish this requires the strengthening of a very important skill related to critical thinking, namely inquiry. It becomes crucial that we ask questions such as: How might the Jain concept help formulate new questions about the assumptions around an ideal pre-existent Truth and its consequences for human ways of knowing? How is knowledge characterized, who has access, and what might this reflect about human experience from these different worldviews? Each story, reflecting different ways of knowing, comes into sharper focus through the process of cross-cultural comparison. Take again for example another central concept in the study of humanities, namely, aesthetics. On the one hand, this term could be seen as having innately westernized constructs, but when we step back and ask, "How do humans create, define, and experience artistic expressions?," many possible approaches create multiple, contextualized case studies and interpretations that illuminate various underlying foundations.

The selections of primary sources included in each Reader reflect our unwavering commitment to the dual values of cross-cultural diverse perspectives and inquiry-focused engagements. We aim to course correct from some of the available humanities textbooks in which the defining narrative remains that of Western liberalism. For example, the ways that humanities' textbooks have treated race and indigeneity have often furthered harm by excluding multiple perspectives on the difficult lived realities of what we now call racial injustices, as well as patronizing or whitewashing the experiences through stilted frameworks and terminology. In these volumes, there are, at times, gaps in source materials focused on experiences of race, slavery, and indigeneity that are curricular growth areas for the program. It is relevant to note here that in spite of coming from a large group of contributors, our selections are still reflective of the group's interests and areas of focus and we know that a different group might have come up with a different set of readings and perspectives. The choices made are a reflection of the times in which the editors and faculty contributors are living. Engaging in collaborative editing processes with faculty contributors provided us opportunities to have conversations about problematic framing, terms, and even the sources we decided to include. For example, we included a footnote about the use of the terms "negro" and "colored" in the sources in which they appear to help our students understand the use of racial terminology that has since shifted, but remains part of the history that we do not want to erase. This process has made us aware that inclusivity need not be pitted against expertise or any of its cousins, such as rigor or standards, that are often used to police boundaries around knowledge. We don't always get it right, but we are working to bring more awareness, with honesty and humility, to correcting mistakes made in the past.

Our sincere attempt has been to anchor the framing narratives of each Reader in cross-cultural and interdisciplinary perspectives where no one single cultural ideology or disciplinary approach is privileged. However, it is important to acknowledge that each Reader is still temporally organized linearly, focused on written and primary source content, and clearly foregrounds a human-centered perspective that might be suspect from certain cultural viewpoints. These choices, especially the chronological framing of content, admittedly presuppose a linear understanding of time sometimes challenged by various cultures. Linear temporal systems value locating dates for events and people based on criteria that at times exclude cultural expressions of humanity in which orality is valued as much as or sometimes more than writing. The emphasis on time has had the impact of undervaluing sources that come to us through oral means because they could not be tied to a particular origin date. We have tried to address this exclusionary tendency by including more sources from oral traditions to honor cultures' own understandings of their ancient roots by not marking particular time periods in the titles of the volumes.

At the moment of compiling the Readers, for many institutional, program, and resource reasons, we moved forward with a chronological framing even though we are aware of ways of understanding time that diverge from this framing. Linda Tuhiwai Smith, for example, draws our attention to the fact that many Indigenous languages don't have a word for time. She takes this to reflect the fact that lineal or linear time does not operate as a foundational organizing principle in these cultures.[3] In order to disrupt a singular linear organizational model, we have included a second suggested grouping of sources by either theme, question, or some other category and included sources in the Readers that are engaged across chronological time frames.

We realize that each of our decisions, however intentional about inclusivity, has blind spots. Instead of treating this realization as a paralyzing hurdle, we want to approach it as an opportunity for self-reflection that makes explicit the reasoning behind and also the implications of our selections/choices. Indeed, this self-awareness commits us to an epistemic humility that is the hallmark of a pedagogy that foregrounds process and meaningful engagement. Thus, while we are confident that this revision project makes huge strides, there is always more work to be done. For example, because of a long-standing commitment to written sources, our introductory Humanities course has struggled to expand its understanding of "primary source" to include artefacts, material cultures, and other aspects from the Global South. We do include these components, but they currently live on an online learning platform rather than in this Reader. It is our hope in the next revision that these materials will be incorporated more directly.

Finally, our ability to ask questions is often taken for granted, as a given without the need for cultivation. It is often assumed that we automatically learn how to ask questions without direct instruction on how we come to ask particular questions, in what contexts, based on what criteria, and for what purposes. The editorial team realized in talking with students that the skill of asking productive questions needed to be made more visible, with opportunities for practice, and thus decided to make it the central pedagogical focus of these Readers. The team began to test out several learning features that would support this noteworthy and transferable skill. In the

---

3. Linda Tuhiwai Smith, *Decolonizing Methodologies: Research and Indigenous People*, 2nd ed. (New York: Zed Books, 2012), 52.

following section we discuss how inquiry-based learning is embedded in the support features of the Readers.

PART II: HOW TO USE THIS READER: INTRODUCING THE LEARNING SUPPORT FEATURES

Over the past several years, faculty and staff collaborated across various disciplines, programs, and areas at UNC Asheville to globalize the content of courses that grew out of a westernized humanities model. In addition, to support effective and meaningful encounters with the ideas in these sources, faculty have embedded the insights of pedagogical research, namely creating learning environments that are culturally aware, active, inquiry-based and draw upon best practices in cultivating reflective spaces. The editorial team, in view of these aims, realized the need to create a thoroughly interactive text that actualizes our commitments to student success.

Like no other revision process in the past, the editorial team engaged in a research-based approach utilizing our faculty's and students' feedback through surveys, focus groups, and pilot feedback cycles. The unique organization of these Readers emerged as a result of this process and we want to specifically mention how central students were to the final product design. Thus, in addition to the brief introductions to each primary source, which was a hallmark of previous Readers, these new Readers now incorporate several intentional learning support features students overwhelmingly identified as useful to their learning process. We hope the descriptions of each of these features serve to enhance your own particular nuanced engagement with the sources in these Readers.[4]

Cross-Cultural Historical Introductions to Each Volume

One of the most unique features that you will encounter in these Readers is a cross-cultural historical introduction at the beginning of each volume. Authored by our colleague Tracey Rizzo from the History Department, these essays provide a perspective on a larger sweep of history during each time period, identifying key moments and concepts that shape a particular chronological era. These introductions are global in focus, weaving examples from various parts of the world together in order to exemplify how humans in different cultures and times experience, shape, and respond to their worlds. In acknowledging the historical orientation of these cross-cultural introductions, we understand that other disciplinary approaches might have used their own framing questions and criteria. What types of questions and criteria might scholars from other disciplines foreground when seeking to discuss human forms of experience, such as religious movements, war, or love?

---

4. The description of learning support features has been edited from a document first drafted by Brian Hook and used to help guide faculty contributors who have written entries.

These introductions are intended to be flexible in how they are used in classrooms. You may be asked to read the essay at the beginning of a semester to provide an historical disciplinary approach and contextualize the semester. You may also be directed to segments as relevant to particular entries for each week, as they provide further context in addition to each entry's dedicated introduction.

Snapshot Boxes with Tags

We have included a small box at the beginning of each entry that provides some basic contextual information, based on scholarly consensus, for reading at a glance. Specific information may vary based on what is appropriate to the source but often includes the following: language of the original document; date; location or origin; genre; and tags.

A unique feature developed for these entries is the set of "tags" listed in the snapshot box. Tags aim to highlight connections, for example, by offering a bird's-eye view of central concepts, within the course and possibly across courses. They are not places, names, and events; they also are not themes or keywords for that matter. Each course also contains a tag glossary that collects all the tags used in that course along with the readings in which they appear. We have come to think of the tags as hubs that offer an initial location for seeing, creating, and facilitating exciting new connections. We welcome you to enjoy exploring the trails that these tags help signpost and to create your own.

Introductions with Bolded Terms

Each course entry is accompanied by an introduction that invites you into the reading and offers a few navigational tools. These introductions are not SparkNotes summaries or comprehensive overviews like an encyclopedia or wikipedia article. Reading the introduction thus cannot replace reading the source itself, and much will be missed if this strategy is attempted. We also bolded a few terms to alert you to key concepts and frameworks.

We have modified the primary focus of these introductions to prioritize inquiry-based learning, and so you will note the inclusion of questions embedded directly in the introduction in order to prompt exploration of both the context and the source itself. Questions as opportunities of reflective pauses are often framed such that readers have an opportunity to make their own connections. Our aim is to provide much-needed contextual support while leaving room for you to engage a source without preemptively providing many of the interpretative possibilities. This moves away from "tell me what to think or what I should know" to "give me parameters that can guide my own productive engagement with the source."

In some cases, you will notice slightly different approaches to readings, especially if they are from typically underrepresented cultures in the curriculum. This might entail more notes to provide access to critical contextual sources, an expanded narrative timeline as part of the introduction, and/or different types of strategies for engaging the text. By allowing for differences in some of the entries, our intention is to provide more inclusive spaces for expert voices from the margins that our students have not usually heard or been able to find, and to build skills for working with multiple perspectives. It is a goal of the liberal arts and this project to put the values into practice that will foster, educate, and engage these skills as part of becoming global citizens.

Timelines

Most Reader entries include a timeline with three different types of chronological information: (1) black points relevant to the source directly; (2) orange points for comparison to other cultures during the same time period; and (3) larger historical time periods, eras, or movements relevant to the context of the source (as blue bands) or as cross-cultural comparisons (as orange bands). Timelines are a way to provide a type of context for each source, but with the important reminder of what else is going on in other parts of the world. Creating a timeline for ancient, oral, storytelling traditions that are not matched to a particular date did not seem effective but rather revealed the assumptions of linear time frames. In a few other cases, we have added a timeline with more modern-day points to raise awareness about present-day contexts that have inherited these storytelling traditions. Sometimes we have also included a more substantial narrative timeline for underrepresented cultures.

At the beginning of each volume you will find a comprehensive timeline noting important points across all the sources in one place. To create a comprehensive timeline is by its very nature an impossible task, as no amount of space or organizational strategy could possibly capture so many concepts visually. However, we hope that the choices we made bring into perspective some of the most prominent chronological points.

Pre-PARs and Post-PARs

You will find a unique feature on either side of the primary source itself: Primed and Ready (PAR) activities placed just before you begin reading (pre-PARs) and again after your first read-through (post-PARs). After getting your contextual and chronological grounding with the introduction and timeline, the pre-PARs are a way for you to pause and spend a few minutes connecting to your prior knowledge of a concept or experience (e.g., "What do you think the role of a teacher is?") or on knowledge already learned in class through previous materials (e.g., "What kinds of models for imitation are the heroes of earlier myths?").

These are not intended to involve research but rather invite you to gather your own thoughts before you start reading. There are no right or wrong answers. The goal is to encourage you to approach the readings with questions in mind and to see in the works a resemblance or distance between your own responses and those you find in the work.

At the end of the source reading, you will often find post-PARs that might ask you to revisit the brief observations noted in the pre-PARs, but through the lens of the source directly. If a pre-PAR asks you to list five ideas that you associate with the "sacred," a post-PAR might ask you to identify how the work presents the "sacred." A second type of post-PAR may ask you to briefly practice a particular skill, such as becoming attentive to a particular feature, or to consider the reading with an analytical tool in mind, to help with comprehension and clarity. Strategies might include outlining a small portion of an argument, identifying evidence, looking for assumptions, listing dominant and missing perspectives, or locating initial comparative patterns.

PARs are not discussion or essay questions, deep-level critical thinking activities, or "busy work." The purpose is to move you from more passive to more active forms of processing the information with which you are engaging so that when you come to class, you have a starting point to enter into the discussion. Faculty may select a particular pre-PAR and/or post-PAR for you to complete prior to class, however they are all available for you to use to support your engagement with the materials.

Inquiry Corners

Another feature comes at the end of most entries: The Inquiry Corner.[5] As part of our commitment to supporting an inquiry-based focus, we developed this feature as a platform to bring awareness to what different types of questions do as pathways of inquiry. It is intended as a model for how to ask more productive questions in relation to inquiry processes and goals. The questions provided are not the only types of questions that can be asked, nor do they need to be asked in any particular order.

You may want to ask what certain questions can help you to do—clarify, compare, connect, or critically engage with a topic in which you can delineate the criteria and assumptions of what that question entails. While you may end up utilizing some of these questions in class discussion or in writing prompts—especially the comparative or critical forms—the idea is that with practice, you will gain facility in formulating your own versions of these questions and other types, including those from various disciplinary contexts.

The Inquiry Corner is not a set assignment meant to "be completed" before class, but your professor may guide you to engage this feature in various ways as a part of

---

5. We are indebted to some inspirational models that supported the development of this inquiry-based learning feature, especially Keya Maitra's "Philosopher's Corner" as found at the end of each chapter in her *Philosophy of the Bhagavad Gita*. We are also grateful to Heather Laine Talley's question prompts that she used in her sociology classes and that served as a useful base for the development of this feature for our Humanities courses.

assignments or class preparation or to practice creating your own questions, or to explore a source on your own. Here are some brief frameworks for the types of questions we chose to include:

- **Content Questions:** Models how to clarify an idea or term in the source, as part of close reading skills. (How is dharma being defined in the source?).
- **Comparative Questions:** Compares a topic between course materials for exploration. (How is nature viewed/depicted in the *Epic of Gilgamesh* and the *Daodejing*?)
- **Critical Questions:** Invites a source-grounded examination of a topic/subtopic with multiple possible perspectives/examples, within a source or across sources. This type of question builds analytical/interpretive/reasoning capacities utilizing evidence. (What forms of authority do leaders rely upon to support their positions of power?)
- **Connection Questions:** Bridges one's own knowledge/experience with ideas in the source; could also connect to student life experiences. (What rhetorical or aesthetic skills do you use when expressing your own authority? Your own doubts or vulnerabilities?)

BEYOND THE CLASSROOM

In collaboration with colleagues from UNC Asheville's Career Center, in 20–25 percent of the entries, we have included questions that arise out of the content and approach of the reading but move into real-life, forward-looking engagement, thus allowing new contexts to explore, practice, and apply the active model of inquiry.

MAPS

Maps are an important aspect of contextualizing our primary source materials. We decided that since there are rich and well-developed online map resources, it would be best to direct our students and faculty to their use, instead of trying to replicate them in not as detailed a form in these Readers. Some of the resources we recommend using are: Ancient World Mapping Center (http://awmc.unc.edu/wordpress/free-maps/), World History Encyclopedia (https://www.ancient.eu/mapselect/), and TimeMaps (https://www.timemaps.com/).

A Few Parting Notes

Finally, the time has come to turn it over to you, dear reader. Our hope is that you have as much fun as we had in compiling this, and we mean all of us—more than sixty people from more than twenty departments/programs/areas were involved in making this series possible. We engaged in a unique collaborative process at every stage, including in the editing of sources that centered dialogue between editors in real time, instead of an individualist approach. We have endeavored to not only bring the elephant into the classroom but to provide strategies to behold more than one aspect—the trunk, the ear, or the side—together and collectively while also becoming aware of the parts of the elephant we don't know how to see from our own cultural perspectives. May we all continue to find more perspectives to engage and respect. Enjoy!

MODERN WORLDS

An Historical Cross-Cultural Introduction

Tracey Rizzo

Images curated by Eva Hericks-Bares

World historians mark the "ancient" world by the gradual integration of Afroeurasia by means of overland transportation; lands separated by deserts and oceans maintained their distinctiveness. The crossing of the Sahara Desert brought sub-Saharan Africa into the orbit of Afroeurasia in the "premodern" period. During the modern era, developments in ship building and navigation across the vast Atlantic Ocean enabled the incorporation of the Americas into a truly global economy and led to massive cultural and ecological exchanges. "Modern," as a historical marker, thus refers to that technology-driven integration of all of the world's population. Taking a birds-eye view of the history of humanity, world historians use the terms "integration" and "interconnectivity" to describe impersonal processes whose impacts are personal, as attested to by the many voices represented in the readings that follow this introduction. Interconnectivity on a global scale was only possible beginning around 1500. Beyond describing global interconnectivity, the terms "modern," "modernization," and "modernity" are highly contested and have been used prejudicially as a synonym for "advanced" or even "Western."

As in the ancient and premodern eras, expansionist territorial states were one of the most destructive and creative forces sparking integration, incidentally or intentionally. Yet resistance to those forces on the part of individuals or groups is almost always intentional. Frequent challenges to those states, sometimes militarized and often populist, brought down empires on almost every continent in the modern era. Ideologically charged, revolutions and social movements prompted change as often as they triggered reactions, and contributed over time to increases in the numbers of representative governments, literacy and mortality rates, and standards of living. Indeed, major global developments such as political liberalism, capitalism, and mod-

2   An Historical Cross-Cultural Introduction

Charles White, *The Contribution of the Negro to Democracy in America*, mural, 1943. Hampton University, Hampton, VA. Permission granted by Hampton University.

Painted more than eighty years after the Emancipation Proclamation, this mural celebrates key contributions of African Americans to US history. With portraits spanning both the nineteenth century (Frederick Douglass, Harriet Tubman) and the twentieth century (Marian Anderson, Paul Robeson) the image focuses on Black leaders and their myriad accomplishments, be they political, social, intellectual, military, athletic, scientific, or artistic. Unlike other public art works during this time, White's painting was funded by a private grant from the Julius Rosenwald Fellowship rather than through WPA monies.

ern science were both cause and consequence of that dynamic between aggrandizing states and popular resistance.

Starting in the sixteenth century, the transatlantic slave trade forced removal and displacement of enslaved African peoples mainly to the Americas. During the modern period this destructive and dehumanizing system became one of the main factors responsible for global economic interconnectedness. Economic interconnectedness not only led to an unprecedented amalgamation of ideas and cultures but also threatened the survival of Indigenous languages, cultures, and epistemologies. Global industrialization resulted in the widespread increase of unregulated pollutants and the burning of fossil fuels, which rapidly increased CO_2 levels and escalated human-caused climate change. Diasporas of millions of indentured laborers, primarily from Asia, contributed to the globalization of populations and cultures around the world and prompted anti-immigration policies and extra-legal actions that took many forms. Reliance on increasingly diverse mass labor forces fueled industrialization in

An Historical Cross-Cultural Introduction 3

Diego Rivera, *The Marriage of the Artistic Expression of the North and of the South on This Continent*, also known as *Pan American Unity*, mural, 1940. City College of San Francisco, CA. Courtesy of City College of San Francisco; © Banco de México Diego Rivera and Frida Kahlo Museums Trust, Mexico City / Artists Rights Society (ARS), New York. Image by Cultural Heritage Imaging.

Public artworks (both sculptures and murals) were among the many projects supported by the Works Progress Administration (WPA), created under President Roosevelt in 1935 as part of the New Deal. These projects were important because they provided an accessible and highly visible emphasis on the importance of art in American culture. This mural, by Mexican artist Diego Rivera, focuses on the past, present, and future of the Americas, and, as the well-known artist himself stated, it is centered on the importance of indigenous traditions to make "a real American art."

Western Europe and the Americas who largely monopolized international trade into the twentieth century. Their rivalries played out on every continent, fueling a commercial and arms race that spurred technological innovation, particularly in naval warfare, to the point of destabilizing empires throughout Asia. But just as consumer products, people, weapons, raw materials, and disease circulated ever more rapidly and widely, so too did ideas, including those about rights and self-determination, leading gradually to international solidarity movements to end slavery, regulate industrial practices, and limit child labor and the exploitation of animals. These ideas and movements include the UN Declaration of Universal Human Rights (1948) and continued work by governments and nongovernmental organizations (NGOs) to advance the rights of communities and individuals across the globe. Continued protest movements, peaceful or armed, attest to the enduring human impetus to stand against injustice and to change the world, even as people dispute the contours and implications of those changes.

Developments in world history have been fashioned by those in power; however the impact of people, especially the marginalized and others, who demanded change have significantly intervened in altering the course of history. As in earlier eras, empires continued to rise and fall, but at a more rapid pace due to internal weaknesses, geopolitical integration, and superior firepower. Even the massive authoritarian empires of Nazi Germany, Imperial Japan, and Soviet Russia in the twentieth century lasted less than one hundred years (the first less than twenty), but the extent of change, including loss of lives on an unprecedented scale, and material and psychological devastation, was magnified due to the very interconnectedness that forged those global communities.

Atlantic Worlds

The integration of the economies of the four continents bordering the Atlantic Ocean between the seventeenth and nineteenth centuries constitutes the first wave of modern globalization. Rooted in the triangular trade in the sixteenth century, of which enslaved Africans were at the center, Caribbean societies constituted a plantation complex whose organization of labor was distinctly modern. Its implications extended beyond the plantation, and gradually across the world, as seen in the spread of the factory system, monocultural agriculture, and scientific racism, defined by the misuse of science to justify dehumanizing people based on race. It destroyed traditional forms of community and rendered millions of people impoverished, dispossessed, and othered. Frequent acts of resistance by marginalized peoples against European settlers and nations underpinned an emerging revolutionary tradition in the Atlantic world beginning in the seventeenth century and bore fruit in the largest successful slave rebellion in history, the Haitian Revolution in 1804. Uprisings by Indigenous people such as the 1680 Pueblo Revolt in New Mexico, and by enslaved people such as Tacky's War in Jamaica in 1760, although initially suppressed, imparted liberation legends and scripts for future generations.

Desire for control over the Americas led to brutal conflicts between the empires of France, Britain, and Spain in the seventeenth and eighteenth centuries. France's aid to North American rebels was in part an act of revenge for Britain's seizure of French colonies in Canada in the Seven Years War, also known as the French and Indian War (1756–1763). Their century-long jostling for colonial dominance in the Caribbean influenced the Haitian Revolution, a war for independence that lasted ten years and resulted in Haitian independence in 1804 and the end of French dominance in the Americas. Conditions for enslaved people in the sugar islands were harsh, leading to the highest death tolls of all plantation economies: enslaved people working the fields seldom lived into their twenties. Thus, plantations in the Caribbean and Brazil imported the largest number of enslaved people, tens of thousands every year in Saint Domingue (later Haiti) alone. Newly arrived people brought their own political and religious beliefs and practices, particularly Kongolese, influencing the development of Caribbean philosophies and ways of life. With far fewer whites than Blacks (40,000 to 400,000 on the eve of the revolution), and with enslaved people recalling their lives in their birthplaces, Saint Domingue was ripe for a revolution. People who escaped formed maroon communities, preserving languages and traditions that

An Historical Cross-Cultural Introduction   5

Jacob Lawrence, *To Preserve Their Freedom*, from the series *The Life of Toussaint L'Ouverture*, screenprint, 1988—inspired by paintings created by the artist between 1936–1938. Museum of Modern Art, NYC. Digital Image © The Museum of Modern Art/Licensed by SCALA / Art © 2021 The Jacob and Gwendolyn Knight Lawrence Foundation, Seattle / Artists Rights Society (ARS), New York.

In this series, Lawrence considers ideas of revolution and rebellion based on the life and leadership of Haitian Toussaint L'Ouverture. The decade-long struggle for freedom (1791–1804) led to an end of French rule and the abolition of slavery in Haiti, and it represents one of the largest successful revolts by the formerly enslaved. The artist uses color to draw our attention to details, while his use of shapes or large areas of color works particularly well for making screen prints (itself a more democratic art form, since it produces multiples instead of unique, single paintings).

enabled organizing. Even those laboring on plantations by day organized at night, including around their sacred ceremonies, known collectively as "vodou." Believing that spirits communicated through religious specialists, usually priestesses, participants in ceremonies pledged to free themselves at any cost. After thirteen years and 300,000 dead, the revolt succeeded. The Haitian Revolution became an inspiration for slave revolts into the nineteenth century and liberation movements throughout the Americas and Africa into the twentieth century.

Yet environmental degradation and indemnity payments to France in restitution for what they perceived as lost property and labor from slavery plagued the new nation. Soil exhaustion from over-planting monocultures was compounded by scorched-earth policies on all sides of the conflict that made the land inarable. Seeking new plots for subsistence farming, farmers rapidly cleared forests, denuding hilly slopes of protective vegetation. Haiti went from being one of the most resource-rich and therefore valuable colonies to one of the poorest countries in the world today. Devastated landscapes and lifeways, especially when combined with indebtedness to rich countries, fostered dictatorships, where the very few rich and powerful used terror to control the masses of the very poor. Even in such desperate circumstances, however, Haitians regularly revolted against dictators, slowly accumulating greater freedoms and a gradual improvement in their standard of living.

Another source of the Atlantic revolutionary tradition derives from English Constitutionalism with its central ideal of separation of powers. The "Glorious Revolution" of 1688, as the culmination of the Puritan attack on Anglican domination in the 1640s in Europe and North America, institutionalized a gradual transition to constitutional, representative government. European political philosophers and activists in the street explored its numerous implications.

One such implication was the "social contract" model of government, which holds that political legitimacy stems only from the consent of the governed, not from birthright, divine right, or military might. Debates ensued as to who should be a party to the contract. Some demanded the inclusion of all, including poor people, racialized others, and women, yet constitutions were initially exclusive; most people would have to fight for more than a century for equal rights. In 1776, demands for representation spurred the American Revolution when some colonists in North America believed the British Crown no longer represented their interests, leading to a civil and foreign revolutionary war that lasted until the British were fully defeated and withdrew from the United States in 1783. A wide array of colonists supported the revolution, regardless of race, class, or gender. A substantial minority remained loyal to the British Crown, including some enslaved people who fought for the British in exchange for manumission. The British also sought support from autonomous Indigenous tribes like the Huron by promising to limit westward expansion. Enthusiasm among the Americans wanting freedom from the British led some to demand more than independence; the more radical of them lobbied for genuine participatory government, others going so far as to abolish slavery (e.g., Vermont) and still others extending voting rights to white men regardless of wealth (e.g., New Hampshire). The US Constitution of 1787 and the subsequent Bill of Rights guaranteed a host of individual rights for male citizens, including speech, assembly, bearing arms, and freedom from arbitrary arrest. But it stopped short of abolishing slavery until 1864, thirty years after the British Empire did.

Following the English and American Revolutions, the French Revolution (1789–1799) was a precondition for the slave revolt in Haiti. Revolutionaries in France itself ended Bourbon rule (1589–1792) with the execution of King Louis XVI and Queen Marie Antoinette in 1793. Radical measures during the Reign of Terror (1793–1794) accompanied civil war and the suspension of due process with tens of thousands of

Jacques-Louis David, *Death of Marat*, oil on canvas, 1793. Royal Museum of Fine Arts of Belgium. Public Domain.

Jean-Paul Marat was a revolutionary leader and radical journalist who was murdered in 1793 in his bath-cum-workplace (where he soaked to get relief from a skin condition). David painted the scenes in the months after Marat's murder, an unusual decision because it took a contemporary, political event as the subject of the work while the French Revolution's Reign of Terror was still in full effect. The painting documents two of the revolution's many factions and actions: Marat, a Montagnard, was assassinated by Charlotte Corday, a Girondin (her name is on the letter in his hand), who blamed Marat for the September Massacre.

political dissidents executed by guillotine. The abolition of slavery in 1794 (revoked in 1802 by Napoleon) reflected the might and legitimacy of the slave rebellion in Haiti, but the government in Paris still could not hold the colony. Government-sponsored attacks on Catholicism led to divorce by mutual consent and secular public schooling. But the forcible closure of churches, seizure of church property, and attacks on priests and nuns turned many against the revolution, especially in Catholic rural areas, as it did some elite commanders, including former slave Toussaint L'Ouverture (1743–1803), a staunch Catholic, who called for the rebuilding of Haiti on the basis of holy matrimony. Battling the monarchs of Europe in addition to counterrevolutionaries in France for more than a decade exhausted French revolutionaries and led to the dictatorship of General Napoleon Bonaparte (1769–1821). His attempt to establish an empire across Europe and North Africa sparked a Pan-European war, fought on several continents. A coalition of monarchs, including those of England, Russia, and Prussia, ended the Napoleonic Wars and forced the restoration of France's monarchy in 1814. But three more revolutions in nineteenth-century France followed until a third republic was established in 1870. Some of those revolutions, especially that of 1848, spread throughout Europe, attesting to the increased ability of protesters to organize on a large scale.

With each progressive revolution, more people joined the ranks of the rebels, some demanding economic rights such as the right to work or to the means of subsistence. In addition to persistent antislavery agitation on the part of Black and white abolitionists, by 1848 an industrial class of urban workers shaped radical thinking and actions for a century to come. The *Communist Manifesto* by Karl Marx (1818–1883) and Friedrich Engels (1820–1895) argued for the abolition of private property to address its critique of capitalist political economies and advocated for the worldwide revolt of working men. On the one hand, most orthodox communists called for violent overthrow, believing that participatory democracy would always serve the interest of capital. On the other hand, some communists and other critics formed or supported political parties that reformed the systems of government from within by sponsoring social safety net legislation, for example. Industrialization led to rapid urbanization as rural workers left the countryside for factories. Protesting working conditions, workers extended their critique to the forces of economic inequality, including the theory and practice of capitalism itself. Some even decried environmental degradation, especially evident in lethal air and water pollution that marred an otherwise improved standard of living for most into the twentieth century. While the overthrow of capitalism did not happen, some workers gained some protections once they organized into labor unions. A number of governments accepted that certain regulations were essential, not just for the benefit of the poor but for the health of the economy and nation as a whole.

French expansion in Europe destabilized the Spanish Empire in the Americas and revolutions erupted in the first decades of the nineteenth century leading to the creation of independent countries in Latin America. Building on centuries-old

An Historical Cross-Cultural Introduction   9

Albert Bierstadt, *Among the Sierra Nevada, California*, oil on canvas, 1868. Smithsonian American Art Museum. Public Domain.

Like many artists of his generation, Bierstadt traveled West with surveyor expeditions, providing visuals of the terrain in the era before landscape photography. From the sketches, the painter would then craft an enormous canvas (6 × 10 feet) and pander to the public's curiosity about the new frontier. While this painting was inspired by Bierstadt's trip to Yosemite, it was painted years later in London, and it is not a faithful rendering of the scene but a composition in which each element was chosen for maximum dramatic effect.

revolutionary traditions, forged by Indigenous and enslaved peoples, insurgents in Mexico fought against oppression. Embracing an early form of liberation theology, Catholic priests Miguel Hidalgo, "Father of Mexican Independence" (1753–1811) and José María Morelos (1765–1815) led poor farmers, their livestock in tow, from the countryside to the capital, protesting land confiscations and food shortages in 1811.

Though numbering in the tens of thousands, and inclusive of mestizo and Indigenous people, they were no match for New Spain's imperial army. As in North America, fears of "revolutions from below" from Indigenous and enslaved populations as well as from poor farmers led to curbing the most grassroots forms of dissent, while the benefits of independence continued to be monopolized by elites. Simón Bolívar (1783–1830), known as "The Liberator" of Latin America, was one such elite who believed that widespread rights would have to evolve gradually as more people became affluent and educated. Revolutionary momentum continued, however, as peasants and poor urban dwellers continued to protest. One hundred years later, under the leadership of Emiliano Zapata (1879–1919), rural and poor people pushed for a program that included secularization and new opportunities for women; indeed women served as commanders in Zapata's forces. By 1920 revolutionaries had ousted a dictator after ten years of civil war and adopted one of the world's most liberal constitutions; it included social rights such as land reform, labor organizing, and free public schooling. Although it guaranteed access to land, this tenet of the constitution was not put into effect until ten years later, under the presidency of the progressive Lázaro Cárdenas (1895–1970).

The new United States applied Manifest Destiny doctrine to justify occupying the entirety of the continent, from the Atlantic to the Pacific. Manifest Destiny was bolstered by distinct undercurrents of American Christian Protestantism, in particular a biblical foundation for chosen-ness, faithfulness to the covenant, and a promised land preserved by God for cultivation by his chosen people as the fulfillment of the covenantal relationship. Settler colonialism evolved from the premise that pioneers must settle "empty lands," bringing them under cultivation to foster material and moral progress. Over the course of the nineteenth century, scientific racism infused Eurocentric notions of progress. Some biologists and pseudoscientists promoted the view that Northern Europeans sat atop a racial hierarchy that ranked peoples and cultures. Some even went so far as to prophesize the extinction of Indigenous peoples whose cultures they saw as incompatible with modernity. Others promoted uplift and assimilation into whiteness. Their belief that these lands were theirs to own and improve erased the practices and identities of many Indigenous peoples and ultimately resulted in their forced removal onto reservations.

Its immediate implications were border wars with Canada (War of 1812) and Mexico (Mexican-American War, 1846–1848). While those conflicts contained north-south expansion, westward expansion could only be checked by the resistance of Native Americans who engaged US forces in armed conflicts regularly, the largest of these being the Battle of Greasy Grass in Montana in 1876. Two thousand Lakota Sioux and Cheyenne forces defeated the US Army who badly miscalculated by assembling a contingent of only six hundred men. Further conflicts reversed gains made by the Sioux and Cheyenne during that battle, inspiring some Native Americans like the Paiute Wovoka (c. 1856–1932) and the Lakota Sioux Sitting Bull (1831–1890) to call for a mystical millenarian movement known as the Ghost Dance. Visions of the return of the buffalo, the defeat of the white man, and the restoration of Native American sovereignty led some to don shirts that were thought to repel bullets. Fearing the movement, US troops fired on the dancers at Wounded Knee in South Dakota on December 29, 1890, killing up to three hundred men, women, and children. In addition to such atrocities, Indigenous people suffered from forced assimilation into boarding schools and discrimination, ongoing treaty violations, and repeated displacement through resettlement, such as the Trail of Tears. By the twentieth century, American Indian activists challenged settler colonialism through mass protests, lawsuits, lobbying, outreach, and education. By the 1970s their acts of civil disobedience included the occupation of historic sites such as Mount Rushmore and the Wounded Knee massacre battle site itself.

As new western states entered the union, fierce debates ensued about whether

Fred Kabotie, *Salt Lake Mural at Painted Desert Inn,* fresco, 1948. Petrified Forest National Park. Public Domain.

This mural tells a story in visual form: It presents two young Hopi men walking hundreds of miles from their home to Zuni Salt Lake to collect salt. It refers to a journey that is both physical and sacred. Kabotie, who had survived the traumatic re-education efforts of an Indian residential school to become a nationally acclaimed Hopi artist, painted the mural to commemorate the fact that the young Hopi's journey would have taken them through the area now known as Petrified Forest.

or not slavery would be legal within them. One result was the Fugitive Slave Act of 1850, which made the federal government responsible for returning enslaved peoples who had escaped, even if in a state that had banned slavery, to their owners. The US Constitution allowed some autonomy to state governments, an arrangement whose ambiguity led to the Civil War (1861–1865) when Southern states seceded from the union over their right to determine whether or not slaveholding would be legal. Although the Confederacy lost and the Thirteenth Amendment to the Constitution abolished slavery in 1865, African Americans had to continually fight for equality and justice. Where they did attain affluence and influence as business owners and political leaders, as in Wilmington, North Carolina, for example, white supremacists invented new forms of disenfranchisement through voter suppression and violence, murdering more than fifty African Americans in one day of violence in 1898. Vigilantism went nearly unchecked for decades as the Ku Klux Klan and other hate groups lynched nearly 5,000 African Americans and other minorities between the 1880s and the 1960s, primarily in the Southern United States. Beyond overt violence, racial

Aaron Douglas, *Into Bondage* (one of four in a series), oil on canvas, 1936. National Gallery of Art, Washington, DC. © 2021 Heirs of Aaron Douglas / Licensed by VAGA at Artists Rights Society (ARS), NY. Digital image courtesy of National Gallery of Art.

This image was a commission, which means it was specifically created for an exhibition that opened Juneteenth 1936 at the Texas Centennial Exposition in Dallas, Texas. Though conceived as a mural, it was actually painted on canvas, which made it easily movable (and also led to the demise of two of the four works). The entire sequence presented in visual form the beginning of slavery through emancipation and into the present (1936). Douglas worked with a modern art approach that featured outlines and layered colors and included symbolism that focused on the freeing of slaves rather than slavery's ominous beginnings.

apartheid, known as "Jim Crow" laws, segregated Blacks and whites across the South for most of the twentieth century. In an attempt to escape poverty and violence, 6 million African Americans relocated to northern and western cities throughout the twentieth century in what has been called the Great Migration. By forming advocacy groups like the National Association for the Advancement of Colored People, African Americans compelled local, state, and the federal government to extend liberty, equality, and justice to all while a concentration of creative energy in New York City resulted in the literary and musical achievements of the Harlem Renaissance. But the legal apparatus of Jim Crow persisted into the 1970s and beyond, even after many decades of civil rights activism, by taking new forms.

The second wave of US imperialism saw expansion beyond the continent into the Caribbean, the Philippines, and elsewhere in Asia, escalating in the twentieth century and including the absorption of Hawai'i and Alaska. Queen Liliuokalani of Hawai'i (1838–1917) attempted to curb the economic might of white American planters and businessmen but they organized a coup against her in 1893. When her defenders organized a counter coup she was forced to abdicate in order to prevent their arrest and execution. Upon her abdication, the monarchy itself was abolished in favor of a Republic, giving the architects of the coup ideological cover. Apologists for overseas imperialism often touted the superiority of purportedly democratic institutions to justify their interventions. They perpetuated the idea of the civilizing mission or "white man's burden," claiming that classic liberal economic, political, and cultural modernization would raise people out of servitude and poverty. Yet continued superpower contests and resource extraction in these regions led to military escalation and complicated narratives of progress and uplift. Regular rebellions against US imperialism led eventually to the end of formal occupation but not to other forms of "soft" imperialism.

The United States extended its sphere of influence starting in 1898 in Spain's former colonies in Latin America and the Philippines. Twentieth-century covert and not so covert actions in Panama, Cuba, Puerto Rico, Guatemala, and later Nicaragua and El Salvador, illustrate the imperial ambitions of the United States. These new forms of empire often rested less on the annexation of territories and more on the exertion of influence through aid, proxies, and threats of sanctions. The United States evoked classic justifications such as national security and protection of financial interests while adding updated ideological justifications to include human rights or free trade. Revolutions against US interests and the local governments that protected them proliferated across Latin America throughout the twentieth century, some of them explicitly communist. As early as 1933, Communists in Cuba played a role in the populist coup by Fulgencio Batista that toppled a US-backed military dictatorship. Two decades later, a more extensive revolution made Cuba the only Communist country in the Western hemisphere.

MEDITERRANEAN WORLD

The Ottoman Empire, its capital in Istanbul, Turkey, was increasingly decentralized. Occupying much of Afroeurasia, it had dominated Mediterranean and Silk Road trade for three centuries but entered into a long period of decline as the global economy shifted to the Atlantic in the seventeenth and eighteenth centuries. Moreover, given its cultural, linguistic, and religious diversity, many subject populations sought independence. Thus when Napoleon's forces occupied Egypt and Syria (1798–1801), rebels saw their chance to enlist the aid of Europeans to modernize their economies in order to achieve independence. After the loss of its American colonies and to fuel its rapid industrialization of textile production, British investors offered loans to Egyptian firms and the government itself, under the leadership of Muhammad Ali (1769–1849), to secure their access to Egypt's cotton exports. By 1831, rebels had secured enough military aid to revolt against the Ottoman Empire and declare independence but the resulting wars deferred formal independence until 1867. Poorer Egyptians protested initiatives undertaken by Ali's Alawiyya dynasty, including mass conscription, increased taxes, and its increasing indebtedness and reliance on British aid and advisors. When one of these protests turned violent, British gunboats amassed at the harbor, unleashing a cycle of further protests and reprisals, some under the banner of anti-Western Islamic pan-nationalism under the leadership of Muhammad Ahmed al-Mahdi (1844–1885). A protracted conflict in neighboring Sudan led to atrocities on both sides during nearly twenty years of fighting. Anglo-Egyptian forces eventually crushed the Mahdist state, with up to half of the population lost to war and disease. Dislocations on this scale helped spread Wahhabism, a form of Sunni Islam originating in central Arabia that called for a return to a particularly selective and narrowly defined view of tradition. While the Alawiyya dynasty remained in power until 1952, it was in effect a client state of Great Britain who had gained greater control of Afroeurasia with the completion of the Suez Canal in 1869. Indeed, Britain maintained control of the canal zone until 1956, but revolutionaries otherwise forced their withdrawal, securing independence and a constitution in 1922. However, an anti-Western Islamic party, the Muslim Brotherhood, won elections, only to have the results annulled by the British, with full self-determination denied.

During the same years, the French deepened their involvement in neighboring Algeria. Superpower contests often hinge on maintaining equivalent zones of influence as a check on rivals' aggrandizement. There, too, local rulers sought independence from the Ottoman Empire, but instead of loans, the French brought a full-scale military occupation that lasted until 1962. By facilitating the relocation of hundreds of thousands of Europeans to Algeria, France effectively established one of the largest settler states in Africa and annexed Algeria as an official department of France. While some elite Algerians became full French citizens involved in colonial administration, for most Algerians the occupation resembled quasi-apartheid (legal and cultural segregation). Regular rebellions against French rule, particularly in the regions bordering the Sahara, founded a resistance tradition almost immediately upon occupation. One hundred and thirty years later it finally succeeded, but only after six years of fighting in the brutal Algerian War of Independence (1956–1962). Assia Djebar (1936–2015) lived on both sides of the war, and both sides of the nation. Seeking mobility for his family, her father taught French and let Assia attend school

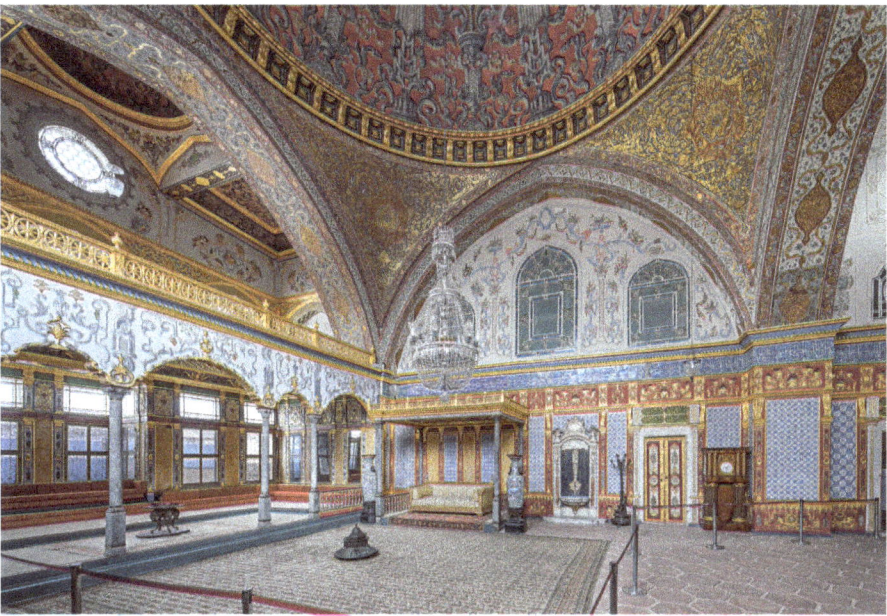

Imperial Hall/Imperial Sofa in Harem of Topkapi Palace, architecture decorated with prestigious imported materials including Dutch tile, Venetian glass, and gilded wood, originally 1580s, remodeled in the seventeenth century. Istanbul, Turkey. Public Domain.

Also known as Seraglio, the Topkapi Palace was the prime residence and administrative center of the Ottoman sultans during the fifteenth to nineteenth centuries. The Imperial Hall or Imperial Sofa served as the throne room and official reception hall for entertaining guests. As a semipublic room, its decorations show off both the luxurious art of Ottoman Turkey (for example, see the blue band of tiles with calligraphic inscription and in the gold-enhanced painting of arabesques all along the arches) and the diplomatic ties with Dutch and Venetian trading companies (for example, see the blue and white Delft tile panels).

in the 1940s. She called French her stepmother-tongue and enjoyed the freedoms her Western education afforded but also described her estrangement from the cloistered world of the women of her family who lived in relative seclusion as devout Muslims. She joined the freedom struggle as a student in France and a journalist; she later interviewed the women who fought in the war. Some provided material aid and shelter, sewing uniforms and hiding partisans. Some joined the partisans and suffered arrest and torture. Others planted bombs in urban areas, hidden in unsuspecting places like handbags and baby carriages. While these rebellions might have begun as Pan-Islamic nationalist movements, they grew to include Western-educated students, bureaucrats, and servicemen.

The loss of one territory after another prompted the Ottoman administration to embark on ambitious reforms, but in the end, these were too little, too late. Modernization attempts, known collectively as the Tanzimat reforms (1839–1876), succeeded in legal and bureaucratic transformations centering a proposed equality between non-Muslims and Muslims and spurred economic and technological innovation, but they also prompted backlash by more conservative Muslims. When Abdulhamid II (1842–1918), the last sultan of the six-hundred-year Ottoman Empire, acceded to the throne, he represented the triumph of Pan-Islamism and the rejection of Western modernity. To overthrow him and gain independence, a group of rebels known as the Young Turks, committed to Western modernization, sought assistance from Germany. Meanwhile, British forces supported rebels elsewhere in Southwest Asia once the Ottoman Empire entered World War I on the side of Germany and the Central Powers. Christian Armenians, victims of increasing persecution, aided the allies during the war. Turkey's government, in retribution, conducted a genocidal campaign against them, killing about 1 million men, women, and children between 1915 and 1922. Loss in World War I finally ended the Ottoman Empire, created an independent and secular Turkey under the leadership of Kemal Atatürk, and left a power vacuum throughout Southwest Asia into which Britain and France rushed, dividing up the region into their spheres of influence, nominally overseen by the newly formed League of Nations.

These developments coalesced to secure a Jewish homeland in Palestine in another instance of settler colonialism. During World War I, Britain aimed to destabilize the Ottoman Empire by supporting rebellion from within, promising Sharif Hussein of Mecca recognition of an independent Arabia after the war. At the same time, it concluded another secret treaty, betraying Hussein by agreeing with the French to divide up Ottoman lands after the war. In a third agreement, the Balfour Declaration (1917), Britain pledged to the World Zionist Organization that it would support the creation of a "national home" for Jews in Palestine. European and North American Zionists had called for the return of diasporic Jews to their biblical homeland proposing settlement. Palestinian Jews and Christians, prejudicially treated by the Muslim Ottoman Empire, experienced the British Mandate as liberation, but a racial hierarchy developed where European and North American immigrants had better access to employment and other benefits. Gradually their numbers climbed through immigration, from 12 percent to 30 percent of the population by 1940. Some socialist settlers created experimental communities, known as *kibbutzim*, in rural areas. Some enjoyed peaceful relations with Palestinians; others did not, and sporadic violence led to full-scale conflict in 1936. For three years the Arab Rebellion pitted Zionists against Palestinians and both against the British. The result, in 1939, was Britain's limitation on Jewish immigration to Palestine, just at the moment when Jews fleeing Nazi persecution sought refuge. That compromise satisfied no one and terrorist attacks on all sides escalated through the war years; a weakened Britain withdrew in 1947 and an all-out Arab war on the Zionists led finally to the creation of the State of Israel in 1948. Some Holocaust survivors relocated there, supported in part by reparations paid by the West German government to the new nation.

SOUTH ASIA

As in the Ottoman Empire, weaknesses in the land-based empires made them vulnerable to revolution from within and invasion from without. This dynamic describes the expanding influence of the British in eighteenth-century India where the Mughal Empire entered a period of decline especially following Aurangzeb (1618–1707) whose reign is often contrasted with his predecessors, for example, that of Akbar who was open to pluralism. Mughals, Central Asian Muslim horsemen from the North, conquered most of the Indian subcontinent in the sixteenth century. While some of their rulers promoted religious toleration or even syncretism, others were less tolerant. Because Indian princes retained some autonomy, those who resented Aurangzeb's taxes and persecutions, including the destruction of their temples, signed treaties with the British East India Company, in part to enjoy privileged access to British markets for Indian goods, particularly textiles, and in part to acquire British arms to be used against the Mughals.

Recognizing this increasing support, the British extended their presence by installing the first governor general of India, Lord William Bentinck, in 1828. With this consolidation of power, Indian reformers like Ram Mohan Roy (1772–1833) pushed for reforms such as women's education and ending child marriage. Roy was one of the founders of the Brahmo Samaj religion, a monotheistic Hindu sect influenced by elements from Islam and Christianity. Yet, the alliance with Christians, who stepped up efforts at proselytization, stoked fears about forced conversions and tainted his reforms as imperialistic. Meanwhile the East India Trading Company and then the British Raj brought the Indian subcontinent under direct rule of the British Crown. Service in the British bureaucracy or army provided opportunities for Indians; indeed, British control of the vastly populated subcontinent depended on the service of local subordinates. High level British officers and successful residential merchants in the 1700s often adopted Indian dress and served as patrons of musicians and dancers—all court habits of local rulers that replicated known systems of power within which networks were sustained. However, increasing disrespect for Hindu and Muslim customs alike, on the part of some British, especially after their British wives relocated to India, added insult to injury. Demands for self-determination spread until the first full-scale war for independence broke out in 1857 when Indian troops, *sepoys*, serving in the British army mutinied against their commanders.

The remaining independent *rajas* and *nabobs*, or local Hindu and Muslim rulers, were reluctant to take sides in the conflict. Lakshmibai (1828–1858), wife of the ruler of still-independent Jhansi in Northern India, had enjoyed tolerable relations with the British. When her husband died in 1853, disputes over the succession emerged and the British did not accept her adopted son as legitimate, but they did allow her to govern as a client and assume the title of Rani, or queen. This cooperation estranged her from some of her deceased husband's troops. Neither a collaborator nor a freedom fighter, the Rani sought to protect the sovereignty of her state and believed negotiations with the British would secure it. Indeed, in the first months of the rebellion she sided with the British, even offering her troops to come to their aid. But they rejected her offer indicating a deepening mistrust. Persuaded by her troops to join the rebellion, she gradually embraced the freedom struggle as atrocities mounted on both sides. Troops welcomed her to lead them as she wielded her husband's sword and dressed as a man, although legend has it that she also led as a mother, with her son strapped to her back in combat. She won victories but was killed in 1858. Her heroism was celebrated across India, particularly her willingness to order the destruction of a Hindu temple that British forces occupied. "Our country before our religion," she is purported to have proclaimed. The loss of the war resulted in India's total absorption into the British Empire and a new phase of the freedom struggle.

Western-educated men who had served in the British Empire, such as Mohandas Gandhi (1869–1948), Muhammad Ali Jinnah (1876–1948), and Jawaharlal Nehru (1889–1964) rose to prominence as organizers who pursued different strategies and ultimately different visions of the future India. Tensions between Muslims and Hindus that had plagued the Mughal Empire over a century before, exploited by the British for their advantage, divided the freedom movement as well, with the Muslim League formed as a response to the perceived dominance of Hindus in the Indian National Congress. Gandhi's philosophy of passive resistance, and his program of *satyagraha* (nonviolence and noncooperation), attracted many thousands of supporters, especially those who embraced his rejection of capitalism and his dream of *swaraj*, a self-ruling India with the self-sufficient villages serving as its economic heart. Indian feminists were more ambivalent and worked closely with international women's organizations, including the YWCA, to intervene in problems of women's poverty and illiteracy. Madras's first woman doctor, Muthulakshmi Reddy (1886–1968), identified women's lack of empowerment as a source of disease and early mortality. She worked in maternity, juvenile, and widows' institutions, some administered by the Children's Aid Society created jointly in 1908 by British and Indian philanthropists. She traced the sources of mental and physical disability to gender-specific neglect and abuse and started a massive slum rehabilitation program in cooperation with the YWCA and the Catholic Bishop of Madras. This multiethnic and transnational cooperation expanded under the auspices of the Women's Indian Association, which she founded and led to the anticolonialist All-Asian Women's Conference in 1931. Women's movements everywhere worked hard to keep women's issues at the center, to varying degrees of success.

More militant rebels formed rival organizations dedicated to violent tactics, including the Communist Party of India and the Congress Socialist Party. More confrontational nationalists existed like V. D. Savarkar (1883–1966) who formulated Hindutva nationalism, or Subhas Chandra Bose (1897–1945) who accepted Japanese weapons to form the Indian National Army (INA). Between 1942 and 1945, 40,000 troops rallied behind Bose who had initially sought Hitler's support for the INA.

Many of these troops were prisoners of war defeated in Malaysia by the Japanese. To give the army a Pan-Indian character, Bose called for volunteers from every religion, caste, region, and gender. To this end, he organized a Rani of Jhansi regiment that would eventually comprise fifteen hundred young women who fought in combat roles alongside men.

Both violent and nonviolent opposition to British rule led eventually to independence in 1947 and the promulgation of a constitution under the direction of B. R. Ambedkar (1891–1956). As a Dalit, a person born to a family outside of the four castes of Hinduism or "outcaste," Ambedkar campaigned against social discrimination based on caste. He instituted a reservation system for scheduled castes and tribes, for example, members of Dalit and Indigenous communities, in the new constitution that guaranteed economic and political rights, such as a decent standard of living, the means of subsistence, and adequate livelihood. Despite political negotiations aimed to guarantee freedom of religion and the secularization of the state, sectarian violence accompanied Indian independence and the creation of Pakistan as a Muslim majority nation in 1947. More than 1 million people were killed in one of the largest population transfers in history called the Partition: some 12 million people were displaced from their homes. The separate states attempted rapprochement, even signing the Delhi Pact allowing refugees to return, but Pakistan's first prime minister, Liaquat Ali Khan (1895–1951), was assassinated by a Muslim extremist and sectarian violence continued. Nehru, India's first prime minister, led the newly independent states to avoid the polarization of the world between the Russian and US spheres of influence, known as the Cold War, by founding the Non-Alignment Movement. His daughter Indira Gandhi (1917–1984), active herself in India's freedom struggle, became one of the world's first female elected heads of state in 1966.

SUB-SAHARAN AFRICA

British involvement in West Africa formally dates to the 1880s, but in fact began with the Atlantic slave trade. Along with other European and North American traders, British captains forcibly relocated 12.5 million Africans, primarily from West Africa to the Americas through the nineteenth century. Millions more were trafficked across the Indian Ocean by Arab slave traders over ten centuries and dispersed throughout Asia. Collectively, this level of depopulation, together with escalating resource extraction, resulted in the economic underdevelopment of Africa. The triangle trade introduced new crops to African cultivators as well, with corn having the most disruptive effects. Originally cultivated in what is now present-day Mexico as many as seven thousand years ago, corn has a higher caloric yield, requires less labor, and matures faster than other staples. Fueled by corn, cultivators in West Africa cleared rainforests more rapidly to enable more cultivation. The combination of guns, corn, and relative depopulation led to the rise of powerful rulers, the Asante in present-day Ghana (1701–1896), and the Oyo and Benin in present-day Nigeria (1400–1895)

Benin Bronze Plaques, brass and bronze, sixteenth–nineteenth centuries, originally from Oba's Palace, Benin City. British Museum, London. Photograph by Joyofmuseums/CC-SA 4.0.

More than 900 of these bronze and brass plaques had originally decorated the palace of the Oba (ruler) of the Kingdom of Benin, until they were looted in a retaliatory military expedition in 1897 and brought to Europe. They had been created to serve as a visual historical record, documenting the members of the royal household, important events, and even trade with the Portuguese. However, without the record of their original location, any chronological or taxonomical order has been lost to us forever.

who consolidated power by annexing territory and founding large cities. Their role in delivering enslaved people to traders on their coasts shifted power away from cultivators and herders to merchants and warrior elites. By the end of the nineteenth century, European forces toppled West African empires seeking to secure access to raw materials and strategic advantage vis-à-vis their European rivals. In West Africa, urban elites undertook a program of selective modernization, retaining distinctive traditions while crafting new forms of education, economy, and governance. African branches of international organizations headquartered in the colonizing West, however, contributed to a global hegemonic homogenization of social reform movements.

By the twentieth century, regular small-scale protests and larger-scale bids for independence erupted across the African continent. Decrying continued land seizures, Indigenous Herero and Nama cultivators and cattle herders in German Southwest Africa (present-day Namibia) rebelled. In what Germany has finally acknowledged was a genocide, German forces ended the rebellion in 1907, killing 80 percent of the population. More typically, local revolts, usually suppressed in the short run, constituted a decades-long fight for independence against imperial control. The case of Nigeria is illustrative. In 1929, Igbo women in the southern Nigerian state of Opobo shamed their countrymen who served the British as tax collectors. After their first demonstration was ignored, they followed the men night and day narrating their grievances in improvised songs saturated with ridicule and satire. As tensions mounted and their numbers grew to nearly ten thousand, they gathered at prisons, liberating prisoners and attacking officials' huts and offices, setting fire to some. Fearing further escalation, British soldiers fired into crowds of women, killing at least forty and wounding many more. Because they were so easily overpowered, violent protests rarely achieved immediate results. But other strategies continued the struggle and saw greater results. In 1941, civil disobedience took many forms. Strikes, boycotts, and marches erupted in almost every colony during World War II. Nigeria's cost of living increased 74 percent between 1939 and 1943 as labor power, access to overseas markets, and agricultural output dwindled. Yoruba women in southern Nigerian cities, especially the capital Lagos, were active merchants and traders who sustained male strikers during the general strike of 1945 by lowering prices, extending credit, or contributing directly to protest funds. During the six weeks of the strike, 150,000 government workers walked off their jobs. It came after four years of strife in which the government instituted price controls and managed food distribution. To subvert price controls, Nigerian men and women alike engaged in acts of sabotage and a brisk black market trade. By 1944, over two-thirds of Nigerians obtained their food on the black market. Over one thousand gathered in August 1945, and, shouting in Yoruba, demanded an end to government-managed markets. Refusing to speak in English was a palpable form of resistance in itself.

Civilian disobedience combined with the demands of veterans after World War II. Fighting the Nazis roused some Nigerians to support the British war effort initially. Youth learned anti-Nazi songs with lyrics like "Hitler that is throwing the world into confusion, push him with a shovel into the grave." British recruiters promised young men they would learn a trade while enlisted. Forty-five thousand ended up serving, not all of them voluntarily, and the irony of fighting fascism as a conscript was not lost on freedom fighters. Isaac Fadoyebo (1925–2012) joined the Royal West African Air Force at age sixteen. Within a year he deployed to Burma where his company was ambushed by the Japanese. Though badly injured, he and David Kagbo from Sierra Leone, were the only survivors. Villagers hid them for ten months before they were finally rescued and repatriated. The powerful image of the African soldiers was essential to cracking the myth of white superiority, reclaiming the sphere of physical agency, and empowering the muscular nationalism of Africa's liberation movements. It took another decade of sometimes peaceful and sometimes violent protest, however, before a wave of decolonization movements could declare 1960 the Year of Africa as seventeen newly independent nations were created.

In East Africa, Great Britain consolidated its influence along the Swahili coast in the 1890s once the Sultanate of Zanzibar capitulated after 15 minutes of bombing. While sincere abolitionists in and outside East Africa saw British involvement as a way to end the Indian Ocean slave trade, its imperial aims included connecting inland Lake Victoria in Uganda to the coast via an extensive railroad. Initially it sought trading concessions from local leaders representing over seventy linguistic groups, predominantly Kikuyu peoples. Ivory, bananas, and a variety of other products shipped to the coast could then be sold throughout the Arab world. After Germany's loss to Britain in World War I, the British took possession of German East Africa and shifted to settler colonialism with the creation of the new colony of Kenya. Coffee plantations dotted the highlands around Nairobi; African labor sustained an aristocratic elite who preserved their superiority by means of eugenics. Funding the research of British eugenicists, planters aimed to preserve their class position by controlling the reproduction of poor whites through sterilization. Meanwhile, ethnopsychiatry preserved white supremacy by describing the "African mind" as childlike and incapable of adapting to Western education although some British reformers and missionaries established educational institutions.

As plantations spread, they monopolized the most productive land, which sparked violent rebellion. By 1946, a resistance movement organized around traditional oathing rituals united disparate groups to fight the British. The resulting Mau Mau Uprising (1952–1960) was a guerrilla campaign based in the forests around Mount Kenya. As with other guerrilla struggles, women participated alongside men. After defeat by the British, colonizers confined over a million Kikuyu in fenced villages and reeducation camps. The detention system classified detainees by color code, from "black" for the recalcitrant, through shades of gray, to "white" for those who were fully reformed. To remind them of their servile status, men were forced to do women's work. The British may have won the battle, but they lost the war. African independence movements spread across the continent in 1960, leading the United Nations to pass the "Declaration on the Granting of Independence to Colonial Countries and Peoples." Former Mau Mau insurgent, Jomo Kenyatta (c. 1897–1978), was elected newly independent Kenya's first president in 1963.

EAST ASIA

China boasted the world's largest contiguous empire and population by the end of the eighteenth century. The Qing dynasty, having wrested the Mandate of Heaven away from the Ming during the seventeenth century, pressed into southernmost China in a series of civil wars and eastward into Taiwan. As Manchurian horsemen from the north, these conquerors were not Han Chinese and insisted on maintaining their ethnic distinctiveness, including wearing the long braid, which they required of all men who served them; they opposed intermarriage with ethnic Chinese as well, positioning themselves atop a racial hierarchy. While interested in European scientific and technological innovations, Qing elites under the direction of Emperor Kang-hsi compiled a five-thousand-volume encyclopedia of Chinese classics. By the end of the century they rejected overtures by the British government to import British goods. Accepting only silver payment for such highly desirable exports as tea and silk, the Qing thus isolated themselves further from the global circulation of goods. Meanwhile, Britain, heavily indebted to China because of this unfavorable balance of payments, sold opium grown in India to an increasingly addicted Chinese populace, especially in port cities such as Guangzhou. As addiction spread, Qing officials took action against opium smugglers, including dumping 1,000 tons of it into the harbor at Humen. Military skirmishes escalated into the 1840s and the first "Opium War" ended in a humiliating defeat for China. It was followed in less than twenty years by another defeat. This time Europeans invaded the imperial palace and looted treasures, including the royal Pekingese dog, whom they named Looty and gifted to Queen Victoria; a craze for the dog breed ensued, leading to a thriving black market in international dog smuggling and breeding.

The Qing remained in power until 1911, but they gradually ceded control over their own economy to foreign interests who conducted business in a growing number of treaty ports. The increasing presence of foreigners, including hundreds of Christian missionaries who established themselves in every major city, delegitimized the Qing in the eyes of many Chinese who openly revolted in the 1850s and 1890s. Taiping rebels, believing their leader was the brother of Jesus Christ, advocated equality for men and women and rejected the wealth and status hierarchies deeply embedded in Chinese tradition. Their target was the Qing dynasty, but its dependence on European military aid elevated the conflict to war in 1850. The rebellion was so widespread and well organized that it was only suppressed after fourteen years and 20 million casualties. Slaughter on that scale only further isolated the Qing and another messianic rebellion broke out in 1899. Believing spirit possession would render them invulnerable to Western firepower, martial artists formed the Heavenly Society of Righteous Fists, or Boxers, to fight Christians and eventually the imperial powers that defended them. The Boxer Rebellion was ultimately crushed by an eight-nation fighting force, half of it Japanese, illustrating to what degree Qing forces were outmatched by the turn of the century.

As early as 1903, Chinese nationalist leader Sun Yat-sen (1866–1925) praised the Boxers for their spirited resistance, seeing them as heroic, if simple-minded, patriots whose sacrifice could only be redeemed by a more modern revolution. Sun was part of a generation of Western-educated students and civil servants who advocated liberal reforms and eventual revolution. Nationalist reformers also embraced women's liberation, arguing that it was impossible for China to become strong as long as half the population was excluded from schooling or work outside the home. Sun Yat-sen's "People's Principles" of nationalism, democracy, and social welfare were embraced by women activists such as revolutionary feminist Qiu Jin (1875–1907). Qiu Jin fled a traditional marriage to study in Japan; as a poet she decried women's subordination in general, and foot binding in particular. After joining Sun's group in 1905, she joined a coup attempt and was executed in 1907. But other reformers continued the fight and sought to ban foot binding, prostitution, and pornography. In 1912, Sun Yat-sen's Revolutionary Alliance successfully overthrew the Qing emperor Puyi (1906–1967).

The alliance was short-lived. Three decades of civil war ensued after Sun's death, fought primarily by Nationalists under Chiang Kai-shek (1887–1975) and Communists under Mao Zedong (1893–1976). A distinctly Chinese form of Communism developed in the early twentieth century. While all communists shared a vision of economic equality achieved through the abolition of private property and capitalism, they disagreed about the best means to achieve these ends. Rooting its vision of a collectivist future in the peasantry, Chinese Communists departed significantly from European Communists who, following Marx and Engels, believed only the industrial working class possessed the organizational skills to overthrow capitalism. Chinese Communists were still battling feudalism and so took aim at the class of elite landowners connected to the disgraced dynasty. Gradually they also targeted the financial class in cosmopolitan port cities, and the urban and rural bureaucrats who defended private property. Mao's greatest successes occurred in rural areas but demands for absolute loyalty led to regular purges of party and military rivals. Only in 1949 did Communists prevail and establish the People's Republic of China. Winning the war did not necessarily mean they had won the hearts of the people, however. The Nationalists retreated to Taiwan and established the parallel Republic of China. Mao launched the Cultural Revolution (1966–1976) to extirpate any remaining non-Communist views, attacking especially artists, educators, and other professionals, including doctors.

Communist consolidation was possible due in part to the devastating impact of Japanese imperialism in China in the previous decades. Japan was largely isolated from globalization until the 1850s. Formerly closed to trade with the United States and Europe, Tokugawa Japan, established in 1603, was ruled by loosely knit shogunates who had preserved Japanese culture by limiting all outside influences, including Christian missionaries and converts. When US gunboats under Commodore Matthew Perry arrived in 1853 to compel trade, a coalition of military commanders agreed to trade treaties and simultaneously organized the restoration of the empire. These Meiji Revolutionaries ended the shogunate, persecuting samurai and rapidly introducing European-inspired systems of governance, commerce, manufacturing, and an army. As in many parts of the world, Japanese culture reflected increased globalization. Business interests adapted capitalism to the *zaibatsu*, meaning clique or cartel model. Wealthy families spread their investments in banking and manu-

Kobayashi Kiyochika, *Fuji with Boat at Miho in Sunshu (Shizuoka)*, triptych of woodblock prints, ink and color on paper, 1878. Metropolitan Museum of Art, New York. Public Domain.

Like the woodblock print by Katsushika Hokusai known as *The Great Wave*, this scene features the iconic Mt. Fuji, high waves, and a boat. Unlike its more famous predecessor, though, Kiyochika's rendition focuses on the changes in Japanese society: no longer are boats and mountain dwarfed by the waves, no longer does Mt. Fuji take the central pride of place. Instead, the boat is a huge paddle steamer—motorized and much larger than anything else in the image—and it flies the newly adopted flag of Japan.

facturing for export: Mitsubishi's diverse investments, for example, included shipping, oil, and insurance. Wartime production helped Mitsubishi become a giant in air and ground transportation. Literature, music, and theater combined Eastern and Western influences while Western-educated intellectuals promoted women's rights, including the right to attend political meetings and join political parties; the right to vote, however, was not granted until 1947. Although their governmental system was representative, it was highly patriarchal and became increasingly autocratic during the Great Depression of the 1930s. Emperor Hirohito (1901–1989), who claimed quasidivinity, launched an empire based on the superiority of the Japanese over all Asians. Their imperial ambitions included dominating Asia and they rapidly occupied parts of China, Vietnam, Korea, and Indonesia. After the so-called Rape of Nanking, China, where Japanese forces destroyed the city and raped up to 80,000 women in 1937, Hirohito ordered the installation of brothels known as comfort stations across the new empire, staffed by tens of thousands of women and girls, forced into sexual slavery. Expanding into the Pacific, the Japanese eventually attacked Pearl Harbor, a US military base in Hawai'i in 1941. After protracted conflicts in the Pacific theater of World War II, the United States dropped two atomic bombs on Japan, killing between 129,000 and 226,000 people, mostly civilians, instantly and others due to after effects of radiation poisoning and war. Revolutions broke out in Japan's former colonies of Korea, Indonesia, and Vietnam, which had been colonized by European powers before that. Many of them were influenced by Communism, which identified Western imperialism and its proxy rulers in its colonies as the enemy. Communist states also advocated for national self-determination, in theory, while expanding their spheres of influence during the Cold War, ushering in a new form of imperialism.

EASTERN AND CENTRAL EUROPE

Russian expansionism in the eighteenth century accelerated under Catherine the Great (r. 1762–1796) who sought to consolidate autocratic rule, securing the loyalty of nobles in exchange for land grants and the serfs who worked that land. Indeed, serfdom expanded considerably in the Urals and Siberia before it was abolished one hundred years later when Alexander II freed 23 million people in 1861. Conscripts in the military also had the status of serf; their ranks grew during the Napoleonic Wars. These forces engaged Persia successfully as Russia absorbed the trans-Caucasus region. International contests over control of the Caucasus, the region of Eurasia between Russia and Turkey, destabilized and impoverished the area in the early nineteenth century and spiked the numbers of enslaved peoples, including debtors who sold themselves or their children, hoping for a better life. Local traders transported their captives across the Black Sea to slave markets in Constantinople. Enslaved white people were trafficked through Constantinople to destinations as far-flung as Latin America and India. Russian expansionism included the Americas as well; fur traders and later Christian missionaries established their influence as far as Alaska, which it retained until it was sold to the United States in 1867 for $7.2 million.

Russia in the early twentieth century had established industrial centers and a nascent representative government, adopting a parliament after the Revolution of 1905. But Communists like Vladimir Lenin (1870–1924) believed that professional revolutionaries could organize in secret cells and proselytize for the revolution throughout the countryside, rousing peasants to defeat aristocrats. While planning a violent revolution, the Bolsheviks also formed a political party that held seats in the parliament and advocated for women's equality in addition to worker's collectives. During World War I, as Russia's position became more desperate, protesting women, striking workers, and mutinous sailors demanded "peace, land, and bread." Military high command and the tsar refused to concede defeat to the Germans, thus becoming isolated from the populace. The Bolshevik promise to end the war led millions to rally when revolution broke out again in 1917. Lenin did surrender, freeing the Central Powers to concentrate their energies on the Western Front in France. But the allies also fought to keep Russia in, to defend the alliance, the tsar, and suppress Communism. Thus, foreign and civil war erupted, ending in 1922 with the establishment of the Soviet Union by the Bolsheviks. The Bolsheviks prevailed in part because few troops rallied to the tsar and the allies had to concentrate on defeating the Central Powers. They attempted to build a new society upon the ruins of the Old Regime by confiscating private property and encouraging collective farming. Under the administration of Alexandra Kollontai (1872–1952), head of the Women's Department, Communists combated women's illiteracy, provided rural healthcare, and spread information about the new liberal divorce law. They experimented with collective nurseries and kitchens to liberate women's labor for the workforce, but their efforts were halting. Indeed, Joseph Stalin (1878–1953) ended these programs and focused on other forms of collectivization. It was not until the first five-year plan that major strides at collectivization and rapid industrialization occurred. The toll was high, however. While scholars debate the exact number, famine alone killed at least 5 million people, while millions of people who resisted collectivization, or were otherwise deemed enemies of the revolution, were killed or deported. The process also resulted in what many call an ecocide, the combined effects of pollution, overgrazing, intensive farming, and massive irrigation projects: for example, the Aral Sea is now one-third of its original size, polluted, and serves as a warning to the world about the risks of losing large bodies of fresh water.

Because they believed the overthrow of capitalism would have to take place on a global scale, Russian Communists promoted revolutions elsewhere, most notably in Germany after World War I. They also expanded their sphere of influence by colonizing parts of Central Asia and Eastern and Central Europe between the 1920s and 1940s. Soviet women's activists passed laws banning child marriage and polygamy, enabled women to access divorce, and expanded educational opportunities. Bourgeois feminist Muslims in other countries such as Turkey and Afghanistan had already instigated similar reforms, more successful to the degree that their reforms were in the service of nationalist modernity. This lent urgency to Soviet efforts, which were made rapidly and forcefully. To overcome resistance, Soviet police prosecuted men who refused to allow wives and daughters to go to school. The mass public unveilings known as the Hujum of 1927 generated the most opposition, where critics likened unveiling to prostitution. These tensions came to a violent head when traditionalists murdered some two thousand women in Uzbekistan who participated in the unveilings. Turkmen women were murdered for attempting to get divorces or for joining the Communist Party. The Soviets alienated local men, defensive of religious and especially family traditions. At the same time, Soviet state centrism also alienated local liberals, among them feminist organizations that were forbidden to meet after the occupation. They even alienated local communists who distanced themselves from the issue, strengthening the impression that women's emancipation was an imposition from Moscow. Despite these missteps, the Soviet Union maintained control of Central Asia, including Afghanistan, until 1989.

Russian expansionism reached nearly every continent but Africa. Germany, however, in the nineteenth century established an overseas empire with colonies in Africa (Namibia, Cameroon, Tanganyika, and Togo). In the twentieth century, the Nazi

Vera Mukhina, *Worker and Kolkhoznitza Woman*, stainless steel, 1937. Originally shown at the World's Fair, Paris, France, now in Moscow, Russia. Public Domain.

The monumental sculpture of a worker and kolkhoz (collective farm) woman was created by a female artist for the Soviet Pavilion of the World's Fair. Standing seventy-eight feet tall, the figures visually tower over the event. Creating an emblem of Soviet Russia, Mukhina combined the socialist hammer-and-sickle symbol (held by the male and female figure respectively), and showcased socialist ideals of gender equality, manual labor, and the powerful representation of the human figure.

An Historical Cross-Cultural Introduction   29

Opening of the Degenerate Art Exhibition, Berlin 1938. Visible from left to right are works by Emil Nolde, *Mulattin* (Mulatto Woman), Karl Schmidt-Rotluff, *Bildnis B. R.* (Berti Rosenberg) (Portrait of B. R.), Otto Müller, *Zigeunerkind mit Esel* (Gypsy child with Donkey), and Emil Nolde, *Akte und Eunuch* (Nudes and Eunuch). Newspaper photo, February 26, 1938, Süddeutsche. Sueddeutsche Zeitung Photo / Alamy Stock Photo.

The inscription above the paintings refers to the popularity of African influences on music, theater, and art in the early twentieth century. In conjunction with the display of paintings, it shows that this "anti-exhibition" of modern art mounted by the Nazi Party was a full-blown propaganda effort to promote ideas of "racial purity" and create a clear divide between who and what is "German" and who and what is not.

regime expanded its land empire. Tensions persisted over its relationship with Austria in particular; only war between Austria and Prussia in 1866 resolved who would dominate the newly formed nation. Desire for German hegemony in Europe itself was one of the triggers for World War I, and the break up of the German Empire after its defeat in 1918 was surely one of the triggers for World War II. The rise of the Nazi Party after the First World War introduced a template for a new version of an old form of land-based empire, Germany's Third Empire or Third Reich. Based on a racial hierarchy atop of which sat Aryans (by whom Nazis meant Nordic—or northern European—people), a master race would dominate all others; but first they must be united under Adolf Hitler's (1889–1945) leadership. This mandate led to the annexation of Austria in 1938; invasions of Czechoslovakia and Poland in 1939;

and the occupations of France, Denmark, and Norway in 1940. Expansion into the Soviet Union provided Aryans with territories in which to expand and slave labor that would support their goal of world domination. Nazis targeted Jews especially, deporting millions of people to labor and concentration camps during the 1940s. They also sought the reform and eventual elimination of other populations: the disabled, homosexuals, other ethnic groups such as the Roma, and political opponents, particularly Communists (the first to be interned in concentration camps). Other eugenic measures included the forced sterilization of Afro-Germans. Despite the degree to which modern authoritarian states circumscribed people's actions, resistance took many forms: assassination attempts by Hitler's own men; rescue of Jews; sabotage by French and Polish resisters; and armed revolt by Jewish partisans, most indefatigably in the Warsaw Ghetto. But ultimately it took a world war to end the empire, with an estimated 80 million lives lost, nearly 3 percent of the world's population.

By some measures, the global catastrophe was followed by a reckoning where the rule of law prevailed with thirteen trials from 1945–1949 of some surviving Nazi leadership at Nuremberg and the establishment of vigorous postwar democracies and demilitarized economies in Japan and Germany. The postwar West German government accepted responsibility for the war, paid reparations, and undertook ambitious Holocaust education campaigns, attacking all forms of hate. The United Nations, formed immediately after the war, passed a Genocide Convention as one of its first acts in 1948. Although this did not put an end to genocide, it did give the international community a means of condemning, intervening, and ultimately punishing perpetrators. Its Declaration of Universal Human Rights, modeled on the French Declaration of the Rights of Man and Citizen (1789), may have originated from the European Enlightenment but is regularly adapted to allow for more culturally specific concepts of rights, freedoms, and protections to individuals and communities.

CONCLUSION

The rise and fall of empires, a characteristic of world history since it was first recorded, can be attributed to many factors, not the least of which are the human strivings for dominance and for freedom. We noted in almost every section the dynamics in which the colonial attempts at dominance through creating spheres of influence were met with the self-determination and resistance of colonized peoples. Although freedom is a culturally relative concept, people in every time and place have challenged, weakened, and even toppled governments in its name. Such popular movements were often overtaken by educated elites planning to modernize their political and economic systems. These revolutions usually occurred against a backdrop of decaying imperial states, their dynastic and internal structures incompatible with the modern bureaucratic nation-state.

The creation of modern nations often emerged from demands for constitutional limitations on autocratic power, including a separation of powers, checks and balances, and individual political rights for at least some members of the citizenry. But these revolutions seldom addressed economic inequality, or the communal rights of groups who sought to preserve their religious or ethnic identities in the framework of modern nationalisms. Because new regimes have usually failed to deliver sufficient freedom to sufficient numbers, popular mobilizations continue. The integration of the world's peoples, accelerated by technological advances dating back to the eighteenth century, continues apace, as do revolutions. Indeed, swifter electronic communications have enabled global organizing and solidarity, even as these methods facilitate surveillance and the largely unfettered spread of disinformation. While global capitalism continues to exploit labor and the environment, and wealth inequality grows, the forms of empire that predominated over five thousand years of world history no longer exist. People toppled them. However, people's continued demands for justice today meet the same cycle of elite takeover of resistance movements, thereby requiring our continued engagement with attempts to write and rewrite resistance at the grassroots levels.

Comprehensive Timeline

Modern Worlds Comprehensive Timeline I (1450 - 1750 CE)

Events	Periods	People
	1450	Leonardo da Vinci (1452 - 1519)
1493: Papal Bull by Pope Alexander VI: the Doctrine of Discovery	1220-1974: Ethiopian Empire ruled by Solomonic Dynasty	Pico (1463 - 1494)
	1299-1922: Ottoman Empire	
	1468-1591: Songhai Empire (West Africa)	Michelangelo (1475 - 1564)
ca. 16th c.: Our Lady of Guadalupe pilgrimage established	**1480**	Ignatius of Loyola (1491 - 1556)
	1493-1810: Spread of Spanish Imperialism in the Americas	Mirabai (ca. 1498 - 1546)
	1501-1722 Safavid Empire (Shiite-Iran)	John Calvin (1509 - 1564)
1517: Martin Luther nails *Ninety-five Theses* to Wittenberg Church door (Protestant Reformation)	**1510**	
1522: Enslaved Africans rebel in Hispaniola	1517-1857: Mughal Empire (South Asia)	Ivan (IV) the Terrible (1530 - 1584)
1524: Spanish forces claim the K'iche' land	**1540**	Akbar (1542 - 1605)
1534: Church of England established		
1550s: K'iche'-Maya nobles compile the *Pop Wuj*		Galileo Galilei (1564 - 1642)
1570: Gaspar Yanga leads first successful slave uprising in Mexico	**1570**	Panditaraja Jagannatha (1572 - 1665)
	1600 1600-1868: Japanese Tokugawa Shogunate	Zera Yacob (1599 - 1692)
1613: Two-Row Wampum ("woven shell belt") Treaty between Iroquois and Dutch	1605-1694: Maroon Quilombo dos Palmares, kingdom founded by fugitive enslaved Africans (Brazil)	
	1630	
1664: Sor Juana invited to be lady-in-waiting in Viceroy's Royal Court		Sor Juana Ines de la Cruz (1648 - 1695)
1668: *Hatata* written	**1660**	Kang-hsi (1654 - 1722)
1669: First known operational reflecting telescope built by Isaac Newton	1680-1692: Puebloan independence period in Spanish colony of Santa Fe de Nuevo México	
1676: The University of San Carlos founded in Antigua, Guatemala	1682-1725: Peter the Great and the Westernization of Russia	
	1690	
1712: Carolina Colony is divided into North and South		Jorge Juan (1713 - 1773)
1716: Kang-hsi publishes *Dictionary of Chinese Characters*	**1720** 1715-1789: European Enlightenment	Antonio de Ulloa (1716 - 1795)
1746: Earthquake levels Lima, related tsunami destroys port city of Callao	1736-1796: Reign of Emperor Qianlong (China)	Benjamin Banneker (1731 - 1806)
1748: First publication of Juan and Ulloa's *Voyage to South America*	**1750**	Olaudah Equiano (1745 - 1797)

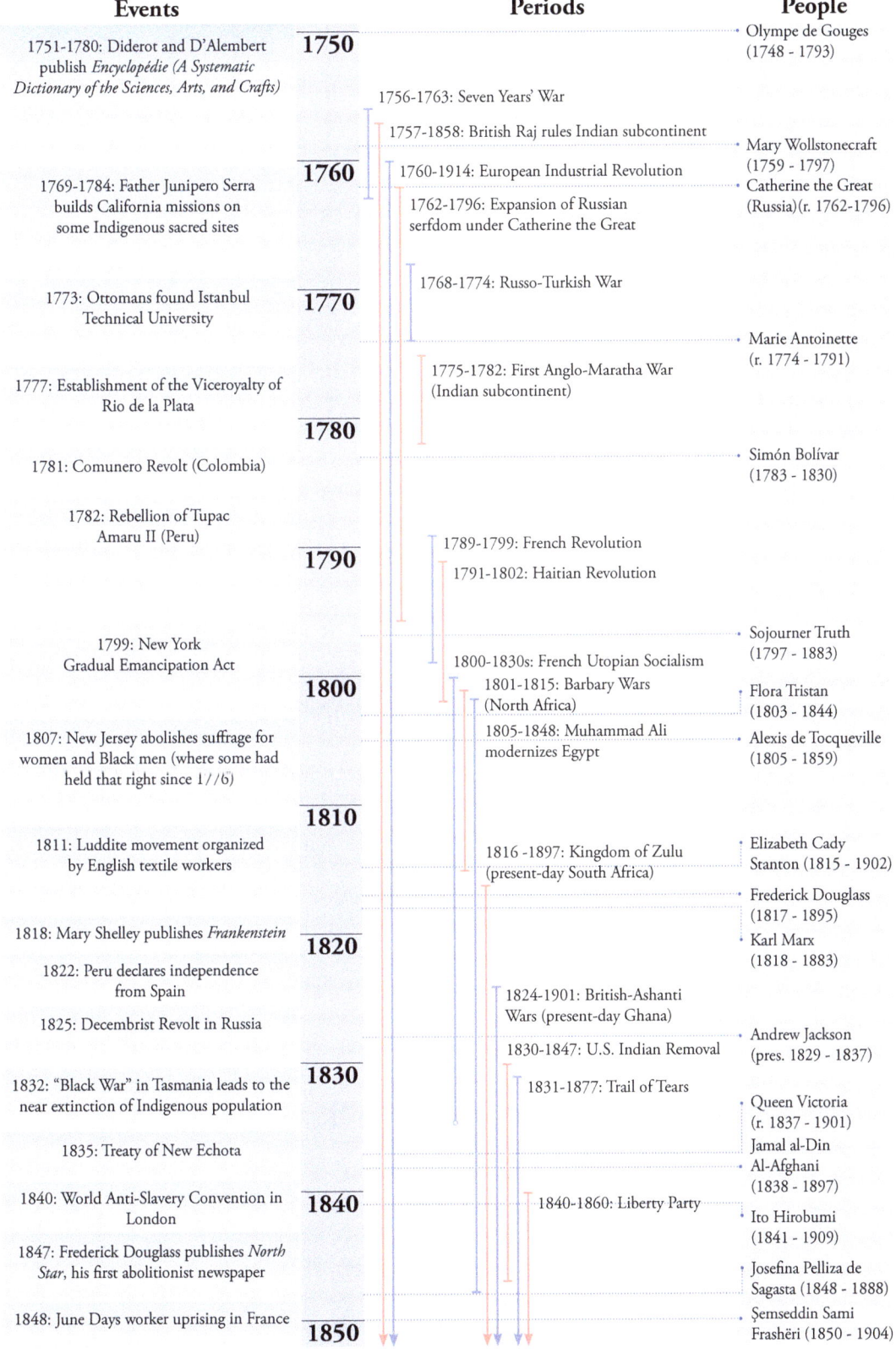

Modern Worlds Comprehensive Timeline III (1850 - 1900 CE)

Events

- 1850: First National Women's Rights Convention (Massachusetts)
- 1853: Argentina adopts earliest version of its current constitution
- 1854: Peru abolishes slavery
- 1857: Sepoy Mutiny in India
- 1861-1865: U.S. Civil War
- 1863: Emancipation Proclamation
- 1864: International Workingmen's Association founded
- 1865 (June 19): Union Army arrives in Galveston, Texas to enforce emancipation, inspiring Juneteenth celebrations
- 1866-1868: Red Cloud leads Lakota Sioux, Arapahoe, & Cheyenne forces to protect homelands
- 1870: U.S. Constitution 15th Amendment grants Black men the right to vote
- 1870-1930: 13 million Europeans immigrate to Latin America
- 1874: Impressionists, first public group art exhibition in Paris
- 1881: Tsar Alexander II assassinated (Russia)
- 1882: Great Britain gains control of Egypt
- 1886: Abolition of slavery in Cuba
- 1887: U.S. Congress passes Dawes Severalty Act
- 1890: Wounded Knee Massacre
- 1894-1895: Sino-Japanese War
- 1897: First Zionist Congress meets in Basel, Switzerland
- 1899-1902: Second Boer War in South Africa

Periods

- 1850-1864: Taiping Rebellion (China)
- 1850-1890: U.S. Golden Age of Railroads
- 1857-1920: Forced assimilation of Indigenous populations in U.S.
- 1858-1947: British Raj
- 1858-1988: Istanbul Girls' High School
- 1862-1877: Tongzhi Hui Revolt (Qing dynasty China)
- 1865-1877: Reconstruction Era (U.S.)
- 1867-1886: Height of Impressionism art movement
- 1868-1912: Meiji period (Japan)
- 1868-1898: Cuban struggle for independence from Spain
- 1871-1912: "Scramble for Africa"
- 1877-1965: Jim Crow Era (U.S.)
- 1879-1883: War of the Pacific (Chile, Peru and Bolivia)
- 1885-1899: Independent Sudan ruled by Mahdi
- 1885-Present: Indian National Congress
- 1890-1915: Period of Armenian Genocides
- 1891-1941: Italy rules Eritrea as a colony

People

- María Eugenia Echenique (1851 - 1878)
- José Martí (1853 - 1895)
- Booker T. Washington (1856 - 1915)
- Ohiyesa (1858 - 1939)
- Rabindranath Tagore (1861 - 1941)
- Ida B. Wells (1862 - 1931)
- Helena Marie Swanwick (1864 - 1939)
- Sun Yat-sen (1866 - 1925)
- W. E. B. DuBois (1868 - 1963)
- Mohandas K. Gandhi (1869 - 1948)
- José Enrique Rodó (1871 - 1917)
- Arturo A. Schomburg (1874 - 1938)
- Zitkala-Ša (1876 - 1938)
- Albert Einstein (1879 - 1955)
- Rokeya Sakhawat Hossain (1880 - 1932)
- Mustafa Kemal (Ataturk) (1881-1938)
- Benito Mussolini (1883 - 1945)
- Halidé Edib (1884 - 1964)
- Marcus Garvey (1887 - 1940)
- Gabriela Mistral (1889 - 1957)
- Ho Chi Minh (1890 - 1969)
- Bhimrao Ramji Ambedkar (1891 - 1956)
- Harry Haywood (1898 - 1985)

Modern Worlds Comprehensive Timeline IV (1900 - 1950 CE)

Events | Periods | People

1900

1904-1908: Herero and Namaqua genocide in German South West Africa (Namibia)

1900-2014: Pan African Congresses and Conferences

- Langston Hughes (1901 - 1967)
- C.L.R. James (1901 - 1989)

1905: Japan defeats Russia

1905-1920: Expressionist Art Movement
1905-1909: Niagara Civil Rights Movement

- Juan José Arévalo (1904 - 1990)

1905

1905: First Partition of Bengal

1905: Founding of *The Chicago Defender*, an African American newspaper

1906-present: National Association for the Advancement of Colored Peoples (NAACP)

- Hannah Arendt (1906 - 1975)
- Simone de Beauvoir (1908 - 1986)

1909: Triangle Shirtwaist Strike by women garment workers in New York

1910

1910-1920: Mexican Revolution

1912-1949: Republic of China

1914: Universal Negro Improvement Association (UNIA) founded

1914-1918: World War I
1916-1940: First Great Migration of African Americans

- Albert Camus (1913 - 1960)
- Sirimavo Bandaranaike (1916 - 2000)

1915

1916: *Journal of African American History* founded at Howard University

1917-1920: Influenza Pandemic
1917-1923: Russian Revolution
1918-1933: Weimar Republic
1918-1937: Harlem Renaissance

- Indira Gandhi (1917 - 1984)
- Monica Sone (1919 - 2011)

1920: Gandhi leads Indian National Congress in Non-Cooperation Movement

1920

1920: Grand National Assembly of Turkey established in Ankara

1920-1946: League of Nations
1921-1940: Mexican Muralists

- Shirley Chisholm (1924 - 2005)
- James Baldwin (1924 - 1987)

1921: Tulsa Race Massacre

1924: U.S. Congress passes Indian Citizenship Act

1925

1924: Society for Human Rights founded, first gay rights organization in Chicago

- Frantz Fanon (1925 - 1961)
- Josef Stalin (r. 1927 - 1953)
- Martin Luther King Jr. (1929 - 1968)

1929: U.S. Stock Market Crash

1931: Japan invades Manchuria (China)

1930

1930-1936: U.S. Dust Bowl

- Sandra Day O'Connor (1930 - Present)
- Ruth Klüger (1931 - 2020)

1931: Brazilian Black Front formed in Sao Paulo

1935: Mary McLeod Bethune founds the National Council for Negro Women

- Nina Simone (1933 - 2003)

1935

1935: Nuremberg Laws bars citizenship for Jewish, Black, and Romani peoples

1936-1939: Spanish Civil War
1937-1945: Estado Novo (Brazil)

1938: South African Press Association founded

- Kofi Annan (1938 - 2018)

1939-1945: World War II

1942: Dine (Navajo) develop code used for encrypted messages by U.S. in WWII

1940

1942: Ethiopian Empire abolishes slavery

- Stephen Hawking (1942 - 2018)

1942: Internment of Japanese-Americans begins

1945: Liberation of Auschwitz

1944-1954: Guatemalan "Ten Years of Spring"

- Wilma Mankiller (1945 - 2010)

1945

1948: Costa Rica abolishes army

1946-1958: French Fourth Republic

1948: United Nations proclaims Universal Declaration of Human Rights

1949: The Nationalist Party adopts Apartheid (South Africa)

1950

from "Books That Have Influenced Me" by Chandrasekhara Venkata Raman

Introduction

Even before Chandrasekhara Venkata Raman (1888–1970) had begun his Nobel Prize–winning study of the scattering of light, he had achieved international renown for his work in physics. The prize would cement his place as one of the founders of modern science, and, as the first Physics Nobel awarded to a non-European (in 1930), it became an important symbol in the struggle for Indian independence. Colonialism, after all, had its roots in scientific racism and an implicit assumption that Western ways of thinking, and thus Western thinkers, were the path to the "true" understanding of nature. Raman's scientific legacy spans multiple fields of physics and his discovery of the "anomalous scattering of light" became a decisive moment in the development of quantum mechanics. However, Raman's legacy also includes a cultural component for creating institutions, journals, and national academies dedicated to the instruction and advancement of science.

In his childhood and early school years, Raman grew up in a comfortable, but humble, home filled with books and music. His father, Chandrasekhara Iyer, broke from his agrarian Brahmin heritage to attend a British school and became a teacher of mathematics and physics. His mother, Parvati Ammal, who Raman credits for his love of languages, came from a family of Sanskrit scholars. Raman completed high

> **SNAPSHOT BOX**
>
> LANGUAGE: English
> PUBLISHED: 1947, India
> GENRE: Magazine essay
> TAGS: Autobiography and Testimony; Education; Poetry, Music, Literature; Science; Ways of Knowing

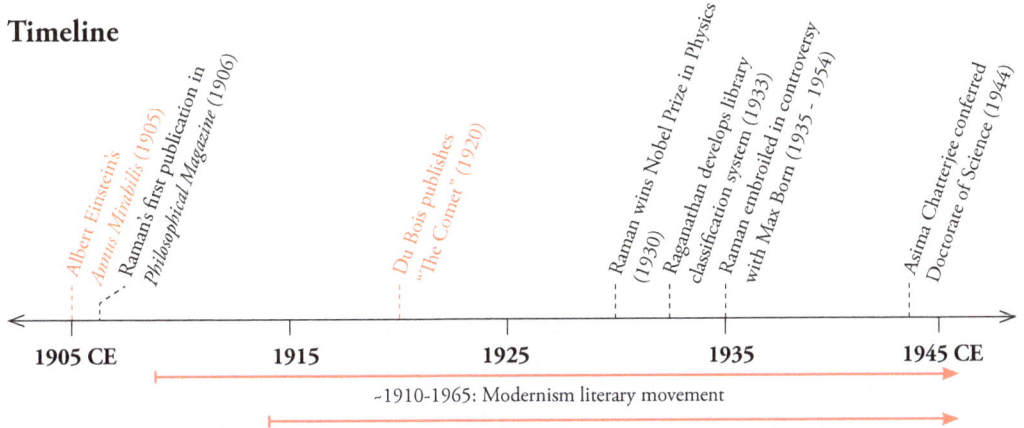

school at eleven and his intermediate exam at thirteen (from the college where his father was lecturer in physics) and in both achieved first rank (equivalent to valedictorian) earning him entrance into the prestigious Presidency College in Madras. There he studied with mostly European teachers and would go on to win gold medals in both English and physics on his way to a bachelor's degree and another first rank at only fifteen years old.

His teachers advised Raman to continue his education in England, but on account of his frail health, his doctor forbade it. Raman, years later, recounted of this moment, "I shall ever be grateful to this man" for allowing him to continue his education and career in the culture and tradition of his native India. So, instead, Raman continued his graduate studies at Presidency College where he enjoyed great academic freedom—attending lectures infrequently and rather making use of open access to the library and laboratory. While still a graduate student, he published two scientific papers in the *Philosophical Magazine* (a prestigious scientific journal in London). His publications attracted the attention of J. W. S. Lord Rayleigh, an influential physicist whose works had been an inspiration for Raman.

In 1907, Raman completed his master's degree. Even though he again earned the highest rank and graduated from the most prestigious college in southern India, there were practically no opportunities for him to pursue his passions as a scientist. Studying in England was also a requirement for working in the Indian Civil Service, leaving Raman to pursue an appointment with the Financial Civil Service (FCS), the second most lucrative and respected position within the colonial government for Indians. In his late teens, Raman was appointed assistant accountant general in the bustling city of Calcutta, capital of British India, a very well-paying position.

But, his love for science could not be deterred. In Calcutta, Raman encountered the Indian Association for the Cultivation of Science (IACS), a private research laboratory. There, Raman arranged to use laboratory space and continue his own research. From 1907–1917, Raman simultaneously ascended the ranks in the FCS and, moonlighting at the IACS, published broadly in the areas of liquids, optics, and acoustics, continuing to draw attention from scientists in Europe. In 1917, Raman accepted a job as professor of physics at Calcutta University.

He used his position to support numerous students' and colleagues' research endeavors and to advocate for the development and creation of institutions of science such as the IACS, Calcutta Physical Society, and the *Indian Journal of Physics*. On February 28, 1928, Raman observed that molecules excited by one color of light emitted light of two colors. Imagine, if you shine a green laser pointer at the wall, green light reflects back and you see a green dot. In what would come to be called the "Raman effect" a small amount of that light changed color. By filtering out the original light, Raman was able to observe the second color, which was characteristic of the scattering material. Raman received the Nobel Prize in Physics in 1930 for this discovery, and February 28 is still celebrated in India as National Science Day.

Raman's legacy does not end with this award; he had a lifetime of research uncovering the mysteries of the physical world as well as a devotion to the improvement of the institutions and appreciation of science in India. In public speeches, Raman declared that the men and women of India were just as capable as the Europeans but were being inhibited only by a "defeatist spirit," which was contrary to their identity and history.[6] His language shows the multilayered nature of colonial Indian science. Raman simultaneously participated in European scientific institutions and infused his own intellectual traditions such as Indian music. Even as he created Indian journals and academies modeled in the British and German styles, he bemoaned having to accept his Nobel Prize standing under the Union Jack (flag of the British Empire). In dealing with his Western colleagues Raman faced prejudicial **orientalism** (patronizing stereotyping toward Asian societies), but he continued, in defiance, to always wear his trademarked turban. How does Raman's strategy reflect a navigation of the impact of colonialism? In this reading, Raman cites several authors who are inheritors and creators of Western forms of knowledge. How does this list reflect an approach to building support for an emerging nationalism?

James Perkins
Department of Physics and Astronomy

---

6. G. Venkataraman, *Journey into Light: Life and Science of C. V. Raman*, Indian Academy of Science (New Delhi: Bangalore and Indian National Science Academy 1988), 503–4. Quote is from Patna University Convocation in 1941.

> **PRE-READING PARS**
>
> 1. Make a list of some books you have been assigned to read, and another of ones you've discovered for yourself. What differences do you note between the two lists?
> 2. What books or other types of media have influenced you? Make a list.

From Books That Have Influenced Me: A Symposium

As has been remarked by Robert Louis Stevenson in a charming little essay on this subject, it is scarcely possible to speak of books that have influenced one without finding oneself engaged on an auto-biographical essay of a sort. A man's outlook on the problems of life is necessarily moulded by the influences to which he has been subject, and especially by the influences brought to bear on him when at an impressionable age. The share which books have had in shaping his mental outlook and ultimately also his career in life, is, I fancy a highly variable one, and to no small extent dependent on the person's environment at home and at school in his early days. Indeed, a good home and a good school may be judged by the kind of books they put in the way of the growing young person for him to feed his mind and his emotions upon. I believe it is the exception rather than the rule for the books which are formally taught at school and at college to exercise any profound influence on the mind of the student. The element of compulsion introduced in the prescription of books for study is usually fatal to that attitude of mind which is necessary for the full appreciation of their contents. It is the books the merits of which you have, so to say, discovered for yourself, that really influence you.

The failure to recognise this elementary fact of human psychology, namely the antithesis between choice and compulsion, is responsible for the unfruitful character of a vast amount of scholastic effort in the way of both teaching and learning. I can tell you here a story about myself or rather against myself in this connection. Forty-five years ago, a well-meaning University prescribed Robert Louis Stevenson's well-known story "Kidnapped" as an English text for the First Arts course. I do not remember the precise number of times this text was taught or lectured upon in class, or the precise number of times I read through the book during the two years' course of study for the examination. The copy I purchased and used disappeared in due course. One evening, a couple of years ago, a copy of Stevenson's "Kidnapped" beautifully printed and bound caught my eye at a Railway bookstall. I was tempted to buy it and took it home and started reading the book before going to bed. Believe it or not, the story or rather the manner of its telling, gripped me so powerfully that I had to finish reading the whole book at a sitting before retiring for the night. I had, so to say, discovered Stevenson's magic charm of writing for myself. Since then, I have read everything that Stevenson wrote with the keenest enjoyment.

I finished my school and college career and my University examinations at the age of eighteen. In this short span of years had been compressed the study of four languages and of a great variety of diverse subjects, in several cases up to the highest University standards. A list of all the volumes I had to study would be of terrifying length. Did these books influence me? Yes, in the narrow sense of making me tolerably familiar with subjects so diverse as Ancient Greek and Roman history, modern Indian and European History, Formal Logic, Economics, Monetary Theory and Public Finance, the later Sanskrit writers and the minor English authors, to say nothing of Physiography, Chemistry and a dozen branches of Pure and Applied Mathematics, and of Experimental and Theoretical Physics. But out of all this welter of subjects and books, can I pick out anything that helped really to mould my mental and spiritual outlook and determine my chosen path in life? Yes, I can and I shall mention three books.

A purposeful life needs an axis or hinge to which it is firmly fixed and yet around which it can freely revolve. As I see it, this axis or hinge has been, in my own case, strangely enough, not the love of science nor even the love of Nature, but a certain abstract idealism or belief in the value of the human spirit and the virtue of human endeavour and achievement. The nearest point to which I can trace this source of ideals is my recollection of reading Edwin Arnold's great book, *The Light of Asia*. I remember being powerfully moved by the story of Siddhartha's great renunciation, of his search for truth and of his final enlightenment. This was at a time when I was young enough to be impressionable, and the reading of the book fixed firmly in my mind the idea that this capacity for renunciation in the pursuit of exalted aims is the very essence of human greatness. This is not an unfamiliar idea to us in India, but it is not easy to live up to. It has always seemed to me a surprising and regrettable fact that the profound teaching of the Buddha has not left a deeper and stronger impress on the life of our country of which he was the greatest son that ever lived.

The next of the books that I have to mention is one of the most remarkable works of all time, namely, *The Elements of Euclid*. Familiarity with some parts of Euclid and a certain dislike of its formalism have dethroned this great work from the apparently unassailable position which it occupied in the esteem of the learned world for an almost incredibly long period of time. Indeed, my own early reactions to the compulsory study of Euclid were anything but favourable. The reason for this is, I think, to be found in the excessive emphasis placed on the subject as an intellectual discipline and the undue attention given to details as distinguished from its broader aspects. To put it a little differently, the student of Euclid is invited to look at the trees and to examine their branches and twigs so minutely, that he ceases even to be conscious of the existence of the wood. The real value of Geometry appears when we consider it as a whole, not as merely as the properties of straight lines, triangles and circles, but of everything else, curves, figures and solids of all kinds. Thus regarded, Geometry makes a profound appeal both to our senses and to our intellect. Indeed, of all branches of Mathematics, it is that which links most closely what we see with the eye with what we perceive by reasoning. The ancient Greeks had a fine sense of the value of intellectual discipline, they had also a fine sense of the beautiful. They loved Geometry just because it had both these appeals. In my early years, it was a great struggle for me to learn to overcome the dislike of the formalism of Euclid and gradually to perceive the fascination and beauty of the subject. Not until many years later, however, did I fully appreciate the central position of Geometry in relation to all natural knowledge. I can illustrate this relationship by a thousand examples but will content myself with remarking that every mineral found in Nature, every crystal made by man, every leaf, flower or fruit that we see growing, every living thing from the smallest to the largest that walks on earth, flies in the air or swims in the waters or lives deep down on the ocean floor, speaks aloud of the fundamental role of Geometry in Nature. The pages of Euclid are like the opening bars of the music in the grand opera of Nature's great drama. So to say, they lift the veil and show to our vision a glimpse of a vast world of natural knowledge awaiting study.

Of all the great names in the world of learning that have come down to us from the remote past, that of Archimedes, by common consent, occupies the foremost place. Speaking of the modern world, the supremest figure, in my judgment is that of Herman Von Helmholtz. In the range and depth of his knowledge, in the clearness and profundity of his scientific vision, he easily transcended all other names I could mention, even including Isaac Newton. Rightly he has been described as the intellectual Colossus of the nineteenth century. It was my great good fortune, while I was still a student at college, to have possessed a copy of an English translation of his great work on "The Sensations of Tone." As is well known, this was one of Helmholtz's masterpieces. It treats the subject of music and musical instruments not only with profound knowledge and insight, but also with extreme clarity of language and expression. I discovered this book for myself and read it with the keenest interest and attention. It can be said without exaggeration that it profoundly influenced my intellectual outlook. For the first time, I understood from its perusal what scientific research really meant and how it could be undertaken. I also gathered from it a variety of problems for research which were later to occupy my attention and keep me busy for many years. Helmholtz had written yet another great masterpiece entitled "The Physiology of Vision." Unfortunately, this was not available to me as it had not then been translated into the English language.

Natesan, B., and C. V. Raman. "II. Sir C. V. Raman." In *Books That Have Influenced Me: A Symposium*, 21–29. Madras: G. A. Natesan, 1947.

POST-READING PARS

1. Revisit your book lists. Now that you have completed this reading, do you notice any new patterns?
2. Are there any books that, seeing them later in your life in a used bookstand, you might want to reread? How do you think that experience will be different having chosen to read it as opposed to it having been assigned?

Inquiry Corner

Content Question:	**Critical Question:**
For Raman, what is the "axis around which purposeful life freely revolves"?	Critically analyze Raman's struggle with compulsion and choice in his intellectual experience.
Comparative Questions:	**Connection Question:**
Consider how Raman's career was not immediately related to his college education and passions. Are there other people you've read in this class or artists who took nonlinear paths in their education, passions, and careers? Compare how their journeys were parts of their success?	How does having a broad set of interests and exposure to diverse perspectives contribute to your interactions in work, family, or other contexts?

BEYOND THE CLASSROOM

» What have you read/learned/experienced so far in college that you think will have a lasting impact on you?
» Do you have a plan for including lifelong learning or other educational pursuits after you graduate? What sources do you think you will seek out in your lifetime that will expand your learning and understanding?

from *Hatata* by Zera Yacob

SNAPSHOT BOX

LANGUAGE: Ge'ez
DATE: 1668
LOCATION: Ethiopia
INFLUENCES: Jewish, Christian, and Muslim scriptures
TAGS: Autobiography and Testimony; Education; Ethics and Morality; Family; Gender and Identity; Psyche; Religion; Tradition; Ways of Knowing

Introduction

Zera Yacob (1599–1692) was born in Axum in what is now present-day Ethiopia. Christianity was practiced in Ethiopia beginning in the fourth century. In 1622, the emperor, Susenyos I (r. 1606–1632), converted to Catholicism and decreed Orthodox Catholicism to be the state religion. By the 1620s, Portuguese **Jesuit** missionaries began to make their presence felt in Ethiopia, especially through building schools. Zera Yacob was from a poor farming family that made sacrifices so that he could attend one of these Jesuit schools. There his teachers noticed him to be thoughtful and "quick to learn" and encouraged him to further study. Excelling at literature and composition Yacob was promoted to a school where he spent ten years studying the Bible and other Christian texts, as well as Jewish and Islamic writings. He became a teacher following this schooling. Following the emperor's decree, those who held ideas that fell outside of the sanctioned canon were subject to persecution. By then, Yacob had become known for teaching that no religion was superior and that reason was the logical underpinning of the **Abrahamic** religions (Christianity, Judaism, and Islam all recognize the prophet Abraham as a forefather). Because his views on religion made him an enemy to some, in 1627 he fled to the countryside. There he eventually made his home in a cave in a secluded valley. Alone for two years (1631–1632) he contemplated what he judged to be the "important questions" of life, such as equality and the true character of religion.

Timeline

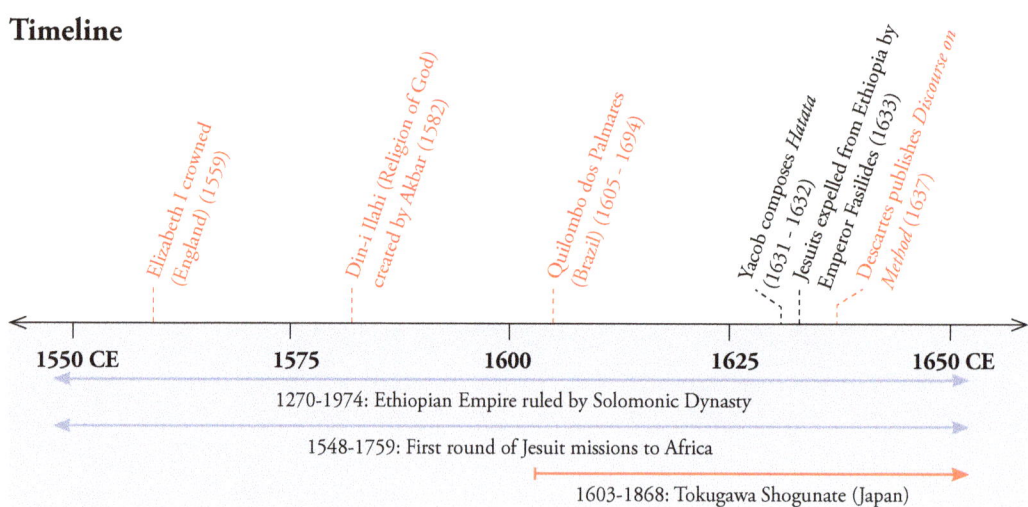

"I have learnt more while living alone in a cave than when I was living with scholars. What I wrote in this book is very little; but in my cave I have meditated on many other such things" (*Hatata*, Chapter 9).

After Emperor Susenyos's death, persecution in Ethiopia declined. Yacob left his seclusion and returned to the outside world. Still, he never revisited his home in Axum, but rather wandered, finally settling in Emfraz in the Amhara District of Ethiopia. There he became the scribe for a rich man and the tutor for his sons. Rejecting the monastic life and the common practice of polygamy, both of which he judged as counter to the reason that he believed underlay religious ethics, he married a servant in his employer's house. One of the sons that he tutored, Walad Heywat, eventually persuaded Yacob to write down the ideas he had developed over the past thirty years in what became known as *Hatata* (*Inquiry*). One has to wonder how that conversation might have gone?

The philosophy Yacob developed during his time withdrawn from society articulated his views on race, gender, and reason and highlighted his rejection of the supremacy of any one religion. Rene Descartes's *Discourse on Methods*, published in 1637 in Paris, is considered by historians as the document that launched the European Enlightenment foregrounding ideas about equality, freedom of religion, and reason. One could argue that Yacob's proposed ideas pushed the logic of religious pluralism the furthest in comparison to others being advanced at, or after, this time. How might you argue for or against this statement? What might be some of the positive and negative considerations in making such associations? What might be some of the pitfalls that anyone making such a comparison should be aware? Unfortunately, Yacob's *Hatata* has not been widely read outside of Ethiopia, probably because it has seldom been translated.

Alvis Dunn
Department of History

> **PRE-READING PARS**
>
> 1. In what ways might being alone and away from society influence a person's thinking? Feelings? Faith?
> 2. Brainstorm one or two examples of when law and religion intersect.

from *Hatata* (*Inquiry*)

Later on I thought, saying to myself: "Is everything that is written in the Holy Scriptures true?" Although I thought much about these things I understood nothing, so I said to myself: "I shall go and consult scholars and thinkers; they will tell me the truth." But afterwards I thought, saying to myself: "What will men tell me other than what is in their heart?" Indeed each one says: "My faith is right, and those who believe in another faith believe in falsehood, and are the enemies of God." These days the Frang [Europeans, Catholics] tell us: "Our faith is right, yours is false." We on the other hand tell them: "It is not so; your faith is wrong, ours is right." If we also ask the Mohammedans and the Jews, they will claim the same thing, and who would be the judge for such a kind of argument? No single human being can judge: for all men are plaintiffs and defendants between themselves. Once I asked a Frang scholar many things concerning our faith; he interpreted them all according to his own faith. Afterwards I asked a well-known Ethiopian scholar and he also interpreted all things according to his own faith. If I had asked the Mohammedans and the Jews, they also would have interpreted according to their own faith; then, where could I obtain a judge that tells the truth? As my faith appears true to me, so does another one find his own faith true; but truth is one. While thinking over this matter, I said: "O my creator, wise among the wise and just among the just, who created me with an intelligence, help me to understand, for men lack wisdom and truthfulness; as David said: 'No man can be relied upon.'"

I thought further and said: "Why do men lie over problems of such great importance, even to the point of destroying themselves?" and they seemed to do so because although they pretend to know all, they know nothing. Convinced they know all, they do not attempt to investigate the truth. As David said: "Their hearts are curdled like milk." Their heart is curdled because they assume what they have heard from their predecessors and they do not inquire whether it is true or false. But I said: "O Lord! who strike me down with such torment, it is fitting that I know your judgement. You chastise me with truth and admonish me with mercy. But never let my head be anointed with the oil of sinners and of masters in lying: make me understand, for you created me with intelligence." I asked myself: "If I am intelligent, what is it I understand?" And I said: "I understand there is a creator, greater than all creatures; since from his overabundant greatness, he created things that are so great. He is intelligent who understands all, for he created us as intelligent from the abundance of his intelligence; and we ought to worship him, for he is the master of all things. If we pray to him, he will listen to us; for he is almighty." I went on saying in my thought: "God did not create me intelligent without a purpose, that is to look for him and to grasp him and his wisdom in the path he has opened for me and to worship him as long as I live." And still thinking on the same subject, I said to myself:

"Why is it that all men do not adhere to truth, instead of believing falsehood?" The cause seemed to be the nature of man which is weak and sluggish. Man aspires to know truth and the hidden things of nature, but his endeavour is difficult and can only be attained with great labour and patience, as Solomon said: "With the help of wisdom I have been at pains to study all that is done under heaven; oh, what a weary task God has given mankind to labour at!" Hence people hastily accept what they have heard from their fathers and shy from any critical examination. But God created man to be the master of his own actions, so that he will be what he wills to be, good or bad. If a man chooses to be wicked he can continue in this way until he receives the punishment he deserves for his wickedness. But being carnal, man likes what is of the flesh; whether they are good or bad, he finds ways and means through which he can satisfy his carnal desire. God did not create man to be evil, but to choose what he would like to be, so that he may receive his reward if he is good or his condemnation if he is bad. If a liar, who desires to achieve wealth or honours among men, needs to use foul means to obtain them, he will say he is convinced this falsehood was for him a just thing. To those people who do not want to search, this action seems to be true, and they believe in the liar's strong faith. I ask you in how many falsehoods do our people believe in? They believe wholeheartedly in astrology and other calculations, in the mumbling of secret words, in omens, in the conjuration of devils and in all kinds of magical art and in the utterances of soothsayers. They believe in all these because they did not investigate the truth but listened to their predecessors. Why did these predecessors lie unless it was for obtaining wealth and honours? Similarly, those who wanted to rule the people said: "We were sent by God to proclaim the truth to you"; and the people believed them. Those who came after them accepted their fathers' faith without question: rather, as a proof of their faith, they added to it by including stories of signs and omens. Indeed, they said: "God did these things"; and so they made God a witness of falsehood and a party to liars.

To the person who seeks it, truth is immediately revealed. Indeed he who investigates with the pure intelligence set by the creator in the heart of each man and scrutinizes the order and laws of creation, will discover the truth. Moses said: "I have been sent by God to proclaim to you his will and his law"; but those who came after him added stories of miracles that they claimed had been wrought in Egypt and on Mount Sinai and attributed them to Moses. But to an inquisitive mind they do not seem to be true. For in the Books of Moses, one can find a wisdom that is shameful and that fails to agree with the wisdom of the creator or with the order and the laws of creation. Indeed, by the will of the creator, and the law of nature, it has been ordained that man and woman would unite in a carnal embrace to generate children, so that human beings will not disappear from the earth. Now this mating, which is willed by God in his law of creation, cannot be impure since God does not stain the work of his own hands. But Moses considered that act as evil; but our intelligence teaches us that he who says such a thing is wrong and makes his creator a liar. Again, they said that the law of Christianity is from God, and miracles are brought forth to prove it. But our intelligence tells and confirms to us with proofs that marriage springs from the law of the creator; and yet monastic law renders this wisdom of the creator ineffectual, since it prevents the generation of children and extinguishes mankind. The law of Christians which propounds the superiority of monastic life over marriage is false and cannot come from God. How can the violation of the law of the creator stand superior to his wisdom, or can man's deliberation correct the word of God? Similarly, Mohammed said: "The orders I pass to you are given to me by God"; and there was no lack of writers to record miracles proving Mohammed's mission, and people believed in him. But we know that the teaching of Mohammed could not have come from God; those who will be born both male and female are equal in number; if we count men and women living in an area, we find as many women as men; we do not find eight or ten women for every man; for the law of creation orders one man to marry one woman. If one man marries ten women, then nine men will be without wives. This violates the order of creation and the laws of nature and it ruins the usefulness of marriage; Mohammed, who taught in the name of God, that one man could marry many wives, is not sent from God. These few things I examined about marriage.

Similarly, when I examine the remaining laws, such as the Pentateuch, the law of the Christians and the law of Islam, I find many things which disagree with the truth and the justice of our creator that our intelligence reveals to us. God indeed has illuminated the heart of man with understanding by which he can see the good and evil, recognize the licit and the illicit, distinguish truth from error, "and by your light we see the light, oh Lord"! If we use this light of our heart properly, it cannot deceive us; the purpose of this light which our creator gave us is to be saved by it, and not to be ruined by it. Everything that the light of our intelligence shows us comes from 'the source of truth, but what men say comes from the source of lies and our intelligence teaches us that all that the creator established is right. The creator in his kind wisdom has made blood to flow monthly from the womb of women. And the life of a woman requires this flow of blood in order to generate children; a woman who has no menstruation is barren and cannot have children, because she is impotent by nature. But Moses and Christians have defiled the wisdom of the creator; Moses even considers impure all the things that such a woman touches; this law of Moses impedes marriage and the entire life of a woman and it spoils the law of mutual help, prevents the bringing up of children and destroys love. Therefore, this law of Moses cannot spring from him who created woman. Moreover, our intelligence tells us that we should bury our dead brothers. Their corpses are impure only if we follow the wisdom of Moses; they are not, however, if we follow the wisdom of our creator who made us out of dust that we may return to dust. God does not change into impurity the order he imposes on all creatures with great wisdom, but man attempts to render it impure that he may glorify the voice of falsehood.

The Gospel also declares: "He who does not leave behind father, mother, wife and children is not worthy of God." This forsaking corrupts the nature of man. God does not accept that his creature destroy itself, and our intelligence tells us that abandoning our father and our mother helpless in their old age is a great sin; the Lord is not a god that loves malice; those who desert their children are worse than the wild animals, that never forsake their offspring. He who abandons his wife abandons her to adultery and thus violates the order of creation and the laws of nature. Hence what the Gospel says on this subject cannot come from God. Likewise, the Mohammedans said that it is right to go and buy a man as if he were an animal. But with our intelligence we understand that this Mohammedan law cannot come from the creator of man who made us equal, like brothers, so that we call our creator our father. But Mohammed made the weaker man the possession of the stronger and equated a rational creature with irrational animals; can this depravity be attributed to God?

God does not order absurdities, nor does he say: "Eat this, do not eat that; today eat, tomorrow do not eat; do not eat meat today, eat it tomorrow," unlike the Christians who follow the laws of fasting. Neither did God say to the Mohammedans: "Eat during the night, but do not eat during the day," nor similar and like things. Our reason teaches us that we should eat of all things which do no harm to our health and our nature, and that we should eat each day as much as is required for our sustenance. Eating one day, fasting the next endangers health; the law of fasting reaches beyond the order of the creator who created food for the life of man and wills that we eat it and be grateful for it; it is not fitting that we abstain from his gifts to us. If there are people who argue that fasting kills the desire of the flesh, I shall answer them: "The concupiscence of the flesh by which a man is attracted to a woman and a woman to a man springs from the wisdom of the creator; it is improper to do away with it; but we should act according to the well-known law that God established concerning legitimate intercourse." God did not put a purposeless concupiscence into the flesh of men and of all animals; rather he planted it in the flesh of man as a root of life in this world and a stabilizing power for each creature in the way destined for it. In order that this concupiscence lead us not to excess, we should eat according to our needs, because overeating and drunkenness result in ill health and shoddiness in work. A man who eats according to his needs on Sunday and during the fifty days does not sin, similarly he who eats on Friday and on the days before Easter does not sin. For God created man with the same necessity for food on each day and during each month. The Jews, the Christians and the Mohammedans did not understand the work of God when they instituted the law of fasting; they lie when they say that God imposed fasting upon us and forbade us to eat; for God our creator gave us food that we support ourselves by it, not that we abstain from it.

I said to myself: "Why does God permit liars to mislead his people?" God has indeed given reason to all and everyone so that they may know truth and falsehood, and the power to choose between the two as they will. Hence if it is truth we want, let us seek it with our reason which God has given us so that with it we may see that which is needed for us from among all the necessities of nature. We cannot, however, reach truth through the doctrine of man, for all men are liars. If on the contrary we prefer falsehood, the order of the creator and the natural law imposed on the whole of nature do not perish thereby, but we ourselves perish by our own error. God sustains the world by his order which he himself has established and which man cannot destroy, because the order of God is stronger than the order of men. Therefore, those who believe that monastic life is superior to marriage are they themselves drawn to marriage because of the might of the order of the creator; those who believe that fasting brings righteousness to their soul eat when they feel hungry; and those who believe that he who has given up his goods is perfect are drawn to seek them again on account of their usefulness, as many of our monks have done. Likewise, all liars would like to break the order of nature: but it is not possible that they do not see their lie broken down. But the creator laughs at them, the Lord of creation derides them. God knows the right way to act, but the sinner is caught in the snare set by himself. Hence a monk who holds the order of marriage as impure will be caught in the snare fornication and of other carnal sins against nature and of grave sickness. Those who despise riches will show their hypocrisy in the presence of kings and of wealthy persons in order to acquire these goods. Those who desert their relatives for the sake of God lack temporal assistance in times of difficulty and in their old age, they begin to blame God and men and to blaspheme. Likewise, all those who violate the law of the creator fall into the trap made by their own hands. God permits error and evil among men because our souls in this world live in a land of temptation, in which the chosen ones of God are put to the test, as the wise Solomon said: "God has put the virtuous to the test and proved them worthy to be with him; he has tested them like gold in a furnace and accepted them as a holocaust." After our death, when we go back to our creator, we shall see how God made all things in justice and great wisdom and that all his ways are truthful and upright. It is clear that our soul lives after the death of our flesh; for in this world our desire for happiness is not fulfilled; those in need desire to possess, those who possess desire more, and though man owned the whole world, he is not satisfied and craves for more. This inclination of our nature shows us that we are created not only for this life, but also for the coming world; there the souls which have fulfilled the will of the creator will be perpetually satisfied and will not look for other things. Without this inclination the nature of man would be deficient and would not obtain that of which it has the greatest need. Our soul has the power of having the concept of God and of seeing him mentally; likewise, it can conceive of immortality. God did not give this power purposelessly; as he gave the power, so did he give the reality. In this world complete justice is not achieved: wicked people are in possession of the goods of this world in a satisfying degree, the humble starve; some wicked men are happy, some good men are sad, some evil men exult with joy;

some righteous men weep. Therefore, after our death there must be another life and another justice, a perfect one, in which retribution will be made to all according to their deeds, and those who have fulfilled the will of the creator revealed through the light of reason and have observed the law of their nature will be rewarded. The law of nature is obvious, because our reason clearly propounds it, if we examine it. But men do not like such inquiries; they choose to believe in the words of men rather than to investigate the will of their creator.

The will of God is known by this short statement from our reason that tells us: "Worship God your creator and love all man as yourself." Moreover, our reason says: "Do not do unto others that which you do not like done to you, but do unto others as you would like others to do unto you." The decalogue of the Pentateuch expresses the will of the creator accepting the precept about the observance of the Sabbath, for our reason says nothing of the observance of the Sabbath. But the prohibitions of killing, stealing, lying, adultery: our reason teaches us these and similar ones. Likewise, the six precepts of the Gospel are the will of the creator. For indeed we desire that men show mercy to us; it therefore is fitting that we ourselves show the same mercy to the others, as much as it is within our power. It is the will of God that we keep our life and existence in this world. It is the will of the creator that we come into and remain in this life, and it is not right for us to leave it against his holy will. The creator himself wills that we adorn our life with science and work; for such an end did he give us reason and power. Manual labour comes from the will of God, because without it the necessities of our life cannot be fulfilled. Likewise, marriage of one man with one woman and education of children. Moreover, there are many other things which agree with our reason and are necessary for our life or for the existence of mankind. We ought to observe them, because such is the will of our creator, and we ought to know that God does not create us perfect but creates us with such a reason as to know that we are to strive for perfection as long as we live in this world, and to be worthy for the reward that our creator has prepared for us in his wisdom. It was possible for God to have created us perfect and to make us enjoy beatitude on earth; but he did not will to create us in this way; instead he created us with the capacity of striving for perfection, and placed us in the midst of the trials of the world so that we may become perfect and deserve the reward that our creator will give us after our death; as long as we live in this world we ought to praise our creator and fulfill his will and be patient until he draws us unto him, and beg from his mercy that he will lessen our period of hardship and forgive our sins and faults which we committed through ignorance, and enable us to know the laws of our creator and to keep them.

Now as to prayer, we always stand in need of it because our rational nature requires it. The soul endowed with intelligence that is aware that there is a God who knows all, conserves all, rules all, is drawn to him so that it prays to him and asks him to grant things good and to be freed from evil and sheltered under the hand of him who is almighty and for whom nothing is impossible, God great and sublime who sees all that is above and beneath him, holds all, teaches all, guides all, our Father, our

Creator, our Protector, the reward for our souls, merciful, kind, who knows each of our misfortunes, takes pleasure in our patience, creates us for life and not for destruction, as the wise Solomon said: "You, Lord, teach all things, because you can do all things and overlook men's sins so that they can repent. You love all that exists, you hold nothing of what you have made in abhorrence, you are indulgent and merciful to all." God created us intelligent so that we may meditate on his greatness, praise him and pray to him in order to obtain the needs of our body and soul. Our reason which our creator has put in the heart of man teaches all these things to us. How can they be useless and false?

Yacob, Zera. "God, Faith, and the Nature of Knowledge." In *The Source of African Philosophy: The Ethiopian Philosophy of Man*, edited by Claude Sumner. Stuttgart, Germany: F. Steiner Verlag Wiesbaden, 1986.

POST READING PARS

1. In what ways might Yacob's time away from society have influenced his thinking? Feelings? Faith?
2. Identify a few critiques of religious practices and laws found in the sacred Abrahamic texts Yacob discusses.

Inquiry Corner

Content Questions:

For Yacob, what is the relationship between truth and intelligence?

What does Yacob suggest is the "Nature of Knowledge"?

Critical Question:

In what ways does the interpretation of scripture influence ethical guidelines in theory and ethical behaviors in practice?

Comparative Questions:

What authors and ideas do you associate with the Enlightenment? How do Yacob and his writings compare?

Connection Questions:

How do the contexts of and foundations for equality today compare with what Yacob says is the foundation for equality?

BEYOND THE CLASSROOM

» For many, it is far easier to do what has always been done rather than thinking critically or creatively about how to do things differently. A liberal arts education cultivates critical thinking and creative problem solving. These are among the top skills that employers look for in job candidates. Think of one or two specific instances where more was accomplished because you, or someone else, went about solving a problem in a different way than it had always been done.

from "Letter to the Grand Duchess Christina" by Galileo Galilei

Introduction

> **SNAPSHOT BOX**
>
> **LANGUAGE:** Latin and Italian
>
> **WRITTEN:** 1615, Grand Duchy of Tuscany, present-day Italy
>
> **GENRE:** Published correspondence
>
> **TAGS:** Education; Religion; Science; Ways of Knowing

Galileo Galilei (1564–1642) was the first-born son of Giulia Ammannati and Vincenzo Galilei. "Galileo" was styled after the family surname, as was typical of naming practices in Renaissance Italy. In one of the many examples of the ways that he self-fashioned his own life, career, and worldview, he preferred to go only by his given name, "Galileo."[7] Vincenzo was a well-connected musician and music theorist who taught his two sons to play the lute and the mathematical underpinnings of music theory. He also connected both to the family's network of patronage through which each would establish their careers. The Italian patronage system at the time was an unwritten social formalism through which artisans, artists, philosophers, and academics could—through connections with wealthy or noble patrons—accrue power, exchange gifts, gain legitimacy, and earn titles.

Galileo was born in Pisa but was educated from ten to fifteen years of age in a Benedictine Monastery in Florence, the capital of the Grand Duchy of Tuscany. After dropping out of medical school, Galileo studied mathematics and physics independently with the help of a social web of academics, patrons, and patronage

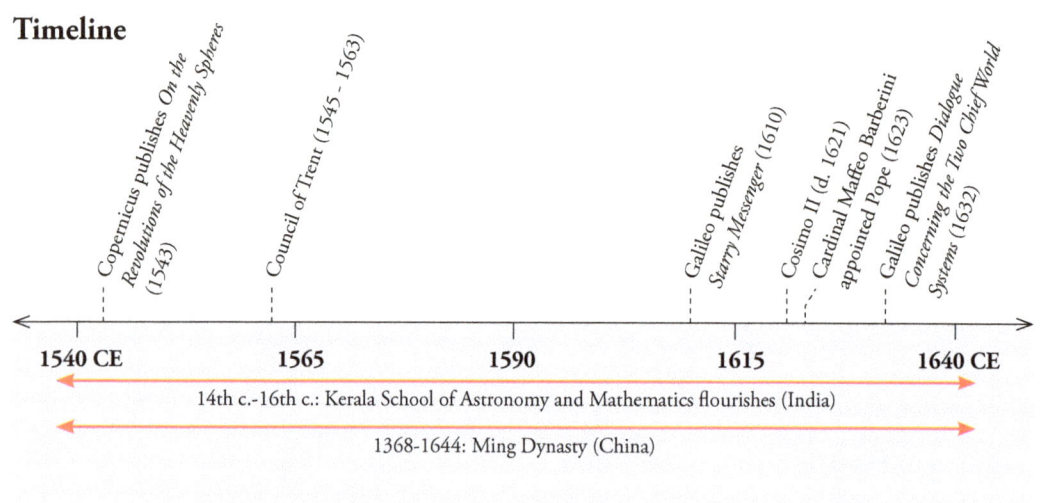

Timeline

---

7. Mario Biagioli, *Galileo, Courtier: The Practice of Science in the Culture of Absolutism* (Chicago, IL: University of Chicago Press, 1994).

brokers. He was able to use his connections to obtain academic appointments as a professor of mathematics at increasingly prestigious universities in Siena, Pisa, and Padua. In 1605, Galileo became the tutor for Prince Cosimo II de' Medici, heir to the Grand Duchy of Tuscany. In 1609 the Grand Duke Ferdinand passed, and Cosimo II ascended to the throne. That same year, Galileo heard about the 1608 patent application for "Dutch perspective glasses"—rudimentary devices made with refracting lenses that could make distant objects appear as if nearby. Galileo, without ever seeing an actual example, was able to construct his own and greatly improve on the design. Turning his newly made instrument—which would come to be known as the telescope—to the sky, Galileo was able to observe properties of our galaxy that had probably never been seen before. Several of these observations made it immediately clear to Galileo, whose mathematical training included astronomy, that there were problems with geocentrism, the prevailing sixteenth-century model of the universe in which the Earth was the stationary center around which all other heavenly bodies revolved.

Only a generation before, in 1543, Nicolas Copernicus had proposed heliocentrism in *On the Revolutions of the Celestial Spheres*, the idea that the sun, and not the Earth, was the center around which all the planets moved. Galileo's observations—particularly that Venus displayed all the lighting variation phases (similar to those commonly seen on the moon), that the sun and the moon had sunspots and craters, respectively, and that Jupiter had moons of its own—all contradicted geocentrism and the accompanying Catholic dogma that said the Earth was stationary, the sun moved, and the heavenly bodies were all "perfect," smooth spheres. The story of Joshua, in particular, from the Bible made it clear that God's miracle was to stop the sun (hence the sun was the thing moving) so that the day lasted longer allowing the Israelites to defeat the armies of the Amorite kings (Joshua 10:13).

Galileo collected his telescopic observations into a pamphlet titled *Starry Messenger*, and dedicated the work to the new Grand Duke. In it, Galileo named one of the most astonishing of his discoveries, the moons of Jupiter, the "Medicean Stars" (one each for Cosimo II and his three brothers). Galileo thus tied his discovery to Cosimo's ascension to the throne, simultaneously legitimizing the discovery and Cosimo's reign. What other strategies do people employ to gain the favor of their benefactors and patrons? Galileo was subsequently promoted to Court Mathematician, and the question of heliocentricity became a topic of debate.

The most important advantage of Galileo's new court position was that the strict disciplinary hierarchical structures of the academy did not apply at court, where the favor of the Grand Duke and his brokers was the most important factor in deciding disputes. Thus, Galileo was able to transcend his identity as mathematician, declare himself a philosopher, and have the possibility of entering into conversations of the physical working of the world. What might have been the implications of discounting mathematical views on nature based solely on disciplinary hierarchies? Today, what disciplines are "allowed" to discuss nature?

One of the most important patronage brokers for Galileo was Cosimo's mother, the Grand Duchess Christina. She was known to host debates over heliocentrism, which was attracting scrutiny from the Roman Inquisition, the punitive arm of the Catholic Church in Italy. Preempting negative attention, Galileo constructed his defense and framed it as a letter to his patroness. Nevertheless, *The Letter to the Grand Duchess* was one of the writings that earned Galileo's censure from the Church in 1616. As a result, he was ordered to abandon the concept of a heliocentric universe.

After several years of compliance, Galileo returned to the question of heliocentrism in 1623 once his ally, Cardinal Maffeo Barberini, was named Pope Urban VIII. As cardinal, Barberini had opposed the original censuring of Galileo. In Galileo's ensuing defense of heliocentrism, the 1632 *Dialog Concerning the Two Chief World Systems*, Galileo made a social miscalculation. The book was a conversation between three characters representing the two celestial models (and an impartial learner). The character representing heliocentrism (who also repeated several of Pope Urban VIII's arguments) was named Simplicio. But, as in English, the name in Italian might have been received as a slight — a simpleton. In debt and under other political pressure, Urban VIII could not permit this perceived insult whether intended or not, and Galileo's ensuing trial with the Inquisition resulted in his conviction for heresy and a sentence to spend the rest of his life under house arrest; all of his books were added to the banned book list alongside Copernicus's.

James Perkins
Department of Physics and Astronomy

Letter to the Grand Duchess Christina of Tuscany

Galileo Galilei to the Most Serene Grand Duchess Mother:

Some years ago, as Your Serene Highness well knows, I discovered in the heavens many things that had not been seen before our own age. The novelty of these things, as well as some consequences which followed from them in contradiction to the physical notions commonly held among academic philosophers, stirred up against me no small number of professors—as if I had placed these things in the sky with my own hands in order to upset nature and overturn the sciences. They seemed to forget that the increase of known truths stimulates the investigation, establishment, and growth of the arts; not their diminution or destruction. Showing a greater fondness for their own opinions than for truth they sought to deny and disprove the new things which, if they had cared to look for themselves, their own senses would have demonstrated to them. To this end they hurled various charges and published numerous writings filled with vain arguments, and they made the grave mistake of sprinkling these with passages taken from places in the Bible which they had failed to understand properly, and which were ill-suited to their purposes.

[...]

I hope to show that I proceed with much greater piety than they do, when I argue not against condemning this book, but against condemning it in the way they suggest—that is, without understanding it, weighing it, or so much as reading it. For Copernicus never discusses matters of religion or faith, nor does he use arguments that depend in any way upon the authority of sacred writings which he might have interpreted erroneously. He stands always upon physical conclusions pertaining to the celestial motions, and deals with them by astronomical and geometrical demonstrations, founded primarily upon sense experiences and very exact observations. He did not ignore the Bible, but he knew very well that if his doctrine were proved, then it could not contradict the Scriptures when they were rightly understood.

[...]

Such are the people who labor to persuade us that an author like Copernicus may be condemned without being read, and who produce various authorities from the Bible, from theologians, and from Church Councils to make us believe that this is not only lawful but commendable. Since I hold these to be of supreme authority, I consider it rank temerity for anyone to contradict them—when employed according to the usage of the holy Church. Yet I do not believe it is wrong to speak out when there is reason to suspect that other men wish, for some personal motive, to produce and employ such authorities for purposes quite different from the sacred intention of the holy Church.

[...]

The reason produced for condemning the opinion that the earth moves and the sun stands still in many places in the Bible one may read that the sun moves and the earth stands still. Since the Bible cannot err, it follows as a necessary consequence that anyone takes an erroneous and heretical position who maintains that the sun is inherently motionless and the earth movable.

With regard to this argument, I think in the first place that it is very pious to say and prudent to affirm that the holy Bible can never speak untruth—whenever its true meaning is understood. But I believe nobody will deny that it is often very abstruse, and may say things which are quite different from what its bare words signify. Hence in expounding the Bible if one were always to confine oneself to the unadorned grammatical meaning, one might fall into error. Not only contradictions and propositions far from true might thus be made to appear in the Bible, but even grave heresies and follies. Thus it would be necessary to assign to God feet, hands and eyes, as well as corporeal and human affections, such as anger, repentance, hatred, and sometimes even the forgetting of things past and ignorance of those to come. These propositions uttered by the Holy Ghost were set down in that manner by the sacred scribes in order to accommodate them to the capacities of the common people, who are rude and unlearned. For the sake of those who deserve to be separated from the herd, it is necessary that wise expositors should produce the true senses of such passages, together with the special reasons for which they were set down in these words. This doctrine is so widespread and so definite with all theologians that it would be superfluous to adduce evidence for it.

Hence I think that I may reasonably conclude that whenever the Bible has occasion to speak of any physical conclusion (especially those which are very abstruse and hard to understand), the rule has been observed of avoiding confusion in the minds of the common people which would render them contumacious toward the higher mysteries. Now the Bible, merely to condescend to popular capacity, has not hesitated to obscure some very important pronouncements, attributing to God himself some qualities extremely remote from (and even contrary to) His essence. Who, then, would positively declare that this principle has been set aside, and the Bible has confined itself rigorously to the bare and restricted sense of its words, when speaking but casually of the earth, of water, of the sun, or of any other created thing? Especially in view of the fact that these things in no way concern the primary purpose of the sacred writings, which is the service of God and the salvation of souls—matters infinitely beyond the comprehension of the common people.

This being granted, I think that in discussions of physical problems we ought to begin not from the authority of scriptural passages but from sense-experiences and necessary demonstrations; for the Holy Bible and the phenomena of nature proceed alike from the divine Word, the former as the dictate of the Holy Ghost and the latter as the observant executrix of God's commands. It is necessary for the Bible, in order to be accommodated to the understanding of every man, to speak many things which appear to differ from the absolute truth so far as the bare meaning of the words is concerned. But Nature, on the other hand, is inexorable and immutable; she never transgresses the laws imposed upon her, or cares a whit whether

her abstruse reasons and methods of operation are understandable to men. For that reason it appears that nothing physical which sense-experience sets before our eyes, or which necessary demonstrations prove to us, ought to be called in question (much less condemned) upon the testimony of biblical passages which may have some different meaning beneath their words. For the Bible is not chained in every expression to conditions as strict as those which govern all physical effects; nor is God any less excellently revealed in Nature's actions than in the sacred statements of the Bible. Perhaps this is what Tertullian[8] meant by these words:

"We conclude that God is known first through Nature, and then again, more particularly, by doctrine; by Nature in His works, and by doctrine in His revealed word."

From this I do not mean to infer that we need not have an extraordinary esteem for the passages of holy Scripture. On the contrary, having arrived at any certainties in physics, we ought to utilize these as the most appropriate aids in the true exposition of the Bible and in the investigation of those meanings which are necessarily contained therein, for these must be concordant with demonstrated truths. I should judge that the authority of the Bible was designed to persuade men of those articles and propositions which, surpassing all human reasoning could not be made credible by science, or by any other means than through the very mouth of the Holy Spirit.

Yet even in those propositions which are not matters of faith, this authority ought to be preferred over that of all human writings which are supported only by bare assertions or probable arguments, and not set forth in a demonstrative way. This I hold to be necessary and proper to the same extent that divine wisdom surpasses all human judgment and conjecture.

But I do not feel obliged to believe that the same God who has endowed us with senses, reason, and intellect has intended us to forego their use and by some other means to give us knowledge which we can attain by them. He would not require us to deny sense and reason in physical matters which are set before our eyes and minds by direct experience or necessary demonstrations. This must be especially true in those sciences of which but the faintest trace (and that consisting of conclusions) is to be found in the Bible. Of astronomy, for instance, so little is found that none of the planets except Venus are so much as mentioned, and this only once or twice under the name of "Lucifer." If the sacred scribes had had any intention of teaching people certain arrangements and motions of the heavenly bodies, or had they wished us to derive such knowledge from the Bible, then in my opinion they would not have spoken of these matters so sparingly in comparison with the infinite number of admirable conclusions which are demonstrated in that science. Far from pretending to teach us the constitution and motions of the heavens and other stars, with their shapes, magnitudes, and distances, the authors of the Bible intentionally forbore to speak of

---

8. An early Church father (ca. 155–220 ce).

these things, though all were quite well known to them. Such is the opinion of the holiest and most learned Fathers, and in St. Augustine we find the following words:

"It is likewise commonly asked what we may believe about the form and shape of the heavens according to the Scriptures, for many contend much about these matters. But with superior prudence our authors have forborne to speak of this, as in no way furthering the student with respect to a blessed life—and, more important still, as taking up much of that time which should be spent in holy exercises. What is it to me whether heaven, like a sphere, surrounds the earth on all sides as a mass balanced in the center of the universe, or whether like a dish it merely covers and overcasts the earth? Belief in Scripture is urged rather for the reason we have often mentioned; that is, in order that no one, through ignorance of divine passages, finding anything in our Bibles or hearing anything cited from them of such a nature as may seem to oppose manifest conclusions, should be induced to suspect their truth when they teach, relate, and deliver more profitable matters. Here let it be said briefly, touching the form of heaven, that our authors knew the truth but the Holy Spirit did not desire that men should learn things that are useful to no one for salvation."

The same disregard of these sacred authors toward beliefs about the phenomena of celestial bodies is repeated to us by St. Augustine in his next chapter. On the question whether we are to believe that the heaven moves or stands still, he writes thus:

"Some of the brethren raise a question concerning the motion of heaven, whether it is fixed or moved. If it is moved, they say, how is it a firmament? If it stands still, how do these stars which are held fixed in it go round from east to west, the more northerly performing shorter circuits near the pole, so that the heaven (if there is another pole unknown to us) may seem to revolve upon some axis, or (if there is no other pole) may be thought to move as a discus? To these men I reply that it would require many subtle and profound reasonings to find out which of these things is actually so; but to undertake this and discuss it is consistent neither with my leisure nor with the duty of those whom I desire to instruct in essential matters more directly conducing to their salvation and to the benefit of the holy Church."

From these things it follows as a necessary consequence that, since the Holy Ghost did not intend to teach us whether heaven moves or stands still, whether its shape is spherical or like a discus or extended in a plane, nor whether the earth is located at its center or off to one side, then so much the less was it intended to settle for us any other conclusion of the same kind. And the motion or rest of the earth and the sun is so closely linked with the things just named, that without a determination of the one, neither side can be taken in the other matters. Now if the Holy Spirit has purposely neglected to teach us propositions of this sort as irrelevant to the highest goal (that is, to our salvation), how can anyone affirm that it is obligatory to take sides on them, that one belief is required by faith, while the other side is erroneous? Can an opinion be heretical and yet have no concern with the salvation of souls? Can the Holy Ghost be asserted not to have intended teaching us something that does concern our salvation? I would say here something that was heard from an ecclesiastic of the most eminent degree: "That the intention of the Holy Ghost is to teach us how one goes to heaven, not how heaven goes."⁹ [...]

Galilei, Galileo. "Galileo Galilei: Letter to the Grand Duchess Christina of Tuscany, 1615." [Original in public domain]. Also found at Internet History Sourcebooks, August 1997. https://sourcebooks.fordham.edu/mod/galileo-tuscany.asp.

---

9. Attributed to Cardinal Baronius (1538–1607).

"The Negro Digs Up His Past" by Arturo (Arthur) Schomburg

SNAPSHOT BOX

LANGUAGE: English
PUBLISHED: 1925, New York
GENRE: Historiographical essay
TAGS: Community; Education; Historiography; Internationalism; Race; Struggle, Resistance, and Revolution; Ways of Knowing

Introduction

Historiography is the study of the methods and approaches of doing and writing history. In 1925 Arturo A. Schomburg (1874–1938) wrote "The Negro Digs Up His Past" and made a "radical intervention in the production of historiographic knowledge"[10] demonstrating that the work of established, white historians had failed to include African and African American histories and was profoundly in need of recasting. Born in Puerto Rico, Arturo Alfonso Schomburg's mother, Mary Joseph, was an Afro-Caribbean woman from St. Croix, and his father, Carlos Federico Schomburg, was Puerto Rican with German ancestors. Identifying as Afro-Puerto Rican, Schomburg remembers asking his early childhood schoolteachers about the history of his ancestors and being told that Black people had no history. He never forgot that disparaging insult and dedicated his life to finding and making available historical sources establishing the depth and breadth of Black history. How might his early experiences have shaped his interest in historiography?

At the age of seventeen he moved to New York City where he studied English and taught Spanish, eventually working clerical jobs. In the city Schomburg also befriended other Puerto Rican and Cuban immigrants and joined in their discussions and activism directed toward the independence and self-determination of their colonized island homes. Among the militants that he worked with in the cause of independence for Antillian self-rule were Jose Martí and Rafael Serra.[11] Those independence movements transformed into a full-blown war of liberation, which, in turn, became the Spanish American War (1895–1898). The US victory in this war did not bring independence to those Spanish colonies but rather recolonization by the United States. Schomburg's radical stance for Puerto Rican self-determination was transformed as he began to work within the legal framework of his new country for equality and civil rights. Still, he never forgot his dedication to African and African American history and much of his time and energy continued to be devoted to the search and acquisition of sources that illuminated the Black past. His quest was an increasingly internationalist, Pan-African one that transcended borders as well as national identities and languages.[12] What could be possible points

---

10. Adalaine Horton, "Decolonizing History: Arthur Schomburg's Afrodisasporic Archive," *Journal of African American History* 92, no. 2 (Spring, 2007): 220.

11. Vanessa Valdés, *Diasporic Blackness: The Life and Times of Arturo Schomburg* (Albany, NY: SUNY Press, 2018).

12. Jesse Hoffnung-Garskoff, "The Migrations of Arturo Schomburg: On Being Antillano, Negro, and Puerto Rican in New York, 1891–1938," *Journal of American Ethnic History* 21, no. 1 (2001): 3–29.

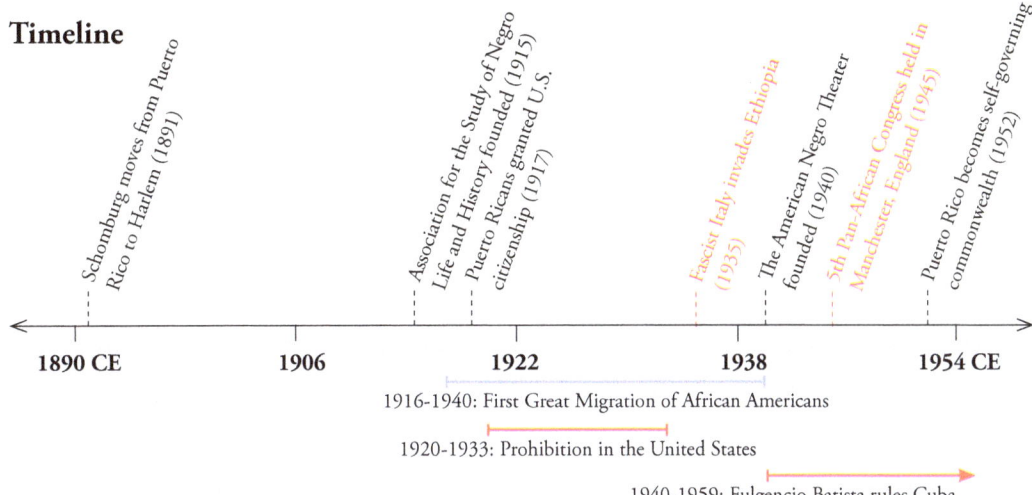

of convergence or tension between a civil rights movement, internationalism, and Pan-Africanism?

In 1911, with historian and journalist John Edward Bruce, Schomburg founded the Negro Society for Historical Research. This brought his work to the attention of other African American scholars and in 1914 he became a member of the American Negro Academy (ANA). The ANA was an organization dedicated to promoting and facilitating scholarly research by African Americans that revealed the true past and refuted racist and white supremacist writings that were very prevalent among established white scholars. Schomburg's friends and collaborators included Black intellectuals like W. E. B. Du Bois, Carter Woodson, and Alain Locke. In 1935, Du Bois's *Black Reconstruction in America* would build upon Schomburg's work and effectively challenge the racist historiography of the Dunning School, perhaps the most entrenched example of bigoted historical writing.[13]

While in New York, Schomburg continued to work his day job as a mail clerk at a bank but his collection of materials related to African, African American, and Afro-Latino histories continued to grow. Schomburg was a member of the Order of Free and Accepted Masons, also known as Freemasonry, the world's largest fraternal secret society and dedicated many hours to serving as the archivist (and translator) for his lodge, one whose membership was made up of Black migrants from the islands of the Caribbean, increasingly English-speaking as well as Spanish. With only a high school education as a foundation, by the age of forty (1914) Schomburg had

---

13. W. E. B. Du Bois, *Black Reconstruction in America: An Essay Toward a History of the Part Which Black Folk Played in the Attempt to Reconstruct Democracy in America, 1860–1880* (New York: Russell & Russell, 1935); see also Eric Foner, "Black Reconstruction: An Introduction," *South Atlantic Quarterly* 112, no. 3 (2013): 409–18.

nevertheless established himself as the intellectual equal of more conventionally credentialed colleagues while simultaneously remaining in touch with working-class learners like his lodge brothers. In the early years of the Harlem Renaissance he already stood as a local and international authority on African American history, art, and culture. By this time, he counted among his friends Langston Hughes, Zora Neale Hurston, and even Marcus Garvey (who was also a Freemason). In New York City Schomburg navigated multiple worlds, maintaining contact with the Spanish-speaking and English-speaking Caribbean, the blossoming African American–US self-discovery, the push for civil rights of the Harlem Renaissance, the working-class concerns of his colleagues in Freemasonry, and the intellectual pursuits and policy-making of the most well-educated Blacks in the nation. What strategies do people typically employ to navigate across such a wide range of contexts and communities?

With the publication of "The Negro Digs Up His Past" in 1925 Schomburg forged ahead with the broadening and the deepening of the field of African American history. By internationalizing Black history while simultaneously casting profoundly into the past, his work resulted in a tour de force listing of scholars and scholarship. "The Negro Digs Up His Past" also served as an "Afrodiasporic archive,"[14] that is, an annotated bibliography of the worth and utility of source after source. Why do you think that, in this essay, Schomburg provides such an exhaustive inventory of scholars and their works? In 1926 the Carnegie Corporation funded the purchase of Schomburg's collection on behalf of the New York Public Library. The collection eventually became The Schomburg Center for Research in Black Culture, today a world-renowned archive encompassing an entire block in Harlem. Schomburg continued to work with books and sources, helping to start a similar library at Fisk University in Nashville in the early 1930s. At Fisk, a top-ranked historically Black university, the focus of the collection was Pan-African and International Black studies. In a very short time he increased Fisk's holdings to more than 4,500 books. Continuing to work until the end of his life, Schomburg died of complications associated with surgery in 1938.

Alvis Dunn
Department of History

14. See Horton, "Decolonizing History."

The Negro Digs Up His Past

The American Negro[15] must remake his past in order to make his future. Though it is orthodox to think of America as the one country where it is unnecessary to have a past, what is a luxury for the nation as a whole becomes a prime social necessity for the Negro. For him, a group tradition must supply compensation for persecution, and pride of race the antidote for prejudice. History must restore what slavery took away, for it is the social damage of slavery that the present generations must repair and offset. So among the rising democratic millions we find the Negro thinking more collectively, more retrospectively than the rest, and apt out of the very pressure of the present to become the most enthusiastic antiquarian of them all.

Vindicating evidences of individual achievement have as a matter of fact been gathered and treasured for over a century: Abbé Gregoire's liberal-minded book on Negro notables in 1808 was the pioneer effort; it has been followed at intervals by lesser-known and often less discriminating compendiums of exceptional men and women of African stock. But this sort of thing was on the whole pathetically overcorrective, ridiculously over-laudatory; it was apologetics turned into biography. A true historical sense develops slowly and with difficulty under such circumstances. But today, even if for the ultimate purpose of group justification, history has become less a matter of argument and more a matter of record. There is the definite desire and determination to have a history, well documented, widely known at least within race circles, and administered as a stimulating and inspiring tradition for the coming generations.

Gradually as the study of the Negro's past has come out of the vagaries of rhetoric and propaganda and become systematic and scientific, three outstanding conclusions have been established:

First, that the Negro has been throughout the centuries of controversy an active collaborator, and often a pioneer, in the struggle for his own freedom and advancement. This is true to a degree which makes it the more surprising that it has not been recognized earlier.

Second, that by virtue of their being regarded as something "exceptional," even by friends and well-wishers, Negroes of attainment and genius have been unfairly disassociated from the group, and group credit lost accordingly.

Third, that the remote racial origins of the Negro, far from being what the race and the world have been given to understand, offer a record of creditable group achievement when scientifically viewed, and more important still, that they are of

---

15. Schomburg uses the term "Negro" to refer to his own African American communities as was a prevalent practice within and outside of Black communities from the nineteenth to mid-twentieth centuries. The term "negro" should not be confused with the derogatory n-word. Likewise another term used during the same timeframe, "colored," is outdated and should not be confused with the current usage of "person of color." Words reflecting African American and Black communities' preferences for self-identification continue to shift in meaning and connotation over time.

vital general interest because of their bearing upon the beginnings and early development of culture.

With such crucial truths to document and establish, an ounce of fact is worth a pound of controversy. So the Negro historian today digs under the spot where his predecessor stood and argued. Not long ago, the Public Library of Harlem housed a special exhibition of books, pamphlets, prints and old engravings, that simply said, to sceptic and believer alike, to scholar and school-child, to proud black and astonished white, "Here is the evidence." Assembled from the rapidly growing collections of the leading Negro bookcollectors and research societies, there were in these cases, materials not only for the first true writing of Negro history, but for the rewriting of many important paragraphs of our common American history. Slow though it be, historical truth is no exception to the proverb.

Here among the rarities of early Negro Americana was Jupiter Hammon's Address to the Negroes of the State of New York, edition of 1787, with the first American Negro poet's famous "If we should ever get to Heaven, we shall find nobody to reproach us for being black, or for being slaves." Here was Phillis Wheatley's Mss. poem of 1767 addressed to the students of Harvard, her spirited encomiums upon George Washington and the Revolutionary Cause, and John Marrant's St. John's Day eulogy to the 'Brothers of African Lodge No. 459' delivered at Boston in 1784. Here too were Lemuel Haynes' Vermont commentaries on the American Revolution and his learned sermons to his white congregation in Rutland, Vermont, and the sermons of the year 1808 by the Rev. Absalom Jones of St. Thomas Church, Philadelphia, and Peter Williams of St. Philip's, New York, pioneer Episcopal rectors who spoke out in daring and influential ways on the Abolition of the Slave Trade. Such things and many others are more than mere items of curiosity: they educate any receptive mind.

Reinforcing these were still rarer items of Africana and foreign Negro interest, the volumes of Juan Latino, the best Latinist of Spain in the reign of Philip V, incumbent of the chair of Poetry at the University of Granada, and author of Poems printed Granatae 1573 and a book on the Escurial published 1576; the Latin and Dutch treatises of Jacobus Eliza Capitein, a native of West Coast Africa and graduate of the University of Leyden, Gustavus Vassa's celebrated autobiography that supplied so much of the evidence in 1796 for Granville Sharpe's attack on slavery in the British colonies, Julien Raymond's Paris expose of the disabilities of the free people of color in the then (1791) French colony of Hayti, and Baron de Vastey's Cry of the Fatherland, the famous polemic by the secretary of Christophe that precipitated the Haytian struggle for independence. The cumulative effect of such evidences of scholarship and moral prowess is too weighty to be missed as exceptional.

But weightier surely than evidence of individual talent and scholarship could ever be, is the evidence of important collaboration and significant pioneer initiative in social service and reform, in the efforts toward race emancipation, colonization and race betterment. From neglected and rust-spotted pages comes testimony to the black men and women who stood shoulder to shoulder in courage and zeal, and often on a parity of intelligence and public talent, with their notable white benefactors. There was the already cited work of Vassa that aided so materially the efforts of Granville Sharpe, the record of Paul Cuffee, the Negro colonization pioneer, associated so importantly with the establishment of Sierra Leone as a British colony for the occupancy of free people of color in West Africa; the dramatic and history-making expose of John Baptist Phillips, African graduate of Edinburgh, who compelled through Lord Bathhurst in 1824 the enforcement of the articles of capitulation guaranteeing freedom to the blacks of Trinidad. There is the record of the pioneer colonization project of Rev. Daniel Coker in conducting a voyage of ninety expatriates to West Africa in 1820, of the missionary efforts of Samuel Crowther in Sierra Leone, first Anglican bishop of his diocese, and that of the work of John Russwurm, a leader in the work and foundation of the American Colonization Society.

When we consider the facts, certain chapters of American history will have to be reopened. Just as black men were influential factors in the campaign against the slave trade, so they were among the earliest instigators of the abolition movement. Indeed there was a dangerous calm between the agitation for the suppression of the slave trade and the beginning of the campaign for emancipation. During that interval colored men were very influential in arousing the attention of public men who in turn aroused the conscience of the country. Continuously between 1808 and 1845, men like Prince Saunders, Peter Williams, Absalom Jones, Nathaniel Paul, and Bishops Varick and Richard Allen, the founders of the two wings of African Methodism, spoke out with force and initiative, and men like Denmark Vesey (1822), David Walker (1828) and Nat Turner (1831) advocated and organized schemes for direct action. This culminated in the generally ignored but important conventions of Free People of Color in New York, Philadelphia and other centers, whose platforms and efforts are to the Negro of as great significance as the nationally cherished memories of Faneuil and Independence Halls. Then with Abolition comes the better documented and more recognized collaboration of Samuel R. Ward, William Wells Brown, Henry Highland Garnett, Martin Delaney, Harriet Tubman, Sojourner Truth, and Frederick Douglass with their great colleagues, Tappan, Phillips, Sumner, Mott, Stowe and Garrison.

But even this latter group who came within the limelight of national and international notice, and thus into open comparison with the best minds of their generation, the public too often regards as a group of inspired illiterates, eloquent echoes of their Abolitionist sponsors. For a true estimate of their ability and scholarship, however, one must go with the antiquarian to the files of the Anglo-African Magazine, where page by page comparisons may be made. Their writings show Douglass, McCune Smith, Wells Brown, Delaney, Wilmot Blyden and Alexander Crummell to have been as scholarly and versatile as any of the noted publicists with whom they were associated. All of them labored internationally in the cause of their fellows; to Scotland, England, France, Germany and Africa, they carried their brilliant offensive of debate and propaganda, and with this came instance upon instance of signal foreign recognition, from academic, scientific, public and official sources. Delaney's *Principia of Ethnology* won public reception from learned societies, Penington's discourses an honorary doctorate from Heidelberg, Wells Brown's three years mission the entree of the salons of London and Paris, and Douglass' tours receptions second only to Henry Ward Beecher's.

After this great era of public interest and discussion, it was Alexander Crummell, who, with the reaction already setting in, first organized Negro brains defensively through the founding of the American Negro Academy in 1874 at Washington. A New York boy whose zeal for education had suffered a rude shock when refused admission to the Episcopal Seminary by Bishop Onderdonk, he had been befriended by John Jay and sent to Cambridge University, England, for his education and ordination. On his return, he was beset with the idea of promoting race scholarship, and the Academy was the final result. It has continued ever since to be one of the bulwarks of our intellectual life, though unfortunately its members have had to spend too much of their energy and effort answering detractors and disproving popular fallacies. Only gradually have the men of this group been able to work toward pure scholarship. Taking a slightly different start, The Negro Society for Historical Research was later organized in New York, and has succeeded in stimulating the collection from all parts of the world of books and documents dealing with the Negro. It has also brought together for the first time cooperatively in a single society African, West Indian and Afro-American scholars. Direct offshoots of this same effort are the extensive private collections of Henry P. Slaughter of Washington, the Rev. Charles D. Martin of Harlem, of Arthur Schomburg of Brooklyn, and of the late John E. Bruce, who was the enthusiastic and far-seeing pioneer of this movement. Finally and more recently. the Association for the Study of Negro Life and History has extended these efforts into a scientific research project of great achievement and promise. Under the direction of Dr. Carter G. Woodson it has continuously maintained for nine years the publication of the learned quarterly, The Journal of Negro History, and with the assistance and recognition of two large educational foundations has maintained research and published valuable monographs in Negro history. Almost keeping pace with the work of scholarship has been the effort to popularize the results, and to place before Negro youth in the schools the true story of race vicissitude, struggle and accomplishment. So that quite largely now the ambition of Negro youth can be nourished on its own milk.

Such work is a far cry from the puerile controversy and petty braggadocio with which the effort for race history first started. But a general as well as a racial lesson has been learned. We seem lately to have come at last to realize what the truly scientific attitude requires, and to see that the race issue has been a plague on both our historical houses, and that history cannot be properly written with either bias or counter-bias. The blatant Caucasian racialist with his theories and assumptions of race superiority and dominance has in turn bred his Ethiopian counterpart—the rash and rabid amateur who has glibly tried to prove half of the world's geniuses to have been Negroes and to trace the pedigree of nineteenth century Americans from the Queen of Sheba. But fortunately today there is on both sides of a really common cause less of the sand of controversy and more of the dust of digging.

Of course, a racial motive remains legitimately compatible with scientific method and aim. The work our race students now regard as important, they undertake very naturally to overcome in part certain handicaps of disparagement and omission too well-known to particularize. But they do so not merely that we may not wrongfully be deprived of the spiritual nourishment of our cultural past, but also that the full story of human collaboration and interdependence may be told and realized. Especially is this likely to be the effect of the latest and most fascinating of all of the attempts to open up the closed Negro past, namely the important study of African cultural origins and sources. The bigotry of civilization which is the taproot of intellectual prejudice begins far back and must be corrected at its source. Fundamentally it has come about from that depreciation of Africa which has sprung up from ignorance of her true role and position in human history and the early development of culture. The Negro has been a man without a history because he has been considered a man without a worthy culture. But a new notion of the cultural attainment and potentialities of the African stocks has recently come about, partly through the corrective influence of the more scientific study of African institutions and early cultural history, partly through growing appreciation of the skill and beauty and in many cases the historical priority of the African native crafts, and finally through the signal recognition which first in France and Germany, but now very generally the astonishing art of the African sculptures has received. Into these fascinating new vistas, with limited horizons lifting in all directions, the mind of the Negro has leapt forward faster than the slow clearings of scholarship will yet safely permit. But there is no doubt that here is a field full of the most intriguing and inspiring possibilities. Already the Negro sees himself against a reclaimed background, in a perspective that will give pride and self-respect ample scope, and make history yield for him the same values that the treasured past of any people affords.

Schomburg, Arturo (Arthur) A. "The Negro Expresses Himself: The Negro Digs Up His Past." *The Survey*, March 1, 1925, 670–72.

"The Painter" by Hannah Höch and from *Negro Sculpture* by Carl Einstein

SNAPSHOT BOX

LANGUAGE: German
DATE: 1920/1915
LOCATION: Germany
GENRE: Art theory and criticism
TAGS: Art; Cross-Cultural Encounters; Poetry, Music, Literature; Race; Ways of Knowing

Introduction

The three decades transitioning the world from the late nineteenth into the early twentieth centuries were some of the most diverse and exciting ones in recent art history: global connections, technological advances, and sociocultural ferment contributed to a very fertile arts environment. Many of the developments that started during this time did not come to full fruition immediately—in fact, some of them would only be effectively addressed in the twenty-first century—but this atmosphere of change was not only palpable in the 1910s, it was also actively propelled forward by the work of artists. Among the challengers who were attempting to overturn the cultural, socioeconomic, and political status quo of the 1800s were Hannah Höch (1889–1978) and Carl Einstein (1885–1940). Three movements had a direct bearing on their work and writings: **women's suffrage**, **decolonization**, and **modern art**. What might have made this turn-of-the-century period such an incubator for change and ferment?

While the activities in the women's suffrage movement ostensibly centered on procuring the right to vote for women, the organizations formed to support this cause pursued a much broader platform of women's rights—extending far beyond the political. Economic equality and social reforms were considered important as well, and the different waves of feminism following later in the twentieth century

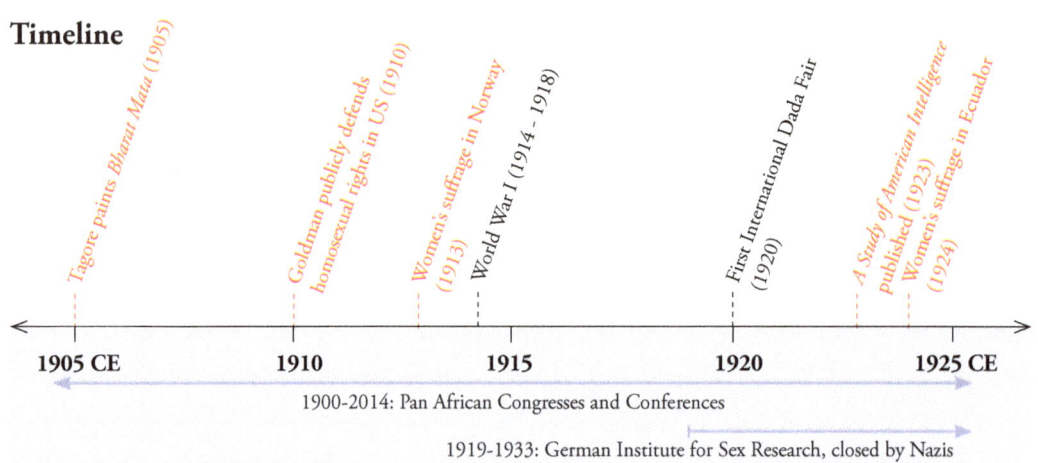

can be seen as logical extensions of a process that was begun but not completed in the century's first decades. Why do you think that the changes advocated by social movements are often multigenerational?

The key colonial powers of Great Britain and France held on to most of their non-European territories through the first half of the twentieth century. However, a major shift toward decolonization occurred with the very public appearance of the first Pan-African Congress (Paris, 1919). The Pan-African Congress was organized by W. E. B. Du Bois and Ida Gibbs Hunt, and its delegates from fifteen countries would petition the concurrently held Versailles Peace Conference for changes to the governing structure in the colonies, including home rule and involving Africans in the governance of their countries. While **Pan-Africanism** (a movement to create solidarity and bonds between those of African descent, both on and off the continent), and the more specifically developed framework of **Négritude** (conceived by francophone intellectuals, who would use this literary theory and critique to foster "Black consciousness" across Africa and its diaspora) did not begin to gain much traction until the 1930s, there were numerous precursor movements and organizations. There were many entities that promoted engagement with African heritage and connection to the homeland, including the first Pan-African Conference (1900), Marcus Garvey's Universal Negro Improvement Association and African Communities League (founded in 1914), and Alain Locke's manifesto *The New Negro* (published 1925).

The third important movement, known as modern art, does not refer to a particular group or event, but describes a general trend in the later nineteenth-century art world. This trend encouraged breaking with tradition and embracing experimentation, especially new ways of "seeing" (e.g., the Impressionists) and working (i.e., using new media, techniques, locations). Artists such as Van Gogh and Paul Cezanne were inspired by working outside in the South of France, where they tried to reveal the particularities of "light" found in different locations, which then also affects how color is experienced. Furthermore, artists sought inspiration by exploiting the artistic achievements of other cultures (especially Pablo Picasso, who created Cubism as a result of his fascination with West African Art), by traveling beyond Europe (for example, Paul Gauguin, who spent much time in Polynesia), or by inventing new artistic media (such as **collage**, which is made up of torn or cut pieces of paper as well as other materials, reconfigured into a new "image"). Photography and mass-produced imagery had changed visual culture in the nineteenth century, and by the time movie theaters started becoming ubiquitous in the 1920s, society was flooded with images. As you read Einstein and Höch, what complex and complicated aspects of these three movements do you see contributing to their writings?

With a background in art history and philosophy, Carl Einstein (1885–1940) became a well-known author and critic in Berlin during the first decades of the twentieth century. Like many of his artist and writer contemporaries, he was swept up in the general excitement for the war (WWI) and actually joined the Imperial German

Army in 1915. When his communist leanings and anarchist views put him at odds with the rising fascist regime, he was forced to leave Berlin in 1928. He settled in Paris, but as a Jew and anti-fascist, he also became a target for the Vichy government, and in 1940 was arrested and incarcerated in a concentration camp near Bordeaux. Though freed that same year, he found himself caught between two equally hostile powers (Francoist Spain and Nazi Germany), and saw his only escape by taking his life jumping off a bridge in the Pyrenees border region of France.

Einstein had several pioneering writings, but "Negerplastik" ("Negro Sculpture," published 1915) stands out and is "considered to be the first account of African art, specifically sculpture, to challenge various prejudices and misconceptions around this subject, by a European critic."[16] His ideas came at a time when—despite the efforts of colonial powers to categorize art of colonized peoples as demonstrating inferior skills and primitive aesthetics—the art works had started to speak for themselves. This process was aided by what had happened to the Benin bronzes. Since 1897, hundreds of looted bronzes and plaques entered Europe as a result of the British "Punitive Expedition," a retaliatory invasion and ransacking of the palace and capital city of the Kingdom of Benin. The Benin bronze works clearly documented both extraordinary craftsmanship and aesthetic features, which resonated with the European art world and which conflicted with the official message of a "degenerate people" propagated by bigoted eyewitness accounts and news media. Yet, most scholars still tried to understand African sculpture through "the system of sculpture production developed by Europeans."[17] This is Einstein's key contribution: he suggests that African sculpture cannot be understood by that system and proposes a radically different and new aesthetic theory. With his particular take on formalism he was able to move away from a "European awareness [that] is fatally flawed by virtue of prejudice and an overweening sense of superiority, a master narrative of the development of art which is exclusionary of other cultures and productions."[18]

German modern artist Hannah Höch (1889–1978) is best known as a member of the **Berlin Dada group**, a circle of mostly male artists in post–World War I Berlin, who used appropriated and recombined images/materials to critique contemporary society, culture, and politics. She is celebrated for her collages and **photomontages**, collages mostly consisting of photos or photographic reproductions. Höch's works generally ridiculed the stodgy, bourgeois culture of the Weimar Republic (first German federal constitutional republic), but they also constructed a brave new world, spliced together from disparate sources all the while questioning her contemporaries' colonial ambitions, ethnographic photography, gender stereotypes, beauty standards, and expectations of women. In addition to being famous for her artistic

---

16. Patrick Healy, "Introduction," in *Carl Einstein: Negro Sculpture*, translated by Patrick Healy (Amsterdam: November Editions, 2016), 2.
17. Healy, "Introduction," 3.
18. Healy, "Introduction," 4.

output, Hannah Höch was involved in two well-known relationships—the first, an extramarital affair (from 1915–1922) with fellow Dada artist Raoul Hausmann, and the second (from 1926–1936) with her lesbian partner, the Dutch author and poet Mathilda Maria Petronella (aka "Til") Brugman. In each instance, the relationship resulted in artistic inspiration and collaborative projects.

From her choice of media and partners, as well as her published writing, Höch challenged both the social and the artistic conventions of her time—by not conforming to anyone's expectations. She wrote "The Painter" shortly after the end of World War I; German women had just received equal suffrage, and she had exhibited her work in the First International Dada Fair. However, all was clearly not well in Germany, and the satirical text highlighted some of the issues: from the creator-god assumptions of the male genius, to the masculine identity crisis resulting from doing "women's work," and the way in which an intensely patriarchal society supported the entrenched beliefs held by the artist. Her protagonist's name, Gotthold Heavenlykingdom, was a curious choice in the secular atmosphere of 1920s Germany: it helped her contrast the lofty ideals of the name with the character's baser ideas and conflicts. Gotthold is a traditional German given name for someone who has received God's favor, is precious to God, or favorably disposed toward God. Höch also picked a rather humble member of the allium (onion) family, the dainty chive (used mostly like an herb), as her tangible, visual, and gustatory counterpart to the abstract and indefinable notion of "the female soul." In German, chives are known as "Schnittlauch" (cutting leeks)—thus allowing the artist to bring into the text her preferred method of working (with a cutting knife). Like Höch's ludicrous comparison of the ethereal soul with the pungent onion, her 1920s collage titled "Cut with the Kitchen Knife Dada through the Last Era of the Weimar Beer-belly Culture" took a scalpel to her contemporary world and showed the turmoil of the time with a jumble of images ranging from machine parts to depiction of crowds, to words, and interspersing the heads of politicians and artists placed on the bodies of dancers, performers, and sculptures.

Eva Hericks-Bares
Department of Art & Art History

> **PRE-READING PARS**
>
> 1. First bring to mind an entrenched stereotype. Outline the steps you could take to evaluate it in an objective and unbiased manner. Also note what might make such an evaluation possible and what gets in the way?
> 2. Recall an instance in which you or another author/artist/creator used satire to deal with a challenging situation/experience. What advantages did the satire format have? (A common definition of satire is "using humor, irony, exaggeration, or ridicule to expose and criticize people's stupidity or vices, particularly in the context of contemporary politics and other topical issues.")

"The Painter" and selection from *Negro Sculpture*

"The Painter"

Once upon a time there was a painter. He wasn't called Dribble, or anything else like that, as he might have been in earlier times. It was around 1920—the painter was a modern painter—so his name was Heavenlykingdom. Unlike the real painters of earlier times, he was not asked to work only with brush and palette. This was his wife's fault: she thwarted the boundless fight of his genius. At least four times in four years, he was forced to wash dishes—the kitchen dishes. The first time, actually, there had been a pressing reason. She was giving birth to the baby Heavenlykingdom, Jr. But he wanted to keep the peace—because after all God had created the male to do just that—and so had no choice but to obey her Xanthippian demand. Yet the matter continued to weigh on him. He felt degraded as a man and as a painter under its dark shadow. On the days of crisis he would suffer nightmares. He kept seeing Michelangelo washing up the cups. He knew enough about psychoanalysis to confront the woman with the truth that such demands always arise out of the desire to dominate, no matter what other reasons there might be. As a modern person he felt that in theory he had to agree with the equality of the sexes—still, if one looked closely at the situation one could not—and then, especially in your own house—her demand seemed to him comparable to an enslavement of his soul . . .

Now one day he began to paint a picture. A dark force moved him, because he was full of dark forces. He wanted to represent, to cube really, the essential likeness between the nature of chives and the female soul. In theory the whole problem was solved. He saw the emptiness that fills both these objects precisely and with total intellectual clarity. There is more to genius that intellect, however, and, when he connected the herb's snake-like form with the previously mentioned soul, his unusually developed instinct gave him mystical knowledge. No genius would deny a certain complement of mysticism.

Our Heavenlykingdom was deeply wounded by something he had also heard about from his fellow men: although these little women are often really tiny, they can still not be shaped and modeled into the form one needs for physical and psychic comfort. Had he been a writer, he would have been compelled to enrich the literature with a ponderous work on the theme, "When you go to Woman, do not forget the whip." But under the circumstances that you know about now, his painting was to be called, "The Chive and the Female Soul: A Comparison." I think it was already announced for exhibition, while the canvas still shone blankly, spotlessly receptive. One has to do everything in good time. Gotthold—that was Heavenlykingdom's first name—suffered under the female soul in the totality of his manhood. And we all need to confront what makes us suffer. No wonder, then, that Heavenlykingdom (secretly) began to think of himself as on a level with a redeemer—let's admit it, with Christ—because of the likeness he has discovered.

But you have to imagine the painting properly—as it were, a scientifically dissected representation—the female soul, totally clear in a segmented cubist painting—so that everyone able to adopt an abstract point of view could read, there she is, that's her innermost being. And next to that the analogy and parallel: chives. Wouldn't everyone see it as clear as day? We also know that when we recognize what ails us, we are cured. So what perspectives would open up with the creation of this painting? Wouldn't the most burning question of our time be solved? Yet we have had to admit too often that theory and practice don't coincide. He had worked on his picture for two years and two days already. He labored and labored mightily, unable to advance beyond the chives. In the first place, the painting remained green. As soon as he used a different color, the disturbance that resulted was so great that he covered it with green again. For a while he thought that the treacherous female soul (treachery no doubt its most important element alongside emptiness) could appear as a cubist lemon-yellow spiral among the green—a shape more or less like one of those sofa-springs that winds crookedly upward. But alas, painting is color as well as form. The yellow refused to meld with the massive green of his chive allegory. He had no choice but to remove the winding spiral. A painter must remain enough of an aesthete to refuse to paint badly for the sake of his idea. The same thing happened with composition. He tried and tried, even falling into trances, but nothing beyond the dull repetitive up-and-down of the chive motif would develop. Over and over again he hoped to fix the damnable female soul in a fluted doughnut-shape. But his eye remained objective and told him the truth without pity: this fretwork muddies the powerful melody of the chive movement. His most intimate friend, looking at the painting, remarked that it had the kind of power that liberated itself in an overwhelming sense of bore.... No, that's not what he said. He said, liberates itself in sameness. Then he decided with a heavy heart to abandon the female soul and to devote himself only to chives from now on.

A month later, and the President, who has just opened the exhibition, is propelling his presidential belly around the myriad chambers that display the works of all the painters of the realm. Suddenly he stops. His face displays emotion. His entourage observes closely. He begins to speak. "A masterpiece," he stammers. "Has my administration ever produced anything better?" He questioned everyone around him. All that green—what can it remind me of? His adjutant (unless an assistant goes by another name in a Republic) suggested helpfully, "Of the revolution? Of the revolution, my President?"

"Absolutely right. The revolution."

They say the State bought the painting for the National Gallery. They say that when its creator was asked for the title, he omitted mention of the chives and proudly called it "The Female Soul." They say Gotthold Heavenlykingdom will be the next candidate for a Nobel Prize.

from *Negro Sculpture*

Remarks on Method

There is probably no art that the European approaches with more suspicion than the art of Africa. [...] The negro[19] [...] is regarded from the outset as an inferior part of humanity that must be ruthlessly developed into something better, and what he has to offer is judged in advance as wanting. Entirely vague evolutionary hypotheses were hastily fashioned to account for him. For some he was pressed into service to provide a misguided concept of primitive man, while others garlanded this hapless object of research with demonstrably false phrases about a people of timeless prehistory. Some hoped to discover in the negro a kind of origin, a condition of life that will never escape its first beginnings. Many of the opinions entertained about African man are largely based on prejudices such as these, prejudices effectively developed to fit some comfortable theory or other. In passing judgement on the negro the European makes one assumption: that of an unqualified and almost fantastical superiority on his part.

In fact our lack of respect for the negro merely expresses an ignorance about him, and one that oppresses him quite unjustly.

[...]

Certain problems arising in connection with modern art, however, have encouraged a less superficial exploration of the art of the African peoples. Here too, as so often, we see how some current development in the world of art has led to the construction of a corresponding history, one in which the art of the African peoples has assumed a central place. What had appeared quite meaningless before now came to acquire special significance in the light of very recent endeavors in the visual arts. We

---

19. Einstein uses the term "Negro" to refer to African communities as was a prevalent practice within and outside of Black communities from the nineteenth to mid-twentieth centuries. The term "negro" should not be confused with the derogatory n-word. Likewise another term used during the same timeframe, "colored," is outdated and should not be confused with the current usage of "person of color." Words reflecting African, African American, and Black communities' preferences for self-identification continue to shift in meaning and connotation over time.

suddenly came to realize that certain problems concerning space, and a certain form of artistic creation as such, were rarely to be found expressed with such purity as they are in negro art. As a result we grasped that our previous judgements concerning the negro and his art revealed far more about the judge than it ever did about the object in question. This new perspective was soon accompanied by a new enthusiasm. Negro art was now being collected precisely as art, and indeed with passion: one began actively and legitimately producing a freshly interpreted object from the old material.

[. . .] In general our knowledge of African art is scant and extremely vague. [. . .] Nonetheless we must begin from fact rather than some surreptitiously introduced substitute for fact. And I think there is one fact which imposes itself more reliably than any conceivable knowledge of an ethnographic or other kind, and that is the African sculptures themselves. We must ignore their 'objective' character, that is, we must ignore them as objects associated with a specific environment, and analyse them precisely as created forms [*Gebilden*]. We must try and see whether analysis of the formal character of these sculptures can lead us towards an overall conception of form commensurate with that found throughout the different forms of art in general. One thing will certainly have to be observed here, and one thing avoided: we must stay with the realm of perception [*Anschauung*], and proceed in accordance with its specific principles. We must never impose the structure of our own thoughts upon the realm of perception or the specific creativity we are attempting here to explore. We must refrain from hypothesizing comforting evolutionary trends or identifying intellectual processes of thought with the creative achievements of art. We must renounce the prejudice that psychological processes can manifest themselves simply under reversed signs, that reflection upon art simply corresponds to the active creation of art. For such reflection is a generally distinct process, one that advances specifically beyond form and the world of form in order to locate the work of art within the realm of process [*Geschehen*] in general.

Describing sculpture in terms of created forms [*Gebilde*] proves much more fruitful than treating it in 'objectivist' terms. For any 'objectively' oriented description necessarily goes beyond the given created form, treats it as pointing to some kind of practice on a different level altogether rather than concentrating upon the created form itself. The proper analysis of forms, on the other hand, stays with what is immediately given as such. The only thing we must assume here are the specific forms in question. Yet these forms serve to facilitate our grasp of reality better than any individual things can do because, as forms, they simultaneously express something about the structures of seeing and the principles of perception, ineluctably leading us therefore precisely to a kind of knowledge that emphatically remains within the sphere of the given.

If it is possible to provide a formal analysis capable of identifying and circumscribing certain specific and unified features with regard to the articulation of space and the nature of vision, this already implicitly demonstrates that the created forms in question are indeed art. One might object here that this conclusion is already secretly dictated by a penchant for generalization and a predetermined intention on our part. This is quite wrong. For individual form [*Einzelform*] already harbours the required elements of spatial perception within itself, indeed explicitly presents these elements since it is only by means of form that they can be presented at all. The purely individual case [*Einzelfall*], on the other hand, fails to capture the specific character of the concept at issue. For the individual case and the general concept are related to one another in a purely dualistic manner. But it is precisely the essential congruence between the universal character of perception and its specific realization that defines the work of art. One should also remember that artistic creation is just as 'spontaneous' as is our inevitable urge to interpret and connect the specific forms of perception in terms of laws and principles. For in both cases we are successfully attempting to organize our own experience.

The Painterly Element

The typical European lack of understanding for African art is directly related to its stylistic power. For this art does indeed represent an exemplary case of sculptural vision.

One can certainly argue that the sculpture of our own continent has been profoundly influenced by surrogate and essentially painterly effects. Hildebrand's *Problem of Form* presents us with an ideal reconciliation of the painterly and the sculptural. But even the striking examples of French sculpture, up to and including Rodin, appear to be struggling towards a dissolution of the sculptural as such. Even the aspect of frontality, which is generally regarded as a rigorous and 'primitive' clarification of the cubic dimension [*des Kubischen*], must properly be interpreted as a painterly conception of the sculptural. For the three-dimensional character of sculpture is here summarized in terms of a few planes that effectively suppress the cubic aspect altogether. The parts closest to the viewer are emphasized and organized into planes, while the more distant parts are presented as incidental modifications of the frontal plane whose own dynamic character is weakened as a result.

[…]

The viewer was drawn into the sculpture; he became in turn an inseparable function of it (as in perspectival sculpture for example); he related himself, through a predominantly psychological exercise of empathy, with the personality of the creator unless he felt forced explicitly to contradict or repudiate the latter. Sculpture thus became little more than a materially embodied conversation between two souls. A sculptor who worked this way was inevitably concerned above all to envisage the effect and the viewer in advance. In order to anticipate and to test the intended effect, he would then naturally try and transform himself into the viewer (as in Futurist sculpture). The resulting sculptures would then have to be defined essentially in terms of the effects they produced. The psychological and temporal aspect thereby completely overshadowed the determinate spatial articulation of the object. This identity between viewer and maker was posited precisely in order to facilitate what was, often even unconsciously, the end and aim of the creative effort. For this was the only way to ensure an unlimited artistic effect for the work.

It is entirely symptomatic that the effect exercised upon the viewer is generally interpreted as the direct inversion of the creative process, even if it is acknowledged to be less intense in character. The sculptor thus abandoned himself to the most relevant psychological processes and thereby transplanted himself into the position of the viewer. He would always assume a certain distance from the work corresponding to that of the prospective viewer and model the desired effect accordingly. He would place the emphasis upon the visual activity of the viewer, and add certain modelling 'touches' to ensure that it was the viewer alone who would effectively generate the authentic form of the object. The constructive configuration of space was sacrificed to the purely secondary, indeed essentially alien, means of material movement. Cubic space, the presupposition of all sculpture, was forgotten.

A few years ago, in France, we witnessed a crisis in art which has redefined our entire perspective. As a result of immense intellectual effort, we finally recognized the quite inappropriate and questionable character of the prevalent artistic procedures. Certain painters were strong enough to turn their backs upon a craft that was muddling along mechanically. Renouncing the prevailing methods, they investigated the fundamental elements involved in spatial perception [*Raumanschauung*], the elements which produce and determine the character of the latter. The results of all this crucial labor are now sufficiently familiar. It was inevitable that we should simultaneously discover negro sculpture and recognize that in isolation it had already learned to cultivate essentially pure sculptural forms.

The efforts of these painters are usually described in terms of 'abstraction,' and it cannot be denied that a genuinely immediate understanding of space could only be approached on the basis of a devastating critique of misguided and entirely descriptive attempts to conceptualize it. This is an essential task, although in this connection we must emphatically distinguish negro sculpture from the art which was inspired by the latter and self-consciously developed its own identity in relation to it. What presents itself here as abstraction, presented itself there as immediately given nature. For we shall see that negro sculpture, in a formal sense, is also the most powerful kind of realism.

The artist of today is not working solely for the cause of pure form, for he is still registering it in terms of a certain opposition to his own earlier history, and his efforts remain entangled in an all too reactive attitude. This critical and necessary posture accentuates the analytical approach to art.

Religion and African Art

Negro art is above all determined and defined by religion. The crafted images are objects of worship, just as they are with any other ancient people. The maker produces his work as the embodiment and preservation of some divinity, and from the first maintains a certain distance from the work which either is the god or ensures the continuing presence of the god. The maker's labour is itself a kind of distanced adoration, and the work he fashions is a priori something which is independent of, and more powerful than, its maker—especially since he concentrates every fibre of his being upon the work and, as the weaker one in this relation, abandons himself entirely to it. His labour must be described in terms of religious dedication. The work itself, qua divinity, is something free that is independent of anything else that might bind it. The maker and the worshipper stand separated from it by an immeasurable distance. The god in the work does not intervene in the human realm, and even if it did, it would do so as the one that is mightier, and thus once again as the one that is essentially distanced and remote. The transcendent power of the work presupposes the religious dimension and is entirely grounded in it. The work is created in a state of adoration, of fearful awe, before the god, and that is similarly the effect produced by the work. The soul of the maker and the worshipper are attuned in advance, i.e. are constituted in an essentially identical manner. The resulting effect lies not in the work of art, but in the incontestably divine character that the work is assumed to possess. The artist himself would never presume to emulate or rival the effect produced by the god, an effect which is ineluctably exercised and whose character is already defined. The notion of the work of art as calculated to produce a certain effect is entirely meaningless in this context, especially when we consider that idols are actually often worshipped in the dark.

For here the artist labors over a work that is essentially independent, transcendent and detached. This transcendent character of the work corresponds to a perception of space which excludes any functional role for the viewer. The space in question must be presented definitively in a total, exhaustive and unfragmented manner. Spatial closure here is not a matter of abstraction, but one of immediate sensory experience. This closure can only be ensured when the cubic character of space, to which nothing further can possibly be added, is fully realized and acknowledged. The activity of the viewer does not come into it. [...]

Negro sculpture typically displays a vigorous independence as far as the parts of the work are concerned. This too is grounded in their religious character. The parts are defined in terms of themselves, not in terms of the viewer. They are experienced in relation to the compact mass of the object, not minimized by distance. This serves to accentuate the parts themselves and their defining contours.

There is also another striking feature to these works: most of them dispense with a base, or any similarly devised platform. This may seem surprising since the statues appear highly decorative in our eyes. But the god is never represented as anything other than an independent being that itself requires no external support. He will not lack for faithful and adoring hands when he is borne in procession by his worshippers.

Art of this kind will seldom explicitly objectify the metaphysical dimension, for the latter is always presupposed as a matter of course. This dimension necessarily manifests itself entirely in the total form of the work where it is concentrated with astonishing intensity. Which is to say that the form is expressly articulated as a most sharply defined totality. This reveals a powerful realism in the formal sense. And this alone can activate the relevant impulses which do not need to assume form in an abstract or reactively polemical fashion because they are immediately identical with form itself. (The metaphysical dimension in the work of contemporary artists continues to betray their antecedent critique of the painterly and has invaded representation as an essential formal and objective principle: the unconditional character of both art and religion, their strictly demarcated but mutual correlation, has therefore been confusingly and destructively collapsed into one.) Formal realism, which is not to be understood as a mimetic naturalism, implies the moment of transcendence. For all thought of imitation or resemblance is excluded here: what human being is a god supposed to resemble, to what human being can a god ever be subjected? The result is thus a consistent realism of transcendent form. The work of art is not regarded as a deliberate or artificial creation of the artist, but rather as mythical reality which in power and strength exceeds all natural reality. The work is emphatically real by virtue of its closed form. Since it is intrinsically independent and exceedingly powerful in its own right, the sense of distance and remoteness involved necessarily inspires art of a tremendous intensity.

Amongst us Europeans the work of art is typically subjected to an emotional and even formal interpretation in so far as the viewer is expressly summoned to active optical participation. The character of the negro work of art, by contrast, is unequivocally defined, and this for more than purely formal reasons, namely religious ones as well. The work does not signify or symbolize anything. The work simply is the god who thus preserves his own self-contained mythical reality, one which draws the worshippers into itself, transforms them likewise into something mythical, and cancels the limits of their human existence.

The formal and the religious character of closure and self-containment correspond to one another. This is at once a formal and a religious realism. The European work of art has simply become a metaphor of the effect which encourages the viewer to respond as freely as he wishes. The Negro religious work of art is categorical and possesses a concentrated kind of being which precludes all limitation.

In order to ensure a clearly delineated and self-contained existence for the work of art, every temporal function must be suspended. In other words, there can be no question of gradually moving around or touching the work. The deity has no conditioning prehistory behind it, for that would contradict its emphatically binding existence. It must be presented directly in solid material without any recourse to modelling (*modelé*), something which would merely betray a personal, impious and interfering hand. The conception of space embodied in such a work of art must absorb cubic space entirely and express it in a rigorously unified manner. Any suggestion of perspective or accustomed frontality are precluded here and it would be impious to employ either. The work of art must present space as a uniform totality. For it can only appear as something timeless if it excludes any temporal approach grounded in notions of movement. The work of art absorbs time by integrating what we normally experience as movement into its very form.

The Cubic Perception of Space

[...]

If we conceive of cubic space as form—and sculpture is properly concerned with this alone rather than with material mass—then we must first determine what cubic space really is. It is made up of parts that are not immediately perceptible at a glance. They must be perceptibly condensed into a single total form which demands a single act of vision on the part of the viewer and corresponds to a fixed three-dimensional spatial field. It is only in this way that the otherwise irrational character of cubic space can present itself as a perceptible configuration at all. The optical naturalism characteristic of western art is not in fact the imitation of external nature. The nature that is passively imitated here is based upon the perspective of the viewer. This is what accounts for the enormously relative and genetical character of most of our art. Our works of art are adapted to the perspective of the viewer (the idea of frontality, the distanced focus on the image), and responsibility for the final optical effect has been entrusted increasingly to the active participation of the viewer.

Form, like the processes of thought and imagination, represents a kind of equivalence [*Gleichung*]. This equivalence possesses an aesthetic character when it is apprehended unconditionally and without reference to anything external. For form is the total identity between spatial perception and individual realization where they coincide structurally and are not related as concept to individual case. The sphere of perception certainly encompasses many particular cases of active realization, but it possesses no superior qualitative reality in its own right. It is evident therefore that art represents a particular case of unconditional intensity and the quality in question must be recreated in it with undiminished power.

The task of sculpture is to produce an equivalence in which the naturally defined sensations of movement and thus of mass are entirely absorbed and in which their temporally articulate differences are transmuted into a formal structure. This equivalence accomplished in the work of art must be a total one if it is to be experienced differently from that produced by other human activities, if it is to be experienced as something unconditional, self-contained and essentially independent.

Hannah Höch. "The Painter." In Lavin, Maud, *Cut With the Kitchen Knife: The Weimar Photomontages of Hannah Hoch*, translated by Anne Halley, 216–18. New Haven: Yale University Press, 1993. Reprinted with permission from the author.

Einstein, Carl. "Negro Sculpture." In *Art in Theory, 1900–2000: An Anthology of Changing Ideas*, edited by Charles Harrison and Paul Wood, 111–16. Malden, MA: Blackwell Publishing, [1992] 2003.

> **POST-READING PARS**
>
> 1. "Reverse outline" (i.e., break each paragraph down into the simplest statement of its purpose) Einstein's article. What obstacles does it appear he is speaking to and what strategies is he using to overcome them?
> 2. Identify instances of each of the elements from the definition of satire in Höch's piece (i.e., humor, irony, exaggeration, ridicule). Are there any other important elements of that reading that are powerful or provocative?

Inquiry Corner

Content Questions:

Einstein: What are some of the key challenges African art and sculpture have faced in its encounter with European scholars?

Höch: How do the struggles of the artist Heavenlykingdom with his masculinity manifest themselves?

Critical Questions:

Einstein: What could be some of the reasons that it will take another seventy years before many of the author's complaints are finally addressed and rectified?

Höch: Why does Höch use religious terms and associations in her construction of the protagonist?

Why do you think the satire ended the way it did?

Comparative Questions:

Einstein: Consider your own contemporary encounters with African art. How does your experience with the twenty-first-century presentation of art differ from the way in which an early twentieth-century audience and reader of this text would have seen African art?

Höch: Put Höch's piece (style, purpose, arguments) into juxtaposition with earlier feminist critiques (such as Wollstonecraft or Tristan).

Connection Questions:

Einstein: What strategies used by Einstein to challenge the status quo are still employed in today's resistance movements?

Höch: Consider translating and adjusting the content of the satire for the twenty-first century. What would change? What would stay the same?

"Response to Ernest Renan's Criticism of Islam" by Jamal al-Din al-Afghani

SNAPSHOT BOX

LANGUAGE: French
WRITTEN: 1883, Paris
GENRE: Open letter
TAGS: Religion; Tradition; Nationalism; Science

Introduction

Many scholars regard Sayyid Jamal al-Din al-Afghani (1838–1897) to be the founder and principal advocate of Islamic Modernism. This movement was the first attempt to address the colonial dominance of European powers in traditionally Islamic areas of Asia and North Africa by adopting elements of modernity such as "Western" science and the concept of evolutionary social progress. With his disciple and Egyptian colleague Muhammad 'Abduh (1849–1905), al-Afghani argued for a united Pan-Islamic response to European imperialism in speeches and in the pages of their short-lived but influential *Al-'Urwah al-Wuthqa* (*The unbreakable bond*), an Arabic-language journal printed in Paris. Al-Afghani's "Answer to Renan," an epistolary response to a lecture delivered by the French writer Ernest Renan, was published in the *Journal de Débats* in 1883. Renan's position reflected **Orientalism**, an orientation proceeding from a fascination with "exotic" Islamic and Asian societies. Al-Afghani sought to counter Renan's claims that, first, science was incompatible with Islam and second, that the vaunted "Arab sciences" of the medieval period were actually the work of Persian Shi'ites, Greek Christians, and other non-Arab "races" and religions. As you read, see if you can identify what assumptions are embedded in Afghani's and Renan's categorization of science. While his defense of the universality of science as a foundational "philosophy" of the modern world won al-Afghani fame in western Europe, his inclination to base his reform

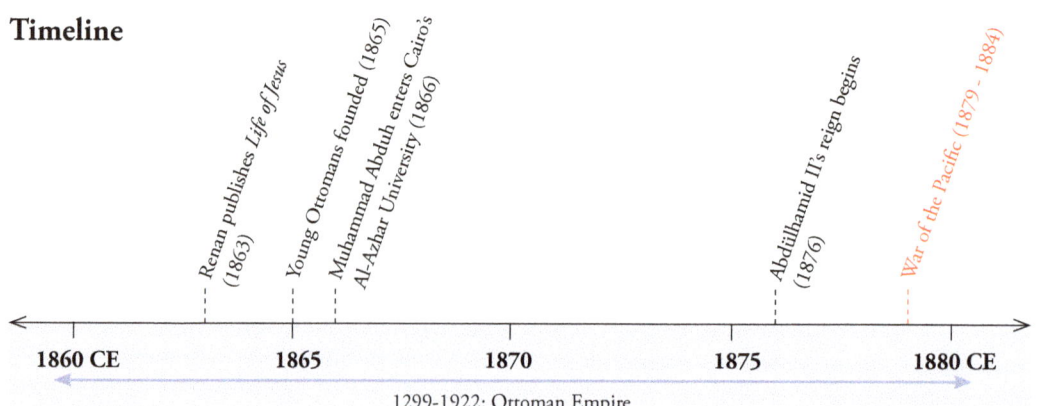

program on such universalism, rather than upon the doctrines of Islam, made him appear too secular to some Muslims.

By Renan's time Orientalism had become very derisive of what was perceived as the "backwardness" and "barbarism" of many non-Western cultures. Al-Afghani agreed with Orientalist critics that the "traditional" expressions of Islam in his day—developed by very conservative jurists (key interpreters of **shari'a**, the "Divine Law") and enforced by what he perceived as despotic and repressive political systems—had contributed to the hostility of contemporary Muslims toward modern European culture. Born in what is now northern Iran, he had taken the surname al-Afghani to separate himself from the Shi'ite faith of his homeland as a means to facilitate his acceptance by Sunni governments. What advantages or costs might be associated with changing one's own name?

Well-educated and well-traveled, al-Afghani was a vocal proponent of religious and political reforms and a determined adversary of European imperialism. While the latter brought him into positions of influence in Egypt, South Asia, and the Ottoman Empire, his opposition to political corruption led to numerous expulsions and forced exiles. His personal religious views were the subject of some speculation, but his speeches and writings illustrate his firm conviction that a renewal of Islamic civilization along rationalist lines could be an effective deterrent against imperialism. His extreme opposition to British colonialism made him an avowed enemy of the Shah of Iran, who al-Afghani viewed as a collaborator with the British. In 1896 he helped to plan the assassination of the shah while he was being "detained" (probably under house arrest) in the Ottoman Empire by order of the sultan, and he died of cancer a little over a year later while still in Constantinople.

In what ways does al-Afghani present his case for Islamic rationalism? How does he challenge the implicit racism of Renan? What historical evidence does he use to support his arguments? What does he understand to be the relationship between science and religion? Where might Renan and al-Afghani agree on the role of religion in society?

Rodger Payne
Department of Religious Studies

Jamal al-Din al-Afghani Answers Ernest Renan's Criticism of Islam

Document 1: Answer of Jamal al-Din to Renan, Journal des Débats, 18 May 1883

Sir,

I have read in your estimable journal of last 29 March, a talk on Islam and Science, given in the Sorbonne before a distinguished audience by the great thinker of our time, the illustrious M. Renan, whose renown has filled the West and penetrated into the farthest countries of the East. Since this speech suggested to me some observations, I took the liberty of formulating them in this letter, which I have the honor of addressing to you with a request that you accommodate it in your columns.

M. Renan wanted to clarify a point of the history of the Arabs which had remained unclear until now and to throw a light on their past, a light that may be somewhat troubling for those who venerate these people, though one cannot say that he has usurped the place and rank that they formerly occupied in the world. M. Renan has not at all tried, we believe, to destroy the glory of the Arabs which is indestructible; he has applied himself to discovering historical truth and making it known to those who do not know it, as well as to those who study the influence of religions in the history of nations, and in particular in that of civilization. I hasten to recognize that M. Renan has acquitted himself marvelously of this very difficult task, in citing certain facts that have passed unnoticed until this time. I find in his talk remarkable observations, new perceptions, and an indescribable charm. However, I have under my eyes only a more or less faithful translation of this talk. If I had had the opportunity to read it in the French text, I could have penetrated better the ideas of this great thinker. He receives my humble salutation as an homage that is due him and as the sincere expression of my admiration. I would say to him, finally, in these circumstances, what Al-Mutanabbi, a poet who loved philosophy wrote several centuries ago to a high personage whose actions he celebrated: "Receive," he said to him, "the praises that I can give you; do not force me to bestow on you the praises that you merit."

M. Renan's talk covered two principal points. The eminent philosopher applied himself to proving that the Muslim religion was by its very essence opposed to the development of science, and that the Arab people, by their nature, do not like either metaphysical sciences or philosophy. This precious plant, M. Renan seems to say, dried up in their hands as if burnt up by the breath of the desert wind. But, after reading this talk one cannot refrain from asking oneself if these obstacles come uniquely from the Muslim religion itself or from the manner in which it was propagated in the world; from the character, manners, and aptitudes of the peoples who adopted this religion, or of those on whose nations it was imposed by force. It is no doubt the lack of time that kept M. Renan from elucidating these points; but the harm is no less for that, and if it is difficult to determine its causes in a precise manner and by irrefutable proof, it is even more difficult to indicate the remedy.

As to the first point, I will say that no nation at its origin is capable of letting itself be guided by pure reason. Haunted by terrors that it cannot escape, it is incapable of distinguishing good from evil, of distinguishing that which could make it happy from that which might be the unfailing source of its unhappiness and misfortune. It does not know, in a word, either how to trace back causes or how to discern effects.

This lacuna means that it cannot be led either by force or persuasion to practice the actions that would perhaps be the most profitable for it, or to avoid what is harmful. It was therefore necessary that humanity looked outside itself for a place of refuge, a peaceful corner where its tormented conscience could find repose. It was then that there arose some educator or other who, not having, as I said above, the necessary power to force humanity to follow the inspiration of reason, hurled it into the unknown and opened it to vast horizons where the imagination was pleased and where it found if not the complete satisfaction of its desires, at least an unlimited field for its hopes. And, since humanity, at its origin, did not know the causes of the events that passed under its eyes and the secrets of things, it was perforce led to follow the advice of its teachers and the orders they gave. This obedience was imposed in the name of the Supreme Being to whom the educators attributed all events, without permitting men to discuss its utility or its disadvantages. No doubt, for man this is one of the heaviest and most humiliating yokes, as I recognize; but one cannot deny that it is by this religious education, whether it be Muslim, Christian, or pagan, that all nations have emerged from barbarism and marched toward a more advanced civilization.

If it is true that the Muslim religion is an obstacle to the development of sciences, can one affirm that this obstacle will not disappear someday? How does the Muslim religion differ on this point from other religions? All religions are intolerant, each one in its way. The Christian religion, I mean the society that follows its inspirations and its teachings and is formed in its image, has emerged from the first period to which I have just alluded; thenceforth free and independent, it seems to advance rapidly on the road of progress and science, whereas Muslim society has not yet freed itself from the tutelage of religion. Realizing, however, that the Christian religion preceded the Muslim religion in the world by many centuries, I cannot keep from hoping that Muhammadan society will succeed in breaking its bonds and marching resolutely in the path of civilization someday after the manner of Western society, for which the Christian faith, despite its rigors and intolerance, was not at all an invincible obstacle. No, I cannot admit that this hope be denied to Islam. I plead here with M. Renan not the cause of the Muslim religion, but that of several hundreds of millions of men, who would thus be condemned to live in barbarism and ignorance.

In truth, the Muslim religion has tried to stifle science and stop its progress. It has thus succeeded in halting the philosophical or intellectual movement and in turning minds from the search for scientific truth. A similar attempt, if I am not mistaken, was made by the Christian religion, and the venerated leaders of the Catholic Church have not yet disarmed, so far as I know. They continue to fight energetically against what they call the spirit of vertigo and error. I know all the difficulties that the Muslims will have to surmount to achieve the same degree of civilization, access to truth with the help of philosophic and scientific methods being forbidden them. A true believer must, in fact, turn from the path of studies that have for their object scientific truth, studies on which all truth must depend, according to an opinion accepted at least by some people in Europe. Yoked, like an ox to the plow, to the dogma whose slave he is, he must walk eternally in the furrow that has been traced for him in advance by the interpreters of the law. Convinced, besides, that his religion contains in itself all morality and all science, he attaches himself resolutely to it and makes no effort to go beyond. Why should he exhaust himself in vain attempts? What would be the benefit of seeking truth when he believes he possesses it all? Will he be happier on the day when he has lost his faith, the day when he has stopped believing that all perfections are in the religion he practices and not in another? Wherefore he despises science. I know all this, but I know equally that this Muslim and Arab child whose portrait M. Renan traces in such vigorous terms and who, at a later age, becomes "a fanatic, full of foolish pride in possessing what he believes to be absolute truth," belongs to a race that has marked its passage in the world, not only by fire and blood, but by brilliant and fruitful achievements that prove its taste for science, for all the sciences, including philosophy (with which, I must recognize, it was unable to live happily for long).

I am led here to speak of the second point that M. Renan treated in his lecture with an incontestable authority. No one denies that the Arab people, while still in the state of barbarism, rushed along the road of intellectual and scientific progress with a rapidity only equaled by the speed of its conquests, since in the space of a century, it acquired and assimilated almost all of the Greek and Persian sciences that had developed slowly during several centuries on their native soil, just as it extended its domination from the Arabian peninsula up to the mountains of the Himalayas and the summit of the Pyrenees.

One might say that during this entire period, the sciences made astonishing progress among the Arabs and in all the countries under their domination. Rome and Byzantium were then the seats of theological and philosophical sciences, as well as the shining center and burning hearth of all human knowledge. Having followed for several centuries the path of civilization, the Greeks and Romans walked with assurance over the vast field of science and philosophy. There came, however, a time when their researches were abandoned and their studies interrupted.

The monuments they had built to science collapsed and their most precious books were relegated to oblivion. The Arabs, ignorant and barbaric as they were in origin, took up what had been abandoned by the civilized nations, rekindled the extinguished sciences, developed them and gave them a brilliance they had never had. Is not this the index and proof of their natural love for sciences? It is true that the Arabs took from the Greeks their philosophy as they stripped the Persians of what made their fame in antiquity; but these sciences, which they usurped by right of conquest, they developed, extended, clarified, perfected, completed, and coordinated with a perfect taste and a rare precision and exactitude. Besides, the French, the Germans, and the English were not so far from Rome and Byzantium as were the Arabs, whose capital was Baghdad. It was therefore easier for the former to exploit the scientific treasures that were buried in these two great cities. They made no effort in this direction until Arab civilization lit up with its reflections the summits of the Pyrenees and poured its light and riches on the Occident. The Europeans welcomed Aristotle, who had emigrated and become Arab; but they did not think of him at all when he was Greek and their neighbor. Is there not in this another proof, no less evident, of the intellectual superiority of the Arabs and of their natural attachment to philosophy? It is true that after the fall of the Arab kingdom in the Orient as in the Occident, the countries that had become great centers of science, like Iraq and Andalusia, fell again into ignorance and became the centers of religious fanaticism; but one cannot conclude from this sad spectacle that the scientific and philosophic progress of the Middle Ages was not due to the Arab people who ruled at that time.

M. Renan does do them this justice. He recognizes that the Arabs conserved and maintained for centuries the hearth of science. What nobler mission for a people! But while recognizing that from about 775 C.E. to near the middle of the thirteenth century, that is to say during about 500 years, there were in Muslim countries very distinguished scholars and thinkers, and that during this period the Muslim world was superior in intellectual culture to the Christian world, M. Renan has said that the philosophers of the first centuries of Islam as well as the statesmen who became famous in this period were mostly from Harran, from Andalusia, and from Iran. There were also among them Transoxianan and Syrian priests. I do not wish to deny the great qualities of the Persian scholars nor the role that they played in the Arab world; but permit me to say that the Harranians were Arabs and that the Arabs in occupying Spain and Andalusia did not lose their nationality; they remained Arabs. Several centuries before Islam, the Arabic language was that of the Harranians. The fact that they preserved their former religion, Sabaeanism, does not mean they should be considered foreign to the Arab nationality. The Syrian priests were also for the most part Ghassanian Arabs converted to Christianity.

As for Ibn-Bajja, Ibn-Rushd (Averroes), and Ibn-Tufail, one cannot say that they are not just as Arab as Al-Kindi because they were not born in Arabia, especially if one is willing to consider that human races are only distinguished by their languages and that if this distinction should disappear, nations would not take long to forget their diverse origins. The Arabs who put their arms in the service of the Muslim religion, and who were simultaneously warriors and apostles, did not impose their language on the defeated, and wherever they established themselves, they preserved it for them with a jealous care. No doubt Islam, in penetrating the conquered countries with the violence that is known, transplanted there its language, its manners, and its doctrine, and these countries could not thenceforth avoid its influence. Iran is an example; but it is possible that in going back to the centuries preceding the appearance of Islam, one would find that the Arabic language was not then entirely unknown to Persian scholars. The expansion of Islam gave it, it is true, a new scope, and the Persian scholars converted to the Muhammadan faith thought it an honor to write their books in the language of the Koran. The Arabs cannot, no doubt, claim for themselves the glory that renders these writers illustrious, but we believe that they do not need this claim; they have among themselves enough celebrated scholars and writers. What would happen if, going back to the first period of Arab domination, we followed step by step the first group from which was formed this conquering people who spread their power over the world, and if, eliminating everything that is outside this group and its descendants, we did not take into account either the influence it exercised on minds or the impulse it gave to the sciences? Would we not be led, thus, no longer to recognize in conquering peoples other virtues or merits than those that flow from the material fact of conquest? All conquered peoples would then regain their moral autonomy and would attribute to themselves all glory, no part of which could be claimed legitimately by the power that fructified and developed these germs. Thus, Italy would come to say to France that neither Mazarin nor Bonaparte belonged to her; Germany or England would in turn claim the scholars who, having come to France, made its professorships illustrious and enhanced the brilliance of its scientific renown. The French, on their side, would claim for themselves the glory of the offspring of those illustrious families who, after [the revocation of] the edict of Nantes, immigrated to all Europe. And if all Europeans belong to the same stock, one can with justice claim that the Harranians and the Syrians, who are Semites, belong equally to the great Arab family.

It is permissible, however, to ask oneself why Arab civilization, after having thrown such a live light on the world, suddenly became extinguished; why this torch has not been relit since; and why the Arab world still remains buried in profound darkness.

Here the responsibility of the Muslim religion appears complete. It is clear that wherever it became established, this religion tried to stifle the sciences and it was marvelously served in its designs by despotism.

Al-Siuti tells that the Caliph al-Hadi put to death in Baghdad 5,000 philosophers in order to destroy sciences in the Muslim countries down to their roots. Admitting that this historian exaggerated the number of victims, nonetheless it remains established that this persecution took place, and it is a bloody stain for the history of a religion as it is for the history of a people. I could find in the past of the Christian religion analogous facts. Religions, by whatever names they are called, all resemble each other. No agreement and no reconciliation are possible between these religions and philosophy. Religion imposes on man its faith and its belief, whereas philosophy frees him of it totally or in part. How could one therefore hope that they would agree with each other when the Christian religion, under the most modest and seductive forms, entered Athens and Alexandria, which were, as everyone knows, the two principal centers of science and philosophy, trying to stifle both under the bushes of theological discussions, to explain the inexplicable mysteries of the Trinity, the Incarnation, and Transubstantiation? It will always be thus. Whenever religion will have the upper hand, it will eliminate philosophy; and the contrary occurs when it is philosophy that reigns as sovereign mistress. So long as humanity exists, the struggle will not cease between dogma and free investigation, between religion and philosophy; a desperate struggle in which, I fear, the triumph will not be for free thought, because the masses dislike reason, and its teachings are only understood by some intelligent members of the elite, and because, also, science, however beautiful it is, does not completely satisfy humanity, which thirsts for the ideal and which likes to exist in such dark and distant regions as the philosophers and scholars can neither perceive nor explore.

Al-Afghani, Jamal al-Din. "Jamal al-Din al-Afghani Answers Ernest Renan's Criticism of Islam." In *An Islamic Response to Imperialism: Political and Religious Writings of Sayyid Jamal al-Din al-Afghani,*" vol. 21. Translated by Nikki R. Keddie, 181–87. Los Angeles: University of California Press, 1983.

from "Response to the Very Illustrious 'Sor Philotea'" by Sor Juana Inés de la Cruz

SNAPSHOT BOX

LANGUAGE: Spanish

WRITTEN: 1691, Mexico, published posthumously in 1700

GENRE: Epistolary, moral philosophy

TAGS: Accessing Rights; Autobiography and Testimony; Education; Ethics and Morality; Gender and Identity; Poetry, Song, Literature; Religion; Science; Struggle, Resistance, and Revolution; Ways of Knowing; Women and Power

Introduction

Sor Juana Inés de la Cruz (1648–1695) was the illegitimate daughter of a **Creole** woman and a **Peninsular** Spanish captain. In the Spanish colonies, Spaniards born in Spain were privileged and called Peninsulars; those of primarily Spanish descent born in the colonies were called Creoles, and in the hierarchy of early Spanish colonial society, held a place just below that of Peninsulars. Young Juana was baptized in 1651 in San Miguel Nepantla, a small town outside of Mexico City. She had access to her grandfather's library where she taught herself to read and write Latin, and soon also learned Greek, Spanish, and Nahuatl—the local Aztec language. She also excelled in her studies of mathematics, philosophy, theology, history, poetry, music, and the sciences.

When her mother sent young Juana to live with relatives in Mexico City she attracted the attention of the Viceroy and Vicereine and soon became a lady-in-waiting at the royal court. She became immediately popular with the educated upper-class Peninsulars, who were astounded by her secular and theological knowledge, her poetic ability, and her rhetorical brilliance. She formed particularly close bonds with her three succeeding patronesses, the Vicereines. The sonnets she wrote to them are in the Petrarchan tradition, expressing loss, jealousy, rejection, and love. The fourteenth-century Italian poet, Petrarch, perfected

this form, which divides a fourteen-line poem into an eight-line stanza rhyming ABBAABBA, and a six-line stanza rhyming CDCDCD or CDECDE. Speculation as to the exact nature of the relationship professed in Sor Juana's poems is ongoing, but certainly the depth of emotion expressed so eloquently rings clearly with profound human truths experienced. What strategies does poetry have for expressing human experience?

Although she was a devout Catholic, Juana's entry into the Hieronymite convent (an order devoted to St. Jerome that began in Spain and traveled to New Spain) in 1669 had more to do with her need to pursue her studies in peace, than with a devotional calling. When she professed her vows, she became *Sor* (sister/nun) Juana, the title she is most commonly known by. She amassed a huge library and a collection of musical instruments, produced plays and wrote poems, and communicated with scholars and theologians on both sides of the Atlantic.

As a vocal female in a social setting that expected silence from women, Sor Juana had enemies. When she took issue with theological points in a forty-year-old sermon by a revered theologian, her essay was published without her consent, and she unwittingly became the scapegoat in a Church debate. In a reply she was admonished by the bishop who disguised his name as Sor Philotea. On March 1, 1691, in what she must have known would be her final burst of rhetorical splendor, ironically addressed to Sor Philotea, she rebutted that admonishment.

The short passage that follows is part of her autobiographical defense of learning for women as well as a scathing criticism of misogyny. As a result of this letter, she was ordered to sequester in the convent and never utter another word. She complied and died a year later while caring for the sisters of her convent during a plague. Her library and musical instruments were seized. Her poems and a play were published posthumously in Spain by her final patroness. What other strategies are used to try and silence people speaking their truth and how successful are they?

Ann Dunn
Humanities Program

> **PRE-READING PARS**
>
> 1. Write down a list of five things you have found yourself curious about as you have moved through your daily life, things that might normally be taken for granted. Perhaps, remember some of your childhood impulses to understand the apparently mysterious workings of things.
> 2. Think of a policy or cultural practice that you are at odds with and note two points of evidence that illustrate your concerns.
> 3. Imagine a situation in which a person atop a hierarchy has complete control over wiser, cleverer, more knowledgeable people. Suggest three techniques that the less powerful could use to get their way.

from "Response to the Very Illustrious 'Sor Philotea'"

Sor Juana writes in 1690:
"This facility of analyzing everything transpired and continues to do so without my willing it; rather, it makes me angry because it makes my head tired. I believed that the same thing, including composing poetry, happened to everyone until experience demonstrated the contrary. This natural inclination or custom is so strong that there is nothing I see that I do not reflect upon. Once I saw two girls playing with a top, and hardly had I seen the movement and the shape when I began, in my insane way, to consider the easy movement of the spherical shape and how long the momentum, once established, remained independent of its original cause, the distant hand of the girl. Not content with this I had flour brought and sprinkled on the floor in order to discover whether the spinning top would describe perfect circles or not. It turned out that they were not perfect circles but spirals that lost their circular shape to the degree that the top lost momentum. Other girls were playing a game of pickup sticks (childhood's most frivolous game). I drew near to examine the figures that they formed. As chance would have it, three sticks fell into a triangle, and I immediately set about linking one thing to another, recalling that this, they say, was the shape of Solomon's mysterious ring, in which could be discerned distant lights and representations and marvels. David's harp whose music cured Saul was said to be the same shape, as is the case with harps even to this day.

What could I tell you, my Lady, of the secrets of nature that I have discovered while cooking? I observed that an egg unifies and fries in butter or oil, but to the contrary dissolves in syrup; that in order to keep sugar liquid it suffices to throw on it a very little bit of water flavored with quince or another bitter fruit; that the yolk and white of the same egg when separated and combined with sugar have an opposite effect, and one different from when they are both used together. I do not mean to tire you with such foolishness, which I only recount to give you a complete picture of my nature and because I think it will amuse you. But, my Lady, what can women know except [the] philosophy of the kitchen? Lupercio Leonardo has said it well: it is possible to philosophize while preparing dinner.[20] As I often say on observing these little things, If Aristotle had cooked, he would have written much more.

[...]

I confess also, this being true, as I have said, that I did not need models, since many books, secular and sacred, have continued to help me.[21] I see Deborah giving laws, both military and political, and governing a people with many learned men (Judges 4–5). I see the wise queen of Sheba, who was so learned that she dared to test the wisdom of the greatest of wise men with riddles and was not reprimanded for doing so; rather, because of it she became the judge of unbelievers (1 Kings 10; 2 Chron 9). I see so many women and so many illustrious women: some adorned with the gift of prophesy, like Abigail (1 Sam 25); others with the gift of persuasion, like Esther; still others with piety, like Rahab (Josh 2); others with perseverance, like Hannah, mother of Samuel (1 Sam 1–2), and an infinite number of others excelling in other types of accomplishments and virtues.

If I turn to the pagans the first that I find are the Sibyls,[22] selected by God to prophesy the principal mysteries of our faith in learned and elegant verses that filled all with admiration. I see a woman like Minerva, daughter of the great Jupiter, expert in all the wisdom of Athens, worshiped as goddess of the sciences. I see Polla Argentaria, who helped her husband, Lucanus, write about the great battle of Pharsalia. I see the daughter of divine Tiresias, more learned than her father. I see Zenobia, queen of the Palmyrans, as wise as she was valiant, and Arete, daughter of Aristippus, a most learned woman; and Nicostrata, who invented Latin Letters and was most erudite in the Greek letters as well. I see Aspasia Milesia, who taught philosophy and rhetoric and was the teacher of the philosopher Pericles; Hypatia, who taught astronomy and lectured for a long time in Alexandria; Greek Leoncia, who challenged the philosopher Theophrastus and convinced him. I see Julia, Corina, Cornelia, and finally the great multitude of those who would merit being named, Greeks, muses, oracles, all those were no more than learned women, recognized, celebrated, and also venerated as such in antiquity, without mentioning the infinite number of others of which books are full. I see the Egyptian Catherine lecturing and confounding the wisdom of the wise men of Egypt. I see Gertrude lecture, write, and teach. So as not to search for examples beyond home, I see my most holy mother Paula, learned in Hebrew, Greek, and Latin, and with a gift for interpreting scripture. As her biographer, the

---

20. According to Salceda, Sor Juana falsely attributes this to Lupercio. The verse is from Bartolome Leonardo de Argensola's *Satira primera*, vv. 143–44.

21. Electa Arenal indicates that Boccaccio's *De Mulieribus Claris* [concerning famous women] and probably Christine de Pizan's *Book of the City of Ladies* are sources (Electa Arenal and Amanda Powell, *The Answer/La Respuesta* (New York: The Feminist Press at the City University of New York, 1994), 124.

22. Isidore of Sevilla, *Etymologies*, VII, 8, lists ten sibyls to whom much was revealed about God, Christ, and the gentiles (OC 4:655).

great St. Jerome, who hardly considered himself worthy to be such, said with the lively praise and efficacious energy characteristic of his style: "If all the members of my body were tongues, they would not suffice to publish the wisdom and virtue of Paula."[23] Blesilla, widow, and the enlightened virgin Eustoquium, daughters of St. Paula, both receive similar praise. The former was called Wonder of the World for her learning. Fabiola of Rome was also very knowledgeable in holy scripture.[24] Proba Falconia, a Roman woman, wrote an elegant book with verses from Virgil that illustrated the mysteries of our holy faith. It is known that our Queen Isabella, wife of Alfonso X, wrote about astrology, not to name others whom I omit so as not to copy what others have said (a vice I have always hated). In our times we see that such women as the greats Christina Alexandra, queen of Sweden, as learned as she is courageous and magnanimous,[25] as well as the most excellent ladies the duchess of Aveyro[26] and the countess of Villaumbrosa, are flourishing.[27]

The venerable doctor Arce (worthy professor of scripture for his virtue and his learning), in his *Studioso Bibliorum* raises this question: *An liceat forminis sacrorum Bibliorum studio incumbere? Eaque interpretari?* [Is it permitted for women to study the holy Bible? To interpret it?][28] As evidence to the contrary, he quotes many opinions from the writings of the saints, especially that of the apostle Paul: *Mulieres in Ecclesiis taceant, non enim permittitur eis loqui, etc.* [Women should be silent in the church. It is not permitted for them to speak there—1 Cor 14:34]). Then he quotes as evidence other opinions, including the passage by the same apostle from his letter to Titus: *Anus similiter in habitu saneto, bene docentes* (Older women likewise of holy demeanor . . . teachers of what is good—Titus 2:3) and interpretations of the holy fathers. Finally, he concludes with all prudence that teaching publicly from the position of a university chair and preaching from the pulpit are not permitted to women.

---

23. St. Jerome, "To Eustochium (Letter 108)," par. 1, in *Handmaids of the Lord: Contemporary Descriptions of Feminine Asceticism in the First Six Christian Centuries*, edited and translated by Joan M. Petersen (Kalamazoo, MI: Cistercian Publications, 1996), 126.

24. St. Jerome praises her in "Letter to Oceanus," Letter CXXVII, par 7, in Frederick Adam Wright, *Select Letters of St. Jerome* (Creative Media Partners, 2018), 327.

25. Queen Christina abdicated on becoming Catholic. She moved to Rome, where she patronized artists and philosophers, including Descartes. Antonio Vieira, SJ, was her confessor while he was in Rome.

26. Maria Guadalupe Alencastre, duchess of Aveyro, to whom Sor Juana dedicated a poem (OC 1:37), was also a relative of her patroness, the countess of Paredes (Arenal and Powell, *The Answer/La Respuesta*, 129).

27. The countess of Villaumbrosa supported a Dominican nun, Sor Maria de la Santisima Trinidad, in founding a convent in Spain. It is not known why Sor Juana would mention her here (Arenal and Powell, *The Answer/La Respuesta*, 130).

28. Dr. Juan Diaz de Arce, *Questionarium expositium pro clariori intelligentia Sacrorum Bibliorum, liber quartus; sive de Studioso Bibliorum*, Quaestio 4 (Mexico, 1648) Arce (1594–1653) taught sacred scripture at the University of Mexico for thirty years.

However, studying, writing, and teaching privately are not only permitted but are very beneficial and useful. Clearly this is not to be understood as being the case for all women, but with those to whom God has given special virtue and prudence, who are very mature, learned, who have the talent and prerequisites necessary for such a sacred task. This does not apply only to women, generally held to be incompetent, but is also true for men who think that they are wise merely by virtue of being men. Men who are not learned, or virtuous, without receptive intellects and good inclinations should be forbidden to interpret sacred scripture. Many such men have become fanatics, and their teachings are at the root of many heresies. For many men study increases their ignorance, especially if they are of an arrogant nature, restless and proud, friends of novelties of the Law, which rejects such novelties, to the point that they are not happy until they have said something no one else has said, even if it is heresy. Of these the Holy Spirit says: *In malevolam animam non introibit sapientia* (In the evil soul wisdom cannot enter—Wis 1:4). Learning causes them more damage than ignorance does. As one wit has said, he who does not know Latin is not a total fool, but he who does can qualify as such. I would add that it would perfect his foolishness (if it possible to speak of perfecting foolishness) to have studied a little philosophy and theology, and to have some knowledge of languages, so that he is able to be foolish in many disciplines and languages. For a great fool the mother tongue is not sufficient. For such as these, study is dangerous because it is like putting a sword in the hands of a raging maniac. What is of itself a noble instrument meant for defense in his hands can cause his own death and the deaths of many others. Such were holy scriptures in the power of the perverse Pelagius and the obstinate Arius, the perverse Luther, and all the other heretics, including our own Doctor Cazalla (who was neither our own nor a doctor). There are those who are harmed by wisdom because, although it is the best food and life source of the soul, if the stomach is of a bad constitution and excessively hot, the better the foods it receives, the more dry, fermented, and perverse are the humors that it creates. So it is with these perverse men; the more they study the worse the opinions they generate. Their mind is obstructed by the very thing that it needs for nourishment. As a result, they study much and digest little, since they do not restrict themselves according to their minds' limited capacity. In this connection the apostle Paul says: *Dico enim per gratiam quae data est mihi, omnibus qui sunt inter vos: Non plus sapere quam oporetet sapere, sed sapere ad sobrietatem; et unicuique sicut Deus divisit mensuram fidei* (I say by the grace that has been given me to all of you: Do not strive to know more than is necessary, but to know what is fitting for you each according to the faith that God has measured out to you—Rom 12:3). In truth, this is what the apostle says not to women, but to men. And so, the *taceant* (being silent) is not only meant for women, but also for all those who are not adept at learning. Should I want to know as much or more than Aristotle or St. Augustine, if I do not have the aptitude of St. Augustine or Aristotle, were I to study more than both of them, not only would I not achieve this goal, but I would weaken and obstruct the operation of my weak mind through the disproportionate greatness of the object of study.

Selection from "Response to the Very Illustrious 'Sor Philotea.'" In *Sor Juana Ines de la Cruz: Selected Writings*, translated by Pamela Kirk Rappaport, 273–78. New York: Paulist Press, 2005.

> **POST-READING PARS**
>
> 1. What does your list say about your habit of mind? What does Sor Juana's list say about her habit of mind? Why would she include her examples of the top and the egg in this rebuttal? What might she be suggesting about her audience's habit of mind?
> 2. Identify two or three statements that Sor Juana cites in her defense of women's abilities? From what areas does she draw her examples? What techniques did Sor Juana use to combat the misogynistic hierarchy she faced?

Inquiry Corner

Content Question:	Critical Question:
Find two examples of poetic prose in the excerpt. What effect do they have on what Sor Juana is communicating?	What can you infer from Sor Juana's response about the bishop's criticism? Incorporate this into a critique of how she decides to reply.
Comparative Question:	**Connection Question:**
In what ways are Sor Juana's style and topics similar and different to other philosophers/theologians/essayists you have read?	The university is a hierarchical system with possible consequences for students who disagree with professors, or with the entire system. How might you respond to perceived injustices in this hierarchical context?

Selections from the Writings of Albert Einstein
by Albert Einstein

Introduction

On May 29, 1919, a total solar eclipse was visible across South America and south-central Africa. During the scant few minutes of total darkness as the sun was blocked by the moon, two teams of researchers—one stationed in Sobral, Brazil, and the other on the West African island of Principe—were able to accurately measure the positions of stars that would have normally been obscured by the brightness of the sun. The path of the light from those stars that passed nearby the sun was—as predicted by Albert Einstein's General Theory of Relativity—bent and thus their apparent positions were altered. When the results were publicized months later, the *New York Times*' famous headline read "Lights All Askew in the Heavens ... Einstein Theory Triumphs, Stars Not Where They Seemed or Were Calculated to Be, but Nobody Need Worry." Overnight Einstein became a household name, and Isaac Newton's seventeenth-century Universal Law of Gravitation—which had been a pillar of the universalism, empiricism, and deterministic optimism of the modern era—had been unseated. What are some things we have to take into account when paradigms in science are radically shifted? Albert Einstein (1879–1955) had been constructing his theory of relativity since he was a sixteen-year-old student, bored by the rote memorization of his formal schoolwork and pursuing for himself advanced mathematics, physics, and philosophy with a tutor. Even before that, in his early childhood, Einstein had a curiosity for the physi-

> **SNAPSHOT BOX**
>
> LANGUAGE: English
> PUBLISHED: 1922, 1930, 1930, 1932
> GENRE: Essays
> TAGS: Ethics and Morality; Internationalism; Religion; Science

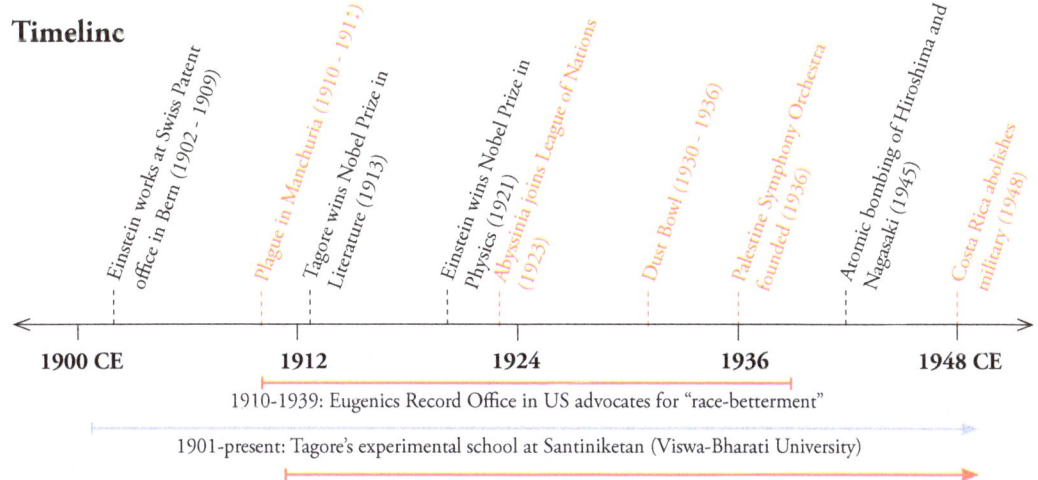

cal world famously symbolized by the wonder and excitement he showed for the compass his father gave him as a toddler. Born in Ulm, but moved at age one to Munich (both part of the German Empire), Einstein had Jewish heritage on both sides, but the family did not practice many religious rites and even sent young Albert to Catholic elementary school. Starting in 1889, the family regularly hosted twenty-one-year-old medical student Max Talmud, who became ten-year-old Albert's tutor and regularly brought him popular illustrated science books and eventually math and physics textbooks. When his family moved to Italy, Einstein, then fifteen, was unable to finish high school while living on his own or pass the entrance exam to begin college early. Instead, he found a home in Aarau, Switzerland, living with one of his teachers and studying for the entrance exam for the prestigious Federal Polytechnic School in Zurich. After completing his degree in Zurich in 1900, Einstein, unsuccessful in finding a graduate teaching job, worked in the patent office in Bern, Switzerland. He continued to pursue his true passions in physics, music, and philosophy extracurricularly through conversations with his self-fashioned book club, "The Olympia Academy," and his new wife, Maria Meric, whom he had met while they were both students in physics and mathematics at Zurich. As a patent officer, Einstein evaluated electromechanical devices, several of which concerned the synchronization of time between distant train stations (or what physicists might call different frames of reference). What facts or myths do you know about Einstein? Why might his education be a source of myths and legends in contemporary popular culture?

In 1905, the year that would come to be called Einstein's "Annus mirabilis" (Miraculous Year), he published four papers, each of which had an impact on some of the most pressing scientific theories of the time, notably atomic theory and nascent quantum theory. The most influential paper, "On the Electrodynamics of Moving Bodies," gave an explanation for the 1887 Michelson-Morley experiment, which had found that the speed of light was the same no matter the frame of reference. This observation, the *invariance* of the speed of light, was inconsistent with Newtonian *relativity*, the idea that measurements of speed depend on the speed of the observer. (For example, when you look out the window of your moving car, the person in the next lane appears stationary to you.) Using illustrations of clocks on trains, Einstein proposed that it was in actuality the measurements of time, length, and mass that were *relative* to the observer, and that the speed of light and laws of physics are *invariant*. One of the consequences of this theory, which came to be called *special relativity* because it only applies to the "special" case of constant velocities, was to show that mass, m, could be exchanged for energy, E, as expressed in the famous formula $E = mc^2$ (where c is the speed of light, a large number, thus making the "exchange rate" tip heavily toward energy).

As the popularity (and controversy) over his special theory spread across the world of physics, Einstein steadily moved through more and more prestigious academic appointments in Europe. Over this time, 1905–1918, he developed his theory of general relativity (applied to all cases, not just the special case of constant velocities), but it would not be until the eclipse measurements of 1919 that this theory gained widespread acceptance and Einstein's fame transcended academia. The experimental confirmation of general relativity was a model of international collaboration and a triumph of modern science, which, in post–World War I Europe, was welcomed as potentially heralding a new era. As the personification of this optimism, Einstein's company was highly sought after by politicians and celebrities as much as scientists. Others, including a growing right-wing, anti-Semitic voice in Germany, sought to distance themselves from Einstein and his controversial theory. As Germany grew more authoritarian, Einstein fled Germany to emigrate to the United States with his second wife and take up residence as professor of mathematics and physics at Princeton University in 1932.

Einstein was a vocal advocate of Zionism (the establishment of a Jewish national state), Democratic Socialism, and pacifism. The selections from Einstein below are all from this inter-war period (1918–1939) where he had become an influential spokesperson for the League of Nations and international cooperation in general. Einstein's thoughts on religion and politics were often the subject of questions from interviewers and dinner guests alike. While the readings will give you an idea of his cosmic religious vision, in other papers and communications he made clear the personal importance of his Jewish heritage.

In his decades-long conversations with Danish colleague Niels Bohr over the emerging theory of quantum mechanics, Einstein rejected the probabilistic nature of the theory. Einstein could not capitulate that some experiments' results were purely random, preferring that all effects must have a preceding cause. Quantum mechanics, for Einstein, was at best incomplete, famously quipping in a personal communication with Bohr that "God does not play dice." Despite his dissension, the symbolism of Einstein's boldness to refute Newtonian physics had paved the way for modern physics. One implication of his relativity soon came to weigh heavily on all humanity. In 1938 Austrian-Swedish physicist Lise Meitner observed the nuclear fission of uranium, and from knowing Einstein's equation, $E=mc^2$, she recognized immediately that this process was capable of producing a weaponizable amount of energy.

Despite his lifetime of pacifism and commitment to human rights, Einstein signed a letter prepared by American physicist Leo Szilard, warning President Franklin Roosevelt of the potential use of nuclear chain reactions in making a bomb and suggesting that the United States should research it before the Germans. This tied his legacy to the use of nuclear weapons in Hiroshima and Nagasaki and to nuclear weapon proliferation, which continues to be an existential threat to humanity.

James Perkins
Department of Physics and Astronomy

> **PRE-READING PARS**
>
> 1. List two or three ways a scientist's training might influence their understanding of spirituality, social concerns, war, or politics?
> 2. Choose an influential scientific discovery or technological innovation. List some of the ramifications of its discovery and use.
> 3. Identify two or three examples in which you see religion and science in conversation with each other.

Selections from the Writings of Albert Einstein

Internationalism of Science

Internationalism of Science, CA. 1922 N & N 1960, 59–60

When nationalism and political passions were reaching a climax during the war, Emil Fischer remarked with emphasis at a session of the Academy: "Whether you like it or not, gentlemen, science is and always will be international."

The great men among scientists have always known this and felt it passionately, even in times of international conflicts when they stood alone amid their narrow-minded colleagues. During the war, the majority of voting members in every country betrayed their sacred trust. The International Association of Academies was destroyed. Congresses were, and still are being, held to which scholars from former enemy countries were not admitted. Political considerations, advanced with pompous solemnity, make it impossible for pure objectivity to prevail, without which great accomplishments cannot mature.

What can be done by well-meaning people who are immune to the emotional temptations of the moment, to restore health to the intellectual community? As long as the majority of intellectual workers remain so embittered, it will not be possible to arrange for an international congress of real significance. Moreover, psychological opposition to the restoration of international associations of scientific workers is still so formidable that the small number of broad-minded people cannot defeat it.

These more enlightened men can make an important contribution to the great task of reviving international societies by keeping in close touch with like-minded men and women the world over, as well as by steadfastly championing the cause of internationalism in their own spheres of influence. Real success will require time, but eventually it will undoubtedly come. I cannot let this opportunity pass without expressing my appreciation to the particularly large number of English colleagues who, throughout these difficult years, have never ceased to manifest a strong desire to preserve the international community of intellectuals.

The attitude of individual citizens is everywhere far superior to official pronouncements. Let men of good will bear this in mind rather than allow themselves to become exasperated or misled: *Senatores boni viri, senatus autem bestia* [the senators are honorable men, but the senate is a monster].

I am extremely hopeful for the progress of a general international organization. My feelings are based not so much on confidence in the intelligence and high-mindedness of scientists as on the inevitable pressure of economic developments. Since these developments are so largely dependent upon the work of even reactionary scientists, they too will have no choice but to assist in the establishment of an international organization.

What I Believe

Forum and Century 84 (October 1930), No. 4, 193–194; Einstein 1954, 8–11

Strange is our situation here upon earth. Each of us comes for a short visit, not knowing why, yet sometimes seeming to divine a purpose.

From the standpoint of daily life, however, there is one thing we do know: that man is here for the sake of other men—above all for those upon whose smiles and well-being our own happiness depends, and also for the countless unknown souls with whose fate we are connected by a bond of sympathy. Many times a day I realize how much my own outer and inner life is built upon the labors of my fellow men, both living and dead, and how earnestly I must exert myself in order to give in return as much as I have received. My peace of mind is often troubled by the depressing sense that I have borrowed too heavily from the work of other men.

I do not believe we can have any freedom at all in the philosophical sense, for we act not only under external compulsion but also by inner necessity. Schopenhauer's saying—"A man can surely do what he wills to do, but he cannot determine what he wills"—impressed itself upon me in youth and has always consoled me when I have witnessed or suffered life's hardships. This conviction is a perpetual breeder of tolerance, for it does not allow us to take ourselves or others too seriously; it makes rather for a sense of humor.

To ponder interminably over the reason for one's own existence or the meaning of life in general seems to me, from an objective point of view, to be sheer folly. And yet everyone holds certain ideals by which he guides his aspiration and his judgment. The ideals which have always shone before me and filled me with the joy of living are goodness, beauty, and truth. To make a goal of comfort or happiness has never appealed to me; a system of ethics built on this basis would be sufficient only for a herd of cattle.

Without the sense of collaborating with like-minded beings in the pursuit of the ever unattainable in art and scientific research, my life would have been empty. Ever since childhood I have scorned the commonplace limits so often set upon human ambition. Possessions, outward success, publicity, luxury—to me these have always been contemptible. I believe that a simple and unassuming manner of life is best for everyone, best both for the body and the mind.

My passionate interest in social justice and social responsibility has always stood in curious contrast to a marked lack of desire for direct association with men and women. I am a horse for single harness, not cut out for tandem or team work. I have never belonged wholeheartedly to country or state, to my circle of friends, or even to my own family. These ties have always been accompanied by a vague aloofness, and the wish to withdraw into myself increases with the years.

Such isolation is sometimes bitter, but I do not regret being cut off from the understanding and sympathy of other men. I lose something by it, to be sure, but I am compensated for it in being rendered independent of the customs, opinions, and prejudices of others, and am not tempted to rest my peace of mind upon such shifting foundations.

My political ideal is democracy. Everyone should be respected as an individual, but no one idolized. It is an irony of fate that I should have been showered with so much uncalled-for and unmerited admiration and esteem. Perhaps this adulation springs from the unfulfilled wish of the multitude to comprehend the few ideas which I, with my weak powers, have advanced.

Full well do I know that in order to attain any definite goal it is imperative that one person should do the thinking and commanding and carry most of the responsibility. But those who are led should not be driven, and they should be allowed to choose their leader. It seems to me that the distinctions separating the social classes are false; in the last analysis they rest on force. I am convinced that degeneracy follows every autocratic system of violence, for violence inevitably attracts moral inferiors. Time has proved that illustrious tyrants are succeeded by scoundrels.

For this reason I have always been passionately opposed to such regimes as exist in Russia and Italy today. The thing which has discredited the European forms of democracy is not the basic theory of democracy itself, which some say is at fault, but the instability of our political leadership, as well as the impersonal character of party alignments.

I believe that you in the United States have hit upon the right idea. You choose a President for a reasonable length of time and give him enough power to acquit himself properly of his responsibilities. In the German Government, on the other hand, I like the state's more extensive care of the individual when he is ill or unemployed. What is truly valuable in our bustle of life is not the nation, I should say, but the creative and impressionable individuality, the personality—he who produces the noble and sublime while the common herd remains dull in thought and insensible in feeling.

This subject brings me to that vilest offspring of the herd mind—the odious militia. The man who enjoys marching in line and file to the strains of music falls below my contempt; he received his great brain by mistake—the spinal cord would have been amply sufficient. This heroism at command, this senseless violence, this accursed bombast of patriotism—how intensely I despise them! War is low and despicable, and I had rather be smitten to shreds [*sic*] than participate in such doings.

Such a stain on humanity should be erased without delay. I think well enough of human nature to believe that it would have been wiped out long ago had not the common sense of nations been systematically corrupted through school and press for business and political reasons.

The most beautiful thing we can experience is the mysterious. It is the source of all true art and science. He to whom this emotion is a stranger, who can no longer pause to wonder and stand rapt in awe, is as good as dead: his eyes are closed. This insight into the mystery of life, coupled though it be with fear, has also given rise to religion. To know that what is impenetrable to us really exists, manifesting itself as the highest wisdom and the most radiant beauty which our dull faculties can comprehend only in their most primitive forms—this knowledge, this feeling, is at the center of true religiousness. In this sense, and in this sense only, I belong in the ranks of devoutly religious men.

I cannot imagine a God who rewards and punishes the objects of his creation, whose purposes are modeled after our own—a God, in short, who is but a reflection of human frailty. Neither can I believe that the individual survives the death of his body, although feeble souls harbor such thoughts through fear or ridiculous egotism. It is enough for me to contemplate the mystery of conscious life perpetuating itself through all eternity, to reflect upon the marvelous structure of the universe which we can dimly perceive, and to try humbly to comprehend even an infinitesimal part of the intelligence manifested in nature.

Religion and Science

New York Times Magazine, 9 November 1930; Einstein 1931B, 43–54

Everything that men do or think concerns the satisfaction of the needs they feel or the escape from pain. This must be kept in mind when we seek to understand spiritual or intellectual movements and the way in which they develop. For feeling and longing are the motive forces of all human striving and productivity—however nobly these latter may display themselves to us.

What, then, are the feelings and the needs which have brought mankind to religious thought and to faith in the widest sense? A moment's consideration shows that the most varied emotions stand at the cradle of religious thought and experience.

In primitive peoples it is, first of all, fear that awakens religious ideas—fear of hunger, of wild animals, of illness and of death. Since the understanding of causal connections is usually limited on this level of existence, the human soul forges a being, more or less like itself, on whose will and activities depend the experiences which it fears. One hopes to win the favor of this being by deeds and sacrifices, which, according to the tradition of the race, are supposed to appease the being or to make him well disposed to man. I call this the religion of fear.

This religion is considerably stabilized—though not caused—by the formation of a priestly caste which claims to mediate between the people and the being they fear, and so attains a position of power. Often a leader or despot, or a privileged class whose power is maintained in other ways, will combine the function of the priesthood with its own temporal rule for the sake of greater security; or an alliance may exist between the interests of the political power and the priestly caste.

A second source of religious development is found in the social feelings. Fathers and mothers, as well as leaders of great human communities are fallible and mortal. The longing for guidance, for love and succor, provides the stimulus for the growth of a social or moral conception of God. This is the God of Providence, who protects, decides, rewards, and punishes. This is the God who, according to man's widening horizon, loves and provides for the life of the race, or of mankind, or who even loves life itself. He is the comforter in unhappiness and in unsatisfied longing, the protector of the souls of the dead. This is the social or moral idea of God.

It is easy to follow in the sacred writings of the Jewish people the development of the religion of fear into the moral religion, which is carried further in the New Testament. The religions of all the civilized peoples, especially those of the Orient, are principally moral religions. An important advance in the life of a people is the transformation of the religion of fear into the moral religion. But one must avoid the prejudice that regards the religions of primitive peoples as pure fear religions and those of the civilized races as pure moral religions. All are mixed forms, though the moral element predominates in the higher levels of social life. Common to all these types is the anthropomorphic character of the idea of God.

Only exceptionally gifted individuals or especially noble communities rise *essentially* above this level; in these there is found a third level of religious experience, even if it is seldom found in a pure form. I will call it the cosmic religious sense. This is hard to make clear to those who do not experience it, since it does not involve an anthropomorphic idea of God: the individual feels the vanity of human desires and aims, and the nobility and marvelous order which are revealed in nature and in the world of thought. He feels the individual destiny as an imprisonment and seeks to experience the totality of existence as a unity full of significance. Indications of this cosmic religious sense can be found even on earlier levels of development—for example, in the Psalms of David and in the Prophets. The cosmic element is much stronger in Buddhism, as, in particular, Schopenhauer's magnificent essays have shown us.

The religious geniuses of all times have been distinguished by this cosmic religious sense, which recognizes neither dogmas nor God made in man's image. Consequently there cannot be a church whose chief doctrines are based on the cosmic religious experience. It comes about, therefore, that we find precisely among the heretics of all ages men who were inspired by this highest religious experience; often they appeared to their contemporaries as atheists, but sometimes also as saints. Viewed from this angle, men like Democritus, Francis of Assisi, and Spinoza are near to one another.

How can this cosmic religious experience be communicated from man to man, if it cannot lead to a definite conception of God or to a theology? It seems to me that the most important function of art and of science is to arouse and keep alive this feeling in those who are receptive.

Thus we reach an interpretation of the relation of science to religion which is very different from the customary view. From the study of history, one is inclined to regard religion and science as irreconcilable antagonists, and this for a reason that is very easily seen. For any one who is pervaded with the sense of causal law in all that happens, who accepts in real earnest the assumption of causality, the idea of a Being who interferes with the sequence of events in the world is absolutely impossible. Neither the religion of fear nor the social-moral religion can have any hold on him. A God who rewards and punishes is for him unthinkable because man acts in accordance with an inner and outer necessity, and would, in the eyes of God, be as little responsible as an inanimate object is for the movements which it makes.

Science, in consequence, has been accused of undermining morals—but wrongly. The ethical behavior of man is better based on sympathy, education, and social relationships, and requires no support from religion. Man's plight would, indeed, be sad if he had to be kept in order through fear of punishment and hope of rewards after death.

It is, therefore, quite natural that the churches have always fought against science and have persecuted its supporters. But, on the other hand, I assert that the cosmic religious experience is the strongest and the noblest driving force behind scientific research. No one who does not appreciate the terrific exertions, and, above all, the devotion without which pioneer creations in scientific thought cannot come into being, can judge the strength of the feeling out of which alone such work, turned away as it is from immediate practical life, can grow. What a deep faith in the rationality of the structure of the world and what a longing to understand even a small glimpse of the reason revealed in the world there must have been in Kepler and Newton to enable them to unravel the mechanism of the heavens, in the long years of lonely work!

Anyone who only knows scientific research in its practical applications may easily come to a wrong interpretation of the state of mind of the men who, surrounded by skeptical contemporaries, have shown the way to kindred spirits scattered over all countries in all centuries. Only those who have dedicated their lives to similar ends can have a living conception of the inspiration which gave these men the power to remain loyal to their purpose in spite of countless failures. It is the cosmic religious sense which grants this power.

A contemporary has rightly said that the only deeply religious people of our largely materialistic age are the earnest men of research.

Letter to Sigmund Freud, 30 July 1932

Einstein/Freud, 11–20; N & N 1960, 188–191

The proposal of the League of Nations and its International Institute of Intellectual Co-operation at Paris that I should invite a person, to be chosen by myself, to a frank exchange of views on any problem that I might select affords me a very welcome opportunity of conferring with you upon a question which, as things now are, seems the most insistent of all the problems civilisation has to face. This is the problem: Is there any way of delivering mankind from the menace of war? It is common knowledge that, with the advance of modern science, this issue has come to mean a matter of life and death for civilisation as we know it; nevertheless, for all the zeal displayed, every attempt at its solution has ended in a lamentable breakdown.

I believe, moreover, that those whose duty it is to tackle the problem professionally and practically are growing only too aware of their impotence to deal with it, and have now a very lively desire to learn the views of men who, absorbed in the pursuit of science, can see world problems in the perspective distance lends. As for me, the normal objective of my thought affords no insight into the dark places of human will and feeling. Thus, in the enquiry now proposed, I can do little more than to seek to clarify the question at issue and, clearing the ground of the more obvious solutions, enable you to bring the light of your far-reaching knowledge of man's instinctive life to bear upon the problem. There are certain psychological obstacles whose existence a layman in the mental sciences may dimly surmise, but whose interrelations and vagaries he is incompetent to fathom; you, I am convinced, will be able to suggest educative methods, lying more or less outside the scope of politics, which will eliminate these obstacles.

As one immune from nationalist bias, I personally see a simple way of dealing with the superficial (i.e., administrative) aspect of the problem: the setting up, by international consent, of a legislative and judicial body to settle every conflict arising between nations. Each nation would undertake to abide by the orders issued by this legislative body, to invoke its decision in every dispute, to accept its judgments unreservedly and to carry out every measure the tribunal deems necessary for the execution of its decrees. But here, at the outset, I come up against a difficulty; a tribunal is a human institution which, in proportion as the power at its disposal is inadequate to enforce its verdicts, is all the more prone to suffer these to be deflected by extrajudicial pressure. This is a fact with which we have to reckon; law and might inevitably go hand in hand, and juridical decisions approach more nearly the ideal justice demanded by the community (in whose name and interests these verdicts are pronounced) in so far as the community has effective power to compel respect of its juridical ideal. But at present we are far from possessing any supranational organisation competent to render verdicts of incontestable authority and enforce absolute submission to the execution of its verdicts. Thus I am led to my first axiom: The quest of international security involves the unconditional surrender by every nation, in a certain measure, of its liberty of action, its sovereignty that is to say, and it is clear beyond all doubt that no other road can lead to such security.

The ill-success, despite their obvious sincerity, of all the efforts made during the last decade to reach this goal leaves us no room to doubt that strong psychological factors are at work, which paralyse these efforts. Some of these factors are not far to seek. The craving for power which characterises the governing class in every nation is hostile to any limitation of the national sovereignty. This political power-hunger is wont to batten on the activities of another group, whose aspirations are on purely mercenary, economic lines. I have specially in mind that small but determined group, active in every nation, composed of individuals who, indifferent to social considerations and restraints, regard warfare, the manufacture and sale of arms, simply as an occasion to advance their personal interests and enlarge their personal authority.

But recognition of this obvious fact is merely the first step toward an appreciation of the actual state of affairs. Another question follows hard upon it: How is it possible for this small clique to bend the will of the majority, who stand to lose and suffer by a state of war, to the service of their ambitions? (In speaking of the majority, I do not exclude soldiers of every rank who have chosen war as their profession, in the belief that they are serving to defend the highest interests of their race, and that attack is often the best method of defence.) An obvious answer to this question would seem to be that the minority, the ruling class at present, has the schools and press, usually the Church as well, under its thumb. This enables it to organise and sway the emotions of the masses, and make its tool of them.

Yet even this answer does not provide a complete solution. Another question arises from it: How is it these devices succeed so well in rousing men to such wild enthusiasm, even to sacrifice their lives? Only one answer is possible. Because man has within him a lust for hatred and destruction. In normal times this passion exists in a latent state, it emerges only in unusual circumstances; but it is a comparatively easy task to call it into play and raise it to the power of a collective psychosis. Here lies, perhaps, the crux of all the complex of factors we are considering, an enigma that only the expert in the lore of human instincts can resolve.

And so we come to our last question. Is it possible to control man's mental evolution so as to make him proof against the psychoses of hate and destructiveness? Here I am thinking by no means only of the so-called uncultured masses. Experience proves that it is rather the so-called "Intelligentzia" that is most apt to yield to these disastrous collective suggestions, since the intellectual has no direct contact with life in the raw, but encounters it in its easiest, synthetic form upon the printed page.

To conclude: I have so far been speaking only of wars between nations; what are known as international conflicts. But I am well aware that the aggressive instinct operates under other forms and in other circumstances. (I am thinking of civil wars, for instance, due in earlier days to religious zeal, but nowadays to social factors; or, again, the persecution of racial minorities.) But my insistence on what is the most typical, most cruel and extravagant form of conflict between man and man was deliberate, for here we have the best occasion of discovering ways and means to render all armed conflicts impossible.

I know that in your writings we may find answers, explicit or implied, to all the issues of this urgent and absorbing problem. But it would be of the greatest service to us all were you to present the problem of world peace in the light of your most recent discoveries, for such a presentation well might blaze the trail for new and fruitful modes of action.

Conversation with Rabindranath Tagore

In the home of Albert Einstein, August 19, 1930, Caputh, Germany.

Tagore: I was discussing with Dr. Mendel today the new mathematical discoveries which tell us that in the realm of infinitesimal atoms chance has its play; the drama of existence is not absolutely predestined in character.

Einstein: The facts that make science tend toward this view do not say good-bye to causality.

Tagore: Maybe not, yet it appears that the idea of causality is not in the elements, but that some other force builds up with them an organized universe.

Einstein: One tries to understand in the higher plane how the order is. The order is there, where the big elements combine and guide existence, but in the minute elements this order is not perceptible.

Tagore: Thus duality is in the depths of existence, the contradiction of free impulse and the directive will which works upon it and evolves an orderly scheme of things.

Einstein: Modern physics would not say they are contradictory. Clouds look as one from a distance, but if you see them nearby, they show themselves as disorderly drops of water.

Tagore: I find a parallel in human psychology. Our passions and desires are unruly, but our character subdues these elements into a harmonious whole. Does something similar to this happen in the physical world? Are the elements rebellious, dynamic with individual impulse? And is there a principle in the physical world which dominates them and puts them into an orderly organization?

Einstein: Even the elements are not without statistical order; elements of radium will always maintain their specific order, now and ever onward, just as they have done all along. There is, then, a statistical order in the elements.

Tagore: Otherwise, the drama of existence would be too desultory. It is the constant harmony of chance and determination which makes it eternally new and living.

Einstein: I believe that whatever we do or live for has its causality; it is good, however, that we cannot see through to it.

Tagore: There is in human affairs an element of elasticity also, some freedom within a small range which is for the expression of our personality. It is like the musical system in India, which is not so rigidly fixed as western music. Our composers give a certain definite outline, a system of melody and rhythmic arrangement, and within a certain limit the player can improvise upon it. He must be one with the law of that particular melody, and then he can give spontaneous expression to his musical feeling within the prescribed regulation. We praise the composer for his genius in creating a foundation along with a superstructure of melodies, but we expect from the player his own skill in the creation of variations of melodic flourish and ornamentation. In creation we follow the central law of existence, but if we do not cut ourselves adrift from it, we can have sufficient freedom within the limits of our personality for the fullest self-expression.

Einstein: That is possible only when there is a strong artistic tradition in music to guide the people's mind. In Europe, music has come too far away from popular art and popular feeling and has become something like a secret art with conventions and traditions of its own.

Tagore: You have to be absolutely obedient to this too complicated music. In India, the measure of a singer's freedom is in his own creative personality. He can sing the composer's song as his own, if he has the power creatively to assert himself in his interpretation of the general law of the melody which he is given to interpret.

Einstein: It requires a very high standard of art to realize fully the great idea in the original music, so that one can make variations upon it. In our country, the variations are often prescribed.

Tagore: If in our conduct we can follow the law of goodness, we can have real liberty of self-expression. The principle of conduct is there, but the character which makes it true and individual is our own creation. In our music there is a duality of freedom and prescribed order.

Einstein: Are the words of a song also free? I mean to say, is the singer at liberty to add his own words to the song which he is singing?

Tagore: Yes. In Bengal we have a kind of song—*kirtan*, we call it—which gives freedom to the singer to introduce parenthetical comments, phrases not in the original song. This occasions great enthusiasm, since the audience is constantly thrilled by some beautiful, spontaneous sentiment added by the singer.

Einstein: Is the metrical form quite severe?

Tagore: Yes, quite. You cannot exceed the limits of versification; the singer in all his variations must keep the rhythm and the time, which is fixed. In European music you have a comparative liberty with time, but not with melody.

Einstein: Can the Indian music be sung without words? Can one understand a song without words?

Tagore: Yes, we have songs with unmeaning words, sounds which just help to act as carriers of the notes. In North India, music is an independent art, not the interpretation of words and thoughts, as in Bengal. The music is very intricate and subtle and is a complete world of melody by itself.

Einstein: Is it not polyphonic?

Tagore: Instruments are used, not for harmony, but for keeping time and adding to the volume and depth. Has melody suffered in your music by the imposition of harmony?

Einstein: Sometimes it does suffer very much. Sometimes the harmony swallows up the melody altogether.

Tagore: Melody and harmony are like lines and colors in pictures. A simple linear picture may be completely beautiful; the introduction of color may make it vague and insignificant. Yet color may, by combination with lines, create great pictures, so long as it does not smother and destroy their value.

Einstein: It is a beautiful comparison; line is also much older than color. It seems that your melody is much richer in structure than ours. Japanese music also seems to be so.

Tagore: It is difficult to analyze the effect of eastern and western music on our minds. I am deeply moved by the western music; I feel that it is great, that it is vast in its structure and grand in its composition. Our own music touches me more deeply by its fundamental lyrical appeal. European music is epic in character; it has a broad background and is Gothic in its structure.

Einstein: This is a question we Europeans cannot properly answer, we are so used to our own music. We want to know whether our own music is a conventional or a fundamental human feeling, whether to feel consonance and dissonance is natural, or a convention which we accept.

Tagore: Somehow the piano confounds me. The violin pleases me much more.

Einstein: It would be interesting to study the effects of European music on an Indian who had never heard it when he was young.

Tagore: Once I asked an English musician to analyze for me some classical music, and explain to me what elements make for the beauty of the piece.

Einstein: The difficulty is that the really good music, whether of the East or of the West, cannot be analyzed.

Tagore: Yes, and what deeply affects the hearer is beyond himself.

Einstein: The same uncertainty will always be there about everything fundamental in our experience, in our reaction to art, whether in Europe or in Asia. Even the red flower I see before me on your table may not be the same to you and me.

Tagore: And yet there is always going on the process of reconciliation between them, the individual taste conforming to the universal standard.

Einstein, Albert. "Internationalism of Science." In *Einstein on Politics: His Private Thoughts and Public Stands on Nationalism Zionism, War, Peace, and the Bomb*, edited by David E. Rowe and Robert J. Schulmann, 192–94. Princeton, NJ: Princeton University Press, 2013.

Einstein, Albert. "What I Believe." In *Einstein on Politics: His Private Thoughts and Public Stands on Nationalism Zionism, War, Peace, and the Bomb*, edited by David E. Rowe and Robert J. Schulmann, 226–30. Princeton, NJ: Princeton University Press, 2013.

Einstein, Albert. "Religion and Science." In *Einstein on Politics: His Private Thoughts and Public Stands on Nationalism Zionism, War, Peace, and the Bomb*, edited by David E. Rowe and Robert J. Schulmann, 231–34. Princeton, NJ: Princeton University Press, 2013.

Einstein, Albert. "Letter to Sigmund Freud, 30 July, 1932." The Albert Einstein Archives. With permission, the Hebrew University of Jerusalem.

Tagore, Rabindranath. "In Conversation with Albert Einstein." In *The Religion of Man*, edited by Rabindranath Tagore, 222–25. George Allen & Unwin, 1953.

POST-READING PARS

1. What does Einstein say that he, or scientists in general, might add to conversations on spirituality, social concerns, war, or politics?
2. How should a scientist/inventor be held accountable for the ramifications of their discovery/innovation? Consider your example in the Pre-PAR or others. How should an artist/author be held accountable?
3. How does Einstein envision the relationship between religion and science?

Inquiry Corner

Content Question:	Critical Questions:
Einstein makes some propositions in his essays as indisputable Truth. These are the starting points (i.e., axioms) on which his arguments and theses are based. Identify examples of Einstein's axioms in each of the readings and connect them to his theses.	In what ways does the scientific method inspire how he writes about the topics in these essays? Critically evaluate how Einstein's discoveries could be considered a product of his cultural milieu and scientific heritage.
Comparative Question:	**Connection Question:**
Hold these readings from Einstein in comparison with each other. Describe possible contradictions, resonances, or common themes.	What shared connections and approach do you find between Einstein's works and movements that call into question the status quo of mathematics, art, literature, social theory, and politics?

> **BEYOND THE CLASSROOM**

» What advantages and challenges are there for localized organizations (NGOs, businesses)? For international organizations? Do the challenges that Einstein noted about international cooperation still apply today?

from "Self Portrait of K'ang-hsi (The Emperor)" by K'ang-hsi

Introduction

At the age of seven, the K'ang-hsi (Kangxi) emperor ascended the throne as the second emperor of the Qing dynasty, which ruled China from 1644–1912. His reign lasted for sixty-one years (1661–1722), the longest of any Chinese emperor, even though he himself was not Chinese. He was a **Manchu**—a minority people from the north who had conquered China much like the Mongols four hundred years earlier. Unlike the Mongols, however, the Manchus devoted themselves to Chinese culture and K'ang-hsi had learned the language as a child. He turned out to be an extraordinarily talented ruler, as were his son and grandson. China had only three emperors in a period of 135 years (1661–1796), which made China one of the most stable, prosperous, and powerful nations in the world at the time. The population grew, art and literature flourished, and the military expanded the borders of the empire. By adopting Confucian ideas, Qing rulers were able to make common cause with Chinese scholars, who filled the ranks of the bureaucracy. How might only having three rulers in 135 years foster stability and at what costs?

The era of K'ang-hsi was also a time when more Westerners began to enter China. Jesuit priests brought European math and science to the imperial court, hoping that their technical skills might persuade the Chinese to adopt their religion as well. Several of the missionaries became quite proficient in both Chinese and Manchu and thus were able to converse freely with K'ang-hsi. The emperor was

> **SNAPSHOT BOX**
>
> **LANGUAGE:** Chinese
>
> **COMPOSED:** Early 1700s China
>
> **GENRE:** Autobiography
>
> **TAGS:** Autobiography and Testimony; Cross-Cultural Encounters; Education; Ethics and Morality; Nationalism; Religion; Science; Statecraft; Ways of Knowing

mildly interested, and there were a few prominent Chinese converts to Christianity, but after his death the mission faltered because of arguments among Catholics about how to treat rituals of filial piety, which were a central part of Chinese culture. The Jesuits viewed these ceremonies as simply a way to show respect to one's parents, while other Catholic orders such as the Dominicans countered that they were "ancestor worship" and thus were unacceptable heathen practices. The pope sided with the Dominicans, which effectively brought an end to proselytizing in China. Similarly, K'ang-hsi was open to foreign trade—though Westerners had little to offer in the way of necessities—but he regulated the travel of Europeans, which later led to foreign merchants being restricted to a single southern city, Canton (near present-day Hong Kong), in an arrangement known as the **Canton System**. K'ang-hsi and his successors felt that Europeans, along with their goods and ideas, were intriguing but potentially dangerous. This limitation on foreigners traveling within China lasted until 1858, the time of the Second Opium War.

K'ang-hsi was something of a workaholic who rose before dawn every day to spend long hours reading and responding to **memorials** (reports) on military, economic, diplomatic, and administrative matters. He personally led two military campaigns and went on six grand tours of inspection to observe conditions around the country. He was curious and energetic. He studied the Confucian Classics diligently, particularly the works of the twelfth-century philosopher Chu Hsi (Zhu Xi); conversed with Jesuits and Buddhists; sponsored the compilation of a massive encyclopedia and an exhaustive dictionary; wrote poetry; and was the first Chinese emperor to learn to play the harpsichord.

Because imperial China was such a highly literate society, in which administrative records were meticulously kept, K'ang-hsi's long reign was documented by daily reports, diaries of court figures, and thousands of pages of the emperor's own writings, including edicts, letters, essays, and handwritten notes on memorials. In 1974, the historian Jonathan Spence read through these materials and selected some of K'ang-hsi's most personal and revealing comments, which he then arranged into a sort of autobiography. The excerpts that follow are from the chapter Spence titled "Thinking." Here we can see the emperor wrestling with new ideas and making judgments. With Spence's assistance, we are able to hear his voice—candid, reflective, inquisitive—on all sorts of topics ranging from epistemology to ethics, natural phenomena to human customs and artifacts, and mathematics to religion. As you read K'ang-hsi's *Self Portrait*, reflect on how his ideas relate to the intellectual and cultural ferment in Europe known as the Scientific Revolution and the Enlightenment. How are they distinctly Chinese?

Grant Hardy
Department of History

from "Self Portrait of K'ang-hsi (The Emperor)"

Too many people claim to know things when, in fact, they know nothing about them. Since my childhood I have always tried to find things out for myself and not to pretend to have knowledge when I was ignorant. Whenever I met older people I would ask them about the experiences they had had, and remember what they said. Keep an open mind, and you'll learn things; you will miss other people's good qualities if you just concentrate on your own abilities. It's my nature to enjoy asking questions, and the crudest or simplest people have something of value to say, something one can check through to the source and remember.

[…]

If you want to really know something you have to observe or experience it in person; if you claim to know something on the basis of hearsay, or on happening to see it in a book, you'll be a laughingstock to those who really know.

[…]

Sometimes an exact answer is hard to find, as with the morning and evening tides. Whenever I was on the seashore—whether in Shan-hai-kuan, or Tientsin, or near the mouth of the Yangtze River—I would observe when the tides rose and fell. But when I would question the locals they generally all gave different answers, and the records of the times kept in different places were also different. Later I found that even water in springs and wells fluctuates slightly in level, though again one can't be precise about the time. I questioned Westerners and ocean sailors; they all disagreed. Clearly Chu Hsi was right that there is a relationship between tides and the moon's waxing and waning, but it's hard to get clearer than that.

So we draw our idea of "principle" from experience rather than from study, though we need to keep aware of both. Many people, after all, call old porcelain vessels "antiques"; but if we think of vessels from the view of principle, then we know that once they were meant to be used. Only now are they grubby-looking and unsuitable for us to drink from, so we end up putting them on our desks or on bookshelves, and look at them once in a while. On the other hand, we can change the function of a given object and thus change its nature, as I did by converting a rustless sword that the Dutch once gave me into a measuring stick that I kept on my desk. As the Jesuit Antoine Thomas observed, this was converting something that gave fear into something that gave pleasure. The rare can become common, as with the lions and other animals that foreign ambassadors like to give us and my children are now accustomed to; though when something new appears, I always take a close look at it, as with the sea lion that the Korean king gave me once on a Northern Tour. I immediately sent riders back to Peking [Beijing] for a copy of the book in which the Westerners said this creature could be identified.

Western skills are a case in point: in the late Ming Dynasty,[29] when the West-

---

29. 1368–1644.

erners first brought the gnomon,[30] the Chinese thought it a rare treasure until they understood its use. And when the Emperor Shun-chih got a small chiming clock in 1653, he kept it always near him; but now we have learned to balance the springs and to adjust the chimes and finally to make the whole clock, so that my children can have ten chiming clocks each to play with, if they want them. Similarly, we learned in a short time to make glassware that is superior to that made in the West, and our lacquer would be better than theirs, too, were it not that their wet sea climate gives a better sheen than the dry and dusty Chinese climate ever could.

[...]

I told Chang Ying once, on a Southern Tour, that there is no need to visit a temple again if you've already been there several times, and I myself like to go to different shrines, whether to the temples in the South, to Wu-t'ai-shan (where I wrote a eulogy in Manchu and had it carved on stone), or to the top of Mount T'ai (where Confucius once stood and surveyed the world below). On that journey, in 1684, I refused my retainers' requests that we visit the precipices where people sometimes killed themselves, hoping that by offering up their own lives they might save those of their dying parents. I refused to condone such acts by visiting the place where they occurred; for even if the suicide was committed in the name of filial piety, by killing himself the victim cut off forever all chances of helping his parents. Instead, I proceeded to Confucius' home at Ch'ü-fu, made the ritual prostrations and offerings, heard the ritual music, and listened to the ritual lectures on the *Great Learning* and the *Book of Changes*. Then I told Confucius' descendant, the Yen-sheng duke, K'ung Yü-ch'i, and his clansman K'ung Shang-jen to show me around.

[...]

The temple grounds were so extensive: where was the Sage's own dwelling? Behind the hall where I heard the lectures were the Lu wall ruins, where Confucius had his home. So I leaned over the railings of Confucius' well and, admiring, drew some water and tasted it. I asked about the ruins, and they said it was in this wall that the ninth-generation descendant of Confucius hid the Classics when the Emperor Ch'in Shih-huang burned the books. They were rediscovered when Emperor Han Ching-ti's fifth son started to pull down the buildings to make way for his own palace [*c.* A.D. 150]. I had them point out the actual places, and looked them over carefully.

Trees and grasses grew on Confucius' tomb, and I faced north and kowtowed before it, offering three libations from the golden bowl of wine that Mingju held. "What are those trees and grasses growing on the tomb? What are the *k'ai* trees used for? Isn't there any *chih* grass? Bring me some to look at. If fifty blades are growing in one clump of *chih* grass, the divinations you make with it will be fulfilled. Is there any of that kind here or not?" Not at present, they said, but some would surely grow in honor of the Emperor's visit. So I had them hunt for what there was, and when they found some I took a double handful and inhaled its strange fragrance.

---

30. Pin on a sundial that casts a shadow indicating the time of day.

[...]

I realized, too, that Western mathematics has its uses. I first grew interested in this subject shortly after I came to the throne, during the confrontations between the Jesuit Adam Schall and his Chinese critic, Yang Kuang-hsien, when the two men argued the merits of their respective techniques by the Wu-men Gate and none of the great officials there knew what was going on. Schall died in prison, but after I had learned something about astronomy I pardoned his friend Verbiest in 1669 and gave him an official position, promoting him in 1682. In 1687 I let the newly arrived Jesuit Fontaney and the others come to Peking, although they had come to China illegally on a Chinese merchant vessel and the Board of Rites had recommended their deportation; and throughout the 1680s I discussed Western skills in Manchu with Verbiest, and I made Grimaldi and Pereira learn the language as well, so they could converse with me.

[...]

But I was careful not to refer to these Westerners as "Great Officials," and corrected Governor Liu Yin-shu when he referred to the Jesuits Régis and Fridelli–whom I had dispatched to make a geographical survey of his province—as if they were honored imperial commissioners. For even though some of the Western methods are different from our own, and may even be an improvement, there is little about them that is new. The principles of mathematics all derive from the *Book of Changes*, and the Western methods are Chinese in origin: this algebra—"A-erh-chu-pa-erh"—springs from an Eastern word. And though it was indeed the Westerners who showed us something our ancient calendar experts did not know—namely how to calculate the angles of the northern pole–this but shows the truth of what Chu Hsi arrived at through his investigation of things: the earth is like the yolk within an egg. The Westerners seem to have principles found in the *Book of Changes*, echoing that book with four axes and four points; and they have magic squares like those in the *Ho-t'u lo-shu*, a sequence of the numbers one, three, nine, seven moving around from the left, and the number five stationary in the center, representing the sum of three for heaven and two for earth–the harmony of mankind.

4	9	2
3	5	7
8	1	6

I did praise their work, saying "the 'new methods' of calculating make basic errors impossible" and "the general principles of Western calendrical science are without error." But I added that they still cannot prevent small errors from occurring, and that over the decades these small errors mount up.

After all, they know only a fraction of what I know, and none of the Westerners is really conversant with Chinese literature—except perhaps for the Jesuit Bouvet, who has read a great deal, and developed the ability to undertake serious study of the *Book of Changes*. Often one can't keep from smiling when they start off on a discussion. How can they presume to talk about "the great principles of China"? Sometimes they act wrongly because they are not used to our ways, sometimes they are misled by ignorant Chinese fellows—the papal legate de Tournon used wrongly elevated characters on his memorials employed improper phrases, implied that the word "emperor" [*huang*] was also used among his own people, wrote his memorials on paper decorated with five-clawed dragons, and so on.

[…]

On the question of the Chinese Rites that might be practiced by the Western missionaries, de Tournon would not speak, though I sent messages to him repeatedly. I had agreed with the formulation the Peking fathers had drawn up in 1700: that Confucius was honored by the Chinese as a master, but his name was not invoked in prayer for the purpose of gaining happiness, rank, or wealth; that worship of ancestors was an expression of love and filial remembrance, not intended to bring protection to the worshiper; and that there was no idea, when an ancestral tablet was erected, that the soul of the ancestor dwelt in that tablet. And when sacrifices were offered to Heaven it was not the blue existent sky that was addressed, but the lord and creator of all things. If the ruler Shang-ti was sometimes called Heaven, T'ien, that had no more significance than giving honorific names to the emperor.

If de Tournon didn't reply, the Catholic Bishop Maigrot did, coming to Jehol and telling me that Heaven is a material thing and should not be worshiped, and that one should invoke only the name "Lord of Heaven" to show the proper reverence. Maigrot wasn't merely ignorant of Chinese literature, he couldn't even recognize the simplest Chinese characters; yet he chose to discuss the falsity of the Chinese moral system. Sometimes, as I pointed out, the emperor is addressed honorifically as "under the steps of the throne"; would Maigrot say this was reverence to a set of steps made by some artisan? I am addressed as "Wan-sui, Ten Thousand Years"; obviously that too is not literal—since from the beginnings of history to the present day only 7,600 years have passed. Even little animals mourn their dead mothers for many days; these Westerners who want to treat their dead with indifference are not even equal to animals. How could they be compared with Chinese? We venerate Confucius because of his doctrines of respect for virtue, his system of education, his inculcation of love for superiors and ancestors. Westerners venerate their own saints because of their actions. They paint pictures of men with wings and say, "These represent heavenly spirits, swift as if they had wings, though in reality there are no men with wings." I do not find it appropriate to dispute this doctrine, yet with superficial knowledge Maigrot discussed Chinese sanctity. He talked for days, with his perverse reason, his poorly concealed anger, and fled the country when he could not get his way, a sinner against the Catholic teaching and a rebel to China. As my son Yin-jeng said to Bouvet on another occasion, "If Buddha and other idols are shown in clothes does that prevent you from wearing clothes? They have temples, yet you build them also to your god. One doesn't blame your attachment to your religion, but one does blame—and rightly—your obstinacy on matters of which you know nothing."

Every country must have spirits that it reveres. This is true for our dynasty, as for Mongols or Mohammedans, Miao or Lolo, or other foreigners. Just as everyone fears something, some snakes but not toads, some toads but not snakes; and as all countries have different pronunciations and different alphabets. But in this Catholic religion, the Society of Peter quarrels with the Jesuits, Bouvet quarrels with Mariani, and among the Jesuits the Portuguese want only their own nationals in their church while the French want only French in theirs. This violates the principles of religion. Such dissension cannot be inspired by the Lord of Heaven but by the Devil, who, I have heard the Westerners say, leads men to do evil since he can't do otherwise.

Spence, Jonathan D. *Emperor of China: Self-Portrait of K'ang-hsi*, 65–72, 74–75, 79–81. New York: Alfred A. Knopf, 1974.

BEYOND THE CLASSROOM

» At the beginning of this reading, K'ang-hsi speaks of the importance of being curious and asking others about their experiences. He also states that if you want to really know something, you have to observe or experience it in person. Today, higher education and career services still believe this to be true. Experiential learning is very important to our personal and professional development. What are some ways you can be intentionally curious and how can this help you learn about potential industries/organizations/careers?

"Teaching and Telling Stories" ("Contar") by Gabriela Mistral

SNAPSHOT BOX

LANGUAGE: Spanish
PUBLISHED: 1929, Costa Rica
GENRE: Essay
TAGS: Art; Community; Education; Historiography; Poetry, Music, Literature; Psyche; Tradition

Introduction

Gabriela Mistral was born Lucila Godoy y Alcayaga in 1889 in Vicuña, Chile (d. 1957). Though her formal education ended when she was about eleven due to the limitations of her rural community and her family's economic poverty, Mistral studied under her sister (a teacher in the local school) and became a teacher herself while still a teenager. She was denied entrance to Normal College, the teacher training facility, most likely due to her writings in the local papers where she had voiced opinions seen by some in authority as unorthodox. Her essays in the local press and her teaching assignments spoke to the need to teach women equal to men.

She taught in rural schools throughout Chile's vast, elongated landscape, including evening classes attended by the poor and working class. By 1921 she had become the director of Liceo #6 in the capital Santiago, one of the nation's most prestigious schools. At the invitation of Jose Vasconcelos, the director of education in post-revolutionary Mexico, Mistral worked for more than a year to advance the cause of rural education and the education of women. Upon her return to Chile in 1923, she was awarded "Teacher of the Nation." In 1925 Chile mandated that all teachers hold university degrees, and despite Mistral's many accomplishments, this was a qualification she herself did not possess. Her knowledge was autodidactic, that is, learned on her own. What role do you think experience should play in enabling the authority to teach? Because she could no longer of-

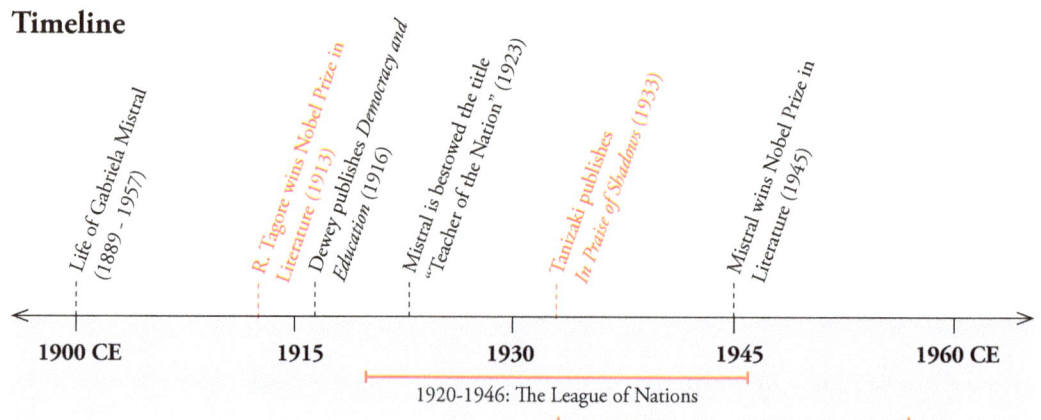

ficially teach in Chile, she began teaching abroad, writing, and practicing diplomacy, holding important posts in North American and European cities.

She dedicated herself to championing the marginalized, especially women, the poor, and the Indigenous. As a youth she sought out the stories of her elders. One sees this in this short excerpt where she extols the value of "ordinary stories" and cites her preference for her sister's renderings of biblical stories over those of the priest.

People have long told stories not only to entertain but to convey important values, ideas, and lessons. By listening to the Anansi stories of West Africa, the proverbs of the Semitic scriptures, the Jataka tales from the Buddhist tradition, or the Jack tales from the Appalachian region, we discern information valued within a culture. In the 1970s Robert Heyman coined the term "**edutainment**" to describe the kind of learning we do while being entertained. This term was picked up and popularized by, among others, the politically conscious rapper KRS-One who named his 1990 album "Edutainment." In what ways has edutainment played a role in your education?

The strong role of narratives in human culture and in education has not been without debate. For years people have grappled with the "authority" of a storyteller (one should not ignore the connection between "author" and "authority"). John Dewey, the early twentieth-century American philosopher and education reformer, thought it important that schools move beyond the didactic "telling" of knowledge to a more hands-on approach to learning, where students construct knowledge through experience. In *The Reader, the Text, the Poem: The Transactional Theory of the Literary Work* (1978), literary theorist Louise Rosenblatt also questioned the role of teacher as expert and student as empty vessel. This **transactional theory of reading response** centered the student as an agent of analysis. Certainly in this text, Mistral seeks to broaden those voices to whom we listen. What about the role of those receiving the story? In what ways does she invite them in to make them a co-creator of knowledge?

In her popular 2009 TedTalk, "The Danger of a Single Story," Chimamanda Ngozi Adichie warns us of drawing too many conclusions from a single narrative. She also encourages us to question whose story is told, whose story is neglected, and how one interprets those stories. In the following excerpt, Mistral presciently calls on the need for all to tell their stories: "Our obligation as writers is to give, with integrity and dignity, our landscape to distant readers." One can see Mistral's pedagogical and socially conscious legacy in the works of Brazilian educator Paulo Freire, author of the *Pedagogy of the Oppressed* (1968), a how-to commentary on empowering the poor and historically unheard and disenfranchised.

Within this very brief essay published in 1929 Mistral addresses many current trends in education, including the need for **multimodal instruction** (for example, visual, auditory, or kinesthetic) and the need to connect new learning to a student's **schema**, a framework that categorizes patterns of thought. As you read, see if you can identify Mistral's language that anticipates these trends.

Gabriela Mistral was the fifth woman and the first Latin American to receive a Nobel Prize when she was recognized for her contributions to literature, notably lyric poetry, in 1945. She also served Chile as a delegate to the League of Nations, the United Nations, and in diplomatic postings in Spain, Italy, and the United States. Instead of getting bogged down in our particular disciplinary fields, Mistral reminds us of the value of storytelling as a conscious act of the humanities.

Reid Chapman
Department of Education

> **PRE-READING PARS**
>
> 1. What is the job of the teacher?
> 2. If one is dedicated to educating the marginalized, how might one go about this? Write three guiding principles that would frame this journey.
> 3. How might a story embody "pure beauty"?

"Teaching and Telling Stories ("Contar")"

The art of storytelling, an essential classroom skill seldom taken into account in the assessment of teachers, is undervalued when one has it and is not demanded when one does not. The same occurs with the rare, precious, and happy vocation of being able to foster play among children. Likewise all instances of grace within the business of teaching. (Philistinism lives comfortably everywhere, but it has established itself as patron to the leaders of the teaching trade).

Yet, half the lesson is in the telling. Half of the day and half of the managing of the children is in the telling—when (like an adagio) to tell a story is to enchant, to let the magic in.

I am referring to primary school, naturally, although this also pertains to the first three years of high school.

Zoology tells the story of the lion-creature, the bird-creature, and the serpent-creature, until one-by-one they walk, fly or climb before the child's eyes, until they get into the child's soul—into that core where the child keeps all of the beings with whom he establishes that lovely animal familiarity that is pure childhood.

Images—all possible images; abundant, numerous images—should be provided first. Without them, the room will be devoid of any real object upon which the child can build knowledge. To this imprint, I would add a colorful adventure or tale—whether an excerpt from a good zoology anthology, or a story about the creature that the teacher might know—describing the animal's habits. Only after receiving this double image of the little creature (one graphic and one oral) would I approach the technical description, keeping it as vigorously lean as the lines of an etcher, because it is always cumbersome for the child. From there I would finally move on to phyllum and genum (which, being exercised in generalization) are quite unrewarding to the little one.

Warmed up with the tale, thrown into the subject like a swimmer plunging head-first, he finds in the bee-creature or the lion-creature an element that gives him pleasure, and from there he will take the necessary steps within the subject, at least to the extent that narration in conjunction with images has aroused his interest.

Botany involves no less storytelling than zoology, contrary to what some believe. The harvest and elaboration of linen can be told with the same beautiful architecture of a tale. The story of the many wonderful American trees can be told so as to provide the child with the same enchantment as an animal fable: thus-and-so is the bread tree, thus-and-so is the palm tree, and thus-and-so is the Ecuadorian *tagua* or the Chilean larch—all comprising a kind of vegetal tribe.

For a great geographer, geography is storytelling; for the mediocre, it is all numbers and squares and figures. The admirable Reclus was a rich and expansive storyteller. Swen Hedin and Humboldt were storytellers. The throngs of authors of geography texts know neither how to tell in their own words nor how to quote generously from the masterful pages of the classics of their field. Hence the ugly and monotonous texts that make up a science which is genuinely beautiful, insofar as her domain is the very panorama.

The American landscape is an untapped source of fine description and narration. [Mexican poet and essayist] Alfonso Reyes began the task a few years ago with *La Visión de Anáhua*, a tour-de-force of lapidary description which should be a model for all Indo-American writers. Our obligation as writers is to give, with integrity and dignity, our native landscape to distant readers....

It is settled, then, that the person who can narrate skillfully has half the battle won.

Now we should clarify what good storytelling is.

I believe that you don't learn this by asking a fable expert (that is, a writer), but rather by recalling those who, when we were children, narrated those important "events" that have remained in our memory for thirty years.

My mother did not know how to tell a story, or did not like to. My father could, but he knew too many things—from his good Latin to his fine decorative drawing. He was an extraordinary man, and I prefer to remember ordinary storytellers. Two or three elderly men from my village taught me the folklore of Elqui (where I come from), and those tales, along with the bible stories that my teacher sister (instead of the priest) taught me, were all of my childhood literature. Since then I have read many masterpieces of childhood literature from all around the world. I must say that the folk tales I heard at age five and those I came upon later in my passion for folklore are, for me, the best. They are what aesthetics professors call "pure beauty," the most intoxicating of fables, and those I like to call classics above all classics.

The narrator of folklore does not use "floweriness," adding neither pedantic flourishes nor saccharine flourishes, and doesn't employ clever adjectives in order to compel interest. This flows naturally and honestly from the very core of the fable. The folkloric storyteller's vitality comes from his sobriety, which always yields something magical, or at least extraordinary, something charged with creative electricity. With repetition over millenia, the tale (like the good gymnast) has lost the fat of superfluous details and only pure muscle remains. Thus, the folktale is not long and is not burdened with digressions. It flies as straight as an arrow to its target and does not tire either the child or the adult. These I think are the main qualities of the popular tale.

And those of the storyteller? Some of them spring from the above.

The storyteller must be simple, even humble, if he is to repeat without additions a master fable that needs no adornment. He should be witty (his words laced with charm, shining with grace), for the child is more receptive to wit than either Goethe or Ronsard. Besides simply narrating, he will have to reduce everything to images, leaving untethered to an image only that which cannot be transmuted into one. He will forgo expansiveness, which in narration is an adult taste rather than that of a child. Within the cluster of fables that has formed, he will have to highlight those elements that bear some living relation to his environment: fresh fruit, tree, creature, or landscape. He will try to use facial expressions and gestures as brotherly aids to the fine tale, because the child likes to see the face of the storyteller animated and alive. If his voice is ugly, there are ways to train it, if only a little, in order to squeeze some sweetness out of it. For a pleasant voice, one that yields like silk to the matter at hand, is a gift the listener is grateful for.

If I were Headmistress of a school, I would create a chair in general and regional folklore. And I wouldn't certify as a teacher anyone who does not narrate with agility, joy, freshness, and even a certain fascination.

Mistral, Gabriela. "Teaching and Telling Stories." In *Keen's Latin American Civilization: History and Society, 1492 to Present*, edited by Benjamin Keen, 397–99. New York: Taylor & Francis Group, 2003.

POST-READING PARS

1. How does Mistral outline the role of the educator? Compare her estimation with your earlier impressions in a short paragraph.
2. How does Mistral intend teachers to reach all of their students?
3. Mistral claims that folktales and fables are "classics above all classics." How does she suggest storytellers emulate these forms in pursuit of "pure beauty"?

Inquiry Corner

Content Questions:

Mistral lists a fairly simple equation for a good story. What is elemental to that equation? What other traits are essential to storytelling?

Access to education was central to Mistral's vision of rural education. In what ways does Mistral seek to reach out to the learner through story?

Critical Questions:

Should anyone be able to tell another's story?

Who gets to interpret a story or to locate its moral?

Comparative Question:

Mistral critiques those who are pedantic in storytelling. She favors the "ordinary" stories. Find two readings, one that epitomizes good storytelling and one that is "pedantic." Compare their impact on you.

Connection Questions:

In what ways do educators continue to fall short in their connection to learners? How might this connect to storytelling?

BEYOND THE CLASSROOM

» The art of storytelling is an important skill. Our resumes and cover letters tell stories. We also tell stories while networking and interviewing. In order to become compelling and effective storytellers, we must know our own stories. What are some of your stories/experiences/events that you would tell during an interview? Have you studied abroad? Did you have an amazing internship experience? Did you play an important role in a group project? How can you take one of these experiences and turn it into an interesting story that highlights your skills and accomplishments and makes the listener want to hear more?

from *A Voice from the South* by Anna Julia Cooper

Introduction

Anna Julia Cooper (1858–1964) was born in Raleigh, North Carolina, to an enslaved woman named Hannah Haywood (or Hayward). It is assumed that Cooper's father was Hannah Haywood's "owner."[31] Freed by the Emancipation Proclamation in 1863, she later was enrolled at the age of nine in the St. Augustine **Normal School** (a school for preparing students to become teachers) in Raleigh, where she began her lifelong commitment to liberal arts education, which she understood in the classical sense of both developing virtue and preparing persons for full participation in civic life (e.g., being capable of serving on juries or in public office, being thoughtful voters, contributing to the social good broadly). She eventually earned bachelor's (1884) and master's (1887) degrees in math from Oberlin College and afterward taught math and other subjects at both the high school and university levels. Later she returned to study at the doctoral level, and in 1925, at the age of sixty-six or sixty-seven, she earned her doctorate degree in "Letters," which is a kind of broad liberal arts category emphasizing the humanities disciplines (in her case, history, philosophy, and languages), from the University of Paris (the Sorbonne), becoming the fourth Black woman in the United States to earn a doctorate. She spent her career

> **SNAPSHOT BOX**
>
> LANGUAGE: English
> DATE: 1892
> LOCATION: Washington, DC
> GENRE: Essay/speech
> TAGS: Race; Struggle, Resistance, and Revolution; Education; Women and Power; Gender and Identity

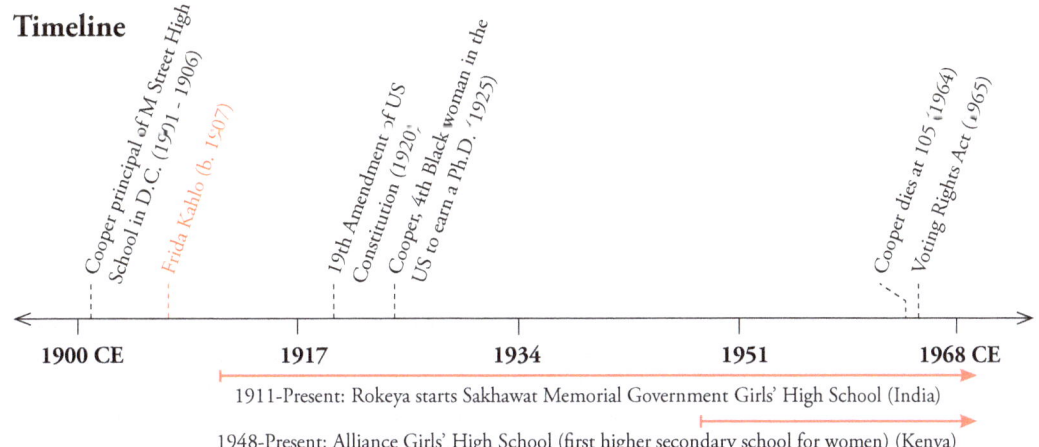

---

31. Quotation marks are used here to acknowledge that claims to ownership of human beings as slaves cannot be considered morally legitimate, regardless of the legal status of the claims at the time.

as an educator and activist, believing that education was the key for improving the status and well-being of Black people in the United States.

Cooper was a well-respected public intellectual and speaker, writing and speaking on many topics connected to the needs and well-being of African Americans, both men and women. She is considered a foundational feminist voice in Black women's history as well as in **Africana** philosophy (having to do with Africa and the African diaspora, or the dispersion of African peoples and their descendants across the globe). In the following reading, which is taken from her book *A Voice from the South: By a Black Woman of the South*, she is clearly strongly concerned with the needs and status of African American women, and how they continue to be treated as "second-class citizens," not just by whites but often by African American men as well.[32] The essay begins with reference to a speech made by Reverend Anna Shaw at the National Woman's Council of 1891, the title of which Cooper takes for her own chapter, "Woman vs. the Indian." However, Cooper disagrees with Shaw about different identity groups competing against each other for recognition of their rights and status as full persons. Rather, Cooper argues strongly that Black women, because they are members of multiple oppressed identity groups, must understand that they are not the only ones who stand in need of liberation. Cooper was thus one of the earliest articulators of "double jeopardy," the idea that oppression against Black women operated on at least two fronts: race and gender. The term more frequently used for this phenomenon today is **intersectionality**, which points to the interlocking nature of multiple forms of oppressions in the lives and identities of people. Where do you see evidence of this kind of intersectional thinking in Cooper's essay?

As an educator and scholar, Cooper was also clearly a strong advocate of critical thinking and offers an extended metaphor of the South as a "little sister" who has bad behavior and multiple, harmful thinking errors, specifically in regard to the practice of slavery and the desire to maintain similar conditions of white supremacy after slavery had officially ended. What examples do you see of the kinds of bad arguments that Southern white women gave to keep Black women "in their place" while simultaneously presenting themselves as advocates for women's freedom, status, and rights?

Although for different reasons, Cooper's philosophy of rights clearly foreshadows later discussions, such as Malcolm X's claim during the civil rights era that African Americans need to argue in terms of *human rights* rather than simply in terms of rights for their own specific group. Whereas Malcolm X was concerned with avoiding the accusation of pleading for "special rights," and with garnering international support for African Americans, Cooper's concern can be seen as an articulation of a

---

32. See "On the Status of Women in America," in *A Voice from the South*, in which Cooper laments that Black men are often "not ready to concede" that Black women are capable of significant contributions to social and political problems and issues of the time (76–78).

later foundational principle of feminism: that no group can be fully free until *all* oppressed groups are free. This is one reason why Cooper is considered such a strong figure in Black feminism, and her book is often cited as the first book-length Black feminist text in the United States.[33] How would you explain the meaning of this feminist principle?

Melissa Burchard
Department of Philosophy

---

33. See Beverly Guy-Sheftall, ed., *Words of Fire: An Anthology of African-American Feminist Thought* (New York: The New Press, 1995), 43.

> **PRE-READING PARS**
>
> 1. What do you see as the meaning of the phrase "social equality"? Give two or three concrete examples of what it means for people to be "social equals."
> 2. What do you think of when you hear the term "good manners"? Give two or three concrete examples of the kinds of behavior you were taught as exhibiting good manners.
> 3. Take three to five minutes to jot down ideas about why it is important to amplify the voices of marginalized groups, or specific members of marginalized groups, to be heard in the broader public and in education.

from *A Voice from the South*

A recent writer on Eastern nations says: "If we take through the earth's temperate zone, a belt of country whose northern and southern edges are determined by certain limiting isotherms, not more than half the width of the zone apart, we shall find that we have included in a relatively small extent of surface almost all the nations of note in the world, past or present. Now, if we examine this belt and compare the different parts of it with one another, we shall be struck by a remarkable fact. *The peoples inhabiting it grow steadily more personal as we go west.* So unmistakable is this gradation, that one is almost tempted to ascribe it to cosmical rather than to human causes. It is as marked as the change in color of the human complexion observable along any meridian, which ranges from black, at the equator to blonde toward the pole. In like manner the sense of self grows more intense as we follow in the wake of the setting sun, and fades steadily as we advance into the dawn. America, Europe, the Levant, India, Japan, each is less personal than the one before.... *That politeness should be one of the most marked results of impersonality* may appear surprising, yet a slight examination will show it to be a fact. Considered *a priori*, the connection is not far to seek. Impersonality by lessening the interest in one's self, induces one to take an interest in others. Looked at *a posteriori*, we find that where the one trait exists the other is most developed, while an absence of the second seems to prevent the full growth of the first. This is true both in general and in detail. *Courtesy increases as we travel eastward round the world, coincidently with a decrease in the sense of self.* Asia is more courteous than Europe, Europe than America. Particular races show the same concomitance of characteristics. France, the most impersonal nation of Europe, is at the same time the most polite." And by inference, Americans, the most personal, are the least courteous nation on the globe.

The Black Woman had reached this same conclusion by an entirely different route; but it is gratifying to vanity, nevertheless, to find one's self sustained by both science and philosophy in a conviction, wrought in by hard experience, and yet too apparently audacious to be entertained even as a stealthy surmise. In fact the Black

Woman was emboldened some time since by a well put and timely article from an Editor's Drawer on the "Mannerless Sex," to give the world the benefit of some of her experience with the *"Mannerless Race"*; but since Mr. Lowell shows so conclusively that the entire Land of the West is a *mannerless continent*, I have determined to plead with our women, the mannerless sex on this mannerless continent, to institute a reform by placing immediately in our national curricula a department for teaching GOOD MANNERS.

Now, am I right in holding the American Woman responsible? Is it true that the exponents of woman's advancement, the leaders in woman's thought, the preachers and teachers of all woman's reforms, can teach this nation to be courteous, to be pitiful, having compassion one of another, not rendering evil for inoffensiveness, and railing in proportion to the improbability of being struck back; but contrariwise, being *all* of one mind, to love as brethren?

I think so.

It may require some heroic measures, and Like all revolutions will call for a determined front and a courageous, unwavering, stalwart heart on the part of the leaders of the reform.

The *"all"* will inevitably stick in the throat of the Southern woman. She must be allowed, please, to except the 'darkey' from the 'all'; it is too bitter a pill with black people in it. You must get the Revised Version to put it, *"love all white people as brethren."* She really could not enter any society on earth, or in heaven above, or in the waters under the earth, on such unpalatable conditions.

The Black Woman has tried to understand the Southern woman's difficulties; to put herself in her place, and to be as fair, as charitable, and as free from prejudice in judging her antipathies, as she would have others in regard to her own. She has honestly weighed the apparently sincere excuse, "But you must remember that these people were once our slaves"; and that other, "But civility towards the Negroes[34] will bring us on *social equality* with them."

These are the two bugbears; or rather, the two humbugbears: for, though each is founded on a most glaring fallacy, one would think they were words to conjure with, so potent and irresistible is their spell as an argument at the North as well as in the South.

One of the most singular facts about the unwritten history of this country is the consummate ability with which Southern influence, Southern ideas and Southern

---

34. Cooper uses (and quotes) the term "Negro" to refer to her own African American communities as was a prevalent practice within and outside of Black communities from the nineteenth to mid-twentieth centuries. The term "negro" should not be confused with the derogatory n-word. Likewise another term used during the same timeframe, "colored," is outdated and should not be confused with the current usage of "person of color." Words reflecting African American and Black communities' preferences for self-identification continue to shift in meaning and connotation over time.

ideals, have from the very beginning even up to the present day, dictated to and domineered over the brain and sinew of this nation. Without wealth, without education, without inventions, arts, sciences, or industries, without well-nigh every one of the progressive ideas and impulses which have made this country great, prosperous and happy, personally indolent and practically stupid, poor in everything but bluster and self-esteem, the Southerner has nevertheless with Italian finesse and exquisite skill, uniformly and invariably, so manipulated Northern sentiment as to succeed sooner or later in carrying his point and shaping the policy of this government to suit his purposes. Indeed, the Southerner is a magnificent manager of men, a born educator. For two hundred and fifty years he trained to his hand a people whom he made absolutely his own, in body, mind, and sensibility. He so insinuated differences and distinctions among them, that their personal attachment for him was stronger than for their own brethren and fellow sufferers. He made it a crime for two or three of them to be gathered together in Christ's name without a white man's supervision, and a felony for one to teach them to read even the Word of Life; and yet they would defend his interest with their life blood; his smile was their happiness, a pat on the shoulder from him their reward. The slightest difference among themselves in condition, circumstances, opportunities, became barriers of jealousy and disunion. He sowed his blood broadcast among them, then pitted mulatto against black, bond against free, house slave against plantation slave, even the slave of one clan against like slave of another clan; till, wholly oblivious of their ability for mutual succor and defense, all became centers of myriad systems of repellent forces, having but one sentiment in common, and that their entire subjection to that master hand.

And he not only managed the black man, he also hoodwinked the white man, the tourist and investigator who visited his lordly estates. The slaves were doing well, in fact couldn't be happier,—plenty to eat, plenty to drink, comfortably housed and clothed—they wouldn't be free if they could; in short, in his broad brimmed plantation hat and easy aristocratic smoking gown, he made you think him a veritable patriarch in the midst of a lazy, well fed, good natured, over-indulged tenantry.

Then, too, the South represented blood—not red blood, but blue blood. The difference is in the length of the stream and your distance from its source. If your own father was a pirate, a robber, a murderer, his hands are dyed in red blood, and you don't say very much about it. But if your great great great grandfather's grandfather stole and pillaged and slew, and you can prove it, your blood has become blue and you are at great pains to establish the relationship. So the South had neither silver nor gold, but she had blood; and she paraded it with so much gusto that the substantial little Puritan maidens of the North, who had been making bread and canning currants and not thinking of blood the least bit, began to hunt up the records of the Mayflower to see if some of the passengers thereon could not claim the honor of having been one of William the Conqueror's brigands, when he killed the last of the Saxon kings and, red-handed, stole his crown and his lands. Thus, the ideal from out the Southland brooded over the nation and we sing less lustily than of yore

'Kind hearts are more than coronets
And simple faith than Norman blood.'

In politics, the two great forces, commerce and empire, which would otherwise have shaped the destiny of the country, have been made to pander and cater to Southern notions. "Cotton is King" meant the South must be allowed to dictate or there would be no fun. Every statesman from 1830 to 1860 exhausted his genius in persuasion and compromises to smooth out her ruffled temper and gratify her petulant demands. But like a sullen younger sister, the South has pouted and sulked and cried: "I won't play with you now; so there!" and the big brother at the North has coaxed and compromised and given in, and ended by letting her have her way. Until 1860 she had as her pet an institution which it was death by the law to say anything about, except that it was divinely instituted, inaugurated by Noah, sanctioned by Abraham, approved by Paul, and just ideally perfect in every way. And when, to preserve the autonomy of the family arrangements, in '61, '62 and '63, it became necessary for the big brother to administer a little wholesome correction and set the obstreperous Miss vigorously down in her seat again, she assumed such an air of injured innocence, and melted away so lugubriously, the big brother has done nothing since but try to sweeten and pacify and laugh her back into a companionable frame of mind.

Father Lincoln did all he could to get her to repent of her petulance and behave herself. He even promised she might keep her pet, so disagreeable to all the neighbors and hurtful even to herself, and might manage it at home to suit herself, if she would only listen to reason and be just tolerably nice. But, no—she was going to leave and set up for herself; she didn't propose to be meddled with; and so, of course, she had to be spanked. Just a little at first—didn't mean to hurt, merely to teach her who was who. But she grew so ugly, and kicked and fought and scratched so outrageously, and seemed so determined to smash up the whole business, the head of the family got red in the face, and said: "Well, now, he couldn't have any more of that foolishness. Arabella must just behave herself or take the consequences." And after the spanking, Arabella sniffed and whimpered and pouted, and the big brother bit his lip, looked half ashamed, and said: "Well, I didn't want to hurt you. You needn't feel so awfully bad about it, I only did it for your good. You know I wouldn't do anything to displease you if I could help it; but you would insist on making the row, and so I just had to. Now, there—there—let's be friends!" and he put his great strong arms about her and just dared anybody to refer to that little unpleasantness—he'd show them a thing or two. Still Arabella sulked,—till the rest of the family decided she might just keep her pets, and manage her own affairs and nobody should interfere.

So now, if one intimates that some clauses of the Constitution are a dead letter at the South and that only the name and support of that pet institution are changed while the fact and essence, minus the expense and responsibility, remain, he is quickly told to mind his own business and informed that he is waving the bloody shirt.

Even twenty-five years after the fourteenth and fifteenth amendments to our

Constitution, a man who has been most unequivocal in his outspoken condemnation of the wrongs regularly and systematically heaped on the oppressed race in this country, and on all even most remotely connected with them—a man whom we had thought our staunchest friend and most noble champion and defender—after a two weeks' trip in Georgia and Florida immediately gives signs of the fatal inception of the virus. Not even the chance traveller from England or Scotland escapes. The arch-manipulator takes him under his special watch-care and training, uses up his stock arguments and gives object lessons with his choicest specimens of Negro depravity and worthlessness; takes him through what, in New York, would be called "the slums," and would predicate there nothing but the duty of enlightened Christians to send out their light and emulate their Master's aggressive labors of love; but in Georgia is denominated "our terrible problem, which people of the North so little understand, yet vouchsafe so much gratuitous advice about." With an injured air he shows the stupendous and atrocious mistake of reasoning about these people as if they were just ordinary human beings, and amenable to the tenets of the Gospel; and not long after the inoculation begins to work, you hear this old-time friend of the oppressed delivering himself something after this fashion: "Ah, well, the South must be left to manage the Negro. She is most directly concerned and must understand her problem better than outsiders. We must not meddle. We must be very careful not to widen the breaches. The Negro is not worth a feud between brothers and sisters."

Lately a great national and international movement characteristic of this age and country, a movement based on the inherent right of every soul to its own highest development, I mean the movement making for Woman's full, free, and complete emancipation, has, after much courting, obtained the gracious smile of the Southern woman—I beg her pardon—the Southern *lady*.

She represents blood, and of course could not be expected to leave that out; and firstly and foremostly she must not, in any organization she may deign to grace with her presence, be asked to associate with "these people who were once her slaves."

Now the Southern woman (I may be pardoned, being one myself) was never renowned for her reasoning powers, and it is not surprising that just a little picking will make her logic fall to pieces even here.

In the first place she imagines that because her grandfather had slaves who were black, all the blacks in the world of every shade and tint were once in the position of her slaves. This is as bad as the Irishman who was about to kill a peaceable Jew in the streets of Cork,—having just learned that Jews slew his Redeemer. The black race constitutes one-seventh the known population of the globe; and there are representatives of it here as elsewhere who were never in bondage at any time to any man,—whose blood is as blue and lineage as noble as any, even that of the white lady of the South. That her slaves were black and she despises her slaves, should no more argue antipathy to all dark people and peoples, than that Guiteau, an assassin, was white, and I hate assassins, should make me hate all persons more or less white. The objection shows a want of clear discrimination.

The second fallacy in the objection grows out of the use of an ambiguous middle, as the logicians would call it, or assigning a double signification to the term "*Social equality.*"

Civility to the Negro implies social equality. I am opposed to associating with dark persons on terms of social equality. Therefore, I abrogate civility to the Negro. This is like

Light is opposed to darkness.

Feathers are light.

Ergo, Feathers are opposed to darkness.

The "social equality" implied by civility to the Negro is a very different thing from forced association with him socially. Indeed it seems to me that the mere application of a little cold common sense would show that uncongenial social environments could by no means be forced on any one. I do not, and cannot be made to associate with all dark persons, simply on the ground that I am dark; and I presume the Southern lady can imagine some whose faces are white, with whom she would no sooner think of chatting unreservedly than, were it possible, with a veritable 'darkey.' Such things must and will always be left to individual election. No law, human or divine, can legislate for or against them. Like seeks like; and I am sure with the Southern lady's antipathies at their present temperature, she might enter ten thousand organizations besprinkled with colored women without being any more deflected by them than by the proximity of a stone. The social equality scare then is all humbug, conscious or unconscious, I know not which. And were it not too bitter a thought to utter here, I might add that the overtures for forced association in the past history of these two races were not made by the manacled black man, nor by the *silent and suffering black woman!*

When I seek food in a public café or apply for first-class accommodations on a railway train, I do so because my physical necessities are identical with those of other human beings of like constitution and temperament, and crave satisfaction, I go because I want food, or I want comfort—not because I want association with those who frequent these places; and I can see no more "social equality" in buying lunch at the same restaurant, or riding in a common car, than there is in paying for dry goods at the same counter or walking on the same street.

The social equality which means forced or unbidden association would be as much deprecated and as strenuously opposed by the circle in which I move as by the most hide-bound Southerner in the land. Indeed I have been more than once annoyed by the inquisitive white interviewer, who, with spectacles on nose and pencil and note-book in hand, comes to get some "points" about "*your people.*" My "people" are just like other people—indeed, too like for their own good. They hate, they love, they attract and repel, they climb or they grovel, struggle or drift, aspire or despair, endure in hope or curse in vexation, exactly like all the rest of unregenerate humanity. Their likes and dislikes are as strong; their antipathies and prejudices too I fear, are as pronounced as you will find anywhere; and the entrance to the inner sanctuary of their homes and hearts is as jealously guarded against profane intrusion.

What the dark man wants then is merely to live his own life, in his own world, with his own chosen companions, in whatever of comfort, luxury, or emoluments his talent or his money can in an impartial market secure. Has he wealth, he does not want to be forced into inconvenient or unsanitary sections of cities to buy a home and rear his family. Has he art, he does not want to be cabined and cribbed into emulation with the few who merely happen to have his complexion. His talent aspires to study without proscription the masters of all ages and to rub against the broadest and fullest movements of his own day.

Has he religion, he does not want to be made to feel that there is a white Christ and a black Christ, a white Heaven and a black Heaven, a white Gospel and a black Gospel,—but the one ideal of perfect manhood and womanhood, the one universal longing for development and growth, the one desire for being, and being better, the one great yearning, aspiring, outreaching, in all the heartthrobs of humanity in whatever race or clime.

[...]

And this is why, as it appears to me, woman in her lately acquired vantage ground for speaking an earnest helpful word, can do this country no deeper and truer and more lasting good than by bending all her energies to thus broadening, humanizing, and civilizing her native land.

"Except ye become as little children" is not a pious precept, but an inexorable law of the universe. God's kingdoms are all sealed to the seedy, moss-grown mind of self-satisfied maturity. Only the little child in spirit, the simple, receptive, educable mind can enter. Preconceived notions, blinding prejudices, and shrivelling antipathies must be wiped out, and the cultivable soul made a tabula rasa for whatever lesson great Nature has to teach.

This, too, is why I conceive the subject to have been unfortunately worded which was chosen by Miss Shaw at the Woman's Council and which stands at the head of this chapter.

Miss Shaw is one of the most powerful of our leaders, and we feel her voice should give no uncertain note. Woman should not, even by inference, or for the sake of argument, seem to disparage what is weak. For woman's cause is the cause of the weak; and when all the weak shall have received their due consideration, then woman will have her "rights," and the Indian will have his rights, and the Negro will have his rights, and all the strong will have learned at last to deal justly, to love mercy, and to walk humbly; and our fair land will have been taught the secret of universal courtesy which is after all nothing but the art, the science, and the religion of regarding one's neighbor as one's self, and to do for him as we would were conditions swapped, that he do for us.

It cannot seem less than a blunder, whenever the exponents of a great reform or the harbingers of a noble advance in thought and effort allow themselves to seem distorted by a narrow view of their own aims and principles. All prejudices, whether of race, sect or sex, class pride and caste distinctions are the belittling inheritance and badge of snobs and prigs.

The philosophic mind sees that its own "rights" are the rights of humanity. That in the universe of God nothing trivial is or mean; and the recognition it seeks is not through the robber and wild beast adjustment of the survival of the bullies but through the universal application ultimately of the Golden Rule.

[...]

The cause of freedom is not the cause of a race or a sect, a party or a class,—it is the cause of human kind, the very birthright of humanity. Now unless we are greatly mistaken the Reform of our day, known as the Woman's Movement, is essentially such an Embodiment, if its pioneers could only realize it, of the universal good. And specially important is it that there be no confusion of ideas among its leaders as to its scope and universality. All mists must be cleared from the eyes of woman if she is to be a teacher of morals and manners: the former strikes its roots in the individual and its training and pruning may be accomplished by classes; but the latter is to lubricate the joints and minimize the friction of society, and it is important and fundamental that there be no chromatic or other aberration when the teacher is settling the point, "Who is my neighbor?"

It is not the intelligent woman vs. the ignorant woman; nor the white woman vs. the black, the brown, and the red,—it is not even the cause of woman vs. man. Nay, 'tis woman's strongest vindication for speaking *that the world needs to hear her voice*. It would be subversive of every human interest that the cry of one-half the human family be stifled. Woman in stepping from the pedestal of statue-like inactivity in the domestic shrine, and daring to think and move and speak,—to undertake to help shape, mold, and direct the thought of her age, is merely completing the circle of the world's vision. Hers is every interest that has lacked an interpreter and a defender. Her cause is linked with that of every agony that has been dumb—every wrong that needs a voice.

It is no fault of man's that he has not been able to see truth from her standpoint. It does credit both to his head and heart that no greater mistakes have been committed or even wrongs perpetrated while she sat making tatting and snipping paper flowers. Man's own innate chivalry and the mutual interdependence of their interests have insured his treating her cause, in the main at least, as his own. And he is pardonably surprised and even a little chagrined, perhaps, to find his legislation not considered "perfectly lovely" in every respect. But in any case his work is only impoverished by her remaining dumb. The world has had to limp along with the wobbling gait and one-sided hesitancy of a man with one eye. Suddenly the bandage is removed from the other eye and the whole body is filled with light. It sees a circle where before it saw a segment. The darkened eye restored, every member rejoices with it.

What a travesty of its case for this eye to become plaintiff in a suit, *Eye vs. Foot*. "There is that dull clod, the foot, allowed to roam at will, free and untrammelled;

while I, the source and medium of light, brilliant and beautiful, am fettered in darkness and doomed to desuetude." The great burly black man, ignorant and gross and depraved, is allowed to vote; while the franchise is withheld from the intelligent and refined, the pure-minded and lofty souled white woman. Even the untamed and untamable Indian of the prairie, who can answer nothing but 'ugh' to great economic and civic questions is thought by some worthy to wield the ballot which is still denied the Puritan maid and the first lady of Virginia.

Is not this hitching our wagon to something much lower than a star? Is not woman's cause broader, and deeper, and grander, than a blue stocking debate or an aristocratic pink tea? Why should woman become plaintiff in a suit versus the Indian, or the Negro or any other race or class who have been crushed under the iron heel of Anglo-Saxon power and selfishness? If the Indian has been wronged and cheated by the puissance of this American government, it is woman's mission to plead with her country to cease to do evil and to pay its honest debts. If the Negro has been deceitfully cajoled or inhumanly cuffed according to selfish expediency or capricious antipathy, let it be woman's mission to plead that he be met as a man and honestly given half the road. If woman's own happiness has been ignored or misunderstood in our country's legislating for bread winners, for rum sellers, for property holders, for the family relations, for any, or all the interests that touch her vitally, let her rest her plea, not on Indian inferiority, nor on Negro depravity, but on the obligation of legislators to do for her as they would have others do for them were relations reversed. Let her try to teach her country that every interest in this world is entitled at least to a respectful hearing, that every sentiency is worthy of its own gratification, that a helpless cause should not be trampled down, nor a bruised reed broken; and when the right of the individual is made sacred, when the image of God in human form, whether in marble or in clay, whether in alabaster or in ebony, is consecrated and inviolable, when men have been taught to look beneath the rags and grime, the pomp and pageantry of mere circumstance and have regard unto the celestial kernel uncontaminated at the core,—when race, color, sex, condition, are realized to be the accidents, not the substance of life, and consequently as not obscuring or modifying the inalienable title to life, liberty, and pursuit of happiness,—then is mastered the science of politeness, the art of courteous contact, which is naught but the practical application of the principal of benevolence, the back bone and marrow of all religion; then woman's lesson is taught and woman's cause is won—not the white woman nor the black woman nor the red woman, but the cause of every man or woman who has writhed silently under a mighty wrong. The pleading of the American woman for the right and the opportunity to employ the American method of influencing the disposal to be made of herself, her property, her children in civil, economic, or domestic relations is thus seen to be based on a principle as broad as the human race and as old as human society. Her wrongs are thus indissolubly linked with all undefended woe, all helpless suffering, and the plenitude of her "rights" will mean the final triumph of all right over might, the supremacy of the moral forces of reason and justice and love in the government of the nation.

    God hasten the day.

Selections from Anna Julia Cooper, *A Voice from the South*, 97–113, 116–18, 120–26. Xenia, Ohio: The Aldine Printing House, 1892.

POST-READING PARS

1. Did your ideas about social equality seem to match what Cooper has to say about the term? Explain how they matched or did not.
2. Does your picture of good manners seem like what Cooper has in mind? State what you see as differences and/or similarities.

Inquiry Corner

Content Questions:

Where in this reading does Cooper emphasize Black women as agents capable of affecting their own lives through their own decisions and actions? What examples does Cooper give of the agency of Black women? Does Black women's agency appear to be different from the agency of white women, according to Cooper?

Critical Question:

Explain the two "bugbears" (or as Cooper says, "humbugbears") that are at work in the arguments of Southern white women for keeping Black women out of their clubs and organizations. What tools of critical thinking does Cooper bring to bear on these arguments to show their flaws?

Comparative Questions:

How would you articulate Cooper's ideas in this reading about the special task that she believes belongs to women generally, and Black women in particular? How does this picture of women's special task compare to the one we find in the reading titled "The Emancipation of Women: Argentina 1876"?

Connection Questions:

What are "morals and manners," and what are the connections that Cooper sees between them? How do they compare with the morals and manners that are currently expected and/or practiced in the United States today?

from *Annihilation of Caste* by Bhimrao Ramji Ambedkar

> **SNAPSHOT BOX**
>
> **LANGUAGE:** English
> **WRITTEN:** 1936, Bombay, India
> **GENRE:** Speech
> **TAGS:** Accessing Rights; Class; Community; Ethics and Morality; Religion; Rhetoric and Persuasion; Struggle, Resistance, and Revolution; Tradition

Introduction

Bhimrao Ramji Ambedkar (1891–1956) was the most distinguished leader of the **Dalit** communities in twentieth-century India. While traditionally referred to as "Untouchables" since their very touch is considered polluting by caste Hindus, the term that members of these communities presently use is "Dalit." *Annihilation of Caste* is one of Ambedkar's most important works. It argues forcefully that India's social reform and by extension, political reform, requires a total dismantling of the **Hindu caste system** along with all the oppressive and dehumanizing practices associated with it.

Who are the Dalits? Dalits occupy the lowest ranks of the hierarchical Hindu caste system and thereby the fateful destiny of being regarded as the "outcaste" by the top three castes—namely, brahmin, kshatriya, and vaisya and their numerous subgroups, referred to as the "caste Hindus" (*savarna*). In spite of worshipping the same Hindu gods and observing the same Hindu festivals, the caste Hindus considered Dalits to be outside of caste, or outcaste. Not only was the physical touch of a Dalit considered polluting, but even the touch of their shadows and sound of their voices were shunned. They were thus forced to live in apartheid-like segregated conditions, while also being denied the use of public wells and often public roads. Their children were not allowed into the public schools reserved exclusively for caste Hindu children.

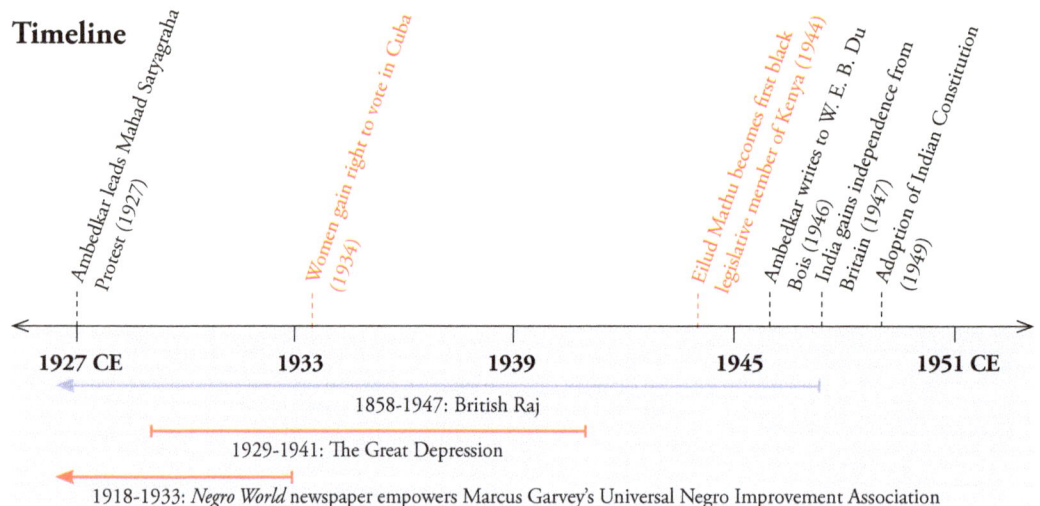

Their many indignities included death from preventable diseases when caste Hindu doctors refused to treat them or hospitals run by caste Hindus refused to admit them. How might you compare the Dalit experience of oppression and segregation in Ambedkar's India to another marginalized community's dehumanization that you are familiar with? Consider the complexities (positive and negative) of this type of comparison.

Ambedkar was born to a family of Mahar, an untouchable caste in the western Indian state of Maharashtra in 1891. Being born to a middle-class family, Ambedkar was educated in the local school where he had to sit by himself in the corner and away from his caste Hindu — "touchable" — classmates or wait for a caste Hindu person to open the water tap if he wanted a drink of water. In spite of suffering humiliations during his formative years that left a lasting imprint, he went on to become the first college graduate in the Mahar community when he graduated from the prestigious Elphinstone College in Bombay. Later, with the financial support from the Maharaja (ruler) of Baroda, a princely state of British India, he studied at Columbia University between 1913 and 1916 where he earned a PhD in economics. All through his education he stayed focused on understanding the sociopolitical underpinnings of the Hindu caste system and changing the plight of his community, Dalits, who were marginalized in every aspect of communal life. Ambedkar served as the minister of law in the first government of independent India and as the chairperson of the drafting committee for the Constitution of Independent India, which abolished untouchability. After becoming convinced that Buddhism is the only avenue for arriving at Dalit equality, Ambedkar, along with hundreds of thousands of his followers, converted to Buddhism in 1956.

Ambedkar characterized the Hindu caste system in terms of a "graded inequality" that becomes "an ascending scale of hatred and a descending scale of contempt." Ambedkar argued that any remedy of this marginalization necessitates the annihilation of the Hindu caste system, which would ultimately result in the disintegration of the Hindu religion. Further, he saw the project of Indian democracy and this annihilation of the existing caste systems as integrally intertwined since the caste system "militates against democracy." Ambedkar's central argument was that in making morality "caste-bound," the Hindu caste system fails to acknowledge our universally shared humanity, and it is this failure that ultimately exposes the Hindu society's essential inability for political reform. What problems do you think a society faces if morality becomes caste-bound or similarly dependent on factors used to categorize human beings into hierarchical groups?

Even though Ambedkar composed his *Annihilation of Caste* as the 1936 presidential address to be delivered at the annual conference of the Jat-Pat-Todak Mandal, a prominent reformist group of upper-caste Hindus, he never delivered the speech. Learning of the content of his address, members of the Reception Committee of the Jat-Pat-Todak Mandal demanded that Ambedkar leave out certain passages where he argued for a "complete annihilation of the Hindu religion." When Ambedkar refused to comply, they disinvited him and cancelled the conference. Ambedkar went ahead and released the printed copies he had prepared for publication and by 1944 this published speech was not only in its third edition but it was also translated into many of the regional languages of India including Gujarati, Tamil, Hindi, and Marathi.

Keya Maitra
Department of Philosophy

Selections from *Annihilation of Caste*

Introduction—[why I am an unlikely President for this Conference]

Friends,

I am really sorry for the members of the Jat-Pat-Todak Mandal who have so very kindly invited me to preside over this Conference. I am sure they will be asked many questions for having selected me as the President. The Mandal will be asked to explain as to why it has imported a man from Bombay to preside over a function which is held in Lahore. I believe the Mandal could easily have found someone better qualified than myself to preside on the occasion. I have criticised the Hindus. I have questioned the authority of the Mahatma whom they revere. They hate me. To them I am a snake in their garden. The Mandal will no doubt be asked by the politically-minded Hindus to explain why it has called me to fill this place of honour. It is an act of great daring. I shall not be surprised if some political Hindus regard it as an insult. This selection of me certainly cannot please the ordinary religiously-minded Hindus. [. . .]

The Mandal knows best the reasons which led it to travel to Bombay to select a president, to fix upon a man so repugnant to the Hindus, and to descend so low in the scale as to select an Antyaja—an untouchable—to address an audience of the Savarnas [caste Hindus]. As for myself, you will allow me to say that I have accepted the invitation much against my will, and also against the will of many of my fellow untouchables. I know that the Hindus are sick of me. I know that I am not a *persona grata* [someone welcome] with them. Knowing all this, I have deliberately kept myself away from them. I have no desire to inflict myself upon them. I have been giving expression to my views from my own platform. This has already caused a great deal of heart burning and irritation. I have no desire to ascend the platform of the Hindus to do within their sight what I have been doing within their hearing. If I am here it is because of your choice and not because of my wish. Yours is a cause of social reform. That cause has always made an appeal to me, and it is because of this that I felt I ought not to refuse an opportunity of helping the cause—especially when you think that I can help it. Whether what I am going to say today will help you in any way to solve the problem you are grappling with, is for you to judge. All I hope to do is to place before you my views on the problem.

2—[Why social reform is necessary for political reform]

The path of social reform like the path to heaven (at any rate, in India), is strewn with many difficulties. Social reform in India has few friends and many critics. The critics fall into two distinct classes. One class consists of political reformers, and the other of the Socialists.

It was at one time recognized that without social efficiency, no permanent progress in the other fields of activity was possible; that owing to mischief wrought by evil customs, Hindu Society was not in a state of efficiency; and that ceaseless efforts must be made to eradicate these evils. It was due to the recognition of this fact that the birth of the National Congress was accompanied by the foundation of the Social Conference. While the Congress was concerned with defining the weak points in the political organisation of the country, the Social Conference was engaged in removing the weak points in the social organisation of the Hindu Society. For some time the Congress and the Conference worked as two wings of one common activity, and they held their annual sessions in the same pandal.[35] But soon the two wings developed into two parties, a 'political reform party' and a 'social reform party,' between whom there raged a fierce controversy. The 'political reform party' supported the National Congress, and the 'social reform party' supported the Social Conference. The two bodies thus became two hostile camps. The point at issue was whether social reform should precede political reform. For a decade the forces were evenly balanced, and the battle was fought without victory to either side. It was, however, evident that the fortunes of the Social Conference were ebbing fast. The gentlemen who presided over the sessions of the Social Conference lamented that the majority of the educated Hindus were for political advancement and indifferent to social reform; and that while the number of those who attended the Congress was very large, and the number who did not attend but who sympathized with it was even larger, the number of those who attended the Social Conference was very much smaller. This indifference, this thinning of its ranks, was soon followed by active hostility from the politicians. Under the leadership of the late Mr. Tilak, the courtesy with which the Congress allowed the Social Conference the use of its pandal was withdrawn, and the spirit of enmity went to such a pitch that when the Social Conference desired to erect its own pandal, a threat to burn the pandal was held out by its opponents. Thus in the course of time the party in favour of political reform won, and the Social Conference vanished and was forgotten. The speech delivered by Mr. W. C. Bonnerji in 1892 at Allahabad, as President of the eighth session of the Congress, sounds like a funeral oration on the death of the Social Conference, and is so typical of the Congress attitude that I venture to quote from it the following extract. Mr. Bonnerji said:

> "I for one have no patience with those who say we shall not be fit for political reform until we reform our social system. I fail to see any connection between the two... Are we not fit (for political reform) because our widows remain unmarried and our girls are given in marriage earlier than in other countries? because our wives and daughters do not drive about with us visiting our friends? because we do not send our daughters to Oxford and Cambridge?" (Cheers [from the audience])

I have stated the case for political reform as put by Mr. Bonnerji. There were many who were happy that the victory went to the Congress. But those who believe in the importance of social reform may ask, is an argument such as that of Mr. Bonnerji

---

35. An open-sided pavilion (typically made with bamboo and canvas fabric) used for large gatherings.

final? Does it prove that the victory went to those who were in the right? Does it prove conclusively that social reform has no bearing on political reform? It will help us to understand the matter if I state the other side of the case. I will draw upon the treatment of the untouchables for my facts.

Under the rule of the Peshwas in the Maratha country, the untouchable was not allowed to use the public streets if a Hindu was coming along, lest he should pollute the Hindu by his shadow. The untouchable was required to have a black thread either on his wrist or around his neck, as a sign or a mark to prevent the Hindus from getting themselves polluted by his touch by mistake. In Poona, the capital of the Peshwa, the untouchable was required to carry, strung from his waist, a broom to sweep away from behind himself the dust he trod on, lest a Hindu walking on the same dust should be polluted. In Poona, the untouchable was required to carry an earthen pot hung around his neck wherever he went—for holding his spit, lest his spit falling on the earth should pollute a Hindu who might unknowingly happen to tread on it. Let me take more recent facts. The tyranny practised by the Hindus upon the Balais, an untouchable community in Central India, will serve my purpose. You will find a report of this in the Times of India of 4th January 1928. The correspondent of the Times of India reported that high-caste Hindus—viz., Kalotas, Rajputs and Brahmins, including the Patels and Patwaris of the villages of Kanaria, Bicholi-Hafsi, Bicholi-Mardana, and about 15 other villages in the Indore district (of the Indore State)—informed the Balais of their respective villages that if they wished to live among them, they must conform to the following rules:

1. Balais must not wear gold-lace-bordered pugrees.
2. They must not wear dhotis with coloured or fancy borders.
3. They must convey intimation [= information] of the death of any Hindu to relatives of the deceased—no matter how far away these relatives may be living.
4. In all Hindu marriages, Balais must play music before the processions and during the marriage.
5. Balai women must not wear gold or silver ornaments; they must not wear fancy gowns or jackets.
6. Balai women must attend all cases of confinement [= childbirth] of Hindu women.
7. Balais must render services without demanding remuneration, and must accept whatever a Hindu is pleased to give.
8. If the Balais do not agree to abide by these terms, they must clear out of the villages.

The Balais refused to comply; and the Hindu element proceeded against them. Balais were not allowed to get water from the village wells; they were not allowed to let go their cattle to graze. Balais were prohibited from passing through land owned by a Hindu, so that if the field of a Balai was surrounded by fields owned by Hindus, the Balai could have no access to his own field. The Hindus also let their cattle graze down the fields of Balais. The Balais submitted petitions to the Darbar [local Court] against these persecutions; but as they could get no timely relief, and the oppression continued, hundreds of Balais with their wives and children were obliged to abandon their homes—in which their ancestors had lived for generations—and to migrate to adjoining States: that is, to villages in Dhar, Dewas, Bagli, Bhopal, Gwalior and other States. What happened to them in their new homes may for the present be left out of our consideration. The incident at Kavitha in Gujarat happened only last year. The Hindus of Kavitha ordered the untouchables not to insist upon sending their children to the common village school maintained by Government. What sufferings the untouchables of Kavitha had to undergo, for daring to exercise a civic right against the wishes of the Hindus, is too well known to need detailed description. Another instance occurred in the village of Zanu, in the Ahmedabad district of Gujarat. In November 1935 some untouchable women of well-to-do families started fetching water in metal pots. The Hindus looked upon the use of metal pots by untouchables as an affront to their dignity, and assaulted the untouchable women for their impudence. A most recent event is reported from the village of Chakwara in Jaipur State. It seems from the reports that have appeared in the newspapers that an untouchable of Chakwara who had returned from a pilgrimage had arranged to give a dinner to his fellow untouchables of the village, as an act of religious piety. The host desired to treat the guests to a sumptuous meal, and the items served included *ghee* (butter) also. But while the assembly of untouchables was engaged in partaking of the food, the Hindus in their hundreds, armed with lathis, rushed to the scene, despoiled the food, and belaboured the untouchables—who left the food they had been served with and ran away for their lives. And why was this murderous assault committed on defenceless untouchables? The reason given is that the untouchable host was impudent enough to serve ghee, and his untouchable guests were foolish enough to taste it. Ghee is undoubtedly a luxury for the rich. But no one would think that consumption of ghee was a mark of high social status. The Hindus of Chakwara thought otherwise, and in righteous indignation avenged themselves for the wrong done to them by the untouchables, who insulted them by treating ghee as an item of their food—which they ought to have known could not be theirs, consistently with the dignity of the Hindus. This means that an untouchable must not use ghee, even if he can afford to buy it, since it is an act of arrogance towards the Hindus. This happened on or about the 1st of April 1936!

Having stated the facts, let me now state the case for social reform. In doing this, I will follow Mr. Bonnerji as nearly as I can, and ask the political-minded Hindus, "Are you fit for political power even though you do not allow a large class of your own countrymen like the untouchables to use public schools? Are you fit for political power even though you do not allow them the use of public wells? Are you fit for political power even though you do not allow them the use of public streets? Are you fit for political power even though you do not allow them to wear what apparel or ornaments they like? Are you fit for political power even though you do not allow them to eat any food they like?" I can ask a string of such questions. But these will suffice. I wonder what would have been the reply of Mr. Bonnerji. I am sure no sensible man will have the courage to give an affirmative answer. Every Congressman who repeats the dogma of Mill that one country is not fit to rule another country, must admit that one class is not fit to rule another class.

How is it then that the Social Reform Party lost the battle? To understand this correctly it is necessary to take note of the kind of social reform which the reformers were agitating for. In this connection it is necessary to make a distinction between social reform in the sense of the reform of the Hindu Family, and social reform in the sense of the reorganization and reconstruction of the Hindu Society. The former has a relation to widow remarriage, child marriage, etc., while the latter relates to the abolition of the Caste System. The Social Conference was a body which mainly concerned itself with the reform of the high-caste Hindu family. It consisted mostly of enlightened high-caste Hindus who did not feel the necessity for agitating for the abolition of Caste, or had not the courage to agitate for it. They felt quite naturally a greater urge to remove such evils as enforced widowhood, child marriages, etc.—evils which prevailed among them and which were personally felt by them. They did not stand up for the reform of the Hindu Society. The battle that was fought centered around the question of the reform of the family. It did not relate to social reform in the sense of the break-up of the Caste System. It was never put in issue by the reformers. That is the reason why the Social Reform Party lost.

[...]

4 — [Caste is not just a division of labour, it is a division of labourers]

It is a pity that Caste even today has its defenders. The defences are many. It is defended on the ground that the Caste System is but another name for division of labour; and if division of labour is a necessary feature of every civilized society, then it is argued that there is nothing wrong in the Caste System. Now the first thing that is to be urged against this view is that the Caste System is not merely a division of labour. It is also a division of labourers. Civilized society undoubtedly needs division of labour. But in no civilized society is division of labour accompanied by this unnatural division of labourers into watertight compartments. The Caste System is not merely a division of labourers which is quite different from division of labour—it is a hierarchy in which the divisions of labourers are graded one above the other. In no other country is the division of labour accompanied by this gradation of labourers. There is also a third point of criticism against this view of the Caste System. This division of labour is not spontaneous, it is not based on natural aptitudes. Social and individual efficiency requires us to develop the capacity of an individual to the point of competency to choose and to make his own career. This principle is violated in the Caste System, in so far as it involves an attempt to appoint tasks to individuals in advance—selected not on the basis of trained original capacities, but on that of the social status of the parents. Looked at from another point of view, this stratification of occupations which is the result of the Caste System is positively pernicious. Industry is never static. It undergoes rapid and abrupt changes. With such changes, an individual must be free to change his occupation. Without such freedom to adjust himself to changing circumstances, it would be impossible for him to gain his livelihood. Now the Caste System will not allow Hindus to take to occupations where they are wanted, if they do not belong to them by heredity. If a Hindu is seen to starve rather than take to new occupations not assigned to his Caste, the reason is to be found in the Caste System. By not permitting readjustment of occupations, Caste becomes a direct cause of much of the unemployment we see in the country. As a form of division of labour, the Caste system suffers from another serious defect. The division of labour brought about by the Caste System is not a division based on choice. Individual sentiment, individual preference, has no place in it. It is based on the dogma of predestination. Considerations of social efficiency would compel us to recognize that the greatest evil in the industrial system is not so much poverty and the suffering that it involves, as the fact that so many persons have callings which make no appeal to those who are engaged in them. Such callings constantly provoke one to aversion, ill will, and the desire to evade. There are many occupations in India which, on account of the fact that they are regarded as degraded by the Hindus, provoke those who are engaged in them to aversion. There is a constant desire to evade and escape from such occupations, which arises solely because of the blighting effect which they produce upon those who follow them, owing to the slight and stigma cast upon them by the Hindu religion. What efficiency can there be in a system under which neither men's hearts nor their minds are in their work? As an economic organization Caste is therefore a harmful institution, inasmuch as it involves the subordination of man's natural powers and inclinations to the exigencies of social rules.

13 — [Caste destroys public spirit, public opinion, and public charity]

The effect of caste on the ethics of the Hindus is simply deplorable. Caste has killed public spirit. Caste has destroyed the sense of public charity. Caste has made public opinion impossible. A Hindu's public is his caste. His responsibility is only to his caste. His loyalty is restricted only to his caste. Virtue has become caste-ridden, and morality has become caste-bound. There is no sympathy for the deserving. There is no appreciation of the meritorious. There is no charity to the needy. Suffering as such calls for no response. There is charity, but it begins with the caste and ends with the caste. There is sympathy, but not for men of other castes. Would a Hindu acknowledge and follow the leadership of a great and good man? The case of a Mahatma apart, the answer must be that he will follow a leader if he is a man of his caste. A Brahmin will follow a leader only if he is a Brahmin, a Kayastha if he is a Kayastha, and so on. The capacity to appreciate merits in a man, apart from his caste, does not exist in a Hindu. There is appreciation of virtue, but only when the man is a fellow caste-man. The whole morality is as bad as tribal morality. My caste-man, right or wrong; my caste-man, good or bad. It is not a case of standing by virtue or not standing by vice. It is a case of standing by, or not standing by, the caste. Have not Hindus committed treason against their country in the interests of their caste?

26 — [The struggle is yours; I have now decided to leave the Hindu fold]

. . . All I claim is to have told you candidly my views. I have little to recommend them but some study and a deep concern in your destiny. If you will allow me to say it, these views are the views of a man who has been no tool of power, no flatterer of greatness. They come from one, almost the whole of whose public exertion has been one continuous struggle for liberty for the poor and for the oppressed, and whose only reward has been a continuous shower of calumny and abuse from national journals and national leaders, for no other reason except that I refuse to join with them in performing the miracle—I will not say trick—of liberating the oppressed with the gold of the tyrant, and raising the poor with the cash of the rich. All this may not be enough to commend my views. I think they are not likely to alter yours. But whether they do or do not, the responsibility is entirely yours. You must make your efforts to uproot Caste, if not in my way, then in your way. I am sorry, I will not be with you. I have decided to change. This is not the place for giving reasons. But even when I am gone out of your fold, I will watch your movement with active sympathy, and you will have my assistance for what it may be worth. Yours is a national cause. Caste is no doubt primarily the breath of the Hindus. But the Hindus have fouled the air all over, and everybody is infected—Sikh, Muslim, and Christian. You, therefore, deserve the support of all those who are suffering from this infection—Sikh, Muslim, and Christian. Yours is more difficult than the other national cause, namely Swaraj.[36] In the fight for Swaraj you fight with the whole nation on your side. In this, you have to fight against the whole nation—and that too, your own. But it is more important than Swaraj. There is no use having Swaraj, if you cannot defend it. More important than the question of defending Swaraj is the question of defending the Hindus under the Swaraj. In my opinion, it is only when Hindu Society becomes a casteless society that it can hope to have strength enough to defend itself. Without such internal strength, Swaraj for Hindus may turn out to be only a step towards slavery. Good-bye, and good wishes for your success.

Ambedkar, Bhimrao Ramji. *Annihilation of Caste: With a Reply to Mahatma Gandhi*, 3rd ed., 1–10, 19–21, 37(?), 80–81. Amritsar: The Ambedkar School of Thoughts, 1945. [Public Domain]. A version can be found at: https://archive.org/details/in.ernet.dli.2015.71655/page/n1/mode/2up.

---

36. This Sanskrit word means "self-rule." It was used commonly by leaders fighting for Indian independence from British rule as capturing the target of their freedom struggle.

"A'n't I a Woman?" and "Address to the First Annual Meeting of the American Equal Rights Association" by Sojourner Truth

SNAPSHOT BOX

LANGUAGE: English

DELIVERED: 1851, Akron, Ohio, and 1867, New York

GENRE: Public addresses

TAGS: Abolition, Slavery, Freedom; Accessing Rights; Autobiography and Testimony; Body; Ethics and Morality; Family; Gender and Identity; Labor; Race; Religion; Rhetoric and Persuasion; Struggle, Resistance, and Revolution; War and Brutality; Women and Power

Introduction

Sojourner Truth (1797–1883) was born Isabella in Hurley, a village in Ulster County, New York. She was the daughter of James and Elizabeth Baumfree, both enslaved by Colonel Johannes Hardenbergh. Upstate New York was predominantly rural, settled by Dutch farmers, and Isabella was born into an Afro-Dutch culture and grew up speaking Dutch. Like many enslaved people across the United States, Isabella had little control over her life. By the age of twelve, Isabella had been bought and sold three times and was enslaved by four different families. Isabella worked in a variety of capacities: she did farm work, brewed beer, cooked, and cleaned. She survived forms of physical and sexual abuse by many of her masters, including Sally Dumont, the wife of her final master John Dumont. It was in the household of the Dumonts that Isabella met her husband Thomas. In New York State, marriage between enslaved people was legally protected. In 1826, Isabella fled the Dumonts with one of her five children, baby Sophia. She found refuge with the Van Wagenens, an abolitionist family. The Van Wagenens protected Isabella and Sophia and purchased her from the Dumonts.

In 1827, New York State abolished slavery and it was during this time that Isabella challenged the enslavement system in court. John Dumont had sold her five-year-old son Peter to a relative, who then transported

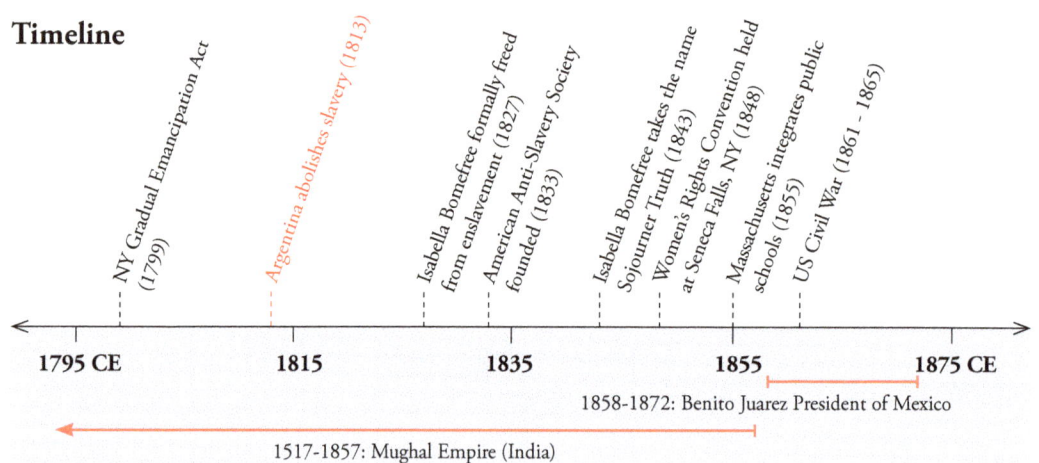

the young boy to Alabama and resold him to a planter. This transaction was illegal under New York State law and Isabella successfully sued for Peter's freedom. As you read Truth's speech, "Ain't I a Woman?," how does she redirect her experiences of enslaved work, hunger, and motherhood as part of her argument for being deserving of rights? While a popular antislavery tract at the time, scholars note that some of this speech was invented by Frances Dana Gage. However, Truth did give a speech in Akron, Ohio, much of which appears in this text. A key difference is that Truth begins the Ohio speech with the statement "I am a woman's rights," not the question "Ain't I a woman?"

In 1828, Isabella moved to New York City. Now a free woman, she became involved in the vibrant evangelical movement that unfolded across the United States. This **Second Great Awakening** fostered an intense religious revival movement that at times challenged gender and racial norms. In the 1830s, Isabella became involved in a religious commune named the Kingdom of Matthias. This community was based on concepts of equality and free love. People participating in the Second Great Awakening believed in the liberation of the body and the spirit, thus enslavement and the oppression of women was a sin before God. Eventually, the community fell apart and it was in those ensuing years that Isabella took up the name Sojourner Truth. In 1843, Isabella contended that she was "called in spirit" during which time the Holy Spirit spoke to her. In this divine revelation, God instructed her to go forth and tell the truth. With the new name Sojourner Truth, she became an itinerant preacher, traveling across the northeast, from camp meetings to town halls, preaching about love and brotherhood. It was during this time that Truth met a number of prominent abolitionists and women's rights activists like William Lloyd Garrison, Lucretia Mott, and Frederick Douglass.

Truth developed the reputation as a powerful and persuasive speaker on behalf of human rights. In her view, equality and freedom were natural rights endowed at birth, not civil qualifications granted by others. Truth's long career as an advocate for African American and women's rights continued until her death in 1883 in Battle Creek, Michigan.

In the following two speeches, Truth reiterates her belief in the fundamental human rights and dignity of all people. Yet, these two speeches are different. Both the abolitionist movement and the women's rights movement raised issues of difference within oppressed groups. This was particularly true among women abolitionists where the issue of race created significant divisions. Black abolitionist and women's rights activists had to contend with not being acknowledged by white women. In the 1851 address, how does Truth challenge the gender politics of white supremacy? In what ways does she challenge the use of reason as a prerequisite of citizenship? The second speech, given in 1867, focuses specifically on women's rights in the context of the Fourteenth and Fifteenth Amendments. The Fourteenth Amendment nationalized US citizenship, while the Fifteenth Amendment protected voting rights for African American men. Following the Civil War, women's rights activists split over whether or not to support African American men's voting rights. Some, like Frederick Douglass, wanted to secure voting rights for African American men before advocating for women's suffrage. In this 1867 speech, how does Truth raise the issue of patriarchal domination? In what ways does Truth think that African American women are disadvantaged by not having voting rights? Finally, why do you think that Truth, despite being a Northerner, is quoted in Southern dialect in the first speech and not in the second?

Sarah Judson
Department of History

> **PRE-READING PARS**
>
> 1. Identify two ways that nineteenth-century slave society might have been different in New York State versus in the American South.
> 2. What kinds of ideas do you think the antislavery movement and the women's rights movement held in common?

"A'n't I A Woman?" and "Address to the First Annual Meeting of the American Equal Rights Association"

A'n't I A Woman?

Delivered 1851. Women's Rights Convention, Old Stone Church (since demolished), Akron, Ohio

Well, children, where there is so much racket there must be something out of kilter. I think that 'twixt the negroes[37] of the South and the women at the North, all talking about rights, the white men will be in a fix pretty soon. But what's all this here talking about?

That man over there says that women need to be helped into carriages, and lifted over ditches, and to have the best place everywhere. Nobody ever helps me into carriages, or over mud-puddles, or gives me any best place! And ain't I a woman? Look at me! Look at my arm! I have ploughed and planted, and gathered into barns, and no man could head me! And ain't I a woman? I could work as much and eat as much as a man—when I could get it—and bear the lash as well! And ain't I a woman? I have borne thirteen children, and seen most all sold off to slavery, and when I cried out with my mother's grief, none but Jesus heard me! And ain't I a woman?

Then they talk about this thing in the head; what's this they call it? [member of audience whispers, "intellect"] That's it, honey. What's that got to do with women's rights or negroes' rights? If my cup won't hold but a pint, and yours holds a quart, wouldn't you be mean not to let me have my little half measure full?

Then that little man in black there, he says women can't have as much rights as men, 'cause Christ wasn't a woman! Where did your Christ come from? Where did your Christ come from? From God and a woman! Man had nothing to do with Him.

---

37. Truth uses the term "Negro" to refer to her own African American communities as was a prevalent practice within and outside of Black communities from the nineteenth to mid-twentieth centuries. The term "negro" should not be confused with the derogatory n-word. Likewise another term used during the same timeframe, "colored," is outdated and should not be confused with the current usage of "person of color." Words reflecting African American and Black communities' preferences for self-identification continue to shift in meaning and connotation over time.

If the first woman God ever made was strong enough to turn the world upside down all alone, these women together ought to be able to turn it back, and get it right side up again! And now they is asking to do it, the men better let them.

Obliged to you for hearing me, and now old Sojourner ain't got nothing more to say.

Address to the First Annual Meeting of the American Equal Rights Association (1867)

My friends, I am rejoiced that you are glad, but I don't know how you will feel when I get through. I come from another field—the country of the slave. They have got their liberty—so much good luck to have slavery partly destroyed; not entirely. I want its root and branch destroyed. Then we will all be free indeed. I feel that if I have to answer for the deeds done in my body just as much as a man, I have a right to have just as much as a man. There is a great stir about colored men getting their rights, but not a word about the colored women; and if colored men get their rights, and not colored women theirs, you see the colored men will be masters over the women, and it will be just as bad as it was before. So I am for keeping the thing going while things are stirring; because if we wait till it is still, it will take a great while to get it going again. White women are a great deal smarter, and know more than colored women, while colored women do not know scarcely anything. They go out washing, which is about as high as a colored woman gets, and their men go about idle, strutting up and down; and when the women come home, they ask for their money and take it all, and then scold because there is no food. I want you to consider on that, chil'n. I call you chil'n; you are somebody's chil'n, and I am old enough to be mother of all that is here. I want women to have their rights. In the courts women have no right, no voice; nobody speaks for them. I wish woman to have her voice there among the pettifoggers. If it is not a fit place for women, it is unfit for men to be there.

I am above eighty years old; it is about time for me to be going. I have been forty years a slave and forty years free, and would be here forty years more to have equal rights for all. I suppose I am kept here because something remains for me to do; I suppose I am yet to help to break the chain. I have done a great deal of work; as much as a man, but did not get so much pay. I used to work in the field and bind grain, keeping up with the cradler; but men doing no more, got twice as much pay; so with the German women. They work in the field and do as much work, but do not get the pay. We do as much, we eat as much, we want as much. I suppose I am about the only colored woman that goes about to speak for the rights of the colored women. I want to keep the thing stirring, now that the ice is cracked. What we want is a little money. You men know that you get as much again as women when you write, or for what you do. When we get our rights we shall not have to come to you for money, for then we shall have money enough in our own pockets; and maybe you will ask us for money. But help us now until we get it. It is a good consolation to know that when we have got this battle once fought we shall not be coming to you any more. You have been having our rights so long, that you think, like a slaveholder, that you own us. I know that it is hard for one who has held the reins for so long to give up; it cuts like a knife. It will feel all the better when it closes up again. I have been in Washington about three years, seeing about these colored people. Now colored men have the right to vote. There ought to be equal rights now more than ever, since colored people have got their freedom. I am going to talk several times while I am here; so now I will do a little singing. I have not heard any singing since I came here.

Truth, Sojourner. "'A'n't I a Woman?" December 1851. [Public Domain]. One version can be found at: https://sourcebooks.fordham.edu/mod/sojtruth-woman.asp.

First Annual Meeting of the American Equal Rights Association. N.p.: New York Tribune, 1867. [Public Domain]. One version can be found at: http://www.self.gutenberg.org/eBooks/WPLBN0100002815-First-Annual-Meeting-of-the-American-Equal-Rights-Association-by-Truth-Sojourner.aspx.

> **POST-READING PARS**
>
> 1. Identify two ways that you see religious beliefs informing Sojourner Truth's vision for equality?
> 2. What are the connections that Sojourner Truth makes between antislavery and women's rights?
> 3. Identify two to three occasions in either speech where Truth critiques patriarchal domination.

Inquiry Corner

Content Questions:

What do you think freedom meant to Sojourner Truth?

In what ways does Sojourner Truth reference her physicality when making claims for equality? Why do you think she included this?

Critical Questions:

Critically evaluate the ways in which Sojourner Truth inspired the antislavery and women's rights activists toward a more inclusive understanding of equality.

How does Sojourner Truth's rights claims challenge the Enlightenment emphasis on reason as the basis for citizenship and personhood?

Comparative Question:

How does Sojourner Truth's perspective on Black women's equal rights compare with other authors' equality claims for women (e.g., Elizabeth Cady Stanton or Maria Eugenia Echenique, etc.)?

Connection Questions:

Truth's writings offer us an opportunity to engage where differently marginalized communities' claims for equality collide. How might you have witnessed or experienced such intersectional tensions? How might they become locations for collaborative coalition building?

How does working with Truth's speeches bring to light the historical invisibility of Black women's labor?

from *The Berlin Stories* by Christopher Isherwood

Introduction

In 1929 the British author Christopher Isherwood (1904–1986) traveled to Berlin, Germany, to meet his friend and fellow author, W. H. Auden, who was there studying German. Isherwood remained in Berlin for four years teaching English, all the while immersing himself in the German capital's culture at the end of Germany's Weimar Republic (the constitutional democratic state from 1919–1933). His daily experiences during this time were first published as two related novels *The Last of Mr. Norris* (1935) and *Goodbye to Berlin* (1939). After emigrating to the United States in 1946, these novels were republished together as *The Berlin Stories* and later formed the basis for the play "I Am a Camera" (1951), the Broadway musical *Cabaret* (1966), and the iconic performance by Liza Minelli in the 1972 film of the same title. Have you found that traveling inspires your creativity? What might the experience of traveling to or living in another culture inspire in someone?

> **SNAPSHOT BOX**
>
> LANGUAGE: English
> PUBLISHED: 1946, United States
> GENRE: Novel
> TAGS: Art; Autobiography and Testimony; Body; Cross-Cultural Encounters; Historiography; Poetry, Music, Literature

Berlin of the 1920s was known for its social and sexual revolutions and its vibrant and experimental cultural productions as much as it is for the economic instability and political unrest resulting from Germany's defeat in World War I that created it. Indeed, Berlin in the 1920s was a global city that had made a name for itself on its social and scientific innovations. *Universum-Film Aktiengesellschaft* or UFA was leading the world in the new medium of film with future classics like *Metropolis* (1926) and *The Blue Angel* (1930). The revolutionary physicists Max Planck and Albert

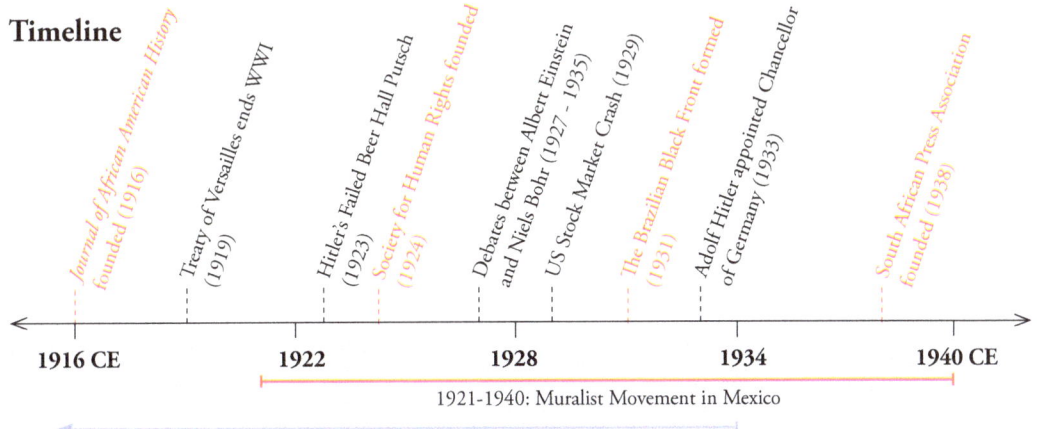

Timeline

- *Journal of African American History* founded (1916)
- Treaty of Versailles ends WWI (1919)
- Hitler's Failed Beer Hall Putsch (1923)
- Society for Human Rights founded (1924)
- Debates between Albert Einstein and Niels Bohr (1927 - 1935)
- US Stock Market Crash (1929)
- The Brazilian Black Front formed (1931)
- Adolf Hitler appointed Chancellor of Germany (1933)
- South African Press Association founded (1938)

1916 CE — 1922 — 1928 — 1934 — 1940 CE

1921-1940: Muralist Movement in Mexico

1915-1934: U.S. occupies Haiti

Einstein also called Berlin home. In nearby Potsdam, the modernist architect Erich Mendelsohn constructed an expressionist astronomy observatory, the *Einsteinturm*, in honor of the latter. Another school of modernist design, *Bauhaus*, relocated its headquarters to Berlin by the 1930s. After the Nazi regime shut down the school in 1933, some of its leaders helped to form the avante-garde Black Mountain College in Western North Carolina. How can science and the arts challenge the social, political, or cultural status quo. What historical or contemporary instances of this are you aware of, and what do you know about government responses to those challenges?

The Weimar Republic also witnessed a shift in formal and informal gender relations and a new openness toward discussions of sexuality. Efforts by German women at gaining the vote were spurred on by World War I, and the 1919 Weimar Constitution introduced female suffrage. Using this new political voice, women protested the government's ban on abortions during the 1920s, extending their newfound political and economic autonomy to the control over their own bodies. Paragraph 175, which had banned male homosexuality since 1871, continued on into the Weimar Republic. Yet, in metropolitan areas and especially Berlin, homosexuality became much more socially acceptable. Berlin itself boasted several guidebooks to the city's gay bars and clubs. Moreover, the openly gay sexologist Magnus Hirschfeld opened the world's first Institute for Sex Research in Berlin in 1919 (also shut down in 1933 with the rise of the Nazis).

When Isherwood arrived in Berlin in 1929, he became part of this milieu, a part of the modern masses who were searching, striving, experimenting, and experiencing the possibilities of the modern world in all of its various permutations. That year also witnessed the great economic downturn in the US economy, and shortly thereafter, a massive economic depression in Germany. With unemployment numbers reaching over 30 percent by 1933, desperation and a further polarization of politics began to take hold in Germany. It is within this context, the end of 1932, and the subsequent appointment of Adolf Hitler as German chancellor in 1933, that Isherwood's final chapter of *The Berlin Stories* takes place. As you read this chapter, note the different social milieus in which Isherwood takes part. What criticisms does he make of the social, cultural, and political climate in which he finds himself? What do we make of his criticisms as an outsider looking in?

Eric Roubinek
Department of History

A Berlin Diary (Winter 1932–3)

To-night, for the first time this winter, it is very cold. The dead cold grips the town in utter silence, like the silence of intense midday summer heat. In the cold the town seems actually to contract, to dwindle to a small black dot, scarcely larger than hundreds of other dots, isolated and hard to find, on the enormous European map. Outside, in the night, beyond the last new-built blocks of concrete flats, where the streets end in frozen allotment gardens, are the Prussian plains. You can feel them all round you, to-night, creeping in upon the city like an immense waste of unhomely ocean—sprinkled with leafless copses and ice-lakes and tiny villages which are remembered only as the outlandish names of battlefields in half-forgotten wars. Berlin is a skeleton which aches in the cold: it is my own skeleton aching. I feel in my bones the sharp ache of the frost in the girders of the overhead railway in the ironwork of balconies, in bridges, tram- lines, lamp-standards, latrines. The iron throbs and shrinks, the stone and the bricks ache dully, the plaster is numb.

Berlin is a city with two centres—the cluster of expensive hotels, bars, cinemas, shops round the Memorial Church, a sparkling nucleus of light, like a sham diamond, in the shabby twilight of the town; and the self-conscious civic centre of buildings round the Unter den Linden, carefully arranged. In grand international styles, copies of copies, they assert our dignity as a capital city—a parliament, a couple of museums, a State bank, a cathedral, an opera, a dozen embassies, a triumphal arch; nothing has been forgotten. And they are all so pompous, so very correct—all except the cathedral, which betrays, in its architecture, a flash of that hysteria which flickers always behind every grave, grey Prussian façade. Extinguished by its absurd dome, it is, at first sight, so startlingly funny that one searches for a name suitably preposterous— the Church of the Immaculate Consumption.

But the real heart of Berlin is a small damp black wood—the Tiergarten. At this time of the year, the cold begins to drive the peasant boys out of their tiny unprotected villages into the city, to look for food, and work. But the city, which glowed so brightly and invitingly in the night sky above the plains, is cold and cruel and dead. Its warmth is an illusion, a mirage of the winter desert. It will not receive these boys. It has nothing to give. The cold drives them out of its streets, into the wood which is its cruel heart. And there they cower on benches, to starve and freeze, and dream of their far-away cottage stoves.

Frl.[38] Schroeder hates the cold. Huddled in her fur-lined velvet jacket, she sits in the corner with her stockinged feet on the stove. Sometimes she smokes a cigarette, sometimes she sips a glass of tea, but mostly she just sits, staring dully at the stove tiles in a kind of hibernation-doze. She is lonely, nowadays. Frl. Mayr is away in Holland, on a cabaret-tour. So Frl. Schroeder has nobody to talk to, except Bobby and myself.

Bobby, anyhow, is in deep disgrace. Not only is he out of work and three months

---

38. Frl. is the abbreviation of Fräulein, German for Miss.

behind with the rent, but Frl. Schroeder has reason to suspect him of stealing money from her bag. "You know, Herr Issyvoo," she tells me, "I shouldn't wonder at all if he didn't pinch those fifty marks from Frl. Kost.... He's quite capable of it, the pig! To think I could ever have been so mistaken in him! Will you believe it, Herr Issyvoo, I treated him as if he were my own son—and this is the thanks I get! He says he'll pay me every pfennig if he gets this job as barman at the Lady Windermere... if, *if*..." Frl. Schroeder sniffs with intense scorn; "I dare say! If my grandmother had wheels, she'd be an omnibus!"

Bobby has been turned out of his old room and banished to the Swedish Pavilion: It must be terribly draughty, up there. Sometimes poor Bobby looks quite blue with cold. He has changed very much during the last year—his hair is thinner, his clothes are shabbier, his cheekiness has become defiant and rather pathetic. People like Bobby are their jobs—take the job away and they partially cease to exist. Sometimes, he sneaks into the living-room, unshaven, his hands in his pockets, and lounges about uneasily defiant, whistling to himself—the dance tunes he whistles are no longer quite new. Frl. Schroeder throws him a word, now and then, like a grudging scrap of bread, but she won't look at him or make for him by the stove. Perhaps she has never really forgiven him for his affair with Frl. Kost. The tickling and bottom-slapping days are over.

Yesterday we had a visit from Frl. Kost herself. I was out at the time: when I got back I found Frl. Schroeder quite excited. "Only think, Herr Issyvoo—I wouldn't have known her! She's quite the lady now! Her Japanese friend has bought her a fur coat—real fur, I shouldn't like to think what he must have paid for it! And her shoes—genuine snakeskin! Well, well, I bet she earned them! That's the one kind of business that still goes well, nowadays.... I think I shall have to take to the line myself!" But however much Frl. Schroeder might affect sarcasm at Frl. Kost's expense, I could see that she'd been greatly and not unfavourably impressed. And it wasn't so much the fur coat or the shoes which had impressed her: Frl. Kost had achieved something higher—the hall-mark of respectability in Frl. Schroeder's world—she had had an operation in a private nursing home. "Oh, not what you think, Herr Issyvoo! It was something to do with her throat. Her friend paid for that, too, of course.... Only imagine—the doctors cut something out of the back of her nose; and now she can fill her mouth with water and squirt it out through her nostrils, just like a syringe! I wouldn't believe it at first—but she did it to show me! My word of honour, Herr Issyvoo, she could squirt it right across the kitchen! There's no denying, she's very much improved, since the time when she used to live here.... I shouldn't be surprised if she married a bank director one of these days. Oh, yes, you mark my words, that girl will go far...."

Herr Krampf, a young engineer, one of my pupils, describes his childhood during the days of the War and the Inflation. During the last years of the War, the straps disappeared from the windows of railway carriages: people had cut them off in order to sell the leather. You even saw men and women going about in clothes made from the carriage upholstery. A party of Krampf's school friends broke into a factory one night and stole all the leather driving-belts. Everybody stole. Everybody sold what they had to sell—themselves included. A boy of fourteen, from Krampf's class, peddled cocaine between school hours, in the streets.

Farmers and butchers were omnipotent. Their slightest whim had to be gratified, if you wanted vegetables or meat. The Krampf family knew of a butcher in a little village outside Berlin who always had meat to sell. But the butcher had a peculiar sexual perversion. His greatest erotic pleasure was to pinch and slap the cheeks of a sensitive, well-bred girl or woman. The possibility of thus humiliating a lady like Frau Krampf excited him enormously: unless he was allowed to realize his fantasy, he refused, absolutely, to do business. So, every Sunday, Krampf's mother would travel out to the village with her children, and patiently offer her cheeks to be slapped and pinched, in exchange for some cutlets or a steak.

At the far end of the Potsdamerstrasse, there is a fairground, with merry-go-rounds, swings and peep-shows. One of the chief attractions of the fair-ground is a tent where boxing and wrestling matches are held. You pay your money and go in, the wrestlers fight three or four rounds, and the referee then announces that, if you want to see any more, you must pay an extra ten pfennigs. One of the wrestlers is a bald man with a very large stomach: he wears a pair of canvas trousers rolled up at the bottoms, as though he were going paddling. His opponent wears black tights, and leather kneelets which look as if they had come off an old cab-horse. The wrestlers throw each other about as much as possible, turning somersaults in the air to amuse the audience. The fat man who plays the part of loser pretends to get very angry when he is beaten, and threatens to fight the referee.

One of the boxers is a negro.[39] He invariably wins. The boxers hit each other with the open glove, making a tremendous amount of noise. The other boxer, a tall, well-built young man, about twenty years younger and obviously much stronger than the negro, is "knocked out" with absurd ease. He writhes in great agony on the floor, nearly manages to struggle to his feet at the count of ten, then collapses again, groaning. After this fight, the referee collects ten more pfennigs and calls for a challenger from the audience. Before any bona fide challenger can apply, another young man, who has been quite openly chatting and joking with the wrestlers, jumps hastily into the ring and strips off his clothes, revealing himself already dressed in shorts and boxer's boots. The referee announces a purse of five marks; and, this time, the negro is "knocked out."

The audience took the fights dead seriously, shouting encouragement to the fight-

---

39. Isherwood uses the term "Negro" to refer to African communities as was a prevalent practice within and outside of Black communities from the nineteenth to mid-twentieth centuries. The term "negro" should not be confused with the derogatory n-word. Likewise another term used during the same timeframe, "colored," is outdated and should not be confused with the current usage of "person of color." Words reflecting African, African American, and Black communities' preferences for self-identification continue to shift in meaning and connotation over time.

ers, and even quarrelling and betting amongst themselves on the results. Yet nearly all of them had been in the tent as long as I had and stayed on after I had left. The political moral is certainly depressing: these people could be made to believe in anybody or anything.

Walking this evening along the Kleiststrasse, I saw a little crowd gathered round a private car. In the car were two girls: on the pavement stood two young Jews, engaged in a violent argument with a large blond man who was obviously rather drunk. The Jews, it seemed, had been driving slowly along the street, on the look-out for a pick-up, and had offered these girls a ride. The two girls had accepted and got into the car. At this moment, however, the blond man had intervened. He was a Nazi, he told us, and as such felt it his mission to defend the honour of all German women against the obscene anti-Nordic menace. The two Jews didn't seem in the least intimidated; they told the Nazi energetically to mind his own business. Meanwhile, the girls, taking advantage of the row, slipped out of the car and ran off down the street. The Nazi then tried to drag one of the Jews with him to find a policeman, and the Jew whose arm he had seized gave him an uppercut which laid him sprawling on his back. Before the Nazi could get to his feet, both young men had jumped into their car and driven away. The crowd dispersed slowly, arguing. Very few of them sided openly with the Nazi: several supported the Jews; but the majority confined themselves to shaking their heads dubiously and murmuring: "*Allerhand!*"

When, three hours later, I passed the same spot, the Nazi was still patrolling up and down, looking hungrily for more German womanhood to rescue.

We have just got a letter from Frl. Mayr: Frl. Schroeder called me in to listen to it. Frl. Mayr doesn't like Holland. She has been obliged to sing in a lot of second-rate cafés in third-rate towns, and her bedroom is often badly heated. The Dutch, she writes, have no culture; she has only met one truly refined and superior gentleman, a widower. The widower tells her that she is really womanly woman—he has no use for young chits of girls. He has shown his admiration for her art by presenting her with a complete new set of underclothes.

Frl. Mayr has also had trouble with her colleagues. At one town, a rival actress, jealous of Frl. Mayr's vocal powers, tried to stab her in the eye with a hatpin. I can't help admiring that actress's courage. When Frl. Mayr had finished with her, she was so badly injured that she couldn't appear on the stage again for a week.

Last night, Fritz Wendel proposed a tour of "the dives." It was to be in the nature of a farewell visit, for the Police have begun to take a great interest in these places. They are frequently raided, and the names of their clients are written down. There is even talk of a general Berlin clean-up.

I rather upset him by insisting on visiting the Salomé, which I had never seen. Fritz, as a connoisseur of night-life, was most contemptuous. It wasn't even genuine, he told me. The management run it entirely for the benefit of provincial sightseers.

The Salomé turned out to be very expensive and even more depressing than I had imagined. A few stage lesbians and some young men with plucked eyebrows lounged at the bar, uttering occasional raucous guffaws or treble hoots—supposed, apparently, to represent the laughter of the damned. The whole premises are painted gold and inferno-red—crimson plush inches thick, and vast gilded mirrors. It was pretty full. The audience consisted chiefly of respectable middle-aged tradesmen and their families, exclaiming in good-humoured amazement: "Do they really?" and "Well, I never!" We went out half-way through the cabaret performance, after a young man in a spangled crinoline and jewelled breast-caps had painfully but successfully executed three splits.

At the entrance we met a party of American youths, very drunk, wondering whether to go in. Their leader was a small stocky young man in pince-nez, with an annoyingly prominent jaw.

"Say," he asked Fritz, "what's on here?"

"Men dressed as women," Fritz grinned.

The little American simply couldn't believe it. "Men dressed as *women*? As *women* hey? Do you mean they're *queer*?"

"Eventually we're all queer," drawled Fritz solemnly, in lugubrious tones. The young man looked us over slowly. He had been running and was still out of breath. The others grouped themselves awkwardly behind him, ready for anything—though their callow, open-mouthed faces in the greenish lamp-light looked a bit scared.

"You *queer*, too, hey?" demanded the little American, turning suddenly on me.

"Yes," I said, "very queer indeed."

He stood before me a moment, panting, thrusting out his jaw, uncertain it seemed, whether he ought not to hit me in the face. Then he turned, uttered some kind of wild college battle-cry, and, followed by the others, rushed headlong into the building.

"Ever been to that communist dive near the Zoo?" Fritz asked me, as we were walking away from the Salomé. "Eventually we should cast an eye in there. . . . In six months, maybe, we'll all be wearing red shirts. . . ."

I agreed. I was curious to know what Fritz's idea of a "communist dive" would be like.

It was, in fact, a small whitewashed cellar. You sat on long wooden benches at big bare tables; a dozen people together—like a school dining-hall. On the walls were scribbled expressionist drawings involving actual newspaper clippings, real playing-cards, nailed-on beer-mats, match-boxes, cigarette cartons, and heads cut out of photographs. The cafe was full of students, dressed mostly with aggressive political untidiness—the men in sailor's sweaters and stained baggy trousers, the girls in ill-fitting jumpers, skirts held visibly together with safety-pins and carelessly knotted gaudy gipsy scarves. The proprietress was smoking a cigar. The boy who acted as a waiter lounged about with a cigarette between his lips and slapped customers on the back when taking their orders.

It was all thoroughly sham and gay and jolly: you couldn't help feeling at home, immediately. Fritz, as usual, recognized plenty of friends. He introduced me to three of them—a man called Martin, an art student named Werner, and Inge, his girl. Inge was broad and lively—she wore a little hat with a feather in it which gave her a kind of farcical resemblance to Henry the Eighth. While Werner and Inge chattered, Martin sat silent: he was thin and dark and hatchet-faced, with the sardonically superior smile of the conscious conspirator. Later in the evening, when Fritz and Werner and Inge had moved down the table to join another party, Martin began to talk about the coming civil war. When the war breaks out, Martin explained, the communists, who have very few machine-guns, will get command of the roof tops. They will then keep the Police at bay with hand-grenades. It will only be necessary to hold out for three days, because the Soviet fleet will make an immediate dash for Swinemünde and begin to land troops. "I spend most of my time now making bombs," Martin added. I nodded and grinned, very much embarrassed—uncertain whether he was making fun of me, or deliberately committing some appalling indiscretion. He certainly wasn't drunk, and he didn't strike me as merely insane.

Presently, a strikingly handsome boy of sixteen or seventeen came into the cafe. His name was Rudi. He was dressed in a Russian blouse, leather shorts and despatch-rider's boots, and he strode up to our table with all the heroic mannerisms of a messenger who returns successful from a desperate mission. He had, however, no message of any kind to deliver. After his whirlwind entry, and a succession of curt, martial handshakes, he sat down quite quietly beside us and ordered a glass of tea.

This evening, I visited the "communist" café again. It is really a fascinating little world of intrigue and counter-intrigue. Its Napoleon is the sinister bomb-making Martin; Werner is its Danton; Rudi its Joan of Arc. Everybody suspects everybody else. Already Martin has warned me against Werner: he is "politically unreliable"—last summer he stole the entire funds of a communist youth organization. And Werner has warned me against Martin: he is either a Nazi agent, or a police spy, or in the pay of the French Government. In addition to this, both Martin and Werner earnestly advised me to have nothing to do with Rudi—they absolutely refused to say why.

But there was no question of having nothing to do with Rudi. He planted himself down beside me and began talking at once—a hurricane of enthusiasm. His favourite word is "knorke": "Oh, *ripping*!" He is a pathfinder. He wanted to know what the boy scouts were like in England. Had they got the spirit of adventure? "All German boys are adventurous. Adventure is ripping. Our Scoutmaster is a ripping man. Last year he went to Lapland and lived in a hut, all through the summer, alone. . . . Are you a communist?"

"No. Are you?"

Rudi was pained.

"Of course! We all are, here. . . . I'll lend you some books, if you like. . . . You ought to come and see our club-house. It's ripping. . . . We sing the Red Flag, and all the forbidden songs. . . . Will you teach me English? I want to learn all languages."

I asked if there were any girls in his pathfinder group. Rudi was as shocked as if I'd said something really indecent.

"Women are no good," he told me bitterly. "They spoil everything. They haven't got the spirit of adventure. Men understand each other much better when they're alone together. Uncle Peter (that's our Scoutmaster) says women should stay at home and mend socks. That's all they're fit for!"

"Is Uncle Peter a communist, too?"

"Of course!" Rudi looked at me suspiciously. "Why do you ask that?"

"Oh, no special reason," I replied hastily. I think perhaps I was mixing him up with somebody else...."

This afternoon I travelled out to the reformatory to visit one of my pupils, Herr Brink, who is a master there. He is a small, broad-shouldered man, with the thin, dead-looking fair hair, mild eyes, and bulging, over-heavy forehead of the German vegetarian intellectual. He wears sandals and an open-necked shirt. I found him in the gymnasium, giving physical instruction to a class of mentally deficient children—for the reformatory houses mental deficients as well as juvenile delinquents. With a certain melancholy pride, he pointed out the various cases: one little boy was suffering from hereditary syphilis—he had a fearful squint; another, the child of elderly drunkards, couldn't stop laughing. They clambered about the wall-bars like monkeys, laughing and chattering, seemingly quite happy.

Then we went up to the workshop, where older boys in blue overalls—all convicted criminals—were making boots. Most of the boys looked up and grinned when Brink came in, only a few were sullen. But I couldn't look them in the eyes. I felt horribly guilty and ashamed: I seemed, at that moment, to have become the sole representative of their gaolers, of Capitalist Society. I wondered if any of them had actually been arrested in the Alexander Casino, and, if so, whether they recognized me.

We had lunch in the matron's room. Herr Brink apologized for giving me the same food as the boys themselves ate—potato soup with two sausages, and a dish of apples and stewed prunes. I protested—as, no doubt, I was intended to protest—that it was very good. And yet the thought of the boys having to eat it, or any other kind of meal, in that building, made each spoonful stick in my throat. Institution food has an indescribable, perhaps purely imaginary, taste. (One of the most vivid and sickening memories of my own school life is the smell of ordinary white bread.)

"You don't have any bars or locked gates here," I said. "I thought all reformatories had them.... Don't your boys often run away?"

"Hardly ever," said Brink, and the admission seemed to make him positively unhappy; he sank his head wearily in his hands. "Where shall they run to? Here it is bad. At home it is worse. The majority of them know that."

"But isn't there a kind of natural instinct for freedom?"

"Yes, you are right. But the boys soon lose it. The system helps them to lose it. I think perhaps that, in Germans, this instinct is never very strong."

"You don't have much trouble here, then?"

"Oh, yes. Sometimes.... Three months ago, a terrible thing happened. One boy stole another boy's overcoat. He asked for permission to go into the town—that is allowed—and possibly he meant to sell it. But the owner of the overcoat followed him, and they had a fight. The boy to whom the overcoat belonged took up a big stone and flung it at the other boy; and this boy, feeling himself hurt, deliberately smeared dirt into the wound, hoping to make it worse and so escape punishment. The wound did get worse. In three days the boy died of blood-poisoning. And when the other boy heard of this he killed himself with a kitchen knife...." Brink sighed deeply: "Sometimes I almost despair," he added. "It seems as if there were a kind of badness, a disease, infecting the world to-day."

"But what can you really do for these boys?" I asked.

"Very little. We teach them a trade. Later, we try to find them work—which is almost impossible. If they have work in the neighbourhood, they can still sleep here at nights.... The Principal believes that their lives can be changed through the teachings of the Christian religion. I'm afraid I cannot feel this. The problem is not so simple. I'm afraid that most of them, if they cannot get work, will take to crime. After all, people cannot be ordered to starve."

"Isn't there any alternative?"

Brink rose and led me to the window.

"You see those two buildings? One is the engineering-works, the other is the prison. For the boys of this district there used to be two alternatives.... But now the works are bankrupt. Next week they will close down."

This morning I went to see Rudi's club-house, which is also the office of a pathfinders' magazine. The editor and scoutmaster, Uncle Peter, is a haggard, youngish man, with a parchment-coloured face and deeply sunken eyes, dressed in corduroy jacket and shorts. He is evidently Rudi's idol. The only time Rudi will stop talking is when Uncle Peter has something to say. They showed me dozens of photographs of boys, all taken with the camera tilted upwards, from beneath, so that they look like epic giants, in profile against enormous clouds. The magazine itself has articles on hunting, tracking, and preparing food—all written in super-enthusiastic style, with a curious underlying note of hysteria, as though the actions described were part of a religious or erotic ritual. There were half-a-dozen other boys in the room with us: all of them in a state of heroic semi-nudity, wearing the shortest of shorts and the thinnest of shirts or singlets, although the weather is so cold.

When I had finished looking at the photographs, Rudi took me into the club meeting-room. Long coloured banners hung down the walls, embroidered with initials and mysterious totem devices. At one end of the room was a low table covered with a crimson embroidered cloth—a kind of altar. On the table were candles in brass candlesticks.

"We light them on Thursdays," Rudi explained, "when we have our camp-fire palaver. Then we sit round in a ring on the floor, and sing songs and tell stories."

Above the table with the candlesticks was a sort of icon—the framed drawing of a young pathfinder of unearthly beauty, gazing sternly into the far distance, a banner in his hand. The whole place made me feel profoundly uncomfortable. I excused myself and got away as soon as I could.

Overheard in a café: a young Nazi is sitting with his girl; they are discussing the future of the Party. The Nazi is drunk.

"Oh, I know we shall win, all right," he exclaims impatiently, "but that's not enough!" He thumps the table with his fist: "Blood must flow!"

The girl strokes his arm reassuringly. She is trying to get him to come home. "But, of *course*, it's going to flow, darling," she coos soothingly, "the Leader's promised that in our programme."

To-day is "Silver Sunday." The streets are crowded with shoppers. All along the Tauentzienstrasse, men, women and boys are hawking postcards, flowers, song-books, hair-oil, bracelets. Christmas-trees are stacked for sale along the central path between the tram-lines. Uniformed S.A. men rattle their collecting-boxes. In the side-streets, lorry-loads of police are waiting; for any large crowd, nowadays, is capable of turning into a political riot. The Salvation Army have a big illuminated tree on the Wittenbergplatz, with a blue electric star. A group of students were standing round it, making sarcastic remarks. Among them I recognized Werner, from the "communist" café.

"This time next year," said Werner, "that star will have changed its colour!" He laughed violently—he was in an excited, slightly hysterical mood. Yesterday, he told me, he'd had a great adventure: "You see, three other comrades and myself decided to make a demonstration at the Labour Exchange in Neuköln. I had to speak, and the others were to see I wasn't interrupted. We went round there at about half-past ten, when the bureau's most crowded. Of course, we'd planned it all beforehand—each of the comrades had to hold one of the doors, so that none of the clerks in the office could get out. There they were, cooped up like rabbits. . . . Of course, we couldn't prevent their telephoning for the Police, we knew that. We reckoned we'd got six or seven minutes. . . . Well, as soon as the doors were fixed, I jumped on to a table. I just yelled out whatever came into my head—I don't know what I said. They liked it, anyhow. . . . In half a minute I had them so excited I got quite scared. I was afraid they'd break into the office and lynch somebody. There was a fine old shindy, I can tell you! But just when things were beginning to look properly lively, a comrade came up from below to tell us the Police were there already—just getting out of their car. So we had to make a dash for it. . . . I think they'd have got us, only the crowd was on our side, and wouldn't let them through until we were out by the other door, into the street. . . ." Werner finished breathlessly. "I tell you, Christopher," he added, "the capitalist system can't possibly last much longer now. The workers are on the move!"

Early this evening I was in the Bülowstrasse. There bad been a big Nazi meeting at the Sportpalast, and groups of men and boys were just coming away from it, in their brown or black uniforms. Walking along the pavement ahead of me were three S.A. men. They all carried Nazi banners on their shoulders, like rifles, rolled tight round the staves—the banner-staves had sharp metal points, shaped into arrowheads.

All at once, the three S.A. men came face to face with a youth of seventeen or eighteen, dressed in civilian clothes, who was hurrying along in the opposite direction. I heard one of the Nazis shout: "That's him!" and immediately all three of them flung themselves upon the young man. He uttered a scream, and tried to dodge, but they were too quick for him. In a moment they had jostled him into the shadow of a house entrance, and were standing over him, kicking him and stabbing at him with the sharp metal points of their banners. All this happened with such incredible speed that I could hardly believe my eyes—already, the three S.A. men had left their victim, and were barging their way through the crowd; they made for the stairs which led up to the station of the Overhead Railway.

Another passer-by and myself were the first to reach the doorway where the young man was lying. He lay huddled crookedly in the corner, like an abandoned sack. As they picked him up, I got a sickening glimpse of his face—his left eye was poked half out, and blood poured from the wound. He wasn't dead. Somebody volunteered to take him to the hospital in a taxi.

By this time, dozens of people were looking on. They seemed surprised, but not particularly shocked—this sort of thing happens too often, nowadays. "*Allerhand....*" they murmured. Twenty yards away, at the Potsdamerstrasse corner, stood a group of heavily armed policemen. With their chests out, and their hands on their revolver belts, they magnificently disregarded the whole affair.

Werner has become a hero. His photograph was in the *Rote Fahne*[40] a few days ago, captioned: "Another victim of the Police blood-bath." Yesterday, which was New Year's day, I went to visit him in hospital.

Just after Christmas, it seems, there was a streetfight near the Stettiner Bahnhof. Werner was on the edge of the crowd, not knowing what the fight was about. On the off-chance that it might be something political, he began yelling: "Red Front!" A policeman tried to arrest him. Werner kicked the policeman in the stomach. The policeman drew his revolver and shot Werner three times through the leg. When he had finished shooting, he called another policeman, and together they carried Werner into a taxi. On the way to the police-station, the policemen hit him on the head with their truncheons, until he fainted. When he has sufficiently recovered he will, most probably, be prosecuted.

He told me all this with the greatest satisfaction, sitting up in bed surrounded by his admiring friends, including Rudi and Inge, in her Henry the Eighth hat. Around him, on the blanket, lay his press-cuttings. Somebody had carefully underlined each mention of Werner's name with a red pencil.

To-day, January 22nd, the Nazis held a demonstration on the Bülowplatz, in front of the Karl Liebknecht House. For the last week the communists have been trying to get the demonstration forbidden: they say it is simply intended as a provocation—as, of course, it was. I went along to watch it with Frank, the newspaper correspondent.

40. *Die Rote Fahne* was the main publication of the German Communist Party.

As Frank himself said afterwards, this wasn't really a Nazi demonstration at all, but a Police demonstration—there were at least two policemen to every Nazi present. Perhaps General Schleicher only allowed the march to take place in order to show who are the real masters of Berlin. Everybody says he's going to proclaim a military dictatorship.

But the real masters of Berlin are not the Police, or the Army, and certainly not the Nazis. The masters of Berlin are the workers—despite all the propaganda I've heard and read, all the demonstrations I've attended, I only realized this, for the first time to-day. Comparatively few of the hundreds of people in the streets round the Bülowplatz can have been organized communists, yet you had the feeling that every single one of them was united against this march. Somebody began to sing the "International," and, in a moment, everyone had joined in—even the women with their babies, watching from top-storey windows. The Nazis slunk past, marching as fast as they knew how, between their double rows of protectors. Most of them kept their eyes on the ground, or glared glassily ahead: a few attempted sickly, furtive grins. When the procession had passed, an elderly fat little S.A. man, who had somehow got left behind, came panting along at the double, desperately scared at finding himself alone, and trying vainly to catch up with the rest. The whole crowd roared with laughter.

During the demonstration nobody was allowed on the Bülowplatz itself. So the crowd surged uneasily about, and things began to look nasty. The police, brandishing their rifles, ordered us back; some of the less experienced ones, getting rattled, made as if to shoot. Then an armoured car appeared, and started to turn its machine-gun slowly in our direction. There was a stampede into house doorways and cafes; but no sooner had the car moved on, than everybody rushed out into the street again, shouting and singing. It was too much like a naughty schoolboy's game to be seriously alarming. Frank enjoyed himself enormously, grinning from ear to ear, and hopping about, in his flapping overcoat and huge owlish spectacles, like a mocking, ungainly bird.

Only a week since I wrote the above. Schleicher has resigned. The monocles did their stuff. Hitler has formed a cabinet with Hugenberg. Nobody thinks it can last till the spring.

The newspapers are becoming more and more like copies of a school magazine. There is nothing in them but new rules, new punishments, and lists of people who have been "kept in." This morning, Göring has invented three fresh varieties of high treason.

Every evening, I sit in the big half-empty artists' café by the Memorial Church, where the Jews and left-wing intellectuals bend their heads together over the marble tables, speaking in low, scared voices. Many of them know that they will certainly be arrested—if not to-day, then to-morrow or next week. So they are polite and mild with each other, and raise their hats and enquire after their colleagues' families. Notorious literary tiffs of several years' standing are forgotten.

Almost every evening, the S.A. men come into the café. Sometimes they are only collecting money; everybody is compelled to give something. Sometimes they have come to make an arrest. One evening a Jewish writer, who was present, ran into the telephone-box to ring up the Police. The Nazis dragged him out, and he was taken away. Nobody moved a finger. You could have heard a pin drop, till they were gone.

The foreign newspaper correspondents dine every night at the same little Italian restaurant, at a big round table, in the corner. Everybody else in the restaurant is watching them and trying to overhear what they are saying. If you have a piece of news to bring them—the details of an arrest, or the address of a victim whose relatives might be interviewed—then one of the journalists leaves the table and walks up and down with you outside, in the street.

A young communist I know was arrested by the S.A. men, taken to a Nazi barracks, and badly knocked about. After three or four days, he was released and went home. Next morning there was a knock at the door. The communist hobbled over to open it, his arm in a sling—and there stood a Nazi with a collecting-box. At the sight of him the communist completely lost his temper. "Isn't it enough," he yelled, "that you beat me up? And you dare to come and ask me for money?"

But the Nazi only grinned. "Now, now, comrade! No political squabbling! Remember, we're living in the Third Reich! We're all brothers! You must try and drive that silly political hatred from your heart!"

This evening I went into the Russian tea-shop in the Kleiststrasse, and there was D. For a moment I really thought I must be dreaming. He greeted me quite as usual, beaming all over his face.

"Good God!" I whispered. "What on earth are you doing here?"

D. beamed. "You thought I might have gone abroad?"

"Well, naturally...."

"But the situation nowadays is so interesting...."

I laughed. "That's one way of looking at it, certainly.... But isn't it awfully dangerous for you?"

D. merely smiled. Then he turned to the girl he was sitting with and said, "This is Mr. Isherwood.... You can speak quite openly to him. He hates the Nazis as much as we do. Oh, yes! Mr. Isherwood is a confirmed anti-fascist!"

He laughed very heartily and slapped me on the back. Several people who were sitting near us overheard him. Their reactions were curious. Either they simply couldn't believe their ears, or they were so scared that they pretended to hear nothing, and went on sipping their tea in a state of deaf horror. I have seldom felt so uncomfortable in my whole life.

(D.'s technique appears to have had its points, all the same. He was never arrested. Two months later, he successfully crossed the frontier into Holland.)

This morning. as I was walking down the Bülowstrasse, the Nazis were raiding the house of a small liberal pacifist publisher. They had brought a lorry and were piling it with the publisher's books. The driver of the lorry mockingly read out the titles of the books to the crowd:

"*Nie Wieder Krieg*!" he shouted, holding up one of them by the corner of the cover, disgustedly, as though it were a nasty kind of reptile. Everybody roared with laughter.

"'No More War!'" echoed a fat, well-dressed woman with a scornful, savage laugh. "What an idea!"

At present, one of my regular pupils is Herr N., a police chief under the Weimar régime. He comes to me every day. He wants to brush up his English, for he is leaving very soon to take up a job in the United States. The curious thing about these lessons is that they are all given while we are driving about the streets in Herr N.'s enormous closed car. Herr N. himself never comes into our house: he sends up his chauffeur to fetch me, and the car moves off at once. Sometimes we stop for a few minutes at the edge of the Tiergarten, and stroll up and down the paths—the chauffeur always following us at a respectful distance.

Herr N. talks to me chiefly about his family. He is worried about his son, who is very delicate, and whom he is obliged to leave behind, to undergo an operation. His wife is delicate, too. He hopes the journey won't tire her. He describes her symptoms, and the kind of medicine she is taking. He tells me stories about his son as a little boy. In a tactful, impersonal way we have become quite intimate. Herr N. is always charmingly polite, and listens gravely and carefully to my explanations of grammatical points. Behind everything he says I am aware of an immense sadness.

We never discuss politics; but I know that Herr N. must be an enemy of the Nazis, and, perhaps, even in hourly danger of arrest. One morning, when we were driving along the Unter den Linden, we passed a group of self-important S.A. men, chatting to each other and blocking the whole pavement. Passers-by were obliged to walk in the gutter. Herr N. smiled faintly and sadly: "One sees some queer sights in the streets nowadays." That was his only comment. Sometimes he will bend forward to the window and regard a building or a square with a mournful fixity, as if to impress its image upon his memory and to bid it good-bye.

To-morrow I am going to England. In a few weeks I shall return, but only to pick up my things, before leaving Berlin altogether.

Poor Frl. Schroeder is inconsolable: "I shall never find another gentleman like you, Herr Issyvoo—always so punctual with the rent.... I'm sure I don't know what makes you want to leave Berlin, all of a sudden, like this...."

It's no use trying to explain to her, or talking politics. Already she is adapting herself, as she will adapt herself to every new régime. This morning I even heard her talking reverently about "Der Führer" to the porter's wife. If anybody were to remind her that, at the elections last November, she voted communist, she would probably deny it hotly, and in perfect good faith. She is merely acclimatizing herself, in accordance with a natural law, like an animal which changes its coat for the winter. Thousands of people like Frl. Schroeder are acclimatizing themselves. After all, whatever government is in power, they are doomed to live in this town.

To-day the sun is brilliantly shining; it is quite mild and warm. I go out for my last morning walk, without an overcoat or hat. The sun shines, and Hitler is master of this city. The sun shines, and dozens of my friends—my pupils at the Workers' School, the men and women I met at the I.A.H.—are in prison, possibly dead. But it isn't of them that I am thinking—the clear-headed ones, the purposeful, the heroic; they recognized and accepted the risks. I am thinking of poor Rudi, in his absurd Russian blouse. Rudi's make-believe, story-book game has become earnest; the Nazis will play it with him. The Nazis won't laugh at him; they'll take him on trust for what he pretended to be. Perhaps at this very moment Rudi is being tortured to death.

I catch sight of my face in the mirror of a shop, and am shocked to see that I am smiling. You can't help smiling, in such beautiful weather. The trams are going up and down the Kleiststrasse, just as usual. They, and the people on the pavement, and the teacosy dome of the Nollendorfplatz station have an air of curious familiarity, of striking resemblance to something one remembers as normal and pleasant in the past—like a very good photograph.

No. Even now I can't altogether believe that any of this has really happened. . . .

Isherwood, Christopher. "A Berlin Diary (Winter 1932–3)." In *The Berlin Stories*, 186–207. New York: New Directions Publishing, [1939, 1935] 2012.

Cherokee Sources during the Removal Period

Introduction

This set of documents provides a glimpse into resistance against the US federal government's policy to forcibly remove Cherokee, Muscogee (Creek), Choctaw, Chickasaw, and Seminole peoples from their ancestral homes in the southeastern United States that is rooted in a **settler-colonial dynamic.**[41] Settler colonialism is an ongoing structural system that promotes the complete replacement of Indigenous populations by any means necessary, whereas settler societies seek permanent occupancy. As alluded to in several of the documents you will read, the **Doctrine of Discovery**, a series of papal bulls, or church edicts, in the fifteenth and sixteenth centuries, laid out the earliest expansionist colonizing framework and religiously sanctioned the rupture of Indigenous people from the lands they had inhabited from time immemorial.[42] Using old Roman laws, such as **terra nullius**, these papal bulls helped establish a legal justification for the genocide and theft of native lands where Indigenous peoples were seen as merely savages, incompatible with a Christian world. As Nanye'hi, known also by her Christian name Nancy Ward, argues in "Cherokee Women Resist Removal," "the Cherokee Nation have been the first settlers of this land; we therefore claim the rights of the soil." The relationship to the land is a sacred one where stories, languages, dances, songs, and kinship patterns are inextricably linked.[43] The removal of people from land is not simply a matter of logistics but a matter of the rupture of a people from their identity and ways of life. What specific ruptures do you think would be included as part of the physical removal from one's place/land?

The Doctrine of Discovery would be brought into US law by the **Marshall Court.** This was a period of the Supreme Court under Chief Justice Marshall in the nineteenth century in which the rulings of the court provided a complicated, often conflicting definition of tribal sovereignty. The ongoing impact of this judicial period can

> **SNAPSHOT BOX**
>
> **LANGUAGES:** English, Tsalagi
>
> **DATES:** Late 18th–early 19th centuries, Hopewell (present-day South Carolina), Cherokee Nation (New Echota, Georgia)
>
> **GENRES:** Government document, petition, treaty, official communications
>
> **TAGS:** Accessing Rights; Colonization; Community; Cross-Cultural Encounters; Family; Race; Struggle, Resistance, and Revolution; Tradition; Women and Power

---

41. To learn more about the settler-colonial framework, see P. Wolfe, "Settler Colonialism and the Elimination of the Native," *Journal of Genocide Research* 8, no. 4 (2007): 387–409. See also E. Tuck and K. W. Yang, "Decolonization Is Not a Metaphor," *Decolonization: Indigeneity, Education & Society* 1, no. 1 (2007): 1–40.

42. For more on the Doctrine of Discovery, see R. Dunbar-Ortiz, *An Indigenous Peoples' History of the United States* (Boston: Beacon Press, 2014). See also S. Newcombe, "Five Hundred Years of Injustice," *Shaman's Drum* (Fall 1992): 18–20.

43. Vine Deloria Jr. provides an excellent framework for understanding sacred places from an Indigenous perspective in chapter 16 of V. Deloria Jr., *God Is Red: A Native View of Religion* (Goldon, CO: Fulcrum Publishing, 1994).

be seen in the Marshall Court ruling in *Johnson v. M'Intosh* (1823), which was used as recently as 2005 in the justification by Ruth Bader Ginsburg in a majority decision against the Oneida Nation. The doctrine continues to inform settler-colonial understanding of the present as can be seen in the development of various pipelines being built across Indigenous territories such as the Energy Transfer Pipeline at Standing Rock, the Coastal GasLink/TC Energy pipeline in Wet'suwet'en territory in Canada, and the Atlantic Coast Pipeline in Virginia and Eastern North Carolina.

These settler-colonial practices, both historically and in contemporary times, undermine the relationship of **nation-to-nation** status built upon four hundred treaties signed by the US government prior to their cessation of making any further treaties with independent tribes in 1871. Treaties should also be seen as living, breathing documents that can be used to leverage autonomy/self-determination in the present. For instance, in 2019 the Cherokee Nation nominated Kimberly Teehee, the vice president of Government Relations for the Cherokee Nation, to represent the Nation as a delegate to the House of Representatives as stipulated in Article XII of the Treaty of Hopewell. This treaty, and others like it, should not be read as simply an artifact of the past but as a portal into the various ways in which Indigenous leaders were negotiating a future. As you read the Hopewell Treaty, identify ways in which it can be used as a portal for future negotiations.

Cherokee resistance to removal is seen throughout these documents. As Nanye'hi of the Cherokee Women's Council lays out in the early part of the nineteenth century in "Cherokee Women Resist Removal," Cherokees adopted Western forms of "civilization" to appeal to the US government for aid. Education was an important part of this effort as many Cherokee leaders supported the sending of their youth to Christian schools, such as the Moravian Springplace Mission in Spring Hill, Georgia. The plea from the Women's Council, led by Nanye'hi, gives insight into the internal dialogue within the Cherokee Nation during an extremely complex time. Nanye'hi was an esteemed leader of the Cherokee having earned the title of "beloved woman." This gave her the right to sit on the War Council and hold the power to determine the fate of captives, whether they be killed, enslaved, released, or adopted into the tribe. Her passionate plea emphasizes the **matrilineal basis**, defined as tracing kinship through the mother's line, and the important role women have played in Cherokee society as clan mothers, knowledge keepers, and political leaders.[44]

During this time of upheaval, Sequoyah was developing a written form of the Cherokee language, which led to high rates of written literacy and the publication in 1828 of the first Native American newspaper printed in an Indigenous language. The *Cherokee Phoenix* became an important source for expressing resistance to removal to a broader audience as can be seen in the final two documents of this set.

---

44. To learn more about Cherokee women and Cherokee matrilineal society, see T. Perdue, *Cherokee Women* (Lincoln: University of Nebraska Press, 1998).

Ultimately, the Cherokee took their lawsuit to the US Supreme Court and in the final case of the **Marshall Trilogy**, *Worcester v. Georgia* (1832), Chief Justice John Marshall works through his often-contradictory position to reaffirm tribal sovereignty.[45] However, President Andrew Jackson subsequently ignored the ruling and enforced the Indian Removal Act of 1830.

In 1838, thousands of Cherokee people were forcibly taken from their homes, incarcerated in stockades, forced to walk more than a thousand miles, and removed to Indian Territory, now Oklahoma. Other Cherokee people, however, resisted by hiding in caves, buying property, and negotiating to remain on their ancestral lands. Some were removed and then walked all the way back from Indian Territory, as Junaluska did, to rebuild. While this group of documents provides insight into the Removal period, this was not the end of the story as commonly depicted. In a testament to their resilience, the Cherokee and other American Indian peoples survived, rebuilt, and continue to thrive.

Trey Adcock
Department of Interdisciplinary Studies and
American Indian and Indigenous Studies

Modern Timeline Cherokee Sources

1802   The Compact of 1802, also known as the Georgia Compact, promised to extinguish American Indian land titles in the state of Georgia.

1803   The Louisiana Purchase: The United States buys the 828,000 square miles of land from France, which doubled the size of the US.

1812   Approximately one-fourth of the Cherokee Nation from the southeastern United States voluntarily migrated to Arkansas Territory (attached to Missouri), settling between the White and Arkansas Rivers in northwest Arkansas.

1817   On July 8 the Turkeytown Treaty was concluded between the Cherokees and representatives of the United States. Though sixty-seven chiefs signed the document, a majority of the tribe opposed it. Those removed to Arkansas Territory are known as "Old Settlers."

1828   Andrew Jackson is elected president. The Western or Old Settler Cherokees removed from Arkansas Territory to Indian Territory. This removal began a protracted war with the Osages, as the Cherokee were encroaching on Osage lands.

---

45. For more on the Removal period, the Marshall Trilogy, and the role of Southern courts, see T. A. Garrison, *The Legal Ideology of Removal: The Southern Judiciary and the Sovereignty of Native American Nations* (Athens: University of Georgia Press, 2009).

1830 The Indian Removal Act fostered by President Jackson passed Congress. The Treaty of Dancing Rabbit Creek stipulated the removal of Choctaws from Mississippi.

1831 The Choctaw Nation began removal from Mississippi to Indian Territory, becoming the first of the Five Tribes to be forcibly removed.

1832 The Treaty of Payne's Landing began the process for removal of the Seminoles of Florida. It would take almost twenty years and 15 million dollars to force the tribe from their lands. The Treaty of Pontotoc in Mississippi required the removal of the Chickasaw Tribe from their lands.

1832 Andrew Jackson was reelected president.

1833 The Muscogee (Creek) tribe began removal.

1835 The Treaty of New Echota provided for the removal of all Cherokees east of the Mississippi River.

1838 Forced removal of 16,000 Cherokees began. Potawatomis of Indiana began forced removal on their Trail of Death.

1839 Cherokee Trail of Tears continued, incurring approximately 4,000 deaths along the way.

1859 The Seminoles of Florida removal era ends.

1887 The General Allotment Act, authored by US senator Henry L. Dawes, passed Congress.

1890 The Oklahoma Territory was organized.

1893 The Dawes Commission was created. The Cherokee Outlet is opened with 100,000 persons making the run for homesteads.

1894 Geronimo's band of Chiricahua Apaches, after being subdued by the military in 1886, removed as prisoners to Florida, then later to Alabama are finally relocated to Fort Sill.

1898 The Curtis Act passes Congress forcing the Five Tribes to treat with the Dawes Commission.

1899 The Muscogees (Creek), Seminoles, Choctaws, and Chickasaws are enrolled by the Dawes Commission.

1900 The Cherokee Nation is enrolled by the Dawes Commission. The Dawes Commission Final Rolls for the Five Tribes is closed.

1907 Oklahoma became a state.

> **PRE-READING PARS**
>
> 1. List three to five things that come to mind when you hear the word "Cherokee." What images and/or ideas come to mind? What do you know about Cherokee people historically and in contemporary society?
> 2. What does it mean to "remove" a people? Identify two ways the "removal" period is remembered in popular culture.
> 3. What does it mean for an entity to be a sovereign power? Identify a few powers that are internally determined within a community/entity and those that are bestowed by external institutions.

Cherokee Sources during the Removal Period

1785 Treaty of Hopewell

Articles concluded at Hopewell, on the Keowee, between Benjamin Hawkins, Andrew Pickens, Joseph Martin, and Lachlan M'Intosh, Commissioners Plenipotentiary of the United States of America, of the one Part, and the headmen and Warriors of all the Cherokees of the other.

The Commissioners Plenipotentiary of the United States in Congress assembled, give peace to all the Cherokees, and receive them into the favor and protection of the United States of America, on the following conditions:

Article I.

The Head-Men and Warriors of all the Cherokees shall restore all the prisoners, citizens of the United States, or subjects of their allies, to their entire liberty. They shall also restore all the Negroes,[46] and all other property taken during the late war from the citizens, to such person, and at such time and place, as the Commissioners shall appoint.

---

46. The authors of the treaty use the term "Negro" to refer to African American communities as was a prevalent practice within and outside of Black communities from the nineteenth to mid-twentieth centuries. The term "negro" should not be confused with the derogatory n-word. Likewise another term used during the same timeframe, "colored," is outdated and should not be confused with the current usage of "person of color." Words reflecting African American and Black communities' preferences for self-identification continue to shift in meaning and connotation over time.

Article II.

The Commissioners of the United States in Congress assembled, shall restore all the prisoners taken from the Indians, during the late war, to the Head-Men and Warriors of the Cherokees, as early as is practicable.

Article III.

The said Indians for themselves and their respective tribes and towns do acknowledge all the Cherokees to be under the protection of the United States of America, and of no other sovereign whosoever.

Article IV.

The boundary allotted to the Cherokees for their hunting grounds, between the said Indians and the citizens of the United States, within the limits of the United States of America, is, and shall be the following, viz. Beginning at the mouth of Duck river, on the Tennessee; thence running north-east to the ridge dividing the waters running into Cumberland from those running into the Tennessee; thence eastwardly along the said ridge to a north-east line to be run, which shall strike the river Cumberland forty miles above Nashville; thence along the said line to the river; thence up the said river to the ford where the Kentucky road crosses the river; thence to Campbell's line, near Cumberland gap; thence to the mouth of Claud's creek on Holstein; thence to the Chimney-top mountain; thence to Camp-creek, near the mouth of Big Limestone, on Nolichuckey; thence a southerly course six miles to a mountain; thence south to the North-Carolina line; thence to the South-Carolina Indian boundary, and along the same south-west over the top of the Oconee mountain till it shall strike Tugaloo river; thence a direct line to the top of the Currohee mountain; thence to the head of the south fork of Oconee river.

Article V.

If any citizen of the United States, or other person not being an Indian, shall attempt to settle on any of the lands westward or southward of the said boundary which are hereby allotted to the Indians for their hunting grounds, or having already settled and will not remove from the same within six months after the ratification of this treaty, such person shall forfeit the protection of the United States, and the Indians may punish him or not as they please: Provided nevertheless, That this article shall not extend to the people settled between the fork of French Broad and Holstein rivers, whose particular situation shall be transmitted to the United States in Congress assembled for their decision thereon, which the Indians agree to abide by.

Article VI.

If any Indian or Indians, or person residing among them, or who shall take refuge in their nation, shall commit a robbery, or murder, or other capital crime, on any citizen of the United States, or person under their protection, the nation, or the tribe to which such offender or offenders may belong, shall be bound to deliver him or them up to be punished Cording to the ordinances of the United States; provided, that the punishment shall not be greater than if the robbery or murder, or other capital crime had been committed by a citizen on a citizen.

Article VII.

If any citizen of the United States, or person under their protection, shall commit a robbery or murder, or other capital crime, on any Indian, such offender or offenders shall be punished in the same manner as if the murder or robbery, or other capital crime, had been committed on a citizen of the United States; and the punishment shall be in presence of some of the Cherokees, if any shall attend at the time and place, and that they may have an opportunity so to do, due notice of the time of such intended punishment shall be sent to some one of the tribes.

Article VIII.

It is understood that the punishment of the innocent under the idea of retaliation, is unjust, and shall not be practiced on either side, except where there is a manifest violation of this treaty; and then it shall be preceded first by a demand of justice, and if refused, then by a declaration of hostilities.

Article IX.

For the benefit and comfort of the Indians, and for the prevention of injuries or oppressions on the part of the citizens or Indians, the United States in Congress assembled shall have the sole and exclusive right of regulating the trade with the Indians, and managing all their affairs in such manner as they think proper.

Article X.

Until the pleasure of Congress be known, respecting the ninth article, all traders, citizens of the United States, shall have liberty to go to any of the tribes or towns of the Cherokees to trade with them, and they shall be protected in their persons and property, and kindly treated.

Article XI.

The said Indians shall give notice to the citizens of the United States, of any designs which they may know or suspect to be formed in any neighboring tribe, or by any person whosoever, against the peace, trade or interest of the United States.

Article XII.

That the Indians may have full confidence in the justice of the United States, respecting their interests, they shall have the right to send a deputy of their choice, whenever they think fit, to Congress.

Article XIII.

The hatchet shall be forever buried, and the peace given by the United States, and friendship re-established between the said states on the one part, and all the Cherokees on the other, shall be universal; and the contracting parties shall use their utmost endeavors to maintain the peace given as aforesaid, and friendship re-established.

In witness of and everything herein determined, between the United States of America and all the Cherokees, we, their underwritten Commissioners, by virtue of Her full powers, have signed this definitive treaty, and have caused our seals to be hereunto affixed.

Done at Hopewell, on the Keowee, this twenty-eighth of November, in the year of our Lord one thousand seven hundred and eighty-five.

> Benjamin Hawkins
> And'w Pickens,
> Jos. Martin
> Lach'n McIntosh
> Koatohee, or Corn Tassel of Toquo, his x mark
> Seholauetta, or Hanging Man of Chota, his x mark
> Tuskegatahu, or Long Fellow of Chistohoe, his x mark
> Ooskvrha, or Abraham of Chilkowa, his x mark
> Kolakusta, or Prince of Noth, his x mark
> Newota, or the Gritzs of Chicamaga his x mark
> Konatota, or the Rising Fawn of Highwassay, his x mark
> Tuckasee, or Young Terrapin of Allajoy, his x mark
> Toostaka, or the Waker of Oostanawa, his x mark
> Untoola, or Gun Rod of Seteco, his x mark
> Unsuokanail, Buffalo White Calf New Cussee, his x mark
> Kostayeak, or Sharp Fellow Wataga, his x mark
> Chonosta, of Cowe, his x mark

Chescoonwho, Bird in Close of Tomotlug, his x mark
Tuckasee, or Terrapin of Hightowa his x mark
Chesetoa, or the Rabbit of Tlaeoa, his x mark
Cheseeotetona, or Yellow Bird of the Pine Log, his x mark
Sketaloska, Second Man of Tillico, his x mark
Chokasatahe, Chiekasaw Killer Tasonta, his x mark
Onanoota, of Koosoate, his x mark,
Ookoseta, or Sower Mush of Kooloque, his x mark
Umatooetha. the Water Hunter Choikamawga, his x mark
Wyuka, of Lookout Mountain, his x mark
Tulco, or Tom of Chatuga, his x mark
Will, of Akoha, his x mark
Neeatee, of Sawta, his x mark
Amokontakona, Kuteloa, his x mark
Kowetatahee, in Frog Town, his x mark
Keukuck, Taleoa, his x mark
Tulatiska, of Chaway, his x mark
Wooaluka, the Waylayer, Chota, his x mark
Tatliusta, or Porpoise of Tilassi, his mark
John, of Little Tallico, his x mark
Skelelak, his x mark
Akonoluchta, the cabin, his x mark
Cheanoka, of Kawetakae, his x mark
Yellow Bird, his x mark

Witness:

Wm. Blount
Sam'l Taylor, Major.,
John Owen,
Jess. Walton,
Jno. Cowan, eapt. eomm'd't,
Thos. Gregg,
W. Hazzard,
James Madison,
Arthur Cooley,
Sworn interpreters.

Petitions of the Cherokee Women's Councils, 1817, 1818[47]

Petition, May 2, 1817

The Cherokee ladies now being present at the meeting of the chiefs and warriors in council have thought it their duty as mothers to address their beloved chiefs and warriors now assembled.

Our beloved children and headmen of the Cherokee Nation, we address you warriors in council. We have raised all of you on the land which we now have, which God gave us to inhabit and raise provisions. We know that our country has once been extensive, but by repeated sales [it] has become circumscribed to a small track, and [we] never have thought it our duty to interfere in the disposition of it till now. If a father or mother was to sell all their lands which they had to depend on, which their children had to raise their living on, which would be indeed bad and to be removed to another country. We do not wish to go to an unknown country [to] which we have understood some of our children wish to go over the Mississippi, but this act of our children would be like destroying your mothers.

Your mothers, your sisters, ask and beg of you not to part with any more of our land. We say ours. You are our descendants; take pity on our request. Keep it for our growing children, for it was the good will of our creator to place us here, and you know our father, the great president, will not allow his white children to take our country away. Only keep your hands off of paper talks for it's our own country. For [if] it was not, they would not ask you to put your hands to paper, for it would be impossible to remove us all. For as soon as one child is raised, we have others in our arms, for such is our situation and will consider our circumstance.

Therefore, children, don't part with any more of our lands but continue on it and enlarge your farms. Cultivate and raise corn and cotton and your mothers and sisters will make clothing for you which our father the president has recommended to us all. We don't charge anybody for selling any lands, but we have heard such intentions of our children. But your talks become true at last; it was our desire to forewarn you all not to part with our lands.

Nancy Ward to her children: Warriors, take pity and listen to the talk of your sisters. Although I am very old, I cannot but pity the situation in which you will hear of their minds. I have a great many grandchildren which [I] wish them to do well on our land.

---

47. First petition located in Presidential Papers Microfilm: Andrew Jackson (Washington, DC, 1961, series 1, reel 22). The second petition was enclosed in a letter from the American Board of Missionaries to their headquarters in Boston. It is included in the Papers of the American Board of Commissioners for Foreign Missions, Houghton Library, Harvard University.

Petition, June 30, 1818

Beloved Children,

We have called a meeting among ourselves to consult on the different points now before the council, relating to our national affairs. We have heard with painful feelings that the bounds of the land we now possess are to be drawn into very narrow limits. The land was given to us by the Great Spirit above as our common right, to raise our children upon, and to make support for our rising generations. We therefore humbly petition our beloved children, the headmen and warriors, to hold out to the last in support of our common rights, as the Cherokee Nation have been the first settlers of this land; we therefore claim the right of the soil.

We well remember that our country was formerly very extensive, but by repeated sales it has become circumscribed to the very narrow limits we have at present. Our father the President advised us to become farmers, to manufacture our own clothes, and to have our children instructed. To this advice we have attended to everything as far as we were able. Now the thought of being compelled to remove to the other side of the Mississippi is dreadful to us, because it appears to us that we, by this removal, shall be brought to a savage state again, for we have, by the endeavor of our father the President, become too much enlightened to throw aside the privileges of a civilized life.

We therefore unanimously join in our meeting to hold our country in common as hitherto. Some of our children have become Christians. We have missionary schools among us. We have heard the gospel in our nation. We have become civilized and enlightened, and are hopeful that in a few years our nation will be prepared for instruction in other branches of sciences and arts, which are both useful and necessary in civilized society.

There are some white men among us who have been raised in this country from their youth, are connected with us by marriage, and have considerable families, who are very active in encouraging the emigration of our nation. These ought to be our truest friends but prove our worst enemies. They seem to be only concerned with how to increase their riches, but do not care what becomes of our Nation, nor even of their own wives and children.

Memorial of the Cherokee Indians, Cherokee Nation (1829)

Cherokee Phoenix and Indians Advocate, *Wednesday, January 20, 1830, Vol. II, no. 40, Page 1, col. 3a–5b.*

To the Honorable Senate and House of Representatives of the United States of America, in Congress assembled;

The undersigned memorialist humbly make known to your honorable bodies, that they are free citizens of the Cherokee Nation. Circumstances of late occurrence have troubled our hearts and induced us at this time to appeal to you, knowing that you are generous and just. As weak and poor children are accustomed to look to their guardians and patrons for protection, so we would come and make our grievances known. Will you listen to us? Will you have pity upon us? You are great and renowned—the nation which you represent is like a mighty man who stands in his strength. But we are small—our name is not renowned. You are wealthy, and have need of nothing; but we are poor in life, and have not the arm and power of the rich.

By the will of our Father in heaven, the Governor of the whole world, the red man of America has become small, and the white man great and renowned. When the ancestors of the people of these United States first came to the shores of America, they found the red man strong—though he was ignorant and savage, yet he received them kindly, and gave them dry land to rest their weary feet. They met in peace, and shook hands in token of friendship. Whatever the white man wanted and asked of the Indians, the latter willingly gave. At that time the Indian was the lord, and the white man the suppliant. But now the scene has changed. The strength of the red man has become weakness. As his neighbors increased in number, his power became less and less, and now, of the many and powerful tribes who once covered these United States, only a few are to be seen—a few whom a sweeping pestilence has left. The Northern tribes who were once as numerous and powerful are now nearly extinct. Thus it has happened to the red man of America. Shall we, who are remnants share the same fate?

Brothers—we address you according to usage adopted by our forefathers, and the great and good men who have successfully directed the Councils of the nation you represent—we now make known to you our grievances. We are troubled by some of your own people. Our neighbor, the State of Georgia is pressing hard upon us, and urging us to relinquish our possessions for her benefit. We are told, if we do not leave the country, which we dearly love, and take ourselves to the western wilds, the laws of the state will be extended over us, and the time, 1st of June 1830, is appointed for the execution of the edict. When we first heard of this we were grieved, and appealed to our father the President, and begged that protection might be extended over us. But we were doubly grieved when we understood, from a letter of the Secretary of War to our Delegation, dated March of the present year, that our father the President had refused us protection, and that he had decided in favor of the extension of the laws of the State over us. This decision induces us to appeal to the immediate representatives of the American people. We love, we dearly love our country, and it is due to your honorable bodies as well as to us, to make known why we think the country is ours, and why we wish to remain in peace where we are.

The land on which we stand we have received as an inheritance from our fathers who possessed it from time immemorial, as a gift from our common father in heaven. We have already said that when the white man came to the shores of America, our ancestors were found in peaceable possession of this very land. They bequeathed it to us as their children, and we have sacredly kept it as containing the remains of our beloved men. This right of inheritance we have never ceded, nor ever forfeited.

Permit us to ask, what better right can a people have to a country, than the right of inheritance and immemorial peaceable possession! We know it is said of late by the State of Georgia, and by the Executive of the United States, that we have forfeited this right—but we think this is said gratuitously. At what time have we made the forfeit? What great crime have we committed, whereby we must forever be divested of our country and rights? Was it when we were hostile to the United States, and took part with the King of Great Britain during the struggle for independence? If so, why was not this forfeiture declared in the first treaty of peace between the United States and our beloved men? Why was not such an article as the following inserted in the treaty: "The United States give peace to the Cherokees, but; for the part they took in the late war, declare them to be but tenants at will, to be removed, when the convenience of the states within whose chartered limits they live shall require it."—That was the proper time to assume such a position. But it was not thought of nor would our forefathers have agreed to any treaty whose tendency was to deprive them of their rights and their country. All that they have conceded and relinquished are inserted in the treaties, open to the investigation of all people. We would repeat, then, the right of inheritance and peaceable possession, which we claim, we have never ceded nor forfeited.

In addition to that first of all rights, the right of inheritance and peaceable possession, we have the faith and pledge of the United States, repeated over and over again in treaties made at various times. By these treaties our rights as a separate people are distinctly acknowledged, and guaranties given that they shall be secured and protected. So we have always understood the treaties. The conduct of the Government towards us, from its organization until very lately, the talks given to our beloved men by the Presidents of the United States, and the speeches of the Agents and Commissioners, all concur to show that we are not mistaken in our interpretation. Some of our beloved men who signed the treaties are still living, and their testimony tends to the same conclusion. We have always supposed that this understanding of the treaties was in accordance with the views of the Government; nor have we ever imagined that anybody would interpret them otherwise. In what light shall we view the conduct of the United States and Georgia, in their intercourse with us in urging us to enter into treaties, and cede lands? If we were but tenants at will, why was it necessary that our consent must first be obtained before these Governments could take lawful possession of our lands? The answer is obvious. These governments perfectly understood our rights—our right to the country, and our right to self government. Our understanding of the treaties is further supported by the intercourse law of the United States, which prohibits all encroachments upon our territory. The undersigned memorialists humbly represent that if their interpretation of the treaties has been different from that of the Government then they have ever been deceived as to how the Government regarded them, and what she has asked and promised. Moreover, they have uniformly misunderstood their own acts.

In view of the strong ground upon which their rights are founded, your memorialists solemnly protest against being considered as tenants at will, or as mere occupants of the soil, without possessing sovereignty. We have already stated to your honorable bodies, that our forefathers were found in possession of this soil, in full sovereignty, by the first European settlers; and as we have never ceded nor forfeited the occupancy of the soil and the sovereignty over it, we do solemnly protest against being forced to leave it either by direct or indirect measures. To the land of which we are now in possession we are attached. It is our fathers gift. It contains their ashes. It is the land of our nativity, and the land of our intellectual birth. We cannot consent to abandon it, for another far inferior and which holds out to us no inducements. We do moreover protest against the arbitrary measures of our neighbor, the state of Georgia, in her attempt to extend her laws over us, in surveying our lands without our consent and in direct opposition to the treaties and the intercourse law of the United States and interfering with our municipal regulations in such a manner as to derange the regular operation of our own laws. To deliver and protect them from all these and every encroachment upon their rights, the undersigned memorialists do most earnestly pray, your honorable bodies. Their existence and future happiness are at stake. Divest them of their liberty and country, and you sink them in degradation, and put a check, if not an end soon to their present progress in the acts of civilized life, and in the knowledge of the Christian religion. Your memorialists humbly conceive that such an act would be in the highest degree oppressive. From the people of these United States, who, perhaps of all those under heaven, are the most religious and free, it cannot be expected. Your memorialists, therefore, cannot anticipate such a result. You represent a virtuous, intelligent and Christian nation. To you they willingly submit their cause for your righteous decision.

Cherokee Nation, December, 1829.

Address of the Committee and Council of the Cherokee Nation, in General Council Convened, to the People of the United States, Lewis Ross et al. (1830)

More than a year ago we were officially given to understand, by the secretary of war, that the president could not protect us against the laws of Georgia. This information was entirely unexpected; as it went upon the principle, that treaties made between the United States and the Cherokee Nation have no power to withstand the legislation of separate states; and of course, that they have no efficacy whatever, but leave our people to the mercy of the neighboring whites, whose supposed interests would be promoted by our expulsion, or extermination. It would be impossible to describe the sorrow, which affected our minds on learning that the chief magistrate of the United States had come to this conclusion, that all his illustrious predecessors had held intercourse with us on principles which could not be sustained; that they had made promises of vital importance to us, which could not be fulfilled—promises made hundreds of times in almost every conceivable manner,—often in the form of solemn treaties, sometimes in letters written by the chief magistrate with his own hand, very often in letters written by the secretary of war under his direction, sometimes orally by the president and the secretary to our chiefs, and frequently and always, both orally and in writing by the agent of the United States residing among us, whose most important business it was, to see the guaranty of the United States faithfully executed.

Soon after the war of the revolution, as we have learned from our fathers, the Cherokees looked upon the promises of the whites with great distrust and suspicion; but the frank and magnanimous conduct of General Washington did much to allay these feelings. The perseverance of successive presidents, and especially of Mr. Jefferson, in the same course of policy, and in the constant assurance that our country should remain inviolate, except so far as we voluntarily ceded it, nearly banished anxiety in regard to encroachments from the whites. To this result the aid which we received from the United States in the attempts of our people to become civilized, and the kind efforts of benevolent societies, have greatly contributed. Of late years, however, much solicitude was occasioned among our people by the claims of Georgia.[48] This solicitude arose from the apprehension, that by extreme importunity, threats, and other undue influence, a treaty would be made, which should cede the territory, and thus compel the inhabitants to remove. But it never occurred to us for a moment that without any new treaty, without any assent of our rulers and people, without even a pretended compact, and against our vehement and unanimous protestations, we should be delivered over to the discretion of those, who had declared by a legislative act, that they wanted the Cherokee lands and would have them.

Finding that relief could not be obtained from the chief magistrate, and not doubting that our claim to protection was just, we made our application to congress. During four long months our delegation waited, at the doors of the national legislature of the United States, and the people at home, in the most painful suspense, to learn in what manner our application would be answered; and, now that congress has adjourned, on the very day before the date fixed by Georgia for the extension of her oppressive laws over the greater part of our country, the distressing intelligence has been received that we have received no answer at all; and no department of the government has assured us, that we are to receive the desired protection. But just at the close of the session, an act was passed, by which an half a million of dollars was appropriated towards effecting a removal of Indians; and we have great reason to fear that the influence of this act will be brought to bear most injuriously upon us. The passage of this act was certainly understood by the representatives of Georgia as abandoning us to the oppressive and cruel measures of the state, and as sanction-

---

48. In December 1829, the Georgia legislature passed a bill that annexed a large section of the Cherokee territory, annulled Cherokee laws, and decreed that Indians were not to be considered competent witnesses in court cases against whites. This stripped the Cherokee people of all legal protection from whites wanting their land.

ing the opinion that treaties with Indians do not restrain state legislation. We are informed by those, who are competent to judge, that the recent act does not admit of such construction; but that the passage of it, under the actual circumstances of the controversy, will be considered as sanctioning the pretensions of Georgia, there is too much reason to fear.

Thus have we realized, with heavy hearts, that our supplication has not been heard; that the protection heretofore experienced is now to be withheld; that the guaranty, in consequence of which our fathers laid aside their arms and ceded the best portions of their country, means nothing; and that we must either emigrate to an unknown region and leave the pleasant land to which we have the strongest attachment, or submit to the legislation of a state, which has already made our people outlaws, and enacted that any Cherokee, who shall endeavor to prevent the selling of his country, shall be imprisoned in the penitentiary of Georgia not less than four years. To our countrymen this has been melancholy intelligence, and with the most bitter disappointment has it been received.

But in the midst of our sorrows, we do not forget our obligations to our friends and benefactors. It was with sensations of inexpressible joy that we have learned that the voice of thousands, in many parts of the United States, has been raised in our behalf, and numerous memorials offered in our favor, in both houses of congress. To those numerous friends, who have thus sympathized with us in our low estate, we tender our grateful acknowledgements. In pleading our cause, they have pleaded the cause of the poor and defenceless throughout the world. Our special thanks are due, however, to those honorable men, who so ably and eloquently asserted our rights, in both branches of the national legislature. Their efforts will be appreciated wherever the merits of this question shall be known; and we cannot but think that they have secured for themselves a permanent reputation among the disinterested advocates of humanity, equal rights, justice, and good faith. We even cherish the hope, that these efforts, seconded and followed by others of a similar character, will yet be available, so far as to mitigate our sufferings, if not to effect our entire deliverance.

Before we close this address, permit us to state what we conceive to be our relations with the United States. After the peace of 1783, the Cherokees were an independent people; absolutely so, as much as any people on earth. They had been allies to Great Britain, and as a faithful ally took a part in the colonial war on her side. They had placed themselves under her protection, and had they, without cause, declared hostility against their protector, and had the colonies been subdued, what might not have been their fate? But her power on this continent was broken. She acknowledged the independence of the United States, and made peace. The Cherokees therefore stood alone; and, in these circumstances, continued the war. They were then under no obligations to the United States any more than to Great Britain, France or Spain. The United States never subjugated the Cherokees; on the contrary, our fathers remained in possession of their country, and with arms in their hands.

The people of the United States sought a peace; and, in 1785, the treaty of

Hopewell was formed, by which the Cherokees came under the protection of the United States, and submitted to such limitations of sovereignty as are mentioned in that instrument. None of these limitations, however, affected, in the slightest degree, their rights of self-government and inviolate territory. The citizens of the United States had no right of passage through the Cherokee country till the year 1791, and then only in one direction, and by an express treaty stipulation. When the federal constitution was adopted, the treaty of Hopewell was confirmed, with all other treaties, as the supreme law of the land. In 1791, the treaty of Holston was made, by which the sovereignty of the Cherokees was qualified as follows: The Cherokees acknowledged themselves to be under the protection of the United States, and of no other sovereign.—They engaged that they would not hold any treaty with a foreign power, with any separate state of the union, or with individuals. They agreed that the United States should have the exclusive right of regulating their trade; that the citizens of the United States should have a right of way in one direction through the Cherokee country; and that if an Indian should do injury to a citizen of the United States he should be delivered up to be tried and punished. A cession of lands was also made to the United States. On the other hand, the United States paid a sum of money; offered protection; engaged to punish citizens of the United States who should do any injury to the Cherokees; abandoned white settlers on Cherokee lands to the discretion of the Cherokees; stipulated that white men should not hunt on these lands, nor even enter the country without a passport; and gave a solemn guaranty of all Cherokee lands not ceded. This treaty is the basis of all subsequent compacts; and in none of them are the relations of the parties at all changed.

The Cherokees have always fulfilled their engagements. They have never reclaimed those portions of sovereignty which they surrendered by the treaties of Hopewell and Holston. These portions were surrendered for the purpose of obtaining the guarantee which was recommended to them as the great equivalent. Had they refused to comply with their engagements, there is no doubt the United States would have enforced a compliance. Is the duty of fulfilling engagements on the other side less binding than it would be, if the Cherokees had the power of enforcing their just claims?

The people of the United States will have the fairness to reflect, that all the treaties between them and the Cherokees were made, at the solicitation, and for the benefit, of the whites; that valuable considerations were given for every stipulation, on the part of the United States; that it is impossible to reinstate the parties in their former situation, that there are now hundreds of thousands of citizens of the United States residing upon lands ceded by the Cherokees in these very treaties; and that our people have trusted their country to the guaranty of the United States. If this guarantee fails them, in what can they trust, and where can they look for protection?

We are aware that some people suppose it will be to our advantage to remove beyond the Mississippi. We think otherwise. Our people universally think otherwise. Thinking that it would be fatal to their interests, they have almost to a man sent their memorial to congress deprecating the necessity of a removal. This question was distinctly before their minds when they signed their memorial. Not an adult person can be found, who has not an opinion on the subject, and if the people were to understand distinctly, that they could be protected against the laws of the neighboring states, there is probably not an adult person in the nation, who would think it best to remove; though possibly a few might emigrate individually. There are doubtless many, who would flee to an unknown country, however beset with dangers, privations and sufferings, rather than be sentenced to spend six years in a Georgia prison for advising one of their neighbors not to betray his country. And there are others who could not think of living as outlaws in their native land, exposed to numberless vexations, and excluded from being parties or witnesses in a court of justice. It is incredible that Georgia should ever have enacted the oppressive laws to which reference is here made, unless she had supposed that something extremely terrific in its character was necessary in order to make the Cherokees willing to remove. We are not willing to remove; and if we could be brought to this extremity, it would be not by argument, not because our judgment was satisfied, not because our condition will be improved; but only because we cannot endure to be deprived of our national and individual rights and subjected to a process of intolerable oppression.

We wish to remain on the land of our fathers. We have a perfect and original right to remain without interruption or molestation. The treaties with us, and laws of the United States made in pursuance of treaties, guarantee our residence and our privileges, and secure us against intruders. Our only request is that these treaties may be fulfilled, and these laws executed.

But if we are compelled to leave our country, we see nothing but ruin before us. The country west of the Arkansas territory is unknown to us. From what we can learn of it, we have no prepossessions in its favor. All the inviting parts of it, as we believe, are preoccupied by various Indian nations, to which it has been assigned. They would regard us as intruders, and look upon us with an evil eye. The far greater part of that region is, beyond all controversy, badly supplied with wood and water; and no Indian tribe can live as agriculturists without these articles. All our neighbors, in case of our removal, though crowded into our near vicinity; would speak a language totally different from ours, and practice different customs. The original possessors of that region are now wandering savages lurking for prey in the neighborhood. They have always been at war, and would be easily tempted to turn their arms against peaceful emigrants. Were the country to which we are urged much better than it is represented to be, and were it free from the objections which we have made to it, still it is not the land of our birth, nor of our affections. It contains neither the scenes of our childhood, nor the graves of our fathers.

The removal of families to a new country, even under the most favorable auspices, and when the spirits are sustained by pleasing visions of the future, is attended with much depression of mind and sinking of heart. This is the case, when the removal is a matter of decided preference, and when the persons concerned are in early youth or vigorous manhood. Judge, then, what must be the circumstances of a removal, when a whole community, embracing persons of all classes and every description, from the infant to the man of extreme old age, the sick, the blind, the lame, the improvident, the reckless, the desperate, as well as the prudent, the considerate, the industrious, are compelled to remove by odious and intolerable vexations and persecutions, brought upon them in the forms of law, when all will agree only in this, that they have been cruelly robbed of their country, in violation of the most solemn compacts, which it is possible for communities to form with each other; and that, if they should make themselves comfortable in their new residence, they have nothing to expect hereafter but to be the victims of a future legalized robbery!

Such we deem, and are absolutely certain, will be the feelings of the whole Cherokee people, if they are forcibly compelled, by the laws of Georgia, to remove; and with these feelings, how is it possible that we should pursue our present course of improvement, or avoid sinking into utter despondency? We have been called a poor, ignorant, and degraded people. We certainly are not rich; nor have we ever boasted of our knowledge, or our moral or intellectual elevation. But there is not a man within our limits so ignorant as not to know that he has the right to live on the land of his fathers, in the possession of his immemorial privileges, and that this right has been acknowledged and guaranteed by the United States; nor is there a man so degraded as not to feel a keen sense of injury, on being deprived of this right and driven into exile.

It is under a sense of the most pungent feelings that we make this, perhaps our last appeal to the good people of the United States. It cannot be that the community we are addressing, remarkable for its intelligence and religious sensibilities, and pre-eminent for its devotion to the rights of man, will lay aside this appeal, without considering that we stand in need of its sympathy and commiseration. We know that to the Christian and to the philanthropist the voice of our multiplied sorrows and fiery trials will not appear as an idle tale. In our own land, on our own soil, and in our own dwellings, which we reared for our wives and for our little ones, when there was peace on our mountains and in our valleys, we are encountering troubles which cannot but try our very souls. But shall we, on account of these troubles, forsake our beloved country? Shall we be compelled by a civilized and Christian people, with whom we have lived in perfect peace for the last forty years, and for whom we have willingly bled in war, to bid a final adieu to our homes, our farms, our streams and our beautiful forests? No. We are still firm. We intend still to cling, with our wonted affection, to the land which gave us birth, and which, every day of our lives, brings to us new and stronger ties of attachment. We appeal to the judge of all the earth, who will finally award us justice, and to the good sense of the American people, whether we are intruders upon the land of others. Our consciences bear us witness that we are the invaders of no man's rights—we have robbed no man of his territory—we have usurped no man's authority, nor have we deprived any one of his unalienable privileges. How then shall we indirectly confess the right of another people to our land by leaving it forever? On the soil which contains the ashes of our beloved men we wish to live—on this soil we wish to die.

We entreat those to whom the foregoing paragraphs are addressed, to remember the great law of love. "Do to others as ye would that others should do to you"—Let them remember that of all nations on the earth, they are under the greatest obligation to obey this law. We pray them to remember that, for the sake of principle, their forefathers were *compelled* to leave, therefore *driven* from the old world, and that the winds of persecution wafted them over the great waters and landed them on the shores of the new world, when the Indian was the sole lord and proprietor of these extensive domains—Let them remember in what way they were received by the savage of America, when power was in his hand, and his ferocity could not be restrained by any human arm. We urge them to bear in mind, that those who would now ask of them a cup of cold water, and a spot of earth, a portion of their own patrimonial possessions, on which to live and die in peace, are the descendants of those, whose origin, as inhabitants of North America, history and tradition are alike insufficient to reveal. Let them bring to remembrance all these facts, and they *cannot,* and we are sure, they will not fail to remember, and sympathize with us in these our trials and sufferings.

Cherokee Nation. 1785 Nov. 28, and Continental Congress Broadside Collection. *Articles of a Treaty, Concluded at Hopewell, on the Keowee, between Benjamin Hawkings, Andrew Pickens, Joseph Martin and Lacklan M'Intosh, Commissioners Plenipotentiary of the United States of America, of the one Part, and the Head-Men and Warriors of all the Cherokees of the other.* New York: s.n., 1786. https://www.loc.gov/resource/bdsdcc.18101/.

Cherokee Indian Women. *"Cherokee Indian/Native American Women to National Council at Amohee, May 2,"* Andrew Jackson Papers (1775–1874), transcribed by Nancy Ward. Manuscript/Mixed Material, 1817. https://www.loc.gov/item/maj007262/. Library of Congress, Manuscript Division, Andrew Jackson Papers.

Cherokee Indian Women. "June 30, 1818." In *Letter to American Board of Missionaries,* 30 June 1818, Papers of the American Board of Commissioners from Foreign Missions, transcribed by Nancy Ward. Boston, Houghton Library, Harvard University, 1818.

Cherokee Nation. "Memorial of the Cherokee Indians." In *Cherokee Phoenix, and Indians' Advocate,* January 20, 1830, vol. 2, no. 40, p. 1, col. 3a–5b. https://gahistoricnewspapers.galileo.usg.edu/lccn/sn83020874/1830-01-20/ed-1/seq-1/.

Cherokee Nation. "Address of the Committee and Council of the Cherokee Nation, in General Council Convened, to the People of the United States." In *Cherokee Phoenix, and Indians' Advocate,* July 24, 1830, p. 1, col. 1b–p. 2, col. 2a. https://www.wcu.edu/library/DigitalCollections/CherokeePhoenix/Vol3/no14/indians-page-1-column-1b-page-2-column-2a.html."

POST-READING PARS

1. How has your perception of the Cherokee people deepened or shifted by reading these documents?
2. Identify two or three ways in which Christianity influenced the writings of the various Cherokee leaders.
3. Locate two or three ways, through the language used and the emotion evoked, in which the various Cherokee leaders were appealing to both leaders in the US government and the larger populace.

Inquiry Corner

Content Questions:

After engaging with the group of documents, what do you find are the three or four most effective arguments laid out against removal?

What role did treaties play in the removal period? How did the Cherokee perceive the various treaties that were signed between themselves and the US government?

Critical Questions:

Look up the United Nation's definition of "genocide." Is this an appropriate term to use when discussing removal? Why or why not?

One concept that ties each of the readings together is that of *rights*. How are rights granted and from whom according to the various Cherokee writers? How is this similar or different than the ways in which rights have been framed in US law and policy?

Comparative Question:

Compare and contrast the ways in which the various Cherokee leaders from the readings discuss ties to land with other sources you are reading in the course that also mention land (e.g., Bolívar, Kangxi, Declaration of Independence, etc.)

Connection Questions:

How are the specific ways in which the various Cherokee leaders evoked emotion through the strategic use of language present in contemporary Indigenous resistance movements, such as #NoDAPL at Standing Rock and the struggle of the Wet'suwet'en Nation in Canada?

An important theme in American Indian and Indigenous Studies is *sacredness of place*. What does this mean to you? What would you define as a sacred place in contemporary American society? To whom is it sacred?

"I, Too" by Langston Hughes

SNAPSHOT BOX

LANGUAGE: English

PUBLISHED: 1925, Harlem, New York City

INFLUENCES: Blues, jazz, Harlem Renaissance

TAGS: Art; Autobiography and Testimony; Community; Poetry, Music, Literature; Psyche; Race; Struggle, Resistance, and Revolution

Introduction

Langston Hughes (1901–1967) was born in Joplin, Missouri, but was raised in Lawrence, Kansas, by his grandmother. She died in 1915, and he then moved to Lincoln, Illinois, where he lived with his mother and stepfather. He completed high school in Cleveland, Ohio, where he began publishing verse and short stories. His parents had separated soon after he was born and his father had moved first to Cuba and then to Mexico to avoid the racial prejudice of the United States. In 1921, when he was only nineteen years old, his poem "The Negro Speaks of Rivers," appeared in the *Crisis*, the magazine of the NAACP, founded and edited by W. E. B. Du Bois. By then, Hughes had found his poetic voice in the **blues and jazz aesthetics** of African American culture. Hughes withdrew from Columbia University due to racial problems on campus and worked his way around West Africa and Europe from 1923 to 1925. When he returned to the United States, his poem "The Weary Blues" won first prize (best poem of the year) in the *Opportunity* magazine literary competition. It is also the title of his first book of published poems in 1926. Soon after, Hughes enrolled at Lincoln University in Chester County, Pennsylvania, and graduated with a bachelor's degree in 1929. His first novel, *Not without Laughter*, was published in 1930 and won the Harmon Foundation Gold Medal Prize for literature. His other literary awards include the Guggenheim Fellowship (1935), Rosenwald Fund Fellowship to write plays (1941), the American Academy of Arts and Letters

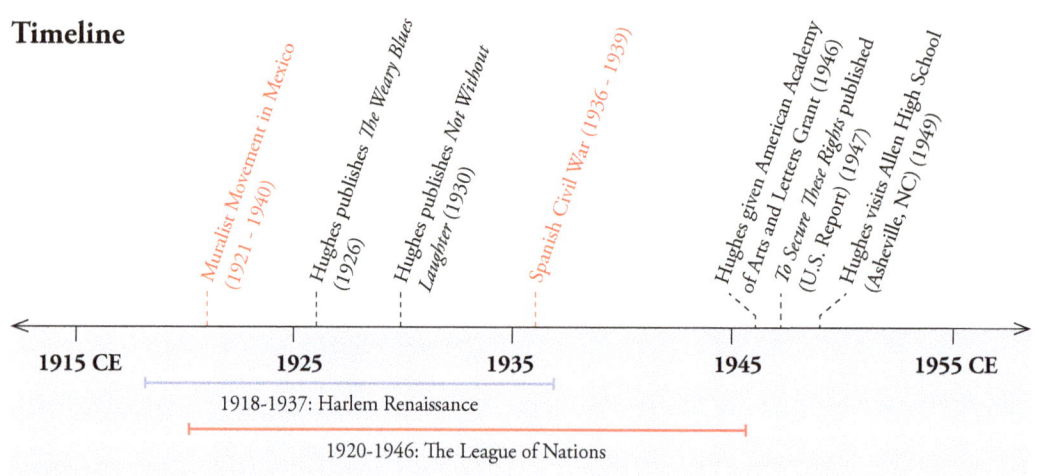

Grant for distinguished service as a writer (1946), and the Spingarn Medal from the National Association for the Advancement of Colored People (NAACP) in 1960.

Throughout his writing career and until his death in 1967, Hughes published poems, short stories, novels, plays, musicals, and nonfiction. His work is popular for portraying realistic experiences of the common people, specifically Black life in America. Although the middle class criticized him for his focus on the impoverished, he maintained that his characters were noble, regardless of status. Hughes embraced the role of poet of the people and his work remains very popular today in America and around the world—what reasons may be contributing to his ongoing popularity? The poem we have selected, "I, Too," was written in 1925 during the **Jim Crow era**, a time of white supremacism, segregation policies, and open lynching in the United States. Antilynching bills failed to pass the Senate, and large numbers of Blacks hoping to find better conditions went north in what became known as **the Great Migration**. New York City was especially attractive to Hughes because of the **Harlem Renaissance**, a period of heightened intellectual, literary, and cultural productivity by Black artists that peaked in the 1920s. Hughes's influence and contributions were central to the Renaissance. He was the first Black poet to make a living as a writer, supplemented by public readings and visiting lectures. Although he settled in Harlem, he traveled widely across the United States and abroad—Russia, Soviet Central Asia, China, Japan, the Caribbean, Mexico, Europe, and Africa. In 1937, Hughes went to Spain to cover the Spanish Civil War for the *Baltimore Afro-American* and other Black newspapers.

In his autobiography, *The Big Sea*, Hughes highlights what first drew him to writing—the beauty and power of language—the way books could express something ordinary with grace and elegance. "Then it was that books began to happen to me," Hughes writes, "and I began to believe in nothing but books and the wonderful world in books—where if people suffered, they suffered in beautiful language, not in monosyllables, as we did in Kansas."[49] Hughes, therefore, was inspired at an early age to turn to writing. In what ways might writing expose the chasm that existed between American social ideals and American social reality? His work has immediacy and demonstrates a racial awareness and keen effort to deal with injustices and negative stereotypes of African Americans that were and still are prevalent.

Mildred Barya
Department of English

---

49. See one of Langston Hughes's autobiographies, *I Wonder as I Wander*, 2nd ed. (Boston: Hill & Wang, 1993), 16. See also Langston Hughes, *The Weary Blues* (New York: Knopf, 1926), and Langston Hughes, *The Big Sea* (Boston: Hill & Wang, 1993).

> **PRE-READING PARS**
>
> 1. Can you think of a time when you went on a trip or journey and it changed your perspective?
> 2. Think of and describe an instance where "place" and "identity" interact.
> 3. Provide two or three examples of the ways in which American ideals might differ from American realities.

"I, Too" (1925)

I, too, sing America.
I am the darker brother.
They send me to eat in the kitchen
When company comes,
But I laugh,
And eat well,
And grow strong.
Tomorrow,
I'll be at the table
When company comes.
Nobody'll dare
Say to me,
"Eat in the kitchen,"
Then.
Besides,
They'll see how beautiful I am
And be ashamed—
I, too, am America.

Hughes, Langston. "I, Too." In *The Collected Poems of Langston Hughes*, 1925. [Public Domain].

> **POST-READING PARS**
>
> 1. In what ways might Hughes's travels across the states and abroad have influenced his writing approach?
> 2. What does the poem say about what it was like to be an African American in 1925?
> 3. From the poem, what ideals and social realities of African American people does Hughes highlight?

Inquiry Corner

Content Questions:

Who is the I? In other words, the speaker?

What is the I's position — in terms of place, class, race, social standing, perspective, and voice?

What is the subject of this poem and what themes can you identify?

Critical Questions:

How does the speaker use time movements to indicate a shift or a visionary perspective?

Identify and elaborate effectively some of the stylistic tools or techniques we recognize as craft elements or rhetorical devices used in this poem (repetition, figures of speech, symbols, metaphors, irony, refrain, etc.)

Comparative Question:

Compare Hughes's theme in "I, Too" with the sense of "double-consciousness" in W. E. B. Du Bois's writings?

Connection Questions:

How do we make meaning in language? In what creative ways can we articulate our experiences (via language) in order to reveal new information and to empower others?

Who are we (as human beings) versus who we are assumed or perceived to be (stereotypes)?

Compare and contrast today's America with Hughes's American in 1925. How much has changed or remained the same in terms of the issues he's addressing?

from *The Interesting Narrative of the Life of Olaudah Equiano or Gustavus Vassa, the African* by Olaudah Equiano

> **SNAPSHOT BOX**
>
> **LANGUAGE:** English
>
> **GENRE:** Autobiography
>
> **PUBLISHED:** 1789, London
>
> **OTHER CONTEXTUAL INFORMATION:** Polemic, abolitionist narrative
>
> **TAGS:** Abolition, Slavery, Freedom; Autobiography and Testimony; Body; Cross-Cultural Encounters; Family; Historiography; Race; Religion; Struggle, Resistance, and Revolution; War and Brutality

Introduction

Olaudah Equiano (1745–1797) was enslaved as a child yet ultimately deployed the tools of modernity to advocate for the abolition of the slave trade. His widely read and translated book galvanized opinion. Due in part to his activism, Britain abolished the slave trade in 1807 and slavery in 1833. At age twenty-one Equiano raised the funds to purchase his freedom from his owner Robert King, a Quaker and merchant in Philadelphia. He had spent most of his teenage years at sea, including service in the British Navy during the Seven Years War and on a scientific expedition to the Arctic. As a free man and Methodist missionary, he traveled extensively, including in Central America where he proselytized among the Indigenous Miskito people of Nicaragua. He settled in London and in 1792 married Susanna Cullen, a white woman.

The Narrative opens with a detailed account of eighteenth-century Nigerian rural life among the Igbo, his community of origin. His descriptions about land tenure, village administration, gender roles, and slave raiding allowed European comprehension of these practices. He likened African male circumcision, for example, to that practiced by Jews. He described the destabilization caused by the slave trade in West Africa, including being captured by local slave raiders. Excerpted here is his account of the Middle Passage in all its horror, both psychological and

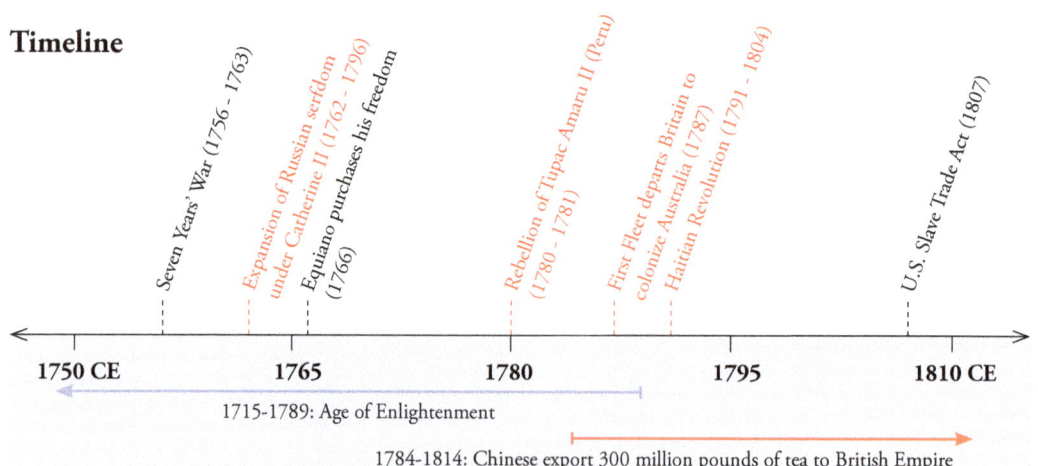

physical. Even though some doubt whether it is a firsthand account, it reflects the experience of thousands, if not millions, of people forcibly transported for nearly three centuries across the Atlantic Ocean, held for three to six weeks in cramped and filthy cargo holds. Treated like chattel, enslaved people survived this first act of dehumanization only to experience further degradation when they were sold, branded, and forced to labor on plantations—the lot of most enslaved people regardless of age or gender. Equiano's experience was different because he worked for the British Navy and, though enslaved, developed basic literacy and numeracy with the help of his tutor and friend Richard Baker. What impact might literacy have for enslaved peoples?

Developing hybrid identities and cultures, some, like Equiano, leveraged knowledge of the new languages and laws, Christianity, and culture to foreground African perspectives into the burgeoning antislavery movement. Once free, Equiano cultivated influential abolitionist allies in London, including Granville Sharp, a prominent member of parliament. Together, they brought bills before parliament to regulate conditions aboard slave ships and raised funds for a back-to-Africa repatriation program. He brought criminal charges against those who sought to re-enslave former enslaved peoples, including himself. His legal actions were usually successful, which emboldened younger abolitionists like William Wilberforce to press for full abolition in a variety of bills he presented between 1800–1833.

The Narrative is replete with biblical passages indicative of Equiano's embrace of Methodism, knowledge of the Gospels, and above all his audience. Like many abolitionists, he appealed to Christians' belief in the humanity of Africans and called out their hypocrisy if they failed to take a stand against slavery. He also attested to the comfort he derived from scripture and his faith in God. His prose appealed to the morality of his readers, their Christian faith, but also their economic self-interest. *The Narrative* ends with an enticement to invest in Africa rather than depopulate it. Does his own identity as a missionary and investor suggest a sincere belief in European uplift or is this appeal to economic interest a tactic to win people to the cause of abolition?

Tracey Rizzo
Department of History

[Content Notice: violence against enslaved peoples]

> **PRE-READING PARS**
>
> 1. How might autobiography be used for polemical purposes?
> 2. Which do you find more persuasive: economic or moral arguments?
> 3. Describe the intersections of race, class, and gender in an enslaved person's experience.

from *The Interesting Narrative of the Life of Olaudah Equiano or Gustavus Vassa, the African*

The first object which saluted my eyes when I arrived on the coast was the sea, and a slave ship, which was then riding at anchor, and waiting for its cargo. These filled me with astonishment, which was soon converted into terror when I was carried on board. I was immediately handled and tossed up to see if I were sound by some of the crew; and I was now persuaded that I had gotten into a world of bad spirits, and that they were going to kill me. Their complexions too differing so much from ours, their long hair, and the language they spoke, (which was very different from any I had ever heard) united to confirm me in this belief. [. . .] Soon after this the blacks who brought me on board went off, and left me abandoned to despair. I now saw myself deprived of all chance of returning to my native country, or even the least glimpse of hope of gaining the shore, which I now considered as friendly; and I even wished for my former slavery in preference to my present situation, which was filled with horrors of every kind, still heightened by my ignorance of what I was to undergo. I was not long suffered to indulge my grief; I was soon put down under the decks, and there I received such a salutation in my nostrils as I had never experienced in my life: so that, with the loathsomeness of the stench, and crying together, I became so sick and low that I was not able to eat, nor had I the least desire to taste any thing.

I now wished for the last friend, death, to relieve me; but soon, to my grief, two of the white men offered me eatables; and, on my refusing to eat, one of them held me fast by the hands, and laid me across I think the windlass, and tied my feet, while the other flogged me severely. I had never experienced any thing of this kind before; and although, not being used to the water, I naturally feared that element the first time I saw it, yet nevertheless, could I have got over the nettings, I would have jumped over the side, but I could not; and, besides, the crew used to watch us very closely who were not chained down to the decks, lest we should leap into the water: and I have seen some of these poor *African* prisoners most severely cut for attempting to do so, and hourly whipped for not eating. This indeed was often the case with myself. In a little time after, amongst the poor chained men, I found some of my own nation, which in a small degree gave ease to my mind. I inquired of these what was to be done with us; they gave me to understand we were to be carried to these white people's country to work for them. I then was a little revived, and thought, if it were no worse than working, my situation was not so desperate: but still I feared I should be put to death, the white people looked and acted, as I thought, in so savage a manner; for I had never seen among any people such instances of brutal cruelty; and this not only shewn towards us blacks, but also to some of the whites themselves. One white man in particular I saw, when we were permitted to be on deck, flogged so unmercifully with a large rope near the foremast, that he died in consequence of it; and they tossed him over the side as they would have done a brute. This made me fear these people the more; and I expected nothing less than to be treated in the same manner. [...]

At last, when the ship we were in had got in all her cargo, they made ready with many fearful noises, and we were all put under deck, so that we could not see how they managed the vessel. But this disappointment was the least of my sorrow. The stench of the hold while we were on the coast was so intolerably loathsome, that it was dangerous to remain there for any time, and some of us had been permitted to stay on the deck for the fresh air; but now that the whole ship's cargo were confined together, it became absolutely pestilential. The closeness of the place, and the heat of the climate, added to the number in the ship, which was so crowded that each had scarcely room to turn himself, almost suffocated us. This produced copious perspirations, so that the air soon became unfit for respiration, from a variety of loathsome smells, and brought on a sickness among the slaves, of which many died, thus falling victims to the improvident avarice, as I may call it, of their purchasers. This wretched situation was again aggravated by the galling of the chains, now become insupportable; and the filth of the necessary tubs, into which the children often fell, and were almost suffocated. The shrieks of the women, and the groans of the dying, rendered the whole a scene of horror almost inconceivable. Happily perhaps for myself I was soon reduced so low here that it was thought necessary to keep me almost always on deck; and from my extreme youth I was not put in fetters. In this situation I expected every hour to share the fate of my companions, some of whom were almost daily brought upon deck at the point of death, which I began to hope would soon put an end to my miseries. Often did I think many of the inhabitants of the deep much more happy than myself. I envied them the freedom they enjoyed, and as often wished I could change my condition for theirs. Every circumstance I met with served only to render my state more painful, and heighten my apprehensions, and my opinion of the cruelty of the whites. One day they had taken a number of fishes; and when they had killed and satisfied themselves with as many as they thought fit, to our astonishment who were on the deck, rather than give any of them to us to eat as we expected, they tossed the remaining fish into the sea again, although we begged and prayed for some as well as we could, but in vain; and some of my countrymen, being pressed by hunger, took an opportunity, when they thought no one saw them, of trying to get a little privately; but they were discovered, and the attempt procured them some very severe floggings.

One day, when we had a smooth sea and moderate wind, two of my wearied countrymen who were chained together (I was near them at the time), preferring death to such a life of misery, somehow made through the nettings and jumped into the sea: immediately another quite dejected fellow, who, on account of his illness, was suffered to be out of irons, also followed their example; and I believe many more would very soon have done the same if they had not been prevented by the ship's crew, who were instantly alarmed. Those of us that were the most active were in a moment put down under the deck, and there was such a noise and confusion amongst the people of the ship as I never heard before, to stop her, and get the boat out to go after the slaves. However two of the wretches were drowned, but they got the other, and afterwards flogged him unmercifully for thus attempting to prefer death to slavery.

[…]

I hope to have the satisfaction of seeing the renovation of liberty and justice resting on the *British* government, to vindicate the honour of our common nature. These are concerns which do not perhaps belong to any particular office: but, to speak more seriously to every man of sentiment, actions like these are the just and sure foundation of future fame; a reversion, though remote, is coveted by some noble minds as a substantial good. It is upon these grounds that I hope and expect the attention of gentlemen in power. These are designs consonant to the elevation of their rank and the dignity of their stations: they are ends suitable to the nature of a free and generous government; and, connected with views of empire and dominion, suited to the benevolence and solid merit of the legislature. It is a pursuit of substantial greatness.— May the time come—at least the speculation to me is pleasing—when the sable people shall gratefully commemorate the auspicious era of extensive freedom. Then shall those persons particularly be named with praise and honour, who generously proposed and stood forth in the cause of humanity; liberty; and good policy; and brought to the ear of the legislature designs worthy of royal patronage and adoption. May Heaven make the *British* senators the dispersers of light, liberty, and science, to the uttermost parts of the earth: then will be glory to God on the highest, on earth peace, and good-will to men.—Glory, honour, peace, etc. to every soul of man that worketh good, to the *Britons* first, (because to them the Gospel is preached) and also to the nations. 'Those that honour their Maker have mercy on the poor.' 'It is righteousness exalteth a nation; but sin is a reproach to any people; destruction shall be to the workers of iniquity, and the wicked shall fall by their own wickedness.' May the blessings of the Lord be upon the heads of all those who commiserated the cases of the oppressed negroes,[50] and the fear of God prolong their days; and may their expectations be filled with gladness! 'The liberal devise liberal things, and by liberal

---

50. Equiano uses the term "Negro" to refer to his own African communities as was a prevalent practice within and outside of Black communities from the nineteenth to mid-twentieth centuries (sometimes earlier). The term "negro" should not be confused with the derogatory n-word. Likewise another term used during the same timeframe, "colored," is outdated and should not be confused with the current usage of "person of color." Words reflecting African, African American, and Black communities' preferences for self-identification continue to shift in meaning and connotation over time.

things shall stand,' Isaiah xxxii. 8. They can say with pious Job, 'Did not I weep for him that was in trouble? was not my soul grieved for the poor?' Job xxx. 25.

As the inhuman traffic of slavery is to be take into the consideration of the *British* legislature, I doubt not, if a system of commerce was established in *Africa*, the demand for manufactures would most rapidly augment, as the native inhabitants will insensibly adopt the *British* fashions, manners, customs, etc. In proportion to the civilization, so will be the consumption of *British* manufactures.

The wear and tear of a continent, nearly twice as large as *Europe*, and rich in vegetable and mineral production, is much easier conceived than calculated.

A case in point. It cost the *Aborigines of Britain*, little or nothing in clothing, etc. The difference between their forefathers and the present generation, in point of consumption, is literally infinite. The supposition is most obvious. It will be equally immense in *Africa*. The same cause, viz. civilization, will ever have the same effect.

It is trading upon safe grounds. A commercial intercourse with *Africa* opens an inexhaustible source of wealth to the manufacturing interests of *Great Britain*, and to all which the slave trade is an objection.

If I am not misinformed, the manufacturing interest is equal, if not superior, to the landed interest, as to the value, for reasons which will soon appear. The abolition of slavery, so diabolical, will give a most rapid extension of manufactures, which is totally and diametrically opposite to what some interested people assert.

The manufactures of this country must and will, in the nature and reason of things, have a full and constant employ by supplying the African markets.[51]

Population, the bowels and surface of *Africa*, abound in valuable and useful returns; the hidden treasures of centuries will be brought to light and into circulation. Industry, enterprise, and mining, will have their full scope, proportionably as they civilize. In a word, it lays open an endless field of commerce to the *British* manufacturer and merchant adventurer. The manufacturing interest and the general interests are synonymous. The abolition of slavery would be in reality an universal good.

Tortures, murder, and every other imaginable barbarity and iniquity, are practised upon the poor slaves with impunity. I hope the slave trade will be abolished. I pray it may be an event at hand. The great body of manufacturers, uniting in the cause, will considerably facilitate and expedite it; and as I have already stated, it is most substantially their interest and advantage, and as such the nation's at large, (except those persons concerned in the manufacturing neck-yokes, collars, chains, handcuffs, leg-bolts, drags, thumb-screws, iron muzzles, and coffins; cats, scourges, and other instruments of torture used in the slave trade.) In a short time one sentiment alone will prevail from motives of interest as well as justice and humanity. *Europe* contains one hundred and twenty millions of inhabitants. Query—How many millions doth *Africa* contain? Supposing the *Africans*, collectively and individually, to expend £5 a

---

51. Not in the original 1815 text.

head in raiment and furniture, yearly, when civilized, etc. an immensity beyond the reach of imagination!

This I conceive to be a theory founded upon facts, and therefore an infallible one. If the blacks were permitted to remain in their own country, they would double themselves every fifteen years. In proportion to such increase, will be the demand for manufactures. Cotton and indigo grow spontaneously in most parts of *Africa*; a consideration this of no small consequence to the manufacturing towns of *Great Britain*. It opens a most immense, glorious, and happy prospect—the clothing, etc. of a continent ten thousand miles in circumference, and immensely rich in productions of every denomination in return for manufactures. [...]

I have only therefore to request the reader's indulgence and conclude. I am far from the vanity of thinking there is any merit in this narrative: I hope censure will be suspended when it is considered that it was written by one who was as unwilling as unable to adorn the plainness of truth by the colouring of imagination. My life and fortune have been extremely chequered and my adventures various. Even those I have related are considerably abridged. If any incident in this little work should appear uninteresting and trifling to most readers, I can only say as my excuse, for mentioning it that almost every event of my life made an impression on my mind and influenced my conduct. I early accustomed myself to look for the hand of God in the minutest occurrence and to learn from it a lesson of morality and religion, and in this light every circumstance I have related was to me of importance. After all, what makes any event important, unless by its observation we become better and wiser, and learn 'to do justly, to love mercy, and to walk humbly before God'? To those who are possessed of this spirit there is scarcely any book of incident trifling that does not afford some profit, while to others the experience of ages seems of no use; and even to pour out to them the treasures of wisdom is throwing the jewels of instruction away.

Equiano, Olaudah. *The Interesting Narrative of the Life of Olaudah Equiano; Or Gustavus Vassa, the African*, 50–53, 55–57, 322–27. Penryn, UK: W. Cock, 1815.

POST-READING PARS

1. In which passages is Equiano's polemic most evident?
2. Are Equiano's economic arguments as effective as his moral arguments, or vice versa?

Inquiry Corner

Content Question:

Describe the intersections of race, class, and gender in Equiano's narrative.

Critical Question:

How might we understand his account of life in Africa and the Middle Passage if he was in fact born in South Carolina?

Comparative Question:

Compare Equiano's strategies for abolitionist activism to those of other authors advocating for freedom.

Connection Questions:

Would you follow Equiano's advice for investing in Africa? How do strategies of investing and divesting enable moral change or social justice?

"Letter from Benjamin Banneker and Thomas Jefferson's Response" by Benjamin Banneker and Thomas Jefferson

SNAPSHOT BOX

LANGUAGE: English
WRITTEN: August 19, 1791, Maryland
GENRE: Epistolary/letter exchange
TAGS: Abolition, Slavery, and Freedom; Accessing Rights; Ethics and Morality; Race; Religion; Science; Struggle, Resistance, and Revolution

Introduction

Benjamin Banneker (1731–1806) was an **Enlightenment** figure. His varied life accomplishments as well as the creative and technical skills he applied across multiple fields of study made him a true "Renaissance Man." The son of a freed slave father and a mixed-race mother, Banneker grew up on his family's farm in Baltimore County, Maryland. Although he was never a slave, Banneker and his family knew the sting of racial animus as public attitudes toward free Blacks deteriorated in the mid-1700s. However, Banneker was able to receive an education denied to most Black people. His Irish grandmother, a formerly indentured servant, taught him to read, and he made the most of his education in an integrated one-room schoolhouse located near the farm. At a young age, Banneker was noticed by Quaker industrialist George Ellicott for his accomplishments and obvious talents. At fifteen, he designed an irrigation system for the farm that carried it through periods of drought. At twenty-one, he designed and built a wooden clock that kept perfect time for forty years. Ellicott, owner of a grist mill and a land surveyor with an interest in the physical and the natural world, loaned Banneker books on astronomy, mathematics, and science, as well as technical books and lunar tables. Banneker was later able to cal-

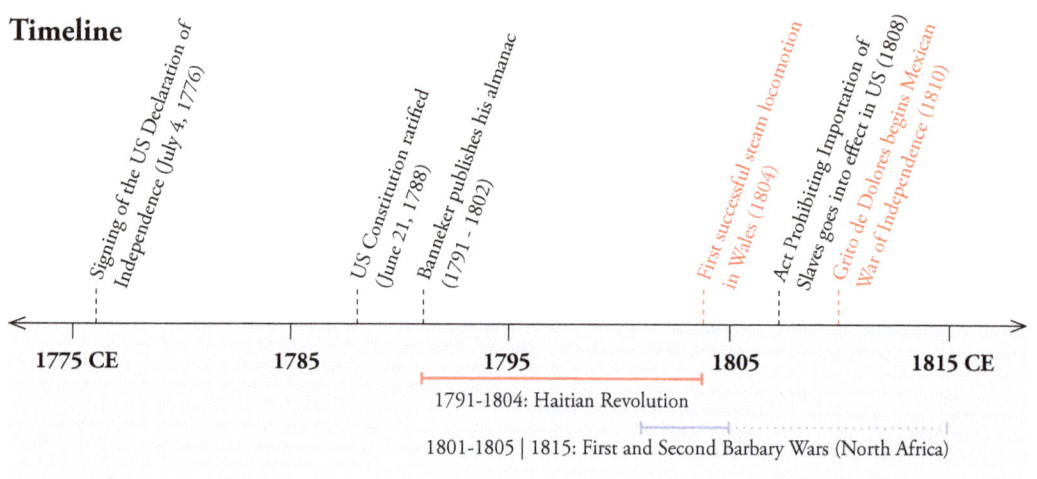

culate a solar eclipse that took place on April 14, 1789, correcting the predictions of other, more prominent, astronomers.

Banneker's most notable accomplishment came with his involvement in the design of the United States Capital. Congress passed the Residence Act on July 16, 1790, authorizing the building of a federal city on the Potomac River. Andrew Ellicott, head engineer of the project and cousin of Banneker's former patron, invited Banneker to help him survey the new capital's boundary. Working with various instruments that maintained the regulator clock used to determine latitude, Banneker worked alongside the French architect Pierre L'Enfant to map out what would become the District of Columbia and the City of Washington.

This reading focuses on a letter that Banneker wrote to Thomas Jefferson (1743–1826), the principal author of the Declaration of Independence and a slaveholder. Pundits and politicians often turn to Jefferson's work for philosophical phrasings on the foundations of democratic republicanism and equal rights before the law. While Jefferson is known as a central figure in Enlightenment principles, he was also one of the foremost promoters of the unfounded lie of African inferiority. How might European Enlightenment principles and hateful stigma reinforce each other?

Banneker's letter highlights Jefferson's inconsistencies around racial bias. In his *Notes on the State of Virginia*, published in 1785 while Secretary of State, Jefferson wrote that Africans were inferior to Europeans in intellectual ability. It is unclear whether his awareness of Banneker's work with Ellicott and L'Enfant was able to change his mind. However, at the time of the survey, an article appeared in the *Georgetown Weekly Ledger* that disagreed with Jefferson's stance: "[Ellicott] is attended by Benjamin Banneker, an Ethiopian, whose abilities, as a surveyor, and an astronomer, clearly prove that Mr. Jefferson's concluding that race of men were void of mental endowments, was without foundation."[52]

Banneker returned to his farm in April 1792 and started work on his first publication, *Benjamin Banneker's Pennsylvania, Delaware, Maryland, and Virginia Almanack of Ephemeris, for the Year of Our Lord 1792*. The almanac contained things of interest to farmers: weather predictions, when to plant, information on the tides, and eclipses based upon Banneker's own astronomical calculations, among other things. The almanac also contained essays, one of them an article by **abolitionist** David Rittenhouse, who called Banneker's calculations "a very extraordinary performance, considering the colour of the Author." Banneker took exception to this, responding, "I am annoyed to find the subject of my race is so much stressed." But Rittenhouse's attitude about race—that white excellence is routine while Black excellence is something of an anomaly—was common among white people. A slight variation was expressed by James McHenry, a Maryland statesman, in his testimonial about

---

52. Silvio A. Bedini, *The Life of Benjamin Banneker* (Rancho Cordova, CA: Landmark Enterprises, 1972), 122.

Banneker: "I consider this Negro[53] as fresh proof that the powers of the mind are disconnected with the colour of the skin."

The assumption that intellect exists independently from racial experience and embodiment remains a prominent one in this attitude about race. Indeed, such an attitude exposes the contradiction of maintaining that all men are created equal while excluding Africans from such equal consideration. This is also reflected in the fact that while Banneker was involved in the technical design of the capital project, the federal project's commissioners allowed the renting of slave laborers for its building the same year. How do people justify the dissonance between their actions and words? The following correspondence between Banneker and Jefferson's brief response mirrors the exchange between Banneker and Rittenhouse. The exchange sheds some light on exploring arguments being levied to work against racial injustices and the ongoing entanglement of enlightenment perspectives in the enslavement of human beings.

Bruce Cahoon
Humanities Program

---

53. McHenry uses the term "Negro" to refer to African American communities as was a prevalent practice within and outside of Black communities from the nineteenth to mid-twentieth centuries. The term "negro" should not be confused with the derogatory n-word. Likewise another term used during the same timeframe, "colored," is outdated and should not be confused with the current usage of "person of color." Words reflecting African American and Black communities' preferences for self-identification continue to shift in meaning and connotation over time.

> **PRE-READING PARS**
>
> 1. How would you characterize the type of writing (tone, style, word choice, etc.) you use when writing physical letters? Emails? Text messages? What content is connected to each of these styles?
> 2. Draft the first three sentences of a letter to your senator, the chancellor, or someone else who holds a position of societal power. Invent your own purpose for writing the letter and note how your purpose influences the tone of your opening.
> 3. Is it important to know the race or ethnic heritage of an author as you read their work? When, how, and why might knowing this kind of context be important? When might it be discriminatory? Outline your thoughts in a five-minute writing.

Letter from Benjamin Banneker and Thomas Jefferson's Response

Letter from Benjamin Banneker

Maryland, Baltimore County, Near Ellicott's Lower Mills,
August nineteenth: 1791

Sir,

I am fully sensible of the greatness of that freedom which I take with you on the present occasion; a liberty which seemed to me scarcely allowable, when I reflected on that distinguished, and dignified station in which you Stand, and the almost general prejudice and prepossession which is so prevalent in the world against those of my complexion.

I suppose it is a truth too well attested to you, to need a proof here, that we are a race of Beings who have long labored under the abuse and censure of the world, that we have long been looked upon with an eye of contempt, and that we have long been considered rather as brutish than human, and scarcely capable of mental endowments.

Sir I hope I may Safely admit, in consequence of that report which hath reached me, that you are a man far less inflexible in Sentiments of this nature, than many others, that you are measurably friendly and well disposed toward us, and that you are willing and ready to lend your aid and assistance to our relief from those many distresses and numerous calamities to which we are reduced.

Now Sir if this is founded in truth, I apprehend you will readily embrace every opportunity to eradicate that train of absurd and false ideas and opinions which so generally prevails with respect to us, and that your Sentiments are concurrent with mine, which are that one universal Father hath given being to us all, and that he hath not only made us all of one flesh, but that he hath also without partiality afforded us all the Same Sensations and endued us all with the same faculties and that however variable we may be in Society or religion, however diversified in Situation or colour, we are all of the Same Family, and Stand in the Same relation to him.

Sir, if these are Sentiments of which you are fully persuaded, I hope you cannot but acknowledge, that it is the indispensible duty of those who maintain for themselves the rights of human nature, and who possess the obligations of Christianity, to extend their power and influence to the relief of every part of the human race, from whatever burthen or oppression they may unjustly labor under, and this I apprehend a full conviction of the truth and obligation of these principles should lead all to.

Sir, I have long been convinced, that if your love for your Selves, and for those inestimable laws which preserved to you the rights of human nature, was founded on Sincerity, you could not but be Solicitous, that every Individual, of whatsoever rank or distinction, might with you equally enjoy the blessings thereof neither could you rest satisfied short of the most active diffusion of your exertions, in order to their promotion from any State of degradation, to which the unjustifiable cruelty and barbarism of men may have reduced them.

Sir I freely and Chearfully acknowledge, that I am of the African race, and in that color which is natural to them of the deepest dye, and it is under a sense of the most profound gratitude to the Supreme Ruler of the universe, that I now confess to you, that I am not under that State of tyrannical thraldom, and inhuman captivity, to which too many of my brethren are doomed; but that I have abundantly tasted of the fruition of those blessings which proceed from that free and unequalled liberty with which you are favoured and which I hope you will willingly allow you have received from the immediate hand of that Being, from whom proceedeth every good and perfect gift.

Sir, Suffer me to recall to your mind that time in which the arms and tyranny of the British Crown were exerted with every powerful effort in order to reduce you to a State of Servitude, look back I entreat you on the variety of dangers to which you were exposed, reflect on that time in which every human aid appeared unavailable, and in which even hope and fortitude wore the aspect of inability to the conflict, and you cannot but be led to a serious and grateful sense of your miraculous and providential preservation; you cannot but acknowledge, that the present freedom and tranquility which you enjoy you have mercifully received, and that it is the peculiar blessing of Heaven.

This, Sir, was a time when you clearly saw into the injustice of a State of Slavery, and in which you had just apprehensions of the horrors of its condition, it was now that your abhorrence thereof was so excited, that you publickly held forth this true and invaluable doctrine, which is worthy to be recorded and remember'd in all succeeding ages. "We hold these truths to be Self evident, that all men are created equal, and that they are endowed by their creator with certain unalienable rights, that among these are life, liberty, and the pursuit of happiness."

Here Sir, was a time in which your tender feelings for your selves had engaged you thus to declare, you were then impressed with proper ideas of the great valuation of liberty, and the free possession of those blessings to which you were entitled by nature; but Sir how pitiable is it to reflect, that altho you were so fully convinced of the benevolence of the Father of mankind, and of his equal and impartial distribution of those rights and privileges which he hath conferred upon them, that you should at the same time counteract his mercies, in detaining by fraud and violence so numerous a part of my brethren under groaning captivity and cruel oppression, that you should at the Same time be found guilty of that most criminal act, which you professedly detested in others, with respect to yourselves.

Sir, I suppose that your knowledge of the situation of my brethren is too extensive to need a recital here; neither shall I presume to prescribe methods by which they may be relieved; otherwise than by recommending to you and all others, to wean yourselves from those narrow prejudices which you have imbibed with respect to them, and as Job proposed to his friends "Put your Soul in their Souls stead" thus shall your hearts be enlarged with kindness and benevolence toward them, and thus shall you need neither the direction of myself or others in what manner to proceed herein.

And now, Sir, altho my sympathy and affection for my brethren hath caused my enlargement thus far, I ardently hope that your candour and generosity will plead with you in my behalf when I make known to you, that it was not originally my design; but that having taken up my pen in order to direct to you as a present, a copy of an Almanack which I have calculated for the succeeding year, I was unexpectedly and unavoidably led thereto.

This calculation, Sir, is the production of my arduous Study in this my advanced Stage of life; for having long had unbounded desires to become acquainted with the Secrets of nature, I have had to gratify my curiosity herein through my own assiduous application to Astronomical Study, in which I need not to recount to you the many difficulties and disadvantages which I have had to encounter.

And altho I had almost declined to make my calculation for the ensuing year, in consequence of that time which I had allotted therefor being taking up at the Federal Territory by the request of Mr. Andrew Ellicott, yet finding myself under several engagements to printers of this state to whom I had communicated my design, on my return to my place of residence, I industriously applied myself thereto, which I hope I have accomplished with correctness and accuracy; a copy of which I have taken the liberty to direct to you, and which I humbly request you will favorably receive, and altho you may have the opportunity of perusing it after its publication, yet I chose to send it to you in manuscript previous thereto, that thereby you might not only have an earlier inspection, but that you might also view it in my own handwriting. And now Sir, I shall conclude and Subscribe my Self with the most profound respect your most Obedient humble Servant,

Benjamin Banneker

To Benjamin Banneker

Philadelphia Aug. 30. 1791

Sir,

    I thank you sincerely for your letter of the nineteenth. instant and for the Almanac it contained. Nobody wishes more than I do to see such proofs as you exhibit, that nature has given to our black brethren, talents equal to those of the other colors of men, and that the appearance of a want of them is owing merely to the degraded condition of their existence both in Africa and America. I can add with truth that nobody wishes more ardently to see a good system commenced for raising the condition both of their body and mind to what it ought to be, as fast as the imbecillity of their present existence, and other circumstances which cannot be neglected, will admit! I have taken the liberty of sending your almanac to Monsieur de Condorcet, Secretary of the Academy of Sciences at Paris, and member of the Philanthropic society because I considered it as a document to which your whole color had a right for their justification against the doubts which have been entertained of them. I am with great esteem, Sir.

Your most obedt. humble servt.,
Th: Jefferson

Banneker, Benjamin, and Thomas Jefferson. "Copy of a Letter from Benjamin Banneker, &c." In *Copy of a Letter from Benjamin Banneker, to the Secretary of State, with His Answer*, 3–12. Philadelphia, PA: Daniel Lawrence, 1792.

POST-READING PARS

1. How would you characterize Jefferson's writing style and response to Banneker? How might it change if the exchange was over text message or in an exchange over public social media?

2. What does Banneker aim to accomplish with the opening (first couple of paragraphs) of his letter? How does it compare to what you drafted in your opening few sentences from the Pre-PAR?

3. Where, how, and why does Banneker disclose his own race in this letter? Does it change your answers in the Pre-PAR if the author discloses their own race?

Inquiry Corner

Content Question:

Why do you think Banneker alludes to the revolutionaries' contention that the British Crown had reduced them to a state of servitude?

Critical Questions:

Evaluate the reasons Banneker offers in support of his assumption that Jefferson would be sympathetic to his arguments.

Why do you think Banneker wanted to send a copy of his Almanac to Jefferson? Interpret and evaluate Jefferson's treatment of this gift? Does Jefferson's unfounded bias/assumptions of African inferiority shape the contours of his response? Why or why not?

Comparative Question:

Compare this letter to other arguments for equal rights that you have studied in this course. What types of strategies do the different authors use? Consider the medium, tone, and audience.

Connection Question:

Articulate how you might rewrite the conversation based on what you know about racial justice today.

BEYOND THE CLASSROOM

» How can colleagues with privilege (e.g., racial, class, and/or power hierarchies, etc.) promote inclusion and equity in the workplace and create an environment where diversity goes beyond being "required" or "accepted" but is truly valued and recognized as crucial for success?

» What is an example of a time when you advocated for yourself or others, or spoke truths that are important to say, but might be difficult to verbalize or hear? How was it received? What might you do differently next time?

from *Narrative of the Life of Frederick Douglass, an American Slave* and from "What to the Slave is the Fourth of July?" by Frederick Douglass

SNAPSHOT BOX

LANGUAGE: English
PUBLISHED: 1845 and 1852, United States
GENRE: Autobiography and speech
TAGS: Abolition, Slavery, and Freedom; Autobiography and Testimony; Body; Education; Family; Historiography; Poetry, Music, Literature; Psyche; Race; Struggle, Resistance, and Revolution

Introduction

Frederick Douglass (1817[54]–1895) was born into slavery in eastern Maryland; his mother was an enslaved person, and his father, his biographers are generally agreed, was his mother's slaveowner. In his narrative, Douglass tells us that he rarely saw his mother as a child and then only at night, without his master's knowledge. For his first seven years, he lived on the plantation of Colonel Edward Lloyd, but was then relocated to the Baltimore home of Hugh Auld, an in-law of Lloyd's. Douglass's experience in the fields of the Lloyd plantation exposed him to all the cruelties of an enslaved person's life; once in Baltimore, he began to sense what might be accomplished in freedom. While still a boy, he was taught to read and write by Sophia Auld, his new master's wife, but when Hugh Auld put an end to this he was forced to finish his education on his own. In 1833, when he was sixteen years old, Douglass was turned over to Edward Covey, a sadistic and ill-tempered man, known for his dehumanizing ability to break the spirits of enslaved persons. After only six months, Douglass had endured enough of Covey's cruel treatment and, in what becomes a primary thematic episode in his narrative, he rebelled physically against his tormenter. Covey never again laid hands on him; for Douglass this was an early taste of freedom.

After a failed escape in 1835, Douglass returned to Baltimore, where Hugh Auld put him to work as a caulker. He began assiduously to cultivate the knowledge and skills necessary to liberate himself and, in 1838, he won his freedom, fleeing to New York and finally settling in New Bedford, Massachusetts. There, he married Anna Murray, a free Black woman who had helped to finance his escape from Baltimore. Within a short time, Douglass became deeply involved in the Black abolition movement, speaking at antislavery conventions and lecturing for the Massachusetts Anti-Slavery Society. In 1845, Douglass published the *Narrative of the Life of Frederick Douglass, an American Slave*, which became a success nearly overnight: within just three years, 11,000 copies were in print, in nine editions, with translations published in France and Holland. In 1846, Douglass received his legal emancipation. Anna and Ellen Richardson, two English women whom he had met during a two-year lecture tour there, bought his freedom from his former master for a sum of

---

54. Douglass writes in his final autobiography, "I suppose myself to have been born in february, 1817." In *The Life and Times of Frederick Douglass: From 1817–1882* (London: Christian Age Office,1882), 2.

Timeline

seven hundred dollars. Moving to Rochester, New York, in 1847, Douglass embarked on a career as a newspaper publisher. One of the excerpts below, now also known by the title, "What to the Slave is the Fourth of July?" was part of an oration he was invited to give at the Rochester Ladies Anti-Slavery Society in 1852. In 1859, he had to leave the United States, first moving to Canada and then to England, after being wrongfully implicated in John Brown's raid at Harper's Ferry, West Virginia.

At the start of the American Civil War in 1861, Douglass became involved in efforts to allow Blacks to serve in the Union army and then to recruit Black enlistees. Until his death in 1895, Douglass worked tirelessly as an advocate for racial equality, women's suffrage, and economic opportunity for the poor.

In the excerpts from the *Narrative* and "What to the Slave is the Fourth of July?" you are about to read, Douglass compels us to examine the patterns of dehumanizing through straightforwardly describing the brutalities endured by enslaved persons. What were the strategies employed by slaveowners to degrade enslaved people? In his speech, what arguments does he refuse to make about slavery, especially in relation to peoples' humanity? How does he contrast the Fourth of July with the experiences of enslaved persons? What, according to Douglass, are the means by which he—and by extension, other enslaved people as well—might escape dehumanized conditions? What does real freedom for all inhabitants entail in the United States?

Humanities Program Faculty

[Content notice: violence against enslaved persons]

from *Narrative of the Life of Frederick Douglass, an American Slave* and from "What to the Slave is the Fourth of July?"

from *Narrative of the Life of Frederick Douglass*, an American Slave

Chapter I

I was born in Tuckahoe, near Hillsborough, and about twelve miles from Easton, in Talbot county, Maryland. I have no accurate knowledge of my age, never having seen any authentic record containing it. By far the larger part of the slaves know as little of their ages as horses know of theirs, and it is the wish of most masters within my knowledge to keep their slaves thus ignorant. I do not remember to have ever met a slave who could tell of his birthday. They seldom come nearer to it than planting-time, harvest-time, cherry-time, springtime, or fall-time. A want of information concerning my own was a source of unhappiness to me even during childhood. The white children could tell their ages. I could not tell why I ought to be deprived of the same privilege. I was not allowed to make any inquiries of my master concerning it. He deemed all such inquiries on the part of a slave improper and impertinent, and evidence of a restless spirit. The nearest estimate I can give makes me now between twenty-seven and twenty-eight years of age. I come to this, from hearing my master say, some time during 1835, I was about seventeen years old.

My mother was named Harriet Bailey. She was the daughter of Isaac and Betsey Bailey, both colored, and quite dark. My mother was of a darker complexion than either my grandmother or grandfather.

My father was a white man. He was admitted to be such by all I ever heard speak of my parentage. The opinion was also whispered that my master was my father; but of the correctness of this opinion, I know nothing; the means of knowing was withheld from me. My mother and I were separated when I was but an infant—before I knew her as my mother. It is a common custom, in the part of Maryland from which I ran away, to part children from their mothers at a very early age. Frequently, before the child has reached its twelfth month, its mother is taken from it, and hired out on some farm a considerable distance off, and the child is placed under the care of an old woman, too old for field labor. For what this separation is done, I do not know, unless it be to hinder the development of the child's affection toward its mother, and to blunt and destroy the natural affection of the mother for the child. This is the inevitable result.

I never saw my mother, to know her as such, more than four or five times in my life; and each of these times was very short in duration, and at night. She was hired by a Mr. Stewart, who lived about twelve miles from my home. She made her journeys to see me in the night, travelling the whole distance on foot, after the performance of her day's work. She was a field hand, and a whipping is the penalty of not being in the field at sunrise, unless a slave has special permission from his or her master to the contrary—a permission which they seldom get, and one that gives to him that gives it the proud name of being a kind master. I do not recollect of ever seeing my mother by the light of day. She was with me in the night. She would lie down with me, and get me to sleep, but long before I waked she was gone. Very little communication ever took place between us. Death soon ended what little we could have while she lived, and with it her hardships and suffering. She died when I was about seven years old, on one of my master's farms, near Lee's Mill. I was not allowed to be present during her illness, at her death, or burial. She was gone long before I knew any thing about it. Never having enjoyed, to any considerable extent, her soothing presence, her tender and watchful care, I received the tidings of her death with much the same emotions I should have probably felt at the death of a stranger.

Called thus suddenly away, she left me without the slightest intimation of who my father was. The whisper that my master was my father, may or may not be true; and, true or false, it is of but little consequence to my purpose whilst the fact remains, in all its glaring odiousness, that slaveholders have ordained, and by law established, that the children of slave women shall in all cases follow the condition of their mothers; and this is done too obviously to administer to their own lusts, and make a gratification of their wicked desires profitable as well as pleasurable; for by this cunning arrangement, the slaveholder, in cases not a few, sustains to his slaves the double relation of master and father.

I know of such cases; and it is worthy of remark that such slaves invariably suffer greater hardships, and have more to contend with, than others. They are, in the first place, a constant offence to their mistress. She is ever disposed to find fault with them; they can seldom do any thing to please her; she is never better pleased than when she sees them under the lash, especially when she suspects her husband of showing to his mulatto children favors which he withholds from his black slaves. The master is frequently compelled to sell this class of his slaves, out of deference to the feelings of his white wife; and, cruel as the deed may strike any one to be, for a man to sell his own children to human flesh-mongers, it is often the dictate of humanity for him to do so; for, unless he does this, he must not only whip them himself, but must stand by and see one white son tie up his brother, of but few shades darker complexion than himself, and ply the gory lash to his naked back; and if he lisp one word of disapproval, it is set down to his parental partiality, and only makes a bad matter worse, both for himself and the slave whom he would protect and defend.

Every year brings with it multitudes of this class of slaves. It was doubtless in consequence of a knowledge of this fact, that one great statesman of the south predicted the downfall of slavery by the inevitable laws of population. Whether this prophecy is ever fulfilled or not, it is nevertheless plain that a very different-looking class of people are springing up at the south, and are now held in slavery, from those originally brought to this country from Africa; and if their increase do no other good, it will do away the force of the argument, that God cursed Ham, and therefore American slavery is right. If the lineal descendants of Ham are alone to be scripturally enslaved, it is certain that slavery at the south must soon become unscriptural; for thousands are ushered into the world, annually, who, like myself, owe their existence to white fathers, and those fathers most frequently their own masters.

from "What to the Slave is the Fourth of July?"

[…] Fellow Citizens, I am not wanting in respect for the fathers of this republic. The signers of the Declaration of Independence were brave men. They were great men too—great enough to give fame to a great age. It does not often happen to a nation to raise, at one time, such a number of truly great men. The point from which I am compelled to view them is not, certainly the most favorable; and yet I cannot contemplate their great deeds with less than admiration. They were statesmen, patriots and heroes, and for the good they did, and the principles they contended for, I will unite with you to honor their memory.

[…]

Fellow-citizens, pardon me, allow me to ask, why am I called upon to speak here to-day? What have I, or those I represent, to do with your national independence? Are the great principles of political freedom and of natural justice, embodied in that Declaration of Independence, extended to us? And am I, therefore, called upon to bring our humble offering to the national altar, and to confess the benefits and express devout gratitude for the blessings resulting from your independence to us?

Would to God, both for your sakes and ours, that an affirmative answer could be truthfully returned to these questions! Then would my task be light, and my burden easy and delightful. For *who* is there so cold, that a nation's sympathy could not warm him? Who so obdurate and dead to the claims of gratitude, that would not thankfully acknowledge such priceless benefits? Who so stolid and selfish, that would not give his voice to swell the hallelujahs of a nation's jubilee, when the chains of servitude had been torn from his limbs? I am not that man. In a case like that, the dumb might eloquently speak, and the "lame man leap as an hart."

But, such is not the state of the case. I say it with a sad sense of the disparity between us. I am not included within the pale of this glorious anniversary! Your high independence only reveals the immeasurable distance between us. The blessings in which you, this day, rejoice, are not enjoyed in common.— The rich inheritance of justice, liberty, prosperity and independence, bequeathed by your fathers, is shared by you, not by me. The sunlight that brought life and healing to you, has brought stripes and death to me. This Fourth July is *yours*, not *mine*. *You* may rejoice, *I* must mourn. To drag a man in fetters into the grand illuminated temple of liberty, and call upon him to join you in joyous anthems, were inhuman mockery and sacrilegious irony. Do you mean, citizens, to mock me, by asking me to speak to-day? If so, there is a parallel to your conduct. And let me warn you that it is dangerous to copy the example of a nation whose crimes, towering up to heaven, were thrown down by the breath of the Almighty, burying that nation in irrecoverable ruin! I can today take up the plaintive lament of a peeled and woe-smitten people!

"By the rivers of Babylon, there we sat down. Yea! We wept when we remembered Zion. We hanged our harps upon the willows in the midst thereof. For there, they that carried us away captive, required of us a song; and they who wasted us required of us mirth, saying, Sing us one of the songs of Zion. How can we sing the Lord's song in a strange land? If I forget thee, O Jerusalem, let my right hand forget her cunning. If I do not remember thee, let my tongue cleave to the roof of my mouth."

Fellow-citizens; above your national, tumultuous joy, I hear the mournful wail of millions! whose chains, heavy and grievous yesterday, are, to-day, rendered more intolerable by the jubilee shouts that reach them. If I do forget, if I do not faithfully remember those bleeding children of sorrow this day, "may my right hand forget her cunning, and may my tongue cleave to the roof of my mouth!" To forget them, to pass lightly over their wrongs, and to chime in with the popular theme, would be treason most scandalous and shocking, and would make me a reproach before God and the world. My subject, then, fellow-citizens, is AMERICAN SLAVERY. I shall see, this day, and its popular characteristics, from the slave's point of view. Standing, there, identified with the American bondman, making his wrongs mine, I do not hesitate to declare, with all my soul, that the character and conduct of this nation never looked blacker to me than on this 4th of July! Whether we turn to the declarations of the past, or to the professions of the present, the conduct of the nation seems equally hideous and revolting. America is false to the past, false to the present, and solemnly binds herself to be false to the future. Standing with God and the crushed and bleeding slave on this occasion, I will, in the name of humanity which is outraged, in the name of liberty which is fettered, in the name of the constitution and the Bible, which are disregarded and trampled upon, dare to call in question and to denounce, with all the emphasis I can command, everything that serves to perpetuate slavery—the great sin and shame of America! "I will not equivocate; I will not excuse;" I will use the severest language I can command; and yet not one word shall escape me that any man, whose judgment is not blinded by prejudice, or who is not at heart a slaveholder, shall not confess to be right and just.

But I fancy I hear some one of my audience say, it is just in this circumstance that you and your brother abolitionists fail to make a favorable impression on the public mind. Would you argue more, and denounce less, would you persuade more, and rebuke less, your cause would be much more likely to succeed. But, I submit, where all is plain there is nothing to be argued. What point in the anti-slavery creed would you have me argue? On what branch of the subject do the people of this country need light? Must I undertake to prove that the slave is a man? That point is conceded already. Nobody doubts it. The slaveholders themselves acknowledge it in the enactment of laws for their government. They acknowledge it when they punish disobedience on the part of the slave. There are seventy-two crimes in the State of Virginia, which, if committed by a black man, (no matter how ignorant he be,) subject him to the punishment of death; while only two of the same crimes will subject a white man to the like punishment.—

What is this but the acknowledgement that the slave is a moral, intellectual and responsible being. The manhood of the slave is conceded. It is admitted in the fact that Southern statute books are covered with enactments forbidding, under severe fines and penalties, the teaching of the slave to read or to write.—When you can point to any such laws, in reference to the beasts of the field, then I may consent to argue the manhood of the slave. When the dogs in your streets, when the fowls of the air, when the cattle on your hills, when the fish of the sea, and the reptiles that crawl, shall be unable to distinguish the slave from a brute, *then* will I argue with you that the slave is a man!

For the present, it is enough to affirm the equal manhood of the negro[55] race. Is it not astonishing that, while we are ploughing, planting and reaping, using all kinds of mechanical tools, erecting houses, constructing bridges, building ships, working in metals of brass, iron, copper, silver and gold; that, while we are reading, writing and cyphering, acting as clerks, merchants and secretaries, having among us lawyers, doctors, ministers, poets, authors, editors, orators and teachers; that, while we are engaged in all manner of enterprises common to other men, digging gold in California, capturing the whale in the Pacific, feeding sheep and cattle on the hill-side, living, moving, acting, thinking, planning, living in families as husbands, wives and children, and, above all, confessing and worshipping the Christian's God, and looking hopefully for life and immortality beyond the grave, we are called upon to prove that we are men!

Would you have me argue that man is entitled to liberty? that he is the rightful owner of his own body? You have already declared it. Must I argue the wrongfulness of slavery? Is that a question for Republicans? Is it to be settled by the rules of logic and argumentation, as a matter beset with great difficulty, involving a doubtful application of the principle of justice, hard to be understood? How should I look to-day, in the presence of Americans, dividing, and subdividing a discourse, to show that men have a natural right to freedom? speaking of it relatively, and positively, negatively, and affirmatively. To do so, would be to make myself ridiculous, and to offer an insult to your understanding.— There is not a man beneath the canopy of heaven, that does not know that slavery is wrong *for him*.

What, am I to argue that it is wrong to make men brutes, to rob them of their liberty, to work them without wages, to keep them ignorant of their relations to their fellow men, to beat them with sticks, to flay their flesh with the lash, to load their limbs with irons, to hunt them with dogs, to sell them at auction, to sunder their families, to

---

55. Douglass uses the term "Negro" to refer to his own African American communities as was a prevalent practice within and outside of Black communities from the nineteenth to mid-twentieth centuries. The term "negro" should not be confused with the derogatory n-word. Likewise another term used during the same timeframe, "colored," is outdated and should not be confused with the current usage of "person of color." Words reflecting African American and Black communities' preferences for self-identification continue to shift in meaning and connotation over time.

knock out their teeth, to burn their flesh, to starve them into obedience and submission to their masters? Must I argue that a system thus marked with blood, and stained with pollution, is *wrong*? Ho! I will not. I have better employment for my time and strength, than such arguments would imply.

What, then, remains to be argued? Is it that slavery is not divine; that God did not establish it; that our doctors of divinity are mistaken? There is blasphemy in the thought. That which is inhuman, cannot be divine! *Who* can reason on such a proposition? They that can, may; I cannot. The time for such argument is past.

At a time like this, scorching irony, not convincing argument, is needed. O! had I the ability, and could I reach the nation's ear, I would, to day, pour out a fiery stream of biting ridicule, blasting reproach, withering sarcasm, and stern rebuke. For it is not light that is needed, but fire; it is not the gentle shower, but thunder. We need the storm, the whirlwind, and the earthquake. The feeling of the nation must be quickened; the conscience of the nation must be roused; the propriety of the nation must be startled; the hypocrisy of the nation must be exposed; and its crimes against God and man must be proclaimed and denounced.

What, to the American slave, is your 4th of July? I answer; a day that reveals to him, more than all other days in the year, the gross injustice and cruelty to which he is the constant victim. To him, your celebration is a sham; your boasted liberty, an unholy license; your national greatness, swelling vanity; your sounds of rejoicing are empty and heartless; your denunciations of tyrants, brass fronted impudence; your shouts of liberty and equality, hollow mockery; your prayers and hymns, your sermons and thanksgivings, with all your religious parade, and solemnity, are, to him, mere bombast, fraud, deception, impiety, and hypocrisy—a thin veil to cover up crimes which would disgrace a nation of savages. There is not a nation on the earth guilty of practices, more shocking and bloody, than are the people of these United States, at this very hour.

Go where you may, search where you will, roam through all the monarchies and despotisms of the old world, travel through South America, search out every abuse, and when you have found the last, lay your facts by the side of the every day practices of this nation, and you will say with me, that, for revolting barbarity and shameless hypocrisy, America reigns without a rival.

[...]

Allow me to say, in conclusion, notwithstanding the dark picture I have this day presented, of the state of the nation, I do not despair of this country. There are forces in operation, which must inevitably, work the downfall of slavery. "*The arm of the Lord is not shortened*," and the doom of slavery is certain. I, therefore, leave off where I began, with *hope*. While drawing encouragement from "the Declaration of Independence," the great principles it contains, and the genius of American Institutions, my spirit is also cheered by the obvious tendencies of the age. Nations do not now stand in the same relation to each other that they did ages ago. No nation can now shut itself up, from the surrounding world, and trot round in the same old path of its fathers without interference. The time *was* when such could be done. Long established customs of hurtful character could formerly fence themselves in, and do their evil work with social impunity. Knowledge was then confined and enjoyed by the privileged few, and the multitude walked on in mental darkness. But a change has now come over the affairs of mankind. Walled cities and empires have become unfashionable. The arm of commerce has borne away the gates of the strong city. Intelligence is penetrating the darkest corners of the globe. It makes its pathway over and under the sea, as well as on the earth. Wind, steam, and lightning are its chartered agents. Oceans no longer divide, but link nations together. From Boston to London is now a holiday excursion. Space is comparatively annihilated.— Thoughts expressed on one side of the Atlantic, are distinctly heard on the other.

The far off and almost fabulous Pacific rolls in grandeur at our feet. The Celestial Empire, the mystery of ages, is being solved. The fiat of the Almighty, "*Let there be Light*" has not yet spent its force. No abuse, no outrage whether in taste, sport or avarice, can now hide itself from the all-pervading light. The iron shoe, and crippled foot of China must be seen, in contrast with nature. *Africa must rise and put on her yet unwoven garment.* "*Ethiopia shall stretch out her hand unto God.*" In the fervent aspirations of William Lloyd Garrison, I say, and let every heart join in saying it:

> God speed the year of jubilee
> The wide world o'er!
> When from their galling chains set free,
> Th' oppress'd shall vilely bend the knee,
> And wear the yoke of tyranny
> Like brutes no more.
> That year will come, and freedom's reign,
> To man his plundered rights again
> Restore.
>
> God speed the day when human blood
> Shall cease to flow!
> In every clime be understood.
> The claims of human brotherhood,
> And each return for evil, good,
> Not blow for blow;
> That day will come all feuds to end,
> And change into a faithful friend
> Each foe.
>
> God speed the hour, the glorious hour,
> When none on earth
> Shall exercise a lordly power,
> Nor in a tyrant's presence cower;

But all to manhood's stature tower,
By equal birth!
That hour will come, to each, to all,
And from his prison-house, the thrall
Go forth.

Until that year, day, hour, arrive,
With head, and heart, and hand I'll strive,
To break the rod, and rend the gyve,
The spoiler of his prey deprive—
So witness Heaven!
And never from my chosen post,
Whate'er the peril or the cost,
Be driven.

Douglass, Frederick. "Chapter 1." In *Narrative of the Life of Frederick Douglass, an American Slave: Written by Himself,* 1–5. Boston: The Anti-Slavery Office, 1846.

Douglass, Frederick. "Oration" also now known as "What to the Slave is the Fourth of July?" 10, 14–21, 37 Rochester: Lee, Mann & Co, 1852.

from *Nisei Daughter* by Monica Sone

SNAPSHOT BOX

LANGUAGE: English
GENRE: Autobiography
PUBLISHED: United States, 1953
TAGS: Abolition, Slavery, and Freedom; Body; Community; Cross-Cultural Encounters; Family; Psyche; Race; Struggle, Resistance, and Revolution; Tradition

Introduction

In December 1941, Seattle native Kasuko Monica Itoi dreamed of attending the University of Washington. She was twenty-one years old and had just returned from a nine-month stay in a sanitarium recovering from tuberculosis when the Empire of Japan attacked the Pearl Harbor naval base in Honolulu, Hawai'i, on December 7, 1941. As President Franklin Roosevelt famously stated, that date would live in "infamy," but for the Japanese American population of the United States, that day forever changed their lives. By mid-February 1942 the enactment of Executive Order 9066 establishing the military Zones of Exclusion on the West Coast of the United States and creating the War Relocation Authority resulted in the removal of more than 120,000 individuals of Japanese descent to temporary encampments located at converted fairgrounds, horse racing tracks, former migrant worker camp sites, former mill worker housing sites, and Civilian Conservation Corps camp sites.

Kasuko Monica Itoi Sone's autobiographical narrative of her life and experience, *Nisei Daughter*, describes her time interned in one such camp. In the following excerpt, **Nisei** (二世, second generation, second-generation Japanese Americans, or the first-generation born in the United States) siblings Henry, Monica, and Sumiko and their **Issei** (一世, first generation, first-generation Japanese Americans) parents Seizo and Benko are forced to leave behind their lives in Seattle in May 1942. They found themselves on a bus bound for the fairgrounds at Pullayup, Washington, and the somewhat ironically named Camp Harmony Assembly Center.

Timeline

- Germany, Japan, and Italy create the Axis Alliance (1940)
- Japanese attack on Pearl Harbor (1941)
- Executive Order 9066 (1942)
- U.S. bombs Hiroshima (1945)
- Creation of India and Pakistan (1947)
- Arendt publishes *The Origins of Totalitarianism* (1951)
- Sone publishes *Nisei Daughter* (1953)

1939–1945: World War II

1944–1954: Guatemalan "Ten Years of Spring"

Sone describes her family's first day and night in the hastily constructed barracks of the internment camp. As the entry progresses, Sone conveys the sense of **shikata ga nai** (仕方がない, it cannot be helped), the mentality shared among the Japanese American internees as they endured less than ideal circumstances—for example, being housed in facilities that resembled chicken farms—and attempted to make the best out of dehumanizing situations for the sake of their families and communities. In the end, legalities were shunted aside and none of the rights afforded to the Nisei as American citizens, nor their parents as legal immigrants, saved them from being forced from their homes and into the so-called War Relocation Authority Assembly Centers and Relocation Camps. As you read the following excerpt, consider the following questions: How does the author reflect on civil rights and more specifically, the legitimacy of her own citizenship and identity? How does this inform ideas of citizenship and identity for other first- and second-generation Americans? How does this inform ideas about identity and belonging for marginalized communities like African Americans?

Nisei Daughter, originally published in 1953, follows Sone's life from her early childhood years, the realization of her ethnicity, her internment, and her college years after the war. Before her death, she worked on a sequel that would cover her careers as a clinical psychologist and social worker and her marriage to Nisei World War II veteran, Geary M. Sone.[56] Few published first-person accounts of the internment exist, and Sone's book went to print to little fanfare. It was not until a subsequent reprint in 1979 by the University of Washington Press that her critical narrative achieved the wider distribution that has continued to the present day. In the introduction to the reprint, Sone writes about the importance of recounting the **Nikkei** ("日系" (Japanese person,) the term used to refer to members of the Japanese diaspora) experience during the war and the **Redress Movement** (the struggle for reparations for Japanese American internees and their families—finally granted in 1989). There she stated, "The Nikkeis hope that this redress movement may discourage similar injustices to others. They aim to work together with white America, to carry out our mutual task which Professor V. Rostow of Yale delineated in his writing: 'Until the wrong is acknowledged and made right, we shall have failed to meet the responsibility of a democratic society . . . the obligation of equal justice.'"[57] How does the acknowledgment of systemic injustice help us meet the responsibilities of a democratic society?

Amanda Glenn-Bradley
Ramsey Library at UNC Asheville

---

56. Nancy Matsumoto, "Monica Sone," Densho Encyclopedia. https://encyclopedia.densho.org/Monica%20Sone/ (accessed March 1, 2020).

57. Monica Sone, *Nisei Daughter* (Seattle: University of Washington Press, 1979), xvii.

from *Nisei Daughter*

Japanese Relocation (1953)

When our bus turned a corner and we no longer had to smile and wave, we settled back gravely in our seats. Everyone was quiet except for a chattering group of university students who soon started singing college songs. A few people turned and glared at them, which only served to increase the volume of their singing. Then suddenly a baby's sharp cry rose indignantly above the hubbub. The singing stopped immediately, followed by a guilty silence. Three seats behind us, a young mother held a wailing red-faced infant in her arms, bouncing it up and down. Its angry little face emerged from multiple layers of kimonos, sweaters and blankets, and it, too, wore the white pasteboard tag pinned to its blanket. A young man stammered out an apology as the mother gave him a wrathful look. She hunted frantically for a bottle of milk in a shopping bag, and we all relaxed when she had found it.

We sped out of the city southward along beautiful stretches of farmland, with dark, newly turned soil. In the beginning we devoured every bit of scenery which flashed past our window and admired the massive-muscled work horses plodding along the edge of the highway, the rich burnished copper color of a browsing herd of cattle, the vivid spring green of the pastures, but eventually the sameness of the country landscape palled on us. We tried to sleep to escape from the restless anxiety which kept bobbing up to the surface of our minds. I awoke with a start when the bus filled with excited buzzing. A small group of straw-hatted Japanese farmers stood by the highway, waving at us. I felt a sudden warmth toward them, then a twinge of pity. They would be joining us soon.

About noon we crept into a small town. Someone said, "Looks like Puyallup, all right." Parents of small children babbled excitedly, "Stand up quickly and look over there. See all the chick-chicks and fat little piggies?" One little city boy stared hard at the hogs and said tersely, "They're *bachi*—dirty!"

Our bus idled a moment at the traffic signal and we noticed at the left of us an entire block filled with neat rows of low shacks, resembling chicken houses. Someone commented on it with awe, "Just look at those chicken houses. They sure go in for poultry in a big way here." Slowly the bus made a left turn, drove through a wire-fenced gate, and to our dismay, we were inside the oversized chicken farm. The bus driver opened the door, the guard stepped out and stationed himself at the door again. Jim, the young man who had shepherded us into the busses, popped his head inside and sang out, "Okay, folks, all off at Yokohama, Puyallup."

We stumbled out, stunned, dragging our bundles after us. It must have rained hard the night before in Puyallup, for we sank ankle deep into gray, gluttinous mud. The receptionist, a white man, instructed us courteously, "Now, folks, please stay together as family units and line up. You'll be assigned your apartment."

We were standing in Area A, the mammoth parking lot of the state fairgrounds. There were three other separate areas, B, C and D, all built on the fair grounds proper, near the baseball field and the race tracks. This camp of army barracks was hopefully called Camp Harmony.

We were assigned to apartment 2—I—A, right across from the bachelor quarters. The apartments resembled elongated, low stables about two blocks long. Our home was one room, about 18 by 20 feet, the size of a living room. There was one small window in the wall opposite the one door. It was bare except for a small, tinny wood-burning stove crouching in the center. The flooring consisted of two by fours laid directly on the earth, and dandelions were already pushing their way up through the cracks. Mother was delighted when she saw their shaggy yellow heads. "Don't anyone pick them. I'm going to cultivate them."

Father snorted, "Cultivate them! If we don't watch out, those things will be growing out of our hair."

Just then Henry stomped inside, bringing the rest of our baggage. "What's all the excitement about?"

Sumi replied laconically, "Dandelions."

Henry tore off a fistful. Mother scolded, "*Arra! Arra!* Stop that. They're the only beautiful things around here. We could have a garden right in here."

"Are you joking, Mama?"

I chided Henry, "Of course, she's not. After all, she has to have some inspiration to write poems, you know, with all the '*nali keli's*.' I can think of a poem myself right now:

Oh, Dandelion, Dandelion,
Despised and uprooted by all,
Dance and bob your golden heads
For you've finally found your home
With your yellow fellows, *nali keli*, amen!"

Henry said, thrusting the dandelions in Mother's black hair, "I think you can do ten times better than that, Mama."

Sumi reclined on her seabag and fretted, "Where do we sleep? Not on the floor, I hope."

"Stop worrying," Henry replied disgustedly.

Mother and Father wandered out to see what the other folks were doing and they found people wandering in the mud, wondering what other folks were doing. Mother returned shortly, her face lit up in an ecstatic smile, "We're in luck. The latrine is right nearby. We won't have to walk blocks."

We laughed, marveling at Mother who could be so poetic and yet so practical. Father came back, bent double like a woodcutter in a fairy tale, with stacks of scrap lumber over his shoulder. His coat and trouser pockets bulged with nails. Father dumped his loot in a corner and explained, "There was a pile of wood left by the carpenters and hundreds of nails scattered loose. Everybody was picking them up, and I hustled right in with them. Now maybe we can live in style with tables and chairs."

The block leader knocked at our door and announced lunchtime. He instructed us to take our meal at the nearest mess hall. As I untied my seabag to get out my pie plate, tin cup, spoon and fork, I realized I was hungry. At the mess hall we found a long line of people. Children darted in and out of the line, skiing in the slithery mud. The young stood impatiently on one foot, then the other, and scowled, "The food had better be good after all this wait." But the Issei stood quietly, arms folded, saying very little. A light drizzle began to fall, coating bare black heads with tiny sparkling raindrops. The chow line inched forward.

Lunch consisted of two canned sausages, one lob of boiled potato, and a slab of bread. Our family had to split up, for the hall was too crowded for us to sit together. I wandered up and down the aisles, back and forth along the crowded tables and benches, looking for a few inches to squeeze into. A small Issei woman finished her meal, stood up and hoisted her legs modestly over the bench, leaving a space for one. Even as I thrust myself into the breach, the space had shrunk to two inches, but I worked myself into it. My dinner companion, hooked just inside my right elbow, was a bald headed, gruff-looking Issei man who seemed to resent nestling at mealtime. Under my left elbow was a tiny, mud-spattered girl. With busy runny nose, she was belaboring her sausages, tearing them into shreds and mixing them into the potato gruel which she had made with water. I choked my food down. We cheered loudly when trucks rolled by, distributing canvas army cots for the young and hardy, and steel cots for the older folks. Henry directed the arrangement of the cots. Father and Mother were to occupy the corner nearest the wood stove. In the other corner, Henry arranged two cots in L shape and announced that this was the combination living room-bedroom area, to be occupied by Sumi and myself. He fixed a male den for himself in the corner nearest the door. If I had had my way, I would have arranged everyone's cots in one neat row as in Father's hotel dormitory.

We felt fortunate to be assigned to a room at the end of the barracks because we had just one neighbor to worry about. The partition wall separating the rooms was only seven feet high with an opening of four feet at the top, so at night, Mrs. Funai next door could tell when Sumi was still sitting up in bed in the dark, putting her hair up. "*Mah, Sumi-chan,*" Mrs. Funai would say through the plank wall, "are you curling your hair tonight again? Do you put it up every night?" Sumi would put her hands on her hips and glare defiantly at the wall.

The block monitor, an impressive Nisei who looked like a star tackle with his crouching walk, came around the first night to tell us that we must all be inside our room by nine o'clock every night. At ten o'clock, he rapped at the door again, yelling, "Lights out!" and Mother rushed to turn the light off not a second later.

Throughout the barracks, there were a medley of creaking cots, whimpering infants and explosive night coughs. Our attention was riveted on the intense little wood stove which glowed so violently I feared it would melt right down to the floor. We soon learned that this condition lasted for only a short time, after which it suddenly turned into a deep freeze. Henry and Father took turns at the stove to produce the harrowing blast which all but singed our army blankets, but did not penetrate through them. As it grew quieter in the barracks, I could hear the light patter of rain. Soon I felt the "splat! splat!" of raindrops digging holes into my face. The dampness on my pillow spread like a mortal bleeding, and I finally had to get out and haul my cot toward the center of the room. In a short while Henry was up. "I've got multiple leaks, too. Have to complain to the landlord first thing in the morning."

All through the night I heard people getting up, dragging cots around. I stared at our little window, unable to sleep. I was glad Mother had put up a makeshift curtain on the window for I noticed a powerful beam of light sweeping across it every few seconds. The lights came from high towers placed around the camp where guards with Tommy guns kept a twenty-four hour vigil. I remembered the wire fence encircling us, and a knot of anger tightened in my breast. What was I doing behind a fence like a criminal? If there were accusations to be made, why hadn't I been given a fair trial? Maybe I wasn't considered an American anymore. My citizenship wasn't real, after all. Then what was I? I was certainly not a citizen of Japan as my parents were. On second thought, even Father and Mother were more alien residents of the United States than Japanese nationals for they had little tie with their mother country. In their twenty-five years in America, they had worked and paid their taxes to their adopted government as any other citizen.

Of one thing I was sure. The wire fence was real. I no longer had the right to walk out of it. It was because I had Japanese ancestors. It was also because some people had little faith in the ideas and ideals of democracy. They said that after all these were but words and could not possibly insure loyalty. New laws and camps were surer devices. I finally buried my face in my pillow to wipe out burning thoughts and snatch what sleep I could.

Sone, Monica. "Life in Camp Harmony." In *Nisei Daughter*, 172–78. Seattle: University of Washington Press, 1979.

from "Speaking Out Against Lynching" by Ida B. Wells

SNAPSHOT BOX

LANGUAGE: English
PUBLISHED: 1895, United States
GENRE: Investigative journalism
TAGS: Accessing Rights; Body; Ethics and Morality; Historiography; Race; Struggle, Resistance, and Revolution; Tyranny; War and Brutality; Women and Power

Introduction

Ida Bell Wells (1862–1931) was born in Mississippi into slavery. Over the next seven decades Wells lead a multidimensional crusade to fight racism, racial violence, and sex, gender, and race discrimination. As a journalist, Wells used her research and writing skills to provide evidence against white supremacy and for African American rights. She was a spokeswoman for an inclusive women's suffrage movement and challenged white suffragists to include Black women in the suffrage movement. She was also a public activist involved in many organizations that fought for the rights of African Americans and women. She is best known for her work exposing the motivations behind white lynch mobs and challenging the myth that Black men were lynched to protect white women.

As a child, Ida B. Wells was exposed to **Reconstruction era** Southern politics since both her parents were politically active. She remembered listening to her father read newspaper articles about African American and **Republican Party** politics in the years following the Civil War. Her childhood ended when both parents died from yellow fever; she then took charge of her younger brothers and sisters and entered the workforce as a teacher. Wells moved her family to Memphis, Tennessee, and there she began her career as a journalist and activist. In 1884, Wells successfully filed a racial segregation suit against the Chesapeake and Ohio Railroad. She recovered $500 in damages; though her vic-

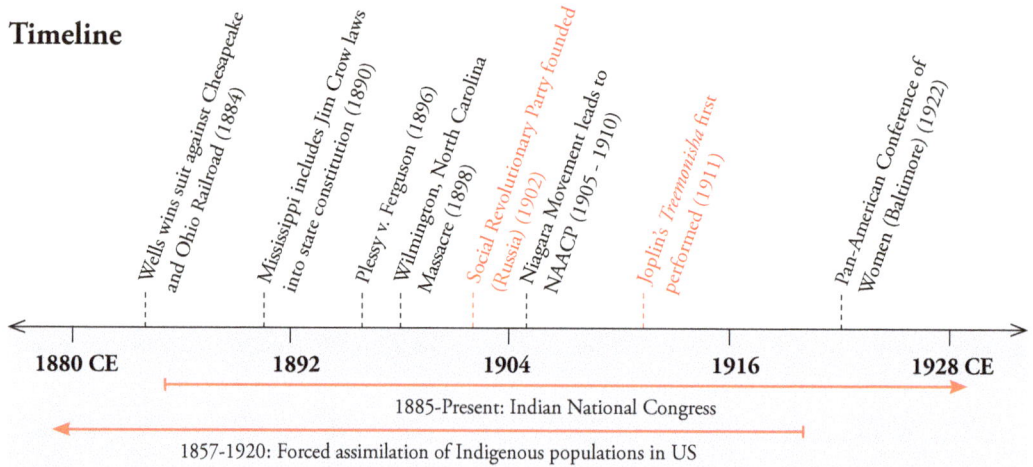

tory was short-lived after a higher court reversed the ruling. Following this event, Wells began to write about racial issues for local African American papers published in Memphis and across the South. What are the differences (e.g., in motivations or ramifications) between pursuing racial justice through legal means versus through journalistic endeavors?

In 1892, Wells wielded the power of her pen when a white mob lynched three of her friends who owned a store that competed successfully with white-owned businesses. This horrific event pushed Wells toward her life's work: documenting and exposing the racial violence of white supremacy and the lies used to justify that violence. As a result of her work, Wells became a target and was forced to leave Memphis for New York City. There, Wells became involved with the African American women's club and women's suffrage movements. In 1895, Wells published *The Red Record: Tabulated Statistics and Alleged Causes of Lynchings in the United States*. The section below is an excerpt from this work. One of the key aspects of Well's analysis is the way she challenges the sexual basis of white supremacy. She posits the question, "If white men claimed to be protecting white women by lynching black men, what about the historic, habitual, and ongoing sexual violence of white men against black women?" As you read, how does Wells confront the ways that the false charge of rape levied against Black men is woven into the late nineteenth-century system of racial domination in the South?

Ida B. Wells was also a prominent advocate for women's suffrage and was active on the national and local levels. She believed that enfranchisement was one way that African American women could protect their communities and elect leaders who would advance African American interests. In the excerpt below, does Wells advance a form of gender justice? After a long life of tireless advocacy, Wells died in 1931 in Chicago, the city she lived in the longest. In 2020, she was awarded a posthumous Pulitzer Prize special citation for her research and reporting on lynching. As you read, consider how Wells's writing acts as a precursor for some of the investigative journalism on racial violence published in the years since?

Sarah Judson
Department of History

[Content notice: mention of rape; racialized violence]

> **PRE-READING PARS**
>
> 1. List two or three main ways that African American men have been portrayed in the media or that you know about from history.
> 2. Why do you think we know more about the lynching of African Americans than about sexual violence aimed at African American women during this time period?
> 3. What are three or four defining features of white supremacy?

Speaking Out Against Lynching

Humanity abhors the assailant of womanhood, and this charge upon the Negro[58] at once placed him beyond the pale of human sympathy. With such unanimity, earnestness and apparent candor was this charge made and reiterated that the world has accepted the story that the Negro is a monster which the Southern white man has painted him. And today, the Christian world feels, that while lynching is a crime, and lawlessness and anarchy the certain precursors of a nation's fall, it can not by word or deed, extend sympathy or help to a race of outlaws, who might mistake their plea for justice and deem it an excuse for their continued wrongs.

The Negro has suffered much and is willing to suffer more. He recognizes that the wrongs of two centuries can not be righted in a day, and he tries to bear his burden with patience for today and be hopeful for tomorrow. But there comes a time when the veriest worm will turn, and the Negro feels today that after all the work he has done, all the sacrifices he has made, and all the suffering he has endured, if he did not, now, defend his name and manhood from this vile accusation, he would be unworthy even of the contempt of mankind. It is to this charge he now feels he must make answer.

If the Southern people in defense of their lawlessness, would tell the truth and admit that colored men and women are lynched for almost any offense, from murder to a misdemeanor, there would not now be the necessity for this defense. But when they intentionally, maliciously and constantly belie the record and bolster up these falsehoods by the words of legislators, preachers, governors and bishops, then the Negro must give to the world his side of the awful story.

---

58. Wells uses the term "Negro" to refer to her own African American communities as was a prevalent practice within and outside of Black communities from the nineteenth to mid-twentieth centuries. The term "negro" should not be confused with the derogatory n-word. Likewise another term used during the same timeframe, "colored," is outdated and should not be confused with the current usage of "person of color." Words reflecting African American and Black communities' preferences for self-identification continue to shift in meaning and connotation over time.

A word as to the charge itself. In considering the third reason assigned by the Southern white people for the butchery of blacks, the question must be asked, what the white man means when he charges the black man with rape. Does he mean the crime which the statutes of the civilized states describe as such? Not by any means. With the Southern white man, any mesalliance existing between a white woman and a colored man is a sufficient foundation for the charge of rape. The Southern white man says that it is impossible for a voluntary alliance to exist between a white woman and a colored man, and therefore, the fact of an alliance is a proof of force. In numerous instances where colored men have been lynched on the charge of rape, it was positively known at the time of lynching, and indisputably proven after the victim's death, that the relationship sustained between the man and woman was voluntary and clandestine, and that in no court of law could even the charge of assault have been successfully maintained.

It was for the assertion of this fact, in the defense of her own race, that the writer hereof became an exile; her property destroyed and her return to her home forbidden under penalty of death, for writing the following editorial which was printed in her paper, the Free Speech, in Memphis, Tenn., May 21, 1892:

> Eight Negroes lynched since last issue of the Free Speech one at Little Rock, Ark., last Saturday morning where the citizens broke(?) into the penitentiary and got their man; three near Anniston, Ala., one near New Orleans; and three at Clarksville, Ga., the last three for killing a white man, and five on the same old racket—the new alarm about raping white women. The same programme of hanging, then shooting bullets into the lifeless bodies was carried out to the letter. Nobody in this section of the country believes the old threadbare lie that Negro men rape white women. If Southern white men are not careful, they will overreach themselves and public sentiment will have a reaction; a conclusion will then be reached which will be very damaging to the moral reputation of their women.

But threats cannot suppress the truth, and while the Negro suffers the soul deformity, resultant from two and a half centuries of slavery, he is no more guilty of this vilest of all vile charges than the white man who would blacken his name.

During all the years of slavery, no such charge was ever made, not even during the dark days of the rebellion, when the white man, following the fortunes of war went to do battle for the maintenance of slavery. While the master was away fighting to forge the fetters upon the slave, he left his wife and children with no protectors save the Negroes themselves. And yet during those years of trust and peril, no Negro proved recreant to his trust and no white man returned to a home that had been dispoiled.

Likewise during the period of alleged "insurrection," and alarming "race riots," it never occurred to the white man, that his wife and children were in danger of assault. Nor in the Reconstruction era, when the hue and cry was against "Negro Domination," was there ever a thought that the domination would ever contaminate a fireside or strike to death the virtue of womanhood. It must appear strange indeed, to every thoughtful and candid man, that more than a quarter of a century elapsed before the Negro began to show signs of such infamous degeneration.

In his remarkable apology for lynching, Bishop Haygood, of Georgia, says: "No race, not the most savage, tolerates the rape of woman, but it may be said without reflection upon any other people that the Southern people are now and always have been most sensitive concerning the honor of their women—their mothers, wives, sisters and daughters." It is not the purpose of this defense to say one word against the white women of the South. Such need not be said, but it is their misfortune that the chivalrous white men of that section, in order to escape the deserved execration of the civilized world, should shield themselves by their cowardly and infamously false excuse, and call into question that very honor about which their distinguished priestly apologist claims they are most sensitive. To justify their own barbarism they assume a chivalry which they do not possess. True chivalry respects all womanhood, and no one who reads the record, as it is written in the faces of the million mulattoes in the South, will for a minute conceive that the Southern white man had a very chivalrous regard for the honor due the women of his own race or respect for the womanhood which circumstances placed in his power. That chivalry which is "most sensitive concerning the honor of women" can hope for but little respect from the civilized world, when it confines itself entirely to the women who happen to be white. Virtue knows no color line, and the chivalry which depends upon complexion of skin and texture of hair can command no honest respect.

Selections from Wells, Ida B. "The Case Stated." In *The Red Record: Tabulated Statistics and Alleged Causes of Lynching in the United States*. N.p., 1895.

POST-READING PARS

1. Does Ida B. Wells believe that there are consensual relationships between African American men and white women? Why would that enrage white Southerners?

2. What does Wells mean by "to justify their own barbarism, they assume a chivalry which they do not possess"?

3. What proof does Wells offer to support her argument against white supremacy?

Inquiry Corner

Content Question:

How does Wells characterize the behavior of white Southern men? How does she call their chivalry into question?

Critical Question:

In today's parlance, we might call Ida B. Wells an intersectional feminist. The theory of intersectional feminism recognizes that barriers to gender equity vary according to other aspects of a woman's identity. How does her critique of white male chivalry reveal how African American and white women experienced victimization differently?

Comparative Question:

How does Wells's view of racial politics contrast with the views held by other African American contemporaries (consider Du Bois, Washington, Douglass, Haywood, or Parsons)?

Connection Question:

How does this excerpt by Ida B. Wells connect with things you may have read or heard about the contemporary Me Too movement started by Tarana Burke?

from Still Alive: *A Holocaust Girlhood Remembered* by Ruth Klüger

SNAPSHOT BOX

LANGUAGE: English
PUBLISHED: 2001, United States
GENRE: Memoir
TAGS: Autobiography and Testimony; Community; Family; Psyche; Race; War and Brutality

Introduction

How do you remember events from your past? How do communities remember their pasts? Who decides which events of the past should be recalled and how they should be remembered? Ruth Klüger's memoir *Still Alive: A Holocaust Girlhood Remembered* forces its readers to confront these questions, while challenging some established approaches in remembering the **Holocaust**.

Born in Vienna, Austria, in 1931, Klüger's childhood—or girlhood as she likes to emphasize—dramatically changed with the annexation of Austria by the Nazis in March 1938 and was henceforth dominated by exclusion, deportation, imprisonment, and escape. Austria became increasingly hostile toward Jews, and as a result Klüger was forced out of her school around the same time that her father lost his license to practice medicine. At eleven years old, Klüger was deported to the Theresienstadt concentration camp with her mother. After one year they were moved to **Auschwitz** and finally to a subcamp of the Gross-Rosen concentration camp, where both Klüger and her mother joined the immense population of forced laborers imprisoned at the camp. As Klüger recounts, she managed to survive by the coincidental overlap of a stranger's kindness and some pure luck. After the end of World War II, Klüger and her mother settled in southern Germany, before emigrating to the United States in 1947.

Published in 2001, her memoir is organized around these different sites of her life, spanning from Vienna to the camps to Germany and finally New York. In con-

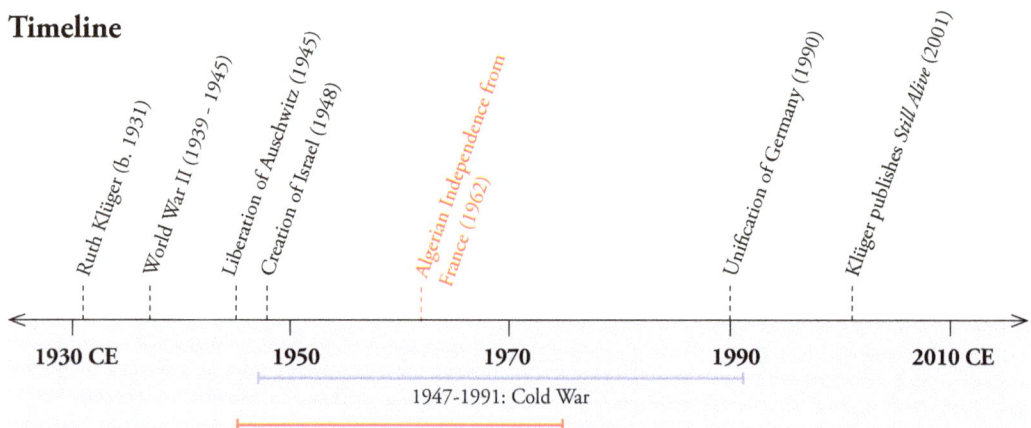

trast to authors such as Primo Levi or Elie Wiesel, who published their firsthand accounts about the Holocaust in 1947 and 1960 respectively, Klüger revisits her experiences of **anti-Semitism** and imprisonment from a significant historical distance, "half a century after the liberation of the camps," as she states. As a result, her text is simultaneously a representation of her life story and a reflection on memory and **memorialization** itself. Throughout her text, Klüger continuously moves between different voices and perspectives: of the child she was, of the adult remembering and writing about her childhood, of the literary scholar and professor of German, and of the Holocaust survivor. While all of these voices are of course united in Klüger, her narrative clearly shifts between them, and she self-reflectively puts the tensions that arise out of these overlapping voices at the center of her text. While Levi's and Wiesel's writings attempt to recount, remember, and memorialize their daily struggles against death during the Holocaust, Klüger's text moves beyond that and toward a critical review of the memorial and remembrance practices put in place in Germany and across the world since the end of World War II. Instead of solely sharing her pain, she forcefully pushes her readers away from the passive stance of pity and sadness toward an active engagement with their respective responsibility in remembering the Holocaust.

As part of her self-reflective writing, Klüger critically engages her ability to actually tell her life story, repeatedly questioning the authenticity and factual correctness of her memories. She is equally critical toward the collective memorialization process. In reading the passage below, consider why is she so discontented with the existing memorials and museums? How do memorial sites and personal experience currently interact, according to Klüger?

Regine Criser
Department of Languages and Literatures

> **PRE-READING PARS**
>
> 1. Name two or three other accounts of the Holocaust you know (books, movies, documentaries, etc.).
> 2. Brainstorm two or three examples of how communities—such as nations, faith communities, universities—remember and celebrate their history.
> 3. Recall a time when you visited a memorial/public monument. What emotions do you remember experiencing?

The Camps

Today more than half a century after the liberation of the camps, Germany is dotted with their carefully tended, unlovely remains: tourist attractions like the ruins of medieval castles. The same people who gather at noon in front of Munich's municipal hall to watch the pretty wooden figures emerge from the bell tower to do their jousting and dancing will take the bus to Dachau in the afternoon, somberly follow a guide, and pay obeisance to the old remains of Hitler's first concentration camp. If you are in the least interested in German literature, you'll want to travel to Weimar, Goethe's town, and once you are there, you feel obligated to trudge up the steep hill of nearby Buchenwald[59] in a show of awe and consternation. The camps are part of a worldwide museum culture of the Shoah, nowhere more evident than in Germany, where every sensitive citizen, not to mention every politician who wants to display his ethical credentials, feels the need to take pictures at these shrines or, even better, have his picture taken.

Yet to what purpose? Of course one is glad that the Germans, who had been in denial for so long that we thought they would never face themselves in the mirror of their past, finally did face up, and once they started, did so with the proverbial German thoroughness. And yet I feel something is missing. In the eighties I happened to spend time at the University of Göttingen, and one afternoon I invited a colleague's class to visit me at home. As I listened to two likable first-semester graduate students who were talking animatedly about Auschwitz, it dawned on me that they were using the name not as shorthand for the Holocaust in general, as has become customary, but concretely, for a place they seemed to know well. I questioned them without letting on that I had a previous acquaintance with the camp, and learned that they had done their alternative national service, their *Zivildienst*, there. Instead of serving in the military, they had whitewashed the fences at Auschwitz. I associate Tom Sawyer and his friends with whitewashed fences, and I wondered aloud whether this cheerful activity made any sense in an extermination camp. My doubts astonished them in turn. Preservation was a form of restitution, they argued. Not that they liked the

---

59. A concentration camp.

tourists (all those Americans!), and they were less than enthusiastic about the noisy schoolchildren with their know-it-all teachers. Nevertheless, the site of suffering has to be preserved.

And I ask myself: Why?

Drunken August, the darling of Viennese legend, spent a besotted night in a ditch full of dead bodies and awoke with only a hangover. He staggered out of the ditch, left it behind him, and continued to play his bagpipe. We are different. We don't get off so cheaply; the ghosts cling to us. Do we expect that our unsolved questions will be answered if we hang on to what's left: the place, the stones, the ashes? We don't honor the dead with these unattractive remnants of past crimes; we collect and keep them for the satisfaction of our own necrophilic desires. Violated taboos, such as child murder and mass murder, turn their victims into spirits, whom we offer a kind of home that they may haunt at will. Perhaps we are afraid they may leave the camps, and so we insist that their deaths were unique and must not be compared to any other losses or atrocities. Never again shall there be such a crime.

The same thing doesn't happen twice anyway. Every event, like every human being and even every dog, is unique. We would be condemned to be isolated monads if we didn't compare and generalize, for comparisons are the bridges from one unique life to another. In our hearts we all know that some aspects of the Shoah have been repeated elsewhere, today and yesterday, and will return in new guise tomorrow; and the camps, too, were only imitations (unique imitations, to be sure) of what had occurred the day before yesterday.

In today's Hiroshima, a busy industrial city, there is a memorial site to the great catastrophe which ushered in the atomic age. It is a park with flowers and temples, where Japanese children, in their English school uniforms, seem to have a thoroughly good time. The Japanese are as frustrated in coping with past horror as we are, because they, too, can think only of the mantra "Never again." It's easier to recognize this helplessness in a strange city. The children, with their history teachers in tow, hang origami toys, cranes, and other symbolic paper objects, on various bushes and trees dedicated to the goddess of peace, and then they romp about the park, screeching and chasing each other. There is the soothing sound of water, so typical of the aesthetics of Japanese landscaping, and tape-recorded messages with humanistic content are released at regular intervals. In the very midst of these efforts to propitiate and tranquilize the visitor, there is *the* monument, the ugliest ruin in the world: the building, we remember, wasn't hit by a bomb in the usual way; the bomb exploded above the building and disfigured it through heat, so that it looks as unnatural as a human face which has been ravaged by fire.

During a discussion with some youngsters in Germany I am asked (as if it was a genuine question and not an accusation) whether I don't think that the Jews have turned into Nazis in their dealings with the Arabs and haven't the Americans always acted like Nazis in their dealings with the Indians? When it gets that aggressive and simple, I just sputter. Or I sit in the student cafeteria with some advanced Ph.D. candidates, and one reports how in Jerusalem he made the acquaintance of an old Hungarian Jew who was a survivor of Auschwitz, and yet this man cursed the Arabs and held them all in contempt. How can someone who comes from Auschwitz talk like that? the German asks. I get into the act and argue, perhaps more hotly than need be. What did he expect? Auschwitz was no instructional institution, like the University of Göttingen, which he attends. You learned nothing there, and least of all humanity and tolerance. Absolutely nothing good came out of the concentration camps, I hear myself saying, with my voice rising, and he expects catharsis, purgation, the sort of thing you go to the theater for? They were the most useless, pointless establishments imaginable. That is the one thing to remember about them if you know nothing else. No one agrees, and no one contradicts me. Who wants to get into an argument with the old bag who's got that number on her arm? Germany's young intellectuals bow their heads over their soup plates and eat what's in front of them. Now I have silenced them, and that wasn't my intention. There is always a wall between the generations, but here the wall is barbed wire. Old, rusty barbed wire.

And yet they could easily have objected. Don't I often insist that I learned something in the camps about what happens to us in extreme situations, which was good to know later on and was usable precisely because I don't reject all comparisons? And don't I resent those who would deny me this knowledge and those who assume, without further inquiry, that we all lost our minds and morals there?

In the late sixties, when I was teaching in Cleveland, a young Jewish political scientist, engaged to a German woman, said to my face, without flinching: "I know what you survivors had to do to stay alive." I didn't know what we had had to do, but I knew what he wanted to say. He wanted to say, "You walked over dead bodies." Should I have answered, "But I was only twelve"? Or said, "But I am a good girl, always have been"? Both answers implicate the others, my fellow prisoners. Or I could have said, "Where do you get off talking like that?" and gotten angry. I said nothing, went home to my children, and was depressed. For in reality the cause of survival was almost pure chance.

So we few survivors are either the best or the worst. And yet, as Bertolt Brecht was fond of saying, the truth is concrete, meaning specific. The role that prison plays in the life of an ex-prisoner cannot be deduced from some shaky psychological rule, for it is different for each one of us, depending on what went before, on what came afterwards, and on what happened to each during his or her time in the camps. Though the Shoah involved millions of people, it was a unique experience for each of them.

The museum culture of the camp sites has been formed by the vagaries and neuroses of our unsorted, collective memory. It is based on a profound superstition, that is, on the belief that the ghosts can be met and kept in their place, where the living ceased to breathe. Or rather, not a profound, but a shallow superstition. A visitor who feels moved even if it is only the kind of feeling that a haunted house conveys, will be proud of these stirrings of humanity. And so the visitor monitors his reactions, examines his emotions, admires his own sensibility, or in other words, turns sentimental. For sentimentality involves turning away from an ostensible object and towards the subjective observer, that is, towards oneself. It means looking into a mirror instead of reality.

In contrast, a German psychiatrist of my generation, who is a good friend, tells me that right after the war she organized a group of other children and took them on an excursion to a nearby concentration camp. The camp was deserted, but the traces of the prisoners could still be seen: rusty objects, bits of clothing, and of course, the living quarters. It had been quickly abandoned after the liberation and had not been revisited. My friend says that there she got a whiff of the Shoah, and it wasn't a Shoah museum. Years later the teachers would shepherd their flocks to the same place, and if possible, steer their reactions along the right channels. But when my friend was there with her group, everything was still fresh; the blood had been shed but hadn't congealed yet. I imagine these children, open-mouthed, giggling with embarrassment, as they held up a tin spoon or stroked a straw mattress. They must have enjoyed the innocently guilty feeling of having pulled one over on the adults, having lifted a curtain and discovered a Bluebeard type of secret,[60] led and seduced by a plucky fellow student.

Or there is Claude Lanzmann, director of the unforgettable documentary *Shoah*, pursuing his tortured search for what happened where, his obsession with place the guiding principle of his film. "Was it three steps to the right or to the left of here?" he asks the natives, "In this or that spot?" "When were these trees planted? Were they part of the old site?" It's a fetish with him, I think, watching him on screen in the dark theater, half of me admiring him while the other half feels ahead of him. You need the places, I tell his image; I need only the names of the places. Yet what is the difference? We are entangled in the same web, only in different meshes.

I once visited Dachau with some Americans who had asked me to come along. It was a clean and proper place, and it would have taken more imagination than your average John or Jane Doe possesses to visualize the camp as it was forty years earlier. Today a fresh wind blows across the central square where the infamous roll calls took place, and the simple barracks of stone and wood suggest a youth hostel more easily than a setting for tortured lives. Surely some visitors secretly figure they can remember times when they have been worse off than the prisoners of this orderly German camp. The missing ingredients are the odor of fear emanating from human bodies, the concentrated aggression, the reduced minds. I didn't see the ghosts of the so-called *Muselmänner* (Muslims)[61] who dragged themselves zombielike through the long, evil hours, having lost the energy and the will to live. Sure, the signs and the

---

60. This is a reference to the Bluebeard folk tale, which has French roots and tells the story of a murderous husband, who hides the bodies of his murdered wives in a locked chamber in his castle. The tale tells the story of his newest wife discovering this horrible secret.

61. The translation in parentheses is problematic. "Muselmänner" was a term specifically used in concentration camps, mostly by Jewish prisoners, to describe those prisoners whose apathy toward their own impending death/fate was viewed derogatorily as a change in their faith.

documentation and the films help us to understand. But the camp as a memorial site? Landscape, seascape—there should be a word like *timescape* to indicate the nature of a place in time, that is, at a certain time, neither before nor after. Lanzmann's greatness, on the other hand, depends on his belief that place captures time and can display its victims like flies caught in amber.

It's all right to believe in ghosts, but you have to know to whom you are praying. One of my two Tom Sawyers is a good Christian and found plenty of opportunity for prayer in Auschwitz One—the core of the sprawling death facility—but he definitely didn't know the difference between the Good Lord and a ghost. For the former is personified serenity and holds all creation in the balance of his imagined hands, whereas the fence in need of refurbishing stood at best in limbo, the realm of the unredeemed. So it is only fitting that on this site a religious war has been raging, Jews against nuns,[62] our victims against your victims. Church dignitaries have a say, but there is no dignity here for the living or the dead. A stalking ground for ghosts, not God's acre.

These two students, who took an unintentional yet voluntary interest in my childhood refused stubbornly to admit the difference between Poles and Jews and to include Polish anti-Semitism in their meditations on good and evil. The Poles had been invaded and mistreated, so they must be good. How else are we to tell victims from victimizers? The camp sites hide as much as they communicate. At Auschwitz the Jewish victims have been so coopted into the Polish losses that my two Tom Sawyers couldn't handle the difference. They believed everything, even the worst, of their own grandfathers, they had unkind thoughts about the Allies, but they couldn't cope with criticism of the victims. That is, they were convinced that the grandparent generation was still in denial, and that the Allies hadn't liberated the concentration camps soon enough, although they could have, or at least bombed the rails that led to the camps. But they categorically refused to believe that the Poles weren't all that averse to getting rid of their Jews. They both energetically rejected my objection to tossing Christian and Jewish Poles into the same kettle, although I pointed out that it was mainly the Jews who went to the gas chambers, and the murdered children had all been Jewish and Gypsy[63] children. I was amazed how sure they were, these thoughtful and excellent specimens of what is best in the new Germany. And yet I hadn't even voiced my nastiest suspicion, about the hard currency which Jewish pilgrims, especially the American variety, bring to Poland and which has presumably made the Auschwitz museum into a lucrative venture for nearby Cracow. But I admit that I am more hard-boiled than I want others to be.

It won't do to pretend that we can evoke the physical reality of the camps as they were when they functioned. Nevertheless, I want my timescapes. Evocations of places

---

62. This refers to an incident from 1984 when Carmelite nuns tried to take over a building in Auschwitz.

63. This is considered a pejorative term for the people now correctly referred to as Roma.

at a time that has passed. I first wanted to call this book *Stations* and tie my diverse memories to the names I connect with them. (It seemed a modest title, until Catholic friends reminded me of the stations of the cross. Cultural differences: I hadn't even thought of it. Once it was pointed out, I was appalled at the unintended hubris.) Now ask myself, why place names, when I am a woman who has never lived anywhere for long? These are not the names of present or former homes; they are more like the piers of bridges that were blown up, only we can't be quite sure of what these bridges connected. Perhaps nothing with nothing. But if so, we have our work cut out for us, as we look out from the old piers. Because if we don't find the bridges, we'll either have to invent them or content ourselves with living in the no-man's-land between past and present. We start with what is left: the names of the places.

Remembering is a branch of witchcraft; its tool is incantation, I often say, as if it were a joke—but it's true—that instead of God I believe in ghosts. To conjure up the dead you have to dangle the bait of the present before them, the flesh of the living, to coax them out of their inertia. You have to grate and scrape the old roots with tools from the shelves of ancient kitchens. Use your best wooden spoons with the longest handles to whisk into the broth of our fathers the herbs our daughters have grown in their gardens. If I succeed, together with my readers—and perhaps a few men will join us in the kitchen—we could exchange magic formulas like favorite recipes and season to taste the marinade which the old stories and histories offer us, in as much comfort as our witches' kitchen provides. It won't get too cozy, don't worry: where we stir our cauldron, there will be cold and hot currents from half-open windows, unhinged doors, and earthquake-prone walls.

Klüger, Ruth. "The Camps." In *Still Alive: A Holocaust Girlhood Remembered*, 63–69. New York: Feminist Press at the City University of New York, 2012.

POST-READING PARS

1. In what ways is Klüger's voice/account similar and different to what you have read or seen about the Holocaust?

2. Klüger challenges contemporary attitudes toward concentration camps and survivors. What is her position and how does she explain her stance?

3. Klüger juxtaposes collective memory and individual experience. Find examples in the text and sort them into each category.

Inquiry Corner

Content Questions:

"Auschwitz was no instructional institution." What expectations does Klüger want to challenge with this statement? Why?

Critical Question:

How is Klüger's concept of "timespace" connected to her perspective on the usefulness of concentration camp memorials?

Comparative Question:

Compare Klüger's memoir to Olaudah Equiano's in terms of how we assess authenticity in each text.

Connection Questions:

What connections do you see between the current discourse in the United States about Confederate memorials and the discourse about concentration camps as memorial sites as represented by Klüger?

Who should decide how a community remembers/commemorates a significant event: those who were present/involved in the event or those who came after? Why?

BEYOND THE CLASSROOM

» We have museums, films, books, and podcasts that present graphic details of the suffering of communities. What are the ethical considerations around what, when, and how to engage with experiences that involve suffering, violence, and death (e.g., museum displays on lynching, holocaust memorials, etc.)? Who benefits from these engagements?

from "Strivings of the Negro People" by W. E. B. Du Bois

Introduction

W. E. B. Du Bois (1868–1963) graduated from Fisk University and, in 1895, became the first African American to receive a doctorate from Harvard. He was a brilliant scholar, trained in history with a broad background in the social sciences. Du Bois was an outspoken critic of Booker T. Washington's accommodationism that argued for African American communities developing vocational skills and economic stability instead of political and social equality with the whites. He believed that only a direct political response was adequate to counter Jim Crow legislation, the barriers to Black voting rights, and the tragic violence of lynching that punctuated the African American experience mostly in the South. At best, he contended, the dominant racist culture would always expect African Americans to do manual and domestic work under the supervision of whites. In the end, Du Bois could not accept the social segregation and restricted educational program advanced in Washington's "Atlanta Compromise."

> **SNAPSHOT BOX**
>
> LANGUAGE: English
>
> PUBLISHED: 1897, United States
>
> GENRE: Journal article
>
> TAGS: Accessing Rights; Autobiography and Testimony; Ethics and Morality; Psyche; Race; Struggle, Resistance, and Revolution; War and Brutality

Du Bois believed that it was necessary to protest racial inequality and to work vigorously through the legal system. He argued for integration, not accommodation, co-founding the National Association for the Advancement of Colored People (NAACP) in 1909. However, the process of achieving integration and political equality was slow. For example, it took until 1954 for the US Supreme

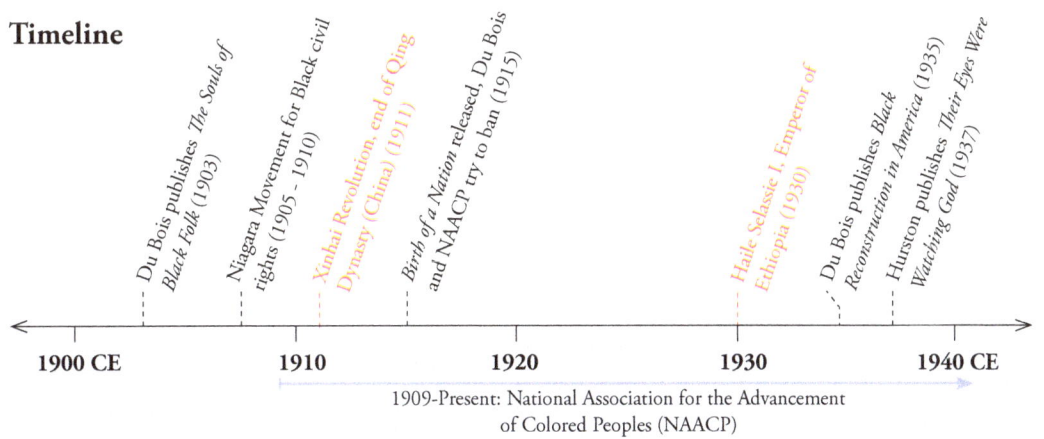

Court in its *Brown v. Board of Education* decision to finally outlaw segregation in the public schools. The Supreme Court ruling was not enforced, and, eventually, having suffered a number of political disappointments and setbacks, Du Bois became frustrated with the American system, drifting instead toward socialism and communism. When he was in his nineties, he renounced his American citizenship and lived the last years of his life in Ghana.

In "Strivings of the Negro People," first published in the *Atlantic Monthly* (1897), Du Bois directly confronts the issue of racial integration and Black identity. The goal of integration, he argues, is neither to Africanize America nor for African Americans to be lost in a sea of white Americanism. How does Du Bois describe the modern Black experience? How does he employ his concept of 'double consciousness' in this description? What sort of balance between the races does he want to achieve in American society? How might different cultural traditions enrich each other? What contributions of African culture does Du Bois find enriching for all Americans? Du Bois writes, "Work, culture and liberty—all these we need, not singly, but together." What are some of the arguments he offers for needing to have political, economic and cultural freedoms together?

Humanities Program Faculty

from "Strivings of the Negro People"

"It dawned upon me with a certain suddenness that I was different from the others; or like, mayhap, in heart and life and longing, but shut out from their world by a vast veil."

Between me and the other world there is ever an unasked question: unasked by some through feelings of delicacy; by others through the difficulty of rightly framing it. All, nevertheless, flutter round it. They approach me in a half-hesitant sort of way, eye me curiously or compassionately, and then, instead of saying directly, How does it feel to be a problem? they say, I know an excellent colored man in my town; or I fought at Mechanicsville; or, Do not these Southern outrages make your blood boil? At these I smile, or am interested, or reduce the boiling to a simmer, as the occasion may require. To the real question, How does it feel to be a problem? I answer seldom a word.

And yet, being a problem is a strange experience,—peculiar even for one who has never been anything else, save perhaps in babyhood and in Europe. It is in the early days of rollicking boyhood that the revelation first burst upon one, all in a day, as it were. I remember well when the shadow swept across me. I was a little thing, away up in the hills of New England, where the dark Housatonic winds between Hoosac and Taghanic to the sea. In a wee wooden schoolhouse, something put it into the boys' and girls' heads to buy gorgeous visiting-cards—ten cents a package—and exchange. The exchange was merry, till one girl, a tall newcomer, refused my card,—refused it peremptorily, with a glance. Then it dawned upon me with a certain suddenness that I was different from the others; or like, mayhap, in heart and life and longing, but shut out from their world by a vast veil. I had thereafter no desire to tear down that veil, to creep through; I held all beyond it in common contempt, and lived above it in a region of blue sky and great wandering shadows. That sky was bluest when I could beat my mates at examination-time, or beat them at a foot-race, or even beat their stringy heads. Alas, with the years all this fine contempt began to fade; for the world I longed for, and all its dazzling opportunities, were theirs, not mine. But they should not keep these prizes, I said; some, all, I would wrest from them. Just how I would do it I could never decide: by reading law, by healing the sick, by telling the wonderful tales that swam in my head,—some way. With other black boys the strife was not so fiercely sunny: their youth shrunk into tasteless sycophancy, or into silent hatred of the pale world about them and mocking distrust of everything white; or wasted itself in a bitter cry, Why did God make me an outcast and a stranger in mine own house? The "shades of the prison-house" closed round about us all: walls strait and stubborn to the whitest, but relentlessly narrow, tall, and unscalable to sons of night who must plod darkly against the stone, or steadily, half hopelessly watch the streak of blue above.

After the Egyptian and Indian, the Greek and Roman, the Teuton and Mongolian, the Negro[64] is a sort of seventh son, born with a veil, and gifted with second-sight

---

64. Du Bois uses the term "Negro" to refer to his own African American communities as was a prevalent practice within and outside of Black communities from the nineteenth to mid-twentieth centuries. The term "negro" should not be confused with the derogatory n-word. Like-

in this American world,—a world which yields him no self-consciousness, but only lets him see himself through the revelation of the other world. It is a peculiar sensation, this double-consciousness, this sense of always looking at one's self through the eyes of others, of measuring one's soul by the tape of a world that looks on in amused contempt and pity. One feels his two-ness—an American, a Negro; two souls, two thoughts, two unreconciled strivings; two warring ideals in one dark body, whose dogged strength alone keeps it from being torn asunder. The history of the American Negro is the history of this strife,—this longing to attain self-conscious manhood, to merge his double self into a better and truer self. In this merging he wishes neither of the older selves to be lost. He does not wish to Africanize America, for America has too much to teach the world and Africa; he does not wish to bleach his Negro blood in a flood of white Americanism, for he believes—foolishly, perhaps, but fervently—that Negro blood has yet a message for the world. He simply wishes to make it possible for a man to be both a Negro and an American without being cursed and spit upon by his fellows, without losing the opportunity of self-development.

This is the end of his striving: to be a co-worker in the kingdom of culture, to escape both death and isolation, and to husband and use his best powers. These powers, of body and of mind, have in the past been so wasted and dispersed as to lose all effectiveness, and to seem like absence of all power, like weakness. The double-aimed struggle of the black artisan, on the one hand to escape white contempt for a nation of mere hewers of wood and drawers of water, and on the other hand to plough and nail and dig for a poverty-stricken horde, could only result in making him a poor craftsman, for he had but half a heart in either cause. By the poverty and ignorance of his people the Negro lawyer or doctor was pushed toward quackery and demagogism, and by the criticism of the other world toward an elaborate preparation that overfitted him for his lowly tasks. The would-be black-savant was confronted by the paradox that the knowledge his people needed was a twice-told tale to his white neighbors, while the knowledge which would teach the white world was Greek to his own flesh and blood. The innate love of harmony and beauty that set the ruder souls of his people a-dancing, a-singing, and a-laughing raised but confusion and doubt in the soul of the black artist; for the beauty revealed to him was the soul-beauty of a race which his larger audience despised, and he could not articulate the message of another people.

This waste of double aims, this seeking to satisfy two unreconciled ideals, has wrought sad havoc with the courage and faith and deeds of eight thousand people, has sent them often wooing false gods and invoking false means of salvation, and has even at times seemed destined to make them ashamed of themselves. In the days of bondage they thought to see in one divine event the end of all doubt and disap-

---

wise another term used during the same timeframe, "colored," is outdated and should not be confused with the current usage of "person of color." Words reflecting African American and Black communities' preferences for self-identification continue to shift in meaning and connotation over time.

pointment; eighteenth-century Rousseauism never worshiped freedom with half the unquestioning faith that the American Negro did for two centuries. To him slavery was, indeed, the sum of all villainies, the cause of all sorrow, the root of all prejudice; emancipation was the key to a promised land of sweeter beauty than ever stretched before the eyes of wearied Israelites. In his songs and exhortations swelled one refrain, liberty; in his tears and curses the god he implored had freedom in his right hand. At last it came,—suddenly, fearfully, like a dream. With one wild carnival of blood and passion came the message in his own plaintive cadences: —

> Shout, O children!
> Shout, you're free!
> The Lord has bought your liberty!

Years have passed away, ten, twenty, thirty. Thirty years of national life, thirty years of renewal and development, and yet the swarthy ghost of Banquo sits in its old place at the national feast. In vain does the nation cry to its vastest problem, —

> Take any shape but that, and my firm nerves
> Shall never tremble!

The freedman has not yet found in freedom his promised land. Whatever of lesser good may have come in these years of change, the shadow of a deep disappointment rests upon the Negro people,—a disappointment all the more bitter because the unattained ideal was unbounded save by the simple ignorance of a lowly folk.

[...]

The first decade was merely a prolongation of the vain search for freedom, the boon that seemed ever barely to elude their grasp,—like a tantalizing will-o'-the wisp, maddening and misleading the headless host. The holocaust of war, the terrors of the Kuklux Klan, the lies of carpet-baggers, the disorganization of industry, and the contradictory advice of friends and foes left the bewildered serf with no new watchword beyond the old cry for freedom. As the decade closed, however, he began to grasp a new idea. The ideal of liberty demanded for its attainment powerful means, and these the Fifteenth Amendment gave him. The ballot, which before he had looked upon as a visible sign of freedom, he now regarded as the chief means of gaining and perfecting the liberty with which war had partially endowed him. And why not? Had not votes made war and emancipated millions? Had not votes enfranchised the freedmen? Was anything impossible to a power that had done all this? A million black men started with renewed zeal to vote themselves into the kingdom. The decade fled away,—a decade containing, to the freedman's mind, nothing but suppressed votes, stuffed ballot-boxes, and election outrages that nullified his vaunted right of suffrage. And yet that decade from 1875 to 1885 held another powerful movement, the rise of another ideal to guide the unguided, another pillar of fire by night after a clouded day. It was the ideal of "book-learning;" the curiosity, born of compulsory ignorance, to know and test the power of the cabalistic letters of the white man, the longing to know. Mission and night schools began in the smoke of battle, ran the gauntlet of reconstruction and at last developed into permanent foundations. Here at last seemed to have been discovered the mountain path to Canaan; longer than the highway of emancipation and law, steep and rugged, but straight, leading to heights high enough to overlook life.

Up the new path the advance guard toiled, slowly, heavily, doggedly; only those who have watched and guided the faltering feet, the misty minds, the dull understandings, of the dark pupils of these schools know how faithfully, how piteously, this people strove to learn. It was weary work. The cold statistician wrote down the inches of progress here and there, noted also where here and there a foot had slipped or some one had fallen. To the tired climbers, the horizon was ever dark, the mists were often cold, the Canaan was always dim and far away. If, however, the vistas disclosed as yet no goal, no resting-place, little but flattery and criticism, the journey at least gave leisure for reflection and self-examination; it changed the child of emancipation to the youth with dawning self-consciousness, self-realization, self-respect. In those sombre forests of his striving his own soul rose before him, and he saw himself,—darkly as through a veil; and yet he saw in himself some faint revelation of his power, of his mission. He began to have a dim feeling that, to attain his place in the world, he must be himself, and not another. For the first time he sought to analyze the burden he bore upon his back, that dead-weight of social degradation partially masked behind a half-named Negro problem. he felt his poverty; without a cent, without a home, without land, tools, or savings, he had entered into competition with rich landed, skilled neighbors. To be a poor man is hard, but to be a poor race in a land of dollars is the very bottom of hardships. He felt the weight of his ignorance,—not simply of letters, but of life, of business, of the humanities; the accumulated sloth and shirking and awkwardness of decades and centuries shackled his hands and feet. Nor was his burden all poverty and ignorance. The red stain of bastardy, which two centuries of systematic legal defilement of Negro women had stamped upon his race, meant not only the loss of ancient African chastity, but also the hereditary weight of a mass of filth from white whoremongers and adulterers, threatening almost the obliteration of the Negro home.

A people thus handicapped ought not to be asked to race with the world, but rather allowed to give all its time and thought to its own social problems. But alas! while sociologists gleefully count his bastards and his prostitutes, the very soul of the toiling, sweating black man is darkened by the shadow of a vast despair. Men call the shadow prejudice, and learnedly explain it as the natural defense of culture against barbarism, learning against ignorance, purity against crime, the "higher" against the "lower" races. To which the Negro cries Amen! and swears that to so much this strange prejudice as is founded on just homage to civilization, culture, righteousness, and progress he humbly bows and meekly does obeisance. But before that nameless prejudice that leaps beyond all this he stands helpless, dismayed, and well-nigh speechless; before that personal disrespect and mockery, the ridicule and systematic humiliation, the distortion of fact and wanton license of fancy, the cynical ignoring of the better and boisterous welcoming of the worse, the all-pervading desire to inculcated disdain for everything black, from Toussaint to the devil,—before this there rises a sickening despair that would disarm and discourage any nation save that black host to whom "discouragement" is an unwritten word.

They still press on, they still nurse the dogged hope,—not a hope of nauseating patronage, not a hope of reception into charmed social circles of stock-jobbers, pork-packers, and earl-hunters, but the hope of a higher synthesis of civilization and humanity, a true progress, with which the chorus "Peace, good will to men,"

May make one music as before,

But vaster.

Thus the second decade of the American Negro's freedom was a period of conflict, of inspiration and doubt, of faith and vain questionings, of Sturm und Drang. The ideals of physical freedom, of political power, of school training, as separate all-sufficient panaceas for social ills, became in the third decade dim and overcast. They were the vain dreams of credulous race childhood; not wrong, but incomplete and over-simple. The training of the schools we need to-day more than ever,—the training of deft hands, quick eyes and ears, and the broader, deeper, higher culture of gifted minds. The power of the ballot we need in sheer self-defense, and as a guarantee of good faith. We may misuse it, but we can scarce do worse in this respect than our whilom masters. Freedom, too, the long-sought, we still seek,—the freedom of life and limb, the freedom to work and think. Work, culture, and liberty—all these we need, not singly, but together; for to-day these ideals among the Negro people are gradually coalescing, and finding a higher meaning in the unifying ideal of race,—the ideal of fostering the traits and talents of the Negro, not in opposition to, but in conformity with, the greater ideals of the American republic, in order that some day, on American soil, two world races may give each to each those characteristics which both so sadly lack. Already we come not altogether empty-handed: there is to-day no true American music but the sweet wild melodies of the Negro slave; the American fairy tales are Indian and African; we are the sole oasis of simple faith and reverence in a dusty desert of dollars and smartness. Will America be poorer if she replace her brutal, dyspeptic blundering with the light-hearted but determined Negro humility; or her coarse, cruel wit with loving, jovial good humor; or her Annie Rooney with Steal Away?

Merely a stern concrete test of the underlying principles of the great republic is the Negro problem, and the spiritual striving of the freedmen's sons is the travail of souls whose burden is almost beyond the measure of their strength, but who bear it in the name of an historic race, in the name of this the land of their fathers' fathers, and in the name of human opportunity.

Du Bois, W. E. Burghardt. "Strivings of the Negro People." *The Atlantic*, August 1897. Atlantic Media Company, republished August 19, 2019. https://www.theatlantic.com/magazine/archive/1897/08/strivings-of-the-negro-people/305446/.

"White Things" by Anne Bethel Spencer

Introduction

SNAPSHOT BOX

LANGUAGE: English
PUBLISHED: 1923, Harlem, New York
GENRE: Poetry
INFLUENCES: Harlem Renaissance
TAGS: Art; Body; Poetry, Music, Literature; Psyche; Race; Struggle, Resistance, and Revolution; Tradition

Anne Bethel Spencer (1882–1975) was born in Henry County, Virginia. The daughter of former slaves, she attended Virginia Theological Seminary and College, now Virginia University-Lynchburg, and graduated as her class's valedictorian. She married Edward Spencer in 1901, and the couple resided in Lynchburg for the remainder of their lives. Until her death in 1975, Spencer played an important role as a poet, activist, and host in the **Harlem Renaissance**—also known as the New Negro Movement (c. 1918–1937)—a period of heightened intellectual and cultural production of African American art, music, stage performances, fashion, literature, and political consciousness. While Harlem served as the symbolic center of this cultural awakening, the renaissance spread widely and became the most influential movement among African American artists seeking to reclaim their identity and racial pride in defiance of racist beliefs and stereotypes.

Spencer made her home much like the **Parisian salons** of the 1700s by bringing together remarkable intellectual and talented personalities such as Mary McLeod Bethune, Paul Robeson, Langston Hughes, Gwendolyn Brooks, George Washington Carver, Martin Luther King Jr., W. E. B. Du Bois, Thurgood Marshall, and Marian Anderson. Black exiles and expatriates from the Caribbean and Africa like Marcus Garvey, Claude McKay, and Léopold Sédar Senghor crossed paths with African Americans moving from rural to urban spaces and from South to North, in what is

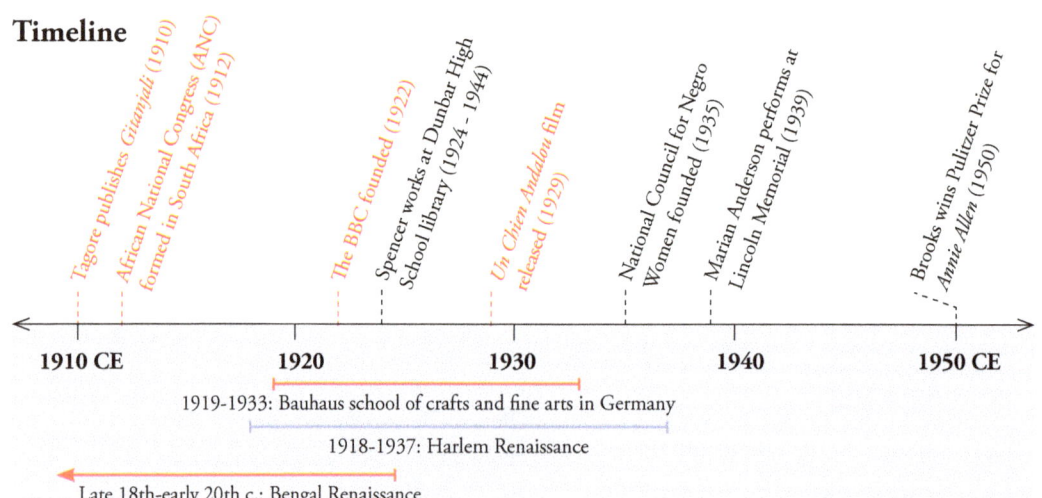

known as the **Great Migration**. Their interactions gave the renaissance a broader international perspective and invigorated Pan-African sensibilities. Since Jim Crow laws prevented Blacks from staying in Lynchburg's hotels, Spencer's hospitable and intellectually stimulating home became a safe haven for cultural, political, and social discussions affecting African American lives. What types of spaces do you think are conducive to fostering dynamic intellectual and cultural pursuits in the face of entrenched social and political marginalization? In 1919, Spencer worked with writer and civil rights activist James Weldon Johnson and others to establish the Lynchburg chapter of the NAACP (National Association for the Advancement of Colored People) and also campaigned to hire Black teachers. From 1924–1944, Spencer worked as the first librarian at Dunbar High School, an African American school named after Black poet Paul Laurence Dunbar. The school was founded in 1923 by an all-white school board as a result of the advocacy of the local African American community.

In her poems, Spencer often used nature imagery inspired by her garden, and themes concerning race, religion, gender, freedom, human relations, values, power, and subjugation, as demonstrated by the poem, "White Things," presented here. This poem was first published in 1923 in the *Crisis*—considered the world's oldest Black publication founded in 1910 and edited by W. E. B. Du Bois. Her poems were anthologized in *The Book of American Negro Poetry* (1922) and *Caroling Dusk* (1927). Spencer was also the first African American woman to be featured in *The Norton Anthology of Modern Poetry* (1973). Posthumous publications include *Time's Unfading Garden: Anne Spencer's Life and Poetry* (1977), *Anne Spencer: "Ah, how poets sing and die!"* (2001), *Half My World: The Garden of Anne Spencer, A History and Guide* (2003), and *Lessons Learned from a Poet's Garden* (2011). What other examples can you list where poetry (word play, imagery, lyrics) and social justice combine?

In 1976, her house and garden were designated a Virginia Historic Landmark, a Friends of the Library USA Literary Landmark, and a Historic Landmark by the Association for the Study for Afro-American Life and History. A selection of Spencer's papers, books, and photographs are archived in the Albert and Shirley Small Special Collections Library at the University of Virginia in Charlottesville, and another collection is maintained at the Beinecke Rare Book and Manuscript Library at Yale University.

Mildred Barya
Department of English

> **PRE-READING PARS**
>
> 1. Make a list of two to four items that symbolize the color white.
> 2. Brainstorm three or four examples of metaphors from your everyday life.
> 3. List three or four social, cultural, environmental, or political issues that you care about and wish to support.

White Things

Most things are colorful things—the sky, earth, and sea.
Black men are most men; but the white are free!
White things are rare things; so rare, so rare
They stole from out a silvered world—somewhere.
Finding earth-plains fair plains, save greenly grassed,
They strewed white feathers of cowardice, as they passed;
The golden stars with lances fine
The hills all red and darkened pine,
They blanched with their wand of power;
And turned the blood in a ruby rose
To a poor white poppy-flower.
They pyred a race of black, black men,
And burned them to ashes white; then,
Laughing, a young one claimed a skull,
For the skull of a black is white, not dull,
But a glistening awful thing;
Made, it seems, for this ghoul to swing
In the face of God with all his might,
And swear by the hell that sired him:
"Man-maker, make white!"

Spencer, Anne B. "White Things." *The Crisis*, March 1923. Copyright The Anne Spencer Memorial Foundation.

> **POST-READING PARS**
>
> 1. How does Spencer use the color white to symbolize subjugation of the Black race?
> 2. Identify three or four examples of metaphors used in the poem.
> 3. List three or four social, cultural, environmental, and political issues that Spencer highlights in the poem.

Inquiry Corner

Content Question:

What are some of the observations that Spencer makes about nature, and relations between whites and Blacks?

Critical Question:

Explore ways in which supremacy of whiteness is maintained through oppression and violent destruction of other colors in the poem.

Comparative Question:

What ideas and principles of the Enlightenment period are expressed in Spencer's poetry in comparison to other works on Enlightenment you have read in this class.

Connection Question:

Using appropriate line breaks, write a short, two-stanza poem describing your values, mood, and setting in a manner that echoes some of the elements in Spencer's poem.

"Declaration of Independence of the Democratic Republic of Vietnam" by Ho Chi Minh

SNAPSHOT BOX

LANGUAGE: Vietnamese

GENRE: Public address

DELIVERED: Hanoi, Vietnam, September 2, 1945

TAGS: Colonization; History and Ideology; Self-Determination; Statecraft

Introduction

From the latter part of the nineteenth century until the 1950s and early 1960s, the Great Powers—Great Britain, France, Germany (until World War I), Belgium, the Netherlands, Portugal, and even the United States—had colonial empires throughout large parts of Africa and Southeast Asia. The commonly used rationale for these practices was that these Great Powers perceived themselves as bringing "civilization" to people in other parts of the globe who were viewed as uncivilized. The reality, of course, was much different, and colonialism was marked by the worst forms of economic exploitation and gross and systemic human rights violations carried out against these subjugated populations. Another factor that complicates all this is the way in which those under colonial rule sought to use Western values, such as political freedom and sovereignty, as a means of achieving independence, but to little avail.

Despite the great damage done by the colonizers, the colonized often employed Western ideals and structures in the construction of their own independence struggles.

Vietnam, which was a French colony from the 1870s until 1954, is a revealing case study of these complicated colonial relationships. At the Paris Peace talks following World War I, President Woodrow Wilson issued his famous Fourteen Points state-

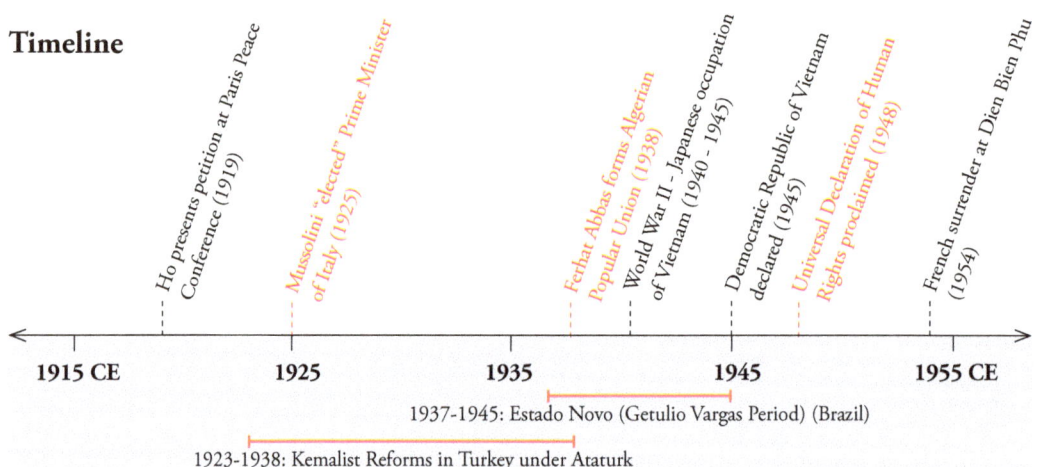

ment of principles, which called for, among other things, the self-determination of all people. Yet, when Ho Chi Minh and others in the Vietnamese resistance movement to colonialism presented a petition at the Paris Conference appealing to the Allied leaders at Versailles to apply President Wilson's ideals to France's colonial territories in Southeast Asia, they were ignored.

In the wake of World War II, in the midst of their recovery from five years of ruthless economic exploitation and brutal human rights violations by the Japanese, the people of Vietnam again sought an end to eighty years of French colonialism. Organized together as the League for the Independence of Vietnam (Vietnam Doc Lap Dong Minh Hoi), better known as the Viet Minh, Vietnamese nationalists fought against the Japanese invaders as well as the defeated French colonial authorities. With the support of rich and poor peasants, workers, businessmen, landlords, students, and intellectuals, the Viet Minh, led by Ho Chi Minh, spread throughout northern Vietnam where it established new local governments, redistributed some lands, and opened granaries to alleviate famine. On September 2, 1945, Ho proclaimed the independent Democratic Republic of Vietnam in Hanoi's Ba Dinh Square. The first lines of his speech repeat verbatim the famous second paragraph of America's 1776 Declaration of Independence. What purposes and/or rhetorical strategies do you think importing a section from the Declaration of Independence served?

This attempt to invoke Western liberal values was disregarded once again. Soon enough, the French returned to Vietnam to reclaim what they viewed as "theirs." The resistance against French rule continued until the decisive battle of Dien Bien Phu in 1954, where the French surrendered. This, of course, is not the end of the story. What soon followed was the American War—or what is referred to in the United States as the Vietnam War—resulting in the deaths of millions of Vietnamese civilians, as well as more than 50,000 US service personnel.

With hindsight, there may have been ways to avoid the great tragedy that occurred in Vietnam. On two separate occasions, Ho Chi Minh invoked not only "Western values," but, more particularly, "American values" as a way of justifying the demand for Vietnam's independence. Yet, both times these entreaties were ignored. Do you think the distinction between "American values" and "Western values" is a viable and/or useful one? What might be some examples of "American values" that are more distinct than those potentially shared more broadly as "Western values"? Why do you think Western states fail to recognize or outright ignore "Western values" when these are adopted by colonized peoples in their struggles for independence?

Mark Gibney
Department of Political Science

Declaration of Independence of the Democratic Republic of Vietnam

"We hold truths that all men are created equal, that they are endowed by their Creator with certain inalienable rights, among them are Life, Liberty, and the pursuit of Happiness."

This immortal statement was made in the Declaration of Independence of the United States of America in 1776. In a broader sense, this means: All the peoples on the earth are equal from birth, all the peoples have a right to live, to be happy and free.

The Declaration of the French Revolution made in 1791 on the Rights of Man and the Citizen also states: "All men are born free and with equal rights, and must always remain free and have equal rights."

Those are undeniable truths.

Nevertheless, for more than eighty years, the French imperialists, abusing the standard of Liberty, Equality, and Fraternity, have violated our Fatherland and oppressed our fellow-citizens. They have acted contrary to the ideals of humanity and justice.

In the field of politics, they have deprived our people of every democratic liberty.

They have enforced inhuman laws; they have set up three distinct political regimes in the North, the Center and the South of Vietnam in order to wreck our national unity and prevent our people from being united.

They have built more prisons than schools. They have mercilessly slain our patriots; they have drowned our uprisings in rivers of blood.

They have fettered public opinion; they have practiced obscurantism against our people.

To weaken our race they have forced us to use opium and alcohol.

In the field of economics, they have fleeced us to the backbone, impoverished our people, and devastated our land.

They have robbed us of our rice fields, our mines, our forests, and our raw materials.

They have monopolized the issuing of bank-notes and the export trade.

They have invented numerous unjustifiable taxes and reduced our people, especially our peasantry, to a state of extreme poverty.

They have hampered the prospering of our national bourgeoisie; they have mercilessly exploited our workers.

In the autumn of 1940, when the Japanese fascists violated Indochina's territory to establish new bases in their fight against the Allies, the French imperialists went down on their bended knees and handed over our country to them.

Thus, from that date, our people were subjected to the double yoke of the French and the Japanese. Their sufferings and miseries increased. The result was that from the end of last year to the beginning of this year, from Quang Tri province to the North of Vietnam, more than two million of our fellow-citizens died from starvation. On March 9, the French troops were disarmed by the Japanese. The French colonialists either fled or surrendered showing that not only were they incapable of "protecting" us, but that, in the span of five years, they had twice sold our country to the Japanese.

On several occasions before March 9, the Vietminh League urged the French to ally themselves with it against the Japanese. Instead of agreeing to this proposal, the French colonialists so intensified their terrorist activities against the Vietminh members that before fleeing they massacred a great number of our political prisoners detained at Yen Bay and Caobang.

Notwithstanding all this, our fellow-citizens have always manifested toward the French a tolerant and humane attitude. Even after the Japanese putsch of March 1945, the Vietminh League helped many Frenchmen to cross the frontier, rescued some of them from Japanese jails, and protected French lives and property.

From the autumn of 1940, our country had in fact ceased to be a French colony and had become a Japanese possession.

After the Japanese had surrendered to the Allies, our whole people rose to regain our national sovereignty and to found the Democratic Republic of Vietnam.

The truth is that we have wrested our independence from the Japanese and not from the French.

The French have fled, the Japanese have capitulated, Emperor Bao Dai has abdicated.

Our people have broken the chains which for nearly a century have fettered them and have won independence for the Fatherland. Our people at the same time have overthrown the monarchic regime that has reigned supreme for dozens of centuries. In its place has been established the present Democratic Republic.

For these reasons, we, members of the Provisional Government, representing the whole Vietnamese people, declare that from now on we break off all relations of a colonial character with France; we repeal all the international obligation that France has so far subscribed to on behalf of Vietnam and we abolish all the special rights the French have unlawfully acquired in our Fatherland.

The whole Vietnamese people, animated by a common purpose, are determined to fight to the bitter end against any attempt by the French colonialists to reconquer their country.

We are convinced that the Allied nations which at Tehran and San Francisco have acknowledged the principles of self-determination and equality of nations, will not refuse to acknowledge the independence of Vietnam.

A people who have courageously opposed French domination for more than eight years, a people who have fought side by side with the Allies against the fascists during these last years, such a people must be free and independent.

For these reasons, we, members of the Provisional Government of the Democratic Republic of Vietnam, solemnly declare to the world that Vietnam has the right to be a free and independent country—and in fact is so already. The entire Vietnamese people are determined to mobilize all their physical and mental strength, to sacrifice their lives and property in order to safeguard their independence and liberty.

"Declaration of Independence of the Democratic Republic of Vietnam." In *Selected Works*, vol. 3, 17–21. Hanoi: Foreign Languages Publishing House, 1960–62.

"Declaration of the Rights of Woman and Citizen" by Olympe de Gouges

Introduction

Although the democratic revolutions of the eighteenth century purported to advance liberty for all, their benefits accrued primarily to white men. Their radicalism inhered in what they destroyed—monarchy, aristocracy—as much as what they created—balanced, representative government. Nonetheless, excluded people have demanded—and sometimes secured—inclusion in the rights of man throughout world history via protest, rebellion, and authorship, especially in the early phases of revolutions. As a playwright and pamphleteer, Marie Gouze (1748–1793), also known as Olympe de Gouges, drew attention to the particular form of revolutionary hypocrisy that perpetuated slavery and women's inequality. Enjoying the momentary opening of opportunities for women to petition, meet, publish, and perform, de Gouges earned some celebrity in the early years of the French Revolution as a feminist and abolitionist until her execution in 1793.

> **SNAPSHOT BOX**
>
> LANGUAGE: French
> GENRE: Manifesto
> PUBLISHED: 1791, Paris
> TAGS: Body; Family; Struggle, Resistance, and Revolution; Women and Power

Copying the spirit and structure of the "Declaration of the Rights of Man and Citizen," promulgated in 1789 as the preamble to a new constitution, de Gouges rendered the revolutionary catechism gender-inclusive in her "Declaration of the Rights of Woman and the Female Citizen," the entirety of which is reprinted here. Merely by including "and woman" in each of the original seventeen articles, de Gouges ex-

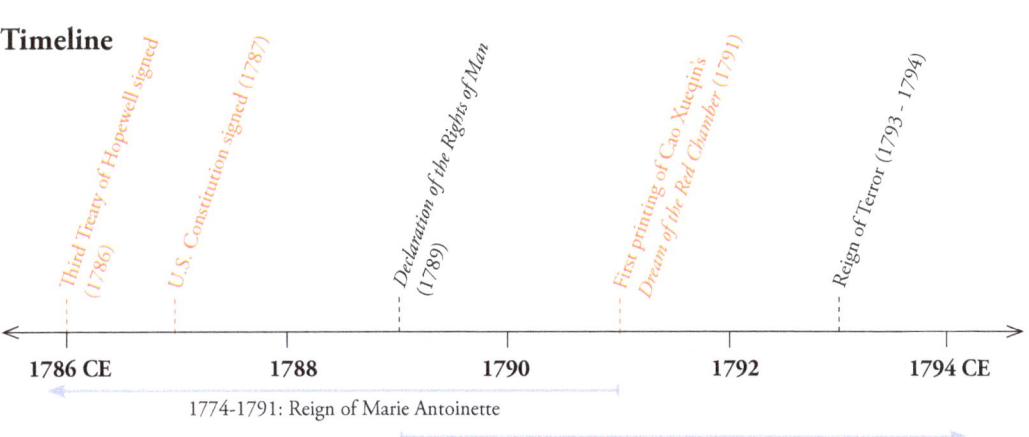

Timeline

- Third Treaty of Hopewell signed (1786)
- U.S. Constitution signed (1787)
- Declaration of the Rights of Man (1789)
- First printing of Cao Xueqin's Dream of the Red Chamber (1791)
- Reign of Terror (1793 - 1794)

1774-1791: Reign of Marie Antoinette
1789-1799: French Revolution

posed how the universal subject "man" was not in fact universal. In some of the articles, the addition of "woman" enables a glimpse at the particular circumstances of women; see, for example, Article Eleven on free speech. How does the act or revising an official document complicate the author's authority and agency? Her most pronounced critique of patriarchy, however, can be found in the pre- and postambles, where she described the connection between the oppression of women and the corruption of the Old Regime.

Born in a small town in Southern France where her father was a butcher, Marie Gouze changed her name when she moved to Paris to "Olympe," recalling classical Athens and "de Gouges," which sounded vaguely aristocratic. What other purposes and connections are made through other instances of changing one's name? Paris in the 1780s attracted aspiring artists, authors, and politicians, women as well as men. De Gouges thus immersed herself in an intellectual milieu where her ideas would be taken seriously. However, as revolutionary politics shifted in a more radical direction by 1792, her affiliation with the moderate Girondin faction of the National Assembly made her loyalty to the revolution suspect. When she addressed the "Declaration" to the queen, however ironically, she set herself against the regicide majority in the government, which put her to death in 1793, the same month that Queen Marie Antoinette was guillotined.

Despite censure of women activists like herself, the radical government implemented many of the progressive ideas she advocated, including abolition of slavery, divorce by mutual consent, equitable inheritance, and erasure of stigmas against "illegitimate" children and their mothers. Indeed, changes to family, status, and property law affected more people than any other legislative acts until reversals under Napoleon and the Restoration stripped away what little gains women had made during the revolution. Women were denied a formal role in politics, for example, only gaining the right to vote in France in 1945. For a century and a half, feminists evoked de Gouges as a visionary and precursor. Even in the United States, advocates for women's rights like Elizabeth Cady Stanton deployed strategies used by earlier feminists across the Atlantic, which included adding "woman" to founding documents; see, for example, Stanton's "Declaration of Sentiments," a feminist's answer to the "Declaration of Independence."

Tracey Rizzo
Department of History

> **PRE-READING PARS**
>
> 1. What unfounded justifications come to mind that blame women for their own oppression?
> 2. What two or three strategies have you seen feminists or other activists use to effect changes in law and in attitudes?

Declaration of the Rights of Woman and Citizen (1791)

To the Queen

Madame,

Little skilled in the language appropriate to addressing royalty, I will not employ a courtesan's adulation to pay you homage with this unique work. Madame, my purpose is to speak to you frankly. I have not awaited the epoch of liberty to express myself thus; I displayed as much energy in a time when the blindness of despots punished such noble audacity.

When the whole empire accused you and held you responsible for its calamities, I alone in a time of trouble and storm, I alone had the strength to take up your defense. I have never been able to persuade myself that a princess raised in the midst of grandeur had all the vices of baseness.

[...]

Madame, may a nobler function [than plotting against the government] characterize you, excite your ambition, and fix your attention. It belongs to one whom chance has elevated to an eminent place to give weight to the progress of the Rights of Woman, and to hasten its success. If you were less well informed, Madame, I would fear that your individual interests would outweigh those of your sex. You love glory: consider, madame, that the greatest crimes become immortal like the greatest virtues, but what a different fame in the annals of history. One is ceaselessly cited as an example, the other is eternally the execration of the human race.

It will never be a crime for you to work for the restoration of morals, to give to your sex all the credit it is due. This is not the work of one day, unfortunately for the new regime. This revolution will happen only when all women fathom the depth of their deplorable fate, and of the rights they have lost in society. Undertake, madame, such a beautiful cause; defend this unfortunate sex and you will soon have one half the kingdom on your side, and at least one third of the other half.

Madame, with the deepest respect I am your most humble and obedient servant.

The Rights of Woman

Man, are you capable of being just? It is a woman who poses the question; at least you will not take away this right. Tell me, what has given you the sovereign empire to oppress my sex? Your strength? Your talents? Observe the Creator in his wisdom; look at nature in all her grandeur, with whom you seem to want to be in harmony, and give me, if you dare, an example of this tyrannical empire.

Go back to the animals, consult the elements, study plants, finally cast a glance over all the modifications of organized matter, and submit to the evidence when I offer it to you; search, probe and distinguish, if you can, the sexes in the administration of nature. Everywhere you will find them mingled, everywhere they cooperate with a unity harmonious to the immortal masterpiece.

Man alone has dressed up this exception as a principle. Bizarre, blind, bloated with science and degenerated-in the century of light and wisdom in the crassest ignorance, he wants to command as a despot this sex which has received all intellectual faculties; he pretends to enjoy the revolution and reclaim his rights to equality only to say nothing more about it.

Declaration of the Rights of Woman and Citizen

Preamble

Mothers, daughters, sisters, representatives of the Nation, demand to be constituted into a national assembly. Considering that ignorance, forgetfulness, or scorn for the rights of woman are the sole causes of public misfortune and corrupt government, [women] have resolved to expose in a solemn declaration the natural, inalienable, and sacred rights of woman in order that this declaration, constantly presented to all members of society, will ceaselessly recall them to their rights and duties; in order that the powerful acts of women and the powerful acts of men can be compared at each instant with the purpose of every political institution, in being more respected, so that the demands of female citizens, henceforth founded on simple and incontestable principles, turn always towards the maintenance of the constitution, good morals, and the happiness of everyone.

Consequently, the sex that is superior in beauty as in the courage of maternal suffering recognizes and declares in the presence and under the auspices of the Supreme Being, the following rights of woman and of female citizens:

Article One

Woman is born free and lives equal to man in her rights. Social distinctions may be founded only upon common utility.

Article Two

The purpose of any political association is the conservation of the natural and imprescriptible rights of woman and man; these rights are liberty, property, security, and above all resistance to oppression.

Article Three

The principle of all sovereignty essentially resides in the Nation, which is nothing more than the union of woman and man: no body, no individual can exercise authority which does not emanate from it.

Article Four

Liberty and justice consist in rendering all that belongs to others; thus the exercise of the natural rights of woman has only been limited by the perpetual tyranny that man opposes to it; these limits should be reformed by the laws of nature and reason.

Article Five

The laws of nature and reason prohibit all actions harmful to society: anything that is not prohibited by these wise and divine laws cannot be prevented, and no one can be constrained to do that which they do not order.

Article Six

The law should be the expression of the general will; all female and male citizens should concur personally, or by their representatives, in its formation it should be the same for all: all female and male citizens, being equal in its eyes, should be equally admissible to every honor, position, and public employment, according to their capacities, and without any distinction than those of their virtues and talents.

Article Seven

No woman is excepted; she is accused, arrested, and detained in cases determined by law. Women, like men, obey this rigorous law.

Article Eight

The law should only establish those penalties strictly and obviously necessary, and no one can be punished except by a law established and promulgated prior to the crime and legally applicable to women.

Article Nine

Any woman found guilty [is subject to] every rigor of the law.

Article Ten

No one should be disquieted for holding basic opinions; woman has the right to mount the scaffold; she should equally have the right to mount the podium, provided that her demonstrations do not trouble the public order established by law.

Article Eleven

The free communication of thoughts and opinions is one of the most precious rights of woman, since that liberty assures the legitimacy of children vis-a-vis their fathers. Every citizen should be able to say freely, "I am the mother of the child who belongs to you," without being forced by a barbarous prejudice to hide the truth; [an exception may be made] to respond to the abuse of this liberty in cases determined by law.

Article Twelve

The guarantee of the rights of woman and citizen entails a major benefit; this guarantee should be instituted for the advantage of all, and not for the particular benefit of those to whom it is entrusted.

For the support of the public force, and for the expenses of administration, the contributions of woman and man are equal; she shares a part in all duties and difficult tasks; she should thus have the same share in the distribution of positions, employment, offices, honors, and jobs.

Female and male citizens have the right to verify by themselves, or by their representatives, the necessity of the public contribution. Women can adhere to this only by the admission of an equal share, not only of wealth, but of public administration, and in the determination of the proportion, base, the collection, and the duration of the tax.

The mass of women, joined for tax purposes to men, has the right to demand of any public agent an account of his administration.

[...]

Article Sixteen

No society in which the guarantee of rights is not assured, nor the separation of powers determined, has a constitution; the constitution is null if the majority of individuals who constitute the Nation has not participated in drafting it.

Article Seventeen

Property belongs to both sexes whether united or separate; it is for everyone an inviolable and sacred right; no one can be deprived of it as it is the veritable patrimony of nature, unless public necessity, legally constituted, obviously needs it, and under the condition of a just and prior indemnity.

Postamble

Women, wake up; the tocsin[65] of reason is heard throughout the whole universe; recognize your rights. The powerful empire of nature is no longer surrounded by prejudice, fanaticism, superstition, and lies. The flame of truth has dissipated all the clouds of folly and usurpation. Enslaved man has multiplied his forces, and needs recourse to yours to break his chains. Having become free, he has become unjust towards his companion. Oh women, women, when will you cease to be blind? What are the advantages you have received from the revolution? A more marked scorn, a more pronounced disdain. In the centuries of corruption you have reigned only over the weaknesses of men. Your empire is destroyed; what remains for you?

[...]

Women have done more harm than good. Constraint and dissimulation have been their portion. That which force ravished from them ruse returned to them; they had recourse to all the resources of their charms, and the most irreproachable could not resist them. Poison and the sword were both subject to them; they commanded in crime as in virtue. The French government, above all, depended for centuries on the nocturnal administration of women; the cabinet kept no secret from their indiscretion; ambassadorial post, command, ministry, presidency, pontificate, cardinalate; finally anything which characterizes the stupidity of men, profane and sacred, all have been submitted to the cupidity and ambition of this sex, formerly contemptible yet respected, and since the revolution respectable and scorned.

De Gouges, Olympe. *Les droits de la femme*. Bibliothèque Nationale, 1790.

> **POST-READING PARS**
>
> 1. Does de Gouges blame women for their own oppression? Find examples in the text to support your answer.
> 2. What are de Gouges's two or three most prominent strategies for effecting change that are demonstrated in the form or content of the declaration?
> 3. How might readers, including other politically active women, have rebutted de Gouges's claims?

---

65. An alarm bell, used as a signal or warning.

Inquiry Corner

Content Questions:

What does de Gouges mean by "nocturnal administration of women"? Why does it merit mention?

Critical Questions:

Did addressing the declaration to the queen make her a royalist? What purposes do you think this choice served and how does this take into consideration the workings of power?

Comparative Question:

How do other such documents that you have read in this course—declarations, petitions, manifestos—define who is eligible for which rights?

Connection Question:

What aspects of the declaration connect to other feminist platforms in other cultures and time periods?

BEYOND THE CLASSROOM

» What can we learn from de Gouges's argument that is still relevant to the gender inequalities that we know still exist in hiring and the workplace (e.g., the pay gap between men and women)?

"Declaration of Sentiments" by Elizabeth Cady Stanton

Introduction

Sometimes big things start in small places. On July 19–20, 1848, in a rural hamlet in the Finger Lakes region of New York State nearly three hundred women and a few men gathered at the Methodist Wesleyan Chapel for what has come to be known as the Seneca Falls Woman's Rights Convention. Participants came to discuss and debate the roles of women and the future of women's rights in US society. Elizabeth Cady Stanton (1815–1902) drafted the convention's seminal document, "Declaration of Sentiments," which is credited with being the first organized platform for the rights of women as citizens in the United States.

> **SNAPSHOT BOX**
>
> LANGUAGE: English
> Delivered: 1848, Seneca Falls, New York
> GENRE: Public address, manifesto
> TAGS: Accessing Rights; Family; Rhetoric and Persuasion; Struggle, Resistance, and Revolution; Women and Power

Stanton, the daughter of a New York State Supreme Court judge and law professor, grew up exposed to lively legal discussions. Early in her activism she worked to reform women's property rights in New York. After attending the London Anti-Slavery Convention in 1840 (and being required to sit as a silent observer behind a curtain), Stanton along with Lucretia Mott resolved to organize in earnest for women's rights. Stanton drafted the "Declaration of Sentiments" as a challenge to the presumption that men have a "right" to govern women. How does this challenge expose the limitations of the idea of "universal male suffrage" as being a matter of human rights?

The year 1848 in the Atlantic world (the Americas, Africa, and Europe) is notable for its revolutionary energy. France ushered in the Second Republic, Karl Marx and Fredrick Engels published *The Communist Manifesto*, the Mexican-American

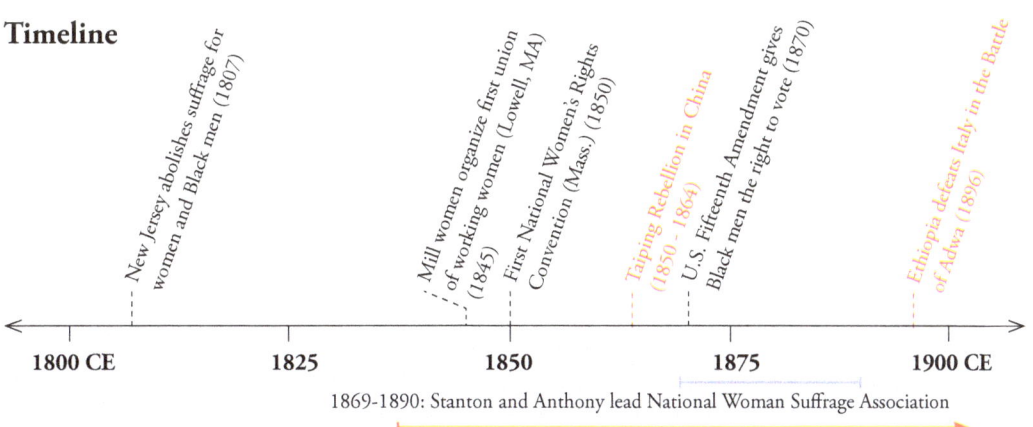

War came to a close, and another approximately fifty smaller revolutionary and reformist movements erupted across Europe. The "Declaration of Sentiments" is often included in the swell of what today is referred to as **first-wave feminism**[66] and the women's rights revolution. Do you think the publication of a proclamation for women's rights in 1848 in the United States was revolutionary (i.e., radical, abrupt), reformist (i.e., moderate, gradual), both, or neither?

The "Declaration of Sentiments" used the US "Declaration of Independence" as a template for outlining grievances and demands. This rhetorical mimicry was considered audacious and sacrilegious by many at the time. Stanton began the "Declaration of Sentiments" with: "We hold these truths to be self-evident, that all men and women are created equal." Jefferson's logical argument against the oppression of colonists, his language in the preamble, his list of grievances, resolutions, and a final declaration established the format for Stanton's women's manifesto. She declared that abusive actions were designed to destroy women's confidence, power, and self-respect; thereby, making women dependent upon men because women were habituated to believe there was no better civic or domestic alternative. Many at the convention objected to one of the proposals, the right to elective franchise, for fear that it pressed too far too fast and would thereby doom the entire document to rejection. Ironically, it is women's suffrage (elective franchise) for which the Declaration of Sentiments is remembered. What might have been gained and what opportunities might have been missed when Stanton modeled her work off of Jefferson's?

The "Declaration of Sentiments" and, by extension, the first-wave feminist movement are not without critiques. The declaration was written by, and for, white, middle-class women and exclusion and prejudice were encoded into the document. Free Black women were not part of the movement at the time and were hardly considered for inclusion. Enslaved Black people in Southern slave society suffered extreme structural violence and were not considered eligible for suffrage or human rights. Indeed, many at the 1848 Women's Convention felt that if the "Declaration of Sentiments" intersected race and gender, then the movement for women would fail entirely. Although many white women were activists for abolition and suffrage, and many Black women were advocates for both as well, Black participation in those movements was rendered invisible by white activists for decades. Stanton and oth-

---

66. First-wave feminism (1848–1920) was activism focused around extending equal opportunities to women including the right to vote, access to higher education, and economic independence through rights to property and career choice. Later "waves" of feminism include a second wave beginning in the 1960s with an emphasis on antidiscrimination and sexual agency. The third wave began in the 1990s as a counter to the perceived privilege of those aligned as white and straight. The metaphor of "waves" is currently under debate because it implies that feminism is a movement which ebbs and flows, peaks and crashes, gains and recedes.

ers believed that less educated, formerly enslaved Black women were not yet prepared for the responsibilities of full franchise and citizenship.

Incidentally, the only Black person and the only male to address the Convention was Frederick Douglass. Douglass was a true advocate for women's rights until he changed his mind later given experiences of the Civil War, Emancipation, and debate over the Fifteenth Amendment (ratified 1870). He concluded that women's suffrage would endanger Black male enfranchisement, so he encouraged women to wait. Stanton and her colleagues similarly prioritized their own political goals and frequently used racialized arguments to advocate that white women's suffrage should come before that of Black men. What was the calculation that might have caused women's rights advocates to make political alliances with anti-Black male suffrage forces?

Suffrage became the focal point and thrust of the "Declaration of Sentiments," yet the document outlines a sentiment against oppression in many forms. Ought not a fight against oppression be a universal struggle? Why was suffrage considered a hinge for how any oppression could be eliminated?

Alison Heston
Humanities Program

Declaration of Sentiments (1848)

When, in the course of human events, it becomes necessary for one portion of the family of man to assume among the people of the earth a position different from that which they have hitherto occupied, but one to which the laws of nature and of nature's God entitle them, a decent respect to the opinions of mankind requires that they should declare the causes that impel them to such a course.

We hold these truths to be self-evident: that all men and women are created equal; that they are endowed by their Creator with certain inalienable rights; that among these are life, liberty, and the pursuit of happiness; that to· secure these rights governments are instituted, deriving their just powers from the consent of the governed. Whenever any form of government becomes destructive of these ends, it is the right of those who suffer from it to refuse allegiance to it, and to insist upon the institution of a new government, laying its foundation on such principles, and organizing its powers in such form, as to them shall seem most likely to effect their safety and happiness. Prudence indeed, will dictate that governments long established should not be changed for light and transient causes; and accordingly all experience hath shown that mankind are more disposed to suffer, while evils are sufferable, than to right them selves by abolishing the forms to which they were accustomed. But when a long train of abuses and usurpations, pursuing invariably the same object evinces a design to reduce them under absolute despotism, it is their duty to throw off such government, and to provide new guards for their future security. Such has been the patient sufferance of the women under this government, and such is now the necessity which constrains them to demand the equal station to which they are entitled.

The history of mankind is a history of repeated injuries and usurpations on the part of man toward woman, having in direct object the establishment of an absolute tyranny over her. To prove this, let facts be submitted to a candid world.

He has never permitted her to exercise her inalienable right to the elective franchise.

He has compelled her to submit to laws, in the formation of which she had no voice.

He has withheld from her rights which are given to the most ignorant and degraded men-both natives and foreigners.

Having deprived her of this first right of a citizen, the elective franchise, thereby leaving her without representation in the halls of legislation, he has oppressed her on all sides.

He has made her, if married, in the eye of the law, civilly dead.

He has taken from her all right in property, even to the wages she earns.

He has made her, morally, an irresponsible being, as she can commit many crimes with impunity, provided they be done in the presence of her husband. In the covenant of marriage, she is compelled to promise obedience to her husband, he becoming, to all intents and purposes, her master-the law giving him power to deprive her of her liberty, and to administer chastisement.

He has so framed the laws of divorce, as to what shall be the proper causes, and in case of separation, to whom the guardianship of the children shall be given, as to be wholly regardless of the happiness of women-the law, in all cases, going upon a false supposition of the supremacy of man, and giving all power into his hands.

After depriving her of all rights as a married woman, if single, and the owner of property, he has taxed her to support a government which recognizes her only when her property can be made profitable to it.

He has monopolized nearly all the profitable employments, and from those she is permitted to follow, she receives but a scanty remuneration. He closes against her all the avenues to wealth and distinction which he considers most honorable to himself As a teacher of theology, medicine, or law, she is not known.

He has denied her the facilities for obtaining a thorough education, all colleges being closed against her.

He allows her in Church, as well as State, but a subordinate position, claiming Apostolic authority for her exclusion from the ministry, and, with some exceptions, from any public participation in the affairs of the Church.

He has created a false public sentiment by giving to the world a different code of morals for men and women, by which moral delinquencies which exclude women from society, are not only tolerated, but deemed of little account in man.

He has usurped the prerogative of Jehovah himself, claiming it as his right to assign for her a sphere of action, when that belongs to her conscience and to her God.

He has endeavored, in every way that he could, to destroy her confidence in her own powers, to lessen her self-respect, and to make her willing to lead a dependent and abject life.

Now, in view of this entire disfranchisement of one-half the people of this country, their social and religious degradation-in view of the unjust laws above mentioned, and because women do feel themselves aggrieved, oppressed, and fraudulently deprived of their most sacred rights, we insist that they have immediate admission to all the rights and privileges which belong to them as citizens of the United States.

In entering upon the great work before us, we anticipate no small amount of misconception, misrepresentation, and ridicule; but we shall use every instrumentality within our power to effect our object. We shall employ agents, circulate tracts, petition the State and National legislatures, and endeavor to enlist the pulpit and the press in our behalf. We hope this Convention will be followed by a series of Conventions embracing every part of the country.

The following resolutions were discussed by Lucretia Mott, Thomas and Mary Ann McClintock, Amy Post, Catharine A F. Stebbins, and others, and were adopted:

WHEREAS, The great precept of nature is conceded to be, that "man shall pursue his own true and substantial happiness." Blackstone in his Commentaries remarks, that this law of Nature being coeval with mankind, and dictated by God himself, is of course superior in obligation to any other. It is binding over all the globe, in all countries, and at all times; no human laws are of any validity if contrary to this, and such of them as are valid, derive all their force, and all their validity, and all their authority, mediately and immediately, from this original; therefore;

Resolved, That such laws as conflict, in any way, with the true and substantial happiness of woman, are contrary to the great precept of nature and of no validity, for this is "superior in obligation to any other."

Resolved, That all laws which prevent woman from occupying such a station in society as her conscience shall dictate, or which place her in a position inferior to that of man, are contrary to the great precept of nature, and therefore of no force or authority.

Resolved, That woman is man's equal-was intended to be so by the Creator, and the highest good of the race demands that she should be recognized as such.

Resolved, That the women of this country ought to be enlightened in regard to the laws under which they live, that they may no longer publish their degradation by declaring themselves satisfied with their present position, nor their ignorance by asserting that they have all the rights they want.

Resolved, That inasmuch as man, while claiming for himself intellectual superiority, does accord to woman moral superiority, it is preeminently his duty to encourage her to speak and teach, as she has an opportunity, in all religious assemblies.

Resolved, That the same amount of virtue, delicacy, and refinement of behavior that is required of woman in the social state, should also be required of man, and the same transgressions should be visited with equal severity on both man and woman.

Resolved, That the objection of indelicacy and impropriety, which is so often brought against woman when she addresses a public audience, comes with a very ill-grace from those who encourage, by their attendance, her appearance on the stage, in the concert, or in feats of the circus.

Resolved, That woman has too long rested satisfied in the circumscribed limits which corrupt customs and a perverted application of the Scriptures have marked out for her, and that it is time she should move in the enlarged sphere which her great Creator has assigned her.

Resolved, That it is the duty of the women of this country to secure to themselves their sacred right to the elective franchise.

Resolved, That the equality of human rights results necessarily from the fact of the identity of the race in capabilities and responsibilities.

Resolved, therefore, That, being invested by the Creator with the same capabilities, and the same consciousness of responsibility for their exercise, it is demonstrably the right and duty of woman, equally with man, to promote every righteous cause by every righteous means; and especially in regard to the great subjects of morals and religion, it is self-evidently her right to participate with her brother in teaching them, both in private and in public, by writing and by speaking, by any instrumentalities proper to be used, and in any assemblies proper to be held; and this being a self-evident truth growing out of the divinely implanted principles of human nature, any custom or authority adverse to it, whether modern or wearing the hoary sanction of antiquity, is to be regarded as a self-evident falsehood, and at war with mankind.

At the last session Lucretia Mott offered and spoke to the following resolution:

Resolved, That the speedy success of our cause depends upon the zealous and untiring efforts of both men and women, for the overthrow of the monopoly of the pulpit, and for the securing to woman an equal participation with men in the various trades, professions, and commerce.

Cady Stanton, Elizabeth. "Declaration of Sentiments." First delivered at the Seneca Falls Convention, 1848.

from "The Emancipation of Women: Argentina 1876" by María Eugenia Echenique and Josefina Pelliza de Sagasta

> **SNAPSHOT BOX**
>
> LANGUAGE: Spanish
> WRITTEN: 1876, Argentina (Córdoba and Buenos Aires)
> GENRE: Public debate
> TAGS: Accessing Rights; Education; Family; Gender and Identity; Struggle, Resistance, and Revolution; Women and Power

Introduction

Throughout the nineteenth century, Argentina struggled to consolidate a sense of its own identity in the wake of independence from Spain (generally dated July 9, 1816), many shifts in political leadership caused by regional conflicts, and the redrawing of its constitution in 1853, in the direction of a stronger federal republic. As part of that process, Argentine women struggled to define and articulate their own identities. In 1876, María Eugenia Echenique (1851–1878) initiated a public debate with Josefina Pelliza de Sagasta (1848–1888) on the rights and roles of Argentine women by publishing letters exchanged on the subject in a women's literary magazine *La Ondina del Plata* (Nymph of the Silver River).[67] Echenique was a young, progressive writer strongly in favor of **emancipation** for women, which was generally understood to refer to equal rights for the women of Argentina as well as full participation in education, the work force, and politics. Her essay was answered in a subsequent volume by Josefina Pelliza de Sagasta, a respected poet and novelist, whose stand on these issues was more traditional and conservative. The literary encounter, lasting from May through October 1876, resulted in an exchange of ideas and arguments, which are sets of premises or statements intended to persuade people to accept a conclusion about what was appropriate for women. This exchange engages in a literary **polemic**, or dispute in which each side expresses strong positions and attempts to undermine the other in order to be determined as the one correct view. Why do you think the topic of women's rights often becomes the location where a nation tries to craft its self-identity?

This excerpt gives you the basic picture of how the two authors disagreed about the roles of women. Pelliza advocated women's rights but not "emancipation," believing that women should be satisfied with a level of education and rights that was sufficient to their work as mothers and "guardians" of morality. She believed that it would be ridiculous for women to claim to be, or want to be, true equals with

---

[67]. The Palouse Translation Project republished this exchange as part of work engaged during a graduate seminar on translation held at Washington State University. Its members were Antonio Cruz, Rich Davies, Jeanette Luján de Molina, Francisco Manzo Robledo, Libardo Mitchell, Juan Carlos Molina Sanjinés, Jennifer Newby, Eugenio Pacelli Villarreal, and Valentine Zimnitsky. The seminar was led by Bonnie Frederick, who served as final editor. The magazine was named for a famous sculpture of a semi-nude woman representing a water nymph, or the personification of spring, which is located in a botanical garden in Buenos Aires. The statue is often understood as an homage to the perfection of womanly form and virtues.

Justice

Timeline

men, because women were both physically different (e.g., weaker) and morally different (e.g., more gentle) than men, and consequently had different tasks to do in creating a strong Argentine society. The primary task of women, she believed, was to teach and guide their children to become good citizens, and she argued strongly that women needed a sophisticated level of education in order to do that work. Echenique, however, argued not that women needed to *gain* rights, but that they must be supported in the *exercise* of rights that she believed had already been granted them in the Constitution of 1853. As she writes in this selection, "When emancipation was given to men, it was also given to women in recognition of the equality of rights, consistent with the principles of nature on which they are founded, that proclaim the identity of soul between men and women." The language that declares the rights of Argentines in the constitution uses the term *habitantes*, which translates as "inhabitants" rather than "men," and Echenique takes that to indicate that the women of the country must be already included. Does this emphasis on inclusive language seem like a good argumentative strategy to persuade her audience to agree that women already had the same rights as men? Does it seem better than the language of "the people," as is used in the US Constitution?

Another interesting piece of information is that although these two authors clearly disagree about many ideas regarding the proper roles of women, they did essentially agree that motherhood was women's special, most honorable and honored role. Like many other women across Latin America, they believed that "to be a mother was to have a social mission, a mission unique to women and different from that of men."[68] What they differed on was what women needed in order to best ful-

---

68. Bonnie Frederick, "Harriet Beecher Stowe and the Virtuous Mother: Argentina, 1852–1910," *Journal of Women's History* 18, no. 1 (Spring 2006): 103.

fill that honored role, especially with regard to the kind of education and freedoms women should have. Echenique believed that a broad education, including the sciences and other practical arts and philosophy, was necessary for women to be the best mothers they could be, capable of meeting whatever challenges might arise for her family. She believed that women should not be prevented from participation in any form of education and should have access to most kinds of work. Pelliza, on the other hand, feared that these emancipated women would simply try to "become" men, taking over men's roles and disrupting the entire social order and leaving motherhood behind. Pelliza believed that women should indeed be educated and should wield social influence, but that it should be of a particular, feminine nature. She believed that women had a special kind of moral authority and responsibility for the moral well-being of the nation, and that emancipation would lead them to reject that responsibility.

Melissa Burchard
Department of Philosophy

> **PRE-READING PARS**
>
> 1. Make a list of three to five roles that you think are generally considered in your culture to be women's roles, and three to five that are considered to be men's roles. Make some notes about what the differences are in those roles and why they are associated with those genders.
> 2. Take three to five minutes to jot down some notes on what you know about Argentina. What do you know about its people, their history, or their culture? The geography, cities, or natural features? If you don't feel like you have a lot of information, what are some things you would like to know?
> 3. This reading is excerpted from an extended argument: a set of statements or premises that should lead to a conclusion the author wants you to accept. Before you read, take three to five minutes to remind yourself what are the "cues" for premises and conclusions? What are the words that indicate what the reasons are, and what the conclusions (or sub-conclusions) are? Look for those words in the reading.

The Emancipation of Women: Argentina 1876

Maria Eugenia Echenique writes:

Our heart rebels against the ideas of spirituality, sensibility, and poetry that, as cultivated by women, have callously contributed until now to women's delay on the road of progress and the improvement of their condition. That remains from those ancient times when women were slaves under the power of absolute masters, subject to the whims and rule of the "heads" of families or of tyrannical husbands, when women had no aspirations nor anything to think about, when they felt a profound emptiness in their hearts that they needed to fill with beautiful daydreams and gilded illusions; the reduced sphere of action to which they had been relegated and the absolute ostracism which surrounded them wherever they were, developed their melancholy feelings to a high degree, making it necessary for them to seek solace for their moments of bitterness and disillusionment.

The ideas of freedom born in this century, by extending the circle of women's prerogatives, have infused them with new aspirations and unveiled great things to think about and occupy themselves with. The women of today are not the women of the past. The change that has taken place within them in these recent times is profound. Instead of poetry, today they need philosophy, practical philosophy that better idealizes life when it saves women from the critical circumstances of a dark and difficult existence, responding to the great interests of humanity.

[...]

Josefina Pelliza de Sagasta responds:

You discuss improving the present condition of women, but in this question of such interest and such serious consequences for South American women, we encounter very grave drawbacks. The emancipation of women, treated with enthusiasm by Argentine and even Peruvian authors, is an unattainable feat in our humble opinion and, moreover, harmful if it were to be attained. Entirely free women, with as much independence as men, would lose their greatest charms and the poetic prestige of their weakness: the prestige which forms the most noble attribute of their sex, the prestige that later, when women are mothers, doubly beautifies them and places them on the sacred throne of the home, where women best belong.

Women, in our opinion, should never even in thought surpass the limits that God when making them—their souls with the softest breaths of divine light and their bodies with the purest of His celestial conceptions—gave them as their path on earth: He pointed out their mission, and gave them a physical and moral constitution different from men and in accordance with the sorrows and sufferings of their destiny as daughters, wives, and mothers. Woman, one celebrated writer has said, "is the poetry of God, and man is His prose." There only remains to admire women's delicate shapes (with some exceptions), their souls susceptible to tender emotions, always gentle and loving, their thoughts, in short their physical beauty, in order to exclaim: the destiny of women is not, as has mistakenly been said, equal to the destiny of men, because the former are weak and tender in their spirit and their bodies cannot endure the difficult hardships to which men are subjected; their dignity would be diminished if they were to attempt to liberate themselves from those sweet attributes of their nature, from those bonds that the propagandist writers of emancipation have been calling guardianship, without realizing that it is precisely that guardianship which makes women more beautiful, that elevates them to their true pedestal without aspirations of glory or applause, that binds them to their husbands, that binds them to the home, and that makes them into the guardian angel of the family. She is a slave, you emancipated women will exclaim—and I in turn will reply to you: not a slave but a companion, man's other half, slave perhaps to her children, but how seductive and poetic is her beautiful sacrifice. Blessed be the woman who is a mother.

[...]

We will add: good women are virtuous, talented, with legitimate aspirations, with freedom of beliefs, educated, with mutual rights between them and their companions for life, energetic, capable of sacrifice, capable of the martyrdom of heroism, well-read, a writer, progressive, an initiator—in short everything but emancipated, less free in independence and rights than men.

Women should be educated; give them a solid education, based on wholesome principles, cemented with moral and sensible beliefs; they should have a general knowledge of everything that awakens ingenuity and determines ideas, but not for them are the calculation and egotism with which they instruct English women, not for them the ridiculous ideas of North American women who pretend in their pride to be equal to men, to be legislators and obtain a seat in Congress or be university professors, as if it were not enough to be a mother, a wife, a housewife, as if her rights as a woman were not enough to be happy and to make others happy, as if it were not enough to carry out her sacred mission on earth: educating her family, cultivating the tender hearts of her children making them useful citizens, laborers of intelligence and progress, with her words and acts; cultivating love in her children and the sentiments that most enhance women: virtue, modesty and humility. Girls, women someday, be tender and loving wives, able to work for the happiness of your life's partner instead of bringing about his disgrace with dreams and aspirations beyond your sphere. We concede to women, if their ability is sufficient, that they be well-read; the woman who writes, when that woman is virtuous, is always useful to society; there are women, wives and mothers, who without forgetting their responsibilities are writers and are the glory of their sex. One only has to look to Europe to see distinguished against a backdrop of light the most passionate and gentle of the poetesses of our era and the most tender and kind of wives—the beautiful Stael,[69] the divine author of Uncle Tom's Cabin, Harriet Beecher Stowe, Madame Gay, her daughter Emilia de Girardin.[70]

Maria Eugenia Echenique responds:

When emancipation was given to men, it was also given to women in recognition of the equality of rights, consistent with the principles of nature on which they are founded, that proclaim the identity of soul between men and women. Thus, Argentine women have been emancipated by law for a long time. The code of law that governs us authorizes a widow to defend her rights in court, just as an educated woman can in North America, and like her, we can manage the interests of our children, these rights being the basis for emancipation. What we lack is sufficient education and instruction to make use of them, instruction that North American women have; it is not just recently that we have proclaimed our freedom. To try to question or to oppose women's emancipation is to oppose something that is almost a fact, it is to attack our laws and destroy the Republic.

The advantages that, from the religious point of view, emancipation offers the young spinster are within reach of even those least able to reflect and study. The luxury and increasing aspirations that rapidly develop in every nascent society that opens its eyes to the light—feeling circulate through its vigorous veins all the energy

---

69. Germaine Necker, Baronne de Staël (1766–1817), French writer whose novel *Corinne* (1807) was probably the most widely read woman-authored novel in Latin America. Apparently Pelliza was unaware that Necker was not an example of marital fidelity.

70. Sophie Gay (1776–1852) and her daughter Delphine (not Emilia) Gay de Girardin (1804–1855) were French writers who were well known and admired in their day. The daughter was indeed considered a model of marital fidelity and felicity.

of life from advanced and ancient peoples while it lacks the necessary organs to elaborate its development—have drawn from the proletariat class in all centuries many victims of immorality and the abandonment of responsibilities. A young woman of humble condition has ambitions, and not having the means to satisfy her aspirations lawfully and honorably, she sets out on the unlawful path, she breaks the ties that subject her to family and society, and there is no rein that can hold her back from the ways of error. Emancipation liberates the young woman from the prejudices that hinder the seed of activity existing in her soul and that deprive her of working in a practical way with dignity and confidence, putting into use all her rights to extend the circle of her abilities to their limits; it gives her the means to satisfy those aspirations honorably, overcoming the obstacles placed in her way to acquire understanding of the material elements of life that can be exploited at all levels of industry and knowledge. Emancipation changes the girl into a worthy and virtuous woman from the moment that she has faith in herself and understands that she can become what she aspires to be, satisfying her needs for herself; from that instant, vice ceases to seem to her an element of necessity, and she sees, as she gains understanding of them, the false shine fade from the objects that dazzle her. In this way, emancipation guards against a young woman losing her way, instilling in her the attitude that by means of work she can satisfy the exigencies of life in such a way as to bring praise to her and to distinguish her.

Emancipate the young woman, that is, let her, once and for all, like a man, have the absolute liberty to work and to forge for herself her position in society, and far from demoralizing her, it will build a wall against corruption. Often men become corrupt because they find the opportunity in women who yield to their seductions, almost always, to have someone to feed them and because they are gripped by the love of luxury. It is necessary to equalize the position between one sex and the other for morality to exist and to avoid these monstrous situations.

In this ill-tempered time of the century in which we are living, the young American woman should not remain any longer in the sphere of actions with her hands tied. She should move, throw off the yoke of the ruinous prejudices that have cut the wings of her spirit, and rise in flight to where she belongs. Young Argentines should not be relegated to inaction and ignorance while a storm rages at their shoulder. We who by the physical conditions of the soil, political traditions, and the special relations of commerce that link us to other nations are destined to always live on a volcano, feeling its rumblings every minute, exposed to the caprice of men who differ in their means of expressing opinions, in religion, in politics, in ambitions. Since we comprise a small world burdened with rude experience in which the sun of tranquility rarely shines for long, the young of the beautiful sex should possess a solid education that would serve them as shield and rampart in its invasions, that protects her in the place of honor whatever may be the events awaiting South America in the coming years.

She needs to be educated and trained beforehand in all the social recourses that useful and practical skills offer in order to distinguish truth from error and to adopt the principles that are to serve as her guidelines for conduct on the harsh road of our turbulent life, to be able to discern, through the dust raised by the ruins of the ancient social edifice, those immovable principles of sacrosanct religion that the young woman should respect because they are her own interests.

The necessity to limit myself to the narrow columns of a newspaper does not permit me to develop my ideas on the emancipation of young, single women to the degree and breadth that I would like nor to demonstrate the advantages that it encompasses from that social point of view and in the arena of progress. Nonetheless, these notes are sufficient to understand what my opinions are in this sphere. Therefore, it can be seen that I have conducted myself with the loyalty that characterizes me, not making use of rather strong words, but rather expressing in all its integrity the truth of my thought. "In the reciprocal expression of ideas is a great source of enlightenment," a wise author has said; this being so, with all my heart I thank you, distinguished friend, for the opportunity you have given me in this polemic to educate myself.

Selections from Echenique, Maria Eugenia, and Josefina Pelliza de Sagasta. "The Emancipation of Women: Argentina 1876," translated by Palouse Translation Project, Baltimore, MD. *Journal of Women's History* 7, no. 3 (1995): 102–26.

POST-READING PARS

1. What do you think Echinique and Pelliza would think of the contemporary gender roles you listed? Write a sentence or two from each of their perspectives.
2. Outline two to four important points you learned about Argentina in the nineteenth century from this reading.
3. Identify three of the most powerful or convincing words or phrases from this reading.

Inquiry Corner

Content Questions:

Pelliza argues that if women were emancipated, they would lose their "greatest charms and the poetic prestige of their weakness." What do you think she means by "greatest charms"? How can weakness have a "poetic prestige"?

Critical Question:

What are the specific reasons or claims that Echenique and Pelliza each raise to try to make their case about whether women should or should not be emancipated? Evaluate their relative merits after reconstructing the main or overarching argument by outlining in your own words the claims that each offer as premises and conclusion.

Comparative Questions:

How do the concerns in this exchange compare with the points made by Tristan, Wollstonecraft, de Gouges, Rokeya Sakhawat Hossein, or Sor Juana?

How does the argument regarding women's special moral authority in this reading compare with Anna Julia Cooper's claim that African American women have a special calling to "uplift the race"?

Connection Questions:

Liberatory movements often give rise to fears about how they will "destroy the social order." What other liberatory movements have given rise to such fears? What commonalities do these movements have? How have liberatory movements overcome and countered this resistance?

"The History of the Chinese Revolution" (Written January 29, 1923) by Sun Yat-sen

Introduction

While Sun Yat-sen (1866–1925) was outside of China, the revolution he had spent his life promoting happened without him. Sun was born during the Qing dynasty, when the non-Chinese Manchu people controlled China through a government headed by a Manchu emperor. In 1878, at the age of twelve, Sun moved to Hawai'i to live with his older brother, where he learned English and received a Western education. He returned to China at seventeen and eventually earned a medical degree in Hong Kong. In the late nineteenth century, China was in serious decline due to civil war, government corruption, drug abuse, and both Western and Japanese imperialism. Important Chinese thinkers were proposing military, economic, and educational reforms that included transitioning to a constitutional monarchy. Sun, by contrast, felt that China needed to overthrow the emperor and become a republic. In the 1880s he quit his medical practice to devote himself full time to revolution by organizing, writing, giving speeches, and raising money. In 1894 Sun founded a secret revolutionary society, but after an unsuccessful uprising in 1895 he fled to Japan and then traveled the world promoting his cause. In London, in 1896, he famously escaped an attempt by Qing agents to kidnap him and return him to China for trial and execution. During the Boxer Rebellion of 1900, Sun launched another unsuccessful uprising. He then spent several years in Southeast Asia, the Americas, and Europe trying to rally the overseas Chinese community.

> **SNAPSHOT BOX**
>
> LANGUAGE: Chinese
> PUBLISHED: 1924, China
> GENRE: Political tract
> TAGS: Nationalism; Self-Determination; Statecraft; Tradition

Timeline

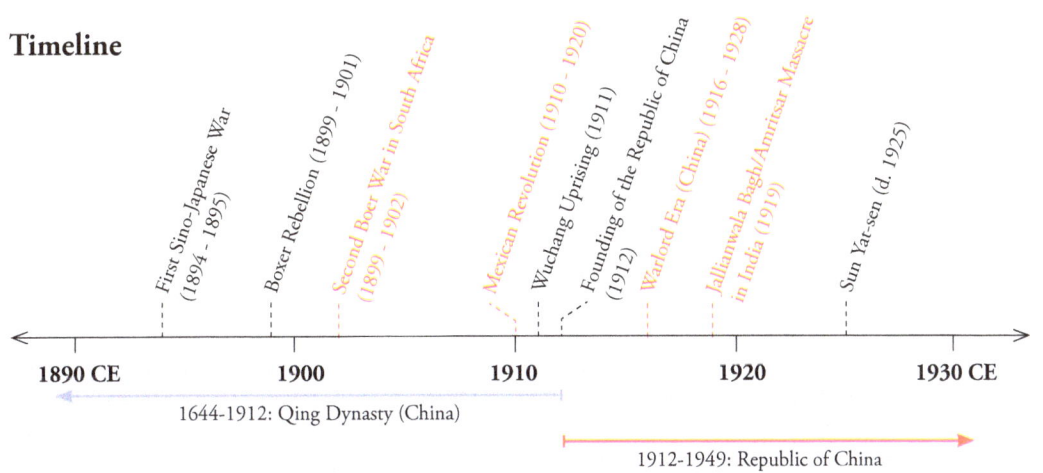

Sun led another failed uprising in 1907, but was in the United States on October 10, 1911, when some of his associates finally began the revolution that brought down the dynasty. What role might failure have in leading to successful revolutionary change?

As a world-renowned, longtime revolutionary leader, Sun Yat-sen became the first provisional president of the Republic of China in 1912. Unfortunately, he did not command an army and after just two months he stepped down so the position could be taken by Yuan Shikai, a military leader with enough troops to hold Beijing and force the abdication of the last Manchu emperor. Sun merged several revolutionary organizations to form a new political party, the **Guomindang**, or Nationalist Party, but after a few years of political turmoil, assassinations, and parliamentary crises, he was again exiled to Japan. In 1915, Yuan Shikai proclaimed a new dynasty with himself as the emperor. That attempt failed and Yuan died six months later. Sun returned to China and throughout World War I and the warlord era that followed he struggled for the military and political support needed to consolidate control of China and stabilize its government. He rejected Marxism but welcomed Soviet advisors and incorporated Chinese Communists into a **United Front** with the Nationalists, allied against the warlords. Two years after he wrote the essay below, Sun died of cancer. Subsequently, hostilities between the Nationalists and the Communists greatly increased and continued through the 1930s and World War II, when the Nationalist leader Chiang Kai-shek led the country. Following the world war, China immediately plunged into a civil war. In 1949, the Communists under Mao Zedong claimed victory and established the People's Republic of China, while two million Nationalist troops followed Chiang to Taiwan, where they declared themselves an independent Republic of China, resulting in an uneasy standoff that continues to this day. Perhaps unexpectedly, Sun Yat-sen is honored by both parties as the father of modern China. This is in part because he died before the decisive split, and also because his ideas were somewhat ambiguous, allowing the Communists and Nationalists to develop them in different ways.

Sun's "Three Principles of the People" consisted of nationalism, democracy, and the people's livelihood. "Nationalism," which at first represented anti-Manchu sentiment, was later redefined as a Chinese identity that included not only the majority Han population but also Mongols, Tibetans, Chinese Muslims, and Manchus who were living in the Chinese province of Manchuria. How might the boundaries and definitions that make up an idea like "nationalism" shift? Sun's ideal of "democracy" was based on a five-branch system of government—the executive, legislative, and judicial branches that he borrowed from Western political theorists, combined with two uniquely Chinese institutions: the **examination branch**, derived from the imperial civil service exams that would impartially recruit government officials; and the **control branch**, derived from the imperial censorate that would audit finances and prevent corruption. (Note that the word "censoring" in the selection does *not* refer to restricting information.) Originally, "the people's livelihood" was a variation on Henry George's idea of taxing increases in land values and later evolved to refer to capitalism with a few nationalized industries and utilities, but the term was ambiguous enough that it was sometimes translated as "socialism." How might the ambiguity of Sun's ideas make them able to be developed differently by Communists and Nationalists? The Nationalists in Taiwan ended up developing a capitalist, democratic nation, while the Communists on the mainland have continued a command economy with single-party rule. In both cases, the implementation of Sun's plan for a transition from military rule to political tutelage to constitutional government has been difficult.

Grant Hardy
Department of History

History of the Chinese Revolution (Written January 29, 1923)

Following China's war with France (1883–1884) I made up my mind to devote myself to the revolution. In 1895 I started the first insurrection in Canton and the revolution of 1911 culminated in the establishment of the Republic. Up to present the task of revolution, however, has not yet been completed. A span of thirty-seven years of my revolutionary work is to be chronicled by future historians from all manner of facts and incidents. An outline sketch is given below.

I. Principles of Revolution

The term *geming*, or revolution, was first used by Confucius. Incidents of a revolutionary nature repeatedly happened in Chinese history after Tang (founder of the Shang Dynasty, 1766 BCE) and Wu (founder of the Zhou Dynasty, 1122 BCE). In Europe revolutionary tides surged in the seventeenth and eighteenth centuries and they have since spread over the whole world. In due course they created republics, they conferred constitutions on monarchies. The principles which I have held in promoting the Chinese revolution were in some cases copied from our traditional ideals, in other cases modeled on European theory and experience and in still others formulated according to original and self-developed theories. They are described as follows:

1. Principle of Nationalism

Revelations of Chinese history prove that the Chinese as a people are independent in spirit and in conduct. Coerced into touch with other people, they could at times live in peace with them by maintaining friendly relations and at others assimilate them as the result of propinquity. During the periods when their political and military prowess declined, they could not escape for the time from the fate of a conquered nation, but they could eventually vigorously reassert themselves. Thus the Mongol rule of China (1260–1333 CE), lasting nearly a hundred years was finally overthrown by Taizu of the Ming dynasty and his loyal followers. So in our own time was the Manchu yoke thrown off by the Chinese. Nationalistic ideas in China did not come from a foreign source; they were inherited from our remote forefathers. Upon this legacy is based my principle of nationalism, and where necessary, I have developed it and amplified and improved upon it. No vengeance has been inflicted on the Manchus and we have endeavored to live side by side with them on a n equal footing. This is our nationalistic policy toward races within our national boundaries. Externally, we should strive to maintain independence in the family of nations, and to spread our indigenous civilization as well as to enrich it by absorbing what is best in world civilization, with the hope that we may forge ahead with other nations towards the goal of ideal brotherhood.

2. Principle of Democracy

In ancient China we had the Emperor Yao (2357–2258 BCE) and Emperor Shun (2258–2206 BCE) who departed from the hereditary system and chose their successors. We also had Tang and Wu who overthrew kingdoms by revolution. Preserved in our books are such sayings as "Heaven sees as the people see; Heaven hears as the people hear."[71] "We have heard of a person named Zhou[72] having been slain, we have not heard of a monarch having been murdered." "The people are most important, while the king is of the least importance." All these sayings ring with democratic sentiments. Since we have had only ideas about popular rights, and no democratic system has been evolved, we have to go to Europe and America for a republican form of government. There some countries have become republics and others have adopted constitutional monarchism, under which royal power has shrunk in the face of the rising demand for popular rights. Though hereditary monarchs have not yet disappeared, they are but vestiges and shadows of their former selves.

All through my revolutionary career I have held the view that China must be made a republic. There are three reasons. First, from a theoretical point of view, there is no ground for preserving a monarchical form of government, since it is widely recognized that the people constitute the foundation of a nation and they are all equal in their own country. In the second place, under Manchu occupation the Chinese were forced into the position of the vanquished, and suffered oppression for more than two hundred and sixty years. While a constitutional monarchy may not arouse deep resentment in other countries and can maintain itself for the time being, it will be an impossibility in China. This is from a historical point of view. A third reason may be advanced with an eye on the future of the nation. That in China prolonged periods of disorder usually followed a revolution was due to the desire of every insurgent to be a king and to his subsequent contention for the throne. If a republican government is adopted, there will be no contention. For these three reasons, I have decided for the republican form of government in order to realize the principle of democracy.

My second decision is that a constitution must be adopted to ensure good government. The true meaning of constitutionalism was discovered by Montesquieu. The threefold separation of the legislative, judicial, and executive powers as advocated by him was accepted in every constitutional country in Europe. On a tour of Europe and America, I made a close study of their governments and laws and took note of their shortcomings as well as their advantages. The shortcomings of election, for instance, are not incurable. In the past China had two significant systems of examination and censoring and they can be of avail where the Western system of government and law falls short. I therefore advocate that the examinative and censorial powers should be placed on the same level with legislative, judicial, and executive, thereby resulting in the five-fold separation of powers. On top of that, the system of the people's direct po-

---

71. Another version reads: The people's ears and eyes are Heaven's ears and eyes.
72. The last emperor of the Shang dynasty, 1154 BCE.

litical powers should be adopted in order that the provision that the sovereign power is vested in the people may become a reality. In this way my principle of democracy may be carried out satisfactorily.

3. Principle of Livelihood

With the invention of modern machines, the phenomenon of uneven distribution of wealth in the West has become all the more marked. Intensified by crosscurrents, economic revolution was flaring up more ferociously than political revolution. This situation was scarcely noticed by our fellow-countrymen thirty years ago. On my tour of Europe and America, I saw with my own eyes the instability of their economic structure and the deep concern of their leaders in groping for a solution. I felt that, although the disparity of wealth under our economic organization is not so great as in the West, the difference is only in degree, not in character. The situation will become more acute when the West extends its economic influence to China. We must form plans beforehand in order to cope with the situation. After comparing various schools of economic thought, I have come to the realization that the principle of state ownership is most profound, reliable, and practical. Moreover, it will forestall in China difficulties which have already caused much anxiety in the West. I have therefore decided to enforce the principle of the people's livelihood simultaneously with the principles of nationalism and democracy, with the hope to achieve our political objective and nip economic unrest in the bud.

To sum up, my revolutionary principles in a nutshell consist in the Three Principles of the People and the Five-Power Constitution. Those who have a clear knowledge of the general tendency of the world and the conditions in China will agree that my views are practical and must be put in practice.

II. Fundamentals of Revolution

In the age of autocracy, the masses of the people were fettered in spirit and body so that emancipation seemed impossible Those who worked for the welfare of the people and were willing to sacrifice themselves for the success of revolution not only did not receive assistance from the people but were also ridiculed and disparaged. Much as they desired to be the guides of the people, they proceeded without followers. Much as they desired to be the vanguards, they advanced without reinforcement. It becomes necessary that, apart from destroying enemy influence, those engaged in revolution should take care to develop the constructive ability of the people. A revolutionary program is therefore indispensable.

According to my plan, the progress of our revolution should be regulated and divided into three stages: First, military rule; second, political tutelage; third, constitutional government. The first stage is a period of destruction, during which military rule is installed. The revolutionary army is to break down (as it did) Manchu despotism, sweep away official corruptions, and reform vicious customs.

The second stage is a transitional period, during which a provisional constitution (not the present one) will be promulgated. Its object is to build a local self-government system for the development of democracy. The *xian* or district will be the unit of self-government. When disbanded troops are disposed of and fighting ceases, every district should accept the provisional constitution, which will regulate the rights and duties of the people and the administrative powers of the revolutionary government. It will be in force for three years, at the end of which period the people will choose their district magistrates. Even before the expiration of the period, the people in a district may be empowered to choose their own magistrate and become a complete self-governing body on the following conditions: That the self-government bureau of the said district has already cleaned the district of its long-standing corruptions; that it has succeeded in getting more than half of its population to understand the Three Principles of the People and devote themselves to the republic; that it has fulfilled the minimum requirements of the provisional constitution in regard to census-taking, residence registration, police, health, education and road-building. In reference to the self-government body, the revolutionary government may exercise the power of political tutelage only in accordance with the provisional constitution. Six years after the whole nation is restored to peace and order, each district which has attained complete self-government may elect one delegate, and these delegates will form the People's Congress to adopt the five-power constitution.

[...]

The third stage, which marks the completion of national reconstruction, will usher in constitutional government. During this period the self-governing bodies in the various districts should exercise the direct political powers of the people. In district political affairs citizens should have the rights of universal suffrage, initiative, referendum, and recall. In national political affairs they should, while directly exercising the right of election, delegate the three other rights to their representatives in the People's Congress. This period of constitutional government marks the completion of national reconstruction and the successful conclusion of the revolution.

If we can proceed according to the revolutionary fundamentals that have been briefly outlined, not only can we clean the Augean stable of autocracy and carry out the rights of the people, but we can also strengthen and safeguard the constructive power of the people against the manipulations of politicians and the unscrupulousness of militarists. It becomes obvious that the principles of revolution must depend upon the fundamentals of revolution for a thorough realization.

Sun Yat-sen. "History of the Chinese Revolution." In *Fundamentals of National Reconstruction*, 76–87. Taipei, Taiwan: China Cultural Service, 1953.

"Letter to United States President Andrew Jackson, 1831" by Tuskeneah

Introduction

> **SNAPSHOT BOX**
>
> **LANGUAGE:** English
> **WRITTEN:** 1831, Creek Nation, Cusiatah Town (Georgia, US)
> **GENRE:** Epistolary, diplomatic correspondence
> **TAGS:** Accessing Rights; Autobiography and Testimony; Colonization; Cross-Cultural Encounters; Historiography; Race; Self-Determination; Struggle, Resistance, and Revolution; War and Brutality

Tuskeneah, principal chief of Cusiatah Town (also spelled Cusseta) and a revered leader of the Creek Nation,[73] emerged as a prominent voice during the early nineteenth century, a period that saw increasing conflict between the Creek people and the United States government. His desire to maintain amicable relations with the US government while protecting Creek national territory and identity led him to send this letter appealing to President Andrew Jackson in May 1831.

It is important to note that the Creek Nation's power was diffused among the headmen who were chosen to lead each town within the Nation. Certain towns carried more authority in the Nation, because of tradition, size of the town, strength of their leadership, and other factors. Towns, factions, and individuals among the Creeks, as well as other American Indigenous groups, pursued their own policies based on their best interests. In general, however, the Creek Nation leveraged its geographic position next to British American, French, and Spanish (stolen) territories to negotiate military, diplomatic, and trade alliances that allowed them to cultivate considerable power in the region. Most Creeks allied with the British in several eighteenth-century wars yet also enjoyed robust trade relationships with all European nations in the area.

After the French lost their North American territory in 1763, the balance of power shifted and the British enacted stricter trade policies, which strained their relationship with Creeks and other Indigenous peoples in the area. White encroachment on Creek territory provoked sporadic violence during the second half of the eighteenth century and further deteriorated relationships between Anglo-Americans and the Creek towns most affected by these conflicts. During the American Revolution (1765–1783), factionalism prevented a unified Creek stance and caused considerable internal strife, as individuals began to consolidate political power around their ability to negotiate trade and military alliances with the British or the Americans. Although they seldom participated in sustained fighting during the war, the majority of the Creeks supported Britain, which put them on the losing side of the revolution, thus subjecting them to the US government's further aggression after the revolution. While the British had seen Indigenous communities as independent nations and military and trade partners, Americans saw them as conquered peoples and potential rivals for territory.

---

73. The birth and death dates of Tuskeneah are not recorded.

Timeline

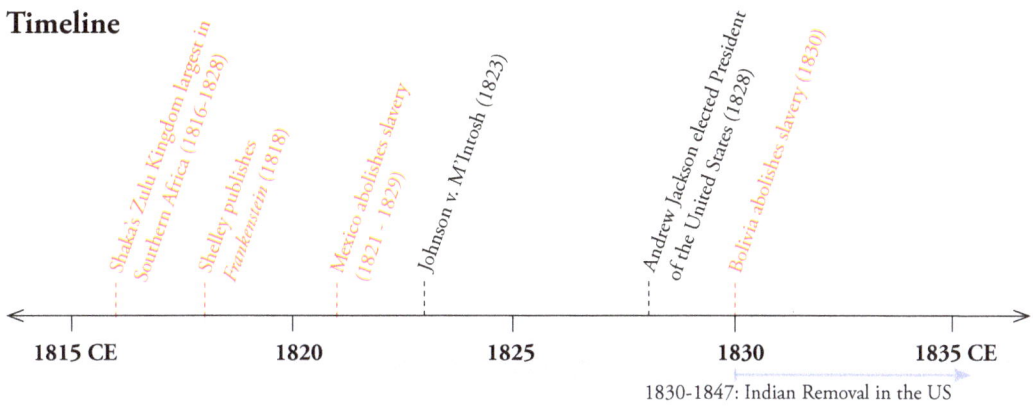

The Creek Nation, like many other Indigenous communities, wished to restore the diplomatic and economic relations that they had settled into before the revolution. Therefore, they adapted their political and economic practices to suit those needs. For example, they incorporated Anglo-American-style property laws and abandoned their matrilineal traditions in favor of a written code of laws institutionalizing the practice of patrilineal inheritance and protecting personal property rights. How might adopting Anglo-American-style practices (like property laws) have helped or harmed the Creek Nation in attempting to create diplomatic relations?

As early nineteenth-century treaties eroded their territory, the Creek National Council also moved to protect the Nation's remaining property, making the unauthorized sale of the Nation's property punishable by death. However, as Alabamans and Georgians encroached on Creek National territory in the 1820s, political divisions between the Lower Creeks and Upper Creeks prevented the Nation from mounting a unified defense. Cusiatah Town was a Lower Creek town, located closer to white settlements and its inhabitants, therefore, were influenced more by white cultural practices. More Lower Creeks spoke English, farmed with Anglo-American methods, and owned enslaved African Americans and Africans. Upper Creeks were more isolated and tended to resist these types of assimilation. How can location, geography, and "place" force and shape adoption or rejection of assimilation pressures?

As tensions grew between Creeks and whites in the 1820s, the US government stepped up pressure to convince the Creeks to be displaced to Indian Territory. In late 1824, the Creek Nation entered into treaty negotiations with the United States to seek resolution to conflicts between Creek citizens and white intruders. Tuskeneah and a few other Lower Creek headmen entered the negotiations convinced that the Creek leadership had already begun secret negotiations for a deal with US officials, and shortly after the talks began, their suspicions were confirmed. They walked out of the negotiations, and shortly thereafter, a spokesman for the Lower Towns, William McIntosh, of Scots-European and Creek ancestry, negotiated the Treaty of Indian Springs, which ceded Creek land in the east in exchange for an equal amount of undeveloped land near the Arkansas River and money to be paid in installments over time to support their forced removal. The Creek National Council condemned McIntosh's unauthorized actions and sentenced him to death. McIntosh was killed during a raid on his plantation, and the Creek headmen — leaders chosen by community consensus — attempted to overturn the Treaty of Indian Springs. Over the next several years, Tuskeneah and his Lower Creek allies attempted to steer a more pragmatic path of compromise, pledging to maintain a cordial relationship with US agents while also pleading for protection from the violence of white squatters. The Lower and Upper Creeks accused one another of misrepresenting the will of the Creek Nation.

The Jackson administration took advantage of this power struggle between the Lower and Upper towns to further divide the two groups. US officials claimed that they could not protect the Creek Nation from white encroachment, and that the reasonable choice would be for the Creeks to move west to Indian Territory to join those who had already shifted. Still, the headmen resisted. Over the next several months, whites escalated their harassment. The headmen of the Lower Creeks sent their own delegation to Washington to complain of white intruders and to secure promised financial support for Creeks displaced by whites. The delegates met with little success, and violent conflict between whites and Creeks intensified. In May 1831, Tuskeneah of Cusiatah Town sent his appeal for relief to the Jackson administration, hoping that his revered position as a Creek elder would persuade the president to help the Creeks maintain their ancestral lands and salvage their political influence in the region.

As you read this letter take note of the distinctive word choices, particularly verbs, made by the author. In writing directly to President Jackson what type of tone does Tuskeneah take? What metaphors does he employ to depict the relationship between the Creek Nation and the United States over time?

Ellen Holmes Pearson
Department of History

Letter to United States President Andrew Jackson, 1831

Creek Nation Cusiatah Town 21st May 1831

Brother

I am very old and feeble and am not able to make a long talk. I have thought for some years I should never make another. But the situation of my country makes it necessary for me again to open my mouth. I have been a Chief for fifty five years. I have witnessed all the Treaties of my Nation with your government since the old British war. I have ever been the friend of the white man. I have never taken up a gun against your white children. I have always taken the presidents of the U. S. by the hand with that friendship which is due from a child to his father. They have always treated me and my people as if though we had been their white children. I have never seen the necessity of complaining until now.

All my white fathers and brothers until now or a few months back have prevented their white sons and daughters from making fields and settling in my country. They have always protected us in the lands that we did not cede away to their government. At this time your white children are fast settling up in my country—they are building houses, mills, making fields and destroying all my timber and game. This I have always been taught by my former fathers and brothers was not a right which your white children were entitled to. We have always required of your government to protect us on the lands that we did not sell. Your government promised to do so. I was informed by the deputation that visited you winter before last that you stated to them that you would not allow of such conduct, that you had placed Soldiers among us that would remove all persons that would settle in our country without our consent and the agents or had an Indian family. This was strictly attended to until a few months back, when to my surprise on application for the removal of some white settlers we were answered by your soldiers that they could not relieve our wants without your consent. This talk was like a clap of thunder upon me. All this we have more than once communicated to you. We have never received any answer. Our deputation told us on their return to the Nation this winter that the Secretary of War had promised to answer us when more at leisure than he was when he was at Washington City. I should not make this talk only, because the situation of my country greatly demands it.[74]

I can only repeat in my talk what we have said to you before your white sons and daughters are moving into my country in abundance. They are spoiling my lands and taking possession of the Red peoples' improvements that they have made with their own labor contrary to the consent of the Nation, and your soldiers have refused to prevent it. This makes me sorry and has caused me to give you this talk, believing at

---

74. In February Eaton had informed a Creek delegation in Washington that he was too busy at present to meet them or attend to their grievances (SDoc 512, 23d Cong., 1st sess., vol. 2, p. 269, Serial 245).

the same time that you will not give a deaf ear to it. For I am contending for nothing but what my People are entitled to and that which your government has promised repeatedly by treaty stipulations.

There are dreadful consequences to be anticipated by the emigration of your white children amongst us. They are bringing whiskey and opening drinking houses. Nothing but what is bad can result. There are bad white people as well as Red. That neither me nor you can control.

These are the kind of characters that settle among us. They steal our property and swear and lie. They make false accounts against us. They sue us in your state courts for that we know nothing of. The Laws that we are judged against immeaneable to are in words that we have no possible means of understanding. Only a few days since an affray took place at an intruders camp who was selling whiskey to the Red people when a white man was severely beaten. Such conduct makes me unhappy—but I cannot help it. I would to the great Spirit above prevent such conduct was it in my power. Affrays alone are not only to be expected, but the shedding of a quantity of blood I am afraid will be the end. This fills my old head with trouble. I talk to you although I am not in person before you. I tell you the truth. My tongue is not forked that such of your white citizens that intrude upon us are of your bad children. They have run away from your laws and they can not live with honest white people. And I don't want them among my Red children. There are a number of my Red children in a dreadful condition without any means of subsistence. They have been compelled to resort to their guns

The Yuchis, a small part of our Tribe, have in small parties crossed into the settlements of Georgia where game they believed more plenty.[75] It is likely such of them as did cross the line may have killed white people stock. The whites have collected themselves in bodies and hunted up such as did cross into Georgia and shot them as though they were deer. From the best information I can learn in the course of the last three months there have been seventeen Red people killed by the whites and nothing thought of more than if they had been so many wild hogs. I can only feel sorry for they have done wrong in crossing the Line. It was contrary to my wishes and orders. But yet such conduct is in your white sons. They drive their [live]stock into our country and they spoil our range. They kill our hogs and cattle. They kill your white childrens' [live]stock running in my Country and blame it on my Red children. The children, they have to bear the blame. They hunt and kill our game. We treat them kindly. I don't wish them [harm.] But still I believe it wrong. When my people cross to the white settlements I don't want them killed. But should they commit a wrong they should suffer in the way your laws point out. I shall endeavour to prevent the Red people from doing anything that will offend you or my white neighbours. All I want is peace and to be protected in what belongs to my Red people, and have

---

75. Once a separate people, the Yuchis now resided among the Creeks.

been solemnly guaranteed to them by your government. With every respect I have the honor to be your unfortunate old brother.

Tuskeneah [his X mark]

Daniel Asburry Inter.[76]

[Endorsed by AJ:] War Dept referred for answer to the chief A. J. June 6th. 1836

Tuskaneah. "From Tuskeneah." In *The Papers of Andrew Jackson*, edited by Daniel Feller, Laura-Eve Moss, Thomas Coens, and Erik B. Alexander, vol. 9, 254–56. Knoxville: University of Tennessee Press, 2013. NB: Lightly edited to aid clarity.

---

76. Daniel B. Asbury (d. 1856) was clerk of the Creek Nation.

from "Message to the Congress of Angostura" by Simón Bolívar

SNAPSHOT BOX

LANGUAGE: Spanish
DELIVERED: February 19, 1819, Angostura, Venezuela
GENRE: Public address, political manifesto
TAGS: Abolition, Slavery, Freedom; Colonization; Cross-Cultural Encounters; History and Ideology; Rhetoric and Persuasion; Self-Determination; Statecraft; Tradition

Introduction

In mid-February 1819, in the city of Angostura (today Ciudad Bolívar, Venezuela) in the Spanish colonial Viceroyalty of New Granada, the Latin American rebel leader Simón Bolívar gathered with twenty-six other like-minded exiles and revolutionaries to create their own sovereign and independent nation. Those attending this **Congress of Angostura** were driven by several motives. For some, ideas made popular by European Enlightenment philosophers like John Locke and Jean Jacques Rousseau led them to seek ways of forming a new type of **social contract**, an agreement between citizen and government establishing sovereignty. For others it was the tyranny of Spanish imperial rule under Ferdinand VII that caused them to consider a drastic severance of their association with Spain, and for yet others the example of the break-away British colonies to the north in forming the United States of America had shone a most specific light on the pathway to self-rule.

Simón Bolívar (1783–1830) was born in Caracas, Venezuela, into a family whose wealth was derived from cacao plantations worked by enslaved Africans. The nineteenth century was a time of increased call for independence in Latin America. Despite his traditional elite status and wealth, as a **Creole** (a Spaniard born in the Americas) rather than a **Peninsular** (a Spaniard born

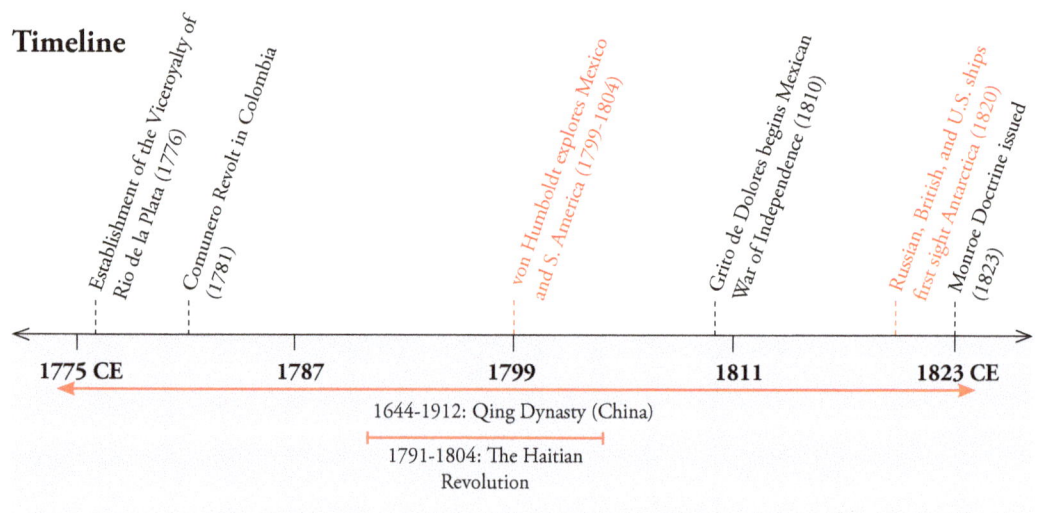

in the Iberian Peninsula), Bolívar was a second-class subject. This subjugation was further exacerbated by the Bourbon Reforms, an effort by the Spanish to streamline the administration of the colonies over the second half of the eighteenth century which, among other policies, eliminated the most tangible benefits of Creoles, such as holding high offices in the colonial administration.

Though he was orphaned by the age of nine, his family fortune and name nevertheless meant that young Bolívar received a rigorous education. Indeed, for years he was tutored by a stream of well-respected educators, most prominent of them, Simón Rodríguez, a well-traveled radical thinker who taught him the works of European Enlightenment philosophers. As a teen, Bolívar spent time in Europe where he experienced the aftermath of the French Revolution and the personal allure and martial prowess of Napoleon Bonaparte. Initially inspired by the possibilities posed by the example of revolutionary France, Bolívar was ultimately disheartened by Napoleon's turn toward political autocracy and warmongering. Can you think of other revolutionary heroes with complicated legacies? How do you navigate your admiration for people who have complicated legacies?

In 1807, the twenty-four-year-old Bolívar returned to Caracas. Soon afterward, Napoleon drove out the Spanish king and placed his brother, Joseph Bonaparte, on the Spanish throne. In 1811, with the French interloper Joseph I wearing the crown and with many in the Spanish colonies uncertain as to where sovereignty actually rested, Bolívar joined the military forces assembling to fight for independence in the northern region of South America. Over the next several years he ascended to command and the fate of the armies that he led rose and fell. Bolívar was a classic **caudillo**, a charismatic leader with followers of religious faith and loyalty.

Caudillos were a fixture in the region's political and military history throughout the nineteenth and into the twentieth centuries and ultimately proved a challenge to constitutional democratic-republican systems, that is, governments of popularly elected representatives. Bolívar was proclaimed by the people as "The Liberator," and as the battles raged, amid the chaos of war, he often assumed dictatorial powers. By the early months of 1819 his armies gained control of much of northern South America, and he called together the Congress of Angostura. Those assembled formed the Republic of Gran Colombia and named Bolívar its president.

In his "Message to the Congress of Angostura," excerpted here, Bolívar called upon the representatives to heed history and consider the natural consequences of the constraints imposed by the Spanish Empire on the colonized. As you read, take note of how Bolívar describes the impact of colonization upon the political acumen of the people of the Spanish colonies, especially the masses. What characteristics fostered by colonialism does Bolívar assert should be taken into consideration as the congress debates the nature of the representative democratic-republican government they should form once independence is achieved?

Bolívar also urges that while learning from the examples of history, the congress should also recognize that the people of the Spanish colonies should consider their own unique pasts as they decide the form of government that they will create. He goes on to emphasize that a large part of that past included lessons infused with "ignorance, tyranny, and vice" taught by "pernicious masters" and corrupted by the "Darkness" of slavery. Indeed, slavery and its malevolent influence had been a constant in his life. Notably, in 1815, military setbacks had forced Bolívar to flee the Spanish colonies, and he was granted asylum by the government of Haiti. There, the leaders of the new nation, the first created by a revolution of the self-liberated and formerly enslaved, provided Bolívar with much-needed supplies and munitions. Accordingly, the caudillo promised his benefactors that abolition would be part of his platform should he ever realize an independent South America. Enslaved people were promised their freedom for fighting on both sides of the independence struggle in South America and the institution had mainly ended in the region prior to its 1865 abolition in the United States. Bolívar did stand against slavery, as we see from his remarks, though that goal was one not easily nor immediately realized. In the "Message to the Congress of Angostura" how does Bolívar describe slavery?

Despite the optimism of the Congress of Angostura, the fight for independence raged on for several more years in South America. Most of the former Spanish colonies began their nationhood with efforts at representative governments, though the variations on that theme were myriad. Most of the region had broken free from Spain by 1825. Bolívar had hoped for a unified northern republic but that was not to be, and by 1830 the Republic of Gran Colombia had fractured into the modern nations of Colombia, Venezuela, and Ecuador. To the south, independence resulted in the creation of the nations of Peru, Bolivia, Chile, Argentina, Paraguay, and Uruguay. The Portuguese colony of Brazil gained its independence in 1822. What might be some of the reasons that South America was not able to stand as a single nation but rather fractured into multiple countries after gaining independence?

Alvis Dunn
Department of History

Address Delivered by the Liberator in Angostura, on the 15th of February, 1819, at the Opening of the Second National Congress of Venezuela.

[...] And, now that by this act of adherence to the Liberty of Venezuela, I can aspire to the glory of being counted among her most faithful lovers, permit me, Sirs, to state with the frankness of a true republican, my respectful opinion regarding the scope of this *Project of a Constitution*, which I take the liberty to submit, as a token of the sincerity and candor of my sentiments. As this is a question involving the welfare of all, I venture to believe that I have the right to be heard by the Representatives of the People. Well I know that in your wisdom you have no need of counsel; I am also aware that my *project* may perhaps appear to you erroneous and impracticable. But, Sirs, receive with benevolence this work which is a tribute of my sincere submission to Congress rather than the outcome of a presumptuous levity. On the other hand, your functions being the creation of a body politic, and, one might say, the creation of an entire community surrounded by all the difficulties offered by a situation—a most peculiar and difficult one—the voice of a citizen may perhaps point out a hidden or unknown danger.

By casting a glance over the past, we shall see what is the basic element of the Republic of Venezuela.

America, on becoming separated from the Spanish monarchy, found itself like the Roman Empire, when that enormous mass fell to pieces in the midst of the ancient world. Each dismembered portion formed then an independent nation in accordance with its situation or its interests, the difference being that those members established anew their former associations. We do not even preserve the vestiges of what once we were; we are not Europeans, we are not Indians, but an intermediate species between the aborigines and the Spaniards—Americans by birth and Europeans in right, we are placed in the dilemma of disputing with the natives our titles of possession and maintaining ourselves in the country where we were born, against the opposition of the invaders. Thus, ours is a most extraordinary and complicated case. Moreover, our part has always been a purely passive one; our political existence has always been null, and we find ourselves in greater difficulties in attaining our liberty than we ever had when we lived on a plane lower than servitude, because we had been robbed not only of liberty but also of active and domestic tyranny. Allow me to explain this paradox.

In an absolute régime, authorized power does not admit any limits. The will of the despot is the supreme law, arbitrarily executed by the subordinates who participate in the organized oppression according to the measure of the authority they enjoy.

They are intrusted with civil, political, military and religious functions; but in the last analysis, the Satraps of Persia are Persians, the Pashas of the Great Master are Turks, the Sultans of Tartary are Tartars. China does not send for her Mandarins to the land of Genghis-khan, her conqueror. America, on the contrary, received all from Spain, which had really deprived her of true enjoyment and exercise of active tyranny, by not permitting us to share in our own domestic affairs and interior administration. This deprivation had made it impossible for us to become acquainted with the course of public affairs; neither did we enjoy that personal consideration which the glamour of power inspires in the eyes of the multitude, so important in the great revolutions. I will say, in short, we were kept in estrangement, absent from the universe and all that relates to the science of government.

The people of America having been held under the triple yoke of ignorance, tyranny and vice, have not been in a position to acquire either knowledge, power or virtue. Disciples of such pernicious masters, the lessons we have received and the examples we have studied, are most destructive. We have been governed more by deception than by force, and we have been degraded more by vice than by superstition. Slavery is the offspring of Darkness; an ignorant people is a blind tool, turned to its own destruction; ambition and intrigue exploit the credulity and inexperience of men foreign to all political, economical or civil knowledge; mere illusions are accepted as reality, license is taken for liberty, treachery for patriotism, revenge for justice. Even as a sturdy blind man who, relying on the feeling of his own strength, walks along with the assurance of the most wideawake man and, striking against all kinds of obstacles, can not steady his steps.

A perverted people, should it attain its liberty, is bound to lose this very soon, because it would be useless to try to impress upon such people that happiness lies in the practice of righteousness; that the reign of law is more powerful than the reign of tyrants, who are more inflexible, and all ought to submit to the wholesome severity of the law; that good morals, and not force, are the pillars of the law and that the exercise of justice is the exercise of liberty. Thus, Legislators, your task is the more laborious because you are to deal with men misled by the illusions of error, and by civil incentives. Liberty, says Rousseau, is a succulent food, but difficult to digest. Our feeble fellow-citizens will have to strengthen their mind much before they will be ready to assimilate such wholesome nourishment. Their limbs made numb by their fetters, their eyesight weakened in the darkness of their dungeons and their forces wasted away through their foul servitude, will they be capable of marching with a firm step towards the august temple of Liberty? Will they be capable of coming close to it, and admiring the light it sheds, and of breathing freely its pure air?

Consider well your decision, Legislators. Do not forget that you are about to lay the foundations of a new people, which may some day rise to the heights that Nature has marked out for it, provided you make those foundations proportionate to the lofty place which that people is to fill. If your selection be not made under the guidance of the Guardian Angel of Venezuela, who must inspire you with wisdom to choose the nature and form of government that you are to adopt for the welfare of the people; if you should fail in this, I warn you, the end of our venture would be slavery.

The annals of past ages display before you thousands of governments. Recall to mind the nations which have shone most highly on the earth and you will be grieved to see that almost the entire world has been, and still is, a victim of bad government.

You will find many systems of governing men, but all are calculated to oppress them, and if the habit of seeing the human race, led by shepherds of peoples, did not dull the horror of such a revolting sight, we would be astonished to see our social species grazing on the surface of the globe, even as lowly herds destined to feed their cruel drivers.

Nature, in truth, endows us at birth with the instinctive desire for liberty; but whether because of negligence, or because of an inclination inherent in humanity, it remains still under the bonds imposed on it. And as we see it in such a state of debasement we seem to have reason to be persuaded that the majority of men hold as a truth the humiliating principle that it is harder to maintain the balance of liberty than to endure the weight of tyranny. Would to God that this principle, contrary to the morals of Nature, were false! Would to God that this principle were not sanctioned by the indolence of man as regards his most sacred rights!

Many ancient and modern nations have cast off oppression; but those which have been able to enjoy a few precious moments of liberty are most rare, as they soon relapsed into their old political vices; because it is the people more often than the government, that bring on tyranny. The habit of suffering domination makes them insensible to the charms of honor and national prosperity, and leads them to look with indolence upon the bliss of living in the midst of liberty, under the protection of laws framed by their own free will. The history of the world proclaims this awful truth!

Only democracy, in my opinion, is susceptible of absolute freedom. But where is there a democratic government that has united at the same time power, prosperity and permanence? Have we not seen, on the contrary, aristocracy, monarchy rearing great and powerful empires for centuries and centuries? What government is there older than that of China? What republic has exceeded in duration that of Sparta, that of Venice? The Roman Empire, did it not conquer the world? Does not France count fourteen centuries of monarchy? Who is greater than England? These nations, however, have been, or still are, aristocracies and monarchies.

Notwithstanding such bitter reflections, I am filled with unbounded joy because of the great strides made by our republic since entering upon its noble career. Loving that which is most useful, animated by what is most just and aspiring to what is most perfect, Venezuela in separating from the Spanish Nation has recovered her independence, her freedom, her equality, her national sovereignty. In becoming a democratic republic, she proscribed monarchy, distinctions, nobility, franchises and privileges; she declared the rights of man, the liberty of action, of thought, of speech, of writing. These preeminently liberal acts will never be sufficiently admired for the sincerity by which they are inspired. The first Congress of Venezuela has impressed upon the annals of our legislation with indelible characters the majesty of the people, so fittingly expressed in the consummation of the social act best calculated to develop the happiness of a Nation.

I need to gather all my strength in order to feel with all the reverence of which I am capable, the supreme goodness embodied in this immortal Code of our rights and our laws! But how can I venture to say it! Shall I dare profane by my censure the sacred tablets of our laws? There are sentiments that no lover of liberty can hold within his breast; they overflow stirred by their own violence, and notwithstanding the efforts of the one harboring such sentiments, an irresistible force will disclose them. I am convinced that the Government of Venezuela must be changed, and while many illustrious citizens will feel as I do, not all possess the necessary boldness to stand publicly for the adoption of new principles. This consideration compels me to take the initiative in a matter of the gravest concern, although there is great audacity in my pretending to give advice to the Counsellors of the People.

The more I admire the excellence of the Federal Constitution of Venezuela, the more I am persuaded of the impossibility of its application in our State. And, in my opinion, it is a wonder that its model in North America may endure so successfully, and is not upset in the presence of the first trouble or danger. Notwithstanding the fact that that people is a unique model of political virtues and moral education; notwithstanding that it has been cradled in liberty, that it has been reared in freedom and lives on pure liberty, I will say more, although in many respects that people is unique in the history of humanity, it is a prodigy, I repeat, that a system so weak and complicated as the federal system should have served to govern that people in circumstances as difficult and delicate as those which have existed. But, whatever the case may be, as regards the American Nation, I must say that nothing is further from my mind than to try to assimilate the conditions and character of two nations as different as the Anglo-American and the Spanish-American. Would it not be extremely difficult to apply to Spain the Code of political, civil and religious liberty of England? It would be even more difficult to adapt to Venezuela the laws of North America. Does not the *Spirit of Laws*[77] state that they must be suited to the people for whom they are made; that it is a great coincidence when the laws of one nation suit another; that laws must bear relation to the physical features of a country, its climate, its soil, its situation, extension and manner of living of the people; that they must have reference to the degree of liberty that their constitution may be able to provide for the religion of the inhabitants, their inclinations, wealth, number, trade, customs and manners? Such is the Code that we should consult, not that of Washington! [...]

Bolívar, Simón. *An Address of Bolívar at the Congress of Angostura: February 15, 1819* (version reprint ordered by the government of the United States of Venezuela, to commemorate the centennial of the opening of the Congress). Washington, DC: B. S. Adams, 1919. https://archive.org/embed/addressofbolivarooboluoft.

---

77. Montesquieu's *The Spirit of the Laws* (1748) offers analyses of forms of government, separation of powers, and the effect of regionalism on politics.

from "A New Guatemala" by Juan José Arévalo

Introduction

Juan José Arévalo (1904–1990) grew up on a farm near the town of Taxisco, in the Guatemalan south Pacific coast Department of Santa Rosa. An excellent student, he was awarded a scholarship to study in Argentina, and while there he earned a doctorate in philosophy. As an educator he was innovative, believing that rote memorization, the most popular way of teaching in early twentieth-century Latin America, did not facilitate critical thinking. Rather than a static classroom where memorization dominated, he promoted engaged and practical hands-on learning. Returning from Argentina, he worked in the Guatemalan Ministry of Education but when General Jorge Ubico took power as a dictator in 1931, he entered a self-imposed exile, returning to Argentina where he taught in various universities. In 1944, upon the overthrow of Ubico, he returned to Guatemala, responding to a call from his countrymen to serve as a candidate in the upcoming presidential election. He won an overwhelming victory, capturing over 80 percent of the vote.

> **SNAPSHOT BOX**
>
> LANGUAGE: Spanish
> DELIVERED: 1945, Guatemala
> GENRE: Public address
> TAGS: Class and Caste; Education; Labor; Psyche; Rhetoric and Persuasion; Self-Determination; Statecraft

The political history of Central America has been complex and troubled. The historic homeland of the Maya, Guatemala gained its independence from Spain in 1821 and has frequently been governed by oligarchs and dictators. A liberal revolution in 1871 brought some progressive policies to the country, but equal rights for the Indigenous population and women remained far from the reality. In 1898 when

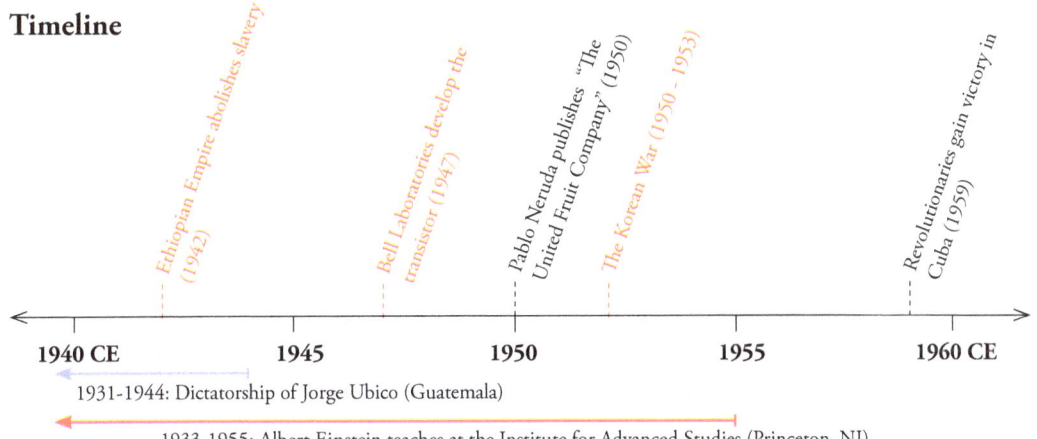

the dictator, José María Reyna Barrios was assassinated, his vice president, Manuel Estrada Cabrera took control of the government and instituted an authoritarian regime that, while continuing with the liberal label, was primarily a kleptocracy (government by thieves), that colluded with one of the world's first multinational corporations (MNC), the United States-based, United Fruit Company (UFC). The UFC constructed infrastructure like railroads and an electrical grid, thus monopolizing transport, energy, and the economy in partnership with a Guatemalan government that controlled the working class and Indigenous farmers by force, keeping wages at poverty levels and conditions deplorable, crushing any attempt by laborers to organize. Estrada Cabrera ruled until 1920 and was followed by a succession of UFC-friendly presidents that rubber-stamped the machinations of the MNC.

In 1931, as the dislocation and desperation of the Great Depression brought unrest, General Jorge Ubico emerged from the elite class and captured a sham election (he was the only candidate). Ubico used the military to enforce unfair and harsh vagrancy laws that essentially extracted unpaid labor from sizable segments of the working class and Indigenous population. Ubico also increased the government's involvement with the UFC, applying his authoritarian policies to facilitate land acquisition and slave-labor wages. From 1931 to 1944 the UFC came to be the country's largest landowner and earned the nickname, "El Pulpo" (The Octopus), because its tentacles reached into every sector of Guatemala's economy and society. What other examples can you think of that create alliances between government and corporate entities?

Guatemala joined with the Allies in World War II (1939–1945) and while it sent no troops to fight, there was considerable joint training between its military and that of the United States. Thanks in part to the Allied propaganda that reached the population, by 1944 the anti-democratic and authoritarian nature of Ubico's regime unmistakably reflected the character of the Axis powers and multiple sectors of Guatemalan society rebelled and overthrew the government. The military was crucial but the participation of the business and educational sectors in the country were equally important, especially the actions of students. Ubico fled the country and an election was held that saw the return from exile of Arévalo and his successful candidacy for the presidency.

Arévalo served a single term (1945–1951) because the new revolutionary constitution forbade re-election of the president. Arévalo pushed through progressive policies like social security, the right for labor to organize, a higher minimum wage, and literacy programs. During his term, the government became an active and positive part of daily life in Guatemala. He also attempted to put the welfare of Guatemalans ahead of foreign investors. As you read Arévalo's speech, take note of the places where he reminds you of an educator/teacher?

When he stepped down in 1951 he was followed into office by Jacobo Arbenz Guzman, who won a resounding election victory by promising to carry on Arévalo's policies. Arbenz's efforts to move the revolutionary legislation into the countryside distressed the interests of the UFC. When his government moved to redistribute land owned by the corporation with compensation, the government led by US president Eisenhower decried the move as "communist." In the tense Cold War atmosphere of the 1950s the United States began a covert operation that in 1954 overthrew Arbenz and installed a friendly and pliable government. Subsequently, Guatemala suffered through thirty-two years of mainly military rule until elections were again held in 1986. Meanwhile, in response to the US-backed coup d'état, a leftist insurgency arose in 1960 that led to a civil war fought from 1960 to 1996, one of the modern era's longest, resulting in between 150,000 and 200,000 dead or "disappeared." What parts of Arévalo's 1945 message in this speech might have caused the US government to begin to scrutinize the actions of the Guatemalan government?

Alvis Dunn
Department of History

> **PRE-READING PARS**
>
> 1. When you are presented with a proposal that you must choose either A or B, what are two or three reasons that would prompt you to ask, "what about C or D?"
> 2. Make a list of some of the legacies of British colonialism in the United States. Can you do the same thing for any two nations in Latin America in regard to Spanish colonialism?

A New Guatemala

The following selection is drawn from a 1945 speech given by Arévalo titled "Conservatives, Liberals, and Socialists."

Conservatism and liberalism are doctrines that in America blossomed and died in the nineteenth century. Conservatism was the political doctrine the Guatemalans of 1821, who received their independence with little effort and as a result ... they installed a republic, or a shell of a republic, the fundamental objective of which was to conserve the Spanish way of life.

... With the ascent to power of liberal ideas in 1871, the neocolonial system of 1821 was neutralized and a sense of national liberation began to form, an authentic Guatemalan independence with the potential for triumph, as the movement counted upon men who were more morally balanced and who had firmer political convictions. But the liberalism of 1871 was just a doctrine; it was simply that doctrine we have all admired since childhood, the doctrine of national emancipation from colonial systems. But in practice, disgracefully, liberalism was from the very beginning—and continued to be until a scant few days ago-a colonial system in disguise, which with pithy words and bombastic rhetoric applied the same methods of rule as had colonialism and conservatism....

Because both doctrines shared the same methods, it became ... impossible to distinguish conservatives from liberals but for their last names. Conservatism had died a natural death, for its dimwitted goal of maintaining the systems of colonialism under the banner of the republic. Liberalism was dying a slow and tortured death by asphyxiation, asphyxiated by the mental, and moral incapacity of its men to install, for once and for all, the republic.... During the entire twentieth century, Guatemala has been neither liberal nor conservative. It has been a people without political expression, governed by men who have been ideologically empty... Because of this, we were slow and suffered from blind spots in our appreciation of Guatemalans' political ideas. And this explains why Guatemala has lived the entire twentieth century, with the exception of a few fleeting interruptions, under dictatorship, isolated from the modern world....

Individualistic liberalism is no longer alive in the world, and conservatism cannot be resuscitated. It has been a century now since the world has been organized according to new social concepts.... And it has been a century since economics, politics, and culture have been reorganized according to socialist ideas, which is to say, according to a new interpretation of history and a new valorizing of man. This socialism began as utopian, continued on as materialistic, and has come to be, in our times, spiritual....

We are socialists because we live in the twentieth century. But we are not socialist materialists. We do not believe that man's essence is his stomach. We believe that man, above all else, desires dignity. To be a man with dignity or to be nothing. For this reason, our socialism is not oriented toward the naive redistribution of material goods, toward the idiotic economic equalizing of men who are economically different. Our socialism seeks to liberate men psychologically, to return to them all of the psychological and spiritual integrity that was denied them by conservatism and liberalism. We will give each citizen not the superficial right to vote but instead the fundamental right to live in peace with his own conscience, with his family, with his possessions, with his destiny. To socialize a republic does not simply mean exploiting industry in cooperation with the workers. Rather, it begins even earlier: to turn every worker into a man who can live as a complete psychological and moral being. A worker who is well-fed and well-dressed is not our goal: the generals' horses have also been well-fed, well-harnessed, and even given hot baths and preventive medicines. Good food and good clothes are indeed needs that should be attended to. But first we must invest the worker with all of his dignities as a man, destroying at the same time the many pretexts that have been used to keep him in humiliation and servitude. Spiritual socialism is a doctrine of psychological and moral liberation....

If we call this postwar socialism "spiritual," it is because in the world—as it is doing in Guatemala today—it will produce a fundamental reversal in human values. Materialistic preachings have been revealed to be a new instrument in the service of totalitarian doctrines. Communism, fascism, and Nazism have also been socialist. But they were socialist in a way that nourished with the left hand while mutilating the moral and civic essence of man with the right. National Socialism, the most modern of all these systems, could only produce a mass of mechanized workers, well-fed and well-clothed, who had lost, as the price for these advantages, their hierarchy as citizens and their authority within the family. Spiritual socialism will transcend the philosophical formula of Nazism, which only recognizes the leader, and it will begin—like liberalism—to invest its majesty in moral and civil virtue. But it will go further than liberalism by breaking the insularity of man, obliging him to integrate himself into the atmosphere of society's values, needs, and goals, simultaneously conceiving of society as an economic organism and a spiritual entity. The spiritual, however, will rule in this conception of the world and in the economic aspects of life, in order to imbue them with national sentiment.

Arévalo, Juan José. "A New Guatemala." In *The Guatemala Reader: History, Culture, Politics*, edited by Greg Grandin, Deborah T. Levenson, and Elizabeth Oglesby. Translated by Kirsten Weld, 206–10. Durham, NC: Duke University Press, 2011.

> **POST-READING PARS**
>
> 1. It is clear that Arévalo's "spiritual socialism" was a different ideology from both the capitalism of the United States and the communism of the Soviet Union. How did Arévalo actually expect this third way to operate?
> 2. What parts of Guatemala's colonial legacy do you learn about in this reading?

Inquiry Corner

Content Question:

What does Arévalo say are the problems with liberalism and conservatism?

Critical Question:

Arévalo calls for "psychological and moral liberation" in Guatemala as a starting point for building a new nation. Critically evaluate the opportunities and challenges of this strategy for a country like Guatemala.

Comparative Questions:

Are there other readings that you have done in this course that also lay out a blueprint for transformation of society? How do the ideas in these sources compare with those presented in Arévalo's "New Guatemala?"

Connection Question:

If you were planning a debate over the design of the ideology undergirding effective political systems, who among the authors that we have read would you invite and why? Think of at least four.

BEYOND THE CLASSROOM

» In many ways Arévalo's concept of "spiritual socialism" sounds like being free to be oneself. How do you see this type of freedom or authenticity being a positive thing in the workplace? Alternately, what challenges may it present?
» In a fast-paced and competitive United States we have a tendency to work toward our own goals as individuals rather than working as a collective. We all have different personal and professional values, so what would it look like to work in an environment where the values and goals of others looked different than your own? How can we work well together even if our values and goals are different?

from "The Rights of Women" by Sayyid Ahmad Khan

SNAPSHOT BOX

LANGUAGE: Urdu

PUBLISHED: 1871, British India

GENRE: Journal article

TAGS: Cross-Cultural Encounters; Gender and Identity; Religion; Tradition

Introduction

Sayyid Ahmad Khan (1817–1898) was an Islamic modernist who lived during the decline of the Mughal Empire in the Indian subcontinent and the establishment of British imperial rule (the **British Raj**). After a brief career in service to the East India Trading Company, he became a writer whose works were instrumental in reforming Islam in South Asia and decreasing tensions between Muslims and the British in India. This document was originally published in the popular Urdu-language journal that Khan founded entitled *Tahzibul Akhlaq* (*Moral Civilization*) that encouraged Indian Muslims to adopt religious and social reforms.

As Western ideas about modernity—such as extending secular education and offering more political and social opportunities to women—began to impact Islamic societies, Muslims responded in a variety of ways to what they viewed as a significant challenge to more conventional ways of life. Some insisted that they should follow the example of the Prophet Muhammad, who, when faced with hostile forces in Mecca, emigrated with his followers (the ***hijra***) to the more welcoming city of Medina. Since such a drastic solution was impractical for most, other voices called simply for noncooperation with colonial governments, while others—notably the Saudi Kingdom in Arabia—enforced more rigidly defined forms of Islam, such as **Wahhabism**, a "fundamentalist" form of Sunni Islam founded by Muhammad ibn Abd al-Wahhab in the eighteenth century. Messianic

Timeline

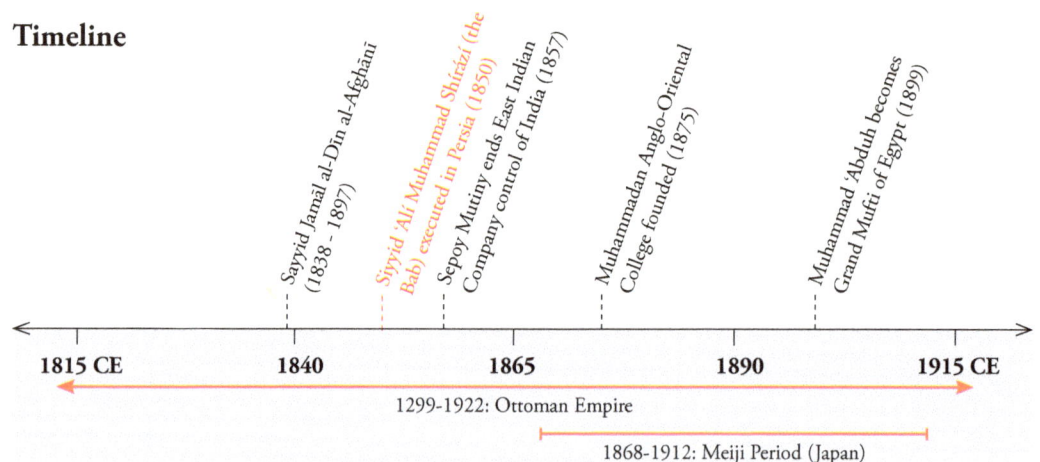

movements gripped some areas of the Muslim world, particularly in majority Shi'ite regions, where many believed the Last Day was about to dawn with the return of the Twelfth Imam, who had mysteriously vanished in the ninth century of the Common Era. For those who termed themselves modernists, however, some form of cooperation between Islam and European-styled modernity was not only possible but was in keeping with the history and development of Islam itself. In fact, the lines between Europe and Islamic worlds had been far more porous in premodern periods than this later more dichotomous framing between so-called modern Europe and the "traditional" Islamic world that became central to the project of European dominance.

Islamic modernists developed several strategies to define the religion in ways that were compatible with ideas and practices derived from secular and humanist approaches. For all practicing Muslims, the Qur'an and the **sunna** (traditions, especially traditions about the Prophet), the two bases of the **sharia** (divine law), were incontrovertible. But rather than impose a restrictive literalism on the Qur'an, modernists, many of whom adopted the legal opinions of medieval Muslim scholars, argued that unless something had been expressly forbidden in the text, then it was allowed. Such a principle had undergirded the practice of rationalist philosophy and empirical sciences in many Islamic scholarly communities in prior centuries, they argued. Indeed, the application of empiricism and reason to the claims of religion was not only acceptable but commended by God in the Qur'an:

> Behold! In the creation of the heavens and the earth; in the alternation of the Night and the Day; in the sailing of ships through the Ocean, for the profit of mankind; in the rain which Allah sends down from the skies, and the life which He gives therewith to an earth that is dead; in the beasts of all kinds that He scatters through the earth; in the change of the winds, and the clouds which they trail like their slaves between the sky and the earth; (here) indeed are Signs for a people that are wise. (2:164)[78]

To examine the history of Islam was to understand that many of the things that seemed novel to strict traditionalists had in fact been developed and utilized previously by Islam. For example, democracy was but a form of the **shura** (consultation) that had been promoted by Muhammad as a way of resolving grievances, and in fact had been used to choose his successor in the Sunni understanding of community-consensus rather than by the Shi'ite understanding of succession to leadership by bloodline to the Prophet. Religious tolerance (but not religious liberty) had been the official policy of Islamic states since the early caliphal period that followed the death of Muhammad. And while the notion of universal human rights was relatively new in Western cultures, Islam had supported many of these principles—such as

---

78. The Qur'an, translation by Abdullah Yusuf Ali (Elmhurst, NY: Tahrike Tarsile Qur'an, 1998).

religious tolerance and greater gender equality in economic affairs—for centuries. How would you describe the interactions between various religious institutions and rights in different contexts? What examples come to mind?

    Sayyid Ahmad Khan (Sir Syed) helped bring these modernist arguments before the government and peoples of British India through his numerous publications and his various educational projects, which included the founding of what became Aligarh Muslim University. How do elements of Islamic modernities shape possible reforms? Why do you think women are often central to reform movements?

Rodger Payne
Department of Religious Studies

The Rights of Women

Developed countries loudly proclaim that men and women are created equal and that both hold equal rights. They also proclaim that there is no reason why women should be thought of as less important or less worthy of respect than men. They do not even accept that, by way of illustration, it can be said that a woman is like the left hand and a man the right hand, or that in value a woman adds up to 12 and a man to a dozen. Nevertheless, even today we observe that in no developed country have women been bestowed with the same stature and parity in rights and authority to men as has been bestowed upon them in the religion of Islam. England greatly favors the freedom of women, yet when its laws relating to women are examined, it is obvious that the English consider women quite insignificant, unintelligent, and valueless.

According to English laws, when a woman marries, she is considered to have lost her separate existence, and her distinctive individuality is absorbed into that of her husband. She does not stand in the capacity of a separate member to a contract, and thus she is not able to hold responsibility for any legal instrument she may have signed according to her own will and without the agreement of her husband. The personal possessions, wealth, cash, and property that were hers before marriage all belong to the husband after marriage. That property that comes to a woman by inheritance either before or after marriage is also possessed by the husband for as long as he lives, and he also receives any earnings produced from it. Her status is like that of a feeble-minded incompetent: She cannot bring a lawsuit against anyone, nor can anyone [directly] bring a lawsuit against her. She cannot buy or sell anything without the permission of her husband. Except for the expenses of food, clothing, and living in one house, that is, the basic expenses necessary for daily living, she cannot spend money on anything without her husband's permission.

In 1870 a bill was presented in Parliament regarding the property of married women. Only this much was desired, that the law be rescinded by means of which after marriage a woman's property becomes lost to her. This bill was presented by the Honorable Mr. Russell Gurney, M. P. On this occasion he made some exquisite remarks. He observed that, according to the law then active, whatever a woman had before marriage and received after marriage, and all that she earned by her ability and hard work, left her hands after marriage. Her husband became the owner of it all. Thus the effect of marriage upon a woman was like that of a crime whose prescribed punishment was the confiscation of property! At this, the whole House of Commons burst into laughter and most of the members supported him. Thus, this is the state of English law regarding women, and probably no other law is more deplorable, damaging, and unjust.

Muslim Law Concerning Women

Now consider how women are honored in Muslim law, and how their rights and authority have been conceded to be equal to those of men. Before adulthood, just like men, women are considered to be without authority and unqualified to enter into official agreements. But upon reaching adulthood she assumes the same authority as a man and is qualified to enter into a contract. Just like men, women have the authority to marry. Just like a man's, a woman's marriage cannot take place without her consent. She herself is the owner and controller of all her personal property, and has full authority over it. She has the capability, like a man, of executing any kind of contract, and her person and her property stand accountable with respect to any contracts and documents that she may have written. She is the owner of any property that may have come into her possession before or after marriage, and she herself is the claimant to its benefits. Like men, women can file suits or be sued in the courts. She can purchase anything she wants to with her wealth, and can sell anything she wishes. Like a man, she can give, will, or donate any kind of inheritance. In accordance with regular procedures she can inherit from the property of her relatives and her husband. She can gain, then, all the materials a man may gain. All of the pious merits a man may gain, she may gain as well. Likewise, she receives the same rewards or punishments for her behavior in this world on Judgment Day.

There is no special restriction placed upon a woman that is not also placed upon a man, except that which she has taken upon herself in terms of the wedding contract, or the restriction relating to the private parts of her body that differ by nature from man's.

Thus, in truth, in no religion and in no nation's law have women and men been considered as equal as in the religion of Islam. But it is a most astonishing fact that all developed countries strongly criticize the condition of women in Islam. Yet there is no doubt that the condition of the women of developed countries is many levels better than that of Muslim women and women of Muslim countries, although the situation ought to be the reverse.

In admitting the superiority of the state of women in developed countries, we have not considered the matter of their freedom from the veil, because in our opinion, to the same extent as there is excess in this respect in India, there is excess [of another kind] in advanced countries. And as far as man can bring his intellect to bear on this matter, the limit set by the shari'ah law certainly seems to be perfectly correct.

At this point, what we wish to argue for is simply: good treatment of women by men; good fellowship; courtesy; consideration; love; encouragement; paying attention to their comfort, ease, happiness, and pleasure; keeping them happy in every way. Instead of considering them servants, to consider them as companions, comrades, and partners in both sorrow and happiness and to consider each other the cause of mutual joy and strength is best. Doubtless, as far as we know considerable progress is being made in areas on these particulars regarding women, in the advanced countries. But in Muslim countries there is no progress in these areas and in India there are perpetrated such unworthy and humiliating events that one can only cry out, "May God have mercy on us!"

People who associate these evils with the religion of Islam are surely mistaken. To the extent that there is deterioration in the condition of women in India, it is due to a failure to observe the regulations of Islam fully. If its principles were brought into practice, no doubt all of these evils would be eliminated.

In addition, there is another important reason for this: Muslims today remain in large part uncivilized. Despite the fact that the laws of the developed nations regarding women were extremely defective and miserable, those nations have elevated the position of their women to an extremely high level while Muslims, despite the fact that the laws of the rest of the world are less generous, on account of being uncivilized have treated women so badly that all the nations laugh at the condition of Muslim women. Because of our inherent evils, and because the whole *ummah*[79] is in a sorry state (with perhaps some minimal exceptions willed by God!), all nations criticize our religion.

Therefore, this is not the time for us to ignore these truths and delay correcting our conduct or to fail to show by the light of our behavior that Islam is an enlightened religion.

Khan, Sayyid Ahmad. "The Rights of Women." In *Maqalat-i Sar Sayyid*, edited by Maulana Muhammad Isma'il Pani Pari, translated by Kamran Talattof, 159–61. Lahaur: Majlis-i Taraqqiyi Adab, 1962.

---

79. The worldwide Islamic community.

from *A Vindication of the Rights of Women* by Mary Wollstonecraft

SNAPSHOT BOX

LANGUAGE: English
PUBLISHED: 1792, London
GENRE: Treatise
TAGS: Body; Education; Ethics and Morality; Family; Gender and Identity; Labor; Struggle, Resistance, and Revolution; Women and Power

Introduction

Mary Wollstonecraft (1759–1797) embodied women's aspirations, capabilities, and struggles during the decades in which revolutions erupted in North America, France, and Haiti. She grew up relatively poor in London, with little support from her family and with no formal education. She knew enough of the Bible and the classics that she could find work as a lady's companion, governess, and eventually as a teacher. But her career as an educator was disrupted by family tragedies and her own bouts of depression and attempted suicide. Tending first her dying mother, then facilitating her sister Eliza's escape from a bad marriage whose infant later died, she developed an analysis of women's suffering and oppression from firsthand experience. In her view, access to education was the first of the rights women must have. How can increased opportunities for education provide a way out of suffering and oppression? How might personal experience with suffering and oppression demonstrate a need for a different kind of education?

Along with two sisters and two friends, she dreamed of opening a girls' school. To attract patrons to the project, Wollstonecraft frequented gatherings of intellectuals, including publishers, one of whom would facilitate the publication of *A Vindication of the Rights of Women* (1792) and her other writings, which included travelogues, translations, and fiction. Wollstonecraft was familiar with the ideol-

ogies and strategies of a generation of activists, including Americans like Phyllis Wheatley and Abigail Adams, and her contemporary Olympe de Gouges in France. She was an eyewitness to the radical phase of the French Revolution, including the execution of King Louis XVI and the Reign of Terror (1792–1794). While in France she gave birth to her first daughter but was soon abandoned by the child's father. Eventually she married William Godwin and gave birth to another daughter, Mary, who survived. Wollstonecraft, however, subsequently died of complications during childbirth. Her daughter, Mary Godwin Shelley, would go on to write *Frankenstein* in 1818. How might being a witness to tumult in history and in life influence an author's subject and/or tone?

Wollstonecraft's *Vindication* contributed to a lively and long-standing philosophical debate with real world applications—how to educate children. Eighteenth-century writers argued that childhood was a distinctive phase of life and proposed a variety of alternatives for cultivating children's minds, bodies, and manners from birth through young adulthood. Most writers assumed that approaches to the education of youth would be gender specific, in part because of the different roles men and women were expected at that time to play as adults, but also in part because of perceived differences in their capabilities. Wollstonecraft particularly objected to Jean Jacques Rousseau's *Emile* (1762), which prescribed a child-centered, free-spirited, and nature-based education for boys only. Indeed, he says little about girls' education, having devoted only one of his six chapters to it and only because the theoretical girl in question, Sophie, was destined to be Emile's companion. As such, "the whole education of women ought to be relative to men . . . to educate them when young, to care for them when grown . . . and to make life agreeable and sweet to them."[80] To which Wollstonecraft replies: "what nonsense!" In the *Vindication*, she describes how the artificial environments and constraints to which girls are subjected stunt their minds and bodies and render them dependent. As you read, consider the following question: How does Wollstonecraft propose to discover if it is their nature or their education that separates men and women? She advocated educating girls similarly to boys even if—especially if—they, as mothers, would oversee the education of young children.

While targeting the proponents of gender-specific education, the *Vindication* also critiques cultural constructs of romantic love and sexual attraction. Associating sexual excess with the fall of the aristocratic regime during the French Revolution, educated and progressive men and women like herself proposed companionate relationships based on friendship and mutual respect as befitting a free people in a democratic society. For them, the personal was political.

Tracey Rizzo
Department of History

80. "Jean Jacques Rousseau, *Emile* (1762)," *Liberty, Equality, Fraternity: Exploring the French Revolution*, accessed April 5, 2021. https://revolution.chnm.org/d/470.

> **PRE-READING PARS**
>
> 1. Do you think social change is better accomplished through reform or revolution? List a couple of pros and cons for each strategy.
> 2. Identify two or three examples of how hardships and life challenges might be perceived as gendered? How might they be formative of one's worldview?

from *A Vindication of the Rights of Woman* (1792)

The Prevailing Opinion of a Sexual Character Discussed

To account for, and excuse the tyranny of man, many ingenious arguments have been brought forward to prove, that the two sexes, in the acquirement of virtue, ought to aim at attaining a very different character; or, to speak explicitly, women are not allowed to have sufficient strength of mind to acquire what really deserves the name of virtue. Yet it should seem, allowing them to have souls, that there is but one way appointed by Providence to lead *mankind* to either virtue or happiness.

If then women are not a swarm of ephemeron triflers,[81] why should they be kept in ignorance under the specious name of innocence? Men complain, and with reason, of the follies and caprices of our sex, when they do not keenly satirise our headstrong passions and grovelling vices. Behold, I should answer, the natural effect of ignorance! The mind will ever be unstable that has only prejudices to rest on, and the current will run with destructive fury when there are no barriers to break its force. Women are told from their infancy, and taught by the example of their mothers, that a little knowledge of human weakness, justly termed cunning, softness of temper, *outward* obedience, and a scrupulous attention to a puerile kind of propriety, will obtain for them the protection of man; and should they be beautiful, everything else is needless, for at least twenty years of their lives.

Thus Milton describes our first frail mother; though when he tells us that women are formed for softness and sweet attractive grace, I cannot comprehend his meaning, unless, in the true Mahometan[82] strain, he meant to deprive us of souls, and insinuate that we were beings only designed by sweet attractive grace, and docile blind obedience, to gratify the senses of man when he can no longer soar on the wing of contemplation.

How grossly do they insult us who thus advise us only to render ourselves gentle, domestic brutes! For instance, the winning softness so warmly and frequently recommended, that governs by obeying. What childish expressions, and how insignificant

---

81. Individuals who engage in short-lived trivialities.
82. Muslim

is the being—can it be an immortal one?—who will condescend to govern by such sinister methods! "Certainly," says Lord Bacon, "man is of kin to the beasts by his body; and if he be not of kin to God by his spirit, he is a base and ignoble creature!" Men, indeed, appear to me to act in a very unphilosophical manner, when they try to secure the good conduct of women by attempting to keep them always in a state of childhood. Rousseau was more consistent when he wished to stop the progress of reason in both sexes, for if men eat of the tree of knowledge, women will come in for a taste; but, from the imperfect cultivation which their understandings now receive, they only attain a knowledge of evil.

Children, I grant, should be innocent; but when the epithet is applied to men, or women, it is but a civil term for weakness. For if it be allowed that women were destined by Providence to acquire human virtues, and, by the exercise of their understandings, that stability of character which is the firmest ground to rest our future hopes upon, they must be permitted to turn to the fountain of light, and not forced to shape their course by the twinkling of a mere satellite. Milton, I grant, was of a very different opinion; for he only bends to the indefeasible right of beauty, though it would be difficult to render two passages which I now mean to contrast, consistent. But into similar inconsistencies are great men often led by their senses:

> To whom thus Eve with *perfect beauty* adorn'd.
> My author and disposer, what thou bids't
> *Unargued* I obey; so God ordains;
> God is *thy law, thou mine*: to know no more
> Is woman's *happiest* knowledge and her praise.

These are exactly the arguments that I have used to children; but I have added, your reason is now gaining strength, and, till it arrives at some degree of maturity, you must look up to me for advice,—then you ought to think, and only rely on God.

Yet in the following lines Milton seems to coincide with me, when he makes Adam thus expostulate with his Maker:

> Hast Thou not made me here Thy substitute,
> And these inferior far beneath me set?
> Among *unequals* what society
> Can sort, what harmony or true delight?
> Which must be mutual, in proportion due
> Given and received; but in *disparity*
> The one intense, the other still remiss
> Cannot well suit with either, but soon prove
> Tedious alike: of *fellowship* I speak
> Such as I seek, fit to participate
> All rational delight—

In treating therefore of the manners of women, let us, disregarding sensual arguments, trace what we should endeavour to make them in order to cooperate, if the expression be not too bold, with the Supreme Being.

By individual education, I mean, for the sense of the word is not precisely defined, such an attention to a child as will slowly sharpen the senses, from the temper, regulate the passions as they begin to ferment, and set the understanding to work before the body arrives at maturity; so that the man may only have to proceed, not to begin, the important task of learning to think and reason.

To prevent any misconstruction, I must add, that I do not believe that a private education can work the wonders which some sanguine writers have attributed to it. Men and women must be educated, in a great degree, by the opinions and manners of the society they live in. In every age there has been a stream of popular opinion that has carried all before it, and given a family character, as it were, to the century. It may then fairly be inferred, that, till society be differently constituted, much cannot be expected from education. It is, however, sufficient for my present purpose to assert that, whatever effect circumstances have on the abilities, every being may become virtuous by the exercise of its own reason; for if but one being was created with vicious inclinations, that is positively bad, what can save us from atheism? or if we worship a God, is not that God a devil?

Consequently, the most perfect education, in my opinion, is such an exercise of the understanding as is best calculated to strengthen the body and form the heart. Or, in other words, to enable the individual to attain such habits of virtue as will render it independent. In fact, it is a farce to call any being virtuous whose virtues do not result from the exercise of its own reason.

This was Rousseau's opinion respecting men; I extend it to women, and confidently assert that they have been drawn out of their sphere by false refinement, and not by an endeavour to acquire masculine qualities. Still the regal homage which they receive is so intoxicating, that until the manners of the times are changed, and formed on more reasonable principles, it may be impossible to convince them that the illegitimate power which they obtain by degrading themselves is a curse, and that they must return to nature and equality if they wish to secure the placid satisfaction that unsophisticated affections impart. But for this epoch we must wait—wait perhaps till kings and nobles, enlightened by reason, and, preferring the real dignity of man to childish state, throw off their gaudy hereditary trappings; and if then women do not resign the arbitrary power of beauty—they will prove that they have less mind than man.

I may be accused of arrogance; still I must declare what I firmly believe, that all the writers who have written on the subject of female education and manners, from Rousseau to Dr. Gregory,[83] have contributed to render women more artificial, weak

---

83. Author of *A Father's Legacy to His Daughters* (1774), a popular book of the day on women and education.

characters, than they would otherwise have been; and consequently, more useless members of society. I might have expressed this conviction in a lower key, but I am afraid it would have been the whine of affectation, and not the faithful expression of my feelings, of the clear result which experience and reflection have led me to draw. When I come to that division of the subject, I shall advert to the passages that I more particularly disapprove of, in the works of the authors I have just alluded to; but it is first necessary to observe that my objection extends to the whole purport of those books, which tend, in my opinion, to degrade one-half of the human species, and render women pleasing at the expense of every solid virtue.

Though, to reason on Rousseau's ground, if man did attain a degree of perfection of mind when his body arrived at maturity, it might be proper, in order to make a man and his wife *one*, that she should rely entirely on his understanding; and the graceful ivy, clasping the oak that supported it, would form a whole in which strength and beauty would be equally conspicuous. But, alas! husbands, as well as their helpmates, are often only overgrown children,—nay, thanks to early debauchery, scarcely men in their outward form,—and if the blind lead the blind, one need not come from heaven to tell us consequence.

Many are the causes that, in the present corrupt state of society, contribute to enslave women by cramping their understanding and sharpening their senses. One, perhaps, that silently does more mischief than all the rest is their disregard of order.

To do everything in an orderly manner is a most important precept, which women, who, generally speaking, receive only a disorderly kind of education, seldom attend to with that degree of exactness that men, who from their infancy are broken into method, observe. This negligent kind of guesswork—for what other epithet can be used to point out the random exertions of a sort of instinctive common sense, never brought to the test of reason?—prevents their generalising matters of fact; so they do to-day what they did yesterday, merely because they did it yesterday.

This contempt of the understanding in early life has more baneful consequences than is commonly supposed; for the little knowledge which women of strong minds attain is, from various circumstances, of a more desultory kind than the knowledge of men, and it is acquired more by sheer observations on real life than from comparing what has been individually observed with the results of experience generalised by speculation. Led by their dependent situation and domestic employments more into society, what they learn is rather by snatches; and as learning is with them in general only a secondary thing, they do not pursue any one branch with that persevering ardour necessary to give vigour to the faculties and clearness to the judgment. In the present state of society, a little learning is required to support the character of a gentleman, and boys are obliged to submit to a few years of discipline. But in the education of women, the cultivation of the understanding is always subordinate to the acquirement of some corporeal accomplishment. Even when enervated by confinement and false notions of modesty, the body is prevented from attaining that grace and beauty which relaxed half-formed limbs never exhibit. Besides, in youth their faculties are not brought forward by emulation; and having no serious scientific study, if they have natural sagacity, it is turned too soon on life and manners. They dwell on effects and modifications, without tracing them back to causes; and complicated rules to adjust behaviour are a weak substitute for simple principles.

As a proof that education gives this appearance of weakness to females, we may instance the example of military men, who are, like them, sent into the world before their minds have been stored with knowledge, or fortified by principles. The consequences are similar; soldiers acquire a little superficial knowledge, snatched from the muddy current of conversation, and from continually mixing with society, they gain what is termed a knowledge· of the world; and this acquaintance with manners and customs has frequently been confounded with a knowledge of the human heart. But can the crude fruit of casual observation, never brought to the test of judgment, formed by comparing speculation and experience, deserve such a distinction? Soldiers, as well as women, practise the minor virtues with punctilious politeness. Where is then the sexual difference, when the education has been the same? All the difference that I can discern, arises from the superior advantage of liberty which enables the former to see more of life.

[...]

It may be further observed that officers are also particularly attentive to their persons, fond of dancing, crowded rooms, adventures, and ridicule. Like the fair sex, the business of their lives is gallantry; they were taught to please, and they only live to please. Yet they do not lose their rank in the distinction of sexes, for they are still reckoned superior to women, though in what their superiority consists, beyond what I have just mentioned, it is difficult to discover.

The great misfortune is this, that they both acquire manners before morals, and a knowledge of life before they have from reflection any acquaintance with the grand ideal outline of human nature. The consequence is natural. Satisfied with common nature, they become a prey to prejudices, and taking all their opinions on credit, they blindly submit to authority. So that if they have any sense, it is a kind of instinctive glance that catches proportions, and decides with respect to manners, but fails when arguments are to be pursued below the surface, or opinions analysed.

May not the same remark be applied to women? Nay, the argument may be carried still further, for they are both thrown out of a useful station by the unnatural distinctions established in civilised life. Riches and hereditary honours have made cyphers of women to give consequence to the numerical figure; and idleness has produced a mixture of gallantry and despotism into society, which leads the very men who are the slaves of their mistresses to tyrannise over their sisters, wives, and daughters. This is only keeping them in rank and file, it is true. Strengthen the female mind by enlarging it, and there will be an end to blind obedience; but as blind obedience is ever sought for by power, tyrants and sensualists are in the right when they endeavour to keep woman in the dark, because the former only want slaves, and the latter a plaything. The sensualist, indeed, has been the most dangerous of tyrants, and women have been duped by their lovers, as princes by their ministers, whilst dreaming that they reigned over them.

[...]

Women are therefore to be considered either as moral beings, or so weak that they must be entirely subjected to the superior faculties of men.

Let us examine this question. Rousseau declares that a woman should never for a moment feel herself independent, that she should be governed by fear to exercise her *natural* cunning, and made a coquettish slave in order to render her a more alluring object of desire, a *sweeter* companion to man, whenever he chooses to relax himself He carries the arguments, which he pretends to draw from the indications of nature, still further, and insinuates that truth and fortitude, the corner-stones of all human virtue, should be cultivated with certain restrictions, because, with respect to the female character, obedience is the grand lesson which ought to be impressed with unrelenting rigour.

What nonsense! When will a great man arise with sufficient strength of mind to puff away the fumes which pride and sensuality have thus spread over the subject! If women are by nature inferior to men, their virtues must be the same in quality, if not in degree, or virtue is a relative idea; consequently their conduct should be founded on the same principles, and have the same aim.

Connected with man as daughters, wives, and mothers, their moral character may be estimated by their manner of fulfilling those simple duties; but the end, the grand end, of their exertions should be to unfold their own faculties, and acquire the dignity of conscious virtue. They may try to render their road pleasant; but ought never to forget, in common with man, that life yields not the felicity which can satisfy an immortal soul. I do not mean to insinuate that either sex should be so lost in abstract reflections or distant views as to forget the affections and duties that lie before them, and are, in truth, the means appointed to produce the fruit of life; on the contrary, I would warmly recommend them, even while I assert, that they afford most satisfaction when they are considered in their true sober light.

Probably the prevailing opinion that woman was created for man, may have taken its rise from Moses' poetical story; yet as very few, it is presumed, who have bestowed any serious thought on the subject ever supposed that Eve was, literally speaking, one of Adam's ribs, the deduction must be allowed to fall to the ground, or only be so far admitted as it proves that man, from the remotest antiquity, found it convenient to exert his strength to subjugate his companion, and his invention to show that she ought to have her neck bent under the yoke, because the whole creation was only created for his convenience or pleasure.

Let it not be concluded that I wish to invert the order of things. I have already granted that, from the constitution of their bodies, men seemed to be designed by Providence to attain a greater degree of virtue. I speak collectively of the whole sex; but I see not the shadow of a reason to conclude that their virtues should differ in respect to their nature. In fact, how can they, if virtue has only one eternal standard? I must therefore, if I reason consequentially, as strenuously maintain that they have the same simple direction as that there is a God.

It follows then that cunning should not be opposed to wisdom, little cares to great exertions, or insipid softness, varnished over with the name of gentleness, to that fortitude which grand views alone can inspire.

I shall be told that woman would then lose many of her peculiar graces, and the opinion of a well-known poet might be quoted to refute my unqualified position. For Pope has said, in the name of the whole male sex:

> Yet ne'er so sure our passion to create,
> As when she touch'd the brink of all we hate.

In what light this sally places men and women I shall leave to the judicious to determine. Meanwhile, I shall content myself with observing, that I cannot discover why, unless they are mortal, females should always be degraded by being made subservient to love or lust.

To speak disrespectfully of love is, I know, high treason against sentiment and fine feelings; but I wish to speak the simple language of truth, and rather to address the head than the heart. To endeavor to reason love out of the world would be to out-Quixote Cervantes, and equally offend against common sense; but an endeavor to restrain this tumultuous passion, and to prove that it should not be allowed to dethrone superior powers, or to usurp the sceptre which the understanding should ever coolly wield, appears less wild.

Youth is the season for love in both sexes; but in those days of thoughtless enjoyment provision should be made for the more important years of life, when reflection takes place of sensation. But Rousseau, and most of the male writers who have followed his steps, have warmly inculcated that the whole tendency of female education ought to be directed to one point—to render them pleasing.

Let me reason with the supporters of this opinion who have any knowledge of human nature. Do they imagine that marriage can eradicate the habitude of life? The woman who has only been taught to please will soon find that her charms are oblique sunbeams, and that they cannot have much effect on her husband's heart when they are seen every day, when the summer is passed and gone. Will she then have sufficient native energy to look into herself for comfort, and cultivate her dormant faculties? or is it not more rational to expect that she will try to please other men, and, in the emotions raised by the expectation of new conquests, endeavor to forget the mortification her love or pride has received? When the husband ceases to be a lover, and the time will inevitably come, her desire of pleasing will then grow languid, or become a spring of bitterness; and love, perhaps, the most evanescent of all passions, gives place to jealously or vanity.

I now speak of women who are restrained by principle or prejudice. Such women, though they would shrink from an intrigue with real abhorrence, yet, nevertheless, wish to be convinced by the homage of gallantry that they are cruelly neglected by their husbands; or, days and weeks are spent in dreaming of the happiness enjoyed by congenial souls, till their health is undermined and their spirits broken by discontent. How then can the great art of pleasing be such a necessary study? it is only useful to a mistress. The chaste wife, and serious mother should only consider her power to please as the polish of her virtues, and the affection of her husband as one of the comforts that render her task less difficult and her life happier. But, whether she be loved or neglected, her first wish should be to make herself respectable, and not to rely for all her happiness on a being subject to like infirmities with herself.

The worthy Dr. Gregory fell into a similar error. I respect his heart, but entirely disapprove of his celebrated *Legacy to his Daughters*.

He advises them to cultivate a fondness for dress, because a fondness for dress, he asserts, is natural to them. I am unable to comprehend what either he or Rousseau mean when they frequently use this indefinite term. If they told us that in a pre-existent state the soul was fond of dress, and brought this inclination with it into a new body, I should listen to them with a half-smile, as I often do when I hear a rant about innate elegance. But if he only meant to say that the exercise of the faculties will produce this fondness, I deny it. It is not natural; but arises, like false ambition in men, from a love of power.

Dr. Gregory goes much further; he actually recommends dissimulation, and advises an innocent girl to give the lie to her feelings, and not dance with spirit, when gaiety of heart would make her feet eloquent without making her gestures immodest. In the name of truth and common sense, why should not one woman acknowledge that she can take more exercise than another? or, in other words, that she has a sound constitution; and why, to damp innocent vivacity, is she darkly to be told that men will draw conclusions which she little thinks of? Let the libertine draw what inference he pleases; but, I hope, that no sensible mother will restrain the natural frankness of youth by instilling such indecent cautions. Out of the abundance of the heart the mouth speaketh; and a wiser than Soloman hath said that the heart should be made clean, and not trivial ceremonies observed, which it is not very difficult to fulfil with scrupulous exactness when vice reigns in the heart.

Women ought to endeavor to purify their heart; but can they do so when their uncultivated understandings make them entirely dependent on their senses for employment and amusement, when no noble pursuits set them above the little vanities of the day, or enables them to curb the wild emotions that agitate a reed, over which every passing breeze has power? To gain the affections of a virtuous man, is affectation necessary? Nature has given woman a weaker frame than man; but, to ensure her husband's affections, must a wife, who, by the exercise of her mind and body whilst she was discharging the duties of a daughter, wife, and mother, has allowed her constitution to retain its natural strength, and her nerves a healthy tone,—is she, I say, to condescend to use art, and feign a sickly delicacy, in order to secure her husband's affection? Weakness may excite tenderness, and gratify the arrogant pride of man; but the lordly caresses of a protector will not gratify a noble mind that pants for and deserves to be respected. Fondness is a poor substitute for friendship!

In a *seraglio*, I grant, that all these arts are necessary; the epicure must have his palate tickled, or he will sink into apathy; but have women so little ambition as to be satisfied with such a condition? Can they supinely dream life away in the lap of pleasure, or the languor of weariness, rather than assert their claim to pursue reasonable pleasures, and render themselves conspicuous by practising the virtues which dignify mankind? Surely she has not an immortal soul who can loiter life away merely employed to adorn her person, that she may amuse the languid hours, and soften the cares of a fellow-creature who is willing to be enlivened by her smiles and tricks, when the serious business of life is over.

Besides, the woman who strengthens her body and exercises her mind will, by managing her family and practising various virtues, become the friend, and not the humble dependent of her husband; and if she, by possessing such substantial qualities, merit his regard, she will not find it necessary to conceal her affection, nor to pretend to an unnatural coldness of constitution to excite her husband's passions. In fact, if we revert to history, we shall find that the women who have distinguished themselves have neither been the most beautiful nor the most gentle of their sex.

Nature, or, to speak with strict propriety, God, has made all things right; but man has sought him out many inventions to mar the work. I now allude to that part of Dr. Gregory's treatise, where he advises a wife never to let her husband know the extent of her sensibility or affection. Voluptuous precaution, and as ineffectual as absurd. Love, from its very nature, must be transitory. To seek for a secret that would render it constant, would be as wild a search as for the philosopher's stone, or the grand panacea; and the discovery would be equally useless, or rather pernicious, to mankind. The most holy band of society is friendship. It has been well said, by a shrewd satirist, "that rare as true love is, true friendship is still rarer."

This is an obvious truth, and, the cause not lying deep, will not elude a slight glance of inquiry.

Love, the common passion, in which chance and sensation take place of choice and reason, is, in some degree, felt by the mass of mankind; for it is not necessary to speak, at present, of the emotions that rise above or sink below love. This passion, naturally increased by suspense and difficulties, draws the mind out of its accustomed state, and exalts the affections; but the security of marriage, allowing the fever of love to subside, a healthy temperature is thought insipid only by those who have not sufficient intellect to substitute the calm tenderness of friendship, the confidence of respect, instead of blind admiration, and the sensual emotions of fondness.

This is, must be, the course of nature. Friendship or indifference inevitably succeeds love. And this constitution seems perfectly to harmonise with the system of government which prevails in the moral world. Passions are spurs to action, and open the mind; but they sink into mere appetites, become a personal and momentary gratification when the object is gained, and the satisfied mind rests in enjoyment. The man who had some virtue whilst he was struggling for a crown, often becomes a voluptuous tyrant when it graces his brow; and, when the lover is not lost in the husband, the dotard, a prey to childish caprices and fond jealousies, neglects the serious duties of life, and the caresses which should excite confidence in his children are lavished on the overgrown child, his wife.

In order to fulfil the duties of life, and to be able to pursue with vigour the various employments which form the moral character, a master and mistress of a family ought not to continue to love each other with passion. I mean to say that they ought not to indulge those emotions which disturb the order of society, and engross the thoughts that should be otherwise employed. The mind that has never been engrossed by one object wants vigour,—if it can long be so, it is weak.

[...]

I own it frequently happens, that women who have fostered a romantic unnatural delicacy of feeling, waste their lives in *imagining* how happy they should have been with a husband who could love them with a fervid increasing affection every day, and all day. But they might as well pine married as single and would not be a jot more unhappy with a bad husband than longing for a good one. That a proper education, or, to speak with more precision, a well-stored mind, would enable a woman to support a single life with dignity, I grant; but that she should avoid cultivating her taste, lest her husband should occasionally shock it, is quitting a substance for a shadow. To say the truth, I do not know of what use is an improved taste, if the individual be not rendered more independent of the casualties of life; if new sources of enjoyment, only dependent on the solitary operations of the mind, are not opened. People of taste, married or single, without distinction, will ever be disgusted by various things that touch not less observing minds. On this conclusion the argument must not be allowed to hinge; but in the whole sum of enjoyment is taste to be denominated a blessing?

The question is, whether it procures most pain or pleasure? The answer will decide the propriety of Dr. Gregory's advice, and show how absurd and tyrannic it is thus to lay down a system of slavery, or to attempt to educate moral beings by any other rules than those deduced from pure reason, which apply to the whole species.

Gentleness of manners, forbearance and long-suffering, are such amiable Godlike qualities, that in sublime poetic strains the Deity had been invested with them; and, perhaps, no representation of His goodness so strongly fastens on the human affections as those that represent Him abundant in mercy and willing to pardon. Gentleness, considered in this point of view, bears on its front all the characteristics of grandeur, combined with the winning graces of condescension; but what a different aspect it assumes when it is the submissive demeanour of dependence, the support of weakness that loves, because it wants protection; and is forbearing, because it must silently endure injurie smiling under the lash at which it dare not snarl. Abject as this picture appears it is the portrait of an accomplished woman, according to the received opinion of female excellence, separated by specious reasoners from human excellence.

Or, they kindly restore the rib, and make one moral being of a man and woman; not forgetting to give her all the "submissive charms."

How women are to exist in that state where there is to be neither marrying nor giving in marriage, we are not told. For though moralists have agreed, that the tenor of life seems to prove that *man* is prepared by various circumstances for a future state, they constantly concur in advising *woman* only to provide for the present. Gentleness, docility, and a spaniel-like affection are, on this ground, consistently recommended as the cardinal virtues of the sex; and, disregarding the arbitrary economy of nature, one writer has declared that it is masculine for a woman to be melancholy. She was created to be the toy of man, his rattle, and it must jingle in his ears, whenever, dismissing reason, he chooses to be amused.

As a philosopher, I read with indignation the plausible epithets which men use to soften their insults; and, as a moralist, I ask what is meant by such heterogeneous associations, as fair defects, amiable weaknesses, etc.? If there be but one criterion of morals, but one architype for man, women appear to be suspended by destiny, according to the vulgar tale of Mahomet's coffin; they have neither the unerring instinct of brutes, nor are allowed to fix the eye of reason on a perfect model. They were made to be loved, and must not aim at respect, lest they should be hunted out of society as masculine.

But to view the subject in another point of view. Do passive indolent women make the best wives? Confining our discussion to the present moment of existence, let us see how such weak creatures perform their part? Do the women who, by the attainment of a few superficial accomplishments, have strengthened the prevailing prejudice, merely contribute to the happiness of their husbands? Do they display their charms merely to amuse them? And have women, who have early imbibed notions of passive obedience, sufficient character to manage a family or educate children? So far from it, that, after surveying the history of woman, I cannot help agreeing with the severest satirist, considering the sex as the weakest as well as the most oppressed half of the species. What does history disclose but marks of inferiority, and how few women have emancipated themselves from the galling yoke of sovereign man? So few that the exceptions remind me of an ingenious conjecture respecting Newton that he was probably a being of superior order, accidentally caged in a human body. Following the same train of thinking, I have been led to imagine that the few extraordinary women who have rushed in eccentrical directions out of the orbit prescribed to their sex, were *male* spirits, confined by mistake in female frames. But if it be not philosophical to think of sex when the soul is mentioned, the inferiority must depend on the organs; or the heavenly fire, which is to ferment the clay, is not given in equal portions.

But avoiding, as I have hitherto done, any direct comparison of the two sexes collectively, or frankly acknowledging the inferiority of woman, according to the present appearance of things, I shall only insist, that men have increased that inferiority till women are almost sunk below the standard of rational creatures. Let their faculties have room to unfold, and their virtues to gain strength, and then determine where the whole sex must stand in the intellectual scale. Yet, let it be remembered, that for a small number of distinguished women I do not ask a place.

It is difficult for us purblind mortals to say to what height human discoveries and improvements may arrive when the gloom of despotism subsides, which makes us stumble at every step; but, when morality shall be settled on a more solid basis, then, without being gifted with a prophetic spirit, I will venture to predict that woman will be either the friend or slave of man. We shall not, as at present, doubt whether she is a moral agent, or the link which unites man with brutes. But should it then appear that like the brutes they were principally created for the use of man, he will let them patiently bite the bridle, and not mock them with empty praise; or, should their rationality be proved, he will not impede their improvement merely to gratify his sensual appetites. He will not, with all the graces of rhetoric, advise them to submit implicitly their understanding to the guidance of man. He will not, when he treats of the education of women, assert that they ought never to have the free use of reason, nor would he recommend cunning and dissimulation to beings who are acquiring, in like manner as himself, the virtues of humanity.

[…]

These may be termed Utopian dreams. Thanks to that Being who impressed them on my soul, and gave me sufficient strength of mind to dare to exert my own reason, till, becoming dependent only on Him for the support of my virtue, I view, with indignation, the mistaken notions that enslave my sex.

I love man as my fellow; but his sceptre, real or usurped, extends not to me, unless the reason of an individual demands my homage; and even then the submission is to reason, and not to man. In fact, the conduct of an accountable being must be regulated by the operations of its own reason; or on what foundation rests the throne of God?

It appears to me necessary to dwell on these obvious truths, because females have been insulated, as it were; and, while they have been stripped of the virtues that should clothe humanity, they have been decked with artificial graces that enable them to exercise a short-lived tyranny. Love, in their bosoms, taking place of every nobler passion, their sole ambition is to be fair, to raise emotion instead of inspiring respect; and this ignoble desire, like the servility in absolute monarchies, destroys all strength of character. Liberty is the mother of virtue, and if women be, by their very constitution, slaves, and not allowed to breathe the sharp invigorating air of freedom, they must ever languish like exotics, and be reckoned beautiful flaws in nature.

As to the argument respecting the subjection in which the sex has ever been held, it retorts on man. The many have always been enthralled by the few; and monsters, who scarcely have shown any discernment of human excellence, have tyrannised over thousands of their fellow-creatures. Why have men of superior endowments submitted to such degradation? For, is it not universally acknowledged that kings, viewed collectively, have ever been inferior, in abilities and virtue, to the same number of men taken from the common mass of mankind—yet have they not, and are they not still treated with a degree of reverence that is an insult to reason? China is not the only country where a living man has been made a God. *Men* have submitted to superior strength to enjoy with impunity the pleasure of the moment; *women* have only done the same, and therefore till it is proved that the courtier, who servilely resigns the birthright of a man, is not a moral agent, it cannot be demonstrated that woman is essentially inferior to man because she has always been subjugated.

Of the Pernicious Effects Which Arise from the Unnatural Distinctions Established in Society

[...]

Besides, when poverty is more disgraceful than. even vice, is not morality cut to the quick? Still to avoid misconstruction, though I consider that women in the common walks of life are called to fulfil the duties of wives and mothers, by religion and reason, I cannot help lamenting that women of a superior cast have not a road open by which they can pursue more extensive plans of usefulness and independence. I may excite laughter, by dropping an hint, which I mean to pursue, some future time, for I really think that women ought to have representatives, instead of being arbitrarily governed without having any direct share allowed them in the deliberations of government.

Selection from Wollstonecraft, Mary. *A Vindication of the Rights of Woman with Strictures on Political and Moral Subjects.* London: J. Johnson, 1792.

POST-READING PARS

1. How does Wollstonecraft demonstrate her erudition? Highlight two instances in the text and comment on how they support Wollstonecraft's thesis.
2. Give two examples from *Vindication* where Wollstonecraft characterizes certain hardships as gendered. How do these hardships shape her worldview?

Inquiry Corner

Content Questions:

What parallels does Wollstonecraft draw between young women and soldiers?

Whom does Wollstonecraft fault for perpetuating women's subordination to men?

Critical Questions:

While Wollstonecraft's Vindication is primarily viewed as a plea for equality, what aspects of hierarchy are also present? How are equality and hierarchy related to each other in this reading?

Comparative Questions:

Wollstonecraft published a favorable review of Equiano's *Interesting Narrative*. How might abolitionists and women's rights advocates find common ground? How might this comparison be problematic?

Connection Questions:

What might contemporary justifications for gender-specific education look like? In the United States, or elsewhere?

"What I Believe" and "Speech Against Conscription and War" by Emma Goldman

SNAPSHOT BOX

PUBLISHED: 1908, *New York World* ("What I Believe")

DELIVERED: June 14, 1917, New York City ("Speech Against Conscription and War")

GENRES: Newspaper editorial, manifesto, public address

TAGS: History and Ideology; Internationalism; Labor; Rhetoric and Persuasion; Statecraft; War and Brutality

Introduction

Emma Goldman (1869–1940) was born in present-day Lithuania, then part of the Russian Empire, but her political renaissance took place in 1886 in the United States in the wake of the Haymarket Incident. Seven anarchists (including Albert Parsons, husband of activist Lucy Parsons) were wrongly convicted of throwing a bomb at the police who were attempting to disperse a labor rally in Chicago's Haymarket Square. These men were martyrs in Emma Goldman's eyes — activists struggling against the oppressive forces of capitalist greed.

Goldman had shown great promise as a young student, but she was discouraged from pursuing further education by her father. Already speaking Yiddish, Russian, and German, and just beginning to learn French, she was not allowed to pursue her studies and began working as a seamstress to help support the family. In 1885, Emma Goldman arrived in the United States to join her older sister in Rochester, New York. Brilliant, but poorly educated, she sought work as a seamstress in the tradition of other Eastern European women immigrants in the area. She married briefly but felt trapped in the relationship and fled to New York City.

Her political awareness of the turmoil in Chicago coincided with her involvement with various groups of labor reformers and anarchists. Almost immediately, she encountered Alexander Berkman, who became her lover

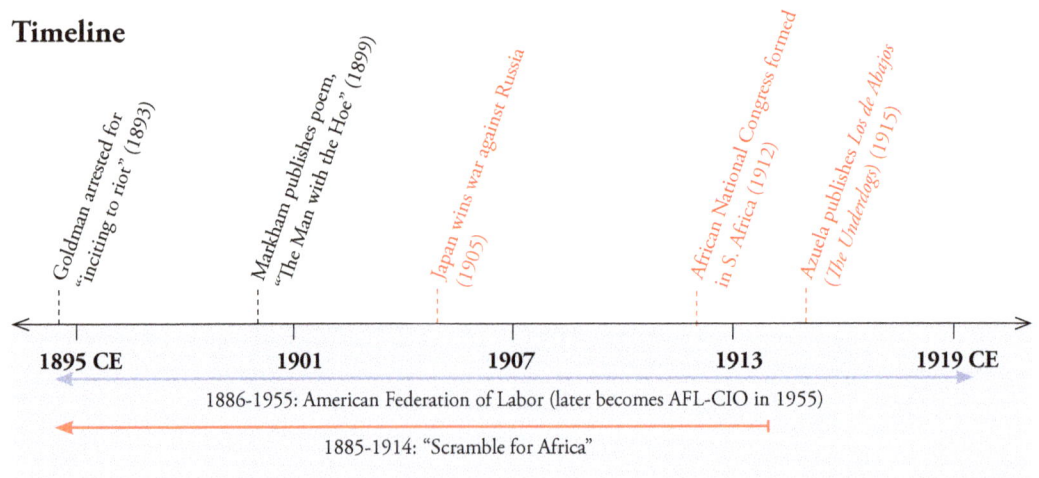

and closest political ally. She was finally free to continue her education on her own among these radical groups, learning political theory, philosophy, medicine, and theater and acquiring English and French with sufficient facility to translate speeches in person from Russian or French into English at political rallies and lectures. Make a few notes of the obstacles society placed in the way of Goldman's aspirations and reflect on your own struggles in getting the education you desire.

She soon began her own distinguished speaking career that carried her across the country, attracting crowds in the thousands in some places, as she defended controversial topics such as anarchism, birth control, free love, and opposition to the draft. She outlines these causes in her 1908 manifesto, "What I Believe." Goldman was already notorious — referred to by authorities as "the most dangerous woman in America." She describes how a soldier was imprisoned merely for shaking hands with her while in uniform. Goldman was involved in many activities that were regarded as seditious. She helped plan Berkman's failed assassination attempt of industrialist Henry Clay Frick, supported violent labor revolts, led huge rallies against capitalist causes, participated in the No Conscription League, and founded the anarchist journal, *Mother Earth*. To you, what is an example of a "capitalist cause?" As you read, try and discern what Goldman might consider a "capitalist cause."

Partially due to her notoriety, she was falsely accused of conspiring with fellow anarchist Leon Czolgosz in his assassination of US president William McKinley in 1901. These accumulated activities created the reputation that she mocks in the opening of our reading, "What I Believe." That persona ultimately led to her deportation at least as much as her crusade against the draft as evidenced in her "Speech Against Conscription and War." What are the implications of weighing someone's reputation as part of the grounds for conviction by the state?

Goldman's recounting of her defense of her anticonscription trial recalls Socrates's "Apology." Socrates, who was fighting with ideological shadows rather than the specific (contradictory) charges levied against him, chose to use his day in court as a teaching moment in defense of the philosophical principles he held dear. Likewise, Goldman was more interested in integrity than exoneration. Goodman recalls the proceedings in her autobiography.

> I pointed out that there had never been an ideal, however humane and peaceful, which in its time had been considered "within the law." I named Jesus, Socrates, Galileo, Giordano Bruno. Were they "within the law"? I asked. And the men who set America free from British rule, the Jeffersons and the Patrick Henrys? The William Lloyd Garrisons, the John Browns, the [Henry] David Thoreaus and Wendell Phillipses — were they "within the law"?[84]

The jury rendered the guilty verdict in only thirty-nine minutes despite the many serious flaws in the prosecution's case. Her persona as a dangerous anarchist was

---

84. Emma Goldman, *Living My Life* (Pantianos Classics, 2018), 415.

being tried. She was already guilty before the trial began, which was more persecution than prosecution.[85] As Goldman noted, the judge even went so far as to instruct the jury that "whether the defendants are right or wrong can have no bearing on the verdict."[86] She and her comrade and lover, Alexander Berkman, were convicted of conspiracy against the draft. The judge opted for the most severe sentence possible: two years in the federal penitentiary, a fine of ten thousand dollars each, and recommendation for deportation as enemies of the state.

Goldman was deported to Soviet Russia in 1920. She had worked hard to support Russian dissidents against the Tsarist rule throughout her years of political activism. The Bolshevik revolution in 1917 inspired her with hope as she arrived to join the struggle there. Goldman soon became disillusioned by the Soviet government, just as she did with the United States. For her the Soviet regime represented another false hope for freedom from persecution of an oppressive state. After leaving the Soviet Union, she took her struggle to France, Germany, Spain, England, and Canada. In addition to her political activities, she worked as a nurse, authored several books, and taught courses in literary theory. Emma Goldman is buried in Forest Home Cemetery in Chicago alongside the Haymarket martyrs she revered, whose cause she fought for indefatigably her entire life.

Duane H. Davis
Department of Philosophy

---

85. Goldman, *Living My Life*, 411.
86. Goldman, *Living My Life*, 415.

Selections by Emma Goldman

What I Believe

"What I believe" has many times been the target of hack writers. Such blood-curdling and incoherent stories have been circulated about me, it is no wonder that the average human being has palpitation of the heart at the very mention of the name Emma Goldman. It is too bad that we no longer live in the times when witches were burned at the stake or tortured to drive the evil spirit out of them. For, indeed, Emma Goldman is a witch! True, she does not eat little children, but she does many worse things. She manufactures bombs and gambles in crowned heads. B-r-r-r!

Such is the impression the public has of myself and my beliefs. It is therefore very much to the credit of *The World* that it gives its readers at least an opportunity to learn what my beliefs really are.

The student of the history of progressive thought is well aware that every idea in its early stages has been misrepresented, and the adherents of such ideas have been maligned and persecuted. One need not go back two thousand years to the time when those who believed in the gospel of Jesus were thrown into the arena or hunted into dungeons to realize how little great beliefs or earnest believers are understood. The history of progress is written in the blood of men and women who have dared to espouse an unpopular cause, as, for instance, the black man's right to his body, or woman's right to her soul. If, then, from time immemorial, the New has met with opposition and condemnation, why should my beliefs be exempt from a crown of thorns?

"What I believe" is a process rather than a finality. Finalities are for gods and governments, not for the human intellect. While it may be true that Herbert Spencer's formulation of liberty is the most important on the subject, as a political basis of society, yet life is something more than formulas. In the battle for freedom, as Ibsen has so well pointed out, it is the *struggle* for, not so much the attainment of, liberty, that develops all that is strongest, sturdiest and finest in human character.

Anarchism is not only a process, however, that marches on with "sombre steps," coloring all that is positive and constructive in organic development. It is a conspicuous protest of the most militant type. It is so absolutely uncompromising, insisting and permeating a force as to overcome the most stubborn assault and to withstand the criticism of those who really constitute the last trumpets of a decaying age.

Anarchists are by no means passive spectators in the theatre of social development; on the contrary, they have some very positive notions as regards aims and methods.

That I may make myself as clear as possible without using too much space, permit me to adopt the topical mode of treatment of "What I Believe":

I. As To Property

"Property" means dominion over things and the denial to others of the use of those things. So long as production was not equal to the normal demand, institutional property may have had some *raison d'être*. One has only to consult economics, however, to know that the productivity of labor within the last few decades has increased so tremendously as to exceed normal demand a hundred-fold, and to make property not only a hindrance to human well-being, but an obstacle, a deadly barrier, to all progress. It is the private dominion over things that condemns millions of people to be mere nonentities, living corpses without originality or power of initiative, human machines of flesh and blood, who pile up mountains of wealth for others and pay for it with a gray, dull and wretched existence for themselves. I believe that there can be no real wealth, social wealth, so long as it rests on human lives—young lives, old lives and lives in the making.

It is conceded by all radical thinkers that the fundamental cause of this terrible state of affairs is

1. that man must sell his labor;
2. that his inclination and judgment are subordinated to the will of a master.

Anarchism is the only philosophy that can and will do away with this humiliating and degrading situation. It differs from all other theories inasmuch as it points out that man's development, his physical well-being, his latent qualities and innate disposition alone must determine the character and conditions of his work. Similarly will one's physical and mental appreciations and his soul cravings decide how much he shall consume. To make this a reality will, I believe, be possible only in a society based on voluntary cooperation of productive groups, communities and societies loosely federated together, eventually developing into a free communism, actuated by a solidarity of interests. There can be no freedom in the large sense of the word, no harmonious development, so long as mercenary and commercial considerations play an important part in the determination of personal conduct.

II. As To Government

I believe government, organized authority, or the State is necessary *only* to maintain or protect property and monopoly. It has proven efficient in that function only. As a promoter of individual liberty, human well-being and social harmony, which alone constitute real order, government stands condemned by all the great men of the world.

I therefore believe, with my fellow-Anarchists, that the statutory regulations, legislative enactments, constitutional provisions, are invasive. They never yet induced man to do anything he could and would not do by virtue of his intellect or temperament, nor prevented anything that man was impelled to do by the same dictates. Millet's pictorial description of "The Man with the Hoe," Meunier's masterpieces of the miners that have aided in lifting labor from its degrading position, Gorki's descriptions of the underworld, Ibsen's psychological analysis of human life, could never have been induced by government any more than the spirit which impels a man to save a drowning child or a crippled woman from a burning building has ever been called into operation by statutory regulations or the policeman's club. I believe—indeed, I know—that whatever is fine and beautiful in the human expresses and asserts itself in spite of government, and not because of it.

The Anarchists are therefore justified in assuming that Anarchism—the absence of government—will insure the widest and greatest scope for unhampered human development, the cornerstone of true social progress and harmony.

As to the stereotyped argument that government acts as a check on crime and vice, even the makers of law no longer believe it. This country spends millions of dollars for the maintenance of her "criminals" behind prison bars, yet crime is on the increase. Surely this state of affairs is not owing to an insufficiency of laws! Ninety percent of all crimes are property crimes, which have their root in our economic iniquities. So long as these latter continue to exist we might convert every lamp-post into a gibbet without having the least effect on the crime in our midst. Crimes resulting from heredity can certainly never be cured by law. Surely we are learning even to-day that such crimes can effectively be treated only by the best modern medical methods at our command, and, above all, by the spirit of a deeper sense of fellowship, kindness and understanding.

III. As To Militarism

I should not treat of this subject separately, since it belongs to the paraphernalia of government, if it were not for the fact that those who are most vigorously opposed to my beliefs on the ground that the latter stand for force are the advocates of militarism.

The fact is that Anarchists are the only true advocates of peace, the only people who call a halt to the growing tendency of militarism, which is fast making of this erstwhile free country an imperialistic and despotic power.

The military spirit is the most merciless, heartless and brutal in existence. It fosters an institution for which there is not even a pretense of justification. The soldier, to quote Tolstoi, is a professional man-killer. He does not kill for the love of it, like a savage, or in a passion, like a homicide. He is a cold-blooded, mechanical, obedient tool of his military superiors. He is ready to cut throats or scuttle a ship at the command of his ranking officer, without knowing or, perhaps, caring how, why or wherefore. I am supported in this contention by no less a military light than Gen. Funston. I quote from the latter's communication to the *New York Evening Post* of June 30, dealing with the case of Private William Buwalda, which caused such a stir all through the Northwest. "The first duty of an officer or enlisted man," says our noble warrior, "is unquestioning obedience and loyalty to the government to which he has sworn allegiance; it makes no difference whether he approves of that government or not."

How can we harmonize the principle of "unquestioning obedience" with the principle of "life, liberty and the pursuit of happiness"? The deadly power of militarism has never before been so effectually demonstrated in this country as in the recent condemnation by court-martial of William Buwalda, of San Francisco, Company A, Engineers, to five years in military prison. Here was a man who had a record of fifteen years of continuous service. "His character and conduct were unimpeachable," we are told by Gen. Funston, who, in consideration of it, reduced Buwalda's sentence to three years. Yet the man is thrown suddenly out of the army, dishonored, robbed of his chances of a pension and sent to prison. What was his crime? Just listen, ye free-born Americans! William Buwalda attended a public meeting, and after the lecture he shook hands with the speaker. Gen. Funston, in his letter to the *Post*, to which I have already referred above, asserts that Buwalda's action was a "great military offense, infinitely worse than desertion." In another public statement, which the General made in Portland, Ore., he said that "Buwalda's was a serious crime, equal to treason."

It is quite true that the meeting had been arranged by Anarchists. Had the Socialists issued the call, Gen. Funston informs us, there would have been no objection to Buwalda's presence. Indeed, the General says, "I would not have the slightest hesitancy about attending a Socialist meeting myself." But to attend an Anarchist meeting with Emma Goldman as speaker—could there be anything more "treasonable"?

For this horrible crime a man, a free-born American citizen, who has given this country the best fifteen years of his life, and whose character and conduct during that time were "unimpeachable," is now languishing in a prison, dishonored, disgraced and robbed of a livelihood.

Can there be anything more destructive of the true genius of liberty than the spirit that made Buwalda's sentence possible—the spirit of unquestioning obedience? Is it for this that the American people have in the last few years sacrificed four hundred million dollars and their hearts' blood?

I believe that militarism—a standing army and navy in any country—is indicative of the decay of liberty and of the destruction of all that is best and finest in our nation. The steadily growing clamor for more battleships and an increased army on the ground that these guarantee us peace is as absurd as the argument that the peaceful man is he who goes well armed.

The same lack of consistency is displayed by those peace pretenders who oppose Anarchism because it supposedly teaches violence, and who would yet be delighted over the possibility of the American nation soon being able to hurl dynamite bombs upon defenseless enemies from flying machines.

I believe that militarism will cease when the liberty-loving spirits of the world say to their masters: "Go and do your own killing. We have sacrificed ourselves and our loved ones long enough fighting your battles. In return you have made parasites and criminals of us in times of peace and brutalized us in times of war. You have separated us from our brothers and have made of the world a human slaughterhouse. No, we will not do your killing or fight for the country that you have stolen from us."

Oh, I believe with all my heart that human brotherhood and solidarity will clear the horizon from the terrible red streak of war and destruction.

IV. As To Free Speech and Press

The Buwalda case is only one phase of the larger question of free speech, free press and the right of free assembly.

Many good people imagine that the principles of free speech or press can be exercised properly and with safety within the limits of constitutional guarantees. That is the only excuse, it seems to me, for the terrible apathy and indifference to the onslaught upon free speech and press that we have witnessed in this county within the last few months.

I believe that free speech and press mean that I may say and write what I please. This right, when regulated by constitutional provisions, legislative enactments, almighty decisions of the Postmaster General or the policeman's club, becomes a farce. I am well aware that I will be warned of consequences if we remove the chains from speech and press. I believe, however, that the cure of consequences resulting from the unlimited exercise of expression is to allow more expression.

Mental shackles have never yet stemmed the tide of progress, whereas premature social explosions have only too often been brought about through a wave of repression.

Will our governors never learn that countries like England, Holland, Norway, Sweden and Denmark, with the largest freedom of expression, have been freest from "consequences"? Whereas Russia, Spain, Italy, France and, alas! even America, have raised these "consequences" to the most pressing political factor. Ours is supposed to be a country ruled by the majority, yet every policeman who is not vested with power by the majority can break up a meeting, drag the lecturer off the platform and club the audience out of the hall in true Russian fashion. The Postmaster General, who is not an elective officer, has the power to suppress publications and confiscate mail. From his decision there is no more appeal than from that of the Russian Czar. Truly, I believe we need a new Declaration of Independence. Is there no modern Jefferson or Adams?

V. As To The Church

At the recent convention of the political remnants of a once revolutionary idea it was voted that religion and vote getting have nothing to do with each other. Why should they? "So long as man is willing to delegate to the devil the care of his soul, he might, with the same consistency, delegate to the politician the care of his rights. That religion is a private affair has long been settled by the Bis-Marxian Socialists of Germany. Our American Marxians, poor of blood and originality, must needs go to Germany for their wisdom. That wisdom has served as a capital whip to lash the several millions of people into the well-disciplined army of Socialism. It might do the same here. For goodness' sake, let's not offend respectability, let's not hurt the religious feelings of the people.

Religion is a superstition that originated in man's mental inability to solve natural phenomena. The Church is an organized institution that has always been a stumbling block to progress.

Organized churchism has stripped religion of its naïveté and primitiveness. It has turned religion into a nightmare that oppresses the human soul and holds the mind in bondage. "The Dominion of Darkness, as the last true Christian, Leo Tolstoi, calls the Church, has been a foe of human development and free thought, and as such it has no place in the life of a truly free people.

VI. As To Marriage And Love

I believe these are probably the most tabooed subjects in this country. It is almost impossible to talk about them without scandalizing the cherished propriety of a lot of good folk. No wonder so much ignorance prevails relative to these questions. Nothing short of an open, frank, and intelligent discussion will purify the air from the hysterical, sentimental rubbish that is shrouding these vital subjects, vital to individual as well as social well-being.

Marriage and love are not synonymous; on the contrary, they are often antagonistic to each other. I am aware of the fact that some marriages are actuated by love, but the narrow, material confines of marriage, as it is, speedily crush the tender flower of affection.

Marriage is an institution which furnishes the State and Church with a tremendous revenue and the means of prying into that phase of life which refined people have long considered their own, their very own most sacred affair. Love is that most powerful factor of human relationship which from time immemorial has defied all man-made laws and broken through the iron bars of conventions in Church and morality. Marriage is often an economic arrangement purely, furnishing the woman with a lifelong life insurance policy and the man with a perpetuator of his kind or a pretty toy. That is, marriage, or the training thereto, prepares the woman for the life of a parasite, a dependent, helpless servant, while it furnishes the man the right of a chattel mortgage over a human life.

How can such a condition of affairs have anything in common with love?—with the element that would forego all the wealth of money and power and live in its own world of untrammeled human expression? But this is not the age of romanticism, of Romeo and Juliet, Faust and Marguerite, of moonlight ecstasies, of flowers and songs. Ours is a practical age. Our first consideration is an income. So much the worse for us if we have reached the era when the soul's highest flights are to be checked. No race can develop without the love element.

But if two people are to worship at the shrine of love, what is to become of the golden calf, marriage? "It is the only security for the woman, for the child, the family, the State." But it is no security to love; and without love no true home can or does exist. Without love no child should be born; without love no true woman can be related to a man. The fear that love is not sufficient material safety for the child is out of date. I believe when woman signs her own emancipation, her first declaration of independence will consist in admiring and loving a man for the qualities of his heart and mind and not for the quantities in his pocket. The second declaration will be that she has the right to follow that love without let or hindrance from the outside world. The third and most important declaration will be the absolute right to free motherhood.

In such a mother and an equally free father rests the safety of the child. They have the strength, the sturdiness, the harmony to create an atmosphere wherein alone the human plant can grow into an exquisite flower.

VII. *As To Acts Of Violence*

And now I have come to that point in my beliefs about which the greatest misunderstanding prevails in the minds of the American public. "Well, come, now, don't you propagate violence, the killing of crowned heads and Presidents?" Who says that I do? Have you heard me, has anyone heard me? Has anyone seen it printed in our literature? No, but the papers say so, everybody says so; consequently it must be so. Oh, for the accuracy and logic of the dear public!

I believe that Anarchism is the only philosophy of peace, the only theory of the social relationship that values human life above everything else. I know that some Anarchists have committed acts of violence, but it is the terrible economic inequality and great political injustice that prompt such acts, not Anarchism. Every institution to-day rests on violence; our very atmosphere is saturated with it. So long as such a state exists we might as well strive to stop the rush of Niagara as hope to do away with violence. I have already stated that countries with some measure of freedom of expression have had few or no acts of violence. What is the moral? Simply this: No act committed by an Anarchist has been for personal gain, aggrandizement or profit, but rather a conscious protest against some repressive, arbitrary, tyrannical measure from above.

President Carnot, of France, was killed by Caserio in response to Carnot's refusal to commute the death sentence of Vaillant, for whose life the entire literary, scientific and humanitarian world of France had pleaded.

Bresci went to Italy on his own money, earned in the silk weaving mills of Paterson, to call King Humbert to the bar of justice for his order to shoot defenseless women and children during a bread riot. Angelino executed Prime Minister Canovas for the latter's resurrection of the Spanish inquisition at Montjuich Prison. Alexander Berkman attempted the life of Henry C. Frick during the Homestead strike only because of his intense sympathy for the eleven strikers killed by Pinkertons and for the widows and orphans evicted by Frick from their wretched little homes that were owned by Mr. Carnegie.

Every one of these men not only made his reasons known to the world in spoken or written statements, showing the cause that led to his act, proving that the unbearable economic and political pressure, the suffering and despair of their fellow-men, women and children prompted the acts, and not the philosophy of Anarchism. They came openly, frankly and ready to stand the consequences, ready to give their own lives.

In diagnosing the true nature of our social disease I cannot condemn those who, through no fault of their own, are suffering from a wide-spread malady.

I do not believe that these acts can, or ever have been intended to, bring about the social reconstruction. That can only be done, first, by a broad and wide education as to man's place in society and his proper relation to his fellows; and, second, through example. By example I mean the actual living of a truth once recognized, not the mere theorizing of its life element. Lastly, and the most powerful weapon, is the conscious, intelligent, organized, economic protest of the masses through direct action and the general strike.

The general contention that Anarchists are opposed to organization, and hence stand for chaos, is absolutely groundless. True, we do not believe in the compulsory, arbitrary side of organization that would compel people of antagonistic tastes and interests into a body and hold them there by coercion. Organization as the result of natural blending of common interests, brought about through voluntary adhesion, Anarchists do not only not oppose, but believe in as the only possible basis of social life.

It is the harmony of organic growth which produces variety of color and form—the complete whole we admire in the flower. Analogously will the organized activity of free human beings endowed with the spirit of solidarity result in the perfection of social harmony—which is Anarchism. Indeed, only Anarchism makes non-authoritarian organization a reality, since it abolishes the existing antagonism between individuals and classes.

Speech Against Conscription and War

Delivered at Forward Hall, New York City, June 14, 1917[87]

The Chairman: The next speaker is one who is well known to you. I shall not waste words or time in introducing her but I want to tell you that before she came to the

---

87. Transcript of meeting (from which Goldman's speech is excerpted here) by public shorthand reporter Charles Pickler, employed by the Stenographic Service Company of New York City, contracted by the No-Conscription League. Copy of original transcript housed at the Tamiment Library, New York University. Permission to reproduce or quote in any form must be obtained from the Tamiment Library. For transcript of court examination of Charles Pickler, see "Goldman & Berkman v. United States: Transcript of Record, 1917 Sept. 25," pp. 163–67, 219–23 (*Emma Goldman Papers* microfilm, reel 59).

meeting tonight somebody telephoned her and told her, "If you go to that meeting you will not get home alive." I simply want to introduce a woman who has more courage than half a dozen regiments (tremendous cheering and applause at 9:12 P.M.) I introduce to you—(interrupted by applause and cheers. Some young man said, "Who loves Emma Goldman? We all do." Great cheering and applause.)

Emma Goldman: This is not the place to applaud or shout Hurrah for Emma Goldman. We have more serious things to talk about and some serious things to do. First of all I wish to say to you, all of you, workers, men and women from the East Side, that I regret deeply that I cannot speak to you in the language I have always spoken from this platform; that I cannot speak to you tonight in Yiddish. I shall speak English because I want those representing the State and Militarism and the Courts and Prisons to understand what I have to say. (Miss Goldman's remarks were so frequently interrupted by cheering and applause that reference to such interruptions will not be made in this report further.) I don't want them to get it secondhand. No language is ever rendered well in translation and I want them to hear what I have to say in the only language they can speak, and speak it poorly.

Friends, tomorrow morning I am sure that you will read the report that a meeting took place on the East Side attended by foreigners, by workmen, and ill-kempt, poorly washed people of the East Side-foreigners who are being jeered at the present time in this country, foreigners who are being ridiculed because they have an idea. Well, friends, if the Americans are to wait until Americans wake up the country they will have to resurrect the Indians who were killed in America and upon whose bodies this so-called democracy was established, because every other American, if you scratch him, you will find him to be an Englishman, Dutchman, Frenchman, Spaniard, a Jew and a German and a hundred and one other nationalities who sent their young men and their women to this country in the foolish belief that liberty was awaiting them at the American Harbor, Liberty holding a torch. That torch has been burning dimly in the United States for a very long time. It is because, the Goddess of Liberty is ashamed of the American people and what they have done in the name of liberty to liberty in the United States. And yet, friends, I am not sorry for the things that are happening in America today. I have come to the conclusion that every nation is like an individual, it must have its own experience and it does not accept the experience of other nations any more than you accept the experience of another individual, for if it were possible for a nation to learn by the bitter and tragic experiences of other nations America today could not be in war and America today could not have inaugurated a reign of terror which is sweeping across the country from one end to another. America had Europe before its face as an example, with all the murders and bloodshed and corpses and millions of lives lost. America had the trenches and the battlefields of the last, nearly, three years of Europe before her. America realized that this war is one of the bloodiest and most criminal wars that has ever been fought by civilized people. America had the lesson that the working people and the sons of working women are being sacrificed in the name of Kultur and they want democracy upon the battlefields of Europe, and if America had been a grown man instead of a child it would have learned the lesson that no matter how great the cause it is never great enough to sacrifice millions of people in the trenches and on the battlefield in the name of democracy or liberty.

Evidently, America has to learn a salutary lesson and it is going to pay a terrible price. It is going to shed oceans of blood, it is going to heap mountains of human sacrifices of men of this country who are able to create and produce, to whom the future belongs. They are to be slaughtered in blood and in sacrifice in the name of a thing which has never yet existed in the United States of America, in the name of democracy and liberty.

My friends, there are people who say and tell you that when they prophecy something the prophecy comes true. I am sorry to say that I am one such and I have to say the same. For thirty years we have pointed out to you that this democratic State which is a government supposedly of the people, by the people and for the people has now become one of the most Imperialistic that the world has ever laid its eyes upon. For twenty-five or thirty years we have told you that the United States of America is appropriating more power every day until the time will come when individual men or women will be nothing but cogs in a machine of this centralized, cruel, blood thirsty government known as the United States. We told you that, and you said, you are alarmists. You said, you are too extreme, that will never happen in the United States. And here you are, friends. It has happened in the United States. A Czar was imposed upon you without the consent of the people. The people were never asked whether they wanted war. Indeed, the people of America placed Mr. Wilson in the White House and in the Chair of the Presidency because he told the people that he would keep them out of war, and as one of his political advertisements billposters were posted all over the city with the picture of a working woman and her children saying, "He has kept us out of war." He promised you heaven, he promised you everything if you would only place him in power. What made you place him in power. You expected peace and not war. The moment you placed him in power, however, he forgot his promises and he is giving you hell. War was imposed upon the people without the people getting a chance to say whether they wanted war or not, and war was imposed upon them, I say, because the gentlemen of power and those who back power want war. And because war has been declared upon you we are told, we men and women of the United States who work and sweat and toil to sustain these gentlemen of power, we are told that there is a law and we must go to war. If war is necessary, only the people must decide whether they want war or not, and as long as the people have not given their consent I deny that the President of the United States has any right to declare it; I deny that the President or those who back the President have any right to tell the people that they shall take their sons and husbands and brothers and lovers and shall conscript them in order to ship them across the seas for the conquest of militarism and the support of wealth and power in the United States. You say that is a law. I deny your law. I don't believe in it.

The only law that I recognize is the law which ministers to the needs of humanity, which makes men and women finer and better and more humane, the kind of law which teaches children that human life is sacred, and that those who arm for the purpose of taking human life are going to be called before the bar of human justice and not before a wretched little court which is called your law of the United States. And so, friends, the people have not yet decided whether they want war and the people are going to say, ultimately, whether they want war or not.

It is not surprising that President Wilson cannot sense the pulse of time. He has been in colleges too long; he has been too long within closed doors; he has been too long at the historical books. He cannot sense the pulse of time. But I tell you, without wishing to be a prophet, that within the next six months—not years but within the next six months—President Wilson will regret deeply that he ever declared war in the United States.

Of course, friends, of course since the war was declared by a country in whose interest it is that the American boy shall be sacrificed it was not to the interest of that country to put the war to a test and therefore conscription had to be imposed upon you. Don't you know that during the Spanish-American War when the people believed in the war there was no need of asking the young men of the country, at the point of the bayonet and gun and club, to put on an American uniform? They flocked to the war because they believed in it. And whether they were American citizens or were residents of America the people of America were all willing to give their lives for something they considered right and just. But because the people of America do not believe in this war, because the people of America have not been asked whether there shall be war, that is why they do not flock to the colors and that is why you in America are doing as the Russians used to do, as the German Kaiser is doing, as all the Imperialistic tyrants are doing. That is why you are going to drag your manhood by force into the uniform. But you are forgetting one thing, gentlemen of the law, you are driving a horse to water but you cannot compel him to drink. You will put the young manhood of America in the uniform, you will drag them to the battlefield and into the trenches, but while they are there there is going to be a bond of anti-militarism among the people of the world (great applause).

No, friends, you cannot compel human beings to take human life, if you give them the chance to reason and to think, to investigate and to analyze. And that is precisely what the authorities of this country don't want. They don't want you to hear anything about conscription; they don't want you to hear anything about the State Military Census. Why don't they want you to hear anything? If their position were correct and logical, if the State Military Census rested upon the need of the people, if conscription rested upon the desire of the people, all the revolutionists and Emma Goldmans and Alexander Berkmans might talk their heads off and the people would not listen to them. But because the people know that conscription is a crime and oppression and an outrage upon reason, because the people know that the Military State Census was determined upon by one of the most reactionary men, we find Mr. Whitman who is on your backs, whom you supported, whom you gave the possibility to live. And the Military State Census, as you have been told, is going to turn every man of you here into a militiaman and into something who is fighting the Kaiser, because it is just as if the Kaiser wanted you to do a thing so that if you are a soldier and I tell you to shoot your mother and father and brother and sister you must obey orders. With the President is Mr. Whitman saying anything else? And then telling you that when you will become militiamen and you shall be ordered to shoot your brothers and fathers and sisters and mothers in the name of democracy that you are going to carry to the poor unfortunate people of Germany. And so, friends, we are here to tell you before you decide what you are going to do, think twice, and remember it is easy to make a mistake but it is very difficult to undo the mistake. You workmen of the East Side; you who have lived in Russia, you who remember the days when you could not meet unless you had detectives and soldiers and police, look about you. See what you have in the United States. See what you have in America.

If the framers of the Declaration of Independence if Jefferson or Henry or the others, if they could look down upon the country and see what their offspring has done to it, how they have outraged it, how they have robbed it, how they have polluted it—why, my friends, they would turn in their graves. They would rise again and they would cleanse this country from its internal enemies, and that is the ruling class of the United States. There is a lesson you are going to learn and terrible as it is for us we nevertheless are glad that you will have to learn that lesson.

And now we come down to the tragedy that was committed in the United States Court in the State of New York yesterday, when two boys were sentenced. It is not only a tragedy because they were sentenced. Such things happen every day, hundreds, thousands of innocent working men are sent to the prison and the penitentiary, thousands of unfortunates throughout the world as well as here in so-called free America and nobody ever hears anything about it. It is an ordinary, commonplace thing to do. But the tragedy of yesterday is in the fact that a Judge, supported as you have been told by your money, protected by public opinion, protected by the President, the tragedy of it is that that Judge had the impudence and audacity to insult Kramer and Becker after he gave them the sentence of such horrible dimensions. Think of a man like that who sits there in judgment on other human beings. Think what must be his character, what must be his mind, what must be his soul, if he can spit human beings in the face, only because he has got the power.

But evidently the Judge knows nothing of history, any more than the ruling class knows. Don't you know there was a time when Marie Antoinette, very much surprised that the people had no bread asked, "Why don't they eat cake"? Don't you know what happened to the fair lady of France, Marie Antoinette? Don't you know what happened to the landowning class of France who said that the people should eat straw? Don't you know what happened to them? The people gave them all the straw they could possibly eat. I consider the action of Judge Mayer an insult and an outrage and I warrant you that he is going to hear about it, not only all over the United States but even from Europe. It may have seemed very insignificant to send two poor workingmen to the penitentiary and to insult them, to send Becker and Kramer, who are both workingmen—that is their crime, they were both honest enough to say they were anarchists. To be condemned in an American Court it is enough that you are an anarchist. The Judge was horrified at the audacity of these people to say it to him, face to face. Don't you know, men, you who are free Americans, the moment you enter an American court you must say, like Dante said, "Ye who enter here leave all hope behind." That is what the American Courts are. And so today you are governed by the bayonet and the police can treat you like dogs. But I say to you, they who live by the sword shall perish by the sword. So I tell you, gentlemen, now is your time. Do whatever you please. But you are forgetting the story and you are forgetting the writing on the wall. You are making a mistake if you think that by sending Kramer and Becker to jail you are going to silence the human voice. You are making a mistake if you believe that by threatening and arresting people you are going to stop the agitation against war. The agitation is in the hearts of the people, the agitation is in the minds of the people, and it only requires the psychological moment to come along, as it did in Russia, and the Judges like Mayer and the other Judges will fly off the bench and into the gutters.

My friends, if we thought for one single minute that the entire agitation is dependent only upon a handful of people we would never bother and endanger your lives, but we know the agitation is in your hearts and souls, we know that the people from the East and West and South and North are opposed to the war, are opposed to conscription, opposed to the Military State Census, and the people will be heard from, I can tell you that. And so, to threaten anyone's life, to say that she will not come back from a meeting alive-how stupid. What is life unless you can live it in freedom and in beauty, and unless you can express yourself, unless you can be true to yourself what is life? I would rather than live the life of a dog to be compelled to sneak about and slink about, to worry that somebody is looking for you ready to take your life—Rather than that I would die the death of a lion any day. Why, what consequence is it if you tell people, we are going to arrest you, Miss Goldman. Just as if arresting Emma Goldman solves all the problems in the world. Prisons have never solved any problems. Guns and bayonets have never solved any problems. Bloodshed has never solved a problem. Never on earth, men and women, have such methods of violence, concentrated and organized violence, ever solved a single problem. Nothing but the human mind, nothing but human emotions, nothing but an intense passion for a great ideal, nothing but perseverance and devotion and strength of character—nothing else ever solved any problem.

And so, men and women, workmen and workwomen, you of the East Side, you who are sweated and bled to create the wealth of this country, you who are being sneered at because you are foreigners—very well, then, if you are good enough to create the wealth of America, if America had to go to Europe for her Art, if America had to go to Europe for her Literature, if America had to go to Europe for her Music and her ideals, by God you will have to go to the foreigners for liberty.

I wish to say here, and I don't say it with any authority and I don't say it as a prophet, I merely tell you—I merely tell you the more people you lock up, the more will be the idealists who will take their place; the more of the human voice you suppress, the greater and louder and the profounder will be the human voice. At present it is a mere rumbling, but that rumbling is increasing in volume, it is growing in depth, it is spreading all over the country until it will be raised into a thunder and people of America will rise and say, we want to be a democracy, to be sure, but we want the kind of democracy which means liberty and opportunity to every man and woman in America (Great and continued applause).

The Chairman: Before we close the meeting I want to call your attention again to the demonstration Saturday, June 23rd, at 2 P.M., in Madison Square. The subject will be Labor and War. Everybody be there. And now, my friends, let the gentlemen of war step out first. They came first; let them leave first, and then you leave the hall gradually, without any disorder. The meeting stands adjourned.

Friends, you will be glad to hear that the collection for Becker and Kramer amounts to $100 (applause).

Meeting adjourned at 9:42 P.M.

Goldman, Emma. "What I Believe." *New York World*, July 19, 1908. One online source can be found at theanarchistlibrary.org. Accessed May 12, 2021.

Goldman, Emma. *Speech Against Conscription and War*. Goldman & Berkman v. United States: Transcript of Record, September 25, 1917.

from *Ariel* by José Enrique Rodó

Introduction

Born in Montevideo, Uruguay, in 1871, José Enrique Rodó (d. 1917) was influenced by the historical events of the nineteenth-century independence movements in other colonies or former colonies of Spain in America and the political and philosophical rhetoric of Latin American contemporary thinkers. He developed relationships with members of the Spanish "generation of 1898," who themselves questioned "Spanishness" and colonialism, and was profoundly influenced stylistically by the *modernista* movement in Latin America, whose founding fathers include Jose Martí (Cuba) and Rubén Darío (Nicaragua). Latin American "modernismo" (c. 1888–c. 1920) is a literary movement principally bound in poetry in which form was heralded above function, and whose exponents influenced the entire Hispanic world. Importantly, unlike most widely studied literary movements in the Western tradition, modernismo was born in America and exported to Europe. Like many liberal philosophers born in newly independent nations of Spanish America, Rodó was intent on breaking away from the traditions of and ties to Spain, which to him and others represented oppression, intolerance, and superstition. Instead he leaned toward the liberal traditions of the French Enlightenment and post-Enlightenment; or as some would say, aspects often assumed as part of dominant frameworks of modernity. Intellectually then, his prose, in particular *Ariel*, is French-oriented, and more or less ignores Latin

> **SNAPSHOT BOX**
>
> LANGUAGE: Spanish
> PUBLISHED: 1900, Uruguay
> GENRE: Essay
> TAGS: Community; Cross-Cultural Encounters; Internationalism; Struggle, Resistance, and Revolution; Tradition

Timeline

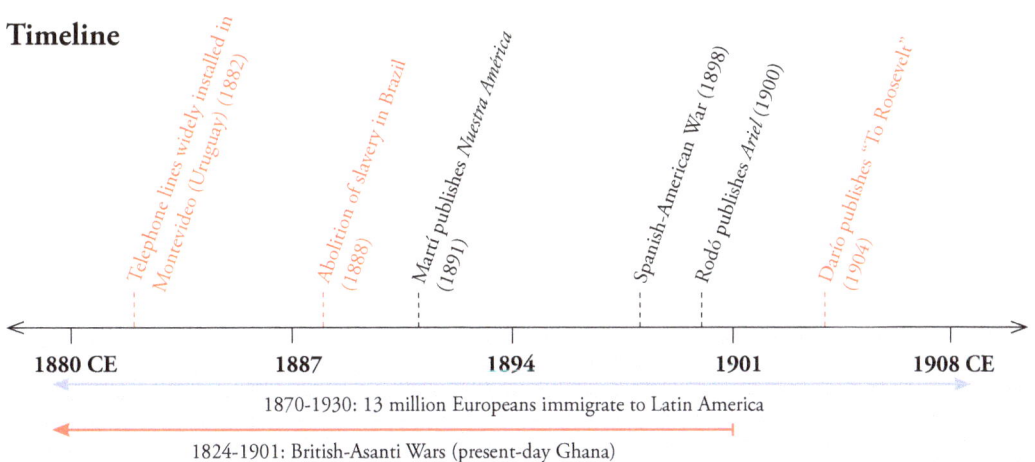

America's historical or cultural ties to Spain, as well as its Indigenous and African heritages. This is not unlike the draw of other philosophers and politicians from nineteenth- and twentieth-century independence movements in America. From Bolívar to Martí, intellectual allegiances with French ideals rather than Spanish traditions formed their philosophies of freedom. *Ariel* fits firmly within the trajectory of philosophy and texts of the nineteenth and twentieth centuries seeking to explain Latin American identity. Uruguay became independent of Spain in 1811; however, it was annexed by Brazil until 1825, and after a three-year federation with Argentina, finally became an independent nation in 1828.

Ariel uses as its global metaphor Shakespeare's *The Tempest*. Although in the form of an essay, its narrative voice, in modernist style, comes through the character of Prospero, a teacher, lecturing to his students about the parallels and divergences of North and Latin America and the different cultural identities he sees in them. Within his discourse, he counsels against the seduction of copying the utilitarianism, mostly understood in this source as materialism, of the North, and warns against *nordomanía*, "USA-mania" (wanting to emulate the United States). In the book, the United States is represented as Caliban (the half monster in *The Tempest*), and Latin America is represented as the fairy, Ariel. Through the voice of Prospero, Rodó encourages a unified, pan-national, romantic sensibility for Latin America. If the North is utilitarian, prosperous, individualistic, and materialistic, then Latin America should seek a unified cultural identity through **cosmopolitanism**; that is, considering all (Latin American) humanity as part of the same community. By dividing the American continent in two, Rodó exemplifies the idea of duality of North and South America that populates much of academic and political rhetoric in the twentieth century. As you read, make note of the metaphors used to describe this duality. The essay's portrayal of what it means and should mean to be Latin American raises important issues about identity. One of the salient problems is that Rodó's notion of one unified "Latin American race" ignores the lived realities and historical truths of Indigenous traditions and communities and the profound influence of the African diaspora in the development of Latin America. How does this absence of important marginalized experiences influence the viability of arguments for Pan-Americanism and/or Pan-Latin-Americanism?

Although Rodó's *Ariel* presents a single, master narrative, it allows us to explore possible reasons behind his strategy. It offers an opportunity to problematize not only Latin American identities and histories, but parallel realities in North American movements such as the **Monroe Doctrine**, or the idea of **Manifest Destiny**. The Monroe Doctrine (1823) insists on the distinct spheres of Europe and America and rejects any continued European colonizing influences in the Americas. Manifest Destiny—a phrase developed in the middle of the nineteenth century—indicates that the United States is divinely destined to expand its territories and dominion over the North American continent. Both of these political platforms influenced the way in which some of the same influences of the French Enlightenment manifested so very differently in the United States in the eighteenth century and many Latin American nations seeking independence in the nineteenth century. What types of interconnectedness might there be between political and cultural developments in the parallel yet profoundly different geopolitical spaces of North and Latin America?

Greta Trautmann
Department of Languages and Literatures

> **PRE-READING PARS**
>
> 1. Do you consider yourself *American*? To you, what does "being an American" mean?
> 2. Come up with adjectives to describe the spirit of the United States (for conversation's sake, feel free to exaggerate). Do the same for the US South. Now do the same for another country/region/continent, perhaps Latin America.

On the Uniqueness of the Latin American Spirit

The inextricably linked concepts of utilitarianism as a concept of human destiny and egalitarian mediocrity as a norm for social relationships compose the formula for what Europe has tended to call the spirit of *Americanism*. It is impossible to ponder either inspiration for social conduct, or to compare them with their opposites, without their inevitable association with that formidable and productive democracy to our North. Its display of prosperity and power is dazzling testimony to the efficacy of its institutions and to the guidance of its concepts. If it has been said that "utilitarianism" is the word for the spirit of the English, then the United States can be considered the embodiment of the word. And the Gospel of that word is spread everywhere through the good graces of its material miracles. Spanish America is not, in this regard, entirely a land of heathens. That powerful federation is effecting a kind of moral conquest among us. Admiration for its greatness and power is making impressive inroads in the minds of our leaders and, perhaps even more, in the impressionable minds of the masses, who are awed by its incontrovertible victories. And from admiring to imitating is an easy step. A psychologist will say that admiration and conviction are passive modes of imitation. "The main seat of the imitative part of our nature is our belief," said Bagehot. Common sense and experience should in themselves be enough to establish this simple relationship. We imitate what we believe to be superior or prestigious. And this is why the vision of an America de-Latinized of its own will, without threat of conquest, and reconstituted in the image and likeness of the North, now looms in the nightmares of many who are genuinely concerned about our future. This vision is the impetus behind an abundance of similar carefully thought-out designs and explains the continuous flow of proposals for innovation and reform. We have our *USA-mania*. It must be limited by the boundaries our reason and sentiment jointly dictate.

When I speak of boundaries, I do not suggest absolute negation. I am well aware that we find our inspirations, our enlightenment, our teachings, in the example of the strong; nor am I unaware that intelligent attention to external events is singularly fruitful in the case of a people still in the process of forming its national entity. I am similarly aware that by persevering in the educational process we hope to modulate the elements of society that must be adapted to new exigencies of civilization and new opportunities in life, thus balancing the forces of heritage and custom with that of innovation. I do not, however, see what is to be gained from denaturalizing the character—the *personality*—of a nation, from imposing an identification with a foreign model, while sacrificing irreplaceable uniqueness. Nor do I see anything to be gained from the ingenuous belief that identity can somehow be achieved through artificial and improvised imitation. Michelet believed that the mindless transferral of what is natural and spontaneous in one society to another where it has neither natural nor historical roots was like attempting to introduce a dead organism into a living one by simple implantation. In a social structure, as in literature and art, forced imitation will merely distort the configuration of the model. The misapprehension of those who believe they have reproduced the character of a human collectivity in its essence, the living strength of its spirit, as well as the secret of its triumphs and prosperity, and have exactly reproduced the mechanism of its institutions and the external from of its customs, is reminiscent of the delusion of naïve students who believe they have achieved the genius of their master when they have merely copied his style and characteristics.

In such a futile effort there is, furthermore, an inexpressible ignobility. Eager mimicry of the prominent and the powerful, the successful and the fortunate, must be seen as a kind of political *snobbery*; and a servile abdication—like that of some snobs condemned by Thackeray in *The Book of Snobs* to be satirized for all eternity—lamentably consumes the energies of those who are not blessed by nature or fortune but who impotently ape the caprices and foibles of those at the peak of society. Protecting our *internal* independence—independence of personality and independence of judgement—is a basic form of self-respect. Treatises on ethics often comment on one of Cicero's moral precepts, according to which one of our responsibilities as human beings is zealously to protect the uniqueness of our personal character—whatever in it that is different and formative—while always respecting Nature's primary impulse: that the order and harmony of the world are based on the broad distribution of her gifts. The truth of this precept would seem even greater when applied to the character of human societies. Perhaps you will hear it said that there is no distinctive mark or characteristic of the present ordering of our peoples that is worth struggling to maintain. What may perhaps be lacking in our collective character is a sharply defined "personality." But in lieu of an absolutely distinct and autonomous particularity, we Latin Americans have a heritage of race, a great ethnic tradition, to maintain, a sacred place in the pages of history that depends upon us for its continuation. Cosmopolitanism, which we must respect as a compelling requisite in our formation, includes fidelity both to the past and to the formative role that the genius of our race must play in recasting the American of tomorrow.

More than once it has been observed that the great epochs of history, the most luminous and fertile periods in the evolution of humankind, are almost always the result of contemporaneous but conflicting forces that through the stimulus of concerted opposition preserve our interest in life, a fascination that would pale in the placidity of absolute conformity. So it was that the most genial and civilizing of cultures turned upon an axis supported by the poles of Athens and Sparta. America must continue to maintain the dualism of its original composition, which re-creates in history the classic myth of the two eagles released simultaneously from the two poles in order that each should reach the limits of its domain at the same moment. Genial and competitive diversity does not exclude but, rather, tolerates, and even in many aspects favors, solidarity. And if we could look into the future and see the formula for an eventual harmony, it would not be based upon the *unilateral imitation*—as Gabriel Tarde would say—of one people by another, but upon a mutual exchange of influences, and the fortuitous fusion of the attributes that gave each its special glory.

Rodó, José Enrique. "On the Uniqueness of the Latin American Spirit." In *Ariel*, translated by Margaret Sayers Peden, 70–74. Austin: University of Texas Press, 1988.

POST-READING PARS

1. Do you feel differently about any of the characterizations of "being an American" you noted earlier?
2. After reading Rodó, identify two or three adjectives each that he might use to describe the spirit of Latin America and America.

Inquiry Corner

Content Questions:

What does Rodó mean by the *natural personality of a nation*?

If Latin America and the United States were to be brought into "eventual harmony," then what are some arguments Rodó offers against "unilateral imitation" and for "mutual exchange" and "fortuitous fusion"?

Critical Questions:

What notions of modernity do you see in this selection? Can you see contradictions arising from these notions?

Comparative Question:

Compare and contrast Rodó's description of utilitarianism and materialism with another account of these concepts that you read in this course.

Connection Question:

Thinking of oneself as a national citizen is an inheritance from nineteenth-century narratives. How do you see the logic of that narrative reflected in our contemporary discussions around citizenship, displacement, and refugee treatment?

"Correspondences between Gandhi and Tagore" by Mohandas Karamchand Gandhi and Rabindranath Tagore

Introduction

Mohandas Karamchand Gandhi (1869–1948) and Rabindranath Tagore (1861–1941) were the two most influential Indians of the twentieth century. Gandhi's conception of **satyagraha** (nonviolent resistance) became a blueprint for protest worldwide. Tagore was the first Asian to receive the Nobel Prize in literature for his book of poems, *Gitanjali* (*An Offering of Songs*), in 1913. These two contemporaries also offered defining voices within the Indian struggle for independence from British rule.

Their lives had divergent beginnings. As the youngest of the fourteen children of one of the most preeminent families of Bengal, which included poets, musicians, painters, novelists, religious reformers, and philosophers, Tagore had a privileged upbringing. Gandhi's childhood, in comparison, was relatively modest. He grew up as the youngest of four children in Gujarat, an eastern state in present-day India, in a devout Hindu family. As he states in his autobiography, his mother's deep devotion and religiosity left a lasting impression on young Gandhi. Both Tagore and Gandhi went to England to become lawyers, as was common practice for many Indian families at the time. While Tagore returned without a degree, Gandhi became a barrister and practiced law in India and South Africa before devoting himself entirely to the Indian independence movement. While the selection below highlights a crucial moment of disagreement between these two men, it also ex-

SNAPSHOT BOX

LANGUAGE: English
PUBLISHED: 1921, British India
GENRE: Published correspondences
TAGS: Accessing Rights; Class; Colonization; Economics; Ethics and Morality; History and Ideology; Poetry, Music, Literature; Psyche; Religion; Self-Determination; Struggle, Resistance, and Revolution; Ways of Knowing; Education; Internationalism; Nationalism

Timeline

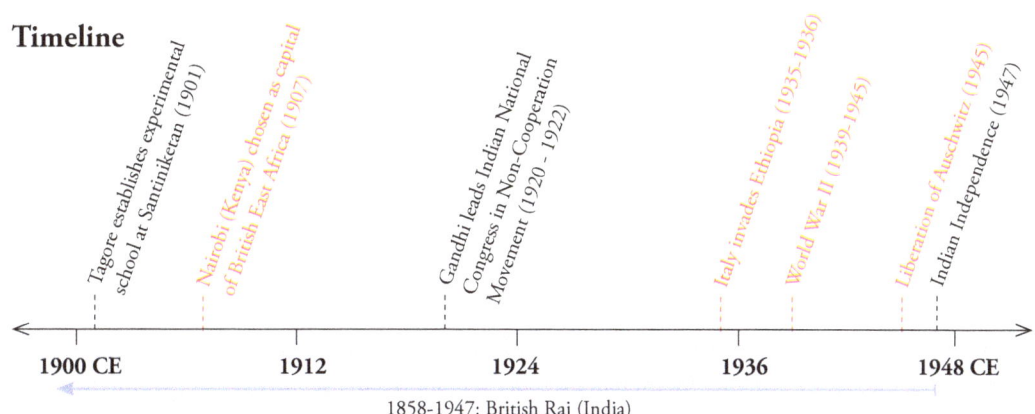

presses the deep admiration they shared for each other. Indeed, according to many scholars, Tagore was the first to use the title *Mahatma* (Great soul) for Gandhi in 1915. As you read the selection, try to identify the occasions that reflect their mutual respect.

The British rule in the Indian subcontinent took definitive shape in 1757 when the East India Trading Company—a British joint-stock venture, predecessor of the modern corporation—defeated a local ruler. Britain's colonial grip grew stronger over time with the subcontinent eventually coming under direct control of the British Crown in 1858. That was the beginning of British Raj, literally, British rule, which lasted until the Indian independence in 1947. Discontent with British rule spanned almost the entire duration of the British presence within the region. However, the call for ***swaraj*** (Indian self-rule) gained momentum after the Jalianwala Bagh Massacre in 1919 when British-led troops fired on unarmed Indians gathered in the field of Jalianwala Bagh, in Punjab, killing hundreds and injuring many more. British failure to prosecute the responsible individuals, for example, General Reginald Dyer who had ordered the troops to fire, laid bare British oppressive strategies and disregard for Indian lives. What are some ways you have read about in this course where colonized peoples have tried to respond to moments of crystalizing oppression?

Gandhi's call for the noncooperation movement in 1920 contained India's response. This nonviolent resistance focused on disobeying the unjust laws of an oppressive government initiated by Gandhi was one of the first examples of a civil disobedience movement. It called on Indians to boycott British goods and participation in British institutions, such as government-run schools, courts, elections, and taxes. Even though immensely successful at first, Gandhi called off the movement in 1922 after an Indian mob turned violent and killed police officers. What might have been some of the reasons behind this decision by Gandhi?

The excerpt below comes from the long course of correspondence, in the form of letters and public debates, between Tagore and Gandhi that started in 1915 after Gandhi's return from South Africa and continued until Tagore's death in 1941. A sense of renewed interest in India's conceptual heritage accompanied Indian nationalism and freedom struggle. As is evident from their correspondence, both Tagore and Gandhi drew from Hindu philosophical and religious concepts. According to a central Hindu belief, a single principle of truth—*brahman*, often characterized as reality, consciousness, and pure joy—permeates the universe thereby uniting everyone and everything. **Mukti**, or freedom in this context, means a realization of this fundamental truth.

Using this conceptual backdrop both Gandhi and Tagore offered a sense of *swaraj* that not only reflected India's demand for political sovereignty but more importantly a perspective reflecting the "power of soul"—identified as that of the East—as opposed to the "power of muscle"—identified as that of the West. Where else have you seen these kinds of narratives of contrast play a role in a people's struggle for self-determination? While Tagore expressed his hesitation and reservations about the various means adopted by the non-cooperationists, Gandhi defended them as necessary. What features of the Indian independence movement are you able to identify as you read through their exchange? What role does education play in their disagreement? Can you imagine ways in which both arguments could have contributed to the Indian call for *swaraj*?

Keya Maitra
Department of Philosophy

Correspondences between Gandhi and Tagore

Tagore's Reflections on the non-cooperation movement, Chicago, March 2, 1921

Your last letter gives wonderful news about our students in Calcutta. I hope that this spirit of sacrifice and willingness to suffer will grow in strength; for to achieve this is an end in itself. This is the true freedom! Nothing is of higher value—be it national wealth, or independence—than disinterested faith in ideals, in the moral greatness of man.

The West has its unshakable faith in material strength and prosperity; and therefore however loud grows the cry for peace and disarmament, its ferocity growls louder, gnashing its teeth and lashing its tail in impatience. It is like a fish, hurt by the pressure of the flood, planning to fly in the air. Certainly the idea is brilliant, but it is not possible for a fish to realize. We, in India, have to show to the world, what is that truth, which not only makes disarmament possible but turns it into strength.

The truth, that moral force is a higher power than brute force, will be proved by the people who are unarmed. Life, in its higher development, has thrown off its tremendous burden of armour and a prodigious quantity of flesh; till man has become the conqueror of the brute world. The day is sure to come, when the frail man of spirit, completely unhampered by air fleets and dreadnoughts, will prove that the meek are to inherit the earth.

It is in the fitness of things, that Mahatma Gandhi, frail in body and devoid of all material resources, should call up the immense power of the meek, that has been lying waiting in the heart of the destitute and insulted humanity of India. The destiny of India has chosen for its ally, *Narayan*, and not the *Narayansena*—the power of soul and not that of muscle. And she is to raise the history of man from the muddy level of physical conflict to the higher moral altitude.

What is Swaraj! It is maya; it is like a mist, that will vanish, leaving no stain on the radiance of the Eternal. However we may delude ourselves with the phrases learnt from the West, Swaraj is not our objective. Our fight is a spiritual fight—it is for Man. We are to emancipate Man from the meshes that he himself has woven round him—these organisations of National Egoism. The butterfly will have to be persuaded that the freedom of the sky is of higher value than the shelter of the cocoon. If we can defy the strong, the armed, the wealthy—revealing to the world the power of the immortal spirit—the whole castle of the Giant Flesh will vanish in the void. And then Man will find his Swaraj.

We, the famished, ragged ragamuffins of the East, are to win freedom for all Humanity. We have no word for 'Nation' in our language. When we borrow this word from other people, it never fits us. For we are to make our league with *Narayan*, and our victory will not give us anything but victory itself; victory for God's world. I have seen the West; I covet not the unholy feast, in which she revels every moment, growing more and more bloated and red and dangerously delirious. Not for us, is this mad orgy of midnight, with lighted torches, but awakening in the serene light of morning.

Tagore, Chicago, March 5, 1921.

Lately I have been receiving more and more news and newspaper cuttings from India, giving rise in my mind to a painful struggle that presages a period of suffering which is waiting for me. I am striving with all my power to tune my mood of mind to be in accord with the great feeling of excitement sweeping across my country. But, deep in my being, why is there this spirit of resistance maintaining its place in spite of my strong desire to remove it? I fail to find a clear answer; and through my gloom of dejection breaks out a smile and a voice saying, "Your place is on 'the seashore of worlds,' with children; there is your peace, and I am with you there."

This is why lately I have been playing with inventing new metres. These are merest nothings that are content to be borne away by the current of time, dancing in the sun and laughing as they disappear. But while I play, the whole creation is amused, for are not flowers and leaves never-ending experiments in metre. Is not my God an eternal waster of time? He flings stars and planets in the whirlwind of changes, he floats paper-boats of ages, filled with his fancies, on the rushing stream of appearance. When I tease him and beg him to allow me to remain his little follower and accept a few trifles of mine as the cargo of his play-boat, he smiles and I trot behind him catching the hem of his robe.

But where am I among the crowd, pushed from behind, pressed from all sides? And what is this noise about me? If it is a song, then my own *sitar* can catch the tune and I join in the chorus, for I am a singer. But if it is a shout, then my voice is wrecked and I am lost in bewilderment. I have been trying all these days to find in it a melody, straining my ear, but the idea of non-co-operation, with its mighty volume of sound, does not sing to me; its congregated menace of negation shouts. And I say to myself, "If you cannot keep step with your countrymen at this great crisis of their history, never say that you are right and the rest of them wrong; only give up your role as a soldier, go back to your corner as a poet, be ready to accept popular derision and disgrace."

R-, in support of the present movement, has often said to me that passion for rejection is a stronger power in the beginning than the acceptance of an ideal. Though I know this to be a fact, I cannot take it as a truth. We must choose our allies once for all; for they stick to us even when we might be glad to be rid of them. If we once claim strength from intoxication, then in the time of reaction our normal strength is bankrupt; and we go back again and again to the demon who lends us resources in a vessel whose bottom it takes away.

Brahma-vidya, the cult of Brahma, the Infinite Being, has for its object *mukti*, emancipation, while Buddhism has *nirvana*, extinction. It may be argued that both have the same idea in different names. But names represent attitudes of mind and emphasize particular aspects of truth. *Mukti* draws our attention to the positive, and *nirvana* to the negative side of truth. Buddha kept silence all through his teachings about the truth of the *Om*, the Everlasting Yes, his implication being that by the negative path of destroying the self we naturally reach that truth. Therefore he emphasized the fact of *dukha*, misery, which had to be avoided. But the *Brahmavidya* emphasized the fact of *Ananda*, Joy, which had to be attained. The latter cult also needs for its fulfilment the discipline of self-abnegation; yet it holds before its view the idea of Brahma, not only at the end, but all through the process of realization.

Therefore the idea of life's training was different in the Vedic period from that of the Buddhistic. In the former it was the purification of life's joy; in the latter it was the eradication of it. The abnormal type of asceticism to which Buddhism gave rise in India revelled in celibacy and mutilation of life in all different forms. Yet the forest life of the Brahmana was not antagonistic to the social life of man, but harmonious with it. It was like our musical instrument *tambura* whose duty is to supply the fundamental notes to the music to save it from straying into discordance. It believed in *Anandam*, the music of the soul, and its own simplicity was not to kill it, but to guide it.

The idea of non-co-operation is political asceticism. Our students are bringing their offering of sacrifices to what? Not to a fuller education, but to non-education. It has at its back a fierce joy of annihilation, which at its best is asceticism, and at its worst is that orgy of frightfulness in which human nature, losing faith in the basic reality of normal life, finds a disinterested delight in an unmeaning devastation, as has been shown in the late war and on other occasions which came nearer to us. 'No' in its passive moral form is asceticism, and in its active moral form is violence. The desert is as much a form of *himsa*, violence, as is the raging sea in storm; they both are against life.

I remember the day, during the Swadeshi movement in Bengal, when a crowd of young students came to see me in the first floor hall of our Vichitra house. They said to me that if I would order them to leave their schools and colleges they would instantly obey. I was emphatic in my refusal to do so, and they went away angry, doubting the sincerity of my love for my motherland. And yet long before this popular ebullition of excitement, I myself had given a thousand rupees, when I had not five rupees to call my own, to open a Swadeshi store and courted banter and bankruptcy.

The reason of my refusing to advise those students to leave their schools was because the anarchy of a mere emptiness never tempts me, even when it is resorted to as a temporary measure. I am frightened of an abstraction which is ready to ignore living reality. These students were no mere phantoms to me. Their life was a great fact to them and to the All. I could not lightly take upon myself the tremendous responsibility of a mere negative programme for them, which would uproot their life from its soil, however thin and poor that soil might be. The great injury and injustice, which had been done to those boys, who were tempted away from their career before any real provision was made, could never be made good to them. Of course that is nothing from the point of view of an abstraction, which can ignore the infinite value even of the smallest fraction of reality. I wish I were the little creature Jack, whose one mission is to kill the giant Abstraction, which is claiming the sacrifice of individuals all over the world under highly painted masks of delusion.

I say again and again that I am a poet; that I am not a fighter by nature. I would give everything to be one with my surroundings. I love my fellow beings and I prize their love. Yet I have been chosen by destiny to ply my boat there, where the current is against me. What irony of fate is this that I should be preaching co-operation of cultures between East and West on this side of the sea just at the moment when the doctrine of non-co-operation is preached on the other side? You know that I do not believe in the material civilization of the West, just as I do not believe the physical body to be the highest truth in man. But I still less believe in the destruction of the physical body, and the ignoring of the material necessities of life. What is needed is establishment of harmony between the physical and spiritual nature of man, the maintaining of balance between the foundation and superstructure. I believe in the true meeting of the East and the West. Love is the ultimate truth of soul. We should do all we can, not to outrage that truth, but to carry its banner against all opposition. The idea of non-co-operation unnecessarily hurts that truth. It is not our hearth-fire, but the fire that burns out our hearth and home.

Tagore, New York, March 19, 1921.

Things that are stationary have no responsibility and need no law. For death, even the tombstone is a useless luxury. But for a world, which is an ever-moving multitude advancing toward an idea, all its laws must have one principle of harmony. This is the law of creation.

Man became great when he found out this law for himself, the law of co-operation. It helped him to move together, to utilize the rhythm and impetus of the world march. He at once felt that this moving together was not mechanical, not an external regulation for the sake of some convenience. It was what the metre is in poetry—not mere system of enclosure for keeping ideas from running away in disorder, but for vitalizing them, making them indivisible in a unity of creation.

So far this idea of co-operation has developed itself into individual communities, within the boundaries of which peace has been maintained and varied wealth of life produced. But outside these boundaries the law of co-operation has not been realized. Consequently the great world of man is suffering from ceaseless discordance. We are beginning to discover that our problem is world wide, and no one people of the earth can work out its salvation by detaching itself from the others. Either we shall be saved together, or drawn together into destruction. This truth has ever been recognized by all the great personalities of the world. They had in themselves the perfect consciousness of the undivided spirit of man. Their teachings were against tribal exclusiveness, and thus we find that Buddha's India transcended geographical India, and Christ's religion broke through the bonds of Judaism.

Today, at this critical moment of the world's history, cannot India rise above her limitations and offer the great ideal to the world that will work towards harmony and co-operation between the different peoples of the earth? Men of feeble faith will say that India requires to be strong and rich before she can raise her voice for the sake of the whole world. But I refuse to believe it. That the measure of man's greatness is in his material resources is a gigantic illusion casting its shadow over the present-day world—it is an insult to man. It lies in the power of the materially weak to save the world from this illusion; and India, in spite of her penury and humiliation, can afford to come to the rescue of humanity.

The freedom of unrestrained egoism in the individual is license and not true freedom. For his truth is in that which is universal in him. Individual human races also attain true freedom when they have the freedom of perfect revelation of Man and not that of their aggressive racial egoism. The idea of freedom which prevails in modern civilization is superficial and materialistic. Our revolution in India will be a true one when its forces are directed against this crude idea of liberty.

The sunlight of love has the freedom that ripens the wisdom of immortal life; but passion's fire can only forge fetters for ourselves. The Spiritual Man has been struggling for its emergence into perfection, and every true cry of freedom is for this emancipation. Erecting barricades of fierce separateness, in the name of national necessity, is offering hindrance to it. Therefore in the long run it is building a prison for the nation itself. For the only path of deliverance for nations is in the ideal humanity.

Creation is an endless activity of God's freedom; it is an end in itself. Freedom is true when it is a revelation of truth. Man's freedom is for the revelation of the truth of Man, which is struggling to express itself. We have not yet fully realized it. But those people who have faith in its greatness, who acknowledge its sovereignty, and have the instinctive urging in their heart to break down obstructions, are paving the way for its coming.

India ever has nourished faith in the truth of the Spiritual Man, for whose realization she has made innumerable experiments, sacrifices and penances, some verging on the grotesque and the abnormal. But the fact is, she has never ceased in her attempt to find it, even though at the tremendous cost of material success. Therefore I feel that the true India is an idea, and not a mere geographical fact. I have come into touch with this idea in far away places of Europe and my loyalty was drawn to it in persons who belonged to countries different from mine. India will be victorious when this idea wins the victory—the idea of *Purusham mahantam aditya varnam tamasah parastat,*—The Infinite Personality whose Light reveals itself through the obstruction of Darkness. Our fight is against this Darkness. Our object is the revealment of the Light of this Infinite Personality in ourselves. This Infinite Personality of Man is not to be achieved in single individuals, but in one grand harmony of all human races. The darkness of egoism which will have to be destroyed is the egoism of the Nation.

The idea of India is against the intense consciousness of the separateness of one's own people from others, which inevitably leads to ceaseless conflicts. Therefore my one prayer is, let India stand for the co-operation of all peoples of the world.

The spirit of rejection finds its support in the consciousness of separateness, the spirit of acceptance in the consciousness of unity. India has ever declared that Unity is Truth, and separateness is *maya*. This unity is not a zero; it is that which comprehends all and therefore can never be reached through the path of negation.

Our present struggle to alienate our heart and mind from the West is an attempt at spiritual suicide. If in the spirit of national vain-gloriousness we shout from our house-tops that the West has produced nothing that has an infinite value for man, then we only create a serious cause of doubt about the worth of any product of the eastern mind. For it is the mind of Man in the East and West which is ever approaching Truth in her different aspects from different angles of vision. If it can be true that the standpoint of the West has betrayed it into an utter misdirection, then we can never be sure of the standpoint of the East. Let us be rid of all false pride and rejoice at any lamp being lit in any corner of the world, knowing that it is a part of the common illumination of our house.

The other day, I was invited to the house of a distinguished art-critic of America who is a great admirer of old Italian art. I questioned him if he knew anything of our Indian pictures, and he brusquely said that most probably he would hate them. I suspected he had seen some of them and hated them already. In retaliation I could have said something in the same language about western art. But I am proud to say it was not possible for me. For I always try to understand western art and never to hate it.

Whatever we understand and enjoy in human products instantly become ours wherever they might have their origin. I should feel proud of my humanity, when I can acknowledge the poets and artists of other countries as my own. Let me feel with unalloyed gladness that all the great glories of man are mine. Therefore it hurts me deeply when the cry of rejection rings loud against the West in my country with the clamor that western education can only injure us.

It cannot be true. What has caused the mischief is the fact that for a long time we have been out of touch with our own culture and therefore western culture has not found its true perspective in our life. Very often it has found a wrong perspective giving our mental eye a squint. When we have intellectual capital of our own, the commerce of thought with the outer world becomes natural and fully profitable. But to say that such commerce is inherently wrong, is to encourage the worst form of provincialism, productive of nothing but intellectual indigence.

The West has misunderstood the East. This is at the root of the disharmony that prevails between them. But will it mend matters if the East in her turn tries to misunderstand the West? The present age has been powerfully possessed by the West; it has only become possible because to her is given some great mission for man. We, from the East, have to come to her to learn whatever she has to teach us; for by doing so we hasten the fulfilment of this age. We know that the East also has her lessons to give, and she has her own responsibility of not allowing her light to be extinguished. The time will come when the West will find leisure to realize, that she has a home of hers in the East where her food is and her rest.

Gandhi's Response, 1st June 1921

Elsewhere the reader will see my humble endeavor in reply to Dr. Tagore's criticism of Non-co-operation. I have since read his letter to the Manager of Shantiniketan. I am sorry to observe that the letter is written in anger and in ignorance of facts. The Poet was naturally incensed to find that certain students in London would not give a hearing to Mr. Pearson, one of the truest of Englishmen, and he became equally incensed to learn that I had told our women to stop English studies. The reasons for my advice, the Poet evidently inferred for himself.

How much better it would have been, if he had not imputed the rudeness of the students to Non-co-operation, and had remembered that Non-co-operators worship Andrews, honor Stokes, and gave a most respectful hearing to Messrs. Wedgwood, Ben Spoor and Holford Knight at Nagpur, that Maulana Mahomed Ali accepted the invitation to tea of an English official when he invited him as a friend, that Hakim Ajmalkhan, a staunch Non-co-operator, had the portraits of Lord and Lady Hardinge unveiled in his Tibbi College and had invited his many English friends to witness the ceremony. How much better it would have been, if he had refused to allow the demon doubt to possess him for one moment, as to the real and religious character of the present movement, and had believed that the movement was altering the meaning of old terms, nationalism and patriotism, and extending their scope.

If he, with a poet's imagination, had seen that I was incapable of wishing to cramp the mind of the Indian women, and I could not object to English learning as such, and recalled the fact that throughout my life I had fought for the fullest liberty for women, he would have been saved the injustice which he has done me, and which, I know, he would never knowingly do to an avowed enemy. The Poet does not know perhaps that English is to-day studied because of its commercial and so-called political value. Our boys think, and rightly in the present circumstances, that without English they cannot get Government service. Girls are taught English as a passport to marriage. I know several instances of women wanting to learn English so that they may be able to talk to Englishmen in English. I know husbands who are sorry that their wives cannot talk to them and their friends in English. I know families in which English is being *made* the mother tongue. Hundreds of youths believe that without a knowledge of English freedom for India is practically impossible. The canker has so eaten into the society that, in many cases, the only meaning of Education is a knowledge of English. All these are for me signs of our slavery and degradation. It is unbearable to me that the vernaculars should be crushed and starved as they have been. I cannot tolerate the idea of parents writing to their children, or husbands writing to their wives, not in their own vernaculars, but in English. I hope I am as great a believer in free air as the great Poet. I do not want my house to be walled in on all sides and my windows to be stuffed. I want the cultures of all the lands to be blown about my house as freely as possible. But I refuse to be blown off my feet by any. I refuse to live in other people's houses as interloper, a beggar or a slave. I refuse to put the unnecessary strain of learning English upon my sisters for the sake of false pride or questionable social advantage. I would have our young men and young women with literary tastes to learn as much of English and other world- languages as they like, and then expect them to give the benefits of their learning to India and to the world, like a Bose, a Roy or the Poet himself. But I would not have a single Indian to forget, neglect or be ashamed of his mother-tongue, or to feel that he or she cannot think or express the best thoughts in his or her own vernacular. Mine is not a religion of the prison house. It has room for the least among God's creation. But it is proof against insolence, pride of race, religion or color. I am extremely sorry for the Poet's misreading of this great movement of reformation, purification and patriotism spelt humanity. If he will be patient, he will find no cause for sorrow or shame for his countrymen. I respectfully warn him against mistaking its excrescences for the movement itself. It is as wrong to judge Non-co-operation by the students' misconduct in London or Malegam's in India, as it would be to judge English men by the Dyers or the O'Dwyers.

Gandhi, The Poet's Anxiety, 1st June, 1921

The Poet of Asia, as Lord Hardinge called Dr. Tagore, is fast becoming, if he has not already become, the Poet of the world. Increasing prestige has brought to him increasing responsibility. His greatest service to India must be his poetic interpretation of India's message to the world. The Poet is therefore sincerely anxious that India should deliver no false or feeble message in her name. He is naturally jealous of his country's reputation. He says he has striven hard to find himself in tune with the present movement. He confesses that he is baffled. He can find nothing for his lyre in the din and the bustle of Non-co-operation. In three forceful letters, he has endeavored to give expression to his misgivings, and he has come to the conclusion that Non co-operation is not dignified enough for the India of his vision, that it is a doctrine of negation and despair. He fears that it is a doctrine of separation, exclusiveness, narrowness and negation.

No Indian can feel anything but pride in the Poet's exquisite jealousy of India's honor. It is good that he should have sent to us his misgivings in language at once beautiful and clear.

In all humility, I shall endeavor to answer to Poet's doubts. I may fail to convince him or the reader who may have been touched by his eloquence, but I would like to assure him and India that Non-co-operation in conception is not any of the things he fears, and he need have no cause to be ashamed of his country for having adopted Non-co-operation. If, in actual application, it appears in the end to have failed, it will be no more the fault of the doctrine, than it would be of Truth, if those who claim to apply it in practice do not appear to succeed. Non-co-operation may have come in advance of its time. India and the world must then wait, but there is no choice for India save between violence and Non-co-operation.

Nor need the Poet fear that Non-co-operation is intended to erect a Chinese wall between India and the West. On the contrary, Non-co-operation is intended to pave the way to real, honorable and voluntary co-operation based on mutual respect and trust. The present struggle is being waged against compulsory co-operation, against one-sided combination, against the armed imposition of modern methods of exploitation masquerading under the name of civilization.

Non-co-operation is a protest against an unwitting and unwilling participation in evil.

The Poet's concern is largely about the students. He is of the opinion that they should not have been called upon to give up Government schools before they had other schools to go to. Here I must differ from him. I have never been able to make a fetish of literary training. My experience has proved to my satisfaction that literary training by itself adds not an inch to one's moral height and that character-building is independent of literary training. I am firmly of the opinion that the Government schools have unmanned us, rendered us helpless and Godless. They have filled us with discontent, and providing no remedy for the discontent, have made us despondent. They have made us what we were intended to become—clerks and interpreters. A government builds its prestige upon the apparently voluntary association of the governed. And if it was wrong to co-operate with the Government in keeping us slaves, we were bound to begin with those institutions in which our association appeared to be most voluntary. The youth of a nation are its hope. I hold that, as soon as we discovered that the system of government was wholly, or mainly evil, it became sinful for us to associate our children with it.

It is no argument against the soundness of the proposition laid down by me that the vast majority of the students went back after the first flush of enthusiasm. Their recantation is proof rather of the extent of our degradation than of the wrongness of the step. Experience has shown that the establishment of national schools has not resulted in drawing many more students. The strongest and the truest of them came out without any national schools to fall back upon, and I am convinced that these first withdrawals are rendering service of the highest order.

But the Poet's protest against the calling out of the boys is really a corollary to his objection to the very doctrine of Non-co-operation. He has a horror of everything negative. His whole soul seems to rebel against the negative commandments of religion. I must give his objection in his own inimitable language. "R, in support of the present 'movement has often said to me that passion for rejection is a stronger power in the beginning than the acceptance of an ideal. Though I know it to be a fact, I cannot take it as a truth.... Brahmavidya in India has for its object *Mukti* (emancipation), while Buddhism has *Nirvana* (extinction). *Mukti* draws our attention to the positive and *Nirvana* to the negative side of truth. Therefore, he emphasized the fact of *duhkha* (misery) which had to be avoided and the Brahmavidya emphasized the fact of *Ananda* (joy) which had to be attained." In these and kindred passages, the reader will find the key to the Poet's mentality. In my humble opinion, rejection is as much an Ideal as the acceptance of a thing. It is as necessary to reject untruth as it is to accept truth. All religions teach that two opposite forces act upon us and that the human endeavor consists in a series of eternal rejections and acceptances. Non-co-operation with evil is as much a duty as co-operation with good. I venture to suggest that the Poet has done an unconscious injustice to Buddhism in describing *Nirvana* as merely a negative state. I make bold to say that *Mukti* (emancipation) is as much a negative state as *Nirvana*. Emancipation from or extinction of the bondage of the flesh leads to *Ananda* (eternal bliss). Let me close this part of my argument by drawing attention to the fact that the final word of the Upanishads (Brahmavidya) is *Not*. *Neti* (not this) was the best description the authors of the Upanishads were able to find for *Brahman*.

I therefore think that the Poet has been unnecessarily alarmed at the negative aspect of Non-co-operation. We had lost the power of saying ' no.' It had become disloyal, almost sacrilegious to say ' no' to the Government. This deliberate refusal to co-operate is like the necessary weeding process that a cultivator has to resort to before he sows. Weeding is as necessary to agriculture as sowing. Indeed, even whilst the crops are growing, the weeding fork, as every husbandman knows, is an instrument almost of daily use. The nation's Non-co-operation is an invitation to the Government to co-operate with it on its own terms as is every nation's right and every good government's duty. Non-co-operation is the nation's notice that it is no longer satisfied to be in tutelage. The nation has taken to the harmless (for it), natural and religious doctrine of Non-co-operation in the place of the unnatural and irreligious doctrine of violence. And if India is ever to attain the Swaraj of the Poet's dream, she will do so only by Nonviolent Non-co-operation. Let him deliver his message of peace to the world, and feel confident that India, through her Non-co-operation, if she remains true to her pledge, will have exemplified his message. Non-co-operation is intended to give the very meaning to patriotism that the Poet is yearning after. An India prostrate at the feel of Europe can give no hope to humanity. An India awakened and free has a message of peace and good will to a groaning world. Non-co-operation is designed to supply her with a platform from which she will preach the message.

Selection from Tagore, Rabindranath. *Letters from Abroad*, 72–85. Madras, India: S. Ganesan, 1924.

Gandhi, Mahatma. "English Learning." In *Young India, 1919–1922*, 459–61. New York: B. W. Huebsch, 1923.

Gandhi, Mahatma. "The Poet's Anxiety." In *Young India, 1919–1922*, 608–13. New York: B. W. Huebsch, 1923.

BEYOND THE CLASSROOM

» There is an African proverb that says: "If you want to go fast, go alone. If you want to go far, go together." What situations can you think of where individualistic leadership is effective? And what situations can you think of where collectivist leadership is effective?
» Think about yourself at work. What aspects of noncooperation, as Gandhi details it, do you think would be effective in today's work environments?

from *Democracy in America* by Alexis de Toqueville

Introduction

Born on July 29, 1805, in Paris, France, Alexis de Tocqueville (1805–1859) was a French aristocrat, diplomat, political scientist, philosopher, and historian. Under the guise of studying the American Penal System, he along with Gustave de Beaumont, a French magistrate and advocate for nineteenth-century prison reform, traveled to the United States in 1830. While a study of the American penal system was published in 1833, Tocqueville's primary desire for visiting the United States was to study firsthand the democratic workings of the young nation. Prior to the visit, Tocqueville intimated to a friend that he had long wanted to go to America to see what a republic is like. In a later letter, he wrote that he and Beaumont were going "with the intention of examining as fully and as scientifically as possible, all the springs of that vast machine—American society; everywhere talked of, and nowhere understood. And if public affairs at home give us time, we expect to bring back the materials for a valuable book, or at least, a new book," he wrote, "for there is nothing whatever extant on the subject."[88]

> **SNAPSHOT BOX**
>
> LANGUAGE: French
> PUBLISHED: 1835/1840, France
> GENRE: Political analysis
> TAGS: Class and Caste; Cross-Cultural Encounters; Historiography; History and Ideology; Statecraft; Tradition

Timeline

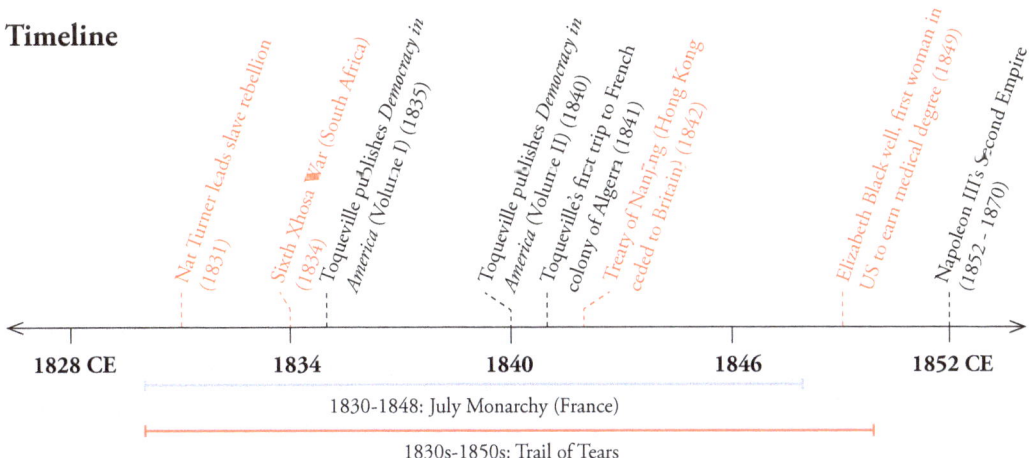

88. Letter from Alexis de Tocqueville to Eugene Stoffels, Feb. 21, 1835. In *Memoir, Letters, and Remains of Alexis de Tocqueville*. Volume 1. Translated form the French by the translator of Napoleon's Correspondence with King Joseph. 2 Volumes. London: Macmillan, 1861, 386–87.

After arriving in New York in the early months of 1830, Tocqueville and Beaumont undertook a nine-month tour of many northern, western, and southern states. The literary result of their extensive tour was the publication of the two-volume work for which Tocqueville is most known, *Democracy in America*. In the excerpts included here, Tocqueville provides his assessment of the developing democratic culture of the United States. At the heart of that culture, he discerns, was a deep and abiding commitment to the idea of "equality," a commitment, he argues, that often meant that an appreciation for the true meaning and value of "liberty" was often lost to many of the nation's citizens. Indeed, Tocqueville asserts that the two concepts of "equality" on one side, and "liberty" on the other, were not one and the same. Despite the nation's expressed commitment to maintaining and securing the blessing of "liberty"—by which he meant freedom from arbitrary or despotic rule—nothing, he writes, struck him "more forcibly than the desire to maintain a sense of the general equality of conditions"[89] among the American populace. "I readily discovered," he adds, "the prodigious influence that this primary fact exercises on the whole course of society. It gives a peculiar direction to public opinion and a peculiar tenor to the laws; it imparts new maxims to the governing authorities and peculiar habits to the governed."[90]

In speaking of a "general equality of conditions," Patrick Deneen notes, Tocqueville was not referring "to the literal material equality of all American citizens, but rather to the universal assumption that no significance was to be accorded any apparent differences—material, social or personal,"[91] among Americans. This is noteworthy because within such a society there exists the idea that no man was above another, and that no man's opinion counted more than another's. In other words, unlike the aristocratic and hierarchical social orders of Europe, the United States, as Tocqueville saw it, was a largely classless society, a place where all opinions were accorded equal respect. Nevertheless, the idea of "liberty" required special guarding in such societies. As Tocqueville argues, there is a tendency in democratic societies to so value "equality of conditions" that differences of any kind might be seen as contemptuous of the democratic social order; especially if the majority deemed it so. "Since everyone's personal judgment is to be regarded as equal to one's own,"[92] Deneen points out that, any claims or suggestions of "aristocratic excellence" or "distinction" was, or at least could be held in suspicion. Thus, if not guarded against, the "sole basis of determining the legitimacy of public issues"[93] could become simply

---

89. Alexis de Tocqueville, *Democracy in America*: Volume 1, translated by Henry Reeve (Auckland: The Floating Press, 2009 [1840]), 31.

90. Tocqueville, *Democracy*, 31.

91. Patrick J. Deneen, "Remembering Alexis de Tocqueville." *The Imaginative Conservative*. Republished March, 2015. https://theimaginativeconservative.org/2017/01/equality-tyranny-despotism-democracy-remembering-alexis-de-tocqueville-timeless-patrick-deneen.html

92. Deneen, "Remembering," 2015.

93. Deneen, "Remembering," 2015.

whatever the majority decided. Tocqueville refers to this **majoritarian** ideal, which was believed to be, according to Deneen, "founded on the apparently benign principle of equality,"[94] or in Tocqueville's words, the "doctrine of the sovereignty of the people."[95] However, Deneen indicates that Tocqueville warns that in such a state there exists the potential for "the opinion of the majority on any specific issue" to be seen as "unassailable,"[96] even if, as in the case of slavery, which Tocqueville found deplorable, the majority opinion is both morally wrong, and ultimately restricting of one's individual liberty.

Would Americans find and ultimately maintain a healthy balance between "liberty" and "equality," a balance that the American founders worked hard to establish in the Constitution? Tocqueville was skeptical and notes that when majoritarianism becomes the rule, which he suspected was already the case in Jacksonian America, people with dissenting views tend to recede into a more individualistic posture. Such individualism, he suggests, was the by-product of a sense of fear that the majority's reaction to dissenting views would result in repression. Thus, as Deneen notes, "a new form of internalized psychological control" develops and rather than engaging in public debate, democratic men and women try to "avoid public commitment to any issue"[97] and adopt a stance that, in Tocqueville's words, leads "each member of the community to sever himself from the mass of his fellow-creatures, and to draw apart with his family and friends."[98] If such an individualism develops, there exists the possibility, Tocqueville feared, that a larger national forgetfulness will occur. He insisted that the memory of the past was important to the maintenance of "liberty."

As Tocqueville assessed the American republic during his visit in 1830, he detected that a loss of a serious, and perhaps critical memory of the past was already afoot. He perceived that rather than thinking about the past and what previous generations had sacrificed to secure the nation's liberty, Americans were becoming more of a present-minded people. Americans seemed to be constantly striving for more from the material world. "A native of the United States," he writes, "clings to this world's goods as if he were certain never to die; and he is so hasty in grasping at all within his reach, that one would suppose he was constantly afraid of not living long enough to enjoy them."[99] Tocqueville goes on to observe that little or no thought is given to either the past or the future—all that seems important is the present moment. As one form of evidence of this, he sees a constant movement happening "which agitates a democratic community, [and thus] the tie that unites one generation to another is relaxed or broken; every man there readily loses all

---

94. Deneen, "Remembering," 2015.
95. Deneen, "Remembering," 2015.
96. Deneen, "Remembering," 2015.
97. Deneen, "Remembering," 2015.
98. Tocqueville, *Democracy*, 963.
99. Tocqueville, *Democracy*, 1026.

trace of the idea of his forefathers or takes no care about them."[100] This, he concludes, poses a great threat to the American republic, and the world would do well to make note of that fact. Written nearly two centuries ago, does Tocqueville's assessment describe who we are today? How might democratic societies ensure a healthy balance between "liberty" and "equality"?

Darin J. Waters
Deputy Secretary for Archives and History, North Carolina State Historian

---

100. Tocqueville, *Democracy*, 798.

from *Democracy in America*

Volume 2: Section II: Influence of Democracy on the Feelings of the Americans

Chapter I: Why Democratic Nations Show a More Ardent and Enduring Love of Equality than of Liberty

The first and most intense passion which is engendered by the equality of conditions is, I need hardly say, the love of that same equality. My readers will therefore not be surprised that I speak of it before all others. Everybody has remarked that in our time, and especially in France, this passion for equality is every day gaining ground in the human heart. It has been said a hundred times that our contemporaries are far more ardently and tenaciously attached to equality than to freedom; but as I do not find that the causes of the fact have been sufficiently analyzed, I shall endeavor to point them out.

It is possible to imagine an extreme point at which freedom and equality would meet and be confounded together. Let us suppose that all the members of the community take a part in the government, and that each one of them has an equal right to take a part in it. As none is different from his fellows, none can exercise a tyrannical power: men will be perfectly free, because they will all be entirely equal; and they will all be perfectly equal, because they will be entirely free. To this ideal state democratic nations tend. Such is the completest form that equality can assume upon earth; but there are a thousand others which, without being equally perfect, are not less cherished by those nations.

The principle of equality may be established in civil society, without prevailing in the political world. Equal rights may exist of indulging in the same pleasures, of entering the same professions, of frequenting the same place—in a word, of living in the same manner and seeking wealth by the same means, although all men do not take an equal share in the government. A kind of equality may even be established in the political world, though there should be no political freedom there. A man may be the equal of all his countrymen save one, who is the master of all without distinction, and who selects equally from among them all the agents of his power. Several other combinations might be easily imagined, by which very great equality would be united to institutions more or less free, or even to institutions wholly without freedom. Although men cannot become absolutely equal unless they be entirely free, and consequently equality, pushed to its furthest extent, may be confounded with freedom, yet there is good reason for distinguishing the one from the other. The taste which men have for liberty, and that which they feel for equality, are, in fact, two different things; and I am not afraid to add that, amongst democratic nations, they are two unequal things.

Upon close inspection, it will be seen that there is in every age some peculiar and preponderating fact with which all others are connected; this fact almost always gives birth to some pregnant idea or some ruling passion, which attracts to itself, and bears away in its course, all the feelings and opinions of the time: it is like a great stream, towards which each of the surrounding rivulets seems to flow. Freedom has appeared in the world at different times and under various forms; it has not been exclusively bound to any social condition, and it is not confined to democracies. Freedom cannot, therefore, form the distinguishing characteristic of democratic ages. The peculiar and preponderating fact which marks those ages as its own is the equality of conditions; the ruling passion of men in those periods is the love of this equality. Ask not what singular charm the men of democratic ages find in being equal, or what special reasons they may have for clinging so tenaciously to equality rather than to the other advantages which society holds out to them: equality is the distinguishing characteristic of the age they live in; that, of itself, is enough to explain that they prefer it to all the rest.

But independently of this reason there are several others, which will at all times habitually lead men to prefer equality to freedom. If a people could ever succeed in destroying, or even in diminishing, the equality which prevails in its own body, this could only be accomplished by long and laborious efforts. Its social condition must be modified, its laws abolished, its opinions superseded, its habits changed, its manners corrupted. But political liberty is more easily lost; to neglect to hold it fast is to allow it to escape. Men therefore not only cling to equality because it is dear to them; they also adhere to it because they think it will last forever.

That political freedom may compromise in its excesses the tranquility, the property, the lives of individuals, is obvious to the narrowest and most unthinking minds. But, on the contrary, none but attentive and clear-sighted men perceive the perils with which equality threatens us, and they commonly avoid pointing them out. They know that the calamities they apprehend are remote, and flatter themselves that they will only fall upon future generations, for which the present generation takes but little thought. The evils which freedom sometimes brings with it are immediate; they are apparent to all, and all are more or less affected by them. The evils which extreme equality may produce are slowly disclosed; they creep gradually into the social frame; they are only seen at intervals, and at the moment at which they become most violent habit already causes them to be no longer felt. The advantages which freedom brings are only shown by length of time; and it is always easy to mistake the cause in which they originate. The advantages of equality are instantaneous, and they may constantly be traced from their source. Political liberty bestows exalted pleasures, from time to time, upon a certain number of citizens. Equality every day confers a number of small enjoyments on every man. The charms of equality are every instant felt, and are within the reach of all; the noblest hearts are not insensible to them, and the most vulgar souls exult in them. The passion which equality engenders must therefore be at once strong and general. Men cannot enjoy political liberty unpurchased by some sacrifices, and they never obtain it without great exertions. But the pleasures of equality are self-proffered: each of the petty incidents of life seems to occasion them, and in order to taste them nothing is required but to live.

Democratic nations are at all times fond of equality, but there are certain epochs at which the passion they entertain for it swells to the height of fury. This occurs at the moment when the old social system, long menaced, completes its own destruction after a last intestine struggle, and when the barriers of rank are at length thrown down. At such times men pounce upon equality as their booty, and they cling to it as to some precious treasure which they fear to lose. The passion for equality penetrates on every side into men's hearts, expands there, and fills them entirely. Tell them not that by this blind surrender of themselves to an exclusive passion they risk their dearest interests: they are deaf. Show them not freedom escaping from their grasp, whilst they are looking another way: they are blind—or rather, they can discern but one sole object to be desired in the universe.

What I have said is applicable to all democratic nations: what I am about to say concerns the French alone. Amongst most modern nations, and especially amongst all those of the Continent of Europe, the taste and the idea of freedom only began to exist and to extend themselves at the time when social conditions were tending to equality, and as a consequence of that very equality. Absolute kings were the most efficient levelers of ranks amongst their subjects. Amongst these nations equality preceded freedom: equality was therefore a fact of some standing when freedom was still a novelty: the one had already created customs, opinions, and laws belonging to it, when the other, alone and for the first time, came into actual existence. Thus the latter was still only an affair of opinion and of taste, whilst the former had already crept into the habits of the people, possessed itself of their manners, and given a particular turn to the smallest actions of their lives. Can it be wondered that the men of our own time prefer the one to the other?

I think that democratic communities have a natural taste for freedom: left to themselves, they will seek it, cherish it, and view any privation of it with regret. But for equality, their passion is ardent, insatiable, incessant, invincible: they call for equality in freedom; and if they cannot obtain that, they still call for equality in slavery. They will endure poverty, servitude, barbarism—but they will not endure aristocracy. This is true at all times, and especially true in our own. All men and all powers seeking to cope with this irresistible passion, will be overthrown and destroyed by it. In our age, freedom cannot be established without it, and despotism itself cannot reign without its support.

Chapter II: Of Individualism in Democratic Countries

I have shown how it is that in ages of equality every man seeks for his opinions within himself: I am now about to show how it is that, in the same ages, all his feelings are turned towards himself alone. Individualism is a novel expression, to which a novel idea has given birth. Our fathers were only acquainted with egotism. Egotism is a passionate and exaggerated love of self, which leads a man to connect everything with his own person, and to prefer himself to everything in the world. Individualism is a mature and calm feeling, which disposes each member of the community to sever himself from the mass of his fellow-creatures; and to draw apart with his family and his friends; so that, after he has thus formed a little circle of his own, he willingly leaves society at large to itself. Egotism originates in blind instinct: individualism proceeds from erroneous judgment more than from depraved feelings; it originates as much in the deficiencies of the mind as in the perversity of the heart. Egotism blights the germ of all virtue; individualism, at first, only saps the virtues of public life; but, in the long run, it attacks and destroys all others, and is at length absorbed in downright egotism. Egotism is a vice as old as the world, which does not belong to one form of society more than to another: individualism is of democratic origin, and it threatens to spread in the same ratio as the equality of conditions.

Amongst aristocratic nations, as families remain for centuries in the same condition, often on the same spot, all generations become as it were contemporaneous. A man almost always knows his forefathers, and respects them: he thinks he already sees his remote descendants, and he loves them. He willingly imposes duties on himself towards the former and the latter; and he will frequently sacrifice his personal gratifications to those who went before and to those who will come after him. Aristocratic institutions have, moreover, the effect of closely binding every man to several of his fellow-citizens. As the classes of an aristocratic people are strongly marked and permanent, each of them is regarded by its own members as a sort of lesser country, more tangible and more cherished than the country at large. As in aristocratic communities all the citizens occupy fixed positions, one above the other, the result is that each of them always sees a man above himself whose patronage is necessary to him, and below himself another man whose co-operation he may claim. Men living in aristocratic ages are therefore almost always closely attached to something placed out of their own sphere, and they are often disposed to forget themselves. It is true that in those ages the notion of human fellowship is faint, and that men seldom think of sacrificing themselves for mankind; but they often sacrifice themselves for other men. In democratic ages, on the contrary, when the duties of each individual to the race are much more clear, devoted service to any one man becomes more rare; the bond of human affection is extended, but it is relaxed.

Amongst democratic nations new families are constantly springing up, others are constantly falling away, and all that remain change their condition; the woof of time is every instant broken, and the track of generations effaced. Those who went before are soon forgotten; of those who will come after no one has any idea: the interest of man is confined to those in close propinquity to himself. As each class approximates to other classes, and intermingles with them, its members become indifferent and as strangers to one another. Aristocracy had made a chain of all the members of the community, from the peasant to the king: democracy breaks that chain, and severs every link of it. As social conditions become more equal, the number of persons increases who, although they are neither rich enough nor powerful enough to exercise any great influence over their fellow-creatures, have nevertheless acquired or retained sufficient education and fortune to satisfy their own wants. They owe nothing to any man, they expect nothing from any man; they acquire the habit of always considering themselves as standing alone, and they are apt to imagine that their whole destiny is in their own hands. Thus not only does democracy make every man forget his ancestors, but it hides his descendants, and separates his contemporaries from him; it throws him back forever upon himself alone, and threatens in the end to confine him entirely within the solitude of his own heart.

[...]

Chapter XIII: Causes of the Restless Spirit of the Americans in the Midst of Their Prosperity

In certain remote corners of the Old World you may still sometimes stumble upon a small district which seems to have been forgotten amidst the general tumult, and to have remained stationary whilst everything around it was in motion. The inhabitants are for the most part extremely ignorant and poor; they take no part in the business of the country, and they are frequently oppressed by the government; yet their countenances are generally placid, and their spirits light. In America I saw the freest and most enlightened men, placed in the happiest circumstances which the world affords: it seemed to me as if a cloud habitually hung upon their brow, and I thought them serious and almost sad even in their pleasures. The chief reason of this contrast is that the former do not think of the ills they endure—the latter are forever brooding over advantages they do not possess. It is strange to see with what feverish ardor the Americans pursue their own welfare; and to watch the vague dread that constantly torments them lest they should not have chosen the shortest path which may lead to it. A native of the United States clings to this world's goods as if he were certain never to die; and he is so hasty in grasping at all within his reach, that one would suppose he was constantly afraid of not living long enough to enjoy them. He clutches everything, he holds nothing fast, but soon loosens his grasp to pursue fresh gratifications.

In the United States a man builds a house to spend his latter years in it, and he sells it before the roof is on: he plants a garden, and lets it just as the trees are coming into bearing: he brings a field into tillage, and leaves other men to gather the crops: he embraces a profession, and gives it up: he settles in a place, which he soon afterwards leaves, to carry his changeable longings elsewhere. If his private affairs leave him any leisure, he instantly plunges into the vortex of politics; and if at the end of a year of unremitting labor he finds he has a few days' vacation, his eager curiosity whirls him over the vast extent of the United States, and he will travel fifteen hundred miles in a few days, to shake off his happiness. Death at length overtakes him, but it is before he is weary of his bootless chase of that complete felicity which is forever on the wing.

At first sight there is something surprising in this strange unrest of so many happy men, restless in the midst of abundance. The spectacle itself is however as old as the world; the novelty is to see a whole people furnish an exemplification of it. Their taste for physical gratifications must be regarded as the original source of that secret inquietude which the actions of the Americans betray, and of that inconstancy of which they afford fresh examples every day. He who has set his heart exclusively upon the pursuit of worldly welfare is always in a hurry, for he has but a limited time at his disposal to reach it, to grasp it, and to enjoy it. The recollection of the brevity of life is a constant spur to him. Besides the good things which he possesses, he every instant fancies a thousand others which death will prevent him from trying if he does not try them soon. This thought fills him with anxiety, fear, and regret, and keeps his mind in ceaseless trepidation, which leads him perpetually to change his plans and his abode. If in addition to the taste for physical well-being a social condition be superadded, in which the laws and customs make no condition permanent, here is a great additional stimulant to this restlessness of temper. Men will then be seen continually to change their track, for fear of missing the shortest cut to happiness. It may readily be conceived that if men, passionately bent upon physical gratifications, desire eagerly, they are also easily discouraged: as their ultimate object is to enjoy, the means to reach that object must be prompt and easy, or the trouble of acquiring the gratification would be greater than the gratification itself. Their prevailing frame of mind then is at once ardent and relaxed, violent and enervated. Death is often less dreaded than perseverance in continuous efforts to one end.

The equality of conditions leads by a still straighter road to several of the effects which I have here described. When all the privileges of birth and fortune are abolished, when all professions are accessible to all, and a man's own energies may place him at the top of any one of them, an easy and unbounded career seems open to his ambition, and he will readily persuade himself that he is born to no vulgar destinies. But this is an erroneous notion, which is corrected by daily experience. The same equality which allows every citizen to conceive these lofty hopes, renders all the citizens less able to realize them: it circumscribes their powers on every side, whilst it gives freer scope to their desires. Not only are they themselves powerless, but they are met at every step by immense obstacles, which they did not at first perceive. They have swept away the privileges of some of their fellow-creatures which stood in their way, but they have opened the door to universal competition: the barrier has changed its shape rather than its position. When men are nearly alike, and all follow the same track, it is very difficult for any one individual to walk quick and cleave a way through the dense throng which surrounds and presses him. This constant strife between the propensities springing from the equality of conditions and the means it supplies to satisfy them, harasses and wearies the mind.

It is possible to conceive men arrived at a degree of freedom which should completely content them; they would then enjoy their independence without anxiety and without impatience. But men will never establish any equality with which they can be contented. Whatever efforts a people may make, they will never succeed in reducing all the conditions of society to a perfect level; and even if they unhappily attained that absolute and complete depression, the inequality of minds would still remain, which, coming directly from the hand of God, will forever escape the laws of man. However democratic then the social state and the political constitution of a people may be, it is certain that every member of the community will always find out several points about him which command his own position; and we may foresee that his looks will be doggedly fixed in that direction. When inequality of conditions is the common law of society, the most marked inequalities do not strike the eye: when everything is nearly on the same level, the slightest are marked enough to hurt it. Hence the desire of equality always becomes more insatiable in proportion as equality is more complete.

Amongst democratic nations men easily attain a certain equality of conditions: they can never attain the equality they desire. It perpetually retires from before them, yet without hiding itself from their sight, and in retiring draws them on. At every moment they think they are about to grasp it; it escapes at every moment from their hold. They are near enough to see its charms, but too far off to enjoy them; and before they have fully tasted its delights they die. To these causes must be attributed that strange melancholy which oftentimes will haunt the inhabitants of democratic countries in the midst of their abundance, and that disgust at life which sometimes seizes upon them in the midst of calm and easy circumstances. Complaints are made in France that the number of suicides increases; in America suicide is rare, but insanity is said to be more common than anywhere else. These are all different symptoms of the same disease. The Americans do not put an end to their lives, however disquieted they may be, because their religion forbids it; and amongst them materialism may be said hardly to exist, notwithstanding the general passion for physical gratification. The will resists—reason frequently gives way.

In democratic ages enjoyments are more intense than in the ages of aristocracy, and especially the number of those who partake in them is larger: but, on the other hand, it must be admitted that man's hopes and his desires are oftener blasted, the soul is more stricken and perturbed, and care itself more keen.

Selections from Tocqueville, Alexis de. *Democracy in America*. Translated by Henry Reeve, 99–106, 144–47. New York: J. & H. G. Langley, 1840.

"An Exhortation to Progress" by Mustafa Kemal (Atatürk)

> **SNAPSHOT BOX**
>
> LANGUAGE: Turkish
> DELIVERED: 1925
> GENRE: Public speech
> PROFESSION: Statesman
> TAGS: Community; History and Ideology; Nationalism; Rhetoric and Persuasion; Self-Determination; Statecraft; Tradition; Tyranny

Introduction

Mustapha Kemal (1881–1938), a military and diplomatic leader whose efforts would make possible the creation of the Republic of Turkey, served as the first president of this newly formed nation that had its roots in the previous Ottoman Empire which had been founded in the late thirteenth century. At its largest extent, the empire ranged from southwestern Asia to northwestern Africa and into eastern Europe. Beginning in the seventeenth century, however, central and western European powers had been chipping away at the empire, establishing colonial regimes in the southern Caucasus, the Balkans, and north Africa, as well as supporting popular dissent against the Turks by the Greeks in southern Europe and the Arabs in the Middle East. Following its defeat in World War I, the remaining territory of the Ottoman Empire was partitioned into several ethnic and colonial enclaves, or "Zones of Influence," by the Treaty of Sèvres in 1920, leaving only the arid plains of the northern sector of Anatolia (Asia Minor) as an ethnic Turkish homeland. For many Turks, the dismemberment of Anatolia was a step too far. A provisional nationalist government was gathered in the city of Ankara, and under the leadership of World War I war hero Mustafa Kemal, a War of Independence nullified the Treaty of Sèvres and reunited Anatolia under Turkish rule. In 1923, the government, now the Turkish National Assembly, proclaimed the creation of the Republic of Turkey and elected Kemal its leader.

Timeline

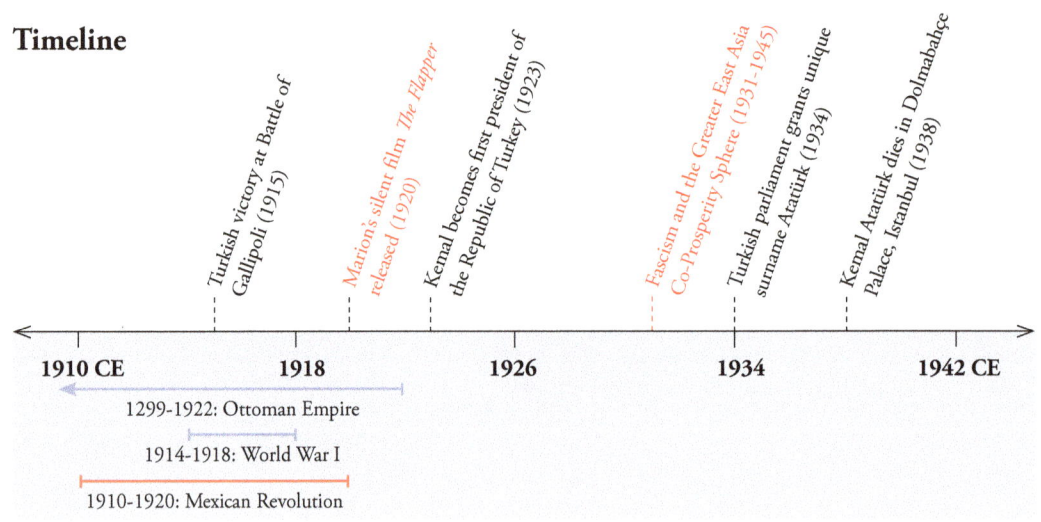

- 1299-1922: Ottoman Empire
- 1914-1918: World War I
- 1910-1920: Mexican Revolution

Kemal quickly set about forming the new Turkish state, but he did not look back to the Islamic Ottomans for his model. Rather, he envisioned a modern and westernized nation, based on a new constitution (written in 1924) that unilaterally abolished the **caliphate**, a position of leadership in the Islamic world that dated back to the period immediately after the Prophet Muhammad's death in the seventh century CE. While most members of the National Assembly supported Kemal's secularization of the Turkish state, many people throughout the country had serious reservations about his program of such radical reform. Thus, in August 1925, Kemal traveled to the cities of Kastamonu and İnebolu in northern Anatolia to encourage the people there to abandon their traditional ways of life and embrace Turkey's emergence into what he labeled "civilization."

Kemal's address in Kastamonu—selections from which were translated into English and published in the popular American magazine *The Living Age* in October 1925 as "An Exhortation to Progress"—urged the new citizens of the Republic to repudiate their Ottoman past, including its overtly Islamic political character (e.g., recognizing the sultan as caliph and use of the Islamic lunar calendar). Holding a wide-brimmed panama hat in his hands, Kemal addressed the crowd as brothers and sisters, appealed passionately to Turkish nationalism, defended his modernist reforms, and attacked many "popular" religious practices—such as the veneration of Sufi saints and dervishes—that dated from the Ottoman era. "He would have the common people adopt Western civilization in their personal lives," wrote one companion who accompanied him on this trip.[101]

Clothing, in particular, became the emblem of such personal change, as Kemal's own hat was meant to demonstrate. Headdress for men (e.g., the **turban** or the **fez**) and the **yashmak** (veil) or **hijab** for women had often been emblems of high social rank during the Ottoman period, and in Kastamonu, Kemal addressed the general public on this issue for the first time. Could something as simple as wearing apparel become an agent for dramatic social, political, and religious reform? What could be the repercussions of trying to transform personal attitudes and practices by governmental edicts?

Headgear and clothing were not superficial issues for Kemal. Three months after his trip to Kastamonu and İnebolu, the National Assembly in Ankara passed the "Hat Law," which mandated that all males had to wear the "Western" style of brimmed headgear while in public or go hatless. Anti-hat riots broke out in parts of the country, often led by conservative **imams**, leaders of the Friday prayers in the mosques, who identified the traditional fez as a part of their Islamic identity. Regarding these protests as political challenges to the national government and its program of modernization, many of the rioters were imprisoned and their leaders executed.[102] What

---

101. D. Vessaz, "The Ghazi on a Tour," *The Living Age*, October 31, 1925, 230–31.
102. "Hanged for Anti-Fez Talk: Turk Suffers Death as Old-Fashioned Natives Oppose Modern Hat," *New York Times*, December 3, 1925.

other complications might arise when democracy and westernized understandings of modernity are imposed by autocratic decree?

Rodger Payne
Department of Religious Studies

An Exhortation to Progress[103]

'The object of the revolution which we have already put on a secure footing, and which we are still carrying on, is to give to the citizens of the Republic a social organization completely modern and progressive in every sense. It is imperative for us to discard every thought that does not fall in line with this true principle. All absurd superstitions and prejudices must be rooted out of our minds and customs. Only thus can we cause the light of truth to shine upon all the people.'

Referring to the practice of some Moslems of praying at the graves of their departed priests and of tying bits of cloth in the grilled windows of their tombs to remind them of their petitions, the Ghazi said: —

'It is shameful for a civilized nation to expect help from the dead. Let the worthy occupants of those tombs rest in the happiness which they have found in a religious life. I can never tolerate the existence, in the bosom of a civilized Turkish society, of those primitive-minded men who seek material or moral well-being under the guidance of a sheik, possibly blind and hostile to the clear light of modern science and art.

'Comrades, gentlemen, fellow countrymen! You well know that the Republic of Turkey can never be a country of dervishes and sheiks and their disciples. *The only true congregation is that of the great international confraternity of civilization.* To be a real man it is necessary to do what civilization commands. The leaders of the *tekkés* (Moslem cloisters, shrines, or "monasteries") will comprehend this truth, which will lead them voluntarily to close those institutions as having already fulfilled their destiny.

'It is my duty to my conscience and to history to set forth openly what I have seen and felt. The Government of the Republic possesses a bureau of religious affairs. This department includes a numerous staff of imams (priests), muftis (chief priests), and scribes. These functionaries are required to have a certain standard of knowledge, training, and morality. But I know that there are also persons who, without being entrusted with such functions, continue to wear priestly garb. I have met many among them who are unlearned, or even illiterate. Yet they set themselves up as guides for the nation! They try to prevent direct contact between the Government and the people. I should like to know from them from what arid from whom they have received the qualities and attributes which they arrogate to themselves. . . .

'It is said that we Turks have a national costume. However that may be, whatever we wear is certainly not of our own invention. The fez is of Greek origin. Very few of us would be able to say what constitutes a national costume. For example, I see in this crowd a man who is wearing a fez wound round with a green turban. He has on a vest with sleeves, and over that a coat like my own. I cannot see what he is wearing

---

103. From *Aakkam* (Evening) (Constantinople independent daily), September 1. The following article is a newspaper report of a speech delivered by the president of Turkey at Kastamuni on August 29, 1925.

below that. What sort of clothing is that anyway? How can a civilized man consent to make himself ridiculous in the eyes of everyone by decking himself out in such outlandish garb? All employees of the Government, and all our fellow citizens, will have to reform such anachronisms in their dress....

'By her great achievements the Turkish nation has proved that she is a nation essentially revolutionary and new. Even before these last few years we had entered upon the path of progress. But all our efforts to advance remained relatively futile. The reason we failed was that we did not pursue our purpose with method. It must be clearly recognized, for instance, that human society is made up of the two sexes. Is it possible for one half of society to progress while the other half is neglected? It is imperative that man and woman march together along the way of progress at the same time and in the same step. We may note with satisfaction that we at last appreciate this necessity. Let us look straight at this question, then, and face the consequences with courage....

'I close with these beautiful verses from our great poet, Namuk Kemal Bey:–

"'This nation cannot die. If the impossible should come to pass, that she should die, the earth itself could not sustain the weight of her casket.'"

Kemal Pasha, Mustapha. "An Exhortation to Progress." In *The Living Age*, October 31, 1925, 232–33. New York: The Living Age Co., 1925.

from "Our América" by José Martí

Introduction

Jose Martí (1853–1895) is considered to be "Cuba's foremost patriotic hero."[104] He is also known as "the Apostle" (el Apóstol). He was born in Cuba and was deported to Spain in 1871 where he studied law, philosophy, and literature. He wrote prolifically while traveling in France, Mexico, Guatemala, and Venezuela. While in Venezuela, in 1881, he authored an anthology of poems titled *Ismaelillo*, considered one of the first examples of Latin American modernism. He lived in the United States (mainly in New York City) from 1880 to 1895. He frequently visited the Cuban tobacco workers exiled in Tampa, as he was organizing the war of 1895 against Spain. In 1892, he founded the Cuban Revolutionary Party and the newspaper *Patria*. Martí died in Dos Ríos, Cuba, on the battlefield, fighting against the Spanish troops.

> **SNAPSHOT BOX**
>
> LANGUAGE: Spanish
> PUBLISHED: 1891, New York, Argentina, Mexico
> GENRE: Newspaper article
> TAGS: Art; Colonization; Community; Cross-Cultural Encounters; Internationalism; Poetry, Music, Literature; Race; Self-Determination; Struggle, Resistance, and Revolution; Tradition; War and Brutality

Martí's "Our América"[105] belongs to a series of narrative testimonies of how intellectuals of the nineteenth century approached and wrote about the struggle for independence in the Americas and the building of a "Latin American identity." "Latin America" is used as an idea/concept that is re-created by authors, governments, or transnational forces with a variety of objectives. We can study these narratives as attempts to wrestle with issues related to the struggle for independence. "Our América" is particularly complex and has become a classical text and José Martí and his work have been **canonized**.[106] What elements does a text have that result in its typically becoming canonical or classical? Does this status create room for multiple interpretations?

In "Our América," Martí is responding to at least two specific and immediate circumstances. First, Martí was involved in the Washington Pan-American Conference (from October 1889 to April 1990), where he became concerned with the at-

---

104. John Charles Chasteen, *Born in Blood and Fire: A Concise History of Latin America* (New York: W. W. Norton, 2016), 223.

105. Experts have recommended Esther Allen's translation, which is the one published in the *Centros de Estudios Martíanos* website. I find it precise, and I agree with most of Allen's choices. I do object to her translation of the sentence "Con los pies en el rosario, la cabeza blanca y el cuerpo pinto de indio y criollo, venimos, denodados, al mundo de las naciones," as "Our feet upon a rosary, our faces white-skinned, and our bodies a motley of Indian and criollo, we boldly entered the community of nations." I believe that the expression "cabezas blancas" becomes a metaphor to signify age / experience. I prefer the translation in Ramos' work: "With our feet in the rosary, our heads white, and our bodies mottled in Indian and Creole, we came, naked into the world of nations" (294).

106. Julio Ramos, *Divergent Modernities* (Durham, NC: Duke University Press, 2001).

Timeline

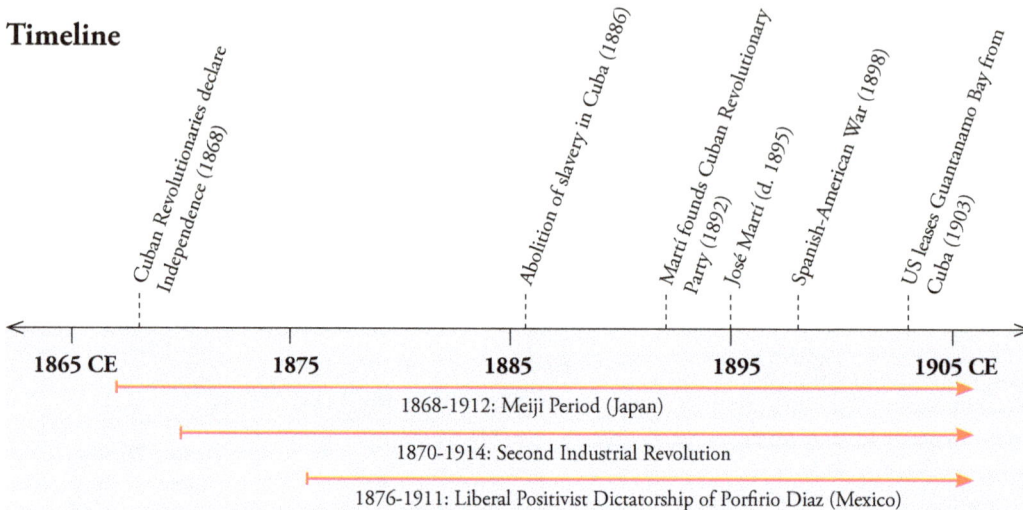

titudes of some of the delegates representing Latin American nations. Martí believed that they were forgetting (perhaps dismissing) the fact that Cuba was still fighting against Spanish colonial rule.[107] Second, concerned about US expansionism and persistent interest in the island, Martí raised his alarm in "Our América." His message is not only a vehement warning against US imperialism but also a fervent and eloquent defense of a form of **Latinamericanism** that needed to be based on the committed unity of all the republics in the South, and on a genuine defense of the "autochthonous"[108] of the Americas (i.e., education, history, etc.).

The relationship between Cuba and the United States presents a complex case study in the Latin American struggle for independence from Spain. For a sector of Cubans, particularly during the mid-nineteenth century, annexation to the United States had been the reasonable and desirable option, given their admiration of their neighbor to the North.[109] The economic relationship between Cuba and the United States had grown steadily during the century, and annexation to the US—as an alternative to Spanish rule—would ensure more solid, simplified, and independent trade between the two neighbors.[110]

José Martí rejected the dichotomy of "civilization" versus "barbarism" popular-

---

107. Enrico Mario Santi, "'Our America' and the Crisis of Latin Americanism," in *Syncing the Americas: José Martí and the Shaping of National Identity*, edited by Ryan Anthony Spangler and Georg Michael Schwarzmann (Lewisburg, PA: Bucknell University Press, 2018), 19–28.

108. The word "autochthonous" in this context refers in very general terms to that which is "American"; to be confronted against anything "foreign" (i.e., European).

109. Ramos, *Divergent Modernities*, 154

110. Louis A. Pérez, *Between Reform and Revolution* (Oxford: Oxford University Press, 2011), 79.

ized by the nineteenth-century Argentine intellectual Domingo Faustino Sarmiento's novel *Civilization and Barbarism: The Life of Facundo Quiroga and the Geography and Customs of the Argentine Republic*. Sarmiento is one among a group of Eurocentric liberal intellectuals who defended the idea that the new American republics should exclude social and political elements that would stagnate their advance toward progress and modernity. Elements aligned with barbarism by Sarmiento were the rural life and its customs, and the worldviews and traditions of all non-European populations. Sarmiento and others proposed that the newly formed nations needed to follow models originating in England, France, or the United States.

José Martí's literary style illustrates what has been termed **modernismo latinoamericano (Latin American modernism)**; a literary movement, originating at the end of the nineteenth century, that embodies some of the contradictions that artists and intellectuals were experiencing at the time. On the one hand, many writers worked for a renewal in literature (mostly poetry) through creative metaphors, and precise and original language. This came as a reaction against the **pragmatism** and **positivism** of the times. On the other hand, there was a realization among those artists and intellectuals of the fact that the geopolitical atmosphere required social, political, and even revolutionary commitment. Martí's poetry and prose (as you can see in "Our América") can be rich, even excessive, with powerful and varied images. The author re-creates those in detail, often employing historical and mythological references. At the same time, though, note how Martí's message is timely, urgent, and even militant. You can thus see in him a celebrated poet and, at the same time, an example of the committed intellectual in the "realm of action." Does an author's willingness to take action change how you read or approach their written work?

Martí's depiction of race is complex. On the one hand, he employs disturbing language and classifications in use within nineteenth-century European discourses in his representation of African-descendent and Indigenous populations. On the other hand, Martí's attentive observation of the racial dynamics in the Jim Crow South made him realize that the United States was not to be the model to follow by a freed Cuba.[111] Many of his writings during the decade of the 1890s are devoted to fighting against racism but deploy the problematic ideal of society as "raceless," or what contemporary analysts might term "colorblind." This "raceless" focus was applied to many nationalist projects in Latin America. Some of those projects, in homogenizing identity, failed to address racism, or have condoned and promoted it. What factors often complicate a person's understanding of race?

Martí's philosophies and political activism have inspired generations of writers, politicians, activists, and revolutionaries. For example, Fidel Castro pointed to José Martí as the "intellectual author" of the revolt that began in 1953 in the fight

---

111. Oleski Miranda Navarro, "José Martí: A Rendering of Black Issues in the United States," in *Syncing the Americas*, 179–94.

against Fulgencio Batista. Martí is also celebrated by the community of Cuban exiles in South Florida. As you read, consider how "Our América" allows us to reflect on the negotiations often involved in navigating complex layers of representation, identity, and inclusion in a nation's struggle for independence.

Elena Adell
Department of Languages and Literatures

> **PRE-READING PARS**
>
> 1. List two intellectuals (writers, politicians, artists, etc.) who inspire you. Under each, make note of what you know of their lives.
> 2. What two or three metaphors come to mind when you think of national identity?
> 3. List as many components or characteristics of colonialism in Latin America as you can in two minutes.

"Our América"

The pompous villager thinks his hometown is the whole world. As long as he can stay on as mayor, humiliate the rival who stole his sweetheart, and watch his nest egg grow in its strongbox, he believes the universe is in good order. He knows nothing of the giants in seven-league boots who can crush him underfoot, the battling comets in the heavens which devour the worlds that lie sleeping in their paths. Whatever is left in América of such drowsy provincialism must awaken. These are not times for lying comfortably in bed. Like Juan de Castellanos'[112] men, we must have no other pillow but our weapons—weapons of the mind, which vanquish all others. Fortifications built of ideas are more valuable than those built of stone.

No armored prow can smash through a cloud of ideas. A vital idea brandished before the world at the right moment like the mystic banner of Judgment Day can stop a fleet of battleships. Nations that remain strangers must rush to know one another, like soldiers about to go into battle together. Those who once shook their fists at each other like jealous brothers quarreling over who has the bigger house or who owns a plot of land must now grip each other so tightly that their two hands become one. Those who took land from a conquered brother—a brother punished far in excess of any crime—and who, under protection of a criminal tradition, smeared their swords in the same blood that flows through their own veins must now return their brother's land if they don't want to be known as a nation of plunderers. A man of honor does not collect a debt of honor in money, at so much per slap. We can no longer be a village of leaves fluttering in the air, crowned in flowers, creaking and buzzing under the caress of capricious sunlight or thrashed and felled by tempests. The trees must line up to block the giant in his seven-league boots. The hour to muster and march in unison is upon us and our ranks must be as compact as the veins of silver in the depths of the Andes.

Only runts—so stunted they have no faith in their own nation—will fail to find the courage. Lacking courage themselves, they'll deny that other men do have it.

---

112. *Juan de Castellanos* (1522–1607): Spanish poet and chronicler of the conquest of New Granada (now Colombia) in which he took part.

Their spindly arms, with clinking bracelets and polished fingernails, shaped by Madrid or Paris, cannot reach the lofty tree, and so they say the tree is unreachable. We must load up the ships with these termites that gnaw away at the core of the patria that nurtured them. If they're Parisians or Madrileños, then let them stroll the Prado by lamplight or take an ice at Tortoni's. These carpenter's sons, ashamed that their father was a carpenter! These men born in América, ashamed of the mother who raised them because she wears an Indian tunic! These scoundrels who disown their sick mother and leave her alone in her sickbed! Who is more truly a man? One who stays with his mother to nurse her through her illness? Or one who curses the bosom that bore him, forces her to work somewhere out of sight, and lives off her sustenance in corrupted lands, sporting a worm for a necktie and a sign that says "traitor" on the back of his paper jacket? These sons of our América, which must save herself through her Indians and is on the rise; these deserters, who ask to take up arms with the forces of North America, which drowns its Indians in blood and is on the wane! These delicate creatures who are men but don't want to do men's work! Did Washington, the founder of their nation, go off to live in England when he saw the English marching against his land? But these incredible creatures drag their honor across foreign soil like the *incroyables* of the French Revolution who danced, primped, and dragged out their Rs.

For what other patria can a man take greater pride in than our long-suffering republics of América?—built by the bloody arms of a hundred apostles, amid mute masses of Indians, to the sound of battle between the book and the monk's candlestick. Never before have such advanced and unified nations been created so rapidly from elements so disparate. The haughty man imagines that because he wields a quick pen and coins vivid phrases the earth was made to be his pedestal; he accuses his native republic of hopeless incapacity because its virgin jungles don't offer him scope for parading about the world like a bigwig, driving Persian ponies and spilling champagne as he goes. The incapacity lies not in the nascent country, which demands forms appropriate to itself and a grandeur that is useful to it, but in those who wish to govern unique populaces, singularly and violently composed, by laws inherited from four centuries of free practice in the United States and nineteen centuries of monarchy in France.[113] A Llanero's bolting colt can't be stopped in its tracks by one of Alexander Hamilton's laws. The sluggish blood of the Indian race can't be quick-

---

113. *Four centuries*: Curiously, Martí exaggerates the period of "free practice" in the United States by locating the nation's origins at the moment of Columbus's discovery of the Americas in 1492, rather than with the first European settlements on the east coast of North America in the early 1600s (less than three centuries before 1891 when this manifesto is written). He also exaggerates the duration of the French monarchy, which began not at the death of Christ but with the establishment of the Kingdom of the Franks in 486, fourteen centuries earlier and not nineteen, as he states. Perhaps the temporal exaggerations are intended to parody the exaggerated authority conceded to US and French ideas against which Martí protests.

ened with a phrase from Sieyès.[114] He who would govern well must attend closely to the place being governed. In América, a good governor isn't one who knows how to govern a German or a Frenchman. It is, rather, one who knows what elements his own country is made up of, and how best to marshal them so as to achieve, by means and institutions arising from the country itself, that desirable state in which every man knows himself and exercises his talents, and all enjoy the abundance that Nature, for the good of all, has bestowed on the land they make fruitful by their labor and defend with their lives. The government must arise from the country. The government's spirit must be the spirit of the country. The government's form must be in harmony with the country's natural constitution. The government is no more than the equilibrium among the country's natural elements.

The natural man has triumphed over the imported book in América; natural men have triumphed over an artificial intelligentsia. The native mestizo has triumphed over the exotic criollo. The battle is not between civilization and barbarity[115] but between false erudition and nature. The natural man is good and will follow and reward a superior intelligence as long as that intelligence doesn't use his submission against him or offend him by ignoring him, which the natural man finds unforgivable. He is prepared to use force to regain the respect of anyone who has wounded his sensibilities or harmed his interests. The tyrants of América have come to power by taking up the cause of these scorned natural elements, and have fallen as soon as they betrayed them. The republics have cured the former tyrannies of their inability to know the true elements of the country, derive the form of government from them, and govern along with them. *Governor*, in a new nation, means *Creator*.

In nations composed of educated and uneducated elements, the uneducated will govern by their habit of attacking and resolving all doubts with their fists, as long as the educated haven't learned the art of governing. The uneducated masses are lazy and timid in matters of the intellect and want to be well-governed, but if a government injures them they shake it off and govern themselves. How can our governors emerge from our universities when there isn't a university in América that teaches the most basic element of the art of governing: the analysis of all that is unique to the peoples of América? Our young men go out into the world wearing Yankee- or French-colored glasses, and aspire to govern by guesswork over a country about which they know nothing. Men who are unacquainted with the rudiments of politics should be barred from a career in politics. The top academic prizes shouldn't go to

---

114. Emmanuel Joseph *Sieyès* (1748–1836): Clergyman, author of the manifesto *What Is the Third Estate?* (1789), and leading figure in the French Revolution, who went on to become one of the central instigators of Napoleon's 1799 coup d'état.

115. *Civilization and barbarity*: Allusion to a key 1845 work by Domingo Faustino Sarmiento titled *Facundo o civilización y barbarie en las pampas argentinas*. In it, Sarmiento, Argentina's president from 1868 to 1874, used a regional caudillo or strongman, Juan Facundo Quiroga, as an example of barbaric forms of government sprung up in the areas beyond the civilization of the capital cities.

the finest ode, but to the best study of the political factors in the country where the student lives. In the newspapers, the lecture halls, and the academies, the study of the country's real factors must advance. Knowing those factors, without blinkers or circumlocution, will suffice. Anyone who deliberately or unknowingly sets aside a part of the truth will ultimately fail because of that missing truth, which expands, under such neglect, to bring down whatever was built without it. Solving a problem in full knowledge of its elements is easier than solving it without knowing them. The natural man, strong and indignant, comes and overthrows an authority accumulated from books because that authority isn't administered in keeping with the manifest needs of the country. To know is to solve. To know the country and govern it in accordance with that knowledge is the only way to free it from tyranny. The European university must yield to the American university. The history of América from the Incas to the present must be taught in its smallest detail, even if the Greek Archons go untaught. Our own Greece is preferable to the Greece that is not ours: we need it more. Statesmen who arise from the nation must replace statesmen who are alien to it. Let the world be grafted onto our republics, but we must be the trunk. And all the vanquished pedants can hold their tongues: there is no patria a man can take greater pride in than our long-suffering American republics.

Our feet upon a rosary, our faces white-skinned, and our bodies a motley of Indian and criollo, we boldly entered the community of nations. Bearing the Virgin's standard, we went forth to conquer our liberty. A priest,[116] a few lieutenants and a woman[117] built a republic in Mexico upon the shoulders of the Indians. A Spanish cleric,[118] under cover of his priestly cape, taught French liberty to a handful of magnificent students who chose a Spanish general to lead Central America against Spain. Still accustomed to monarchy, but with the sun blazing in their chests, the Venezuelans to the north and the Argentines to the south set out to build nations. When the two heroes clashed[119] and the continent was about to erupt, one of them, not the lesser of the two, turned back. But heroism is less glorious in peacetime than

---

116. *A priest*: Miguel Hidalgo y Costilla (1778–1850), who launched Mexico's war of independence from Spain in 1810.

117. *A woman*: Josefa Ortíz de Domínguez (1773–1829), also known as *la corregidora* because she was the wife of Miguel Domínguez, *corregidor* or chief magistrate of the northern Mexican town of Guanajuato. She worked with Miguel Hidalgo (see note 115 above) to organize and promote Mexico's independence insurgency.

118. *Spanish cleric*: José María Castillo (1785–1848), who promoted Central American unity, as well as education and equality in Guatemala.

119. *Two heroes clashed*: General José de San Martín (1778–1850), leader of the revolution against Spanish colonial rule in the Southern Cone, and General Simón Bolívar (1783–1830) who led the revolution in the upper regions of the South American continent. The clash occurred at the famous Guayaquil interview (1822), after which San Martín ceded command of all his forces to Bolívar and left for France, never to return.

in war, and thus rarer; it's easier for a man to die with honor than to think in an orderly way. Exalted and unanimous sentiments are more readily governed than the divergent, arrogant, ambitious, and foreign ideas that emerge when the battle is over. Confronted with the population's cat-like wariness and the sheer weight of reality, the same powers once swept up in the epic struggle began to undermine the governing edifice, which had raised the standard of lands sustained by wise governance in the continual practice of reason and freedom above the crude and singular regions of our mestizo América, in lands where bare legs alternate with Parisian dress-coats. The hierarchical character of the colonies resisted the democratic organization of the republic. The capital city, in its elegant cravat, left the countryside, in its horsehide boots, waiting at the door. The redeemers born from books didn't understand that a revolution that triumphed when the soul of the land was unleashed by a savior's voice had to govern with the soul of the land, and not against or without it. For all these reasons, América began enduring and still endures the weary task of reconciling the discordant and hostile elements inherited from its perverse, despotic colonizer with the imported forms and ideas that have, in their lack of local reality, delayed the advent of a logical form of government. Deformed by three centuries of a rule that denied men the right to exercise their reason, and overlooking or refusing to listen to the ignorant masses that helped it redeem itself, the continent entered into new kind of government based on reason—which should have meant the reason of all directed towards things of concern to all, and not the university-schooled reason of the few imposed upon the rustic reason of others. The problem with independence was not the change in form, but the change in spirit.

Common cause had to be made with the oppressed, in order to consolidate a system that opposed the interests and governmental habits of the oppressor. But the tiger frightened away by the flash of gunfire will creep back in the night to find his prey. He will die with flames shooting from his eyes, his claws unsheathed, but now his step is inaudible for he comes on velvet paws, and when the prey awakens, the tiger is upon him. The colony lived on in the republic. But our América is saving itself from its gravest failings—the arrogance of the capital cities, the blind triumph of the scorned campesinos, the excessive importation of foreign ideas and formulas, the wicked and impolitic disdain for the native race—through the superior virtue, authenticated by necessary bloodshed, of the republic that struggles against the colony. The tiger lurks behind every tree, crouches in every corner. He will die, his claws unsheathed, flames shooting from his eyes.

"These countries will save themselves," as the Argentine Rivadavia,[120] who erred

---

120. Bernardino *Rivadavia* (1780–1845): Argentine politician who defended the Spanish colony against English invaders and subsequently fought Spain for its independence. Elected as the first president of the United Provinces of Río de la Plata in 1826, he was forced to resign by the caudillo Juan Facundo Quiroga (see note 114 above), and went into exile in Spain.

on the side of urbanity during uncouth times, once proclaimed. A machete won't fit in a silken scabbard, nor can the *lanzón* be repudiated in a nation won by the *lanzón*,[121] for the nation will go into a rage and stand at the doorway of Iturbide's Congress demanding that "the white man become emperor."[122] These countries will save themselves. Through the serene harmony of nature, the genius of moderation seems to be prevailing on the continent of light. Under the influence of the critical reading which, in Europe, has replaced the blundering ideas about phalansteries[123] that the previous generation was steeped in, the real man is being born to América in these very real times.

What a sight we were, with an athlete's chest, a dandy's hands, and a child's forehead. We were a veritable fancy dress ball, wearing British trousers, a Parisian waistcoat, and a North American overcoat, topped with a Spanish bullfighter's montera. The Indian circled us mutely and went to the mountaintop to christen his children. The black man, spied upon from above, sang his heart's music in the night, alone and unknown, between waves and wild beasts. The campesinos, men of the land, creators, rose up in blind indignation against the disdainful city, their own creation. We wore military epaulets and judges' robes in countries that came into the world wearing rope sandals and Indian headbands. The wise course would have been to unite—with the charity in our hearts and our founders' audacity—the Indian headband and the judicial robe, to disentrammel the Indian, make a place for the able black, and tailor liberty to the bodies of those who rose up and triumphed in its name. What we had were the judge, the general, the man of letters, and the cleric. Our angelic youth, as if struggling to escape the grasping tentacles of an octopus, cast their minds into the heavens and fell back in sterile glory, crowned in clouds. The natural people, driven by instinct, blind with triumph, overwhelmed their gilded rulers. No Yankee or European book could furnish the key to the Hispano-American enigma. So people tried hatred instead, and each year our countries amounted to less and less. Weary now of useless hatred and the struggle of book against sword, reason against the monk's candlestick, city against countryside, and the quarreling urban castes' impossible empire against the tempestuous or inert natural nation, we begin, almost without realizing it, to try love. The nations arise and salute one another.

---

121. *Lanzón*: a short, thick spear with a large metal grip used by campesinos to protect their fields.

122. *Iturbide's Congress*: Agustín de Iturbide (1783–1824) was a general who initially fought with Spain against Mexico's independence movement, then later joined forces with insurgent general Guerrero to assure Mexico's independence. However, instead of the liberal state envisioned by the insurgents, Iturbide ushered in a conservative one. When his soldiers proclaimed him emperor, the newly independent Mexican Congress, angry but cowed, ratified the proclamation (1822). A revolution soon broke out against him and in 1823 he was forced to abdicate.

123. *Phalansteries*: The French socialist philosopher Charles Fourier (1772–1837) designed a structure called a phalanstery, intended to house self-contained utopian communities of 500–2000 inhabitants. Few of them were ever built.

"What are we?" they ask, and begin telling each other what they are. When a problem arises in Cojímar, the solution is no longer sought in Danzig. The frock-coats are still French but the thinking is starting to be American. The young men of América are rolling up their sleeves and plunging their hands into the dough to make it rise with the leavening of their sweat. They understand that there is too much imitation, that salvation lies in creating. *Create* is the password of this generation. Make wine from plantains. It may be sour, but it is our wine! It is finally understood that a country's form of government must adapt to the country's natural elements, that unless absolute ideas are expressed in relative forms, an error of form will cause them to collapse; that liberty, in order to be viable, must be sincere and complete, that if the republic does not open its arms to all and include all in its progress, it dies. The tiger that lurks inside us attacks through the rents in our social fabric, and the tiger that lurks outside us does, too. The general holds the cavalry to the pace of the infantry; if he leaves the infantry too far behind, the enemy will surround the cavalry. Politics is strategy. Nations must continually criticize themselves—for criticism is health—but with a single heart and a single mind. Go down amidst the unfortunate and raise them up in your arms! Let the heart's fires thaw all that is frozen and motionless in América, and let the country's natural blood surge and throb through its veins! Standing tall, and with the joy of those who work in their eyes, the new men of América salute each other from one country to the next. Natural statesmen are emerging from the direct study of nature. They read in order to apply what they read, not copy it. Economists study problems at their origins. Orators speak in measured tones. Dramatists put native characters onstage.

Academies debate practical subjects. Poetry snips off its wild, Zorilla-esque locks and leaves its red waistcoat hanging from the tree of past glories.[124] Prose, polished and gleaming, is replete with ideas. The governors of Indian republics learn Indian languages.[125]

América is saving herself from all her dangers. Over some republics the octopus sleeps still. Others, by the law of equilibrium, run with mad, sublime speed to the sea, to recover the lost centuries. Others, forgetting that Juárez[126] traveled in a coach drawn by mules, hitch their coaches to the wind and take soap bubbles as their coachmen—as the poison of luxury, liberty's enemy, corrupts the frivolous and opens the door to foreigners. The virile character of other nations is being refined by the

---

124. *Zorilla-esque locks. . . red waistcoat*: José Zorilla (1817–1893) was a Spanish romantic poet. The waistcoat is the famous *gilet rouge* worn by French romantic poet Theophile Gautier (1811–1872) to the opening performance of Victor Hugo's romantic play *Hernani* in 1830. By snipping off the wild locks and abandoning the red waistcoat, Latin American poetry leaves Romanticism behind.

125. *Learn Indian languages*: Perhaps a tacit reference to Benito Juárez (1806–1872), Mexico's president from 1858 to 1872, who was of Zapotec Indian origins. Juárez's first language was Zapotec; he did not learn Spanish until he went to school.

126. Benito Juárez (1806–1872): See note 125 above.

epic spirit of a threatened independence. And others, in rapacious wars against their neighbors, nurture an unruly soldier caste that may one day devour them. But our América may also face another danger, which does not come from within it, but from the differing origins, methods, and interests of the continent's two factions. The hour is near when she will be approached by an enterprising and forceful nation that will demand intimate relations with her, though it does not know her and disdains her. And virile nations, self-made by the rifle and the law, love other virile nations, and only those. The hour of unbridled passion and ambition from which North America may escape by the ascendency of the purest elements in its blood—or into which its vengeful and sordid masses, its tradition of conquest, and the self-interest of a cunning leader could plunge it—is not yet so near, even to the most apprehensive eye, that there is no time left for it to be confronted and averted by the manifestation of a discreet and unswerving pride. Its dignity as a republic, in the eyes of the watchful nations of the Universe, places a brake upon North America that our América must not remove by puerile provocation, ostentatious arrogance, or patricidal discord. Therefore the urgent duty of our América is to show herself as she is, united in soul and intent, fast overcoming the crushing weight of her past, and stained only with the fertilizing blood shed by hands that do battle against ruins, or by veins opened by our former masters. The disdain of the formidable neighbor who does not know her is the greatest danger that faces our América. It is urgent—for the day of the visit draws close—that her neighbor come to know her, and quickly, so he will not disdain her. Out of ignorance, he may begin to covet her. But when he knows her, he will remove his hands from her in respect. One must have faith in the best in man, and distrust the worst. One must give the best every opportunity to reveal itself and prevail over the worst. For if not, the worst will prevail. Nations should have one special pillory for those who incite them to futile hatreds, and another for those who do not tell them the truth until it is too late.

There is no racial hatred because there are no races. Low, weak minds working in dim light, have cobbled together and kept in circulation the library-shelf races that the honest traveler and cordial observer search for in vain within the justice of Nature, where triumphant love and turbulent appetite demonstrate again and again the universal identity of mankind. The soul, equal and eternal, emanates from bodies that are diverse in form and color. Anyone who promotes and disseminates opposition or hatred among races is committing a sin against humanity. But within the jumble of peoples that lives in close proximity to our peoples, certain peculiar and dynamic characteristics are condensed—ideas and habits of expansion, acquisition, vanity, and greed—that could, in a period of internal disorder or precipitation of the nation's cumulative character, cease to be latent national preoccupations and become a serious threat to the neighboring, isolated and weak lands that the strong country declares to be perishable and inferior. To think is to serve. We must not, out of a villager's antipathy, impute some lethal and congenital wickedness to the continent's light-skinned nation simply because it does not speak our language or share our view of what home life should be or resemble us in its political failings, which are different from ours, or because it does not think highly of quick-tempered, swarthy men, or look with charity, from its still uncertain eminence, upon those less favored by history who, in heroic stages are ascending the path that all republics travel. But neither should we seek to conceal the obvious facts of the problem which can, for the peace of the centuries, be resolved by timely study and the urgent, wordless union of the continental soul. For the hymn of unanimity is already ringing forth. The present generation bears industrious América along the road sanctioned by our sublime forefathers. From the Río Bravo[127] to the Straits of Magellan, the Great Cemi,[128] riding high astride a condor, has scattered the seeds of the new América across the romantic nations of the continent and the suffering islands of the sea!

Martí, J. *Nuestra América* (versión inglés), translated by Esther Allen. N.d. Retrieved August 11, 2020, from http://www.josemarti.cu/publicacion/nuestra-america-version-ingles/. Reprinted by permission of the translator (their notes included).

> **POST-READING PARS**
>
> 1. Reread the first two paragraphs only, and list the metaphors. How do you interpret them? What do you think Martí's purpose was in writing this way?
> 2. What prominent metaphors does Martí use throughout to describe Latin American identity?
> 3. Now that you have read "Our América" what would you like to add, edit, or remove from the list you made earlier about colonialism in Latin America?

---

127. *Rio Bravo*: Known as the Rio Grande in the United States, and as the *Rio Bravo del norte* in Spanish, this river marks a long stretch of the southern border of the United States and northern border of Mexico, before it flows into the Gulf of Mexico.

128. *Cemi*: A deity or ancestral spirit worshiped by the Taino, an Indigenous people of the Caribbean. The cemi (or zemi) was often represented as a tricornered clay object, which was believed to house the spirit.

Inquiry Corner

Content Questions:

What is José Martí's idea of Latin America? How does his idea differ from previously existing interpretations of Latin America?

What is the urgent message that the author is transmitting to his audience? Who is Martí's interlocutor?

Critical Questions:

Critically evaluate the sense of the identity or identities of Latin America you get from this reading.

How do you understand Martí's claims about the pervasiveness of colonialism in Latin America? What strategies related to language, religion, economics, and institutions, for example, might be harnessed for independence movements against colonialism?

Comparative Question:

Consider other texts that "build a narrative" around a nation or group of nations. Compare the strategies employed and the values and concerns highlighted in Martí's text with those in other texts.

Connection Question:

What two or three strategies does Martí utilize to persuade his readers? Compose a poem or song lyric (or annotate one you already know) that utilizes these strategies of persuasion.

from "Reminiscences of the Drafting of the New Constitution" by Itō Hirobumi

Introduction

Around 1600, the warlord Tokugawa Ieyasu gained control of Japan and began to rule the country from Edo (present-day Tokyo) as the **shogun**, or head of the military government. During the Edo period (1600–1868), also known as the Tokugawa Shogunate, Japan was not a unified, centralized state but rather a feudal system in which the shogun's allies (**daimyo**) were hereditary rulers in their local territories (**han**) with their own laws and armies. There was still an emperor in Kyoto, but it was a ceremonial, religious position with few resources and little political power. For the next two and a half centuries, Japan's culture and economy flourished, even though the populace was tightly controlled; occupations, including **samurai**, or warriors, were hereditary; and Japan expelled foreigners and closed its borders to the outside world. What might have been reasons for or implications of closed borders?

In 1853, American Commodore Matthew C. Perry sailed into Tokyo Bay with several gunships and demanded that the Japanese end their isolationist policies or face the type of military action that had already opened China in the Opium War of 1839–1842. Realizing the gravity of the threat, the shogun eventually signed unequal treaties with Western powers, in which Westerners forced Japan to open several of its cities to trade, as well as guarantee **extraterritoriality**, an exemption from the local judicial system, for foreigners. Many of

> **SNAPSHOT BOX**
>
> LANGUAGE: Japanese
>
> PUBLISHED: Japan, 1909
>
> GENRE: Memoir
>
> TAGS: Autobiography and Testimony; Community; Cross-Cultural Encounters; Historiography; Nationalism; Self-Determination; Statecraft; Ways of Knowing

Timeline

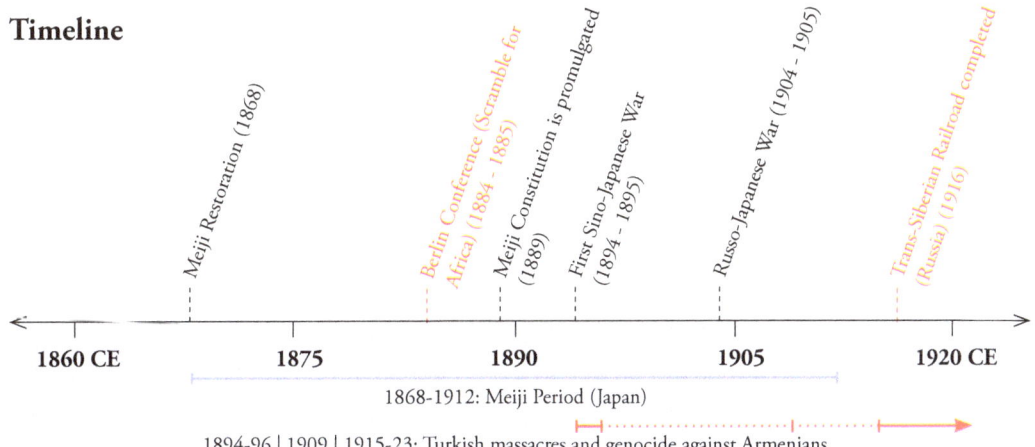

the samurai were furious with the shogun for giving in to Western pressure and in 1868 they revolted in the name of the fifteen-year-old Meiji emperor. The shogunate quickly collapsed and the emperor was installed as the head of the state, though actual power was held by the samurai who served as his advisors. Itō Hirobumi was one of these men.

Over the next few decades, known as the Meiji period (1868–1912), Japan undertook what is probably the most rapid, most successful modernization in world history. The emperor's samurai advisors implemented a series of wide-ranging reforms as they brought in Western education, technology, industry, finance, and military techniques, including conscript armies, which undercut the traditional basis for samurai social status. Ex-samurai were encouraged to shift their ideals of discipline, self-sacrifice, and loyalty—ideals at the center of **bushido**, or the way of warriors—to serving their country as administrators and entrepreneurs. How might samurai have been convinced to become bureaucrats? What benefits or challenges might occur from transferring bushido into business or government contexts? As Japan saw the introduction of railways, telegraphs, and factories, many of the emperor's subjects wanted to become citizens, with rights and more opportunities for participation in government decision-making. Popular calls for democracy were met by an official edict in 1882 to produce a constitution. Itō Hirobumi, who had studied in England as a young man, was appointed to lead an eighteen-month mission to Europe to learn about Western models. After his return, he served as Japan's first prime minister, while he continued to work on a constitution.

Itō was a monarchist, believing that the authority of the emperor was an essential element of Japanese civilization. As a result, he rejected the American constitution as too liberal and was more attracted to German and British models. He eventually put together a proposal that included an independent judiciary and a bicameral legislature (the Diet) consisting of a lower house of elected representatives and an upper house of peers (just over 1 percent of the population was eligible to vote). The emperor, however, remained head of the state and was held to be "sacred and inviolable." It was the emperor, not voters, who appointed the prime minister as the head of the government, along with his cabinet ministers. The military reported directly to the emperor rather than to elected representatives, which would lead to terrible consequences in the 1930s and 40s with Japanese imperialism and World War II. The Meiji Constitution was accepted by the emperor in 1889 and promulgated as a grant, or gift, to his people. Why have an emperor who is only ceremonial? The Meiji Constitution remained in place until 1947, when a new constitution, written under the influence of Allied occupation forces, was adopted. In spite of its flaws, we should remember that the Japanese Constitution of 1889 resulted in the first popularly elected legislative assembly in Asian history.

In the excerpt below, Itō offers a rather rosy remembrance of how all this came about. After the new constitution was put in place, Japan continued its rapid modernization, defeating China in the Sino-Japanese War of 1894–1895, and then defeating Russia in 1905 in a war fought over influence in Manchuria and Korea — the first time in modern history that an Asian country had overpowered a Western nation. (This is the "recent war" that Ito refers to below.) Ito served several terms as prime minister and became one of the emperor's most powerful informal advisors. He was assassinated by a Korean nationalist shortly after he wrote this account.

Grant Hardy
Department of History

> **PRE-READING PARS**
>
> 1. Do you have a sense for what has historically made a country "modern"? List three to five characteristics that might classify a country as "modern" from your perspective.
> 2. Quickly list some pros and cons of monarchy, three of each.

from "Reminiscences of the Drafting of the New Constitution"

[. . .] The advent of Commodore Perry,[129] followed by a rapid succession of great events too well known to be repeated here, roughly awakened us to the consciousness of mighty forces at work to change the face of the outside world. We were ill-prepared to bear the brunt of these forces, but once awakened to the need, were not slow to grapple with them. So, first of all the whole fabric of the feudal system, which with its obsolete shackles and formalities hindered us in every branch of free development, had to be uprooted and destroyed. The annihilation of centrifugal forces taking the form of autocratic feudal provinces was a necessary step to the unification of the country under a strong central government, without which we would not have been able to offer a united front to the outside forces or stand up as a united whole to maintain the country's very existence.

Sources of Japanese Civilization and Culture

I must, however, disabuse my readers of the very common illusion that there was no education and an entire absence of public spirit during feudal times. It is this false impression which has led superficial observers to believe that our civilization has been so recent that its continuance is doubtful—in short, that our civilization is nothing but a hastily donned, superficial veneer. On the contrary, I am not exaggerating when I say that, for generations and centuries, we have been enjoying a moral education of the highest type. The great ideals offered by philosophy and by historical examples of the golden ages of China and India, Japanicized in the form of a "crust of customs," developed and sanctified by the continual usage of centuries under the comprehensive name *bushido*, offered us splendid standards of morality, rigorously enforced in the everyday life of the educated classes. The result, as everyone who is acquainted with Old Japan knows, was an education which aspired to the attainment of Stoic heroism, a rustic simplicity and a self-sacrificing spirit unsurpassed in Sparta, and the aesthetic culture and intellectual refinement of Athens. Art, delicacy of sentiment,

---

129. Commodore Matthew Perry negotiated a treaty with Japan, opening the country to trade with the United States in 1854.

higher ideals of morality and of philosophy, as well as the highest types of valor and chivalry—all these we have tried to combine in the man as he ought to be. We laid great stress on the harmonious combination of all the known accomplishments of a developed human being, and it is only since the introduction of modern technical sciences that we have been obliged to pay more attention to specialized technical attainments than to the harmonious development of the whole. Let me remark, *en passant*, that the humanitarian efforts which in the course of the recent war were so much in evidence and which so much surprised Western nations were not, as might have been thought, the products of the new civilization, but survivals of our ancient feudal chivalry. If further instance were needed, we may direct attention to the numbers of our renowned warriors and statesmen who have left behind them works of religious and moral devotions, of philosophical contemplations, as well as splendid specimens of calligraphy, painting, and poetry, to an extent probably unparalleled in the feudalism of other nations.

Thus it will be seen that what was lacking in our countrymen of the feudal era was not mental or moral fiber, but the scientific, technical, and materialistic side of modern civilization. Our present condition is not the result of the ingrafting of a civilization entirely different from our own, as foreign observers are apt to believe, but simply a different training and nursing of a strongly vital character already existent.

Draft of the New Constitution

It was in the month of March, 1882, that His Majesty ordered me to work out a draft of a constitution to be submitted to his approval. No time was to be lost, so I started on the 15th of the same month for an extended journey to different constitutional countries to make as thorough a study as possible of the actual workings of different systems of constitutional government, of their various provisions, as well as of theories and opinions actually entertained by influential persons on the actual stage itself of constitutional life. I took young men with me, who all belonged to the elite of the rising generation, to assist and to cooperate with me in my studies. I sojourned about a year and a half in Europe, and having gathered the necessary materials, in so far as it was possible in so short a space of time, I returned home in September, 1883. Immediately after my return I set to work to draw up the Constitution. I was assisted in my work by my secretaries, prominent among whom were the late Viscount K. Inouye, and the Barons M. Ito and K. Kaneko, and by foreign advisors, such as Professor Roesler, Mr. Piggott, and others.

Peculiar Features of the National Life

It was evident from the outset that mere imitation of foreign models would not suffice, for there were historical peculiarities of our country which had to be taken into consideration. For example, the Crown was, with us, an institution far more deeply rooted in the national sentiment and in our history than in other countries. It was indeed the very essence of a once theocratic State, so that in formulating the restrictions on its prerogatives in the new Constitution, we had to take care to safeguard the future realness or vitality of these prerogatives, and not to let the institution degenerate into an ornamental crowning piece of the edifice. At the same time, it was also evident that any form of constitutional regime was impossible without full and extended protection of honor, liberty, property, and personal security of citizens, entailing necessarily many important restrictions on the powers of the Crown.

Emotional Elements in Social Life of People

On the other hand, there was one peculiarity of our social conditions that is without parallel in any other civilized country. Homogeneous in race, language, religion, and sentiments, so long secluded from the outside world, with the centuries-long traditions and inertia of the feudal system, in which the family and quasi-family ties permeated and formed the essence of every social organization, and moreover with such moral and religious tenets as laid undue stress on duties of fraternal aid and mutual succor, we had during the course of our seclusion unconsciously become a vast village community where cold intellect and calculation of public events were always restrained and even often hindered by warm emotions between man and man. Those who have closely observed the effects of the commercial crises of our country—that is, of the events wherein cold-blooded calculation ought to have the precedence of every other factor—and compared them with those of other countries, must have observed a remarkable distinction between them. In other countries they serve in a certain measure as the scavengers of the commercial world, the solid undertakings surviving the shock, while enterprises founded solely on speculative bases are sure to vanish thereafter. But, generally speaking, this is not the case in our country. Moral and emotional factors come into play. Solid undertakings are dragged into the whirlpool, and the speculative ones are saved from the abyss—the general standard of prosperity is lowered for the moment, but the commercial fabric escapes violent shocks. In industry, also, in spite of the recent enormous developments of manufactures in our country, our laborers have not yet degenerated into spiritless machines and toiling beasts. There still survives the bond of patron and protege between them and the capitalist employers. It is this moral and emotional factor which will, in the future, form a healthy barrier against the threatening advance of socialistic ideas. It must, of course, be admitted that this social peculiarity is not without beneficial influences. It mitigates the conflict, serves as the lubricator of social organisms, and tends generally to act as a powerful lever for the practical application of the moral principle of mutual assistance between fellow citizens. But unless curbed and held in restraint, it too may exercise baneful influences on society, for in a village community, where feelings and emotions hold a higher place than intellect, free discussion is apt to be smothered, attainment and transference of power liable to become a family question of a powerful oligarchy, and the realization of such a regime as constitutional monarchy to become an impossibility, simply because in any representative regime free discussion is a matter of prime necessity, because emotions and passions have to be stopped for the sake of the cool calculation of national welfare, and even the best of friends have often to be sacrificed if the best abilities and highest intellects are to guide the helm. Besides, the dissensions between brothers and relatives, deprived as they usually are of safety-valves for giving free and hearty vent to their own opinions or discontents, are apt to degenerate into passionate quarrels and overstep the bounds of simple differences of opinion. The good side of this social peculiarity had to be retained as much as possible, while its baneful influences had to be safeguarded. These and many other peculiarities had to be taken into account in order to have a constitution adapted to the actual condition of the country.

Conflict between the Old and New Thoughts

Another difficulty equally grave had to be taken into consideration. We were just then in an age of transition. The opinions prevailing in the country were extremely heterogeneous, and often diametrically opposed to each other. We had survivors of former generations who were still full of theocratic ideas, and who believed that any attempt to restrict an imperial prerogative amounted to something like high treason. On the other hand there was a large and powerful body of the younger generation educated at the time when the Manchester theory[130] was in vogue, and who in consequence were ultra-radical in their ideas of freedom. Members of the bureaucracy were prone to lend willing ears to the German doctrinaires of the reactionary period, while, on the other hand, the educated politicians among the people having not yet tasted the bitter significance of administrative responsibility, were liable to be more influenced by the dazzling words and lucid theories of Montesquieu, Rousseau, and other similar French writers. A work entitled *History Of Civilization*, by Buckle, which denounced every form of government as an unnecessary evil, became the great favorite of students of all the higher schools, including the Imperial University. On the other hand, these same students would not have dared to expound the theories of Buckle before their own conservative fathers. At that time we had not yet arrived at the stage of distinguishing clearly between political opposition on the one hand and treason to the established order of things on the other. The virtues necessary for the smooth working of any constitution, such as love of freedom of speech, love of publicity of proceedings, the spirit of tolerance for opinions opposed to one's own, etc., had yet to be learned by long experience.

130. A nineteenth-century English ideology that advocated free trade, pacifism, freedom of speech, separation of church and state, and the abolition of slavery.

Draft of the Constitution Completed

It was under these circumstances that the first draft of the Constitution was made and submitted to His Majesty, after which it was handed over to the mature deliberation of the Privy Council. The Sovereign himself presided over these deliberations, and he had full opportunities of hearing and giving due consideration to all the conflicting opinions above hinted at. I believe nothing evidences more vividly the intelligence of our august Master than the fact that in spite of the existence of strong undercurrents of an ultra-conservative nature in the council, and also in the country at large, His Majesty's decisions inclined almost invariably towards liberal and progressive ideas, so that we have been ultimately able to obtain the Constitution as it exists at present.

Selection by Itō Hirobumi in Tsunoda Ryūsaku, ed. *Sources of the Japanese Tradition* 2, 2:164–69. New York: Columbia University Press, 1965.

POST-READING PARS

1. Is there a general model for modernization, or must each country find its own way? Explain whether any of the characteristics you listed earlier might not apply to all countries?
2. How does Itō justify or praise monarchy? Does this help explain why some countries still retain constitutional monarchs with little real political power?

Inquiry Corner

Content Questions:	Critical Questions:
How does Itō portray the Western models and precedents that he cites?	Itō places a great deal of emphasis on the need for a "united" Japan. Why might he feel this way? What are the dangers in insisting too much on conformity?
According to Itō, what was new in modern Japan, and what aspects were continued from feudal times? What makes Japan different from other countries, in Ito's opinion?	
Comparative Question:	**Connection Question:**
What were some of the differences between the modernization of Japan and the experience of European nations?	Itō presents his position as a balance between liberalism and conservatism (or even anarchy), when in fact he was promoting extremely conservative ideas. Can you think of other historical instances when people portrayed their partisan ideas as being somewhere in the middle?

BEYOND THE CLASSROOM

» In working with a group of people whose opinions and approaches are vastly different than your own based on experience, age, or something else, how can the group come together to create an effective and respectful work environment? What specific actions (e.g., procedures and policies) could be taken to ensure that people working on the same project share a common purpose of achieving the project goals, even if individuals have different thoughts on how to get there?

» The text mentions "masters and proteges." How do apprenticeship training and education opportunities differ from traditional classroom settings? What is the value of on-the-job training programs like co-ops and internships?

from *The Soul of the Indian* by Ohiyesa

> **SNAPSHOT BOX**
>
> LANGUAGE: English
> PUBLISHED: 1911, United States
> GENRE: Autobiography
> TAGS: Autobiography and Testimony; Body; Colonization; Community; Cross-Cultural Encounters; Ethics and Morality; Family; Poetry, Music, Literature; Psyche; Race; Religion; Struggle, Resistance, and Revolution; Tradition; War and Brutality

Introduction

Ohiyesa (1858–1939), which means "the Winner" in his native **Santee Sioux** language, was one of the first American Indian doctors, an **American Indian** rights activist, and the author of eleven books, including *The Soul of the Indian*. Ohiyesa, later also known as Charles Alexander Eastman, was born in Redwood Falls, Minnesota, to Ite Wakanhdi Ota and Wakantankawin (Mary Nancy Eastman). His mother's father, Captain Seth Eastman, was a white man in the US Army. In 1862, the **Sioux Uprising** against the United States dramatically changed young Ohiyesa's life.

The Sioux Uprising, also known as the Dakota War, began on August 17, 1862. Government agents continued to withhold annuity payments to Sioux peoples due to ongoing disputes throughout the 1850s with white merchants, causing extreme hardship to many Sioux communities. This led to several bands of Dakota (Sioux) attacking white settlers along the Minnesota River. During the uprising, Ohiyesa's maternal grandmother and other family members took Ohiyesa to Canada, but his father was captured. For the next eleven years, Ohiyesa lived in Sioux culture and society in Canada with his uncle and grandmother, believing his father and thirty-eight other Sioux warriors had been executed. His mother had died shortly after childbirth. It was during this time that Ohiyesa became immersed in Sioux **cosmology**, acquiring the skills and spiritual values that would guide his life and writings. His father, Ite Wakanhdi Ota, however, survived. His death sentence was commuted by Abraham Lincoln, and instead

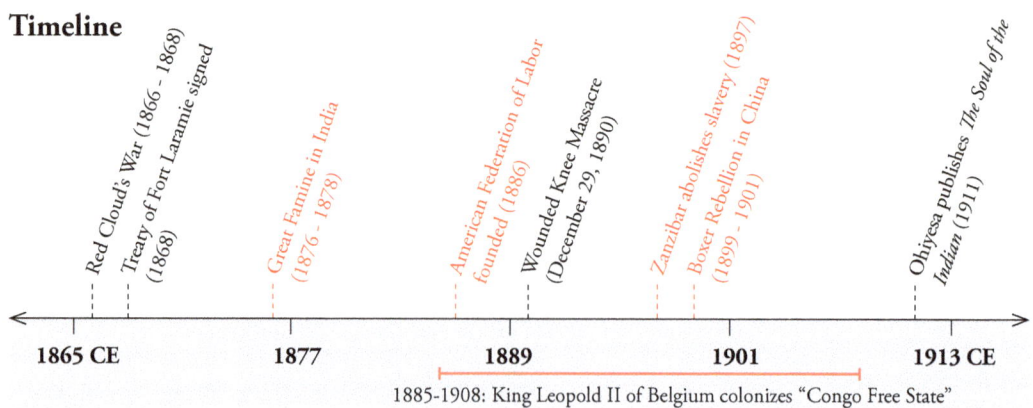

he served three years in prison. During his prison stay and after, Ite Wakanhdi Ota began his assimilation into the dominant white culture, converted to Christianity, and changed his name to Jacob Eastman. At fifteen Ohiyesa was just entering Sioux manhood and preparing to join a war party aimed at avenging his father's death when Ite Wakanhdi Ota—now calling himself Jacob—reappeared. Soon after his return to the family, Jacob took Ohiyesa to an Indian community in Flandreau, Dakota Territory. Jacob had Ohiyesa baptized and changed his name to Charles Alexander Eastman. What significance might a name change, whether by others or one's own choice, have on a person? What examples of changing names can you think of and what implications did those changes have from your perspective?

Jacob then sent Charles, against his will, to a mission school where the unhappy boy thought of running away, back to the traditions and life he had known. But, on his father's insistence, Charles cut his hair and did his best to integrate himself into the white world. Even though he was unhappy, Charles applied himself to his studies, eventually moving to Beloit College in Wisconsin, then Dartmouth University, where he graduated in 1887. He continued his studies at Boston University where he earned a medical degree in 1890.

Dr. Eastman was named government physician for the Pine Ridge Reservation in South Dakota. He was there during the **Ghost Dance Movement** of 1890–1891 and the **Wounded Knee Massacre** in 1890. The Ghost Dance Movement, a spiritual revival among Plains Indians that had Christian and Indigenous elements, was started by a Paiute named Wavoka, who had a vision sent by the Great Spirit that would bring about a return to the Indigenous way of life as it was before colonialism. Believers danced to the point of exhaustion, bringing them spiritual renewal, and wore a special shirt that was said to have the property of deflecting bullets, making the wearer invincible. On December 29, 1890, while performing the Ghost Dance, a Sioux warrior's rifle accidentally discharged, causing the US 7th Cavalry to open fire on a large group of Sioux men, women, and children with Hotchkiss guns, an early form of machine gun, killing 250 Sioux. The massacre at Wounded Knee on the Pine Ridge Reservation was one of the most infamous of the atrocities committed against Indigenous people by the US military.

Dr. Eastman married Elaine Goodale, a white woman involved with tribal education. Elaine would later collaborate with Eastman on several of his fourteen books. Shortly after the wedding, Dr. Eastman was forced out of his job for trying to expose a corrupt government agent. He then accepted a position as a field agent for the International Committee for the YMCA (Young Men's Christian Association) where he established programs and camps for American Indian youths. In 1897, he became a lobbyist for the Sioux community in Washington and from 1899 to 1902 returned to being a physician at the Crow Creek Agency in South Dakota.

This was the period of the **Progressive Movement** in American history, the time when many laws, such as the child labor laws and food processing laws were passed. The women's suffrage movement was gaining momentum and advocacy organizations, like the **Niagara Movement**, headed by W. E. B. Du Bois, were founded. In the spirit of the times, Dr. Eastman continued his advocacy work, and his involvement in organizations connected to the Progressive Movement brought him to the presidency of the Society of American Indians in 1910. After running a camp for girls in New Hampshire from 1915 to 1920, he and his wife separated in 1921 over their differences involving the assimilation of Indigenous peoples. Eastman saw Sioux traditions and Christianity as compatible, a controversial opinion, one to which many Christians took offense. Why might Ohiyesa find these systems compatible? Why might dominant perspectives find such proposed compatibility threatening? *The Soul of the Indian* brings to life the inner struggles of American Indigenous communities as their cultures were systematically destroyed in the relentless westward onslaught of **Manifest Destiny**.

Bruce Cahoon
Humanities Program

> **PRE-READING PARS**
>
> 1. List two or three reasons that colonizing powers have used to justify their destruction of Indigenous societies?
> 2. List two or three ways you might characterize silence.

from *The Soul of the Indian*

I. The Great Mystery

The original attitude of the American Indian toward the Eternal, the "Great Mystery" that surrounds and embraces us, was as simple as it was exalted. To him it was the supreme conception, bringing with it the fullest measure of joy and satisfaction possible in this life.

The worship of the "Great Mystery" was silent, solitary, free from all self-seeking. It was silent, because all speech is of necessity feeble and imperfect; therefore the souls of my ancestors ascended to God in wordless adoration. It was solitary, because they believed that He is nearer to us in solitude, and there were no priests authorized to come between a man and his Maker. None might exhort or confess or in any way meddle with the religious experience of another. Among us all men were created sons of God and stood erect, as conscious of their divinity. Our faith might not be formulated in creeds, nor forced upon any who were unwilling to receive it; hence there was no preaching, proselyting, nor persecution, neither were there any scoffers or atheists.

There were no temples or shrines among us save those of nature. Being a natural man, the Indian was intensely poetical. He would deem it sacrilege to build a house for Him who may be met face to face in the mysterious, shadowy aisles of the primeval forest, or on the sunlit bosom of virgin prairies, upon dizzy spires and pinnacles of naked rock, and yonder in the jeweled vault of the night sky! He who enrobes Himself in filmy veils of cloud, there on the rim of the visible world where our Great-Grandfather Sun kindles his evening camp-fire, He who rides upon the rigorous wind of the north, or breathes forth His spirit upon aromatic southern airs, whose war-canoe is launched upon majestic rivers and inland seas—He needs no lesser cathedral!

That solitary communion with the Unseen which was the highest expression of our religious life is partly described in the word *bambeday*, literally "mysterious feeling," which has been variously translated "fasting" and "dreaming." It may better be interpreted as "consciousness of the divine."

The first *bambeday*, or religious retreat, marked an epoch in the life of the youth, which may be compared to that of confirmation or conversion in Christian experience.

[...]

In every religion there is an element of the supernatural, varying with the influence of pure reason over its devotees. The Indian was a logical and clear thinker upon matters within the scope of his understanding, but he had not yet charted the vast field of nature or expressed her wonders in terms of science. With his limited knowledge of cause and effect, he saw miracles on every hand,—the miracle of life in seed and egg, the miracle of death in lightning flash and in the swelling deep! Nothing of the marvelous could astonish him; as that a beast should speak, or the sun stand still. The virgin birth would appear scarcely more miraculous than is the birth of every child that comes into the world, or the miracle of the loaves and fishes excite more wonder than the harvest that springs from a single ear of corn.

Who may condemn his superstition? Surely not the devout Catholic, even Protestant missionary, who teaches Bible miracles as literal fact! The logical man must either deny all miracles or none, and our American Indian myths and hero stories are perhaps, in themselves, quite as credible as those of the Hebrews of old. If we are of the modern type of mind, that sees in natural law a majesty and grandeur far more impressive than any solitary infraction of it could possibly be, let us not forget that, after all, science has not explained everything. We have still to face the ultimate miracle,—the origin and principle of life! Here is the supreme mystery that is the essence of worship, without which there can be no religion, and in the presence of this mystery our attitude cannot be very unlike that of the natural philosopher, who beholds with awe the Divine in all creation.

It is simple truth that the Indian did not, so long as his native philosophy held sway over his mind, either envy or desire to imitate the splendid achievements of the white man. In his own thought he rose superior to them! He scorned them, even as a lofty spirit absorbed in its stern task rejects the soft beds, the luxurious food, the pleasure-worshiping dalliance of a rich neighbor. It was clear to him that virtue and happiness are independent of these things, if not incompatible with them.

There was undoubtedly much in primitive Christianity to appeal to this man, and Jesus' hard sayings to the rich and about the rich would have been entirely comprehensible to him. Yet the religion that is preached in our churches and practiced by our congregations, with its element of display and self-aggrandizement, its active proselytism, and its open contempt of all religions but its own, was for a long time extremely repellent. To his simple mind, the professionalism of the pulpit, the paid exhorter, the moneyed church, was unspiritual and unedifying, and it was not until his spirit was broken and his moral and physical constitution undermined by trade, conquest, and strong drink, that Christian missionaries obtained any real hold upon him. Strange as it may seem, it is true that the proud pagan in his secret soul despised the good men who came to convert and to enlighten him!

Nor were its publicity and its Phariseeism the only elements in the alien religion that offended the red man. To him, it appeared shocking and almost incredible that there were among this people who claimed superiority many irreligious, who did not even pretend to profess the national faith. Not only did they not profess it, but they stooped so low as to insult their God with profane and sacrilegious speech! In our own tongue His name was not spoken aloud, even with utmost reverence, much less lightly or irreverently.

More than this, even in those white men who professed religion we found much inconsistency of conduct. They spoke much of spiritual things, while seeking only the material. They bought and sold everything: time, labor, personal independence, the love of woman, and even the ministrations of their holy faith! The lust for money, power, and conquest so characteristic of the Anglo-Saxon race did not escape moral condemnation at the hands of his untutored judge, nor did he fail to contrast this conspicuous trait of the dominant race with the spirit of the meek and lowly Jesus.

He might in time come to recognize that the drunkards and licentious among white men, with whom he too frequently came in contact, were condemned by the white man's religion as well, and must not be held to discredit it. But it was not so easy to overlook or to excuse national bad faith. When distinguished emissaries from the Father at Washington, some of them ministers of the gospel and even bishops, came to the Indian nations, and pledged to them in solemn treaty the national honor, with prayer and mention of their God; and when such treaties, so made, were promptly and shamelessly broken, is it strange that the action should arouse not only anger, but contempt? The historians of the white race admit that the Indian was never the first to repudiate his oath.

It is my personal belief, after thirty-five years' experience of it, that there is no such thing as "Christian civilization." I believe that Christianity and modern civilization are opposed and irreconcilable, and that the spirit of Christianity and of our ancient religion is essentially the same.

IV. Barbarism and the Moral Code

Long before I ever heard of Christ, or saw a white man, I had learned from an untutored woman the essence of morality. With the help of dear Nature herself, she taught me things simple but of mighty import. I knew God. I perceived what goodness is. I saw and loved what is really beautiful. Civilization has not taught me anything better!

As a child, I understood how to give; I have forgotten that grace since I became civilized. I lived the natural life, whereas I now live the artificial. Any pretty pebble was valuable to me then; every growing tree an object of reverence. Now I worship with the white man before a painted landscape whose value is estimated in dollars! Thus the Indian is reconstructed, as the natural rocks are ground to powder, and made into artificial blocks which may be built into the walls of modern society.

The first American mingled with his pride a singular humility. Spiritual arrogance was foreign to his nature and teaching. He never claimed that the power of articulate speech was proof of superiority over the silent creation; on the other hand, it is to him a perilous gift. He believes profoundly in silence—the sign of a perfect equilibrium. Silence is the absolute poise or balance of body, mind, and spirit. The man who preserves his selfhood ever calm and unshaken by the storms of existence—not a leaf, as it were, astir on the tree; not a ripple upon the surface of shining pool—his, in the mind of the unlettered sage, is the ideal attitude and conduct of life.

If you ask him: "What is silence?" he will answer: "It is the Great Mystery! The holy silence is His voice!" If you ask: "What are the fruits of silence?" he will say: "They are self-control, true courage or endurance, patience, dignity, and reverence. Silence is the corner-stone of character."

"Guard your tongue in youth," said the old chief, Wabashaw, "and in age you may mature a thought that will be of service to your people!"

The moment that man conceived of a perfect body, supple, symmetrical, graceful, and enduring—in that moment he had laid the foundation of a moral life! No man can hope to maintain such a temple of the spirit beyond the period of adolescence, unless he is able to curb his indulgence in the pleasures of the senses. Upon this truth the Indian built a rigid system of physical training, a social and moral code that was the law of his life.

There was aroused in him as a child a high ideal of manly strength and beauty, the attainment of which must depend upon strict temperance in eating and in the sexual relation, together with severe and persistent exercise. He desired to be a worthy link in the generations, and that he might not destroy by his weakness that vigor and purity of blood which had been achieved at the cost of much self-denial by a long line of ancestors.

He was required to fast from time to time for short periods, and to work off his superfluous energy by means of hard running, swimming, and the vapor-bath. The bodily fatigue thus induced, especially when coupled with a reduced diet, is a reliable cure for undue sexual desires.

Personal modesty was early cultivated as a safeguard, together with a strong self-respect and pride of family and race. This was accomplished in part by keeping the child ever before the public eye, from his birth onward. His entrance into the world, especially in the case of the first-born, was often publicly announced by the herald, accompanied by a distribution of presents to the old and needy. The same thing occurred when he took his first step; when his ears were pierced, and when he shot his first game, so that his childish exploits and progress were known to the whole clan as to a larger family, and he grew into manhood with the saving sense of a reputation to sustain.

The youth was encouraged to enlist early in the public service, and to develop a wholesome ambition for the honors of a leader and feastmaker, which can never be his unless he is truthful and generous, as well as brave, and ever mindful of his personal chastity and honor. There were many ceremonial customs which had a distinct moral influence; the woman was rigidly secluded at certain periods, and the young husband was forbidden to approach his own wife when preparing for war or for any religious event. The public or tribal position of the Indian is entirely dependent upon his private virtue, and he is never permitted to forget that he does not live to himself alone, but to his tribe and his clan. Thus habits of perfect self-control were early established, and there were no unnatural conditions or complex temptations to beset him until he was met and overthrown by a stronger race.

[...]

Ohiyesa (Eastman, Charles A.). *The Soul of the Indian: An Interpretation*, 3–7, 16–24, 87–95. New York: Houghton Mifflin, 1911.

POST-READING PARS

1. Identify two critiques Ohiyesa presents on the American or Christian colonizing strategies toward Indigenous communities?
2. List two characteristics of silence that Ohiyesa offers.

Inquiry Corner

Content Question:	Critical Question:
What qualities or characteristics (of humans, nature, communities, interactions, social institutions, etc.) does Ohiyesa value?	In what ways does nature feature in the ways that Ohiyesa navigates his multiple religious and cultural identities?
Comparative Question:	**Connection Questions:**
How does Ohiyesa's idea of the "Great Mystery" compare/contrast with other concepts of the sacred or gods?	What criteria do you use for reflecting and possibly critiquing your own cultures and communities? What might that engagement look like from a different perspective?

from "Transferring the New Civilization to the Islamic Peoples" by Şemseddin Sami Frashëri

SNAPSHOT BOX

LANGUAGE:
Ottoman Turkish

PUBLISHED:
1883, Ottoman Constantinople (Istanbul)

GENRE: Newspaper editorial

TAGS: Education; Historiography; Religion; Science; Ways of Knowing

Introduction

By the middle of the nineteenth century, the once-dominant Ottoman Empire was collapsing due to the imperialist and colonialist activities of the European powers such as Britain, France, and Russia. Societal responses to this slow dissolution of the Islamic Ottoman state varied from self-exile (in imitation of the Prophet Muhammad's *hijra*, or emigration, to Medina), to the rise of ethnic nationalisms within the fragmenting empire, to numerous programs of reform. In 1839, Sultan Abdulmejid I officially adopted a reform movement known as **Tanzimat** that sought to modernize Ottoman society and to westernize its political policies. Although reactionary religious forces opposed such reforms, a diverse movement known as **Islamic Modernism**, led by figures such as Sayyid Jamal al-Din al-Afghani (1838–1897) in South Asia and his disciple Muhammad 'Abduh (1849–1905) in Egypt, held that Islam could adapt itself to many modern reforms so long as these did not directly contradict the Qur'an or the *sunna* (traditions) of the Prophet.

Şemseddin Sami Frashëri (1850–1904) was one of the great proponents of such modernist reforms.[131] An ethnic Albanian, Sami Bey—as he was popularly known—was a prolific writer, who composed novels, plays, popular essays, and multiple newspaper articles, as well as Turkish language encyclopedias, lexicons, and dictionaries. Although Sunni Muslims, his politically active family was also affiliated with the influential Bektashi Sufi order, which blended forms of intense devotion with Shi'ite practices (such as reverence toward Ali and the Twelve Imams) and initiated women into their ranks. Şemseddin Sami Frashëri's earliest education was at a Bektashi *tekke* (religious lodge), followed by his enrollment at a Greek gymnasium (high school), where he learned several European languages including Greek, Italian, and French, in addition to his private tutoring at a nearby **madrassa** (Islamic school) in Turkish, Arabic, and Persian. How might studying a wide range of subjects and cultures inform a learner's attitude toward the world?

During this period, Şemseddin Sami Frashëri also became acquainted with European science and philosophy, and after moving to Constantinople (later Istanbul) in 1871, he began his prolific career as a writer, journalist, and publisher of periodicals. He presented and promoted his own ideas about how to bring "modern civilization" to the empire and its peoples. Many of his earliest works promoted gender equality, including opposition to polygamy, the elimination of the veil, and the superiority of

---

131. The author is known by different names, depending on whether it is an Albanian or Turkish perspective.

Timeline

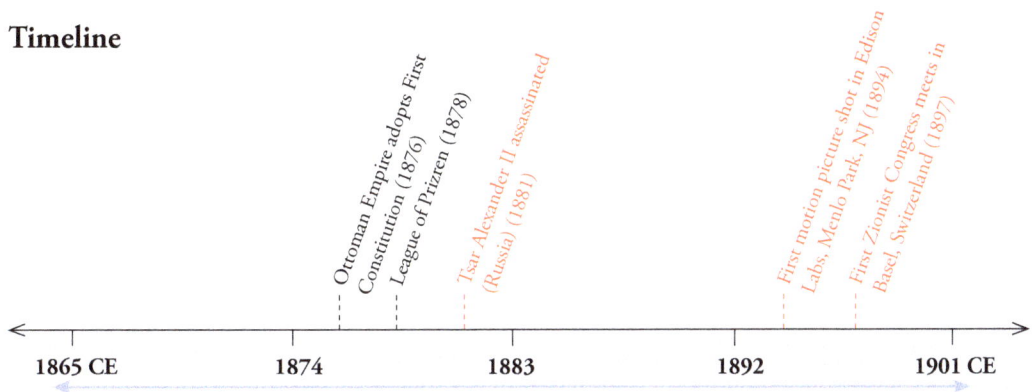

romantic love over arranged marriages. This last idea provided the plot of *Taaşşuk-ı Talat ve Fitnat* (*The Romance of Talat and Fitnat*), considered by scholars to be the first novel written in Turkish. His many writings helped to standardize the Ottoman Turkish language, promoted Turkish arts and culture, and contributed to the rise of Pan-Turkish nationalism in opposition to imperial Ottomanism. He later turned his attention to Albanian nationalist aspirations and argued that Albania should become an autonomous state within the empire, with its own ethnic identity, culture, and language. Indeed, Albanians had maintained a separate identity despite being occupied or ruled by the Ottomans for centuries. How might navigating multiple nationalist possibilities (e.g., Ottoman, Turkish, Albanian) influence a person's worldview? In what ways do ethnicity and nationalism interact as a part of the strategies of modernity? Ultimately, Şemseddin Sami Frashëri's progressive ideas and political activities placed him under the suspicion of Ottoman authorities, and he died while under house arrest in Istanbul at the age of fifty-four.

This selection was originally published in the Istanbul newspaper *Güneş* (*The Sun*) and illustrates Şemseddin Sami Frashëri's lifelong attempt to introduce modern civilization into the Ottoman state. Against what ideas does Frashëri argue? In what ways do his attitudes regarding the role of Islam in promoting progress and modernity reflect the influence of Islamic modernism? Why does he use light as a metaphor for his program of reform?

Rodger Payne
Department of Religious Studies

from "Transferring the New Civilization to the Islamic Peoples"

As may be understood from our previous articles on [Europe's] history and state, although civilization passed through many hands before reaching those of the Europeans, in comparison to modern-day European civilization those ancient civilizations—for all that the later ones were always more perfect than the earlier—are like mere drawings made on a wall with coal by a child in comparison to a painting by the artist Raphael [Italy, 1483–1520]. In addition, those old civilizations have already been destroyed; dealing with them is a duty reserved to history and to the science of archaeology. Many works of Islamic civilization—the latest of the ancient civilizations—and of its predecessor Greek civilization are extant, but given the existence of [modern] works and beacons, whose number is increasing daily, having recourse to these ancient works, or contenting oneself with them, is tantamount to trying to benefit from the wick of an oil lamp in the presence of sunlight. Thus the scholars and philosophers of present day civilization consider Aristotle [Greece, 384–322 B.C.] and Ibn Rushd [Andalusia-Morocco, 1126–1198] as two great mentors of civilization and hold them in high esteem; yet in today's schools they do not teach Aristotle's *History of Animals* or *The Canon of Medicine* by Ibn Sina [Iran, 980–1037]. They rendered great services to humanity; they each lit a lamp in gloomy centuries enveloped in the darkness of ignorance. Gradually people left this environment of darkness, finding the way with the help of their lamps. At last the sun rose, the light of education flooded the world. The duty we owe to those lamps today is simply to cherish and respect them for their role in getting us out the darkness. To go beyond this and to draw a curtain of ignorance and fanaticism in front of the light of the sun, and to content ourselves with the weak light of those lamps, is sheer folly.

Therefore, saving the Muslim peoples from ignorance and once again bringing them to civilization are among the most important priorities of any zealous person who loves his religious community and fatherland, since the survival and glory of Islam are contingent upon this alone.

It is true that religious zeal would impel a man to be content with the lamp which he knows to have been lit by his ancestors; yet it is essential that reason and wisdom should overcome any such feeling. Today, however much effort and expense is required to revive the medicine of Ibn Sina, the wisdom of Ibn Rushd, and the chemistry of Jahiz [Iraq, circa 776–869], to extract their books from underneath the dust of libraries and translate them into the various Muslim languages, to publish them, and to found schools and colleges devoted to teaching them, we must make the same effort and go to the same expense to put into circulation among us the best scientific works of our own century. For just as we cannot cure even malaria with the medicine of Ibn Sina, so we can neither operate a railroad engine or steamship, nor use the telegraph, with the chemistry of Jahiz and the wisdom of Ibn Sina. For this reason, if we wish to become civilized, we must do so by borrowing science and technology from the contemporary civilization of Europe, and leave the study of the works of Islamic scholars to the students of history and antiquity.

It is a regrettable circumstance that, because today civilization seems to belong exclusively to the Christian nations, ignorant masses of our own nation take it to be a symbol or requisite of Christianity, and thus deem distancing themselves from it and guarding themselves against it to be a religious duty.

We can affirm that it is not the religion of Islam which prevents Muslim nations from becoming civilized; rather the cause is the religious difference and conflict which exists between the Muslim and the civilized nations—in other words, the fact that present-day civilization is in the hands of the Christian nations.

To avoid such fanatical reactions on the part of the people, some of our literary figures who are unhappy with this situation have attempted to make European civilization seem less loathsome in the eyes of the people, and so to make them warm to the new sciences and pave the way to transfer contemporary civilization to the Islamic nations. In order to achieve this goal, they used newspapers, books, pamphlets, sermons, and all available means to spread the view that European civilization was borrowed from the Muslims, that Islam is no obstacle to true civilization, and that most of science and technology which we see in the hands of the Europeans today is made up of Muslim discoveries. This effort of these people is a most worthy one. But because there is as much exaggeration as truth in what they assert, one senses that alongside the good they have done, they have also done some harm. This effort has gone to extremes by exceeding the limits of necessity. Just as a large dose of medicine intended to cure an illness creates a new one, so a new idea has arisen from this exaggeration, and although it is less detrimental than the first, its harmfulness cannot be denied. The number of people among the Muslims who view European civilization as a product of unbelief contrary to and incompatible with Islam has decreased, thanks to the efforts of these preachers of civilization. Yet as a result of their exaggerations, the number of those people who have acquired a new fanaticism—viewing European civilization as something stolen from us, imperfect, and an imitation, and insulting that civilization while maintaining that the true civilization is ours—has correspondingly increased.

This new fanaticism is like an illness arising from an overzealous physician's treatment. Shattering this fanaticism is a most weighty duty for those who want to be of service in civilizing the Muslim nations. This duty compels us to say the following to those who have acquired this new fanaticism: The Europeans borrowed many things from us, that is to say from our ancestors or more precisely our coreligionists who lived eight or ten centuries ago; however, none of the things in their hands today is something that was borrowed from our ancestors. Europe borrowed a seed of civilization from the Islamic world, and planted that seed. It is natural that a seed should decompose in the earth in order to bear fruit. That seed decomposed; the cycle has been repeated many times, with the result that its very genus has changed. The knowledge that Europe derived from the scholars of Islam was very considerable by [the standards of] the time, but by present-day standards it is nothing. At that time she borrowed a lamp from us in order to escape from the darkness of ignorance which surrounded her; but once she had reached a bright place with the help of the light of that lamp, she no longer needed it, and threw it away. Can we wax proud of this? There is nothing here to be proud of; rather we should be ashamed of it, because, after dropping this lamp and allowing it to go out, we do not even desire to benefit from a sun of civilization which rises and shines before our very eyes. Some among us say "this is not a sun but a time just before dawn," while some of us say "this is an imitation of our old lamp," thereby preferring to remain in darkness by closing our eyes!

Had the pioneers of Islamic civilization such as [caliph Abu] Ja'far [al-]Mansur [reigned 754–775], [caliph] Harun al-Rashid [reigned 786–809], and the caliph Ma'mun [reigned 813–833], who established the caliphate on the ruins of Babylon, viewed Greek civilization with similar contempt, maintained that that civilization was derived from, and a mere imitation of, the civilization of their ancestors the Chaldeans, or that depending on works of Greek pagans contradicted Islam, would the Islamic civilization of which we are so proud today have materialized? Although Greek civilization was no longer an ongoing enterprise at that time, and had ceased to exist, children of the Companions of the Messenger of God (may God bless him and grant him salvation) borrowed it in its entirety, revived it, and held Greek sages, in whose footsteps they proudly followed, in high esteem and paid tribute to them. Why then do we not want to benefit from European civilization, accusing it sometimes of blasphemy and polytheism and sometimes of being an imitation? Are the European people of the book [Christians and Jews] more profligate in their religion than the ancient Greek pagans, or are we more pious than the children of the Companions of the Prophet who had the honor of conversing with the Messenger of God?

In Europe, too, fanaticism was often an obstacle on the road to civilization, Islamic scholars were viewed as sorcerers, and those cultivating the sciences were accused of heresy and severely punished. There too at first appeared some scholars who tried to reconcile religious texts with science, and to eliminate fanaticism by appeasing it. But because fanaticism is not the sort of monster that can be won over with kindness, it has brutally destroyed those who have attempted to appease it. Finally, the intellectuals gathered together, hand in hand, and waged a war against fanaticism with axes, crowbars, and gunpowder; they demolished it, and only then did civilization begin to move forward. In our society, too, in order to achieve progress in civilization and save the Muslim nations from the ignorance and Bedouinism that are precipitating their annihilation, for all intents and purposes a war must be declared against fanaticism to crush it by force and thus open the road to civilization.

Far from damaging religion, this would in fact greatly benefit it; for fanaticism is the rust of religion, and just as within a short time rust eats up and destroys even the best steel, so also fanaticism stains even the most truthful religion and rots it. The rust of fanaticism must be removed from religion so it shines with its true and essential luster, and its future is secured. There is as great a difference between religion and fanaticism as there is between light and darkness. The darkness of ignorance and fanaticism must be removed so that the light of knowledge and true religion together illuminate and reinvigorate people's minds and hearts. There is no alternative.

Frashëri, Şemseddin Sami. "Transferring the New Civilization to the Islamic Peoples." In *Modernist Islam, 1840–1940: A Sourcebook*, edited by Charles Kurzman, 149–51. Oxford: Oxford University Press, 2002.

> **BEYOND THE CLASSROOM**
>
> » Imagine innovation in two frameworks: creating something from scratch, or improving and adapting an existing model. Which of these is more conducive to your own worldview, values, and skillset?

from *Turkey Faces West* by Halidé Edib

SNAPSHOT BOX

LANGUAGE: English
PUBLISHED: 1930, United States
GENRE: Sociopolitical critique
TAGS: Cross-Cultural Encounters; Psyche; Religion; Statecraft; Tradition; Women and Power

Introduction

Halidé Edib (1884–1964) was a Turkish novelist, writer, educator, feminist, activist, reformer, and politician. An ardent nationalist, she supported the establishment of the Turkish Republic under the leadership of Mustafa Kemal (Atatürk), but she later turned against his dictatorial policies and the haste with which he instituted his modernist reforms.

Edib (also spelled Edip) was born in 1884 in Ottoman Constantinople (later Istanbul), the daughter in a prominent and wealthy Turkish family who provided her with a broad education. Married soon after her graduation in 1901 from the Christian missionary American College for Girls in Üsküdar, she began her career as an essayist and novelist, eventually becoming one of Turkey's most famous and most prolific authors. In spite of a life filled with war, politics, and exile, Edib published over twenty novels (in Turkish, English, and French), two plays, and a number of short stories, in addition to a two-volume memoir and other forms of nonfiction. Two primary themes predominated in both her fiction and nonfiction works: Turkish nationalism and female emancipation from social and religious oppression. In her novels and short stories—many of them somewhat autobiographical—Edib presented resolute female protagonists courageously struggling against outdated patriarchal systems. Similarly, in her personal life, she divorced her first husband after nine years of marriage when he decided to take a second wife, as was allowed under both Islamic and civil law. In 1917, she married physician and prominent re-

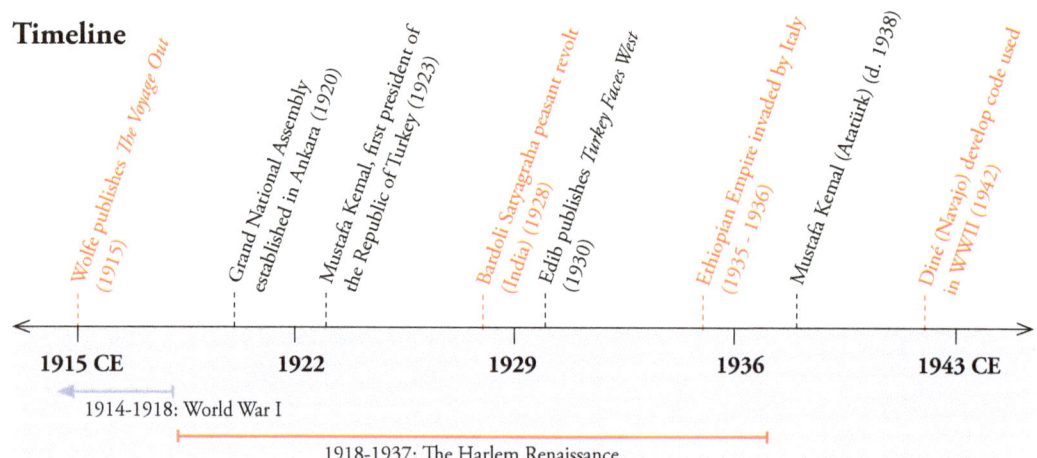

Timeline

- Woolf publishes *The Voyage Out* (1915)
- Grand National Assembly established in Ankara (1920)
- Mustafa Kemal, first president of the Republic of Turkey (1923)
- Bardoli Satyagraha peasant revolt (India) (1928)
- Edib publishes *Turkey Faces West* (1930)
- Ethiopian Empire invaded by Italy (1935 - 1936)
- Mustafa Kemal (Atatürk) (d. 1938)
- Diné (Navajo) develop code used in WWII (1942)

1914-1918: World War I
1918-1937: The Harlem Renaissance

formist politician Dr. Abdülhak Adnan Adıvar, who would become the minister of health in the new republic.

During World War I, Edib worked at an orphanage in Turkish Syria (present-day Lebanon) where she was later accused of supporting the program of **Turkification**, a controversial ideology that sought to erase the ethnic distinctions of Arabs, Kurds, Armenians, and others in **Anatolia** ("Asia Minor") and the Caucasus region, through force if necessary. As a type of ethnic cleansing, Turkification contributed to the massacre of over 1 million Christian Ottomans during the Armenian Genocide of 1914–1923.[132] Additionally, at orphanages throughout the region, Armenian children were stripped of their heritage and identity, forced to convert to Islam, and then given for adoption to Turkish families. Although her personal involvement in this process is contested, Edib's association with the orphanage stands in sharp contrast to a career otherwise dedicated to dignity and human rights. What factors may have contributed to Edib's possible involvement in Turkification related to orphanages? Since this involvement is contested, what questions would we need to ask and how do those questions impact how we engage with her writing?

Alliance with Germany and the Central Powers during World War I, and their subsequent defeat, led to the final dismemberment of the Ottoman Empire between 1918–1920. Anatolia was divided into "zones of influence" by the victorious allies (France, Britain, and Italy) and annexed to neighboring states (Greece, Armenia), leaving only the arid plains around Ankara as a homeland for the Turks. In 1919, Edib gave a patriotic speech in the Sultanahmet Mosque in Constantinople urging resistance to the occupying Greek army in nearby Izmir; the speech made her a national hero and the most recognized female leader in the nationalist movement. Under the threat of capture and exile by the British army in Constantinople, Edib and her husband fled to Ankara to join the Turkish National Resistance led by Mustafa Kemal. They were active in the War of Liberation (1919–1923) and later were among the most important architects of the new Turkish state.

In many of her writings, Edib critiqued what she understood to be the peculiar role of Turkey being caught between the "East" (its Islamic and Ottoman heritage) and the "West" (secular, European worldviews). Arguing that Islam had provided economic freedoms for women that the West had only begun to adopt, she feared that Kemal, now the president of the Republic, was destroying too much of the religious heritage of Turkey in a mad rush to westernize the nation. Accordingly, she and her husband formed an opposition political party that led to their being charged with treason, forcing them in 1926 to flee the country that they had helped to create. What might attract a person (like Edib) to Atatürk's policies? In what ways

---

132. There were Armenians who accepted Turkification, although they continued clandestinely to follow Armenian customs and even to practice their Christianity in secret. The Armenian genocide can be understood as the most vicious form of Turkification, if not of those who were massacred then of the region itself where the massacres took place.

are religion and nationalism in conflict with each other? How might they serve as mutually reinforcing components of communal identity formation? Edib and Adıvar refused to return to Turkey until Kemal's death, living until 1939 in Europe, India, and the United States. Upon her return, Edib taught English literature at the University of Istanbul and served a term in the Turkish Grand National Assembly (1950–1954).

This reading, excerpted from *Turkey Faces West*, is based on a series of lectures that Edib delivered in English at the prestigious Williamstown Institute of Politics in Massachusetts in 1929. In its twelve chapters, Edib rehearses the history of the late Ottoman period and what she believes to be its continuity with the initial reforms promoted by Kemal. Influenced as a child by her grandmother's partiality for **Sufism** (Islamic mysticism) Edib argued that Islam had contributed to the emancipation of women and thus should remain a part of a modern and democratic Turkey. This selection comes from her penultimate chapter entitled "The Turkish Republic."

Rodger Payne
Department of Religious Studies

from *Turkey Faces West*

No other country in the world stands more in need of "doing" than Turkey. In such a country a strong, centralized government, if not a dictatorship, with stabilized forces backing it, is inevitable and perhaps necessary. This fundamental psychology in the world and in Turkey will tend to create and to maintain strong, centralized governments in Turkey, although the dictatorial form is a passing phase.

The continuation of reforms in Turkey under the dictatorial *régime* from 1925 to 1929, and especially their nature, are more interesting and significant than the terrorist methods by which they were supposed to be made possible.

This process of reform has been going on for nearly a century, but within the last twenty years it has moved with tremendous rapidity. The version in the western press, usually the outcome of the most superficial and hurried observation after a pleasant and short Mediterranean trip, is that Turkey was changed overnight from an eastern into a western country. This is worse than superficial; it is false. Whether the recent reforms could have been carried out by other than terrorist methods is a question to be seriously considered. And there is no doubt that they were bound to be carried through—but whether in three years or in thirteen or thirty years, no one can tell. Naturally one includes among the reforms which were sure to be realized only the fundamental ones that will endure. The nature of the leading reforms effected by the dictatorial *régime* confirms the assumption that they are the continuation of earlier tendencies to westernization and are not departures from the fundamental line of progress that the Turks have taken.

The first and most spectacular of these reforms was the "Hat Law," passed in 1925. It was also the most futile and superficial in comparison to the others which followed. But it was the only one which accomplished an external change overnight. In a week it made the Turks don European hats (the only part of the city dwellers' outfit which had not been westernized) and made them look like westerners, although the manner in which it was accomplished was utterly un-western. The westernization of Turks is not and should not be a question of mere external imitation and gesture. It is a much deeper and more significant process. To tell the Turk to don a certain headdress and "get civilized" or be hanged or imprisoned, is absurd, to say the least. The opposition of individuals among the men in the street, really much more westernized than those who carried the measure through, had a note of wounded self-respect rather than of objection to wearing hats. Among all the recent measures, this was the most seriously opposed in the country itself. Any opposition to the "Hat Law" was labeled as reactionary. The interesting fact connected with the substitution of the hat for the Turkish fez is that it attracted the greatest attention in the western world. Other more fundamental changes taking place in Turkey were either entirely unnoticed, or criticized, or neglected as unimportant items of foreign news in the western papers. But the moment the Turks put hats on their heads the general cry in the West was, "At last the Turks are civilized; they wear hats." Hence those who enacted the "Hat

Law" might say: "We have killed a few, and imprisoned a large number, but it was good psychology; has anything in the past brought the Turks so much into the limelight? Has anything brought them nearer to the European in the European mind?"

On the whole the dictatorships have probably sensed the mob psychology of the West more keenly than anyone, especially the Turkish dictatorship and dictator. Count Keyserling says: "Now that the fez, together with other external distinguishing marks, has disappeared, it is easier to get a true picture of this people." Count Keyserling personally does not need to see the Turk wear a hat in order to get a true picture of him. For he declares later:

> To him who knows what psychic atmosphere means, it is *a priori* clear that the contact with the life and spirit of the Greeks during a period of seven centuries, and the intimate relationship with Europe during a period of five, produced of necessity a state of psychological unification.[133]

Evidently for men outside the class of Count Keyserling, it is necessary to see an outward similarity in a people in order to classify them with this or that trend of thought. This represents the kind of new superficial, "doing" western mind that has created the "Boy Scout" type of institution.

The chief result of the "Hat Law" was that it enriched European hat factories at the expense of the already impoverished Turks. Broadly one can say that it could not have been passed without a *régime* of terror. The Islamic reactionaries, the liberals, the people who understood the spirit of the West, were all opposed to it for different reasons. What would have happened was this: The very small number of Turks who wore hats in the summer in Constantinople would have increased gradually and in a generation hat wearers would have been in a majority in the cities. But the Turkish peasant would have stuck to his old headdress.

The adoption of the Swiss code in place of the Islamic family law in 1926 was a reform of a much more serious nature. It could have been put through without much coercion, although there would have been some bitter criticism.

A year after the Sultan's Government had been abolished in Constantinople there was serious discussion whether the revised family law of 1916, abrogated by the Sultan's Government in 1919, should be restored with or without alterations. In 1924 the National Assembly took up the question, and it aroused great interest, especially among the women of the cities and of Constantinople in particular. At a large meeting of women in the Nationalist Club there was elected a committee of women to study the situation and send a petition to the National Assembly. The committee made a selection of the family laws of Sweden, France, England, and Russia, and having found the Swedish law most desirable it sent a translated copy with a petition attached to it to the National Assembly. Their petition had at the time no definite

---

133. Count Hermann Keyserling, *Europe*, translated by Maurice Samuel (Harcourt Brace & Company, 1928).

result. But there was a group of very keenly interested young deputies working for the adoption of a western code rather than the restoration of the revised family law of 1916. Mahmoud Essad Bey, the young deputy of Smyrna who became Minister of Justice in 1925, was one of the leading spirits in the movement. In 1926 the law following the Swiss code was passed. It can be termed perhaps one of the two most significant and important changes that have taken place during the dictatorship. This particular law will mean the final unification of the Turk with the family of European nations, by giving the Turkish family that kind of stability which constitutes the western ideal of the family.

The adoption of the Swiss law, which is entirely western, instead of revision and alteration of the Islamic family law which could have made marriage a freer if a less stable institution and brought it nearer to the present Russian family law, was one more triumph in Turkey of the Western Ideal over the Eastern Ideal, and one of more permanent import than is realized at present.

The educational rights that Turkish women have gained are no longer questioned even by the smallest minority, and the sphere of women's work has been constantly widening. It is perhaps a blessing that they have not obtained the vote. Thus they have been protected from the danger of being identified with party politics, and their activities outside the political world could not be stopped for political reasons.

In the Turkish home, women continue to be the ruling spirit, more so, perhaps, because the majority contribute to the upkeep by their labor. At the present time, offices, factories, and shops are filled with women workers in the cities; and in addition to their breadwinning jobs, and sometimes in connection with them, women have interested themselves in child welfare and hygiene, and in organizing small associations to teach poor women embroidery, sewing, weaving, and so on. The favorite profession of Turkish women today, after teaching, is medicine. All this is the city aspect of the situation. In the rural districts, women still continue to live their old life with its drudgery, and will continue to live under these conditions until a more up-to-date agricultural system is adopted and the rudiments of education can be given in those districts. It would not be an underestimate to say that something like 90 per cent of the Turkish women are very hard workers; the question is not how to provide more work for them but how to train them better for their work and to give them more leisure. The small percentage of the idle rich (much smaller in Turkey than elsewhere) do on a miniature scale what the idle rich of other countries do. Unfortunately Turkey is judged by the life and attitude of these idlers, who are conspicuous to the eyes of the traveler, rather than by the hard-working majority.

On the whole, within the last twenty years women in Turkey as elsewhere have profited by changes more than men. It has been fortunate for Turkey that the emancipation of women there was the result of an all-party program rather than a sex struggle. The contribution of the Republic to women's social emancipation in the introduction of the new civil code has brought the movement to its highest and historically its most important stage. But a generation at least must pass before its full effects can be seen. The general criticism that with westernization a great deal of evil and western immorality has penetrated into Turkish customs is not very important. The evil affects a small number of the idle, while the good penetrates into the majority, although more slowly.

In 1928 the clause in the Constitution which declared Islam the state religion was abolished. In the foreign press this step was criticized very severely, on the ground that it amounted to the abolition of religion in Turkey. This criticism was not only superficial but inaccurate. If religion, in the best sense, is in any danger of losing its hold on the Turkish people, it is not due to absence of governmental interference but to governmental interference itself. The men who sponsored this measure may or may not have been atheists, but the measure itself does not do away with religion. No secular state can logically have a basic law which establishes a state religion. The abolition of the clause from the Constitution was therefore in true and necessary accord with the nature of the new Turkish state at its last stage of secularization. "Render therefore unto Caesar the things which are Caesar's, and unto God the things that are God's." The Turks have at last rendered up the things that were Caesar's or the state's; but Caesar or the state still keeps things which belong to God. Unless the Presidency of Religious Affairs is made free, unless it ceases to be controlled by the office of the Prime Minister, it will always be a governmental instrument. In this respect the Moslem community is less privileged and less free than the Christian Patriarchates. These are free institutions which decide upon all questions of dogma and religion according to the convictions of their particular group. The Islamic community is chained to the policy of the Government. This situation is a serious impediment to the spiritual growth of Islam in Turkey, and there is always a danger in it of the use of religion for political ends.

Now that the state has freed itself entirely from religious control, it should in turn leave Islam alone. Not only should it declare, "Every major Turkish citizen is free to adopt the religion he (or she) wishes to adopt," but it should also allow the Moslem community to teach its religion to its youth. Now that the schools give no religious instruction, and the religious institutions are abolished, the Islamic community, if it is going to last as a religious community, must create its own means of religious teaching, its own moral and spiritual sanctions. Further, in the ritual and in the fundamentals of worship, there are likely to be changes among the Moslems in Turkey. Those changes should be allowed to take place without governmental interference. The occasional proposals by the university professors of new forms of worship in Islam—such as substituting organ music for vocal music, entering the mosques without taking off the shoes, placing benches so that the faithful may pray seated, and doing away with a number of complicated body movements in prayer—have met with profound displeasure. All these changes might take place by the wishes of the people, but governmental interference in this most sacred part of men's rights would constitute a dangerous precedent. It would fetter the religious life of the Turks and bring politics into religion. The fundamental meaning of the long and very interesting phases of secularization is that Turkish psychology separates this world from the next. To take religion out of the political state but at the same time to keep the state in religious affairs, is one of the contradictory aspects of the last phase which must be corrected.

Not only in Turkey but wherever religion is interfered with by governments, it becomes a barrier, and an unremovable one, to peace and understanding. Yet the fundamental doctrine of every religion is peace and the brotherhood of men. If only religions could be freed from political influences all over the world, the barriers between peoples of different creeds would break down sooner than one supposes.

Selection from Edib, Halidé. *Turkey Faces West: A Turkish View of Recent Changes and Their Origin*, 223–32. New Haven: Yale University Press, 1930.

from "Why I Am a Pagan?" by Zitkala-Ša

SNAPSHOT BOX

LANGUAGE: English

GENRE: Autobiography, essay

PUBLISHED: 1902, United States

TAGS: Autobiography and Testimony; Body; Community; Ethics and Morality; Psyche; Race; Religion; Tradition; Ways of Knowing

Introduction

Zitkala-Ša (1876–1938) was born on the Yankton Sioux reservation in South Dakota. Her Lakota name means Red Bird but she is also known by her Christian name, Gertude Simmons Bonnin. Raised by her mother after her white father abandoned the family, she lived on the reservation until she was eight years old and then attended a boarding school in Indiana run by Quaker missionaries. During her three years there, she learned to read, write and play the violin—skills she described with delight that would infuse her activism with prose and music. She also lamented the erasure of her culture of origin and the forced assimilation she experienced at the Indiana Manual Labor Institute, including the mandatory cutting of her long hair. Even after returning to her family home, she described inner conflict about the impact of assimilation on her own identity and others in her community. This resulted in her decision to return to the school at age fifteen where she eventually became a music teacher. She attended the New England Conservatory of Music where she honed music and oratory skills that she would apply throughout her career as an advocate for Indigenous cultures. She revisited Yankton several times as part of her work with the Bureau of Indian Affairs. She published essays in the *Atlantic Monthly* and *Harper's Monthly*, including "Why I Am a Pagan," describing the changes wrought by the bureau that paralleled her own difficult experiences traversing two cultures. What difficulties might be experienced by people navigat-

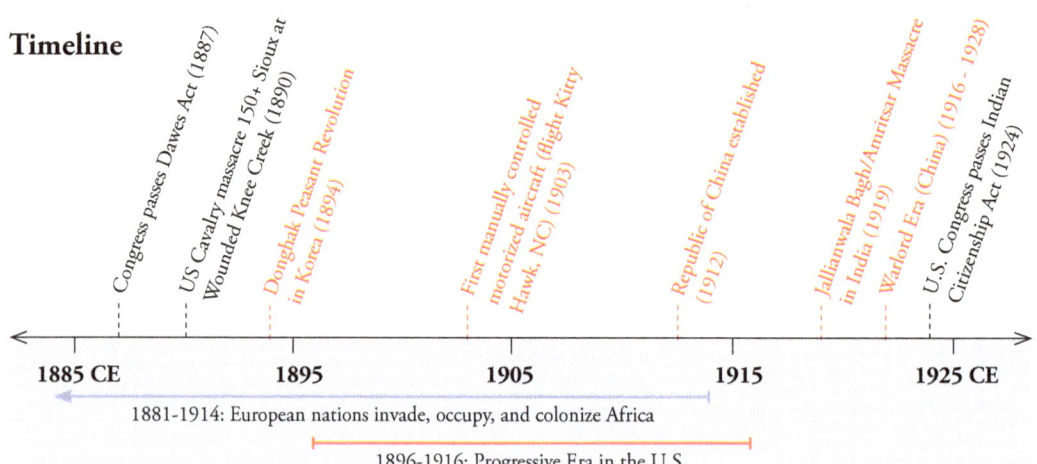

ing two or more different cultural contexts? What strategies might be employed to mitigate the impact of these difficulties?

Over the next three decades, at the height of the Progressive era in US history during which activists mobilized to improve conditions for poor people, Zitkala-Ša joined national women's groups and Indigenous groups that published, lobbied, and raised awareness of the barriers to full citizenship that women and other marginalized people faced. She published autobiographical, fictitious, and journalistic essays that combated stereotypes of Indigenous peoples and their diverse cultures. She criticized boarding schools, such as the Carlisle Indian School where she worked as a music teacher, for **epistemicide**—the deliberate erasure of Indigenous epistemologies, including ways of knowing and being, languages, beliefs, and cultural practices. In 1901, Carlisle fired her despite her tremendous talent as a musician and teacher. Shortly thereafter, she married an army captain and worked for the Bureau of Indian Affairs at the Uintah-Ouray Reservation in Utah. There she met William F. Hanson, a composer with whom she collaborated for over a decade. They wrote and produced *The Sundance Opera* in 1913. This production allowed her to express the multiple cultures in which she lived and worked and is an exemplar of the strategies colonized individuals use to navigate their own identities and subtly undermine oppressive structures. Why might colonized individuals use art to communicate resistance? By the 1920s, she had distanced herself from the Bureau of Indian Affairs and founded the National Council of American Indians, over which she presided until her death.

In this reading, Zikala-Ša, then in her mid-twenties, describes a fictionalized encounter with a missionary and tribal member on the reservation who pressured her to renounce her paganism in favor of Christianity. For her, paganism describes her connection to nature as spiritual and alive, a hallmark of many earth-centered religions. She practices patience when she condemns the old ways. What role does patience play in resistance, art, or spirituality? Although her later writings more explicitly called out prejudices against Indigenous epistemologies, this essay emphasizes the positive aspects of engaging in multiple and different religious worldviews at the same time.

Tracey Rizzo
Department of History

> **PRE-READING PARS**
>
> 1. Outline two ways that an autobiography could be used for polemical purposes.
> 2. Describe three key characteristics that illustrate your understanding of paganism.
> 3. Do you have a pet? What does your relationship with animals or pets say about you?

Why I Am a Pagan (1902)

When the spirit swells my breast I love to roam leisurely among the green hills; or sometimes, sitting on the brink of the murmuring Missouri, I marvel at the great blue overhead. With half closed eyes I watch the huge cloud shadows in their noiseless play upon the high bluffs opposite me, while into my ear ripple the sweet, soft cadences of the river's song. Folded hands lie in my lap, for the time forgot. My heart and I lie small upon the earth like a grain of throbbing sand. Drifting clouds and tinkling waters, together with the warmth of a genial summer day, bespeak with eloquence the loving Mystery round about us. During the idyll while I sat upon the sunny river brink, I grew somewhat, though my response be not so clearly manifest as in the green grass fringing the edge of the high bluff back of me.

At length retracing the uncertain footpath scaling the precipitous embankment, I seek the level lands where grow the wild prairie flowers. And they, the lovely little folk, soothe my soul with their perfumed breath.

Their quaint round faces of varied hue convince the heart which leaps with glad surprise that they, too, are living symbols of omnipotent thought. With a child's eager eye I drink in the myriad star shapes wrought in luxuriant color upon the green. Beautiful is the spiritual essence they embody.

I leave them nodding in the breeze but take along with me their impress upon my heart. I pause to rest me upon a rock embedded on the side of a foothill facing the low river bottom. Here the Stone-Boy, of whom the American aborigine tells, frolics about, shooting his baby arrows and shouting aloud with glee at the tiny shafts of lightning that flash from the flying arrowbeaks. What an ideal warrior he became, baffling the siege of the pests of all the land till he triumphed over their united attack. And here he lay,—Invan, our great-great-grandfather, older than the hill he rested on, older than the race of men who love to tell of his wonderful career.

Interwoven with the thread of this Indian legend of the rock, I fain would trace a subtle knowledge of the native folk which enabled them to recognize a kinship to any and all parts of this vast universe. By the leading of an ancient trail, I move toward the Indian village.

With the strong, happy sense that both great and small are so surely enfolded in His magnitude that, without a miss, each has his allotted individual ground of opportunities, I am buoyant with good nature.

Yellow Breast, swaying upon the slender stem of a wild sunflower, warbles a sweet assurance of this as I pass near by. Breaking off the clear crystal song, he turns his wee head from side to side eyeing me wisely as slowly I plod with moccasined feet. Then again he yields himself to his song of joy. Flit, flit hither and yon, he fills the summer sky with his swift, sweet melody. And truly does it seem his vigorous freedom lies more in his little spirit than in his wing.

With these thoughts I reach the log cabin whither I am strongly drawn by the tie of a child to an aged mother. Out bounds my four-footed friend to meet me, frisking about my path with unmistakable delight. Chan is a black shaggy dog, "a thorough-bred little mongrel," of whom I am very fond. Chan seems to understand many words in Sioux, and will go to her mat even when I whisper the word, though generally I think she is guided by the tone of the voice. Often she tries to imitate the sliding inflection and long drawn out voice to the amusement of our guests, but her articulation is quite beyond my ear. In both my hands I hold her shaggy head and gaze into her large brown eyes. At once the dilated pupils contract into tiny black dots, as if the roguish spirit within would evade my questioning.

Finally resuming the chair at my desk I feel in keen sympathy with my fellow creatures, for I seem to see clearly again that all are akin.

The racial lines, which once were bitterly real, now serve nothing more than marking out a living mosaic of human beings. And even here men of the same color are like the ivory keys of one instrument where each represents all the rest, yet varies from them in pitch and quality of voice. And those creatures who are for a time mere echoes of another's note are not unlike the fable of the thin sick man whose distorted shadow, dressed like a real creature, came to the old master to make him follow as a shadow. Thus with a compassion for all echoes in human guise, I greet the solemn-faced "native preacher" whom I find awaiting me. I listen with respect for God's creature, though he mouth most strangely the jangling phrases of a bigoted creed.

As our tribe is one large family, where every person is related to all the others, he addressed me:—

"Cousin, I came from the morning church service to talk with you."

"Yes," I said interrogatively, as he paused for some word from me.

Shifting uneasily about in the straight-backed chair he sat upon, he began: "Every holy day (Sunday) I look about our little God's house, and not seeing you there, I am disappointed. This is why I come to-day. Cousin, as I watch you from afar, I see no unbecoming behavior and hear only good reports of you, which all the more burns me with the wish that you were a church member. Cousin, I was taught long years ago by kind missionaries to read the holy book. These godly men taught me also the folly of our old beliefs.

"There is one God who gives reward or punishment to the race of dead men. In the upper region the Christian dead are gathered in unceasing song and prayer. In the deep pit below, the sinful ones dance in torturing flames.

"Think upon these things, my cousin, and choose now to avoid the afterdoom of hell fire!" Then followed a long silence in which he clasped tighter and unclasped again his interlocked fingers.

Like instantaneous lightning flashes came pictures of my own mother's making, for she, too, is now a follower of the new superstition.

"Knocking out the chinking of our log cabin, some evil hand thrust in a burning taper of braided dry grass, but failed of his intent, for the fire died out and the half burned brand fell inward to the floor. Directly above it, on a shelf, lay the holy book. This is what we found after our return from a several days' visit. Surely some great power is hid in the sacred book!"

Brushing away from my eyes many like pictures, I offered midday meal to the converted Indian sitting wordless and with downcast face. No sooner had he risen from the table with "Cousin, I have relished it," than the church bell rang.

Thither he hurried forth with his afternoon sermon. I watched him as he hastened along, his eyes bent fast upon the dusty road till he disappeared at the end of a quarter of a mile.

The little incident recalled to mind the copy of a missionary paper brought to my notice a few days ago, in which a "Christian" pugilist commented upon a recent article of mine, grossly perverting the spirit of my pen. Still I would not forget that the pale-faced missionary and the hoodooed aborigine are both God's creatures, though small indeed their own conceptions of Infinite Love. A wee child toddling in a wonder world, I prefer to their dogma my excursions into the natural gardens where the voice of the Great Spirit is heard in the twittering of birds, the rippling of mighty waters, and the sweet breathing of flowers. If this is Paganism, then at present, at least, I am a Pagan.

Zitkala-Ša. "Why I Am a Pagan." *Atlantic Monthly* 90 (1902): 801–3.

POST-READING PARS

1. How is this reading polemical? Does its autobiographical nature make it more or less effective?
2. Identify any quotes from the text that help illustrate what Zitkala-Ša sees as pagan? Might any of these be characterized as animistic or pantheistic?
3. What role do animals, and in particular the dog, play in Zitkala-Ša's narrative?

Inquiry Corner

Content Question:	**Critical Question:**
Why do the preacher's words fail to convince Zitkala-Ša?	How central are Zitkala-Ša's spiritual views to her activism and art?
Comparative Question:	**Connection Questions:**
Consider Du Bois's concept of double-consciousness as a way to approach Zitkala-Ša's cultural identity.	Reverence for nature runs through American countercultures. What other examples of this can you think of? How do activists and artists engage with nature in order to respond to exploitative practices?

"Address at the World's Fair in Atlanta" by Booker T. Washington

SNAPSHOT BOX

LANGUAGE: English
GENRE: Public address
DELIVERED: September 18, 1895, Atlanta, Georgia
TAGS: Accessing Rights; Economics; Education; Labor; Race; Rhetoric and Persuasion; Struggle, Resistance, and Revolution

Introduction

Booker T. Washington was born into slavery in Franklin County, Virginia, on April 5, 1856 (d. 1915). He and his family lived in the kitchen of a plantation for much of his early childhood. At the conclusion of the Civil War and the abolition of slavery, Washington and his family left Virginia and resettled in West Virginia. Though he labored in the salt furnaces, he yearned for an education, an ambition realized when his mother made arrangements for him to be tutored in the evenings. He eventually seized the opportunity to attend school during the day, though his work commitments remained. Washington later attended the Hampton Institute (now Hampton University) in Virginia, where he eventually taught before becoming the head of the Tuskegee Institute (now Tuskegee University) in Alabama in 1881. At Tuskegee, a school attended by African American students especially from the region, Washington helped set the foundation for the development of one of the nation's premier historically Black colleges (HBCUs). By the early twentieth century, given his stature as a national leader in the African American community, Washington was invited to serve as an advisor on race relations for the administrations of presidents Theodore Roosevelt and William Howard Taft.

His educational and professional achievements made him a well-known spokesman on issues that concerned African Americans. The prestige (and success) that

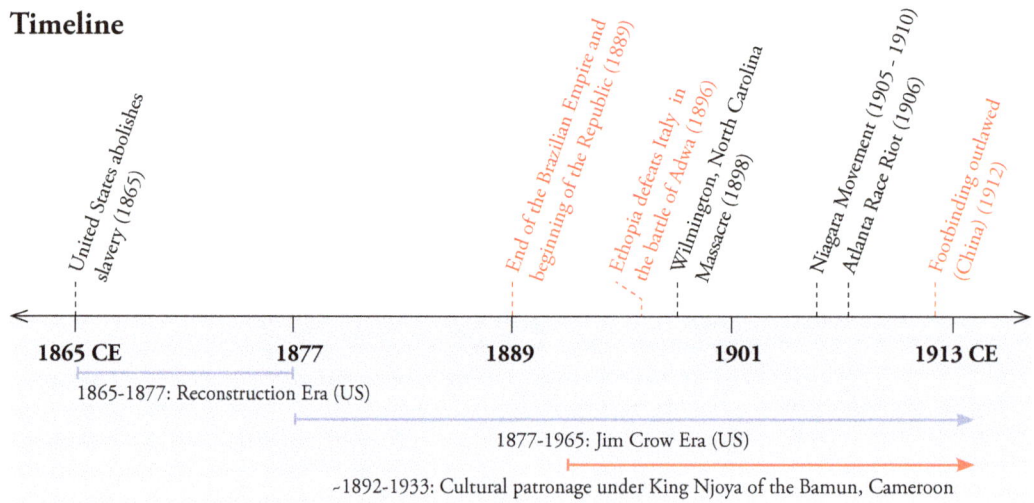

gave him this prominent platform differed from the day-to-day experience of an average African American person at this time in our history. In post–Civil War and Reconstruction America, African Americans were discriminated against and treated as second-class citizens both by way of law and by historically oppressive white social custom. To solidify this condition, new racist and discriminatory laws, eventually termed **Jim Crow laws**, were beginning to take shape across the South. As African Americans were increasingly silenced by legal and extra-legal means, Washington was one of the most sought-after voices by white elites. Indeed, Reconstruction had formally ended two decades before Washington was invited to Atlanta to give his famous address. Washington gave this speech during a period when Jim Crow laws were being considered by white-dominated legislative bodies across the South, and mere months removed from the infamous *Plessy v. Ferguson* (1896) ruling. This Supreme Court decision established the separate-but-equal doctrine making legal the segregationist realities that people in American society were living through at the time. How might this sociopolitical context have impacted Washington's thinking on race relations at the time?

In the fall of 1895 Washington traveled to attend the Cotton States and International Exposition in Atlanta, Georgia. At this exposition, he presented what has been dubbed by some the "Atlanta Compromise Speech," before a predominantly white and affluent audience. This speech was Washington's attempt at providing a means to improve the dire state of race relations between the Black and white populations in American society. Washington's approach was an embodiment of the accommodationist perspective advanced by some at the time; a sentiment echoed in the speech's most famous line: "In all things that are purely social we can be as separate as the fingers, yet one as the hand in all things essential to mutual progress." What is the logic behind this approach? What might be the advantages and disadvantages of taking such a route to address the racial tensions during this time period? With whom might this approach have resonated?

This now-famous speech was well received in some circles and viewed by many as the solution to the racial tensions at the time. This perspective did not go unchallenged, however. W. E. B. Du Bois—one of the period's other intellectual leaders in the Black community—fundamentally disagreed with Washington's viewpoint and challenged his accommodationist approach. For Du Bois, and others that shared his perspective, economic and political rights went hand in hand; Blacks could not advance in a society where they were viewed and treated as second-class citizens. As you read this speech, try to think about what the consequences of Washington's plan would be and how it would have impacted the lives of members of both groups.

Giovanny Pleites-Hernandez
Department of Political Science

> **PRE-READING PARS**
>
> 1. How do our backgrounds influence our decision-making in the political arena? Free write for three minutes on this question.
> 2. To what extent are political and economic rights intertwined? List two or three examples that illustrate your opinion.

Address at the World's Fair in Atlanta (1895)

Mr. President[134] and Gentlemen of the Board of Directors and Citizens: One-third of the population of the South is of the Negro[135] race. No enterprise seeking the material, civil, or moral welfare of this section can disregard this element of our population and reach the highest success. I but convey to you, Mr. President and Directors, the sentiment of the masses of my race when I say that in no way have the value and manhood of the American Negro been more fittingly and generously recognized than by the managers of this magnificent Exposition at every stage of its progress. It is a recognition that will do more to cement the friendship of the two races than any occurrence since the dawn of our freedom.

Not only this, but the opportunity here afforded will awaken among us a new era of industrial progress. Ignorant and inexperienced, it is not strange that in the first years of our new life we began at the top instead of at the bottom; that a seat in Congress or the state legislature was more sought than real estate or industrial skill; that the political convention or stump speaking had more attractions than starting a dairy farm or truck garden.

A ship lost at sea for many days suddenly sighted a friendly vessel. From the mast of the unfortunate vessel was seen a signal, "Water, water; we die of thirst!" The answer from the friendly vessel at once came back, "Cast down your bucket where you are." A second time the signal, "Water, water; send us water!" ran up from the distressed vessel, and was answered, "Cast down your bucket where you are." The captain of the distressed vessel, at last heeding the injunction, cast down his bucket, and it came up full of fresh, sparkling water from the mouth of the Amazon River. To those of my race who depend on bettering their condition in a foreign land or who underestimate the importance of cultivating friendly relations with the Southern

---

134. President of the Atlanta Exposition (Cotton States Exposition).

135. Washington uses the term "Negro" to refer to his own African American communities as was a prevalent practice within and outside of Black communities from the nineteenth to mid-twentieth centuries. The term "negro" should not be confused with the derogatory n-word. Likewise another term used during the same timeframe, "colored," is outdated and should not be confused with the current usage of "person of color." Words reflecting African American and Black communities' preferences for self-identification continue to shift in meaning and connotation over time.

white man, who is their next-door neighbour, I would say: "Cast down your bucket where you are"—cast it down in making friends in every manly way of the people of all races by whom we are surrounded.

Cast it down in agriculture, mechanics, in commerce, in domestic service, and in the professions. And in this connection it is well to bear in mind that whatever other sins the South may be called to bear, when it comes to business, pure and simple, it is in the South that the Negro is given a man's chance in the commercial world, and in nothing is this Exposition more eloquent than in emphasizing this chance. Our greatest danger is that in the great leap from slavery to freedom we may overlook the fact that the masses of us are to live by the productions of our hands, and fail to keep in mind that we shall prosper in proportion as we learn to dignify and glorify common labour, and put brains and skill into the common occupations of life; shall prosper in proportion as we learn to draw the line between the superficial and the substantial, the ornamental gewgaws of life and the useful. No race can prosper till it learns that there is as much dignity in tilling a field as in writing a poem. It is at the bottom of life we must begin, and not at the top. Nor should we permit our grievances to overshadow our opportunities.

To those of the white race who look to the incoming of those of foreign birth and strange tongue and habits for the prosperity of the South, were I permitted I would repeat what I say to my own race, "Cast down your bucket where you are." Cast it down among the eight millions of Negroes whose habits you know, whose fidelity and love you have tested in days when to have proved treacherous meant the ruin of your firesides. Cast down your bucket among these people who have, without strikes and labour wars, tilled your fields, cleared your forests, built your railroads and cities, and brought forth treasures from the bowels of the earth, and helped make possible this magnificent representation of the progress of the South. Casting down your bucket among my people, helping and encouraging them as you are doing on these grounds, and to education of head, hand, and heart, you will find that they will buy your surplus land, make blossom the waste places in your fields, and run your factories. While doing this, you can be sure in the future, as in the past, that you and your families will be surrounded by the most patient, faithful, law-abiding, and unresentful people that the world has seen. As we have proved our loyalty to you in the past, in nursing your children, watching by the sick-bed of your mothers and fathers, and often following them with tear-dimmed eyes to their graves, so in the future, in our humble way, we shall stand by you with a devotion that no foreigner can approach, ready to lay down our lives, if need be, in defense of yours, interlacing our industrial, commercial, civil, and religious life with yours in a way that shall make the interests of both races one. In all things that are purely social we can be as separate as the fingers, yet one as the hand in all things essential to mutual progress.

There is no defense or security for any of us except in the highest intelligence and development of all. If anywhere there are efforts tending to curtail the fullest growth of the Negro, let these efforts be turned into stimulating, encouraging, and making him the most useful and intelligent citizen. Effort or means so invested will pay a thousand per cent interest. These efforts will be twice blessed—"blessing him that gives and him that takes."

There is no escape through law of man or God from the inevitable:—

The laws of changeless justice bind
Oppressor with oppressed;
And close as sin and suffering joined
We march to fate abreast.

Nearly sixteen millions of hands will aid you in pulling the load upwards, or they will pull against you the load downward. We shall constitute one-third and more of the ignorance and crime of the South, or one-third its intelligence and progress; we shall contribute one-third to the business and industrial prosperity of the South, or we shall prove a veritable body of death, stagnating, depressing, retarding every effort to advance the body politic.

Gentlemen of the Exposition, as we present to you our humble effort at an exhibition of our progress, you must not expect overmuch. Starting thirty years ago with ownership here and there in a few quilts and pumpkins and chickens (gathered from miscellaneous sources), remember the path that has led from these to the inventions and production of agricultural implements, buggies, steam-engines, newspapers, books, statuary, carving, paintings, the management of drug stores and banks, has not been trodden without contact with thorns and thistles. While we take pride in what we exhibit as a result of our independent efforts, we do not for a moment forget that our part in this exhibition would fall far short of your expectations but for the constant help that has come to our educational life, not only from the Southern states, but especially from Northern philanthropists, who have made their gifts a constant stream of blessing and encouragement.

The wisest among my race understand that the agitation of questions of social equality is the extremest folly, and that progress in the enjoyment of all the privileges that will come to us must be the result of severe and constant struggle rather than of artificial forcing. No race that has anything to contribute to the markets of the world is long in any degree ostracized. It is important and right that all privileges of the law be ours, but it is vastly more important that we be prepared for the exercise of these privileges. The opportunity to earn a dollar in a factory just now is worth infinitely more than the opportunity to spend a dollar in an opera-house.

In conclusion, may I repeat that nothing in thirty years has given us more hope and encouragement, and drawn us so near to you of the white race, as this opportunity offered by the Exposition; and here bending, as it were, over the altar that represents the results of the struggles of your race and mine, both starting practically empty-handed three decades ago, I pledge that in your effort to work out the great and intricate problem which God has laid at the doors of the South, you shall have at all times the patient, sympathetic help of my race, only let this be constantly in mind, that, while from representations in these buildings of the product of field, of forest, of mine, of factory, letters, and art, much good will come, yet far above and beyond material benefits will be that higher good, that, let us pray God, will come, in a blotting out of sectional differences and racial animosities and suspicions, in a determination to administer absolute justice, in a willing obedience among all classes to the mandates of law. This, coupled with our material prosperity, will bring into our beloved South a new heaven and a new earth.

Washington, Booker T. "Address at the World's Fair in Atlanta (1895)"

POST-READING PARS

1. In your reading, can you identify two or three factors that influenced Washington's accommodationist approach?
2. What was the basis for Washington's thinking that economic and all other rights could be granted to the African American people separately? Identify them in the reading and restate them in your own words.

Inquiry Corner

Content Questions:

Why does Washington ask Black and white individuals to "Cast down [their] buckets where [they] are"? What does that mean? How is the accompanying story used to make (and develop) his argument?

Critical Questions:

Do you think that the role of government (federal, state, and local) in Washington's vision for Black and white relations moving forward would be effective? Why or why not?

Comparative Question:

How does Washington's approach compare and contrast with those of other advocates of racial equality?

Connection Question:

To what extent do you still see some of the inequities that Washington and other individuals at the time were addressing in their speeches and writing?

BEYOND THE CLASSROOM

» It has been more than a century since Booker T. Washington made his address at the World's Fair in Atlanta, yet racism and white privilege are still rampant in today's society and can be seen and felt in the workplace and throughout the hiring process. In what ways can diversity, equity, and inclusion foster more effective work environments? Why, in the twenty-first century, do we still prefer and exclude individuals based on race?

from *Black Bolshevik* by Harry Haywood

Introduction

Harry Haywood (1898–1985) is the nom de guerre of Haywood Hall. Haywood's work is instrumental in understanding the intersection of alienations of class and race. Haywood thought that economic oppression and racial oppression against African Americans were fundamentally intertwined, and he dedicated his entire adult life to understanding the intricacies of their interrelation and finding ways to eliminate them. Though his family had previously suffered from racist attacks, his political awakening occurred in 1919 shortly after his return from World War I, where he fought in the African American Eighth Regiment of the United States Army. In this excerpt from his autobiography, *Black Bolshevik*,[136] Haywood describes the race riots in Chicago in terms that resemble civil war. He had risked his life for his country to return to lynchings, racist mob violence, and systemic racist police oppression. Haywood went on to fight in the Spanish Civil War (1936–39) against the fascists,[137] and later served in the Merchant Marine during World War II.

Haywood was intrigued by the approach to African American independence advocated by Marcus Garvey,[138] but soon broke with Garveyism when he became convinced that capitalism was part of the problem of the oppression of African Americans and could offer no solution to it. He joined the Communist Party of the United States of America (CPUSA), where he tirelessly directed the attention of fellow Marxists to the racial oppression of African Americans as integral to the class conflict at the heart of Marxism. He rose to prominent positions in the party both nationally and internationally and studied in the International Lenin School in the Soviet Union. Haywood became a delegate of the CPUSA to the International Communist Party, where there was interest in enlisting those who were fighting against racism to join the Marxist cause focused on class struggle.

SNAPSHOT BOX

LANGUAGE: English
PUBLISHED: 1978, Chicago
GENRE: Autobiography
TAGS: Autobiography and Testimony; Class and Caste; Community; Economics; Historiography; History and Ideology; Internationalism; Labor; Race; Struggle, Resistance, and Revolution; War and Brutality

---

136. Harry Haywood, *Black Bolshevik: Autobiography of an Afro-American Communist* (Chicago: Liberator Press, 1978).

137. The United States did not contribute to the fight against the fascist coup that deposed the legally elected Spanish socialist republic. Some Americans, mostly Marxists like Haywood, made the effort independently to fight alongside their Spanish comrades. Compare also the 2002 documentary *Into the Fire* about a group of heroic nurses who were part of the struggle against fascism when their countries ignored the conflict. https://www.imdb.com/title/tt1196180/.

138. Garvey advocated for emancipation of African Americans through separatism. He thought that capitalism could provide the means to the end of freedom through economic success in a separate economy, where Black patrons dealt exclusively with Black-owned businesses.

Timeline

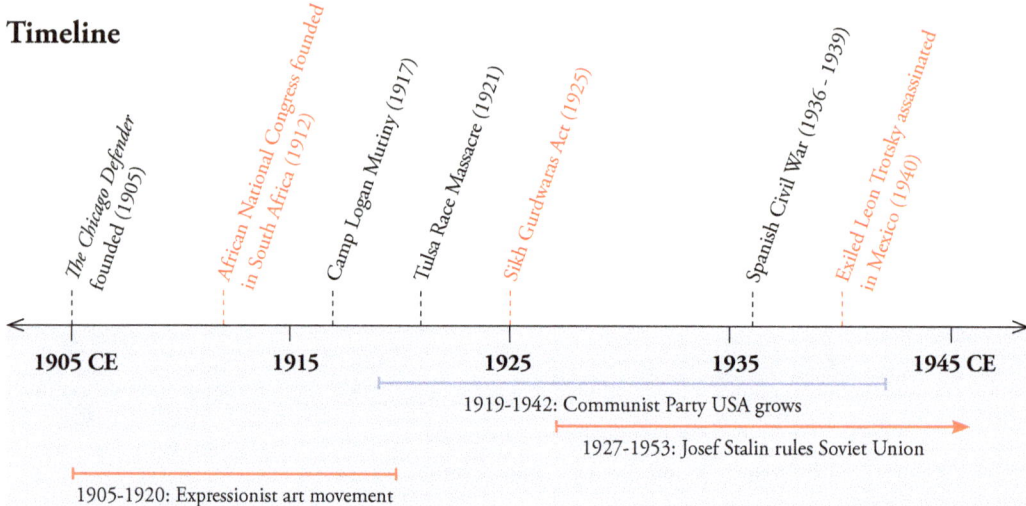

Haywood participated in the internal struggles within Soviet Marxism between Josef Stalin and Leon Trotsky. He ultimately sided with Stalin against the revisionism advocated by the Trotskyites.[139] This alliance with Stalin put Haywood in a powerful position to accomplish his goals of advocating for African American self-sufficiency as part of an international Marxist agenda. He wrote,

> Nowhere, with the exception of apartheid in Southern Africa, had race been made to play such a decisive role [as it was in the United States]. Nowhere had it served for such a long period as an instrument of ruling class oppression. The prominence of racial ideologies in Black oppression in the United States arose from the necessity of white rulers to maintain the degradation of Blacks in the midst of the most modern and advanced capitalist society in the world.[140]

Haywood wanted to establish an independent state in the "Black Belt" region of the Southern United States, where he saw a society in which slaves had been freed only to become wage-slaves or sharecroppers. These unfairly compensated and alienated African American workers lived in poverty even as their labor was recognized as essential by white landowners and business owners to create the highest profit margin for themselves on Southern agriculture and textiles. Haywood sought to organize this potentially powerful group of laborers to fight for economic and

---

139. After the death of Vladimir Lenin, who led the Bolshevik revolution that founded the Union of Soviet Socialist Republics, there was a struggle for leadership of the party. Leon Trotsky led the "left opposition" committed to international revolution and concerned with capitulation to capitalist countries to further internal Soviet industrialization. Stalin kept the focus of the revolution on Soviet matters — partially due to his accurate prediction of turmoil in the next decade of European politics.

140. Haywood, *Black Bolshevik*, 323.

racial equality. However, after Stalin died, Haywood's loyalty to Stalin resulted in his expulsion from the party, which had decided that issues of race were to be addressed after the revolution rather than as part of it. As the CPUSA slowly weakened during the Red Scare of the 1950s, Haywood was instrumental in founding other communist groups in alliance with Maoists and later with the Black Panthers. In creating such alliances, what do you think these groups offer to each other in terms of their focus points and approaches? How might Haywood's alliances reflect an awareness of intersectionality that grounds theorizing in overlapping and interdependent systems of discrimination?

Duane H. Davis
Department of Philosophy

[Content Notice: racial violence, mention of lynching]

from *Black Bolshevik*

Back home in Chicago, I was soon working again as a waiter on the Michigan Central Railroad. As I have already mentioned, the first day of the bloody Chicago race riot (July 28, 1919) came while I was working on the Wolverine run up through Michigan. When I arrived home from work that afternoon, the whole family greeted me emotionally. We were all there except for Otto. The disagreements I had had with my Father in the past were forgotten. Both my Mother and sister were weeping. Everyone was keyed up and had been worrying about my safety in getting from the station to the house.

Following our brief reunion, I tore loose from the family to find out what was happening outside. I went up to the Regimental Armory at Thirty-fifth and Giles Avenue because I wanted to find some of my buddies from the regiment. The street, old Forrest Avenue, had recently been renamed in honor of Lt. Giles, a member of our outfit killed in France. I knew they would be planning an armed defense and I wanted to get in on the action. I found them and they told me their plans. It was rumored that Irishmen from the west of the Wentworth Avenue dividing line were planning to invade the ghetto that night, coming in across the tracks by way of Fifty-first Street. We planned a defensive action to meet them.

It was not surprising that defensive preparations were under way. There had been clashes before, often when white youths in 'athletic clubs' invaded the Black community. These "clubs" were really racist gangs, organized by the city ward heelers and precinct captains.

One of the guys from the regiment took us to the apartment of a friend. It had a good position overlooking Fifty-first Street near State. Someone had brought a Browning submachine gun; he'd gotten it sometime before, most likely from the Regiment Armory. We didn't ask where it had come from, or the origin of the 1903 Springfield rifles (Army issue) that appeared. We set to work mounting the submachine gun and set up watch for the invaders. Fortunately for them, they never arrived and we all returned home in the morning. The following day it rained and the National Guard moved into the Black community, so overt raids by whites did not materialize.

Ours was not the only group which used its recent Army training for self-defense of the Black community. We heard rumors about another group of veterans who set up a similar ambush. On several occasions groups of whites had driven a truck at breakneck speed up south State Street, in the heart of the Black ghetto, with six or seven men in the back firing indiscriminately at the people on the sidewalks.

The Black veterans set up their ambush at Thirty-fifth and State, waiting in a car with the engine running. When the whites on the truck came through, they pulled in behind and opened up with a machine gun. The truck crashed into a telephone pole at Thirty-ninth Street; most of the men in the truck had been shot down and the others fled. Among them were several Chicago police officers – "off duty," of course!

I remember standing before the Angeles Flats on Thirty-fifth and Wabash where the day before four Blacks had been shot by police. It appeared that enraged Blacks had set fire to the building and were attacking some white police officers when the latter fired on them.

Along with other Blacks, I gloated over the mysterious killing of two Black cops with a history of viciousness in the Black community. They had been found dead in an alley between State and Wabash. Undoubtedly they had been killed by Blacks who had taken advantage of the confusion to settle old scores with these Black enforcers of the white man's law.

Bewilderment and shock struck the Black community as well. I had seen Blacks standing before the burned-out buildings of their former homes, trying to salvage whatever possible. Apparent on their faces was bewilderment and anger.

The Chicago rebellion of 1919 was a pivotal point in my life. Always I had been hot-tempered and never took any insults lying down. This was even more true after the war. I had walked out of a number of jobs because of my refusal to take any crap from anyone. My experiences abroad in the Army and at home with the police left me totally disillusioned about being able to find any solution to the racial problem through the help of the government; for I had seen that official agencies of the country were among the most racist and most dangerous to me and my people.

I began to see that I had to fight; I had to commit myself to struggle against whatever it was that made racism possible. Racism, which erupted in the Chicago riot – and the bombings and terrorist attacks which preceded it – must be eliminated. My spirit was not unique – it was shared by many young Blacks at that time. The returned veterans and other young militants were all fighting back. And there was a lot to fight against. Racism reached a high tide in the summer of 1919. This was the "Red Summer" which involved twenty-six race riots across the country – "red" for the blood that ran in the streets. Chicago was the bloodiest.

The holocaust in Chicago was the worst race riot in the nation's post-war history. But riots took place in such widely separate places as Long View, Texas; Charleston, South Carolina; Elaine, Arkansas; Knoxville, Tennessee, and Omaha, Nebraska. The flareup of racial violence in Omaha, my old home town, followed the Chicago riots by less than two months. It resulted in the lynching of Will Brown, a packing house worker, for an alleged assault on a white woman. When Omaha's mayor, Edward P. Smith, sought to intervene, he was seized by the mob. They were close to hanging the mayor from a trolley pole when the police cut the rope and rushed him to a hospital, badly injured.

The common underlying cause of riots in most of the northern cities was the racial tension caused by the migration of tens of thousands of Blacks into these centers and the competition for jobs, housing and the facilities of the city. Rather than being at a temporary peak, this outbreak of racism was more like the rising of a plateau—it never got any higher, but it never really went down, either. Writing in the middle of a riot in Washington, D.C., that summer, the Black poet Claude McKay caught the bitter and belligerent mood of many Blacks:

> *If we must die, let it not be like hogs*
> *Hunted and penned in an inglorious spot,*
> *While round us bark the mad and hungry dogs,*
> *Making their mock at our accursed lot.*
> *If we must die, O let us nobly die*
> *So that our precious blood my not be shed*
> *In vain; then even the monsters we defy*
> *Shall be constrained to honor us though dead!*
> *O kinsmen! We must meet the common foe!*
> *Though far outnumbered let us show us brave,*
> *And for their thousand blows deal one death blow!*
> *What though before us lies the open grave?*
> *Like men we'll face the murderous, cowardly pack,*
> *Pressed to the wall, dying, but fighting back.*

Haywood, Harry. "Searching for Answers." In *Black Bolshevik: Autobiography of an Afro-American Communist*, 81–84. Minneapolis: University of Minnesota Press, 1978. Copyright 1978 by Harry Haywood.

"Grinding Song" (Tigrayan)

Introduction

In most African cultures, singing and drumming is not art for art's sake; it is functional, it is interwoven in the social fabric, it reveals hidden cultural construction, and it displays often unacknowledged forms of creativity. As an artist, educator, and accomplished researcher of many sub-Saharan Africa dance forms, and Ghanaian born and bred, I concur with this idea. To us, singing while working is not ordinary, but a verbal art form. Songs, chants, and ululations (a type of trilling sound connected to both grief and celebration) can be creative participatory expressions that are prevalent during chores and farming as a means of entertainment to essentially ease hard work. Those who are working choose songs selectively as the songs reflect an assessment of the particular experiences of the moment, which may speak directly to one's current relationships, observations, grievances, and other life matters.

Tigray is a group of people residing in northern Ethiopia and Eritrea. They speak the **Tigrinya** language and are referred to as Tigrayans. The countries of Eritrea and Ethiopia and the Tigray people are often neglected in scholarship; only a small amount of information about their culture is accurately represented by historians, anthropologists, linguists, and other researchers. Southern Ethiopia, where famine is now beginning to strike, had a **feudal land system** imposed in the nineteenth century. A feudal land system is a dominant social system

> **SNAPSHOT BOX**
>
> LANGUAGE: Tigrinya
> DATE: Oral history
> LOCATION: Present-day northern Ethiopia and Eritrea
> GENRE: Song
> TAGS: Art; Body; Class; Community; Labor; Poetry, Music, Literature; Self-Determination; Struggle, Resistance, and Revolution

Timeline

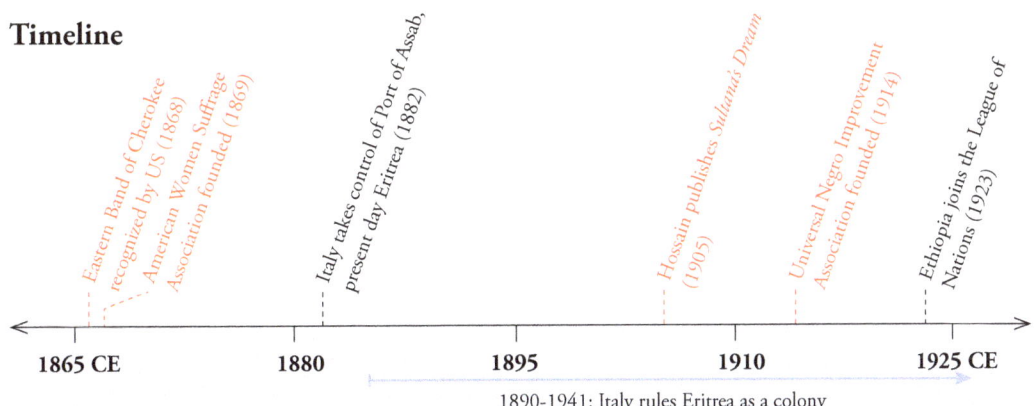

1890-1941: Italy rules Eritrea as a colony

where land is owned and controlled by a monarch or a queen/king. The queen/king only allowed select individuals access as tenants in exchange for service. The service one rendered in exchange for farming or any form of "ownership" of the land could be military service to the monarch, or it could be a sergeantry, such as delivering grain and other duties and demands as assigned by the queen/king. Legitimate personal land ownership was impossible because the titles held were always subservient to the monarch.

The northern provinces, where famine had been historically common, had a system where there were lords of the land, but no landlords, and peasants had the security of access to land even though they paid tithes (percentage of payment or tax of one's income determined by the ruler). The commercialization and mechanization of agriculture in the last generation have eroded those rights. Landlords have become capitalist farmers and a landless class has grown. The famine has accelerated these processes, just as it has been exacerbated by them. What have you heard about Eritrea, Ethiopia, or the Tigray people — in history, art or contemporary news?

"The Grinding Song" is structured in four stanzas, each representing an idea that reflects Tigray cultural norms and contemporary issues they have lived with for centuries. However, this song is set in the nineteenth century. It is performed while grinding grains, on a grinding stone, by a woman within a Tigray family dealing with patriarchy and feudalism in her culture. The frustration, pain, and hurt of the woman fuels the performance of this song with a rhythmic pattern rooted in the grinding process.

Tigray culture is predominantly **patrilineal** and **patrilocal** in inheritance and residence patterns, which puts women in a subordinate position in relation to men. It allows little to no opportunity for women to express themselves in most public venues, especially during decision-making. However, the role of the woman is central in Tigray culture and cannot go unnoticed; it is ingrained in their history and cosmology. They wield social and economic power and influence within their family, especially in the lives of their children. This grinding song sung by a woman, for example, is a response to the social macrocosm in the era of the feudal system in northern Ethiopia and Eritrea. In particular, a large number of the rural population have traditionally been tenants who pay one-third to one-half of their crop production to the landowner depending on such factors as land pressure and fertility. Until land and agrarian reforms are implemented, tenancy exploitation will continue to be one of the principal characteristics of northern Ethiopia and the Eritrea land tenure system.

Women who grind grains consciously incorporate singing and rhythmic elements into the process to alleviate boredom while addressing their burning societal concerns. Grinding is done almost every time a meal is being prepared in a typical Tigray home. Because of its association with food, and the association of food shortages with land tenure, this song is used as a medium to communicate the hunger and discomfort of her family to perpetrators and supporters of feudalism. The words in the song underscore the unhappy conditions feudalism brings to their society and ultimately their culture. In the first stanza, the singer personifies the grains while she grinds. Typically, she echoes this line when she realizes the presence of a feudal landlord, their collaborator or any person of their ilk. Looking on while grinding, the narrator sings of how much harder she has to work and how little food on which she has to survive as compared to the wife of the feudal landlord who sits idle—adorned with gold and henna (a decorative form of body ornamentation).

In the third stanza, she discusses her ideal wish and questions why she was born a woman. She calls out her hardships that follow from the overlap of patriarchy and feudalism, and how she has to work harder for fewer grains, which can only provide food for a single square meal. She laments that *"I can open my heart to no one near, whether they are home or the house is empty, no one speaks to me. My priest is a hen and my friend a grindstone."* This is a sign of loneliness and weariness. She is mostly with her grindstone—and the hen, rooster, and their chicks gather around to peck on the grains fallen on the floor.

The last stanza speaks directly to the husband. She shares despondently the sweat and hard work of her husband, who labors for nothing. The singer is frustrated with her husband, and patrilineality does not give her the leverage to express her frustration to her husband or any man within their society. The wife thus tries to have a rapport with her husband, letting him know that she is there for him and has her support. She is doing this while suggesting a resolution in the form of asking the husband some critical questions to get him to reconsider working within the feudal system.

The song concludes with a vivid description of daily life in this feudal system within the Tigray culture. The song becomes a remorse-filled ballad to her husband asking, *"How do you feel my husband, as you labor for nothing on the land."* Through the song, support and healing is offered to women like her by the singer. This support extends to the men or husbands in their households. What will typically trigger this song is a state of unhappiness, loneliness, and hopelessness that evokes the feeling of vulnerability, injustice, frustration, humiliation, disappointment, and sheer terror of being at someone else's mercy.

Mustapha Braimah
Center for Dance, Music and Theatre, Goucher College

> **PRE-READING PARS**
>
> 1. How do you recuperate after a hard day of work? How do you persevere during a hard day of work?
> 2. What avenues are typically available in society to speak to power and affect change?

Grinding Song (*Tigrayan*)

Hear me, my grains, my grains of wheat—
While I tell my tale.
When we brought you from the harvest fields
You filled the basket to the brim;
But after all that labour on the land,
When you come to the grindstone,
Instead of ten donkey-loads,
You are only a few handfuls.
The feudals have taken it all.

My hands, hear me as you grind,
Not to let fall the smallest grain
And waste it on the floor.
The Lady in the feudal's house
Sits idle, with her hands
Adorned with gold and henna.
But my hands are ground down
With work, and fighting
With this stone—
To ward off hunger.

Why am I born a woman?
For a priest, I make do with a hen;
My grindstone is my only friend.
I can open my heart to no one near,
Whether they are home or the house is empty,
No one speaks to me.
My priest is a hen and my friend a grindstone.

How do you feel, my husband,
As you labour for nothing on the land?
The fire burns bright in the feudal's home,
Where there is soup and meat and milk;

Coming home from the fields
To a house cold and dark
With no fire and no food—
How do you feel, my husband?

"Grinding Song." In *Daughters of Africa: An International Anthology of Words and Writings by Women of African Descent: From the Ancient Egyptian to the Present*, edited by Margaret Busby, 8–9. New York: Ballantine Books, 1994.

> **POST-READING PARS**
>
> 1. What rhetorical strategies does the singer use to respond to hard labor?
> 2. What is your favorite song of resistance? Does it share themes with "Grinding Song?"

Inquiry Corner

Content Question:	**Critical Questions:**
Identify the literary devices used in "Grinding Song" (e.g., alliteration, metaphor, imagery, etc.).	Critically evaluate the strategies of agency this song employs. What is the role of freedom in this song?
Comparative Question:	**Connection Question:**
Consider other readings that focus on gender, class, and/or labor. How does this source compare? Contrast?	In your experience, how might you characterize the relationship between land, food, and work?

from *Manifesto of the Communist Party* by Karl Marx

SNAPSHOT BOX

LANGUAGE: German

PUBLISHED: 1848, Brussels and London

GENRE: Manifesto

TAGS: Class and Caste; Economics; Historiography; History and Ideology; Internationalism; Labor

Introduction

Along with Charles Darwin's *On the Origin of Species* (1859), the *Manifesto for the Communist Party* by Karl Marx (1818–1883) is one the most influential intellectual documents of the nineteenth century. To get an idea of its impact, consider that what is now commonly referred to as *The Communist Manifesto* is one of the four best-selling books of all time (500 million-plus copies), and that in the 1980s, one-third of the world's population lived in countries with governments self-identified as Marxist-Leninist. A strong case can be made that these repressive regimes used the label **communism** as an ideological cover. Some thinkers influenced by Marx have argued that instead of following communism's goal to liberate the working masses, the Soviet Union represented a form of state capitalism in which party bureaucrats, or **apparatchiks**, served as the ruling class. One clue to what Marx himself might have thought of the nominally Marxist bloc comes from his longtime collaborator and financial supporter, Friedrich Engels, who reported that Marx quipped, "What is certain is that I am not a Marxist."

What, then, is **Marxism**? Marx composed *The Communist Manifesto* in 1848, a year remembered as the "Springtime of the Peoples," named for a series of political upheavals that swept across every European state except Russia and England (and from which the Arab Spring of the early 2010s takes its name). Communist ideas started to spread in the 1840s, and the Communist League, an organized left-wing political party, commissioned Marx to write a pamphlet-sized book outlining

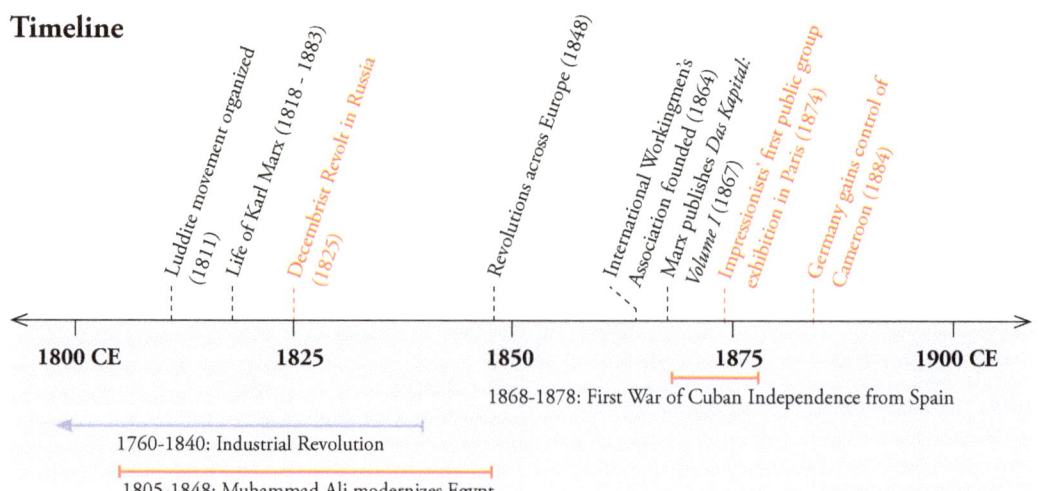

its principles and program. Pressure from local authorities in response to Marx's radical journalism and political writings would force him to renounce his Prussian citizenship and emigrate several times between Paris, Brussels, and Cologne, before eventually settling in London in 1849. Here as a stateless person he wrote his magnum opus, *Das Kapital: Volume I* (1867). Engels published the next two volumes from Marx's notes in 1885 and 1894. While this book represents Marx's most systematic analysis of the contradictions that plague capitalism, *The Communist Manifesto* introduces many of the key ideas that will come to define Marxism. "**Manifesto**," from the Italian *manifestare*, to demonstrate or display, is a genre of writing in which a group or individual publicly declares their beliefs and goals. *The Communist Manifesto* makes clear the theory of **historical materialism**, the modern mode of production called **capitalism**, and the reasons why the **proletariat** will play a revolutionary role in its overthrow.

According to the theory of historical materialism, historical epochs are distinguished by their dominant **mode of production,** and historical change occurs when a new mode of production renders an older one obsolete. In Marxism, the mode of production refers to the material and technical forces that produce a certain kind of society and the social relations that accompany these forces, that is, who does and who gets what. In the capitalist mode of production, for example, human labor and machines transform natural resources into marketable commodities. The social relations in capitalist production, according to Marx, involve two major classes: the capitalists, or **bourgeoisie**, who own the forces of production, from which they must profit, and the proletariat who own nothing but their labor power, which they must sell for wages to buy life's necessities like food, shelter, and leisure. While historical change is constant, the replacement of one mode of production by another has only occurred a handful of times in human history. Much of the early part of *The Communist Manifesto* excerpted here discusses capitalism's overcoming of and distinctness from the feudalist mode of production, an agricultural economy with a strict class system based on heredity. Many commentators have noted how Marx's description of capitalist dynamics not only remains relevant but also rings truer today in the era of globalization. Nevertheless, Marx witnessed antagonisms in mid-nineteenth-century capitalism that he believed threatened the integrity of the entire system, namely the class conflict between the bourgeoisie and proletariat. What examples of conflict between companies and their employees, or property owners and their tenants, are you aware of?

Marx claims that communists "bring to the front . . . the property question," and this distinguishes them from **classical liberals**, like John Locke, for whom ownership of private property forms the basis of freedom (modern liberals, by contrast, believe the government should play an active role in ensuring everyone's basic freedoms). Like Enlightenment thinkers, communists value freedom, but they see its meaning subverted by the private property regime of capitalism. "In place of the numberless indefeasible chartered freedoms," Marx writes, "the present bourgeois conditions of production . . . has set up that single, unconscionable freedom—Free Trade." In other words, the right to own and trade property tends to undermine the vast majority of people's freedoms to be considered equal under the law, to exercise their democratic rights, and to pursue happiness, among others. *The Communist Manifesto* rouses workers of the world to unite in a common struggle to form a mode of production that generates genuine liberty. What do you see as the relationship between private property and freedom and what factors contribute to your view?

Kirk Boyle
Department of English

> **PRE-READING PARS**
>
> 1. What social classes exist in your contemporary society? List a couple of characteristics of each class that set it apart from the others.
> 2. In three sentences, how would you define "capitalism"? What, to you, makes a society capitalist?
> 3. Have you ever felt alienated at a job? What aspects of paid employment make it alienating?

from *Manifesto of the Communist Party*

A spectre is haunting Europe—the spectre of communism. All the powers of old Europe have entered into a holy alliance to exorcise this spectre: Pope and Tsar, Metternich and Guizot, French Radicals and German police-spies.

Where is the party in opposition that has not been decried as communistic by its opponents in power? Where is the opposition that has not hurled back the branding reproach of communism, against the more advanced opposition parties, as well as against its reactionary adversaries?

Two things result from this fact:

I. Communism is already acknowledged by all European powers to be itself a power.

II. It is high time that Communists should openly, in the face of the whole world, publish their views, their aims, their tendencies, and meet this nursery tale of the Spectre of Communism with a manifesto of the party itself.

To this end, Communists of various nationalities have assembled in London and sketched the following manifesto, to be published in the English, French, German, Italian, Flemish and Danish languages.

Chapter I. Bourgeois and Proletarians[141]

The history of all hitherto existing society[142] is the history of class struggles.

Freeman and slave, patrician and plebeian, lord and serf, guild-master[143] and journeyman, in a word, oppressor and oppressed, stood in constant opposition to one another, carried on an uninterrupted, now hidden, now open fight, a fight that each time ended, either in a revolutionary reconstitution of society at large, or in the common ruin of the contending classes.

In the earlier epochs of history, we find almost everywhere a complicated arrangement of society into various orders, a manifold gradation of social rank. In ancient Rome we have patricians, knights, plebeians, slaves; in the Middle Ages, feudal lords, vassals, guild-masters, journeymen, apprentices, serfs; in almost all of these classes, again, subordinate gradations.

The modern bourgeois society that has sprouted from the ruins of feudal society has not done away with class antagonisms. It has but established new classes, new conditions of oppression, new forms of struggle in place of the old ones.

Our epoch, the epoch of the bourgeoisie, possesses, however, this distinct feature: it has simplified class antagonisms. Society as a whole is more and more splitting up into two great hostile camps, into two great classes directly facing each other—Bourgeoisie and Proletariat.

From the serfs of the Middle Ages sprang the chartered burghers of the earliest towns. From these burgesses the first elements of the bourgeoisie were developed.

The discovery of America, the rounding of the Cape, opened up fresh ground for the rising bourgeoisie. The East-Indian and Chinese markets, the colonisation of America, trade with the colonies, the increase in the means of exchange and in commodities generally, gave to commerce, to navigation, to industry, an impulse never

---

141. By bourgeoisie is meant the class of modern capitalists, owners of the means of social production and employers of wage labour. By proletariat, the class of modern wage labourers who, having no means of production of their own, are reduced to selling their labour power in order to live. [Engels, 1888 English edition]

142. That is, all written history. In 1847, the pre-history of society, the social organisation existing previous to recorded history, all but unknown. Since then, August von Haxthausen (1792–1866) discovered common ownership of land in Russia, Georg Ludwig von Maurer proved it to be the social foundation from which all Teutonic races started in history, and, by and by, village communities were found to be, or to have been, the primitive form of society everywhere from India to Ireland. The inner organisation of this primitive communistic society was laid bare, in its typical form, by Lewis Henry Morgan's (1818–1881) crowning discovery of the true nature of the gens and its relation to the tribe. With the dissolution of the primeval communities, society begins to be differentiated into separate and finally antagonistic classes. I have attempted to retrace this dissolution in *The Origin of the Family, Private Property, and the State*, second edition, Stuttgart, 1886. [Engels, 1888 English edition and 1890 German edition (with the last sentence omitted)]

143. Guild-master, that is, a full member of a guild, a master within, not a head of a guild. [Engels, 1888 English edition]

before known, and thereby, to the revolutionary element in the tottering feudal society, a rapid development.

The feudal system of industry, in which industrial production was monopolised by closed guilds, now no longer sufficed for the growing wants of the new markets. The manufacturing system took its place. The guild-masters were pushed on one side by the manufacturing middle class; division of labour between the different corporate guilds vanished in the face of division of labour in each single workshop.

Meantime the markets kept ever growing, the demand ever rising. Even manufacture no longer sufficed. Thereupon, steam and machinery revolutionised industrial production. The place of manufacture was taken by the giant, Modern Industry, the place of the industrial middle class by industrial millionaires, the leaders of the whole industrial armies, the modern bourgeois.

Modern industry has established the world market, for which the discovery of America paved the way. This market has given an immense development to commerce, to navigation, to communication by land. This development has, in its turn, reacted on the extension of industry; and in proportion as industry, commerce, navigation, railways extended, in the same proportion the bourgeoisie developed, increased its capital, and pushed into the background every class handed down from the Middle Ages.

We see, therefore, how the modern bourgeoisie is itself the product of a long course of development, of a series of revolutions in the modes of production and of exchange.

Each step in the development of the bourgeoisie was accompanied by a corresponding political advance of that class. An oppressed class under the sway of the feudal nobility, an armed and self-governing association in the medieval commune[144]: here independent urban republic (as in Italy and Germany); there taxable "third estate" of the monarchy (as in France); afterwards, in the period of manufacturing proper, serving either the semi-feudal or the absolute monarchy as a counterpoise against the nobility, and, in fact, cornerstone of the great monarchies in general, the bourgeoisie has at last, since the establishment of Modern Industry and of the world market, conquered for itself, in the modern representative State, exclusive political sway. The executive of the modern state is but a committee for managing the common affairs of the whole bourgeoisie.

The bourgeoisie, historically, has played a most revolutionary part.

The bourgeoisie, wherever it has got the upper hand, has put an end to all feu-

---

144. This was the name given their urban communities by the townsmen of Italy and France, after they had purchased or conquered their initial rights of self-government from their feudal lords. [Engels, 1890 German edition]

"Commune" was the name taken in France by the nascent towns even before they had conquered from their feudal lords and masters local self-government and political rights as the "Third Estate." Generally speaking, for the economical development of the bourgeoisie, England is here taken as the typical country, for its political development, France. [Engels, 1888 English edition]

dal, patriarchal, idyllic relations. It has pitilessly torn asunder the motley feudal ties that bound man to his "natural superiors," and has left remaining no other nexus between man and man than naked self-interest, than callous "cash payment." It has drowned the most heavenly ecstasies of religious fervour, of chivalrous enthusiasm, of philistine sentimentalism, in the icy water of egotistical calculation. It has resolved personal worth into exchange value, and in place of the numberless indefeasible chartered freedoms, has set up that single, unconscionable freedom—Free Trade. In one word, for exploitation, veiled by religious and political illusions, it has substituted naked, shameless, direct, brutal exploitation.

The bourgeoisie has stripped of its halo every occupation hitherto honoured and looked up to with reverent awe. It has converted the physician, the lawyer, the priest, the poet, the man of science, into its paid wage labourers.

The bourgeoisie has torn away from the family its sentimental veil, and has reduced the family relation to a mere money relation.

The bourgeoisie has disclosed how it came to pass that the brutal display of vigour in the Middle Ages, which reactionaries so much admire, found its fitting complement in the most slothful indolence. It has been the first to show what man's activity can bring about. It has accomplished wonders far surpassing Egyptian pyramids, Roman aqueducts, and Gothic cathedrals; it has conducted expeditions that put in the shade all former Exoduses of nations and crusades.

The bourgeoisie cannot exist without constantly revolutionising the instruments of production, and thereby the relations of production, and with them the whole relations of society. Conservation of the old modes of production in unaltered form, was, on the contrary, the first condition of existence for all earlier industrial classes. Constant revolutionising of production, uninterrupted disturbance of all social conditions, everlasting uncertainty and agitation distinguish the bourgeois epoch from all earlier ones. All fixed, fast-frozen relations, with their train of ancient and venerable prejudices and opinions, are swept away, all new-formed ones become antiquated before they can ossify. All that is solid melts into air, all that is holy is profaned, and man is at last compelled to face with sober senses his real conditions of life, and his relations with his kind.

The need of a constantly expanding market for its products chases the bourgeoisie over the entire surface of the globe. It must nestle everywhere, settle everywhere, establish connexions everywhere.

The bourgeoisie has through its exploitation of the world market given a cosmopolitan character to production and consumption in every country. To the great chagrin of Reactionists, it has drawn from under the feet of industry the national ground on which it stood. All old-established national industries have been destroyed or are daily being destroyed. They are dislodged by new industries, whose introduction becomes a life and death question for all civilised nations, by industries that no longer work up indigenous raw material, but raw material drawn from the remotest zones;

industries whose products are consumed, not only at home, but in every quarter of the globe. In place of the old wants, satisfied by the production of the country, we find new wants, requiring for their satisfaction the products of distant lands and climes. In place of the old local and national seclusion and self-sufficiency, we have intercourse in every direction, universal inter-dependence of nations. And as in material, so also in intellectual production. The intellectual creations of individual nations become common property. National one-sidedness and narrow-mindedness become more and more impossible, and from the numerous national and local literatures, there arises a world literature.

The bourgeoisie, by the rapid improvement of all instruments of production, by the immensely facilitated means of communication, draws all, even the most barbarian, nations into civilisation. The cheap prices of commodities are the heavy artillery with which it batters down all Chinese walls, with which it forces the barbarians' intensely obstinate hatred of foreigners to capitulate. It compels all nations, on pain of extinction, to adopt the bourgeois mode of production; it compels them to introduce what it calls civilisation into their midst, i.e., to become bourgeois themselves. In one word, it creates a world after its own image.

The bourgeoisie has subjected the country to the rule of the towns. It has created enormous cities, has greatly increased the urban population as compared with the rural, and has thus rescued a considerable part of the population from the idiocy of rural life. Just as it has made the country dependent on the towns, so it has made barbarian and semi-barbarian countries dependent on the civilised ones, nations of peasants on nations of bourgeois, the East on the West.

The bourgeoisie keeps more and more doing away with the scattered state of the population, of the means of production, and of property. It has agglomerated population, centralised the means of production, and has concentrated property in a few hands. The necessary consequence of this was political centralisation. Independent, or but loosely connected provinces, with separate interests, laws, governments, and systems of taxation, became lumped together into one nation, with one government, one code of laws, one national class-interest, one frontier, and one customs-tariff.

The bourgeoisie, during its rule of scarce one hundred years, has created more massive and more colossal productive forces than have all preceding generations together. Subjection of Nature's forces to man, machinery, application of chemistry to industry and agriculture, steam-navigation, railways, electric telegraphs, clearing of whole continents for cultivation, canalisation of rivers, whole populations conjured out of the ground—what earlier century had even a presentiment that such productive forces slumbered in the lap of social labour?

We see then: the means of production and of exchange, on whose foundation the bourgeoisie built itself up, were generated in feudal society. At a certain stage in the development of these means of production and of exchange, the conditions under which feudal society produced and exchanged, the feudal organisation of agriculture and manufacturing industry, in one word, the feudal relations of property became no longer compatible with the already developed productive forces; they became so many fetters. They had to be burst asunder; they were burst asunder.

Into their place stepped free competition, accompanied by a social and political constitution adapted in it, and the economic and political sway of the bourgeois class.

A similar movement is going on before our own eyes. Modern bourgeois society, with its relations of production, of exchange and of property, a society that has conjured up such gigantic means of production and of exchange, is like the sorcerer who is no longer able to control the powers of the nether world whom he has called up by his spells. For many a decade past the history of industry and commerce is but the history of the revolt of modern productive forces against modern conditions of production, against the property relations that are the conditions for the existence of the bourgeois and of its rule. It is enough to mention the commercial crises that by their periodical return put the existence of the entire bourgeois society on its trial, each time more threateningly. In these crises, a great part not only of the existing products, but also of the previously created productive forces, are periodically destroyed. In these crises, there breaks out an epidemic that, in all earlier epochs, would have seemed an absurdity—the epidemic of over-production. Society suddenly finds itself put back into a state of momentary barbarism; it appears as if a famine, a universal war of devastation, had cut off the supply of every means of subsistence; industry and commerce seem to be destroyed; and why? Because there is too much civilisation, too much means of subsistence, too much industry, too much commerce. The productive forces at the disposal of society no longer tend to further the development of the conditions of bourgeois property; on the contrary, they have become too powerful for these conditions, by which they are fettered, and so soon as they overcome these fetters, they bring disorder into the whole of bourgeois society, endanger the existence of bourgeois property. The conditions of bourgeois society are too narrow to comprise the wealth created by them. And how does the bourgeoisie get over these crises? On the one hand by enforced destruction of a mass of productive forces; on the other, by the conquest of new markets, and by the more thorough exploitation of the old ones. That is to say, by paving the way for more extensive and more destructive crises, and by diminishing the means whereby crises are prevented.

The weapons with which the bourgeoisie felled feudalism to the ground are now turned against the bourgeoisie itself.

But not only has the bourgeoisie forged the weapons that bring death to itself; it has also called into existence the men who are to wield those weapons—the modern working class—the proletarians.

In proportion as the bourgeoisie, i.e., capital, is developed, in the same proportion is the proletariat, the modern working class, developed—a class of labourers, who live only so long as they find work, and who find work only so long as their labour increases capital. These labourers, who must sell themselves piecemeal, are a commodity, like every other article of commerce, and are consequently exposed to all the vicissitudes of competition, to all the fluctuations of the market.

Owing to the extensive use of machinery, and to the division of labour, the work of the proletarians has lost all individual character, and, consequently, all charm for the workman. He becomes an appendage of the machine, and it is only the most simple, most monotonous, and most easily acquired knack, that is required of him. Hence, the cost of production of a workman is restricted, almost entirely, to the means of subsistence that he requires for maintenance, and for the propagation of his race. But the price of a commodity, and therefore also of labour, is equal to its cost of production. In proportion, therefore, as the repulsiveness of the work increases, the wage decreases. Nay more, in proportion as the use of machinery and division of labour increases, in the same proportion the burden of toil also increases, whether by prolongation of the working hours, by the increase of the work exacted in a given time or by increased speed of machinery, etc.

Modern Industry has converted the little workshop of the patriarchal master into the great factory of the industrial capitalist. Masses of labourers, crowded into the factory, are organised like soldiers. As privates of the industrial army they are placed under the command of a perfect hierarchy of officers and sergeants. Not only are they slaves of the bourgeois class, and of the bourgeois State; they are daily and hourly enslaved by the machine, by the overlooker, and, above all, by the individual bourgeois manufacturer himself. The more openly this despotism proclaims gain to be its end and aim, the more petty, the more hateful and the more embittering it is.

The less the skill and exertion of strength implied in manual labour, in other words, the more modern industry becomes developed, the more is the labour of men superseded by that of women. Differences of age and sex have no longer any distinctive social validity for the working class. All are instruments of labour, more or less expensive to use, according to their age and sex.

No sooner is the exploitation of the labourer by the manufacturer, so far, at an end, that he receives his wages in cash, than he is set upon by the other portions of the bourgeoisie, the landlord, the shopkeeper, the pawnbroker, etc.

The lower strata of the middle class—the small tradespeople, shopkeepers, and retired tradesmen generally, the handicraftsmen and peasants—all these sink gradually into the proletariat, partly because their diminutive capital does not suffice for the scale on which Modern Industry is carried on, and is swamped in the competition with the large capitalists, partly because their specialised skill is rendered worthless by new methods of production. Thus the proletariat is recruited from all classes of the population.

The proletariat goes through various stages of development. With its birth begins its struggle with the bourgeoisie. At first the contest is carried on by individual labourers, then by the workpeople of a factory, then by the operative of one trade, in one locality, against the individual bourgeois who directly exploits them. They direct their attacks not against the bourgeois conditions of production, but against the instruments of production themselves; they destroy imported wares that compete with their labour, they smash to pieces machinery, they set factories ablaze, they seek to restore by force the vanished status of the workman of the Middle Ages.

At this stage, the labourers still form an incoherent mass scattered over the whole country, and broken up by their mutual competition. If anywhere they unite to form more compact bodies, this is not yet the consequence of their own active union, but of the union of the bourgeoisie, which class, in order to attain its own political ends, is compelled to set the whole proletariat in motion, and is moreover yet, for a time, able to do so. At this stage, therefore, the proletarians do not fight their enemies, but the enemies of their enemies, the remnants of absolute monarchy, the landowners, the non-industrial bourgeois, the petty bourgeois. Thus, the whole historical movement is concentrated in the hands of the bourgeoisie; every victory so obtained is a victory for the bourgeoisie.

But with the development of industry, the proletariat not only increases in number; it becomes concentrated in greater masses, its strength grows, and it feels that strength more. The various interests and conditions of life within the ranks of the proletariat are more and more equalised, in proportion as machinery obliterates all distinctions of labour, and nearly everywhere reduces wages to the same low level. The growing competition among the bourgeois, and the resulting commercial crises, make the wages of the workers ever more fluctuating. The increasing improvement of machinery, ever more rapidly developing, makes their livelihood more and more precarious; the collisions between individual workmen and individual bourgeois take more and more the character of collisions between two classes. Thereupon, the workers begin to form combinations (Trades' Unions) against the bourgeois; they club together in order to keep up the rate of wages; they found permanent associations in order to make provision beforehand for these occasional revolts. Here and there, the contest breaks out into riots.

Now and then the workers are victorious, but only for a time. The real fruit of their battles lies, not in the immediate result, but in the ever expanding union of the workers. This union is helped on by the improved means of communication that are created by modern industry, and that place the workers of different localities in contact with one another. It was just this contact that was needed to centralise the numerous local struggles, all of the same character, into one national struggle between classes. But every class struggle is a political struggle. And that union, to attain which the burghers of the Middle Ages, with their miserable highways, required centuries, the modern proletarian, thanks to railways, achieve in a few years.

This organisation of the proletarians into a class, and, consequently into a political party, is continually being upset again by the competition between the workers themselves. But it ever rises up again, stronger, firmer, mightier. It compels legislative recognition of particular interests of the workers, by taking advantage of the divisions among the bourgeoisie itself. Thus, the ten-hours' bill in England was carried.

Altogether collisions between the classes of the old society further, in many ways, the course of development of the proletariat. The bourgeoisie finds itself involved in a constant battle. At first with the aristocracy; later on, with those portions of the bourgeoisie itself, whose interests have become antagonistic to the progress of industry; at all time with the bourgeoisie of foreign countries. In all these battles, it sees itself compelled to appeal to the proletariat, to ask for help, and thus, to drag it into the political arena. The bourgeoisie itself, therefore, supplies the proletariat with its own elements of political and general education, in other words, it furnishes the proletariat with weapons for fighting the bourgeoisie.

Further, as we have already seen, entire sections of the ruling class are, by the advance of industry, precipitated into the proletariat, or are at least threatened in their conditions of existence. These also supply the proletariat with fresh elements of enlightenment and progress.

Finally, in times when the class struggle nears the decisive hour, the progress of dissolution going on within the ruling class, in fact within the whole range of old society, assumes such a violent, glaring character, that a small section of the ruling class cuts itself adrift, and joins the revolutionary class, the class that holds the future in its hands. Just as, therefore, at an earlier period, a section of the nobility went over to the bourgeoisie, so now a portion of the bourgeoisie goes over to the proletariat, and in particular, a portion of the bourgeois ideologists, who have raised themselves to the level of comprehending theoretically the historical movement as a whole.

Of all the classes that stand face to face with the bourgeoisie today, the proletariat alone is a really revolutionary class. The other classes decay and finally disappear in the face of Modern Industry; the proletariat is its special and essential product.

The lower middle class, the small manufacturer, the shopkeeper, the artisan, the peasant, all these fight against the bourgeoisie, to save from extinction their existence as fractions of the middle class. They are therefore not revolutionary, but conservative. Nay more, they are reactionary, for they try to roll back the wheel of history. If by chance, they are revolutionary, they are only so in view of their impending transfer into the proletariat; they thus defend not their present, but their future interests, they desert their own standpoint to place themselves at that of the proletariat.

The "dangerous class," [*lumpenproletariat*] the social scum, that passively rotting mass thrown off by the lowest layers of the old society, may, here and there, be swept into the movement by a proletarian revolution; its conditions of life, however, prepare it far more for the part of a bribed tool of reactionary intrigue.

In the condition of the proletariat, those of old society at large are already virtually swamped. The proletarian is without property; his relation to his wife and children has no longer anything in common with the bourgeois family relations; modern industry labour, modern subjection to capital, the same in England as in France, in America as in Germany, has stripped him of every trace of national character. Law, morality, religion, are to him so many bourgeois prejudices, behind which lurk in ambush just as many bourgeois interests.

All the preceding classes that got the upper hand sought to fortify their already acquired status by subjecting society at large to their conditions of appropriation. The proletarians cannot become masters of the productive forces of society, except by abolishing their own previous mode of appropriation, and thereby also every other previous mode of appropriation. They have nothing of their own to secure and to fortify; their mission is to destroy all previous securities for, and insurances of, individual property.

All previous historical movements were movements of minorities, or in the interest of minorities. The proletarian movement is the self-conscious, independent movement of the immense majority, in the interest of the immense majority. The proletariat, the lowest stratum of our present society, cannot stir, cannot raise itself up, without the whole superincumbent strata of official society being sprung into the air.

Though not in substance, yet in form, the struggle of the proletariat with the bourgeoisie is at first a national struggle. The proletariat of each country must, of course, first of all settle matters with its own bourgeoisie.

In depicting the most general phases of the development of the proletariat, we traced the more or less veiled civil war, raging within existing society, up to the point where that war breaks out into open revolution, and where the violent overthrow of the bourgeoisie lays the foundation for the sway of the proletariat.

Hitherto, every form of society has been based, as we have already seen, on the antagonism of oppressing and oppressed classes. But in order to oppress a class, certain conditions must be assured to it under which it can, at least, continue its slavish existence. The serf, in the period of serfdom, raised himself to membership in the commune, just as the petty bourgeois, under the yoke of the feudal absolutism, managed to develop into a bourgeois. The modern labourer, on the contrary, instead of rising with the process of industry, sinks deeper and deeper below the conditions of existence of his own class. He becomes a pauper, and pauperism develops more rapidly than population and wealth. And here it becomes evident, that the bourgeoisie is unfit any longer to be the ruling class in society, and to impose its conditions of existence upon society as an over-riding law. It is unfit to rule because it is incompetent to assure an existence to its slave within his slavery, because it cannot help letting him sink into such a state, that it has to feed him, instead of being fed by him. Society can no longer live under this bourgeoisie, in other words, its existence is no longer compatible with society.

The essential conditions for the existence and for the sway of the bourgeois class is the formation and augmentation of capital; the condition for capital is wage-labour. Wage-labour rests exclusively on competition between the labourers. The advance of industry, whose involuntary promoter is the bourgeoisie, replaces the isolation of the labourers, due to competition, by the revolutionary combination, due to association. The development of Modern Industry, therefore, cuts from under its feet the very foundation on which the bourgeoisie produces and appropriates products. What the bourgeoisie therefore produces, above all, are its own grave-diggers. Its fall and the victory of the proletariat are equally inevitable.

Chapter II. Proletarians and Communists

In what relation do the Communists stand to the proletarians as a whole?

The Communists do not form a separate party opposed to the other working-class parties.

They have no interests separate and apart from those of the proletariat as a whole.

They do not set up any sectarian principles of their own, by which to shape and mould the proletarian movement.

The Communists are distinguished from the other working-class parties by this only: 1. In the national struggles of the proletarians of the different countries, they point out and bring to the front the common interests of the entire proletariat, independently of all nationality. 2. In the various stages of development which the struggle of the working class against the bourgeoisie has to pass through, they always and everywhere represent the interests of the movement as a whole.

The Communists, therefore, are on the one hand, practically, the most advanced and resolute section of the working-class parties of every country, that section which pushes forward all others; on the other hand, theoretically, they have over the great mass of the proletariat the advantage of clearly understanding the line of march, the conditions, and the ultimate general results of the proletarian movement.

The immediate aim of the Communists is the same as that of all other proletarian parties: formation of the proletariat into a class, overthrow of the bourgeois supremacy, conquest of political power by the proletariat.

The theoretical conclusions of the Communists are in no way based on ideas or principles that have been invented, or discovered, by this or that would-be universal reformer.

They merely express, in general terms, actual relations springing from an existing class struggle, from a historical movement going on under our very eyes. The abolition of existing property relations is not at all a distinctive feature of communism.

All property relations in the past have continually been subject to historical change consequent upon the change in historical conditions.

The French Revolution, for example, abolished feudal property in favour of bourgeois property.

The distinguishing feature of Communism is not the abolition of property generally, but the abolition of bourgeois property. But modern bourgeois private property is the final and most complete expression of the system of producing and appropriating products, that is based on class antagonisms, on the exploitation of the many by the few.

In this sense, the theory of the Communists may be summed up in the single sentence: Abolition of private property.

We Communists have been reproached with the desire of abolishing the right of personally acquiring property as the fruit of a man's own labour, which property is alleged to be the groundwork of all personal freedom, activity and independence.

Hard-won, self-acquired, self-earned property! Do you mean the property of petty artisan and of the small peasant, a form of property that preceded the bourgeois form? There is no need to abolish that; the development of industry has to a great extent already destroyed it, and is still destroying it daily.

Or do you mean the modern bourgeois private property?

But does wage-labour create any property for the labourer? Not a bit. It creates capital, i.e., that kind of property which exploits wage-labour, and which cannot increase except upon condition of begetting a new supply of wage-labour for fresh exploitation. Property, in its present form, is based on the antagonism of capital and wage labour. Let us examine both sides of this antagonism.

To be a capitalist, is to have not only a purely personal, but a social *status* in production. Capital is a collective product, and only by the united action of many members, nay, in the last resort, only by the united action of all members of society, can it be set in motion.

Capital is therefore not only personal; it is a social power.

When, therefore, capital is converted into common property, into the property of all members of society, personal property is not thereby transformed into social property. It is only the social character of the property that is changed. It loses its class character.

Let us now take wage-labour.

The average price of wage-labour is the minimum wage, i.e., that quantum of the means of subsistence which is absolutely requisite to keep the labourer in bare existence as a labourer. What, therefore, the wage-labourer appropriates by means of his labour, merely suffices to prolong and reproduce a bare existence. We by no means intend to abolish this personal appropriation of the products of labour, an appropriation that is made for the maintenance and reproduction of human life, and that leaves no surplus wherewith to command the labour of others. All that we want to do away with is the miserable character of this appropriation, under which the labourer lives merely to increase capital, and is allowed to live only in so far as the interest of the ruling class requires it.

In bourgeois society, living labour is but a means to increase accumulated labour. In Communist society, accumulated labour is but a means to widen, to enrich, to promote the existence of the labourer.

In bourgeois society, therefore, the past dominates the present; in Communist society, the present dominates the past. In bourgeois society capital is independent and has individuality, while the living person is dependent and has no individuality.

And the abolition of this state of things is called by the bourgeois, abolition of individuality and freedom! And rightly so. The abolition of bourgeois individuality, bourgeois independence, and bourgeois freedom is undoubtedly aimed at.

By freedom is meant, under the present bourgeois conditions of production, free trade, free selling and buying.

But if selling and buying disappears, free selling and buying disappears also. This talk about free selling and buying, and all the other "brave words" of our bourgeois about freedom in general, have a meaning, if any, only in contrast with restricted selling and buying, with the fettered traders of the Middle Ages, but have no meaning when opposed to the Communistic abolition of buying and selling, of the bourgeois conditions of production, and of the bourgeoisie itself.

You are horrified at our intending to do away with private property. But in your existing society, private property is already done away with for nine-tenths of the population; its existence for the few is solely due to its non-existence in the hands of those nine-tenths. You reproach us, therefore, with intending to do away with a form of property, the necessary condition for whose existence is the non-existence of any property for the immense majority of society.

In one word, you reproach us with intending to do away with your property. Precisely so; that is just what we intend.

From the moment when labour can no longer be converted into capital, money, or rent, into a social power capable of being monopolised, i.e., from the moment when individual property can no longer be transformed into bourgeois property, into capital, from that moment, you say, individuality vanishes.

You must, therefore, confess that by "individual" you mean no other person than the bourgeois, than the middle-class owner of property. This person must, indeed, be swept out of the way, and made impossible.

Communism deprives no man of the power to appropriate the products of society; all that it does is to deprive him of the power to subjugate the labour of others by means of such appropriations.

It has been objected that upon the abolition of private property, all work will cease, and universal laziness will overtake us.

According to this, bourgeois society ought long ago to have gone to the dogs through sheer idleness; for those of its members who work, acquire nothing, and those who acquire anything do not work. The whole of this objection is but another expression of the tautology: that there can no longer be any wage-labour when there is no longer any capital.

All objections urged against the Communistic mode of producing and appropriating material products, have, in the same way, been urged against the Communistic mode of producing and appropriating intellectual products. Just as, to the bourgeois, the disappearance of class property is the disappearance of production itself, so the disappearance of class culture is to him identical with the disappearance of all culture.

That culture, the loss of which he laments, is, for the enormous majority, a mere training to act as a machine.

But don't wrangle with us so long as you apply, to our intended abolition of bourgeois property, the standard of your bourgeois notions of freedom, culture, law, &c. Your very ideas are but the outgrowth of the conditions of your bourgeois production and bourgeois property, just as your jurisprudence is but the will of your class made into a law for all, a will whose essential character and direction are determined by the economical conditions of existence of your class.

The selfish misconception that induces you to transform into eternal laws of nature and of reason, the social forms springing from your present mode of production and form of property—historical relations that rise and disappear in the progress of production—this misconception you share with every ruling class that has preceded you. What you see clearly in the case of ancient property, what you admit in the case of feudal property, you are of course forbidden to admit in the case of your own bourgeois form of property.

Abolition [*Aufhebung*] of the family! Even the most radical flare up at this infamous proposal of the Communists.

On what foundation is the present family, the bourgeois family, based? On capital, on private gain. In its completely developed form, this family exists only among the bourgeoisie. But this state of things finds its complement in the practical absence of the family among the proletarians, and in public prostitution.

The bourgeois family will vanish as a matter of course when its complement vanishes, and both will vanish with the vanishing of capital.

Do you charge us with wanting to stop the exploitation of children by their parents? To this crime we plead guilty.

But, you say, we destroy the most hallowed of relations, when we replace home education by social.

And your education! Is not that also social, and determined by the social conditions under which you educate, by the intervention direct or indirect, of society, by means of schools, etc.? The Communists have not invented the intervention of society in education; they do but seek to alter the character of that intervention, and to rescue education from the influence of the ruling class.

The bourgeois clap-trap about the family and education, about the hallowed co-relation of parents and child, becomes all the more disgusting, the more, by the action of Modern Industry, all the family ties among the proletarians are torn asunder, and their children transformed into simple articles of commerce and instruments of labour.

But you Communists would introduce community of women, screams the bourgeoisie in chorus.

The bourgeois sees his wife as a mere instrument of production. He hears that the instruments of production are to be exploited in common, and, naturally, can come to no other conclusion than that the lot of being common to all will likewise fall to the women.

He has not even a suspicion that the real point aimed at is to do away with the status of women as mere instruments of production.

For the rest, nothing is more ridiculous than the virtuous indignation of our bourgeois at the community of women which, they pretend, is to be openly and officially established by the Communists. The Communists have no need to introduce community of women; it has existed almost from time immemorial.

Our bourgeois, not content with having wives and daughters of their proletarians at their disposal, not to speak of common prostitutes, take the greatest pleasure in seducing each other's wives.

Bourgeois marriage is, in reality, a system of wives in common and thus, at the most, what the Communists might possibly be reproached with is that they desire to introduce, in substitution for a hypocritically concealed, an openly legalised community of women. For the rest, it is self-evident that the abolition of the present system of production must bring with it the abolition of the community of women springing from that system, i.e., of prostitution both public and private.

The Communists are further reproached with desiring to abolish countries and nationality.

The working men have no country. We cannot take from them what they have not got. Since the proletariat must first of all acquire political supremacy, must rise to be the leading class of the nation, must constitute itself *the* nation, it is so far, itself national, though not in the bourgeois sense of the word.

National differences and antagonism between peoples are daily more and more vanishing, owing to the development of the bourgeoisie, to freedom of commerce, to the world market, to uniformity in the mode of production and in the conditions of life corresponding thereto.

The supremacy of the proletariat will cause them to vanish still faster. United action, of the leading civilised countries at least, is one of the first conditions for the emancipation of the proletariat.

In proportion as the exploitation of one individual by another will also be put an end to, the exploitation of one nation by another will also be put an end to. In proportion as the antagonism between classes within the nation vanishes, the hostility of one nation to another will come to an end.

The charges against Communism made from a religious, a philosophical and, generally, from an ideological standpoint, are not deserving of serious examination.

Does it require deep intuition to comprehend that man's ideas, views, and conception, in one word, man's consciousness, changes with every change in the conditions of his material existence, in his social relations and in his social life?

What else does the history of ideas prove, than that intellectual production changes its character in proportion as material production is changed? The ruling ideas of each age have ever been the ideas of its ruling class.

When people speak of the ideas that revolutionise society, they do but express that fact that within the old society the elements of a new one have been created, and that the dissolution of the old ideas keeps even pace with the dissolution of the old conditions of existence.

When the ancient world was in its last throes, the ancient religions were overcome by Christianity. When Christian ideas succumbed in the eighteenth century to rationalist ideas, feudal society fought its death battle with the then revolutionary bourgeoisie. The ideas of religious liberty and freedom of conscience merely gave expression to the sway of free competition within the domain of knowledge.

"Undoubtedly," it will be said, "religious, moral, philosophical, and juridical ideas have been modified in the course of historical development. But religion, morality, philosophy, political science, and law, constantly survived this change."

"There are, besides, eternal truths, such as Freedom, Justice, etc., that are common to all states of society. But Communism abolishes eternal truths, it abolishes all religion, and all morality, instead of constituting them on a new basis; it therefore acts in contradiction to all past historical experience."

What does this accusation reduce itself to? The history of all past society has consisted in the development of class antagonisms, antagonisms that assumed different forms at different epochs.

But whatever form they may have taken, one fact is common to all past ages, viz., the exploitation of one part of society by the other. No wonder, then, that the social consciousness of past ages, despite all the multiplicity and variety it displays, moves within certain common forms, or general ideas, which cannot completely vanish except with the total disappearance of class antagonisms.

The Communist revolution is the most radical rupture with traditional property relations; no wonder that its development involved the most radical rupture with traditional ideas.

But let us have done with the bourgeois objections to Communism.

We have seen above, that the first step in the revolution by the working class is to raise the proletariat to the position of ruling class to win the battle of democracy.

The proletariat will use its political supremacy to wrest, by degree, all capital from the bourgeoisie, to centralise all instruments of production in the hands of the State, i.e., of the proletariat organised as the ruling class; and to increase the total productive forces as rapidly as possible.

Of course, in the beginning, this cannot be effected except by means of despotic inroads on the rights of property, and on the conditions of bourgeois production; by means of measures, therefore, which appear economically insufficient and untenable, but which, in the course of the movement, outstrip themselves, necessitate further inroads upon the old social order, and are unavoidable as a means of entirely revolutionising the mode of production.

These measures will, of course, be different in different countries.

Nevertheless, in most advanced countries, the following will be pretty generally applicable.

1. Abolition of property in land and application of all rents of land to public purposes.
2. A heavy progressive or graduated income tax.
3. Abolition of all rights of inheritance.
4. Confiscation of the property of all emigrants and rebels.

5. Centralisation of credit in the hands of the state, by means of a national bank with State capital and an exclusive monopoly.
6. Centralisation of the means of communication and transport in the hands of the State.
7. Extension of factories and instruments of production owned by the State; the bringing into cultivation of waste-lands, and the improvement of the soil generally in accordance with a common plan.
8. Equal liability of all to work. Establishment of industrial armies, especially for agriculture.
9. Combination of agriculture with manufacturing industries; gradual abolition of all the distinction between town and country by a more equable distribution of the populace over the country.
10. Free education for all children in public schools. Abolition of children's factory labour in its present form. Combination of education with industrial production, etc, etc.

When, in the course of development, class distinctions have disappeared, and all production has been concentrated in the hands of a vast association of the whole nation, the public power will lose its political character. Political power, properly so called, is merely the organised power of one class for oppressing another. If the proletariat during its contest with the bourgeoisie is compelled, by the force of circumstances, to organise itself as a class, if, by means of a revolution, it makes itself the ruling class, and, as such, sweeps away by force the old conditions of production, then it will, along with these conditions, have swept away the conditions for the existence of class antagonisms and of classes generally, and will thereby have abolished its own supremacy as a class.

In place of the old bourgeois society, with its classes and class antagonisms, we shall have an association, in which the free development of each is the condition for the free development of all.

Marx, Karl. "Chapter I. Bourgeois and Proletarians," and "Chapter II. Proletarians and Communists." In *Manifesto of the Communist Party*. Translated by Samuel Moore and Frederick Engels. https://www.marxists.org/archive/marx/works/1848/communist-manifesto/.

POST-READING PARS

1. Based on Marx's distinctions, which of the "social classes" you listed previously would be bourgeois and which would be proletarian? Why?
2. How does Marx complicate your understanding of capitalism? Based on this reading, what makes a society capitalist?
3. What would work that is fulfilling look like? How might a society de-alienate labor so that "the free development of each is the condition for the free development of all"?

Inquiry Corner

Content Question:

Marx's stance on the "revolutionary part" the bourgeoisie has played in its modernizing influence on world history is ambivalent. What does he applaud the bourgeoisie for accomplishing, and what blame does he place on this class?

Critical Question:

One theory, according to Marx, is that intrinsic contradictions within an existing mode of production will lead to its inevitable downfall. For example, "the feudal relations of property became no longer compatible with the already developed productive forces" and "they had to be burst asunder." With the ongoing continual struggle, and apparent contradictions, between capital and labor, why has capitalism not been rendered obsolete?

Comparative Question:

How do the ten measures Marx advocates in *Manifesto for the Communist Party* compare with the list of rights found in liberal declarations of human rights like the National Assembly of France's "Declaration of the Rights of Man and Citizen" (1798), the United States' "The Bill of Rights" (1789), or the United Nations' "Universal Declaration of Human Rights" (1948)?

Connection Questions:

Many thinkers have argued that *The Communist Manifesto* is more relevant today than it was in the nineteenth century, that the changes wrought by the bourgeoisie that Marx outlines have only become more pronounced in the twenty-first century. Do you agree? Why or why not?

"The Principles of Anarchism" by Lucy Parsons

Introduction

Lucy Parsons (1851–1942) was an American radical whose life crossed a number of significant boundaries, both literally and in the abstract. She is best remembered as being **Tejana** and of Indigenous descent, an identity she claimed throughout her life. In fact, the Chicago park named for her, on a plaque, calls her the "first Chicana socialist labor organizer." Until the twentieth century, it was thought that her name was Lucia Eldine Gonzalez. Now, historians know that she was in fact born an enslaved African American in Virginia named Lucia Carter. During the Civil War, Lucia and her mother were brought to Waco, Texas, where Lucia did household work for white families. While still a teenager, Lucia met and formed a union with a formerly enslaved older man, Oliver Gathing. Lucia and Oliver Gathing were not lawfully married, but lived as a married couple in the years immediately following the Civil War.

In 1869, Lucia's life changed fundamentally when she met Albert Parsons. Parsons was a white Southerner from Alabama who had served for the Confederacy during the Civil War. Antithetically, at war's end, Parsons joined the Republican Party and was involved in **Reconstruction era** politics and journalism in Waco, Texas. Lucia and Albert met, fell in love, and by 1872 they were married. Their marriage occurred on the eve of the re-establishment of Democratic Party rule in Texas, just weeks before a state law that banned interracial marriages passed. The

> **SNAPSHOT BOX**
>
> LANGUAGE: English
> PUBLISHED: 1905, United States
> GENRE: Public address, pamphlet
> TAGS: Class; History and Ideology; Internationalism; Labor; Psyche; Rhetoric and Persuasion Statecraft

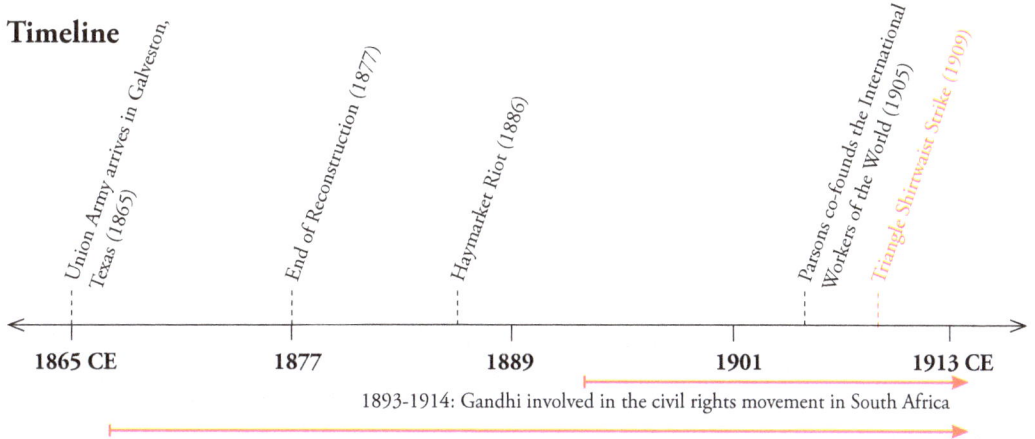

Parsonses left Texas in 1873 and headed to Chicago. Along the way, Lucia changed her name to Lucy.

In Chicago, Lucy opened a dress shop and soon became involved with the Chicago Working Women's Union. The union fought for women's suffrage, equal pay for women, and an eight-hour work day. During the 1880s, Lucy Parsons became committed to the cause of **anarchism**, a set of ideas that viewed government as a form of coercive hierarchy. In Parsons's viewpoint, government protected the interests of the moneyed class and was diametrically opposed to protecting workers' rights. As it has been true in many places and times, and definitely during this time period, government and private industry often collude to suppress labor activism. For Lucy Parsons, even the system of democracy, especially as it existed in her experience living in the United States, could not ensure justice and fairness for working people. Anarchists like Parsons believed that the most just social contract was voluntary and nonhierarchical. What connotations does the word "anarchist" carry for you today?

Lucy and Albert Parsons were involved on the side of workers in the 1886 Haymarket Riot in Chicago where seven people were killed and dozens injured in a violent clash between police and protestors. Albert Parsons was falsely charged and then executed as a conspirator. This miscarriage of justice galvanized radicals across the country and made Lucy Parsons a public figure in the world of American radicalism. Over the next several decades, Lucy Parsons expanded her career as a labor spokesperson, author, and advocate for class struggle. Unlike some labor radicals, most notably Emma Goldman, Parsons focused almost exclusively on class struggle over gender and sex equality. What might be an argument in defense of her decision here? What might be a critique? She wrote extensively for radical and labor publications and was one of the founders of the International Workers of the World (IWW). Later in life she joined the International Labor Defense Fund, the Communist Party–led legal organization famous for defending the "Scottsboro Boys" in the 1930s. Lucy Parsons died in 1942 in a house fire in Chicago.

In "The Principles of Anarchism," Lucy Parsons explored the ways that anarchism might create the conditions for individuals to express and experience their full potential. Critiquing other systems like democracy and socialism, Parsons believed that all government restrictions were a violation of personal liberty. Unlike contemporary Libertarians, anarchists believed that cooperation and mutual aid were fundamental to human nature. Therefore, humans did not need a **social contract** (an agreement between the ruler and the ruled) to build community in a just and fair fashion.

Sarah Judson
Department of History

> **PRE-READING PARS**
>
> 1. Hypothesize three reasons that anarchists might offer for their position that a system of democracy would lead to injustice against the working class.
> 2. Think of two or three examples from our contemporary world where the system of capitalism might block human flourishing.
> 3. What two ways might you use to determine whether working-class people today see themselves as a separate social, political, and economic group?

"The Principles of Anarchism"

Comrades and Friends: I think I cannot open my address more appropriately than by stating my experience in my long connection with the reform movement.

It was during the great railroad strike of 1877 that I first became interested in what is known as the "Labor Question." I then thought as many thousands of earnest, sincere people think, that the aggregate power operating in human society, known as government, could be made an instrument in the hands of the oppressed to alleviate their sufferings. But a closer study of the origin, history and tendency of governments convinced me that this was a mistake.

I came to understand how organized governments used their concentrated power to retard progress by their ever-ready means of silencing the voice of discontent if raised in vigorous protest against the machinations of the scheming few, who always did, always will and always must rule in the councils of nations where majority rule is recognized as the only means of adjusting the affairs of the people.

I came to understand that such concentrated power can be always wielded in the interest of the few and at the expense of the many. Government in its last analysis is this power reduced to a science. Governments never lead; they follow progress. When the prison, stake or scaffold can no longer silence the voice of the protesting minority, progress moves on a step, but not until then.

I will state this contention in another way: I learned by close study that it made no difference what fair promises a political party, out of power, might make to the people in order to secure their confidence, when once securely established in control of the affairs of society that they were after all but human with all the human attributes of the politician. Among these are: First, to remain in power at all hazards; if not individually, then those holding essentially the same views as the administration must be kept in control. Second, in order to keep in power, it is necessary to build up a powerful machine; one strong enough to crush all opposition and silence all vigorous murmurs of discontent, or the party machine might be smashed and the party thereby lose control.

When I came to realize the faults, failings, shortcomings, aspirations and ambitions of fallible man, I concluded that it would not be the safest nor best policy for society, as a whole, to entrust the management of all its affairs, with all their manifold deviations and ramifications in the hands of finite man, to be managed by the party which happened to come into power, and therefore was the majority party, nor did it then, nor does it now make one particle of difference to me what a party, out of power may promise; it does not tend to allay my fears of a party, when entrenched and securely seated in power might do to crush opposition, and silence the voice of the minority, and thus retard the onward step of progress.

My mind is appalled at the thought of a political party having control of all the details that go to make up the sum total of our lives. Think of it for an instant, that the party in power shall have all authority to dictate the kind of books that shall be used in our schools and universities, government officials editing, printing, and circulating our literature, histories, magazines and press, to say nothing of the thousand and one activities of life that a people engage in, in a civilized society.

To my mind, the struggle for liberty is too great and the few steps we have gained have been won at too great a sacrifice, for the great mass of the people of this 20th century to consent to turn over to any political party the management of our social and industrial affairs. For all who are at all familiar with history know that men will abuse power when they possess it. For these and other reasons, I, after careful study, and not through sentiment, turned from a sincere, earnest, political Socialist to the non-political phase of Socialism – Anarchism – because in its philosophy I believe I can find the proper conditions for the fullest development of the individual units in society, which can never be the case under government restrictions.

The philosophy of anarchism is included in the word "Liberty," yet it is comprehensive enough to include all things else that are conducive to progress. No barriers whatever to human progression, to thought, or investigation are placed by anarchism; nothing is considered so true or so certain, that future discoveries may not prove it false; therefore, it has but one infallible, unchangeable motto, "Freedom": Freedom to discover any truth, freedom to develop, to live naturally and fully. Other schools of thought are composed of crystallized ideas—principles that are caught and impaled between the planks of long platforms, and considered too sacred to be disturbed by a close investigation. In all other "issues" there is always a limit; some imaginary boundary line beyond which the searching mind dare not penetrate, lest some pet idea melt into a myth. But anarchism is the usher of science—the master of ceremonies to all forms of truth. It would remove all barriers between the human being and natural development. From the natural resources of the Earth, all artificial restrictions, that the body might be nurtured, and from universal truth, all bars of prejudice and superstition, that the mind may develop symmetrically.

Anarchists know that a long period of education must precede any great fundamental change in society, hence they do not believe in vote-begging, nor political campaigns, but rather in the development of self-thinking individuals.

We look away from government for relief, because we know that force (legalized) invades the personal liberty of man, seizes upon the natural elements and intervenes between man and natural laws; from this exercise of force through governments flows nearly all the misery, poverty, crime and confusion existing in society.

So, we perceive, there are actual, material barriers blockading the way. These must be removed. If we could hope they would melt away, or be voted or prayed into nothingness, we would be content to wait and vote and pray. But they are like great frowning rocks towering between us and a land of freedom, while the dark chasms of a hard-fought past yawn behind us. Crumbling they may be with their own weight and the decay of time, but to quietly stand under until they fall is to be buried in the crash. There is something to be done in a case like this—the rocks must be removed. Passivity while slavery is stealing over us is a crime. For the moment we must forget that we are anarchists—when the work is accomplished we may forget that we were revolutionists—hence most anarchists believe the coming change can only come through a revolution, because the possessing class will not allow a peaceful change to take place; still we are willing to work for peace at any price, except at the price of liberty.

And what of the glowing beyond that is so bright that those who grind the faces of the poor say it is a dream? It is no dream, it is the real, stripped of brain-distortions materialized into thrones and scaffolds, miters and guns. It is nature acting on her own interior laws as in all her other associations. It is a return to first principles; for were not the land, the water, the light, all free before governments took shape and form? In this free state we will again forget to think of these things as "property." It is real, for we, as a race, are growing up to it. The idea of less restriction and more liberty, and a confiding trust that nature is equal to her work, is permeating all modern thought.

From the dark years—not so long gone by—when it was generally believed that man's soul was totally depraved and every human impulse bad; when every action, every thought and every emotion was controlled and restricted; when the human frame, diseased, was bled, dosed, suffocated and kept as far from nature's remedies as possible; when the mind was seized upon and distorted before it had time to evolve a natural thought—from those days to these years the progress of this idea has been swift and steady. It is becoming more and more apparent that in every way we are "governed best where we are governed least."

Still unsatisfied perhaps, the inquirer seeks for details, for ways and means, and whys and wherefores. How will we go on like human beings—eating and sleeping, working and loving, exchanging and dealing—without government? So used have we become to "organized authority" in every department of life that ordinarily we cannot conceive of the most common-place avocations being carried on without their interference and "protection." But anarchism is not compelled to outline a complete organization of a free society. To do so with any assumption of authority would be to place another barrier in the way of coming generations. The best thought of today may become the useless vagary of tomorrow, and to crystallize it into a creed is to make it unwieldy.

We judge from experience that man is a gregarious animal, and instinctively affiliates with his kind—co-operates, unites in groups, works to better advantage combined with his fellow men than when alone. This would point to the formation of co-operative communities, of which our present trades-unions are embryonic patterns. Each branch of industry will no doubt have its own organization, regulations, leaders, etc.; it will institute methods of direct communication with every member of that industrial branch in the world, and establish equitable relations with all other branches. There would probably be conventions of industry which delegates would attend, and where they would transact such business as was necessary, adjourn and from that moment be delegates no longer, but simply members of a group. To remain permanent members of a continuous congress would be to establish a power that is certain sooner or later to be abused.

No great, central power, like a congress consisting of men who know nothing of their constituents' trades, interests, rights or duties, would be over the various organizations or groups; nor would they employ sheriffs, policemen, courts or jailers to enforce the conclusions arrived at while in session. The members of groups might profit by the knowledge gained through mutual interchange of thought afforded by conventions if they choose, but they will not be compelled to do so by any outside force.

Vested rights, privileges, charters, title deeds, upheld by all the paraphernalia of government—the visible symbol of power—such as prison, scaffold and armies, will have no existence. There can be no privileges bought or sold, and the transaction kept sacred at the point of the bayonet. Every man will stand on an equal footing with his brother in the race of life, and neither chains of economic thralldom nor menial drags of superstition shall handicap the one to the advantage of the other.

Property will lose a certain attribute which sanctifies it now. The absolute ownership of it—"the right to use or abuse"—will be abolished, and possession, use, will be the only title. It will be seen how impossible it would be for one person to "own" a million acres of land, without a title deed, backed by a government ready to protect the title at all hazards, even to the loss of thousands of lives. He could not use the million acres himself, nor could he wrest from its depths the possible resources it contains.

People have become so used to seeing the evidences of authority on every hand that most of them honestly believe that they would go utterly to the bad if it were not for the policeman's club or the soldier's bayonet. But the anarchist says, "Remove these evidences of brute force, and let man feel the revivifying influences of self-responsibility and self-control, and see how we will respond to these better influences."

The belief in a literal place of torment has nearly melted away; and instead of the direful results predicted, we have a higher and truer standard of manhood and womanhood. People do not care to go to the bad when they find they can as well as not. Individuals are unconscious of their own motives in doing good. While acting out their natures according to their surroundings and conditions, they still believe they are being kept in the right path by some outside power, some restraint thrown around them by church or state. So the objector believes that with the right to rebel and secede, sacred to him, he would forever be rebelling and seceding, thereby creating constant confusion and turmoil.

Is it probable that he *would*, merely for the reason that he *could* do so? Men are to a great extent creatures of habit, and grow to love associations; under reasonably good conditions, he would remain where he commences, if he wished to, and, if he did not, who has any natural right to force him into relations distasteful to him? Under the present order of affairs, persons do unite with societies and remain good, disinterested members for life, where the right to retire is always conceded.

What we anarchists contend for is a larger opportunity to develop the units in society, that mankind may possess the right as a sound being to develop that which is broadest, noblest, highest and best, unhandicapped by any centralized authority, where he shall have to wait for his permits to be signed, sealed, approved and handed down to him before he can engage in the active pursuits of life with his fellow being. We know that after all, as we grow more enlightened under this larger liberty, we will grow to care less and less for that exact distribution of material wealth, which, in our greed-nurtured senses, seems now so impossible to think upon carelessly. The man and woman of loftier intellects, in the present, think not so much of the riches to be gained by their efforts as of the good they can do for their fellow creatures.

There is an innate spring of healthy action in every human being who has not been crushed and pinched by poverty and drudgery from before his birth, that impels him onward and upward. He cannot be idle, if he would; it is as natural for him to develop, expand, and use the powers within him when not repressed, as it is for the rose to bloom in the sunlight and fling its fragrance on the passing breeze.

The grandest works of the past were never performed for the sake of money. Who can measure the worth of a Shakespeare, an Angelo or Beethoven in dollars and cents? Agassiz said, "he had no time to make money," there were higher and better objects in life than that. And so will it be when humanity is once relieved from the pressing fear of starvation, want, and slavery, it will be concerned, less and less, about the ownership of vast accumulations of wealth. Such possessions would be but an annoyance and trouble. When two or three or four hours a day of easy, of healthful labor will produce all the comforts and luxuries one can use, and the opportunity to labor is never denied, people will become indifferent as to who owns the wealth they do not need.

Wealth will be below par, and it will be found that men and women will not accept it for pay, or be bribed by it to do what they would not willingly and naturally do without it. Some higher incentive must, and will, supersede the greed for gold. The involuntary aspiration born in man to make the most of one's self, to be loved and appreciated by one's fellow-beings, to "make the world better for having lived in it," will urge him on to nobler deeds than ever the sordid and selfish incentive of material gain has done.

If, in the present chaotic and shameful struggle for existence, when organized society offers a premium on greed, cruelty, and deceit, men can be found who stand aloof and almost alone in their determination to work for good rather than gold, who suffer want and persecution rather than desert principle, who can bravely walk to the scaffold for the good they can do humanity, what may we expect from men when freed from the grinding necessity of selling the better part of themselves for bread? The terrible conditions under which labor is performed, the awful alternative if one does not prostitute talent and morals in the service of mammon; and the power acquired with the wealth obtained by ever-so-unjust means, combine to make the conception of free and voluntary labor almost an impossible one.

And yet, there are examples of this principle even now. In a well-bred family each person has certain duties, which are performed cheerfully, and are not measured out and paid for according to some pre-determined standard; when the united members sit down to the well-filled table, the stronger do not scramble to get the most, while the weakest do without, or gather greedily around them more food than they can possibly consume. Each patiently and politely awaits his turn to be served, and leaves what he does not want; he is certain that when again hungry plenty of good food will be provided. This principle can be extended to include all society, when people are civilized enough to wish it.

Again, the utter impossibility of awarding to each an exact return for the amount of labor performed will render absolute communism a necessity sooner or later. The land and all it contains, without which labor cannot be exerted, belong to no one man, but to all alike. The inventions and discoveries of the past are the common inheritance of the coming generations; and when a man takes the tree that nature furnished free, and fashions it into a useful article, or a machine perfected and bequeathed to him by many past generations, who is to determine what proportion is his and his alone? Primitive man would have been a week fashioning a rude resemblance to the article with his clumsy tools, where the modern worker has occupied an hour. The finished article is of far more real value than the rude one made long ago, and yet the primitive man toiled the longest and hardest.

Who can determine with exact justice what is each one's due? There must come a time when we will cease trying. The Earth is so bountiful, so generous; man's brain is so active, his hands so restless, that wealth will spring like magic, ready for the use of the world's inhabitants. We will become as much ashamed to quarrel over its possession as we are now to squabble over the food spread before us on a loaded table.

"But all this," the objector urges, "is very beautiful in the far off future, when we become angels. It would not do now to abolish governments and legal restraints; people are not prepared for it."

This is a question. We have seen, in reading history, that wherever an old-time restriction has been removed the people have not abused their newer liberty. Once it was considered necessary to compel men to save their souls, with the aid of governmental scaffolds, church racks and stakes. Until the foundation of the American republic it was considered absolutely essential that governments should second the efforts of the church in forcing people to attend the means of grace; and yet it is found that the standard of morals among the masses is raised since they are left free to pray as they see fit, or not at all, if they prefer it. It was believed the chattel slaves would not work if the overseer and whip were removed; they are so much more a source of profit now that ex-slave owners would not return to the old system if they could.

So many able writers have shown that the unjust institutions which work so much misery and suffering to the masses have their root in governments, and owe their whole existence to the power derived from government, we cannot help but believe that were every law, every title deed, every court, and every police officer or soldier abolished tomorrow with one sweep, we would be better off than now. The actual, material things that man needs would still exist; his strength and skill would remain and his instinctive social inclinations retain their force and the resources of life made free to all the people that they would need no force but that of society and the opinion of fellow beings to keep them moral and upright.

Freed from the systems that made him wretched before, he is not likely to make himself more wretched for lack of them. Much more is contained in the thought that conditions make man what he is, and not the laws and penalties made for his guidance, than is supposed by careless observation. We have laws, jails, courts, armies, guns and armories enough to make saints of us all, if they were the true preventives of crime; but we know they do not prevent crime; that wickedness and depravity exist in spite of them, nay, increase as the struggle between classes grows fiercer, wealth greater and more powerful and poverty more gaunt and desperate.

To the governing class the anarchists say: "Gentlemen, we ask no privilege, we propose no restriction; nor, on the other hand, will we permit it. We have no new shackles to propose, we seek emancipation from shackles. We ask no legislative sanction, for co-operation asks only for a free field and no favors; neither will we permit their interference.["] It asserts that in freedom of the social unit lies the freedom of the social state. It asserts that in freedom to possess and utilize soil lie social happiness and progress and the death of rent. It asserts that order can only exist where liberty prevails, and that progress leads and never follows order. It asserts, finally, that this emancipation will inaugurate liberty, equality, fraternity. That the existing industrial system has outgrown its usefulness, if it ever had any, is, I believe, admitted by all who have given serious thought to this phase of social conditions.

The manifestations of discontent now looming upon every side show that society is conducted on wrong principles and that something has got to be done soon or the wage class will sink into a slavery worse than was the feudal serf. I say to the wage class: Think clearly and act quickly, or you are lost. Strike not for a few cents more an hour, because the price of living will be raised faster still, but strike for all you earn, be content with nothing less.

Parsons, Lucy Eldine Gonzales. "The Principles of Anarchism." In *Freedom, Equality and Solidarity*. Chicago: Charles H. Kerr, 2004. Published as a pamphlet, circa 1905–1910.

> **POST-READING PARS**
>
> 1. In Lucy Parsons's view, what is the goal of anarchism? What would an anarchist society achieve?
> 2. Outline one argument Parsons presents for her position that capitalism blocks human flourishing.
> 3. Why does Parsons think that people have internalized the idea that authority is a positive force in society?

Inquiry Corner

Content Question:

How is anarchism the highest expression of freedom and liberty, according to Parsons?

Critical Questions:

In US political culture, both in the past and present, there is the prevailing belief that capitalism and democracy are intertwined and provide the best possible system. According to Parsons, how do capitalism and democracy obstruct freedom?

Do you think that Parsons makes a compelling argument against coercive government authority? If so, list the points of her argument. If not, which arguments fail for you?

Comparative Question:

How does Parsons's theory of anarchism compare to Enlightenment theories of the social contract?

Connection Question:

How does technology add another dimension to the problems and potentials that Parsons identifies?

Selections from the Writings of Marcus Garvey

Introduction

Born in Jamaica, Marcus Garvey (1887–1940) became one of the leading African American political thinkers of the early twentieth century. These thinkers represented a range of approaches to improve access to resources and rights for Black individuals and communities. For example, Booker T. Washington was an accommodationist arguing for working within white power structures, including maintaining some segregated components; Anna Julia Cooper and W. E. B. Du Bois employed integrationist ideas, promoting the creation of shared institutional structures including equal access to education. Garvey, in contrast, conceived of himself as a separatist, heading the Black Nationalist movement of the 1920s. **Black Nationalism** celebrates African cultural identity, encouraging economic independence and political self-governance within Black communities. The more extreme separatist positions call for a Black nation either in the United States or as part of a relocation to Africa. W. E. B. Du Bois had entertained Pan-African ideas, whereby individuals of African descent but living in different continents would work together for a common cause. However, Garvey developed a Black nationhood movement with the founding of the Universal Negro Improvement Association (UNIA) in 1916.

Garvey established the Black Star Line, a shipping company that was intended to promote trade, internationally, between Black communities, with the aim of establishing a foundation for a worldwide Black Pan-African economy. The shipping

> **SNAPSHOT BOX**
>
> LANGUAGE: English
> PUBLISHED: 1929, 1930, 1930, 1935
> GENRE: Essays
> TAGS: Economics; Internationalism; Struggle, Resistance, and Revolution; Nationalism; Self-determination; Race

Timeline

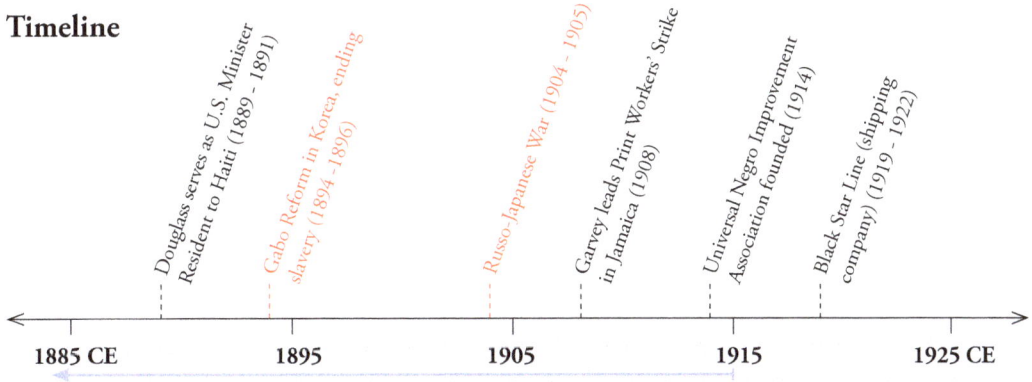

1881-1915: Booker T. Washington president of Tuskegee University

company also planned to transport African American passengers who intentionally were choosing to go back to Africa. His beliefs, including his views in favor of racial purity, made him unpopular with many other African American leaders. After a controversial mail fraud conviction, and subsequent jail term, President Calvin Coolidge pardoned Garvey but deported him back to Jamaica in 1927. Garvey's movement lost momentum; however, Black religious movements, such as the Moorish Science Temple of America, founded in 1913 by Noble Drew Ali, and the Nation of Islam, founded in 1930 by Wallace Fard Muhammad, would take on this grassroots work of incorporating and building forms of Black nationalism within religious organizations. Garveyism also would resurge in political Black nationalism movements, such as the Black Panther Party, in the decades following World War II (1939–1945).

The sources below all are written by Marcus Garvey after he was deported back to Jamaica (1927–1935) and reflect his experiences not only living in a segregated United States but also living again within a majority Black community. As you read, consider the following questions: How is Black nationalism reflected in Garvey's "Negro Progress Postulates Negro Government" (1929)? What social perceptions work against a unified Black cultural identity, as Garvey articulates this problem in his essays "The World as It Is: Insulting Negro Womanhood" (1930) and "The World as It Is: The Internal Prejudices of Negroes" (1930)? What is the value of self-determination as Garvey conceives it in "Let the Negro Accumulate Wealth: It Will Bring Him Power" (1935)?

Humanities Program Faculty

Selections from the Writings of Marcus Garvey

Negro Progress Postulates Negro Government (1929)

Whether it be viewed from the moral, legal, industrial and economic, social or political standpoint, there is no reasonable ground of objection to the establishment of a system of government by Negroes[145] for Negroes. And such a system will not be characterized, as some persons fear, by the primitivism of intertribal strife and savage, perpetual warfare for temporary supremacy of this or that tribal leader. For the race is endowed with the instincts of government that bore the marks of a high standard of civilization, to which, in certain features, our boasted Western Culture has not made a worthy approach.

The Race has fallen but her instincts are not dead. The silence of centuries has been broken. Her winter has passed and her springtime is here with the promise of a bountiful harvest, for Negro genius has again been fanned into activity, and is ready to infuse into Negro life the qualities and characteristics that made Negroes great in their institutions of the past.

The Seat of Empire Northward Moves was true to history and poetry during the period of Negro decline. But its Northern limit has been reached, and with the revival of Negro activity its path has again turned South. For Empire has not only a Seat but a Home and that Home is Africa.

It is well for black men to think on these things and to notice the movements that are contributory to this end. Jamaica is to be favored in August with the General Convention of the UNIA movement. And while we can make only the briefest reference to that subject today we would ask Negroes to say what is their mind upon the matter. What do they expect to see and hear? They possibly have read concerning former conventions held in New York. These have been wonderful happenings in a wonderful country. What is their conjecture concerning that to be held in Jamaica? Hundreds and hundreds of Negro delegates from all parts of the world will meet from day to day for a whole month in discussion on Negro problems, and world issues as they affect the Negro. What is the aim? What will be the effect? Can Jamaica Negroes and the Jamaica community be the same after the convention?

And will not this convention in its implications and bearings be significant in regard to the growing consciousness of kinship of Negroes in whatever part of the world they are found? Can it leave us without a strong, irresistible urge to realize the meaning of a common, permanent government, with a fixed habitation and a name?

---

145. Garvey uses the term "Negro" to refer to his own African American and Afro-Caribbean communities as was a prevalent practice within and outside of Black communities from the nineteenth to mid-twentieth centuries. The term "negro" should not be confused with the derogatory n-word. Likewise another term used during the same timeframe, "colored," is outdated and should not be confused with the current usage of "person of color." Words reflecting African American, Afro-Caribbean, and Black communities' preferences for self-identification continue to shift in meaning and connotation over time.

The convention will be a demonstration of the possibilities of Negro Government that no one can deny.

The World as It Is: Insulting Negro Womanhood (1930)

It is an unfortunate thing that the Negro womanhood of Jamaica in particular and of the West Indies in general can be abused without any protection given them or interest taken in the matter. We have before us the case of a prominent man, who is only one of many, who has taken gross advantage of a Negro girl, yet he continues to enjoy public respect. Unfortunately, the man himself is a Negro; his action toward a member of his own race is worse than if it were committed by a man of any other race. This man is wealthy, he was not always so, he was once a poor man. When he was poor, he got engaged to a colored girl probably with the best intention; when he started to get rich, he started to ignore this colored fiancee, to "put her off" and tell her all kinds of false tales with the object of breaking his pledge. According to the man's way of thinking he had become sufficiently prominent and rich to enter "into society" and so he wanted a white wife, apparently, as most successful Negro men of a certain turn of mind do after amassing fortunes. The colored girl refused to release him from his obligation and so because he feared a suit for breach of promise he has not yet married a white woman but he doesn't want to marry a colored girl any more, yet during the time he has been taking advantage of colored girls and in one instance has made one a mother.

The World as It Is: The Internal Prejudices of Negroes (1930)

According to the arrangement of the "colored" leaders, the following plan is decided and acted upon; it is made very successful in the West Indies and is now being successfully fostered in America and elsewhere. In countries where the blacks outnumber the whites, the "colored" build up a buffer society through the financial assistance and patronage of the minority whites. They convince the minority whites that the blacks are dangerous and vicious, and that their only chance of successfully living among them is to elevate to positions of trust, superiority and overseership of the "colored" element who will directly deal with the blacks and exploit them for the general benefit of the whites. The whites being not strong enough to stand alone accept our acquiescence and thus the "colored" element is elevated to a superior position and naturally becomes attached to the whites. The skillful group, however, by its ability to acquire wealth through the privileged position allowed, immediately starts out to socially equip itself educationally and culturally to meet the whites on equal terms. They also skillfully strengthen their positions by stirring up the blacks against the whites explaining to the former that all their ills are caused by the whites, then they go back to the whites and intimidate them by drawing their attention to the great danger of the dissatisfied blacks, and offer as a solution the uniting of the whites and "colored" in a social and economic union to offset the supposed common danger from the blacks. By this artful method the "colored" elements of the colonies have socially subdued the white man, who now looks on and sees the prosperous "colored" gentleman leading away his sister or daughter in the bonds of marriage without the ability to raise the voice of protest.

The "colored" elements have arranged it so that the blacks are always kept down, so that they can use their dissatisfaction and disaffection as an argument to strengthen and further perpetuate their positions of social equality and economic privilege and preferment with the whites.

Such is the game that is being played over in America by the Du Bois-Weldon Johnson group of "colored" persons of the National Association for the Advancement of Colored People. The Universal Negro Improvement Association stands in opposition to this association on the miscegenation question, because we believe in the racial purity of both the Negro and white races. We feel that the moral disadvantage of slavery should not be perpetuated. That where our slave masters were able to abuse our slave mothers and thereby create a hybrid bastardy, we ourselves, at this time of freedom and culture, should not perpetuate the crime of nature.

We desire to standardize our race morally, hence our advocacy of all elements and shades within the race coming together and by well understood and defined codes build up a strong and healthy Negro race with pride and respect in itself, rather than seeking, as the Du Bois group does, to practice an unrestricted intercourse of miscegenation.

All the hate that the leaders of the small "colored" group can find has been levied at me for my interference with and interruption of their plans. My indictment, conviction and imprisonment are but a small effort of theirs to help destroy and ruin me because of my effort to save the Negro race from extinction through miscegenation.

That "colored" group has scientifically arranged their method of propaganda. In America and the colonies, they hold out certain baits and hopes to the educated and financially prosperous men of the darker groups, such as encouraging them to marry the very lightest element of their women and adopting them into their society. These darker men for the special privilege and "honor" are used as active propagandists to deceive the great mass of dark people so that they would not suspect the motive or the design of the "colored" element. Generally the darker men, who marry the very lightest "colored" women who sometimes pass off as white, become more hostile to their kind in the mass as well as by individual contact than the very leaders, as the leaders are generally careful not to attract or arouse suspicion of their motive. The majority of the "colored" leaders who seek after white women and the darker men who marry very light "colored" women are seldom on social terms with their own mothers if they are dark. If they have their mothers in their homes, which is generally never so, they hide them away either in the kitchen or a back room where they do not come in contact with either their light "colored" or white guests. Such is the great problem that I have sought to solve, and no one will wonder why I have been made a criminal in the struggle to rescue and save the Negro race from itself and from continuous suffering and ultimate extermination.

This treatment to colored girls is common among us and it is time a halt be called if by no one else, by the Blackman in exposing such cases to the public. It is a dirty trick on the part of successful Negroes to spend two-thirds of their lives amassing wealth from among the Negro people, [that] then when they become rich they marry people outside of their own race to die shortly after, leaving their fortunes, made from the Negro people, to go into the coffers of other people who are sufficiently independent and provided for, while the Negro race still remains in poverty. It is a shame, and so we shall make it a point of our duty to at all times bring any abuse of our womanhood to the attention of the public.

Not long ago a prominent doctor died and left a fortune. The fortune went to the white lady he married and, naturally, to her relatives. The doctor, like most of our successful men, came up through difficulties; his poor Negro parents labored hard to give him an education. Nearly everything he got by way of education and start in life came through Negroes. The success of his profession was insured through Negroes because all his patients were Negroes, yet when he became rich instead of marrying a Negro woman like his mother, he married a white woman, and now that he is dead all of his wealth is gone out of the race.

There is one thing that we have to admire the white man for and that is he is never found disloyal to his race. We find isolated cases where individuals of the white race marry Negro women, but not where they have to give their fortunes to these women or their relatives; it is always the case [that] the Negro women are rich when marriages take place between them and white men. We hope that public sentiment will be stirred as to make it impossible for successful Negro men to so insult our womanhood, and we hope the gentleman we have in mind will marry the poor nurse he has dishonored.

Let the Negro Accumulate Wealth: It Will Bring Him Power (1935)

Our economic condition seems, to a great extent, to affect our general status. When it is considered that twentieth century civilization pays homage to and worships peoples and nations only on the basis of wealth, it should not be surprising to understand why the Negro is universally ignored. Economic independence or wealth is the recommendation of a people in the full consideration of others. With all that may be said of the morals and ethics of our time, carrying with it the suggestion of rights, liberty and justice, the whole fabric is based upon economic wealth. Either the wealth of the individual, the race, or the nation. So it behooves the Negro to think in terms of economic expansion through which he may enforce the consideration that is necessary for his political, social and other betterment.

The Universal Negro Improvement Association, as everyone will admit—the most thoughtful Negro movement in the world is now, according to the need of time, emphasizing economic expansion and solidarity among Negroes. We have to make more conquests in the economic field. We have to bring under control every available resource to which the Negro is allied on his natural ground or wheresoever he happens to find himself in its midst. Be assured of this, that in the Negro's rise to wealth will come the adjustment of most of the wrongs inflicted upon him. We must have wealth in culture, wealth in education and solidly wealth of real economic values.

The program laid down by the last Convention of the Universal Negro Improvement Association in Jamaica, 1934, covers a wide range of economic expansion. This is a program that every sensible Negro, in affiliation with the Universal Negro Improvement Association, must work for, and so the urge is for greater loyalty to the work, because it is only through proper organization that the real work can be done. Be not deceived, wealth is strength, wealth is power, wealth is influence, wealth is justice, is liberty, is real human rights. The system of our world politics suggests such and as a fact it is. Show wealth to your statesmen and they will couch their language in terms satisfactory, show wealth to the soldiers and they will enlist in your army, show wealth to the neutral populations and they will turn on your side. It is by the accumulated wealth of the Jew that he is winning support from a hostile world, it is the accumulated wealth of the Negro that will force him to the front and compel men and nations to think of him in terms of human justice. All this is achievable through a greater economic expansion. That must be our purpose and to this the Universal Negro Improvement Association dedicates itself.

P.S. No message of mine would be complete to the Negro peoples of the world without again reminding them of their obligations to the parent body of the Universal Negro Improvement Association. Divisions, branches, chapters and members must do their duty. The greatest duty now is to report regularly each month and for each member to pay in his Assessment Tax; if not convenient to pay it to the divisions pay it direct to the parent body, Universal Negro Improvement Association, 2, Beaumont Crescent, West Kensington, London, W 14, England.

Clarke, John Henrik, ed., with the assistance of Amy Jacques Garvey. *Marcus Garvey and the Vision of Africa*, 300–301, 307–11. New York: Random House, 1974. Garvey's writings excerpted here are in public domain, cleared by permission of Penguin Random House.

from "The Structure of Class and Caste" by Jorge Juan and Antonio de Ulloa

SNAPSHOT BOX

LANGUAGE: Spanish
PUBLISHED: 1748, Spain
GENRE: Travelogue
TAGS: Abolition, Slavery, Freedom; Class and Caste; Colonization; Cross-Cultural Encounters; Historiography; Labor; Race; Science

Introduction

In 1734, Philip V, the Bourbon king of Spain ordered his subjects, Jorge Juan (1713–1773) and Antonio de Ulloa (1716–1795) to join the Geodesic Mission organized by the French Academy of Sciences and commissioned by Louis XV, the king of France. The Bourbon royal family controlled both the Spanish and French thrones at the time. In fact, Philip V was the uncle of Louis XV. The goal of the mission was to measure the span of a meridian arc at the Equator, and by doing so, determine the shape of the Earth. Spanish control of key territory in the Andes mountain range drew the geopolitical interests of the two nations together. This was a crucial measurement given the importance of precision maritime navigation for the colonizing powers of Europe in their intense competition for the wealth to be gained from overseas territories. On May 26, 1735, the delegation left the Spanish port of Cadiz in the company of the Marquess of Villagarcia, who had just been appointed the Viceroy of Peru. The expedition traveled to Quito, in present-day Ecuador, and after nine years of trials, travails, and methodical study, correctly calculated that the Earth is not a sphere but oblate, that is, level at the poles.

Jorge Juan was born in Novelda, in the Spanish province of Alicante. His family was well off but his father died when he was three years old at which time he came under the care of the religious order of the Society of Jesus, or the Jesuits. As a teen he entered the military religious order the Knights of Malta. Later he was enlisted

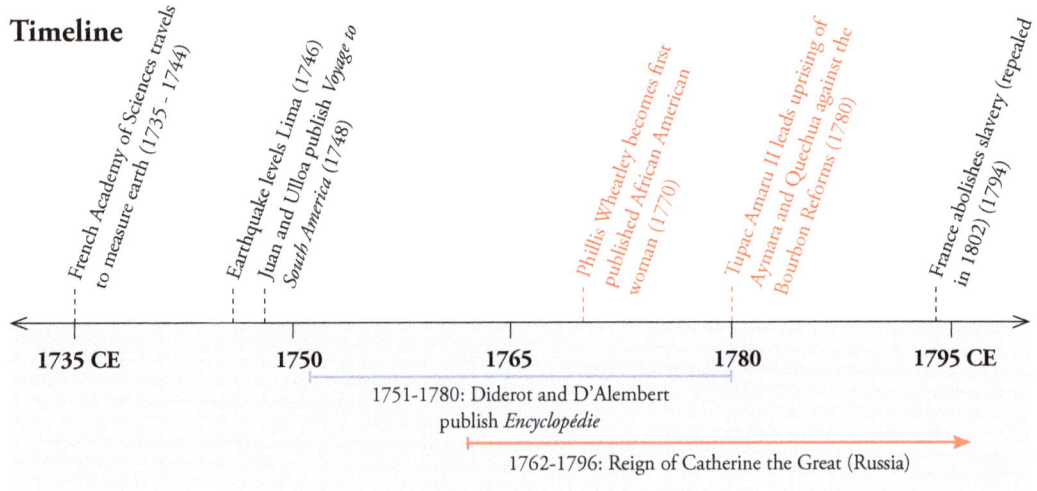

into the Royal Company of Marine Guards where he studied mathematics and naval science and met Antonio de Ulloa. Ulloa was born in Sevilla and his father was an economist to the Spanish Royal Court. As a youth he studied mathematics as well as astronomy and the art of navigation. At thirteen he shipped out to sea to study to become a master mariner. Between fourteen and sixteen years of age he sailed to the Americas at least once.

Juan and Ulloa stayed in the Americas from 1735 until 1744. The French mission resulted in extremely accurate measurements of the Earth and the Spaniards were instrumental participants in the investigation. When Juan and Ulloa returned to Spain they penned their own account of the expedition titled, *Relación histórica del viaje a la América Meridional* (*A Voyage to South America*), which was published in 1748. German, Dutch, and English translations were all available by 1771. During the two Spanish scientists' nine years in South America they were not only engaged in scientific research but were also studying the political and social situation in the Spanish territories. In fact, upon their return to Spain the Spanish Crown charged the two with writing *noticias secretas* or a secret report on the state of the Viceroyalty of Peru. *A Voyage to South America*, however, was published quite quickly after their return and it is an excerpt from that travelogue that we read here. As you read, think about the kind of information you appreciate in a travel publication. Does this reading contain that type of material? What kind of particulars do you think the authors included that were very specific to their anticipated early eighteenth-century audience?

"The Structure of Class and Caste" excerpt consists of Jorge Juan and Antonio de Ulloa's specific observations on Cartagena de las Indias (in modern Colombia) in the Viceroyalty of New Granada, a Spanish colony. As this subtitle indicates, class is one focus of their reporting but so too are the complexities of race and ethnicity, or caste (*casta*), the term used by the Spanish to categorize people of different combinations of races and ethnicities. Also note the often underlying role played by gender in the reflections of the two observers. Even the location al birth of a person was important in this European Enlightenment era obsession with inventorying everything, including people. Do you observe continued correlations between birthplace, gender, and class in contemporary times or other historical eras? Of course, human hierarchies were also imagined by the Spaniards, and it is those observations that make this reading so indicative of a European worldview not only of those conquering societies but of the manner in which those ways of seeing were imposed on the enslaved, colonized, and even colonizing people of the Atlantic world. Such rules, written and unwritten, created legacies that have endured long beyond colonial times. How do the impressions of Juan and Ulloa reverberate in other readings (Equiano? Sor Juana? Zera Yacob?) from the seventeenth and eighteenth centuries?

Alvis Dunn
Department of History

[Content Notice: racism, use of outdated racialized language, casteism]

from "The Structure of Class and Caste"

The inhabitants may be divided into different castes or tribes, who derive their origin from a coalition of Whites, Negroes,[146] and Indians. Of each of these we shall treat particularly.

The Whites may be divided into two classes, the Europeans, and Creoles, or Whites born in the country. The former are commonly called Chapetones, but are not numerous; most of them either return into Spain after acquiring a competent fortune, or remove up into inland provinces in order to increase it. Those who are settled at Carthagena, carry on the whole trade of that place, and live in opulence; whilst the other inhabitants are indigent, and reduced to have recourse to mean and hard labour for subsistence. The families of the White Creoles compose the landed interest; some of them have large estates, and are highly respected, because their ancestors came into the country invested with honorable posts, bringing their families with them when they settled here. Some of these families, in order to keep up their original dignity, have either married their children to their equals in the country, or sent them as officers on board the galleons; but others have greatly declined. Besides these, there are other Whites, in mean circumstances, who either owe their origin to Indian families, or at least to an intermarriage with them, so that there is some mixture in their blood; but when this is not discoverable by their colour, the conceit of being Whites alleviates the pressure of every other calamity.

Among the other tribes which are derived from an intermarriage of the Whites with the Negroes, the first are the Mulattos. Next to these, the Tercerones, produced from a white and a Mulatto, with some approximation to the former, but not so near as to obliterate their origin. After these follow the Quarterones, proceeding from a White and a Tercerone. The last are the Quinterones, who owe their origin to a White and Quarteron. This is the last gradation, there being no visible difference between them and the Whites, either in color or features; nay they are often fairer than the Spaniards. The children of a White and Quinteron are also called Spaniards, and consider themselves as free from all taint of the Negro race. Every person is so jealous of the order of their tribe or caste, that if, through inadvertence, you call them by a degree lower than what they actually are, they are highly offended, never suffering themselves to be deprived of so valuable a gift of fortune.

Before they attain the class of the Quinterones, there are several intervening circumstances which throw them back; for between the Mulatto and the Negro, there is an intermediate race, which they call Sambos, owing their origin to a mixture

---

146. Juan and Ulloa use the term "Negro" to refer to African communities as was a prevalent practice within and outside of Black communities from the nineteenth to mid-twentieth centuries (sometimes earlier). The term "negro" should not be confused with the derogatory n-word. Likewise another term used during the same timeframe, "colored," is outdated and should not be confused with the current usage of "person of color." Words reflecting African and Black communities' preferences for self-identification continue to shift in meaning and connotation over time.

between one of these with an Indian, or among themselves. They are also distinguished according to the castes their fathers were of. Between the Tercerones and the Mulattos, the Quarterones and the Tercerones, etc., are those called Tente en el Ayre, suspended in the air, because they neither advance nor recede. Children, whose parents are a Quarteron or Quinteron, and a Mulatto or Terceron, are Salto atras retrogrades; because, instead of advancing towards being Whites, they have gone backwards towards the Negro race. The children between a Negro and Quinteron are called Sambos de Negro, de Mulatto, de Terceron, etc.

These are the most known and common tribes or castes; there are indeed several others proceeding from their intermarriages; but, being so various, even they themselves cannot easily distinguish them; and these are the only people one sees in the city, the estancias,[147] and the villages; for if any Whites, especially women, are met with, it is only accidental; these generally reside in their houses; at least, if they are of any rank or character.

These castes, from the Mulattos, all affect the Spanish dress, but wear very slight stuffs on account of the heat of the climate. These are the mechanics of the city; the Whites, whether Creoles or Chapitones, disdaining such a mean occupation, follow nothing below merchandize. But it being impossible for all to succeed, great numbers not being able to procure sufficient credit, they become poor and miserable from their aversion to those trades they follow in Europe; and, instead of the riches which they flattered themselves with possessing in the Indies, they experience the most complicated wretchedness.

The class of Negroes is not the least numerous, and is divided into two parts; the free and the slaves. These are again subdivided into Creoles and Bozares, part of which are employed in the cultivation of the haziandes,[148] or estancias. Those in the city are obliged to perform the most laborious services, and pay out of their wages a certain quota to their masters, subsisting themselves on the small remainder. The violence of the heat not permitting them to wear any clothes, their only covering is a small piece of cotton about their waist; the female slaves go in the same manner. Some of these live at the estancias, being married to the slaves who work there; while those in the city sell in the markets all kinds of eatables, and cry fruits, sweetmeats, cakes made of the maize, and cassava, and several other things about the streets.

Ulloa, A. D., J. Juan, and J. Adams. "Of the Inhabitants of Carthagena." In *A voyage to South America: Describing at large, the Spanish cities, towns, provinces, &c. on that extensive continent, undertaken by command of the King of Spain, by Don George Juan, and Don Antonio de Ulloa, both captains of the Spanish Navy; fellows of the Royal Society of London; Members of the Royal Academy at Paris, &c. &c.*, 29–32. London, Holborn: Printed for Lockyer Davis, 1772.

147. Estancia properly signifies a mansion, or place where one flops to rest; but at Carthagena it implies a country house, which, by reason of the great number of slaves belonging to it, often equals a considerable village. [Footnotes 147 and 148 from original translated source.]

148. Hazianda in this place signifies a country house, with the lands belonging to it.

from *The War and Its Effect upon Women* by Helena Marie Swanwick

SNAPSHOT BOX

LANGUAGE: English
PUBLISHED: 1915, Great Britain
GENRE: Essay
TAGS: Economics; Ethics and Morality; Family; Gender and Identity; Internationalism; Labor; Psyche; Struggle, Resistance, and Revolution; War and Brutality; Women and Power

Introduction

Helena Maria Sickert Swanwick (1864–1939) was born in Munich, Germany, the daughter of Danish artist Oswald Sickert, and a professional dancer, Eleanor Louisa Moravia Henry. Swanwick moved with her family to the United Kingdom when she was four years old and graduated from one of England's first women's colleges (Girton) and later attended Cambridge University. Following her formal education she began a career as a journalist, eventually writing for the new, liberal paper, the *Manchester Guardian*. As the reading below exemplifies, much of Swanwick's life and journalistic publications focused on the issue of women's rights. She was an activist in the National Union of Women's Suffrage Societies and even worked as the editor of *The Common Cause* (the main British suffragists' publication) until the outbreak of World War I.

The war challenged calls for women's suffrage in Britain—as it did for other suffrage and labor movements across the globe. Internal, domestic unity was seen as a precondition to victory over foreign aggressors. For example, in Britain some suffragists, such as Emmeline Pankhurst and her followers, ceased their calls for the women's vote during the military conflict. Others, such as Swanwick, saw the war as an opportunity to continue to use women and motherhood to call for peace and raise the importance of women's voices.

In the following selection, Swanwick acknowledges the social construction of separate, gendered spheres of life (the public gendered as male and the domestic

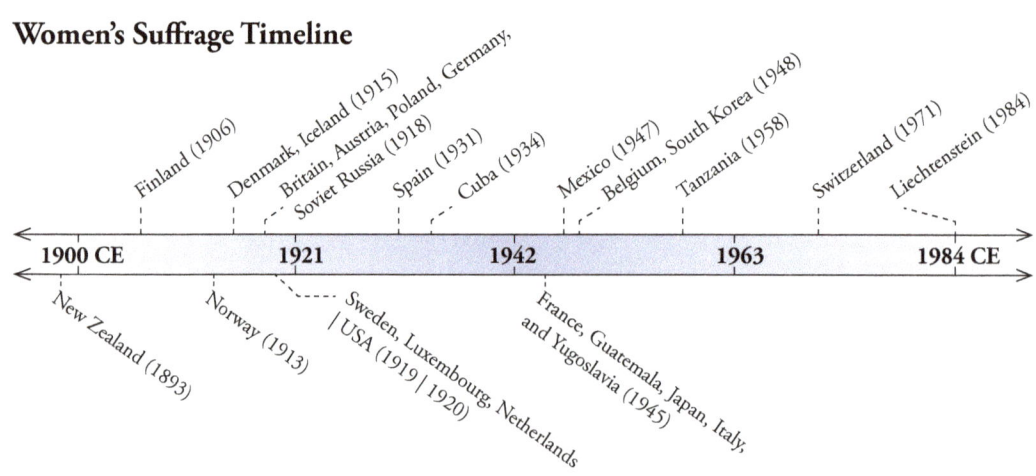

Women's Suffrage Timeline

as female) even as she seeks to move beyond these "peculiarities." For her, the war drew acute attention to the way in which both men and women suffer the violence of warfare, as mothers, fathers, sons, daughters, and siblings. As she notes, "In fact, life would be far more truly envisaged if we dropped the silly phrases 'men's and women's questions'; for, indeed, there are no such matters, and all human questions affect all humanity." In making such an argument, what previous ideas and rhetorical strategies is Swanwick building upon? How does her argument move beyond them? What intersections between other calls for equality (racial, economic, etc.) do you see here?

British women were finally granted the right to vote through acts of parliament in 1918 and 1928, and again in 1932 with the Reform Act. World War I proved to be the turning point for other women's suffrage movements, as illustrated by the timeline accompanying this reading.

Eric Roubinek
Department of History

from *The War and Its Effect upon Women* (1915)

How has the war affected women? How will it affect them? Women, as half the human race, are compelled to take their share of evil and good with men, the other half. The destruction of property, the increase of taxation, the rise of prices, the devastation of beautiful things in nature and art–these are felt by men as well as by women. Some losses doubtless appeal to one or the other sex with peculiar poignancy, but it would be difficult to say whose sufferings are the greater, though there can be no doubt at all that men get an exhilaration out of war which is denied to most women. When they see pictures of soldiers encamped in the ruins of what was once a home, amidst the dead bodies of gentle milk cows, most women would be thinking too insistently of the babies who must die for need of milk to entertain the exhilaration which no doubt may be felt at "the good work of our guns." When they read of miles upon miles of kindly earth made barren, the hearts of men may be wrung to think of wasted toil, but to women the thought suggests a simile full of an even deeper pathos; they will think of the millions of young lives destroyed, each one having cost the travail and care of a mother, and of the millions of young bodies made barren by the premature death of those who should have been their mates. The millions of widowed maidens in the coming generation will have to turn their thoughts away from one particular joy and fulfillment of life. While men in war give what is, at the present stage of the world's development, the peculiar service of men, let them not forget that in rendering that very service they are depriving a corresponding number of women of the opportunity of rendering what must, at all stages of the world's development, be the peculiar service of women. After the war, men will go on doing what has been regarded as men's work; women, deprived of their own, will also have to do much of what has been regarded as men's work. These things are going to affect women profoundly, and one hopes that the reconstruction of society is going to be met by the whole people—men and women—with a sympathetic understanding of each other's circumstances. When what are known as men's questions are discussed, it is generally assumed that the settlement of them depends upon men only; when what are known as women's questions are discussed, there is never any suggestion that they can be settled by women independently of men. Of course they cannot. But, then, neither can "men's questions" be rightly settled so. In fact, life would be far more truly envisaged if we dropped the silly phrases "men's and women's questions"; for, indeed, there are no such matters, and all human questions affect all humanity.

Now, for the right consideration of human questions, it is necessary for humans to understand each other. This catastrophic war will do one good thing if it opens our eyes to real live women as they are, as we know them in workaday life, but as the politician and the journalist seem not to have known them....

Women are, through the war, becoming good "copy." But women have not suddenly become patriotic, or capable, or self-sacrificing; the great mass of women have always shown these qualities in their humble daily life. Now that their services are asked for in unfamiliar directions, attention is being attracted to them, and many more people are realising that, with extended training and opportunity, women's capacity for beneficent work would be extended. The fiction of women's incapacity must have indeed bitten deep, when it could be supposed that it required a "super-woman" to clip a ticket![149]

There never was any justification for that sort of sentimentalism, but we are now in some danger of sentimentalism of the opposite kind. Extravagant writers are filling the papers with assertions that women in engineering works can do two or three times as much work as men, and that raw female hands can plough a straighter and deeper furrow in heavy soil than practised men are able. All this does nothing but harm. If unpractised women have turned out more work at a lathe than practised men, it is most assuredly not because the men could not have turned out more than they did; we must seek for other reasons. The problem of the readjustment of men's and women's work after the war is going to be so difficult and so great that we want none of this frivolous sentimentality in dealing with it. We want facts. We want a sober judgment. We want an alert mind, which will meet the problems with no dead obstructive prejudices, but with the single intention to make the very best use of the men and women who will emerge from this ghastly catastrophe. To condemn any section of the people to inaction, to restrict or cramp their powers of production and of healing, is going to cripple the nation and be the most unpatriotic course conceivable.

It is often forgotten that for full prosperity a country needs to be producing as much wealth as possible, consistently with the health, freedom, and happiness of its people. To arrive at this desired result, it is quite clear that as many people as possible should be employed productively, and it is one of the unhappy results of our economic anarchy that employers have found it profitable to have a large reserve class of unemployed and that wage-earners have been driven to try and diminish their own numbers and to restrict their own output. To keep women out of the "labour market" (by artificial restrictions, such as the refusal to work with them, or the refusal to allow them to be trained, or the refusal to adapt conditions to their health requirements) is in truth anti-social. But it is easy to see how such anti-social restrictions have been forced upon the workers, and it is futile to blame them. A way must be found out of industrial war before we can hope that industry will be carried on thriftily. Men and women must take counsel together and let the experience of the war teach them how to solve economic problems by co-operation rather than conflict. Women have been increasingly conscious of the satisfaction to be got from economic independence, of the sweetness of earned bread, of the dreary depression of subjection. They have felt the bitterness of being "kept out"; they are feeling the exhilaration of being "brought in." They are ripe for instruction and organisation in working for the good of the whole....

149. A published snapshot of the first women ticket collectors on English buses had been captioned "Superwomen."

The return of millions of men to civil life and work will tax the goodwill and organising capacity of the whole nation. The change from war production to peace production will possibly be even greater. The readjustments required must necessarily be slow and difficult, and unless there can be co-operation between employers and employed, and between all sections of employed, there will be friction to the raw and many disastrous mistakes.

Because it will obviously be impossible for all to find work quickly (not to speak of the right kind of work), there is almost certain to be an outcry for the restriction of work in various directions, and one of the first cries (if we may judge from the past) will be to women: "Back to the Home!" This cry will be raised whether the women have a home or not. All who care for the good of the whole must meet this cry and all that it implies with a sympathetic understanding of all sides of the problem, and a grasp, not only of present difficulties, but of the needs of the future, and there must be no hurried rushing into emergency measures which will seriously cripple future development. We must understand the unimpeachable right of the man who has lost his work and risked his life for his country, to find decent employment, decent wages and conditions, on his return to civil life. We must also understand the enlargement and enhancements of life which women feel when they are able to live by their own productive work, and we must realise that to deprive women of the right to live by their work is to send them back to a moral imprisonment (to say nothing of physical and intellectual starvation), of which they become now for the first time fully conscious. And we must realise the exceeding danger that conscienceless employers may regard women's labour as preferable, owing to its cheapness and its docility, and that women, if unsympathetically treated by their male relatives and fellow workers, may be tempted to continue to be cheap and docile in the hands of those who have no desire except that of exploiting them and the community. The kind of man who likes "to keep women in their place" may find he has made slaves who will be used by his enemies against him. Men need have no fear of free women; it is the slaves and the parasites who are a deadly danger.

The demand for equal wage for equal work has been hotly pressed by men since the war began, and it is all to the good so far as it goes. But most men are still far from realising the solidarity of their interests with those of women in all departments of life, and are still too placidly accepting the fact that women are sweated over work which is not the same as that of men. They don't realise yet that starved womanhood means starved manhood, and they don't enough appreciate the rousing and infectious character of a generous attitude on the part of men, who, in fighting the women's battles unselfishly and from a love of right, would stimulate the women to corresponding generosity. There are no comrades more staunch and loyal than women, where men have engaged their truth and courage. But men must treat them as comrades; they must no longer think only of how they can "eliminate female labour"; they must take the women into their trade unions and other organisations, and they must understand that the complexities of a woman's life are not of her invention or choosing, but are due to her function as mother of men.

The sexual side of a woman's life gravely affects the economic side, and we can never afford to overlook this. As mothers and home-makers women are doing work of the highest national importance and economic value, but this value is one which returns to the nation as a whole and only in small and very uncertain part to the women themselves. The fact that a woman is a wife and mother diminishes her value in the "labour market," and even the fact that she is liable to become a wife and mother has done so in the past. Unless men are prepared to socialise the responsibilities of parenthood, one does not see how women's labour is ever to be organised for the welfare of the whole, nor does one see how women are to perform their priceless functions of motherhood as well as possible if they are to be penalised for them in the future as they have been in the past. I do not overlook the complexity of the problem of the reconcilement of women's work as mothers with their work as home-makers and wage-earners, but I plead that the problem should be treated as a whole and not in scraps, as hitherto. . . .

Selection from Swanwick, Helena Marie. *The War and Its Effect upon Women (1915)*. London: Women's International League, 1916.

BEYOND THE CLASSROOM

» Consider one of the leading economic indicators of a country's overall economic health, namely, its gross domestic product (one way of understanding GDP is in terms of the total final goods produced within a country in a year).[150] What Swanwick calls "women's work" does not factor in a calculation of GDP. What would be a more equitable measure of an economy? What factors should and should not be considered?

---

150. For more information about GDP, visit https://www.investopedia.com/terms/g/gdp.asp.

from "The Worker's Union" by Flora Tristán

SNAPSHOT BOX

LANGUAGE: French
GENRE: Essay
PUBLISHED: 1843, France
TAGS: Class and Caste; Community; Economics; Family; Gender and Identity; History and Ideology; Internationalism; Labor; Struggle, Resistance, and Revolution; Women and Power

Introduction

Five years before *The Communist Manifesto* (1848) rallied workers of the world to unite, Flora Tristán (1803–1844) called for a "universal union of working men and women" in her own manifesto, *L'Union Ouvrière* (*The Worker's Union*, 1843).[151] She campaigned throughout France to establish an international union that would guarantee "man and woman the enjoyment of their rights as workers," speaking with workers and labor leaders at factories and organizing meetings and political societies. Her proposal included the construction of "Palaces for the Workers' Union, where children of the working class will be instructed, intellectually and professionally, and where working men and women who have been injured at their jobs, and those who are infirm or aged, will be cared for"[152]—concerns with which the modern welfare state (which provides basic public services like healthcare, education, housing, and the like) is still occupied. On her tour she fell ill and died in Bordeaux, France, where 8,000 people attended her funeral. She was only forty-one.

Tristán was a product of the **Atlantic Revolutions**. Born Flore-Celestine-Thérèse-Henriette-Tristan-Moscoso, she was the daughter of a Frenchwoman and an aristocratic Peruvian colonel in the Spanish navy who died when she was a child. Because her parents' marriage was religious and not legal (a government-sanctioned union), she was disinherited and subsequently rejected by her first lover's parents for being an unsuitable match. Instead, she worked as a lithographer and married her employer. The marriage proved abusive, and she left to become a salesclerk in a candy shop. Tristán was only granted a legal separation years later after her husband shot her over custody of their three children. An 1833 trip to Peru failed to procure her paternal inheritance but resulted in two publications about her marital experience and the state of women during Peru's fight for independence: *Peregrinations of a Pariah* and *Of the Necessity of Welcoming Foreign Women*, both appearing in France in 1835. Influenced by the revolutionary ideals of France, she believed that the status of women indicated the progress of society. "Women's rights are human rights" is a feminist aphorism, made most famous by former US secretary of state Hillary Clinton in a 1995 speech at the United Nations. What do you think this statement means in the context of our contemporary, global society?

---

151. The title is sometimes translated as "The Female Worker's Union" due to specification of gender in the original French title.

152. Flora Tristan, *The Worker's Union*, 2nd ed. Quoted in Nancy Holmstrom's *The Socialist Feminist Project: A Contemporary Reader in Theory and Politics* (New York: Monthly Review Press, 2002), 15.

Timeline

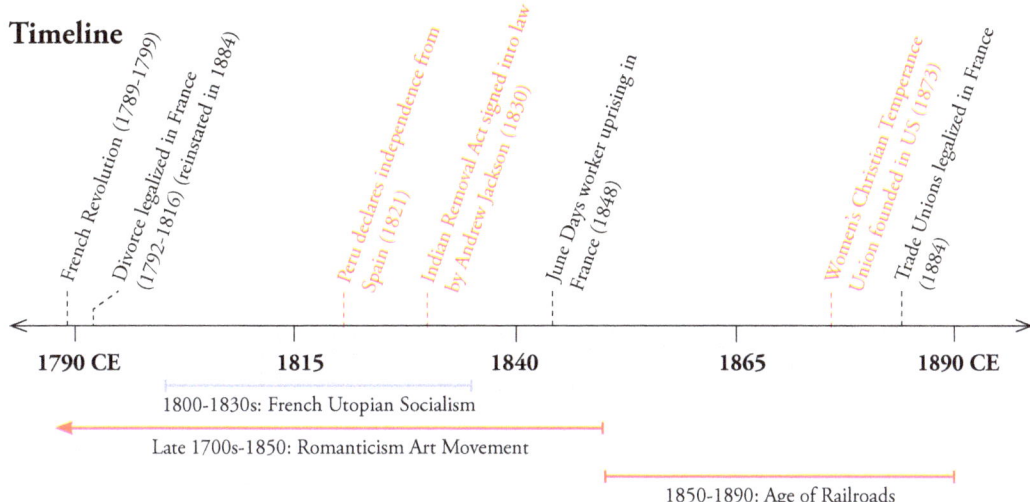

Today Tristán is considered one of the first to combine **feminism** with **socialism**. To put her work in contemporary terms, Tristan is thinking intersectionally about identity as the interactive confluence of multiple positionalities like gender and socioeconomic class.[153] Tristán's labor politics were inspired by French utopian socialists like Charles Fourier and Saint-Simone and her own travels to England, which she wrote about in the 1840 work, *Walks Through London*. In the slums of England's capital, she witnessed the immiseration of working peoples, much like Friedrich Engels would in his famous *The Condition of the Working Class in England* (1845). She also prefigured Engels in her conception of prostitution as the plight of both poor women compelled into sex work and bourgeois women trafficked between fathers and husbands. Women need equality under the law and a right to earn a living wage in order to avoid such a fate. Likewise, because women are "the proletarian of the proletarian," Tristán argues that the **proletariat** (working class) can only be unified as a class opposed to the **bourgeoisie** (capital-owning class) if working men recognize women as equals. You will notice that *The Worker's Union* specifically addresses men who labor. In what ways do Tristán's appeals raise issues ignored by bourgeois women's rights discourse and the values it espouses? In what ways has contemporary feminist socialism progressed beyond Tristán's thinking? What value do you find in reading Tristán today?

Kirk Boyle
Department of English

153. For more, see Marie M. Collins and Sylvie Weil-Sayre's "Flora Tristan: Forgotten Feminist and Socialist," *Nineteenth-Century French Studies* 1, no. 4 (Summer 1973): 229–34. https://www.jstor.org/stable/23535978.

from *The Workers Union* (1843)

Woman is everything in the life of the worker: as mother she an influence over him during his childhood, it is from her and her alone that he learns the first notions of the science of life, so important to master because it teaches us to live decently for ourselves and for others in whatever walk of life fate has placed us. As lover she has an influence over him during his youth, and what powerful influence has a beautiful girl who is loved! As wife she has an influence on three-quarters of his life, and finally, as daughter she has an influence on his old age.

You will observe that the workers' position is quite different from that of the rich. If a rich child's mother is incapable of raising him, he is sent to a boarding school or given a governess. If a rich young man has no mistress, he can study art or science to keep his heart and imagination occupied. If a rich man has no wife, he will easily find pleasures in society. If a rich old man has no daughter, he can find some old friends or young nephews who will gladly come and play cards with him. Whereas the worker, to whom all these advantages are denied, has only the company of the women of his family—his fellow sufferers—for his sole joy and comfort.

As a result it is imperative, in order to improve the intellectual, moral, and material condition of the working class, that women of the lower classes be given a rational and solid education, conducive to the development of their good inclinations, so that they may become skillful workers, good mothers capable of raising and guiding their children, and of tutoring them in their school work, and so that they may also act as moralizing agents in the life of the men on whom they exert an influence from the cradle to the grave.

Do you begin to understand, you, men, who cry shame before even looking into the question, why I demand rights for woman? Why I should like her to be placed on a footing of absolute equality with man in society, and that she should be so by virtue of the legal right every human being brings at birth?

I demand rights for women because I am convinced that all the misfortunes in the world result from the neglect and contempt in which woman's natural and inalienable rights have so far been held. I demand rights for woman because it is the only way she will get an education, and because the education of man in general and man of the lower classes in particular depends on the education of woman. I demand rights for woman because it is the only way to obtain her rehabilitation in the Church, the law, and society, and because this preliminary rehabilitation is necessary to achieve the rehabilitation of the workers themselves. All the woes of the working class can be summed up in these two words: poverty and ignorance, ignorance and poverty. Now, I see only one way out of this labyrinth: begin by educating women, because women have the responsibility for educating male and female children.

Workers, the way things stand now, you know what is going on in your homes. You, man–the master–with rights over your wife, do you like living with her? Tell me: are you happy? No, no, it is easy to see that despite your rights you are neither content nor happy. Between master and slave there can be nothing but the weariness caused by the weight of the chain that binds them together. Whenever freedom is lacking there can be no happiness.

Men keep on complaining about the surliness, the sly and underhandedly mean character that woman reveals in nearly all her relationships. Oh, I would indeed have a very poor opinion of the female race if, in the state of abjection in which the law and customs have maintained them, women submitted to the yoke that weighs upon them without uttering a word. Thank heavens, it is not so; their protest has been continuous since the beginning of time. But since the *Declaration of the Rights of Man*—a solemn act that proclaimed the neglect and contempt of the new men for them—their protest has become vigorous and vehement, which proves that the exasperation of the slave has reached its peak.

Workers, you have good sense and one can reason with you because your minds are not stuffed with a bunch of systems, as Fourier[154] says, would you imagine for a moment that woman is by right the equal of man? Well, what would happen?

As soon as the dangerous consequences of the development of the moral and physical faculties of women—dangerous because of women's current slave status—are no longer feared, woman can be taught with great care so as to make the best possible use of her intelligence and work. Then, you, men of the lower classes, will have as mothers skillful workers who earn a decent salary, are educated, well brought up, and quite capable of raising you, of educating you, the workers, as is proper for free men. You will have well brought up and well educated sisters, lovers, wives, friends, with whom daily contacts will be most pleasant for you. Nothing is sweeter or more agreeable to a man's heart than the sensible and gracious conversation of good and well educated women. We have given a brief outline of what takes place currently in workers' households. Let us now see what will take place in these same households when woman is equal to man.

The husband who knows that his wife's rights are equal to his does not treat her with the disdain and scorn that are shown to inferiors; on the contrary, he treats her with the respect and regard due to one's equal. Then, the woman has no more cause for irritation, and once the cause of irritation is removed the woman is no longer brutal, sly, surly, angry, exasperated, or mean. She is no longer considered as the husband's servant in the house, but rather as the man's partner, his friend and companion. She naturally takes an interest in their association and does her best to make the household prosper. Thanks to her practical experience and theoretical knowledge, she runs her house intelligently, economically, and methodically. Because she is well educated and aware of the usefulness of education, her highest ambition is to raise her children well, she lovingly instructs them herself, supervises their school work, and apprentices them to good employers. Finally she guides them in all manner of things with solicitude, affection, and good judgment.

---

154. Charles Fourier (1772–1837), socialist.

The man, the worker, the husband who has such a wife, enjoys great peace of mind, satisfaction, and happiness. Aware of his wife's intelligence, good sense, and high-mindedness, he is able to discuss important matters with her, communicate his plans, work with her on ways to improve their position. Flattered by his trust, she helps him in his undertakings and business either with good advice or by her activity. The worker, who is himself well educated and well brought up, finds great joy in educating and developing the minds of his children. Workers, in general, are quite warm-hearted and love children.

[...]

Workers, I have barely sketched a picture of the life the proletarian class would enjoy if woman were recognized as the equal of man. This should make you think about the existing evil and about the well-being that could exist. It should make you greatly determined.

Workers, you have no power to repeal old laws and make new ones; no, indeed; but you have the power to protest against the inequity and absurdity of laws that hinder the progress of humanity and make you suffer, you in particular. Thus you can—it is even your sacred duty—you can protest strongly with your ideas, your words, and your writings against all the laws that oppress you. Now, be sure you understand this well: the law that enslaves woman and deprives her of an education also oppresses you, proletarian men.

To raise him, educate him, and teach him the science of the world, the son of the rich has learned governesses and teachers, clever head-mistresses, and finally, beautiful marquises, witty and elegant women, whose function consists in educating the youths of the upper class when they leave college. It is a most useful function for the well-being of those gentlemen of the high nobility. The ladies teach them politeness, tact, subtlety, open-mindedness, and good manners; in a word, they make of them men who know how to live, men of good breeding. If a young man shows any ability, if he has the good fortune to be under the protection of one of those lovely ladies, his success is assured. At thirty-five, he is certain to be an ambassador or a minister. Meanwhile, you, poor workers, to raise you, to educate you, you have only your mothers; to make of you men who know how to live, you have only the women of your class, your companions in ignorance and poverty.

Therefore it is not in the name of the superiority of woman (of which I shall no doubt be accused) that I tell you to demand rights for woman; no, indeed. To begin with, woman must be recognized as a full member of society before we can discuss her superiority. I rely on more solid arguments than that. It is in the name of your own interest, men, of your own improvement, men, and lastly, it is in the name of the universal well-being of all men and women that I urge you to demand rights for women and, in the meantime, to acknowledge them yourselves, at least in principle.

Thus, it is up to you, workers, victims of de facto inequality and injustice, finally to establish on earth the reign of justice and absolute equality between woman and man. Give a great example to the world, an example that will show your oppressors that you wish to triumph by right and not by brute force; you, the 7, 10, 15 millions of proletarians who could use that brute force.

While demanding justice for yourselves, show that you are just and fair; proclaim—you, the strong men, the men with bare arms—that you recognize woman as your equal, and that, as such, you recognize for her an equal right to the benefits of the Universal Union of Working Men and Women.

Tristán, Flora. "The Female Worker's Union (1843)." In *Women, the Family, and Freedom*, vol. 1, translated by Giselle Pincetl, 212–15. Palo Alto, CA: Stanford University Press, 1983.

from *Imperialism: The Highest Stage of Capitalism* by Vladimir Lenin

> **SNAPSHOT BOX**
>
> **LANGUAGE:** Russian
> **PUBLISHED:** 1917, Petrograd, Russia
> **GENRE:** Social theory
> **TAGS:** Class and Caste; Colonization; Economics; History and Ideology; Nationalism; War and Brutality

Introduction

Vladimir Ilich Ulianov—better known by the alias Lenin (1870–1924)—went from being an imprisoned communist dissident to leading Soviet Russia through the Russian Revolution and serving as the first premier of the Union of Soviet Socialist Republics (USSR). One of the most influential people of the twentieth century, Lenin remains a divisive figure today, at once a revolutionary hero of the **proletariat**, the waged laborers under capitalism, and founder of an **authoritarian**, one-party state.

From an educated, noble family, Lenin became radicalized when his brother was executed by the absolutist state of Tsar Alexander III in 1887. The Russian Empire remained autocratic and feudalist despite Alexander II's emancipation of the serfs in 1861, and Alexander III had initiated a series of repressive measures opposed to liberal reforms and revolutionary elements. Lenin joined the forces of political opposition and discovered Marxism when he was a student at Kazan University. In 1897, he was arrested for sedition and exiled to Siberia for three years. He then moved to Europe to study, write, and organize before returning to Russia in 1917 to help lead the October Revolution and usher the Bolsheviks—the more radical faction of the Russian Socialist Democratic Labor Party and predecessor to the Communist Party—into power.

Capitalism is a political and economic system in which the means of production are privately owned. By contrast, **communism** argues that companies, factories,

Timeline

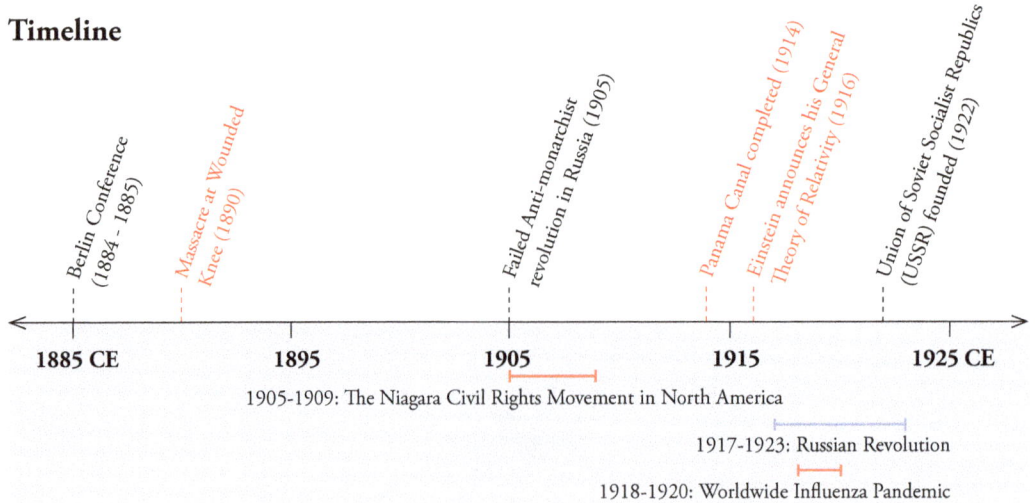

utilities, and the like should be collectively owned and operated because wealth is socially produced. However, Lenin's communist politics, which came to be known as Leninism, departed from orthodox Marxism in two major ways. First, he believed that revolutionary change required leadership by a well-trained **vanguard party** (e.g., the Bolsheviks), as opposed to Marx's positioning of the **proletariat**—the industrial working class—as the political agent that would usher in a post-capitalist society. Lenin's top-down, as opposed to Marx's bottom-up approach to creating a communist state can be understood within the context of the Russian Empire, which was behind its European counterparts in the **capitalist modernization** process and lacked a class-conscious proletariat. Second, Lenin also deviated from Marx's belief that the seeds of communism required the advances of a highly developed capitalist society to take root. Lenin believed, to the contrary, that Russia and its neighboring republics could, with the guidance of the revolutionary vanguard, leap from feudalism to communism, hence his famous motto: "communism is Soviet power plus the electrification of the whole country." Does revolutionary change require both a vanguard party and the presence of advanced forces of modernization like universal broadband or renewable energy? Might a post-capitalist society arise on its own without being instituted by a political party, perhaps due to technological changes rendering capitalism obsolete?

While Lenin remained a stalwart communist, he was a pragmatic political leader willing to alter his beliefs and strategies depending on circumstances. His written work reflects his solidarity with Marxism and his willingness to develop its analytical tools to new topics. The excerpt here from *Imperialism: The Highest Stage of Capitalism* (written in 1916 while in exile in Switzerland) argues that the class struggle between the **bourgeoisie** and proletariat has gone global, with imperialist countries assuming the role of the capitalist class exploiting the labor and resources of working-class colonies. Furthermore, the tendency in capitalism for profits to increase and power to centralize has substituted free market, laissez-faire principles with "international capitalist monopolies." How does Lenin connect imperialism to monopoly behavior? How might his understanding of competition between "advanced countries" help us reconsider the roots of global conflict and war? Does Lenin's description of the usury between rentier and debtor states ring true today?

Kirk Boyle
Department of English

from *Imperialism: The Highest Stage of Capitalism*

Chapter VII: Imperialism as a Special Stage of Capitalism

We must now try to sum up and put together what has been said above on the subject of imperialism. Imperialism emerged as the development and direct continuation of the fundamental attributes of capitalism in general. But capitalism only became capitalist imperialism at a definite and very high stage of its development, when certain of its fundamental attributes began to be transformed into their opposites, when the features of a period of transition from capitalism to a higher social and economic system began to take shape and reveal themselves all along the line. Economically, the main thing in this process is the substitution of capitalist monopolies for capitalist free competition. Free competition is the fundamental attribute of capitalism, and of commodity production generally. Monopoly is exactly the opposite of free competition; but we have seen the latter being transformed into monopoly before our very eyes, creating large-scale industry and eliminating small industry, replacing large-scale industry by still larger-scale industry, finally leading to such a concentration of production and capital that monopoly has been and is the result: cartels, syndicates and trusts, and merging with them, the capital of a dozen or so banks manipulating thousands of millions. At the same time monopoly, which has grown out of free competition, does not abolish the latter, but exists over it and alongside of it, and thereby gives rise to a number of very acute, intense antagonisms, friction and conflicts. Monopoly is the transition from capitalism to a higher system.

If it were necessary to give the briefest possible definition of imperialism we should have to say that imperialism is the monopoly stage of capitalism. Such a definition would include what is most important, for, on the one hand, finance capital is the bank capital of a few big monopolist banks, merged with the capital of the monopolist combines of manufacturers; and, on the other hand, the division of the world is the transition from a colonial policy which has extended without hindrance to territories unoccupied by any capitalist power, to a colonial policy of monopolistic possession of the territory of the world which has been completely divided up.

But very brief definitions, although convenient, for they sum up the main points, are nevertheless inadequate, because very important features of the phenomenon that has to be defined have to be especially deduced. And so, without forgetting the conditional and relative value of all definitions, which can never include all the concatenations of a phenomenon in its complete development, we must give a definition of imperialism that will embrace the following five essential features:

1. The concentration of production and capital developed to such a high stage that it created monopolies which play a decisive role in economic life.
2. The merging of bank capital with industrial capital, and the creation, on the basis of this "finance capital," of a "financial oligarchy."

3. The export of capital, which has become extremely important, as distinguished from the export of commodities.
4. The formation of international capitalist monopolies which share the world among themselves.
5. The territorial division of the whole world among the greatest capitalist powers is completed.

Imperialism is capitalism in that stage of development in which the dominance of monopolies and finance capital has established itself; in which the export of capital has acquired pronounced importance; in which the division of the world among the international trusts has begun; in which the division of all territories of the globe among the great capitalist powers has been completed.

[…]

Capitalism is growing with the greatest rapidity in the colonies and in overseas countries. Among the latter, new imperialist powers are emerging (e.g., Japan). The struggle of world imperialism is becoming more acute. The tribute levied by finance capital on the most profitable colonial and overseas enterprises is increasing. In sharing out this "booty," an exceptionally large part goes to countries which, as far as the development of productive forces is concerned, do not always stand at the top of the list.

[…]

Chaper VIII: The Parasitism and Decay of Capitalism

As we have seen, the most deep-rooted economic foundation of imperialism is monopoly. This is capitalist monopoly, i.e., monopoly which has grown out of capitalism and exists in the general environment of capitalism, commodity production and competition, and remains in permanent and insoluble contradiction to this general environment. Nevertheless, like all monopoly, this capitalist monopoly inevitably gives rise to a tendency to stagnation and decay. As monopoly prices become fixed, even temporarily, so the stimulus to technical and, consequently, to all progress, disappears to a certain extent, and to that extent, also, the *economic* possibility arises of deliberately retarding technical progress. For instance, in America, a certain Mr. Owens invented a machine which revolutionised the manufacture of bottles. The German bottle manufacturing cartel purchased Owens' patent, but pigeonholed it, refrained from utilising it. Certainly, monopoly under capitalism can never completely, and for a long period of time, eliminate competition in the world market (and this, by the by, is one of the reasons why the theory of ultra-imperialism is so absurd). Certainly the possibility of reducing cost of production and increasing profits by introducing technical improvements operates in the direction of change. Nevertheless, the *tendency* to stagnation and decay, which is the feature of monopoly, continues, and in certain branches of industry, in certain countries, for certain periods of time, it becomes predominant.

The monopoly of ownership of very extensive, rich or well-situated colonies, operates in the same direction.

Further, imperialism is an immense accumulation of money capital in a few countries, which, as we have seen, amounts to 100–150 billion francs in various securities. Hence the extraordinary growth of a class, or rather of a category, of *bondholders (rentiers)*, i.e., people who live by "clipping coupons," who take no part whatever in production, whose profession is idleness. The export of capital, one of the most essential economic bases of imperialism, still more completely isolates the *rentiers* from production and sets the seal of parasitism on the whole country that lives by the exploitation of the labour of several overseas countries and colonies.

[…]

The income of the bondholders is *five times greater* than the income obtained from the foreign trade of the greatest "trading" country in the world. This is the essence of imperialism and imperialist parasitism.

For that reason the term, "rentier state" (*Rentnerstaat*), or usurer state, is passing into current use in the economic literature that deals with imperialism. The world has become divided into a handful of usurer states on the one side, and a vast majority of debtor states on the other.

[…]

Chapter X: The Place of Imperialism in History

We have seen that the economic quintessence of imperialism is monopoly capitalism. This very fact determines its place in history, for monopoly that grew up on the basis of free competition, and precisely out of free competition, is the transition from the capitalist system to a higher social-economic order. We must take special note of the four principal forms of monopoly, or the four principal manifestations of monopoly capitalism, which are characteristic of the epoch under review.

Firstly, monopoly arose out of the concentration of production at a very advanced stage of development. This refers to the monopolist capitalist combines, cartels, syndicates and trusts. We have seen the important part that these play in modern economic life. At the beginning of the twentieth century, monopolies acquired complete supremacy in the advanced countries. And although the first steps towards the formation of the cartels were first taken by countries enjoying the protection of high tariffs (Germany, America), Great Britain, with her system of free trade, was not far behind in revealing the same basic phenomenon, namely, the birth of monopoly out of the concentration of production.

Secondly, monopolies have accelerated the capture of the most important sources of raw materials, especially for the coal and iron industries, which are the basic and most highly cartelised industries in capitalist society. The monopoly of the most important sources of raw materials has enormously increased the power of big capital, and has sharpened the antagonism between cartelised and non-cartelised industry.

Thirdly, monopoly has sprung from the banks. The banks have developed from modest intermediary enterprises into the monopolists of finance capital. Some three or five of the biggest banks in each of the foremost capitalist countries have achieved the "personal union" of industrial and bank capital, and have concentrated in their hands the disposal of thousands upon thousands of millions which form the greater part of the capital and income of entire countries. A financial oligarchy, which throws a close net of relations of dependence over all the economic and political institutions of contemporary bourgeois society without exception—such is the most striking manifestation of this monopoly.

Fourthly, monopoly has grown out of colonial policy. To the numerous "old" motives of colonial policy, finance capital has added the struggle for the sources of raw materials, for the export of capital, for "spheres of influence," i.e., for spheres for profitable deals, concessions, monopolist profits and so on; in fine, for economic territory in general. When the colonies of the European powers in Africa, for instance, comprised only one-tenth of that territory (as was the case in 1876), colonial policy was able to develop by methods other than those of monopoly-by the "free grabbing" of territories, so to speak. But when nine-tenths of Africa had been seized (approximately by 1900), when the whole world had been divided up, there was inevitably ushered in a period of colonial monopoly and, consequently, a period of particularly intense struggle for the division and the redivision of the world.

The extent to which monopolist capital has intensified all the contradictions of capitalism is generally known. It is sufficient to mention the high cost of living and the oppression of the cartels. This intensification of contradictions constitutes the most powerful driving force of the transitional period of history, which began from the time of the definite victory of world finance capital.

Monopolies, oligarchy, the striving for domination instead of the striving for liberty, the exploitation of an increasing number of small or weak nations by an extremely small group of the richest or most powerful nations—all these have given birth to those distinctive characteristics of imperialism which compel us to define it as parasitic or decaying capitalism. More and more prominently there emerges, as one of the tendencies of imperialism, the creation of the "bondholding" (rentier) state, the usurer state, in which the bourgeoisie lives on the proceeds of capital exports and by "clipping coupons." It would be a mistake to believe that this tendency to decay precludes the possibility of the rapid growth of capitalism. It does not. In the epoch of imperialism, certain branches of industry, certain strata of the bourgeoisie and certain countries betray, to a more or less degree, one or other of these tendencies. On the whole, capitalism is growing far more rapidly than before. But this growth is not only becoming more and more uneven in general; its unevenness also manifests itself, in particular, in the decay of the countries which are richest in capital (such as England).

Selection from Lenin, Vladimir. *Imperialism: The Highest Stage of Capitalism*, 88–89, 97, 99–101, 123–25. New York: International Publishers, [1939] 1988. Originally published by Progress Publishers. www.progresspublishers.org.

from *Mein Kampf* by Adolf Hitler

SNAPSHOT BOX

LANGUAGE: German
PUBLISHED: 1925–1926, Germany
GENRE: Manifesto
TAGS: History and Ideology; Nationalism; Statecraft; Tyranny; War and Brutality

Introduction

Adolf Hitler (1889–1945) was born in 1889 outside the town of Linz, Austria—then a part of the Austro-Hungarian Empire. Never a strong student, Hitler left Linz after completing his technical schooling (*Realschule*) at the age of sixteen and moved to Vienna to pursue his passion for art. Twice denied entry into the Academy of Fine Arts in Vienna, Hitler was forced to live a bohemian lifestyle, living off the sale of the watercolors and postcards he painted. At the outbreak of World War I, he was conscripted by the Austro-Hungarian Army but failed to pass his medical examination. Returning to Munich, where he had moved in 1913, he enlisted in the Bavarian army of the German Empire in 1914.

Hitler, already a German nationalist in his youth, was struck particularly hard by Germany's defeat in World War I and the subsequent dissolution of the German Empire. That it was succeeded by the liberal democratic Weimar Republic—the same that was responsible for signing the Versailles Peace Treaty that brought World War I to an end—only further inflamed Hitler's anger. He, like many on the right and radical right, believed Germany had been "stabbed in the back" by liberals, democrats, and Jews on the home front, denying Germany a victory in the war. As a result, Hitler joined the German Workers' Party (*Deutsche Arbeiterpartei* or DAP) after the war. The DAP was one of many new parties on the radical right that sought to capitalize on the economic and political instability in the postwar period. After a rebranding of the DAP into the National Socialist German Workers' Party

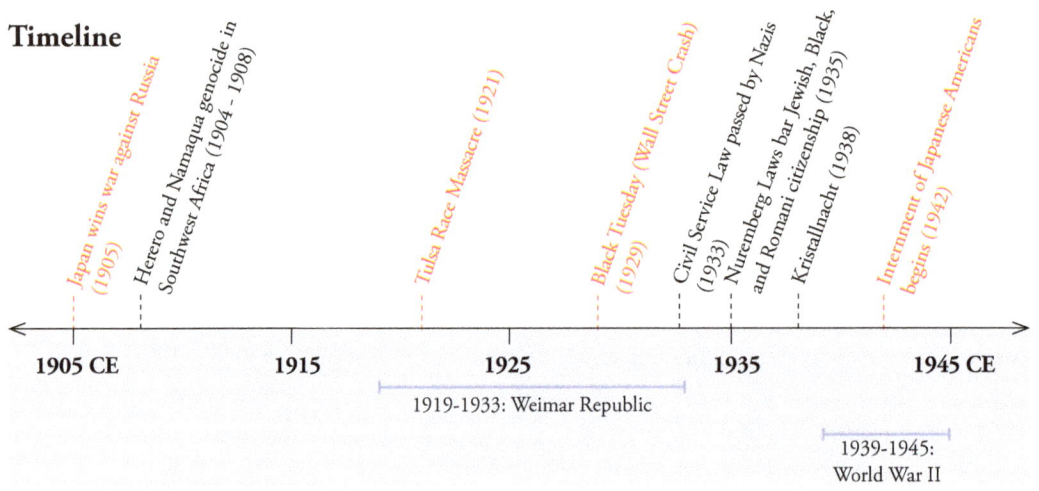

(*Nationalsozialistische Deutsche Arbeiterpartei* or NSDAP, abbreviated Nazi) in 1920, Hitler soon rose through its ranks to become president of the party by 1921. How might suffering a political or economic setback, such as the German defeat in World War I or the international economic downturn of the late 1920s, influence the nature of national identity or foster radical ideologies?

Mein Kampf (*My Struggle*) is the personal manifesto of the Nazi leader Adolf Hitler that was conceived while he was imprisoned for a failed 1923 coup d'état. Inspired by Benito Mussolini's "March on Rome" the previous year, Hitler was convinced that his "brown shirts"—the militia of the Nazis—could first march to the Bavarian armory in Munich and then north to the German capital in Berlin. The "Beer Hall Putsch" of November 9, 1923, was stopped by the police before it ever made it to the armory and Hitler was subsequently arrested and imprisoned. While the police demonstrated their loyalty to the laws of the new Weimar Republic by arresting many of the actors in the coup, the court proved more sympathetic to Hitler's antidemocratic cause: he was sentenced to five years in Landsberg prison and served only nine months. Although his coup attempt was a failure, his subsequent imprisonment taught Hitler an important lesson: he would have to come to power through legal means. As you read, what are some of his machinations on how to harness power through legal means that you can identify?

Hitler's manifesto consists of two volumes, the first published in 1925 and the latter in 1926. Throughout the 1920s its popularity was limited; only after Hitler was able to secure his legal appointment to chancellor in 1933 did its presence on German bookshelves and coffee tables become ubiquitous. As such, *Mein Kampf* does more to tell us how Hitler and the Nazis came to power than it does in providing us with a blueprint for what they would do once there. Nonetheless, it does lay out some of Nazism's ideological themes: propaganda as a necessary tool of the state, a biologically reductionist and racist understanding of the nation, and the creation of a common enemy in Jews and communists.

Eric Roubinek
Department of History

[Content Notice: racism, anti-Semitism]

> **PRE-READING PARS**
>
> 1. When was the last time you were part of a crowd—maybe at a theater, concert, sporting event, or house of worship? Describe what it was like to be a part of that group. How did you, as an individual, act?
> 2. List the forms of media (print, film, television, etc.) that you consume on a daily basis. For what purpose do you consume them (information, entertainment, etc.)?
> 3. In a sentence or two, define the following two terms: "race" and "nation." How are your definitions of these words different or similar?

from *Mein Kampf* (1925–1926)

Volume One: A Reckoning

III. General Political Considerations Based on My Vienna Period

[...] But the power which has always started the greatest religious and political avalanches in history rolling has from time immemorial been the magic power of the spoken word, and that alone.

Particularly the broad masses of the people can be moved only by the power of speech. And all great movements are popular movements, volcanic eruptions of human passions and emotional sentiments, stirred either by the cruel Goddess of Distress or by the firebrand of the word hurled among the masses; they are not the lemonade-like outpourings of literary aesthetes and drawing-room heroes.

[...]

A movement with great aims must therefore be anxiously on its guard not to lose contact with the broad masses.

It must examine every question primarily from this standpoint and make its decisions accordingly.

It must, furthermore, avoid everything which might diminish or even weaken its ability to move the masses, not for 'demagogic' reasons, but in the simple knowledge that without the mighty force of the mass of a people, no great idea, however lofty and noble it may seem, can be realized.

[...]

In general the art of all truly great national leaders at all times consists among other things primarily in not dividing the attention of a people, but in concentrating it upon a single foe. The more unified the application of a people's will to fight, the greater will be the magnetic attraction of a movement and the mightier will be the impetus of the thrust. It belongs to the genius of a great leader to make even adversaries far removed from one another seem to belong to a single category, because in weak and uncertain characters the knowledge of having different enemies can only too readily lead to the beginning of doubt in their own right.

[…]

VI. War Propaganda

[…] The second really decisive question was this: To whom should propaganda be addressed? To the scientifically trained intelligentsia or to the less educated masses?

It must be addressed always and exclusively to the masses.

[…]

All propaganda must be popular and its intellectual level must be adjusted to the most limited intelligence among those it is addressed to. Consequently, the greater the mass it is intended to reach, the lower its purely intellectual level will have to be. But if, as in propaganda for sticking out a war, the aim is to influence a whole people, we must avoid excessive intellectual demands on our public, and too much caution cannot be exerted in this direction.

The more modest its intellectual ballast, the more exclusively it takes into consideration the emotions of the masses, the more effective it will be. And this is the best proof of the soundness or unsoundness of a propaganda campaign, and not success in pleasing a few scholars or young aesthetes.

The art of propaganda lies in understanding the emotional ideas of the great masses and finding, through a psychologically correct form, the way to the attention and thence to the heart of the broad masses. The fact that our bright boys do not understand this merely shows how mentally lazy and conceited they are.

Once we understand how necessary it is for propaganda to be adjusted to the broad mass; the following rule results:

It is a mistake to make propaganda many-sided, like scientific instruction, for instance.

The receptivity of the great masses is very limited, their intelligence is small, but their power of forgetting is enormous. In consequence of these facts, all effective propaganda must be limited to a very few points and must harp on these in slogans until the last member of the public understands what you want him to understand by your slogan. As soon as you sacrifice this slogan and try to be many-sided, the effect will piddle away, for the crowd can neither digest nor retain the material offered. In this way the result is weakened and in the end entirely cancelled out.

[…]

X. Causes of the Collapse

[…] It required the whole bottomless falsehood of the Jews and their Marxist fighting organization to lay the blame for the collapse on that very man who alone, with superhuman energy and will power, tried to prevent the catastrophe he foresaw and save the nation from its time of deepest humiliation and disgrace. By branding Ludendorff [155] as guilty for the loss of the World War, they took the weapon of moral right from the one dangerous accuser who could have risen against the traitors to the fatherland. In this they proceeded on the sound principle that the magnitude of a lie always contains a certain factor of credibility, since the great masses of the people in the very bottom of their hearts tend to be corrupted rather than consciously and purposely evil, and that, therefore, in view of the primitive simplicity of their minds, they more easily fall a victim to a big lie than to a little one, since they themselves lie in little things, but would be ashamed of lies that were too big.

[...]

XI. Nation and Race

[...] No more than Nature desires the mating of weaker with stronger individuals, even less does she desire the blending of a higher with a lower race, since, if she did, her whole work of higher breeding, over perhaps hundreds of thousands of years, night be ruined with one blow.

Historical experience offers countless proofs of this. It shows with terrifying clarity that in every mingling of Aryan blood with that of lower peoples the result was the end of the cultured people. North America, whose population consists in by far the largest part of Germanic elements who mixed but little with the lower colored peoples, shows a different humanity and culture from Central and South America, where the predominantly Latin immigrants often mixed with the aborigines on a large scale. By this one example, we can clearly and distinctly recognize the effect of racial mixture. The Germanic inhabitant of the American continent, who has remained racially pure and unmixed, rose to be master of the continent; he will remain the master as long as he does not fall a victim to defilement of the blood.

The result of all racial crossing is therefore in brief always the following:

(a) lowering of the level of the higher race;
(b) physical and intellectual regression and hence the beginning of a slowly but surely progressing sickness.

To bring about such a development is, then, nothing else but to sin against the will of the eternal creator.

[...]

Everything we admire on this earth today—science and art, technology and inventions—is only the creative product of a few peoples and originally perhaps of *one* race. On them depends the existence of this whole culture. If they perish, the beauty of this earth will sink into the grave with them.

---

155. Erich Ludendorff (1865–1937), a high-ranking World War I German military commander who insisted on an armistice after it became clear to him that Germany would lose the war.

However much the soil, for example, can influence men, the result of the influence will always be different depending on the races in question. The low fertility of a living space may spur the one race to the highest achievements; in others it will only be the cause of bitterest poverty and final undernourishment with all its consequences. The inner nature of peoples is always determining for the manner in which outward influences will be effective. What leads the one to starvation trains the other to hard work.

All great cultures of the past perished only because the originally creative race died out from blood poisoning.

The ultimate cause of such a decline was their forgetting that all culture depends on men and not conversely; hence that to preserve a certain culture the man who creates it must be preserved. This preservation is bound up with the rigid law of necessity and the right to victory of the best and stronger in this world.

Those who want to live, let them fight, and those who do not want to fight in this world of eternal struggle do not deserve to live.

[...]

If we were to divide mankind into three groups, the founders of culture, the bearers of culture, the destroyers of culture, only the Aryan could be considered as the representative of the first group. From him originate the foundations and walls of all human creation, and only the outward form and color are determined by the changing traits of character of the various peoples. He provides the mightiest building stones and plans for all human progress and only the execution corresponds to the nature of the varying men and races.

[...]

Thus, the Jew of all times has lived in the states of other peoples, and there formed his own state, which, to be sure, habitually sailed under the disguise of 'religious community' as long as outward circumstances made a complete revelation of his nature seem inadvisable. But as soon as he felt strong enough to do without the protective cloak, he always dropped the veil and suddenly became what so many of the others previously did not want to believe and see: the Jew.

The Jew's life as a parasite in the body of other nations and states explains a characteristic which once caused Schopenhauer, as has already been mentioned, to call him the 'great master in lying.' Existence impels the Jew to lie, and to lie perpetually, just as it compels the inhabitants of the northern countries to wear warm clothing.

His life within other peoples can only endure for any length of time if he succeeds in arousing the opinion that he is not a people but a 'religious community,' though of a special sort.

And this is the first great lie.

[...]

But even more: all at once the Jew also becomes liberal and begins to rave about the necessary progress of mankind.

Slowly he makes himself the spokesman of a new era.

Also, of course, he destroys more and more thoroughly the foundations of any economy that will really benefit the people. By way of stock shares he pushes his way into the circuit of national production which he turns into a purchasable or rather tradable object, thus robbing the enterprises of the foundations of a personal ownership. Between employer and employee there arises that inner estrangement which later leads to political class division.

Finally, the Jewish influence on economic affairs grows with terrifying speed through the stock exchange. He becomes the owner, or at least the controller, of the national labor force.

[...]

Since the Jew is not the attacked but the attacker, not only anyone who attacks passes as his enemy, but also anyone who resists him. But the means with which he seeks to break such reckless but upright souls is not honest warfare, but lies and slander.

Here he stops at nothing, and in his vileness he becomes so gigantic that no one need be surprised if among our people the personification of the devil as the symbol of all evil assumes the living shape of the Jew.

The ignorance of the broad masses about the inner nature of the Jew, the lack of instinct and narrow-mindedness of our upper classes, make the people an easy victim for this Jewish campaign of lies.

[...]

With satanic joy in his face, the black-haired Jewish youth lurks in wait for the unsuspecting girl whom he defiles with his blood, thus stealing her from her people. With every means he tries to destroy the racial foundations of the people he has set out to subjugate. Just as he himself systematically ruins women and girls, he does not shrink back from pulling down the blood barriers for others, even on a large scale. It was and it is Jews who bring the Negroes[156] into the Rhineland, always with the same secret thought and dear aim of ruining the hated white race by the necessarily resulting bastardization, throwing it down from its cultural and political height, and himself rising to be its master.

For a racially pure people which is conscious of its blood can never be enslaved by the Jew. In this world he will forever be master over bastards and bastards alone.

And so he tries systematically to lower the racial level by a continuous poisoning of individuals.

And in politics he begins to replace the idea of democracy by the dictatorship of the proletariat.

In the organized mass of Marxism he has found the weapon which lets him dis-

---

156. Hitler uses the term "Negro" to refer to African communities as was a prevalent practice within and outside of Black communities from the nineteenth to mid-twentieth centuries. The term "negro" should not be confused with the derogatory n-word. Likewise another term used during the same timeframe, "colored," is outdated and should not be confused with the current usage of "person of color." Words reflecting African and Black communities' preferences for self-identification continue to shift in meaning and connotation over time.

pense with democracy and in its stead allows him to subjugate and govern the peoples with a dictatorial and brutal fist.

[…]

Volume Two: The Socialist Movement

I. Philosophy and Party

[…] Human culture and civilization on this continent are inseparably bound up with the presence of the Aryan. If he dies out or declines, the dark veils of an age without culture will again descend on this globe.

The undermining of the existence of human culture by the destruction of its bearer seems in the eyes of a folkish philosophy the most execrable crime. Anyone who dares to lay hands on the highest image of the Lord commits sacrilege against the benevolent creator of this miracle and contributes to the expulsion from paradise.

And so the folkish philosophy of life corresponds to the innermost will of Nature, since it restores that free play of forces which must lead to a continuous mutual higher breeding, until at last the best of humanity, having achieved possession of this earth, will have a free path for activity in domains which will lie partly above it and partly outside it.

We all sense that in the distant future humanity must be faced by problems which only a highest race, become master people and supported by the means and possibilities of an entire globe, will be equipped to overcome.

[…]

Selection from Hitler, Adolf. *Mein Kampf*, translated by Ralph Manheim, 106–7, 118, 179, 180–81, 231, 286, 288–90, 305, 314, 324–26, 383–84. Boston: Houghton Mifflin Company, [1943] 1971.

POST-READING PARS

1. How well do Hitler's claims about the power of the spoken word fit with the example you listed above from your experience of being a part of a crowd?

2. *Mein Kampf* outlines the power of propaganda and the simple message. In what ways might we consider the forms of media you consume to be propaganda?

3. How does Hitler define the concepts of race and nation? How do your definitions differ? How do Hitler's definitions differ from previous understandings of these terms as put forth during the age of revolutions?

Inquiry Corner

Content Question:

How does Hitler see propaganda functioning, its role, and its target?

Critical Question:

Identify strategies of fascism being employed in this excerpt.

Comparative Question:

Many scholars have deemed Nazism a scavenger ideology, one that pulled from different strands of thought and practice while creating little of its own. At the same time, others have considered Nazism's rabid anti-Semitism beyond comparison. In these selections from *Mein Kampf*, can you identify any strands of thought or practice that are similar to other texts we have read?

Connection Question:

Mein Kampf was born out of a specific historical context following the German defeat in World War I. When and where have similar ideas manifested since the defeat of Nazism in World War II?

from *The Origins of Totalitarianism* by Hannah Arendt

Introduction

Hannah Arendt (1906–1975) was one of the most important political thinkers of the twentieth century. She is highly regarded by theorists in political science and philosophy, though she adamantly refused the label of "philosopher."[157] Much of Arendt's political analysis was a critique of European modernity. By Arendt's analysis, totalitarianism is a completely new and modern phenomenon, and the greatest evil of our time. It was an evil she had encountered personally as a Jew in Nazi Germany. She escaped Nazi persecution of Jews by moving to France after defending her doctorate in philosophy. When France was occupied by the Nazis, she was arrested and escaped, fleeing to the United States in 1941. In the "Affidavit of Identity in Lieu of a Passport" that Arendt completed in 1946 to return to Germany for a few months to help with Jewish cultural reconstruction after the war, she describes herself as "a stateless person" at the time of her analysis of totalitarianism.[158] Arendt was suspicious of modern ideals of the nation-state.

> **SNAPSHOT BOX**
>
> LANGUAGE: English
> PUBLISHED: 1951
> GENRE: Sociopolitical critique, philosophical treatise
> TAGS: Ethics and Morality; History and Ideology; Nationalism; Tyranny; Ways of Knowing

She offered an intricate analysis and critique of totalitarianism, focusing upon what she regarded as the two most important examples in her time, Nazi Germany and the Stalinist Soviet Union. Arendt speaks of two complementary aspects of totalitarianism that, at first, might seem to be contradictory: atomization and nebulous unifiers. Atomization of the people into isolated individuals eliminates all other allegiances and renders them vulnerable to the totalitarian regime's demand for complete and absolute loyalty. The totalitarian state demands to be the sole source of all value in one's life. In place of former obligations to family, religion, friends, and other political groups, the totalitarian regime rallies the atomized individuals through nebulous unifiers that secure complete loyalty. These illusory, arbitrary, and meaningless unifiers allow the totalitarian regime to secure a fanatical devotion in place of any substantial political goal or conviction. Hitler and Stalin implemented these unifiers to create "mass organizations of atomized, isolated individuals." The resulting mob mentality, characterized by its zeal and its potential for violence, was most effective when unified by slogans or unfounded ideas that were not suscep-

---

157. Günter Gaus, "Hannah Arendt Zur Person [im Gespräch with Günter Gaus]," video of interview on West German Television "Zur Person," October 28, 1964, https://www.youtube.com/watch?v=dsoImQfVsO4. The comment is at the 0:57 mark.

158. Hannah Arendt, "Affidavit of Identity in Lieu of a Passport" (1946). Library of Congress, "From Haven to Home: 350 Years of Jewish Life in America." https://www.loc.gov/exhibits/haventohome/haven-century.html#obj27.

Timeline

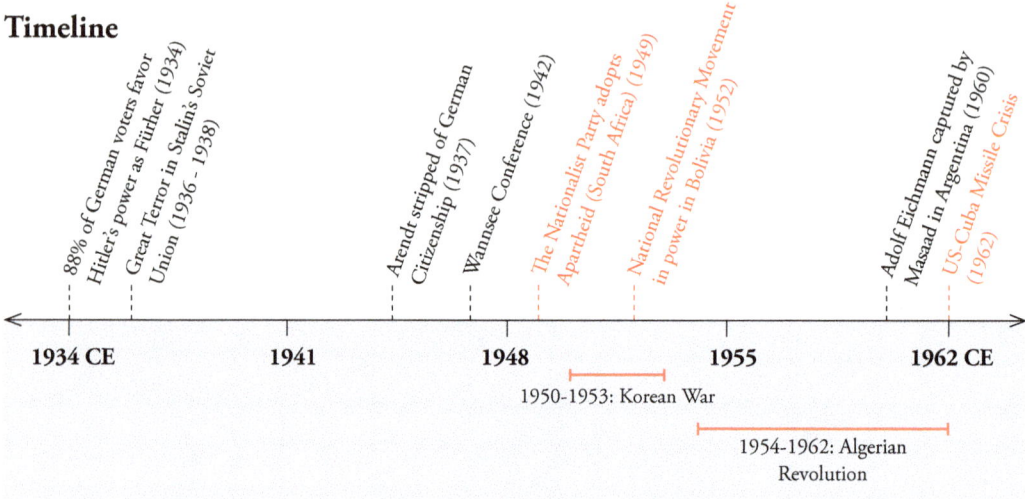

tible to critique.¹⁵⁹ In what ways do you see atomization or nebulous unifiers within institutions or communities?

Arendt describes how a totalitarian regime depends upon such a mass movement. "The totalitarian movements aim at organizing masses not classes."¹⁶⁰ Classes have clearly defined identities often associated with ideologies. Masses are comprised of disaffected people whose identity can be molded by loyalty to the regime. In the case of Nazi Germany, Hitler rose to power by manipulating a mass movement that was already in place. His use of what Arendt frames as atomization and nebulous unifiers separated the Nazi party from its original platform, as discussed in the excerpt you will be reading, simply by never addressing the original ideals, in favor of fiery rhetoric demanding loyalty, fabricating false history, and laying claim to a destiny. Stalin's case was different, according to Arendt. Stalin had to create the mass movement that wrested control of the party — creating and flexing the muscle

---

159. I witnessed such a mass movement in Paris in 2019, with the mass protests of the "*gilets jaunes*" [yellow vests]. Anyone with a motor vehicle in France is required by law to have a yellow vest in the car in case of incident, so it was the perfect "uniform" to adopt for the mass movement. Everyone with a car already has one, regardless of political affiliation, social standing, religion, etc. The yellow vests organized mass protests throughout France for many months. As an example of what Arendt describes as a "nebulous unifier," I witnessed ultra-left and ultra-right protesters marching arm-in-arm, chanting "*Macron: la France n'est pas à vendre!*" [Macron: France is not for sale!] To the ultra-leftists, these words meant that French president Macron should not continue to reduce the strong social network in France; to the ultra-rightists, this same slogan meant that France should withdraw from the European Union and expel immigrants. The point is, these atomized individuals were unified by a meaningless slogan.

160. Hannah Arendt, *Totalitarianism* (Part III of *The Origins of Totalitarianism* (New York: Harcourt, Brace, Jovanovich, 1968), 6.

at the same time. Arendt writes, "To change Lenin's revolutionary dictatorship into full totalitarian rule, Stalin had first to create artificially that atomized society which had been prepared for the Nazis in Germany by historical circumstances."[161] In the cases of Hitler and Stalin, the vilification and persecution of Jews unified the totalitarian movements.

It is interesting that Arendt did not consider Lenin or Mussolini to be totalitarians. She describes them as "single party dictators" distinguished by their relations to mass movements. Lenin's penchant for analysis and self-critique was "against the rules of even ordinary demagogy."[162] Mussolini, "who was so fond of the term 'totalitarian state,' [still] did not attempt to establish a full-fledged totalitarian regime," as she demonstrates through the possibility of judicial innocence once one was accused of disloyalty.[163]

Perhaps the most controversial moment in Arendt's career came when she covered the trial of Adolf Eichmann in Jerusalem in 1962.[164] Eichmann was the principal organizer of the logistics of shipping millions of Jews, homosexuals, communists, Roma, and others to their deaths in extermination camps—the so-called final solution. Eichmann had escaped to Argentina, where he was arrested about fifteen years after the end of World War II. He was extradited to Israel where he was tried, convicted, and executed. Arendt was alarmed at some traits of totalitarianism on display by Israel, where Eichmann's conviction was a "show trial" not unlike those orchestrated by Stalin during his purges in 1938 in the Soviet Union. Arendt adamantly refused that Eichmann or any of the Nazis were monsters or unlike anyone else (for which she was banned from Israel). She thought the real danger of totalitarianism was in the capacity of the everyday person to succumb to it. The phrase in the subtitle of her book, "the banality of evil," points out that the capacity for the greatest evils of modernity is present in everyday modern life. Arendt reveals that the troubling potential for totalitarianism is intertwined with the foundations of Western modernities. As you read the excerpt below, consider how our contemporary experience might offer us a way to evaluate Arendt's ideas.

Duane H. Davis
Department of Philosophy

161. Arendt, *Totalitarianism*, 16.
162. Arendt, *Totalitarianism*, 16.
163. Arendt, *Totalitarianism*, 6.
164. She published her account serially in the *New Yorker*, and as a book in 1963. Hannah Arendt, *Eichmann in Jerusalem: A Report on the Banality of Evil* (New York: Penguin Classics, 2006).

from *The Origins of Totalitarianism*

Totalitarian movements are mass organizations of atomized, isolated individuals. Compared with all other parties and movements, their most conspicuous external characteristic is their demand for total, unrestricted, unconditional, and unalterable loyalty of the individual member. This demand is made by the leaders of totalitarian movements even before they seize power. It usually precedes the total organization of the country under their actual rule and it follows from the claim of their ideologies that their organization will encompass, in due course, the entire human race. Where, however, totalitarian rule has not been prepared by a totalitarian movement (and this, in contradistinction to Nazi Germany, was the case in Russia), the movement has to be organized afterward and the conditions for its growth have artificially to be created in order to make loyalty—the psychological basis for total domination—at all possible. Such loyalty can be expected only from the completely isolated human being who, without any other social ties to family, friends, comrades, or even mere acquaintances, derives his sense of having a place in the world only from his belonging to a movement, his membership in the party.

Total loyalty is possible only when fidelity is emptied of all concrete content, from which changes of mind might naturally arise. The totalitarian movements, each in its own way, have done their utmost to get rid of the party programs which specified concrete content and which they inherited from earlier, nontotalitarian stages of development. No matter how radically they might have been phrased, every definite political goal which does not simply assert or circumscribe the claim to world rule, every political program which deals with issues more specific than "ideological questions of importance for centuries" is an obstruction to totalitarianism. Hitler's greatest achievement in the organization of the Nazi movement, which he gradually built up from the obscure crackpot membership of a typically nationalistic little party, was that he unburdened the movement of the party's earlier program, not by changing or officially abolishing it, but simply by refusing to talk about it or discuss its points, whose relative moderateness of content and phraseology were very soon outdated.[165] Stalin's task in this as in other respects was much more formidable; the socialist program of the Bolshevik party was a much more troublesome burden[166]

---

165. Hitler stated in *Mein Kampf* (2 vols., 1st German ed., 1925 and 1927 respectively. Unexpurgated translation, New York, 1939) that it was better to have an antiquated program than to allow a discussion of program (Book II, chapter v). Soon he was to proclaim publicly: "Once we take over the government, the program will come of itself. . . . The first thing must be an inconceivable wave of propaganda. That is a political action which would have little to do with the other problems of the moment." See Hitler, op. cit., 203.

166. Souvarine, in our opinion wrongly, suggests that Lenin had already abolished the role of a party program: "Nothing could show more clearly the nonexistence of Bolshevism as a doctrine except in Lenin's brain; every Bolshevik left to himself wandered from 'the line' of his faction . . . for these men were bound together by their temperament and by the ascendancy of Lenin rather than by ideas" (op. cit., 85).

than the 25 points of an amateur economist and a crackpot politician.[167] But Stalin achieved eventually, after having abolished the factions of the Russian party, the same result through the constant zigzag of the Communist Party lines, and the constant reinterpretation and application of Marxism which voided the doctrine of all its content because it was no longer possible to predict what course or action it would inspire. The fact that the most perfect education in Marxism and Leninism was no guide whatsoever for political behavior—that, on the contrary, one could follow the party line only if one repeated each morning what Stalin had announced the night before—naturally resulted in the same state of mind, the same concentrated obedience, undivided by any attempt to understand what one was doing, that Himmler's ingenious watchword for his SS-men expressed: "My honor is my loyalty."[168]

Lack of, or ignoring of, a party program is by itself not necessarily a sign of totalitarianism. The first to consider programs and platforms as needless scraps of paper and embarrassing promises, inconsistent with the style and impetus of a movement, was Mussolini with his fascist philosophy of activism and inspiration through the historical moment itself.[169] Mere lust for power combined with contempt for "talkative" articulation of what they intend to do with it is characteristic of all mob leaders, but does not come up to the standards of totalitarianism. The true goal of fascism was only to seize power and establish the fascist "elite" as uncontested ruler over the country. Totalitarianism is never content to rule by external means, namely, through the state and a machinery of violence; thanks to its peculiar ideology and the role assigned to it in this apparatus of coercion, totalitarianism has discovered a means of dominating and terrorizing human beings from within. In this sense it eliminates the distance between the rulers and the ruled and achieves a condition in which power and the will to power, as we understand them, play no role, or at best, a secondary role. In substance, the totalitarian leader is nothing more nor less than the functionary of the masses he leads; he is not a power-hungry individual imposing a tyrannical and arbitrary will upon his subjects. Being a mere functionary, he can be replaced at

---

167. Gottfried Feder's Program of the Nazi Party with its famous twenty-five points has played a greater role in the literature about the movement than in the movement itself.

168. The impact of the watchword, formulated by Himmler himself, is difficult to render. Its German equivalent: "*Meine Ehre heisst Treue,*" indicates an absolute devolution and obedience which transcends the meaning of mere discipline or personal faithfulness. *Nazi Conspiracy*, whose translations of German documents and Nazi literature are indispensable source material but, unfortunately, are very uneven, renders the SS watchword: "My honor signifies faithfulness" (V, 346).

169. Mussolini was probably the first party leader who consciously rejected a formal program and replaced it with inspired leadership and action alone. Behind this act lay the notion that the actuality of the moment itself was the chief element of inspiration, which would only be hampered by a party program. The philosophy of Italian Fascism has been expressed by Gentile's "actualism" rather than by Sorel's "myths." Compare also the article "Fascism" in the *Encyclopedia of the Social Sciences*. The Program of 1921 was formulated when the movement had been in existence two years and contained, for the most part, its nationalist philosophy.

any time, and he depends just as much on the "will" of the masses he embodies as the masses depend on him. Without him they would lack external representation and remain an amorphous horde; without the masses the leader is a nonentity. Hitler who was fully aware of this interdependence, expressed it once in a speech addressed to the SA:[170] "All that you are, you are through me; all that I am, I am through you alone."[171] We are only too inclined to belittle such statements or to misunderstand them in the sense that acting is defined here in terms of giving and executing orders, as has happened too often in the political tradition and history of the West.[172] But this idea has always presupposed someone in command who thinks and wills, and then imposes his thought and will on a thought- and will-deprived group—be it by persuasion, authority, or violence. Hitler, however, was of the opinion that even "thinking . . . [exists] only by virtue of giving or executing orders,"[173] and thereby eliminated even theoretically the distinction between thinking and acting on one hand, and between the rulers and the ruled on the other.

Neither National Socialism nor Bolshevism has ever proclaimed a new form of government or asserted that its goals were reached with the seizure of power and the control of the state machinery. Their idea of domination was something that no state and no mere apparatus of violence can ever achieve, but only a movement that is constantly kept in motion: namely, the permanent domination of each single individual in each and every sphere of life.[174] The seizure of power through the means of violence is never an end in itself but only the means to an end, and the seizure of power in any given country is only a welcome transitory stage but never the end of the movement. The practical goal of the movement is to organize as many people as possible within its framework and to set and keep them in motion; a political goal that would constitute the end of the movement simply does not exist.

Selection from Arendt, Hannah. *The Origins of Totalitarianism*. New York: Harcourt Brace Jovanovich, 1973 [1979].

---

170. Editor's note: SA, an abbreviation for *die Sturmabteilung*, or Brownshirts, Hitler's infamous storm troops.

171. Ernst Bayer, *Die SA*, Berlin, 1938. Translation quoted from Nazi Compiracy, N, 783.

172. For the first time in Plato's *Statesman*, 305, where acting is interpreted in terms of *archein* and *prattein*—of ordering the start of an action and of executing this order.

173. Henry Picker, ed., *Hitlers Tischgespräche im Führerhauptquartier* (Goldman Verlag, 1976), 198.

174. *Mein Kampf*, Book I, chapter xi. See also, for example, Dieter Schwarz, *Angriffe auf die nationalsozialistische Weltanschauung*. Aus dem Schwarzen Korps, No. 2, 1936, who answers the obvious criticism that National Socialists after their rise to power continued to talk about "a struggle": "National Socialism as an ideology [Weltanschauung] will not abandon its struggle until . . . the way of life of each individual German has been shaped by its fundamental values and these are realized every day anew."

from *The Political and Social Doctrine of Fascism* by Benito Mussolini

Introduction

Benito Mussolini (1883–1945) was born in 1883 to a blacksmith father and schoolteacher mother in the province of Forlí in Romagna, Italy. By the age of thirty he had worked as a teacher, journalist, and active member of Italy's socialist party. Although Mussolini's support for Marxist ideals led him to become editor of the socialist newspaper *Avanti!* he also maintained—a seemingly paradoxical—support for Italian nationalism. While in 1911 he joined the other rioting socialists against the imperialist war Italy was waging in Libya; by 1914 he was expelled from the socialist party for his support of Italian intervention in World War I.

The Great War (WWI) represented a turning point for much of the world, and particularly for Mussolini and Italy. France and Britain had lured Italy to side with the Triple Entente (an alliance between Britain, France, and Russia) by promising territorial gains in the Mediterranean and Africa, but despite concluding the war on the victorious side, none of these promises came to fruition. Betrayed by socialists upon entering the war and liberal democrats upon its conclusion, Mussolini now endeavored to find a third way to circumvent the social, political, and economic uncertainty brought about by the war. Building upon his prior journalistic experience with his newspaper, *Il Popolo d'Italia* (created in 1914), he became a strong orator and effective propagandist for his new

> **SNAPSHOT BOX**
>
> LANGUAGE: Italian
> PUBLISHED: 1935, Italy
> GENRE: Manifesto
> TAGS: Class and Caste; Community; History and Ideology; Nationalism; Psyche; Statecraft; Tyranny; War and Brutality

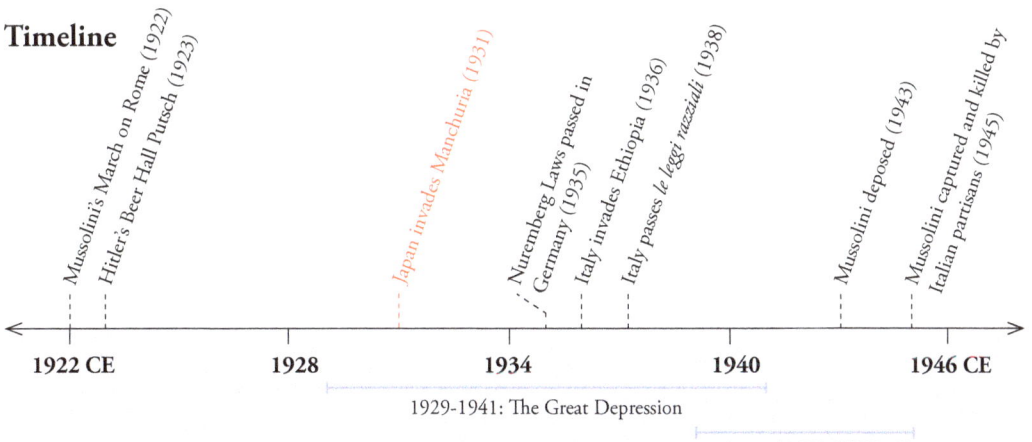

Timeline

ideas, attracting anarchists, frustrated republicans, veterans, and radicals from all sides of the political spectrum. Why would such a nationalist appeal garner support after the sacrifices of World War I?

Beyond Mussolini's broad appeal, he was further supported by the *Camicie Nere* (Blackshirts) who were the Italian Fascist Party's militia and who later became self-styled soldiers for the Italian state. The Fascist movement's militarized appearance and name were intended to hark back to the greatness of the Roman Empire even as they claimed to solidly represent Italy in the twentieth century. Mussolini was able to use this spectacle of myth and order in these times of instability to great effect. In October 1922 Mussolini and his Blackshirts marched on Rome to demand that the king appoint him prime minister. With some 30,000 fascists converging on the capital city, King Victor Emmanuel III agreed to their demands. In this moment of crisis, Mussolini was initially granted limited dictatorial powers as prime minister, but by 1923 he had passed the Acerbo Law that changed election policies and essentially guaranteed his indefinite dictatorship.

Mussolini's National Fascist Party (the name his movement took in 1921) rejected orthodox socialism with its privileging of class conflict and instead focused on the nation. But Fascism for Mussolini was also populist and recognized the needs and desires of the "little man." Fascism claimed that the state was the ultimate guarantor and protector of both needs and desires. Toward this end, Mussolini and the Fascist Party initiated massive social and political reforms, public works projects, and grand constructions to immortalize their achievements within the built landscape. Mussolini's Fascist revolution called for nothing less than the creation of a "new Fascist man and woman." What arguments might you find convincing to re-create yourself?

Italian Fascism was the first of many similar movements across Europe: Oswald Moseley's British Union of Fascists, Codreanu's Legion of the Archangel Michael in Romania, the Arrow Cross in Hungary, Croatia's Ustaše, and, of course, National Socialism in Germany. While Hitler was inspired by Mussolini's march on Rome (see his failed Beer Hall Putsch, 1923), the other movements were largely inspired by Nazism, or at least shared Nazism's anti-Semitism (the prejudice and discrimination against Jewish people), something that was not predominant within Italian Fascism. Indeed, Italian Fascism and German National Socialism were relatively antagonistic until Mussolini decided to invade Ethiopia (a member state of the League of Nations) in 1935 and found himself without international support — except for Hitler's Germany. Uniting over imperial claims, the two states soon came together in the Rome-Berlin Treaty (Axis) and Anti-Comintern Pact, both in 1936. By 1938 Fascist Italy had adopted a version of Nazi Germany's anti-Semitic Nuremberg Laws. By 1939 both states had entered into World War II and would be joined by Japan in 1940 with the signing of the Tripartite Pact forming the Axis. Their major opponents in the war, the Allies, consisted primarily of Britain, France, China, and later the Soviet Union and the United States.

Less prepared for another great conflict than its Axis partners, Fascist Italy became the Western Allies' successful point of invasion from northern Africa in 1943. As a result Mussolini was deposed and imprisoned. Soon rescued by the Nazis, Mussolini was subsequently installed as the leader of the Republic of Saló (a puppet state created by Nazi Germany after Mussolini's rescue) in northern Italy. Yet, by this time the National Fascist Party had already been dissolved and the new Italian government was pursuing peace with the Allies. In 1945 Mussolini was captured and executed by Italian partisans.

In *The Political Doctrine of Fascism*, Mussolini glorifies war, violence, and the state. In many ways this seems to go against the grain of the Enlightenment thinkers and their emphasis on the recognition and protection of natural rights. On the other hand, can you think of examples that ground his ideas within the Enlightenment and modern thought? What failures of Marxist and liberal democratic ideals does he highlight? How does Mussolini argue that the Fascist state is the best guarantor of individual rights? Why do you think that it took thirteen years from the Fascist revolution in 1922 to outline the "doctrine" of Fascism as understood within the Italian context?

Eric Roubinek
Department of History

from *The Political and Social Doctrine of Fascism* (1935)

[. . .] The years which preceded the march to Rome were years of great difficulty, during which the necessity for action did not permit of research or any complete elaboration of doctrine. The battle had to be fought in the towns and villages. There was much discussion, but—what was more important and sacred—men died. They knew how to die. Doctrine, beautifully defined and carefully elucidated, with headlines and paragraphs, might be lacking; but there was to take its place something more decisive—Faith. Even so, anyone who can recall the events of the time through the aid of books, articles, votes of congresses and speeches of great and minor importance—anyone who knows how to research and weigh evidence—will find that the fundamentals of doctrine were cast during the years of conflict. It was precisely in those years that Fascist thought armed itself, was refined, and began the great task of organization. The problem of the relation between the individual citizen and the State; the allied problems of authority and liberty; political and social problems as well as those specifically national—a solution was being fought for all these while at the same time the struggle against Liberalism, Democracy, Socialism, and the Masonic bodies was being carried on, contemporaneously with the "punitive expedition." But, since there was inevitably some lack of system, the adversaries of Fascism have disingenuously denied that it had any capacity to produce a doctrine of its own, though that doctrine was growing and taking shape under their very eyes, even though tumultuously; first, as happens to all ideas in their beginnings, in the aspect of a violent and dogmatic negation, and then in the aspect of positive construction which has found its realization in the laws and institutions of the regime as enacted successively in the years 1926, 1927, and 1928.

Fascism is now a completely individual thing, not only as a regime but as a doctrine. And this means that to-day Fascism, exercising its critical sense upon itself and upon others, has formed its own distinct and peculiar point of view, to which it can refer and upon which, therefore, it can act in the face of all problems, practical or intellectual, which confront the world.

And above all, Fascism, the more it considers and observes the future and the development of humanity quite apart from political considerations of the moment, believes neither in the possibility nor the utility of perpetual peace. It thus repudiates the doctrine of Pacifism—born of a renunciation of the struggle and an act of cowardice in the face of sacrifice. War alone brings up to its highest tension all human energy and puts the stamp of nobility upon the peoples who have the courage to meet it. All other trials are substitutes, which never really put men into the position where they have to make the great decision—the alternative of life or death. Thus a doctrine which is founded upon this harmful postulate of peace is hostile to Fascism. And thus hostile to the spirit of Fascism, though accepted for what use they can be in dealing with particular political situations, are all the international leagues and societies which, as history will show, can be scattered to the winds when once strong national feeling is aroused by any motive—sentimental, ideal, or practical. This anti-Pacifist spirit is carried by Fascism even into the life of the individual; the proud motto of the *Squadrista*, "Me ne frego,"[175] written on the bandage of the wound, is an act of philosophy not only stoic, the summary of a doctrine not only political—it is the education for combat, the acceptation of the risks which combat implies, and a new way of life for Italy. Thus the Fascist accepts life and loves it, knowing nothing of and despising suicide: he rather conceives of life as duty and struggle and conquest, life which should be high and full, lived for oneself, but above all for others—those who are at hand and those who are far distant, contemporaries, and those who will come after.

This "demographic" policy of the regime is the result of the above premise. Thus the Fascist loves in actual fact his neighbor, but this "neighbor" is not merely a vague and undefined concept, this love for one's neighbor puts no obstacle in the way of necessary educational severity, and still less to differentiation of status and to physical distance. Fascism repudiates any universal embrace, and in order to live worthily in the community of civilized peoples watches its contemporaries with vigilant eyes, takes good note of their state of mind and, in the changing trend of their interests, does not allow itself to be deceived by temporary and fallacious appearances.

Such a conception of life makes Fascism the complete opposite of that doctrine, the base of so-called scientific and Marxian Socialism, the materialist conception of history; according to which the history of human civilization can be explained simply through the conflict of interests among the various social groups and by the change and development in the means and instruments of production. That the changes in the economic field—new discoveries of raw materials, new methods of working them, and the inventions of science—have their importance no one can deny; but that these factors are sufficient to explain the history of humanity excluding all others is an absurd delusion. Fascism, now and always, believes in holiness and in heroism; that is to say, in actions influenced by no economic motive, direct or indirect. And if the economic conception of history be denied, according to which theory men are no more than puppets, carried to and fro by the waves of chance, while the real directing forces are quite out of their control, it follows that the existence of an unchangeable and unchanging class-war is also denied—the natural progeny of the economic conception of history. And above all Fascism denies that class-war can be the preponderant force in the transformation of society. These two fundamental concepts of Socialism being thus refuted, nothing is left of it but the sentimental aspiration—as old as humanity itself—towards a social convention in which the sorrows and sufferings of the humblest shall be alleviated. But here again Fascism repudiates the conception of "economic" happiness, to be realized by Socialism and, as it were, at a given moment in economic evolution to assure to everyone the maximum of well-being. Fascism denies the materialist conception of happiness as a possibility, and abandons it to its inventors, the economists of the first half of the nineteenth century: that is to say, Fas-

---

175. A Blackshirt slogan that translates as "I don't give a damn."

cism denies the validity of the equation, well-being-happiness, which would reduce men to the level of animals, caring for one thing only—to be fat and well-fed—and would thus degrade humanity to a purely physical existence.

After Socialism, Fascism combats the whole complex system of democratic ideology, and repudiates it, whether in its theoretical premises or in its practical application. Fascism denies that the majority, by the simple fact that it is a majority, can direct human society; it denies that numbers alone can govern by means of a periodic consultation, and it affirms the immutable, beneficial, and fruitful inequality of mankind, which can never be permanently leveled through the mere operation of a mechanical process such as universal suffrage. The democratic regime may be defined as from time to time giving the people the illusion of sovereignty, while the real effective sovereignty lies in the hands of other concealed and irresponsible forces. Democracy is a regime nominally without a king, but it is ruled by many kings—more absolute, tyrannical, and ruinous than one sole king, even though a tyrant. This explains why Fascism, having first in 1922 (for reasons of expediency) assumed an attitude tending towards republicanism, renounced this point of view before the march to Rome; being convinced that the question of political form is not to-day of prime importance, and after having studied the examples of monarchies and republics past and present reached the conclusion that monarchy or republicanism are not to be judged, as it were, by an absolute standard; but that they represent forms in which the evolution—political, historical, traditional, or psychological—of a particular country has expressed itself. Fascism supersedes the antithesis monarchy or republicanism, while democracy still tarries beneath the domination of this idea, forever pointing out the insufficiency of the first and forever praising the second as the perfect regime. To-day, it can be seen that there are republics innately reactionary and absolutist, and also monarchies which incorporate the most ardent social and political hopes of the future.

[...]

The foundation of Fascism is the conception of the State, its character, its duty, and its aim. Fascism conceives of the State as an absolute, in comparison with which all individuals or groups are relative, only to be conceived of in their relation to the State. The conception of the Liberal State is not that of a directing force, guiding the play and development, both material and spiritual, of a collective body, but merely a force limited to the function of recording results: on the other hand, the Fascist State is itself conscious, and has itself a will and a personality—thus it may be called the "ethic" State. In 1929, at the first five-yearly assembly of the Fascist regime, I said:

"For us Fascists, the State is not merely a guardian, preoccupied solely with the duty of assuring the personal safety of the citizens; nor is it an organization with purely material aims, such as to guarantee a certain level of wellbeing and peaceful conditions of life; for a mere council of administration would be sufficient to realize such objects. Nor is it a purely political creation, divorced from all contact with the complex material reality which makes up the life of the individual and the life of the people as a whole. The State as conceived of and as created by Fascism, is a spiritual and moral fact in itself, since its political, juridical, and economic organization of the nation is a concrete thing: and such an organization must be in its origins and development a manifestation of the spirit. The State is the guarantor of security both internal and external, but it is also the custodian and transmitter of the spirit of the people, as it has grown up through the centuries in language, in customs, and in faith. And the State is not only a living reality of the present, it is also linked with the past and above all with the future, and thus transcending the brief limits of individual life, it represents the immanent spirit of the nation. The forms in which States express themselves may change, but the necessity for such forms is eternal. It is the State which educates its citizens in civic virtue, gives them a consciousness of their mission and welds them into unity; harmonizing their various interests through justice, and transmitting to future generations the mental conquests of science, of art, of law and the solidarity of humanity. It leads men from primitive tribal life to that highest expression of human power which is Empire: it links up through the centuries the names of those of its members who have died for its existence and in obedience to its laws, it holds up the memory of the leaders who have increased its territory and the geniuses who have illumined it with glory as an example to be followed by future generations. When the conception of the State declines, and disunifying and centrifugal tendencies prevail, whether of individuals or of particular groups, the nations where such phenomena appear are in their decline."

From 1929 until to-day, evolution, both political and economic, has everywhere gone to prove the validity of these doctrinal premises. Of such gigantic importance is the State. It is the force which alone can provide a solution to the dramatic contradictions of capitalism, and that state of affairs which we call the crisis can only be dealt with by the State, as between other States. Where is the shade of Jules Simon,[176] who in the dawn of Liberalism proclaimed that, "The State must labor to make itself unnecessary, and prepare the way for its own dismissal"? Or of McCulloch,[177] who, in the second half of the last century, affirmed that the State must guard against the danger of governing too much? What would the Englishman, Bentham, say today to the continual and inevitably-invoked intervention of the State in the sphere of economics, while according to his theories industry should ask no more of the State than to be left in peace? Or the German, Humboldt,[178] according to whom the "lazy" State should be considered the best? It is true that the second wave of Liberal economists were less extreme than the first, and Adam Smith himself opened the door—if only very cautiously—which leads to State intervention in the economic field: but whoever says Liberalism implies individualism, and whoever says Fascism implies the

---

176. Jules Simon (1814–1896), French premier (1876–1877) who favored the establishment of a republic.

177. John Ramsey McCulloch (1789–1864), political economist who argued for laissez-faire.

178. Wilhelm von Humboldt (1767–1835), statesman and Prussian scholar who was critical of state control of education and religion.

State. Yet the Fascist State is unique, and an original creation. It is not reactionary, but revolutionary, in that it anticipates the solution of the universal political field by the rivalry of parties, the excessive power of the parliamentary regime and the irresponsibility of political assemblies; while it meets the problems of the economic field by a system of syndicalism which is continually increasing in importance, as much in the sphere of labor as of industry: and in the moral field enforces order, discipline, and obedience to that which is the determined moral code of the country. Fascism desires the State to be a strong and organic body, at the same time reposing upon broad and popular support. The Fascist State has drawn into itself even the economic activities of the nation, and, through the corporative social and educational institutions created by it, its influence reaches every aspect of the national life and includes, framed in their respective organizations, all the political, economic and spiritual forces of the nation. A State which reposes upon the support of millions of individuals who recognize its authority, are continually conscious of its power and are ready at once to serve it, is not the old tyrannical State of the medieval lord nor has it anything in common with the absolute governments either before or after 1789. The individual in the Fascist State is not annulled but rather multiplied, just in the same way that a soldier in a regiment is not diminished but rather increased by the number of his comrades. The Fascist State organizes the nation, but leaves a sufficient margin of liberty to the individual; the latter is deprived of all useless and possibly harmful freedom, but retains what is essential; the deciding power in this question cannot be the individual, but the State alone.

Selection from Mussolini, Benito. *The Political and Social Doctrine of Fascism*, translated by Jane Soames, 10–15, 21–24. London: Hogarth Press, 1933.

BEYOND THE CLASSROOM

» In your work experience, how has the leader been chosen? What leadership style did they employ? How was their authority created among those they were leading?

"The Revolution and the Negro" by C. L. R. James

Introduction

Cyril Lionel Richard James (1901–1989), most popularly known as C. L. R., was born into a middle-class Afro-Trinidadian family. His father was a teacher and school administrator and in his earliest days he recalled that he had two passions: books and the game of cricket. He became a teacher, historian, activist, literary critic, cultural interpreter, Pan-Africanist, Black liberationist, Marxist, cricket player, playwright, journalist, and sports writer. A small sampling of his voluminous literary production includes: *Minty Alley* (1936), an acclaimed novel set in Trinidad and the first book by a Black West Indian author to be published in England; *Notes on Dialectics: Hegel, Marx, and Lenin* (1948), an analysis of the writings of three of the most significant authors connected to Marxist theory; *Mariners, Renegades and Castaways: The Story of Herman Melville and the World We Live In* (1953), a postcolonial critique of Moby Dick; and *The Black Jacobins: Toussaint L'Ouverture and the San Domingo Revolution* (1938), the definitive activist chronicle of the Haitian Revolution. A prodigious writer and a voracious reader who lived a transnational life and was acquainted with famous radicals, intellectuals, and figures around the world, James left a wide-ranging legacy of books and essays.

"Revolution and the Negro" was published in 1939 in the *New International*, the

> **SNAPSHOT BOX**
>
> LANGUAGE: English
> PUBLISHED: 1939, United States
> GENRE: Essay
> TAGS: Historiography; Internationalism; Race; Self-Determination; Struggle, Resistance, and Revolution

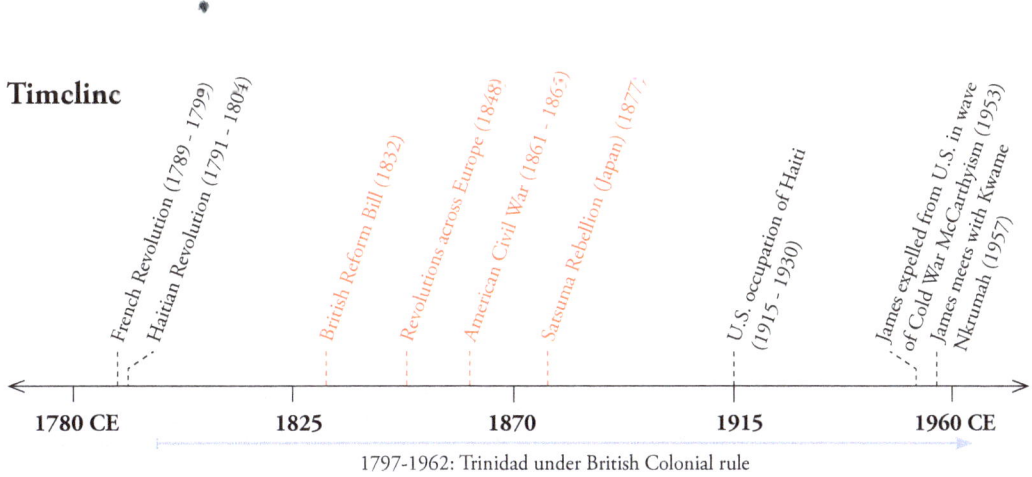

magazine of the US Socialist Workers Party.[179] The year before, James had published both *The Black Jacobins* and *The History of Negro Revolt*. *The Black Jacobins* was the first historical effort to write about the Haitian Revolution (1791–1804), the first successful, modern slave rebellion, from the point of view of the rebels themselves. In particular, James follows closely the actions and perspectives of the revolutionary leader Toussaint L'Ouverture, himself formerly enslaved. In the "Introduction" to *The Black Jacobins*, James wrote: "The transformation of slaves, trembling in hundreds before a single white man, into a people able to organize themselves and defeat the most powerful European nations of their day, is one of the great epics of revolutionary struggle and achievement. Why and how this happened is the theme of this book."[180] *The History of Negro Revolt*, written very soon afterward, addresses that same theme, internationalizing it. "Revolution and the Negro," a far shorter piece that appears here as your reading, is intended to synopsize these ideas.

By the early 1930s James became a Marxist, as evident in the ways he engaged in ideas about class struggle, dialectical materialism (the concept that over time humanity passes through phases of conflicts between economic classes), and how ultimately the working class, or **proletariat**, would triumph over the **bourgeoisie** (the owners of the means of production) and bring a classless, stateless, and more equal society into being. In 1939, as James published "Revolution and the Negro," the fascist regime of Benito Mussolini in Italy had conquered Ethiopia. Hitler had consolidated power in Germany and the fascists there had begun their own aggressive efforts at territorial expansion. Fascist antipathy for Marxists was a sentiment they held in equal firmness for capitalists. Indeed, at that time the world was still reeling from the economic devastation of the Great Depression, xenophobia and racism were increasingly prevalent, and nationalism was proliferating. How do you see these factors contributing to World War II (1939–1945)?

In "Revolution and the Negro," James points to the forgotten, ignored history of resistance, revolt, and revolution of Black people throughout history. The essay relies heavily on historical intricacies and details of the French Revolution (1789–1799), the Haitian Revolution (1791–1804), the American Revolution (1765–1783), the British Reform Bill (1832), the revolutionary year of 1848, and the American Civil War (1861–1865). For our purposes, however, the foremost consideration of the essay should be focused on James's theme of the mid-twentieth-century potential for insurgency and self-determination through the unified and revolutionary Pan-African struggle of the world's Black populations. James wrote history for the present in an activist mode, with the intent of moving the reader to action. In particular, as the world stood on the precipice of global war, James, in keeping with his Marxist

---

179. During those years, James often wrote under the pseudonym, J. R. Johnson, including for this reading.

180. C. L. R. James, *The Black Jacobins: Toussaint L'Ouverture and the San Domingo Revolution*, 2nd ed. (New York, Vintage Books, 1989 [1938]), ix.

view of history, anticipated a conflict that would bring the world closer to the next stage, a consequence of the Marxist concept of dialectical materialism.[181] As you read "Revolution and the Negro" take note of ways that James writes of patterns of recurring behavior. James also sees the working class as being connected by social forces that transcend borders, race, and ethnicities. How would you characterize the criteria and/or approach for writing history today? How is James's approach similar or different to your characterization?

Alvis Dunn
Department of History

---

181. C. L. R. James, *Beyond a Boundary* (Durham, NC: Duke University Press, 2013), 151. Accessed May 31, 2021. https://www.jstor.org/stable/j.ctv1220md2.19. "Fiction-writing drained out of me and was replaced by politics. I became a Marxist, a Trotskyist. I published large books and small articles on these and kindred subjects. I wrote and spoke. Like many others I expected war, and during or after the war, social revolution. In 1938 a lecture tour took me to the United States and I stayed there fifteen years."

"Revolution and the Negro"

The Negro's[182] revolutionary history is rich, inspiring, and unknown. Negroes revolted against the slave raiders in Africa; they revolted against the slave traders on the Atlantic passage. They revolted on the plantations.

The docile Negro is a myth. Slaves on slave ships jumped overboard, went on vast hunger strikes, attacked the crews. There are records of slaves overcoming the crew and taking the ship into harbor, a feat of tremendous revolutionary daring. In British Guiana during the eighteenth century the Negro slaves revolted, seized the Dutch colony, and held it for years. They withdrew to the interior, forced the whites to sign a treaty of peace, and have remained free to this day. Every West Indian colony, particularly Jamaica and San Domingo and Cuba, the largest islands, had its settlements of maroons, bold Negroes who had fled into the wilds and organized themselves to defend their freedom. In Jamaica the British government, after vainly trying to suppress them, accepted their existence by treaties of peace, scrupulously observed by both sides over many years, and then broken by British treachery. In America the Negroes made nearly 150 distinct revolts against slavery. The only place where Negroes did not revolt is in the pages of capitalist historians. All this revolutionary history can come as a surprise only to those who, whatever International they belong to, whether Second, Third, or Fourth, have not yet ejected from their systems the pertinacious lies of Anglo-Saxon capitalism. It is not strange that the Negroes revolted. It would have been strange if they had not.

But the Fourth International, whose business is revolution, has not to prove that Negroes were or are as revolutionary as any group of oppressed people. That has its place in agitation. What we as Marxists have to see is the tremendous role played by Negroes in the transformation of Western civilization from feudalism to capitalism. It is only from this vantage-ground that we shall be able to appreciate (and prepare for) the still greater role they must of necessity play in the transition from capitalism to socialism.

What are the decisive dates in the modern history of Great Britain, France, and America? 1789, the beginning of the French Revolution; 1832, the passing of the Reform Bill in Britain; and 1865, the crushing of the slave-power in America by the Northern states. Each of these dates marks a definitive stage in the transition from feudal to capitalist society. The exploitation of millions of Negroes had been a basic factor in the economic development of each of these three nations. It was reason-

---

182. James uses the term "Negro" to refer to his own African and African diasporic communities as was a prevalent practice within and outside of Black communities from the nineteenth to mid-twentieth centuries. The term "negro" should not be confused with the derogatory n-word. Likewise another term used during the same timeframe, "colored," is outdated and should not be confused with the current usage of "person of color." Words reflecting African, Afro-Caribbean, American American, and Black communities' preferences for self-identification continue to shift in meaning and connotation over time.

able, therefore, to expect the Negro question to play no less an important role in the resolution of the problems that faced each society. No one in the pre-revolutionary days, however, even faintly foresaw the magnitude of the contributions the Negroes were to make. Today Marxists have far less excuse for falling into the same mistake.

The Negro and the French Revolution

The French Revolution was a bourgeois revolution, and the basis of bourgeois wealth was the slave trade and the slave plantations in the colonies. Let there be no mistake about this. "Sad irony of human history," says Jaures, "the fortunes created at Bordeaux, at Nantes by the slave-trade gave to the bourgeoisie that pride which needed liberty and contributed to human emancipation." And Gaston-Martin the historian of the slave trade sums up thus: though the bourgeoisie traded in other things than slaves, upon the success or failure of the traffic everything else depended. Therefore when the bourgeoisie proclaimed the Rights of Man in general, with necessary reservations, one of these was that these rights should not extend to the French colonies. In 1789 the French colonial trade was eleven million pounds, two-thirds of the overseas trade of France. British colonial trade at that time was only five million pounds. What price French abolition? There was abolitionist society to which Brissot, Robespierre, Mirabeau, Lafayette, Condorcet, and many such famous men belonged even before 1789. But liberals are liberal. Face to face with the revolution, they were ready to compromise. They would leave the half million slaves in their slavery, but at least the Mulattoes, men of property (including slaves) and education, should be given equal rights with the white colonials. The white colonial magnates refused concessions and they were people to be reckoned with, aristocrats by birth or marriage, bourgeois their trade connections with the maritime bourgeoisie. They opposed all change in the colonies that would diminish their social and political domination. The maritime bourgeosie, concerned about their millions of investments, supported the colonials, and against eleven million pounds of trade per year the radical politicians were helpless. It was the revolution that kicked them from behind and forced them forward.

First of all the revolution in France. The Gironde right wing of the Jacobin club overthrew the pro-royalist Feuillants and came to power in March, 1792.

And secondly the revolution in the colonies. The Mulattoes in San Domingo revolted in 1790, followed a few months later by the slave revolt in August 1791. On April 4, 1792 the Girondins granted political and social rights to the Mulattoes. The big bourgeoisie agreed, for the colonial aristocrats, after vainly trying to win Mulatto support for independence, decided to hand the colony over to Britain rather than tolerate interference with their system. All these slave owners, French nobility and French bourgeoisie, colonial aristocrats and Mulattoes, were agreed that the slave revolt should be suppressed and the slaves remain in their slavery.

The slaves, however, refused to listen to threats, and no promises were made to them. Led from beginning to end by men who had themselves been slaves and were unable to read or write, they fought one of the greatest revolutionary battles in history. Before the revolution they had seemed subhuman. Many a slave had to be whipped before he could be got to move from where he sat. The revolution transformed them into heroes.

The island of San Domingo was divided into two colonies, one French, the other Spanish. The colonial government of the Spanish Bourbons supported the slaves in their revolt against the French republic, and many rebel bands took service with the Spaniards. The French colonials invited Pitt to take over the colony, and when war was declared between France and England in 1793, the English invaded the island.

The English expedition, welcomed by all the white colonials, captured town after town in the south and west of French San Domingo. The Spaniards, operating with the famous Toussaint Louverture, an ex-slave, at the head of four thousand black troops, invaded the colony from the east. British and Spaniards were gobbling up as much as they could before the time for sharing came. "In these matters," wrote the British minister, Dundas, to the governor of Jamaica, "the more we have, the better our pretensions." On June 4th, Port-au-Prince, the capital of San Domingo, fell. Meanwhile another British expedition had captured Martinique, Guadeloupe, and the other French islands. Barring a miracle, the colonial trade of France, the richest in the world, was in the hands of her enemies and would be used against the revolution. But here the French masses took a hand.

August 10, 1792 was the beginning of the revolution triumphant in France. The Paris masses and their supporters all over France, in 1789 indifferent to the colonial question, were now striking in revolutionary frenzy at every abuse of the old regime and none of the former tyrants were so hated as the "aristocrats of the skin." Revolutionary generosity, resentment at the betrayal of the colonies to the enemies of the revolution, impotence in the face of the British navy—these swept the Convention off its feet. On February 4, 1794, without a debate, it decreed the abolition of Negro slavery and at last gave its sanction to the black revolt.

The news trickled through somehow to the French West Indies. Victor Hugues, a Mulatto, one of the great personalities produced by the revolution, managed to break through the British blockade and carried the official notice of the manumission to the Mulattoes and blacks of the West Indian islands. Then occurred the miracle. The blacks and Mulattoes dressed themselves in the revolutionary colors and, singing revolutionary songs, they turned on the British and Spaniards, their allies of yesterday. With little more from revolutionary France than its moral support, they drove the British and Spaniards from their conquests and carried the war into enemy territory. The British, after five years of trying to reconquer the French colonies, were finally driven out in 1798.

Few know the magnitude and the importance of that defeat sustained at the hands of Victor Hugues in the smaller islands and of Toussaint Louverture and Rigaud in San Domingo. Fortescue, the Tory historian of the British army, estimates the total loss to Britain at 100,000 men. Yet in the whole of the Peninsular War Wellington lost from all causes—killed in battle, sickness, desertions—only 40,000 men. British blood and British treasure were poured out in profusion in the West Indian campaign. This was the reason for Britain's weakness in Europe during the critical years 1793–1798. Let Fortescue himself speak: "The secret of England's impotence for the first six years of the war may be said to lie in the two fatal words St. Domingo." British historians blame chiefly the fever, as if San Domingo was the only place in the world that European imperialism had met fever.

Whatever the neglect or distortions of later historians, the French revolutionaries themselves knew what the Negro question meant to the revolution. The Constituent, the Legislature, and the Convention were repeatedly thrown into disorder by the colonial debates. This had grave repercussions in the internal struggle as well as in the revolutionary defense of the Republic. Says Jaures, "Undoubtedly but for the compromises of Barnave and all his party on the colonial question, the general attitude of the Assembly after the flight to Varennes would have been different." Excluding the masses of Paris, no portion of the French empire played, in proportion to its size, so grandiose a role in the French Revolution as the half million blacks and Mulattoes in the remote West Indian islands.

The Black Revolution and World History

The black revolution in San Domingo choked at its source one of the most powerful economic streams of the eighteenth century. With the defeat of the British, the black proletarians defeated the Mulatto Third Estate in a bloody civil war. Immediately after, Bonaparte, representative of the most reactionary elements of the new French bourgeoisie, attempted to restore slavery in San Domingo. The blacks defeated an expedition of some 50,000 men, and with the assistance of the Mulattoes, carried the revolution to its logical conclusion. They changed the name of San Domingo to Haiti and declared the island independent. This black revolution had a profound effect on the struggle for the cessation of the slave trade.

We can trace this close connection best by following the development of abolition in the British Empire. The first great blow at the Tory domination of Britain (and at feudalism in France for that matter) was struck by the Declaration of Independence in 1776. When Jefferson wrote that all men are created equal, he was drawing up the death-warrant of feudal society, wherein men were by law divided into unequal classes. Crispus Attucks, the Negro, was the first man killed by the British in the war that followed. It was no isolated or chance phenomenon. The Negroes thought that in this war for freedom, they could win their own. It has been estimated that of the 30,000 men in Washington's army 4,000 were Negroes. The American bourgeoisie did not want them. They forced themselves in. But San Domingo Negroes fought in the war also.

The French monarchy came to the assistance of the American Revolution. And Negroes from the French colonies pushed themselves into the French expeditionary force. Of the 1,900 French troops who recaptured Savannah, 900 were volunteers from the French colony of San Domingo. Ten years later some of these men—Rigaud, André, Lambert, Beauvais and others (some say Christophe also)—with their political and military experience will be foremost among the leaders in the San Domingo revolution. Long before Karl Marx wrote, "Workers of the world, unite," the revolution was international.

The loss of the slave-holding American colonies took much cotton out of the ears of the British bourgeoisie. Adam Smith and Arthur Young, heralds of the industrial revolution and wage-slavery, were already preaching against the waste of chattel-slavery. Deaf up to 1783, the British bourgeois now heard, and looked again at the West Indies. Their own colonies were bankrupt. They were losing the slave trade to French and British rivals. And half the French slaves that they brought were going to San Domingo, the India of the eighteenth century. Why should they continue to do this? In three years, the first abolitionist society was formed and Pitt began to clamor for the abolition of slavery—"for the sake of humanity, no doubt," says Gaston-Martin, "but also, be it well understood, to ruin French commerce." With the war of 1793, Pitt, cherishing a prospect of winning San Domingo, piped down on abolition. But the black revolution killed the aspirations of both France and Britain.

The Treaty of Vienna in 1814 gave to France the right to recapture San Domingo: the Haitians swore that they would rather destroy the island. With the abandonment of the hopes for regaining San Domingo, the British abolished the slave trade in 1807. America followed in 1808.

If the East Indian interest in Britain was one of the great financial arsenals of the new bourgeoisie (whence the diatribes of Burke, Whig spokesman, against Hastings and Clive), the West Indian interest, though never so powerful as in France, was a cornerstone of the feudal oligarchy. The loss of America was the beginning of their decline. But for the black revolution, San Domingo would have strengthened them enormously. The reformist British bourgeoisie belabored them, the weakest link in the oligarchic chain. A great slave revolt in Jamaica in 1831 helped to convince those who had doubts. In Britain "Better emancipation from above than from below" anticipated the Tsar by thirty years. One of the first acts of the victorious reformers was to abolish slavery in the British colonies. But for the black revolution in San Domingo, abolition and emancipation might have been postponed another thirty years.

Abolition did not come to France until the revolution of 1848. The production of beet-sugar, introduced into France by Bonaparte, grew by leaps and bounds, and placed the cane sugar interests, based on slavery in Martinique and Guadeloupe, increasingly on the defensive. One of the first acts of the revolutionary government of 1848 was to abolish slavery. But as in 1794, the decree was merely the registration of an accomplished fact. So menacing was the attitude of the slaves that in more than one colony the local government, in order to head off the servile revolution, proclaimed abolition without waiting for authorization from France.

The Negro and the Civil War

1848, the year following the economic crisis of 1847, was the beginning of a new cycle of revolutions all over the Western world. The European revolutions, Chartism in England, were defeated. In America the irrepressible conflict between capitalism in the North and the slave system in the South was headed off for the last time by the Missouri Compromise of 1850. The political developments following the economic crisis of 1857 made further compromise impossible.

It was a decade of revolutionary struggle the world over in the colonial and semi-colonial countries. 1857 was the year of the first war of Indian independence, commonly miscalled the Indian Mutiny. In 1858 began the civil war in Mexico, which ended with the victory of Juarez three years later. It was the period of the Taiping revolution in China, the first great attempt to break the power of the Manchu dynasty. North and South in America moved to their predestined clash unwillingly, but the revolutionary Negroes helped to precipitate the issue. For two decades before the Civil War began, they were leaving the South in thousands. The revolutionary organization known as the Underground Railway, with daring, efficiency and dispatch, drained away the slave owners' human property. Fugitive slaves were the issue of the day. The Fugitive Slave Law of 1850 was a last desperate attempt by the Federal Government to stop this illegal abolition. Ten Northern states replied with personal liberty laws which nullified the heavy penalties of the 1850 law. Most famous perhaps of all the whites and Negroes who ran the Underground Railway is Harriet Tubman, a Negro who had herself escaped from slavery. She made nineteen journeys into the South and helped her brothers and their wives and three hundred other slaves to escape. She made her depredations in enemy territory with a price of $40,000 on her head. Josiah Henson, the original of Uncle Tom, helped nearly two hundred slaves to escape. Nothing so galled the slave owners as this twenty-year drain on their already bankrupt economic system.

It is unnecessary to detail here the causes of this, the greatest civil war in history. Every Negro schoolboy knows that the last thing Lincoln had in mind was the emancipation of Negroes. What is important is that, for reasons both internal and external, Lincoln had to draw them into the revolutionary struggle. He said that without emancipation the North might not have won, and he was in all probability right. Thousands of Negroes were fighting on the Southern side, hoping to win their freedom that way. The abolition decree broke down the social cohesion of the South. It was not only what the North gained but, as Lincoln pointed out, what the South lost. On the Northern side 220,000 Negroes fought with such bravery that it was impossible to do with white troops what could be done with them. They fought not only with revolutionary bravery but with coolness and exemplary discipline. The best of them were filled with revolutionary pride. They were fighting for equality. One company stacked arms before the tent of its commanding officer as a protest against discrimination.

Lincoln was also driven to abolition by the pressure of the British working class. Palmerston wanted to intervene on the side of the South but was opposed in the cabinet by Gladstone. Led by Marx, the British working class so vigorously opposed the war, that it was impossible to hold a pro-war meeting anywhere in England. The British Tories derided the claim that the war was for the abolition of slavery: hadn't Lincoln said so many times? The British workers, however, insisted on seeing the war as a war for abolition, and Lincoln, for whom British non-intervention was a life and death matter, decreed abolition with a suddenness which shows his fundamental unwillingness to take such a revolutionary step.

Abolition was declared in 1863. Two years before, the movement of the Russian peasants, so joyfully hailed by Marx, frightened the Tsar into the semi-emancipation of the serfs. The North won its victory in 1865. Two years later the British workers won the Second Reform Bill, which gave the franchise to the workers in the towns. The revolutionary cycle was concluded with the defeat of the Paris Commune in 1871. A victory there and the history of Reconstruction would have been far different.

The Negro and World Revolution

Between 1871 and 1905 the proletarian revolution was dormant. In Africa the Negroes fought vainly to maintain their independence against the imperialist invasions. But the Russian Revolution of 1905 was the forerunner of a new era that began with the October Revolution in 1917. While half a million Negroes fought with the French Revolution in 1789, today the socialist revolution in Europe has as its potential allies over 120 million Negroes in Africa. Where Lincoln had to seek an alliance with an isolated slave population, today millions of Negroes in America have penetrated deep into industry, have fought side by side with white workers on picket lines, have helped to barricade factories for sit-down strikes, have played their part in the struggles and clashes of trade unions and political parties. It is only through the spectacles of historical perspective that we can fully appreciate the enormous revolutionary potentialities of the Negro masses today.

Half a million slaves, hearing the words Liberty, Equality, and Fraternity shouted by millions of Frenchmen many thousands of miles away, awoke from their apathy. They occupied the attention of Britain for six years and, once again to quote Fortescue, "practically destroyed the British army." What of the Negroes in Africa today? This is a bare outline of the record.

French West Africa: 1926–1929, 10,000 men fled into the forest swamps to escape French slavery.

French Equatorial Africa: 1924, uprising. 1924–1925, uprising, 1000 Negroes killed. 1928, June to November, rising in Upper Sangha and Lai. 1929, a rising lasting four months; the Africans organized an army of 10,000.

British West Africa: 1929, a revolt of women in Nigeria, 30,000 in number; 83 killed, 87 wounded. 1937, general strike of the Gold Coast. Farmers, joined by dockers and truck drivers.

Belgian Congo: 1929, revolt in Ruanda Urundi; thousands killed. 1930–1931, revolt of the Bapendi, 800 massacred in one place, Kwango.

South Africa: 1929, strikes and riots in Durban; the Negro quarter was entirely surrounded by troops and bombarded by planes.

Since 1935 there have been general strikes, with shooting of Negroes, in Rhodesia, in Madagascar, in Zanzibar. In the West Indies there have been general strikes and mass action such as those islands have not seen since the emancipation from slavery a hundred years ago. Scores have been killed and wounded.

The above is only a random selection. The Negroes in Africa are caged and beat against the bars continually. It is the European proletariat that holds the key. Let the workers of Britain, France, and Germany say, "Arise, ye children of starvation" as loudly as the French revolutionaries said Liberty, Equality, and Fraternity and what force on earth can hold these Negroes back? All who know anything about Africa know this.

Mr. Norman Leys, a government medical officer in Kenya for twenty years, a member of the British Labour Party, and about as revolutionary as the late Ramsay MacDonald, wrote a study of Kenya in 1924. Seven years later he wrote again. This time he entitled his book *A Last Chance in Kenya*. The alternative, he said, is revolution.

In *Caliban in Africa,* Leonard Barnes, another milk and water socialist, writes as follows: "So he [the South African white] and the native he holds captive go spinning down the stream fatally, madly spinning together along the rapids above the great cataract, both yoked to one omnipotent hour." That is the revolution, wrapped in silver paper.

The revolution haunts this conservative Englishman. He writes again of the Bantu, "They crouch in their corner, nursing a sullen anger and desperately groping for a plan. They will not be many years making up their minds. Time and fate, even more prevailing than the portcullis of the Afrikaner, are driving them on from the rear. Something must give; it will not be fate or time. Some comprehensive social and economic reconstruction must take place. But how? By reason or by violence?..."

He poses as alternatives what are in reality one. The change will take place, by violence and by reason combined.

"We Have a False Idea of the Negro"

Let us return again to the San Domingo revolution with its paltry half a million slaves. Writing in 1789, the very year of the revolution, a colonist said of them that they were "unjust, cruel, barbarous, half-human, treacherous, deceitful, thieves, drunkards, proud, lazy, unclean, shameless, jealous to fury and cowards."

Three years later Roume, the French Commissioner, noted that even though fighting with the royalist Spaniards, the black revolutionaries, organizing themselves into armed sections and popular bodies, rigidly observed all the forms of republican organization. They adopted slogans and rallying cries. They appointed chiefs of sections and divisions who, by means of these slogans, could call them out and send them back home again from one end of the province to the others. They threw up from out of their depths a soldier and a statesman of the first rank, Toussaint Louverture, and secondary leaders fully able to hold their own with the French in war, diplomacy, and administration. In ten years they organized an army that fought Bonaparte's army on level terms. "But what men these blacks are! How they fight and how they die!" wrote a French officer looking back at the last campaign after forty years. From his dying bed, Leclerc, Bonaparte's brother-in-law and commander-in-chief of the French expedition, wrote home, "We have . . . a false idea of the Negro." And again, "We have in Europe a false idea of the country in which we fight and the men whom we fight against. . . ." We need to know and reflect on these things to-day.

Menaced during its whole existence by imperialism, European and American, the Haitians have never been able to overcome the bitter heritage of their past. Yet that revolution of a half million not only helped to protect the French Revolution but initiated great revolutions in its own right. When the Latin American revolutionaries saw that half a million slaves could fight and win, they recognised the reality of their own desire for independence. Bolivar, broken and ill, went to Haiti. The Haitians nursed him back to health, gave him money and arms with which he sailed to the mainland. He was defeated, went back to Haiti, was once more welcomed and assisted. And it was from Haiti that he sailed to start on the final campaign, which ended in the independence of the five states.

Today 150 million Negroes, knit into the world economy infinitely more tightly than their ancestors of a hundred years ago, will far surpass the work of that San Domingo half million in the work of social transformation. The continuous risings in Africa; the refusal of the Ethiopian warriors to submit to Mussolini; the American Negroes who volunteered to fight in Spain in the Abraham Lincoln Brigade, as Rigaud and Beauvais had volunteered to fight in America, tempering their swords against the enemy abroad for use against the enemy at home—these lightnings announce the thunder. The racial prejudice that now stands in the way will bow before the tremendous impact of the proletarian revolution.

In Flint during the sit-down strike of two years ago seven hundred Southern whites, soaked from infancy in racial prejudice, found themselves besieged in the General Motors building with one Negro among them. When the time came for the first meal, the Negro, knowing who and what his companions were, held himself in the background. Immediately it was proposed that there should be no racial discrimination among the strikers. Seven hundred hands went up together. In the face of the class enemy the men recognized that race prejudice was a subordinate thing which could not be allowed to disrupt their struggle. The Negro was invited to take his seat first, and after the victory was won, in the triumphant march out of the factory, he was given the first place. That is the prognosis of the future. In Africa, in America, in the West Indies, on a national and international scale, the millions of Negroes will raise their heads, rise up from their knees, and write some of the most massive and brilliant chapters in the history of revolutionary socialism.

James, C. L. R. "The Revolution and the Negro." In *New International*, vol. 5, December 1939, transcribed by Ted Crawford, 339–43. Chicago: J. R. Johnson, 1939.

from *The Second Sex* by Simone de Beauvoir

Introduction

> **SNAPSHOT BOX**
>
> **LANGUAGE:** French
> **GENRE:** Treatise, social critique
> **PUBLISHED:** 1949, Paris
> **TAGS:** Ethics and Morality; Family; Gender and Identity; Psyche; Struggle, Resistance, and Revolution; Tyranny; Women and Power

Parisian Simone de Beauvoir (1908–1986) was a teacher, editor, fiction writer, activist, and award-winning author. Raised Catholic and middle class, Beauvoir was more likely to lead her life in the domestic sphere, as a wife and mother, than as a celebrity intellectual. But strained family finances meant the family was unable to provide a wedding dowry, and her father instead supported her advanced education. Beauvoir became critical of marriage and bourgeois morality, led an unconventional life, and devoted her career as a writer and activist to developing a feminist theory—one that continues to influence the development of diverse feminist perspectives and theories today. Beauvoir lived through two world wars and the collapse of the French Empire, including brutal conflicts that led to Vietnamese and Algerian independence (1954 and 1962 respectively). As a leftist (i.e., one opposed to France's colonial holdings), she participated actively in these events and, as a philosopher, theorized their impact on French and European cultures. She was part of a close circle of existentialist philosophers, including her lifelong companion Jean Paul Sartre (1905–1980), whose postwar writings explored human nature itself. By deploying dichotomies, as in Sartre's *Being and Nothingness* (1943), existentialists described the process of othering, whereby people in all cultures and eras, in their view, have categorized those who are different as opposite from themselves, most especially

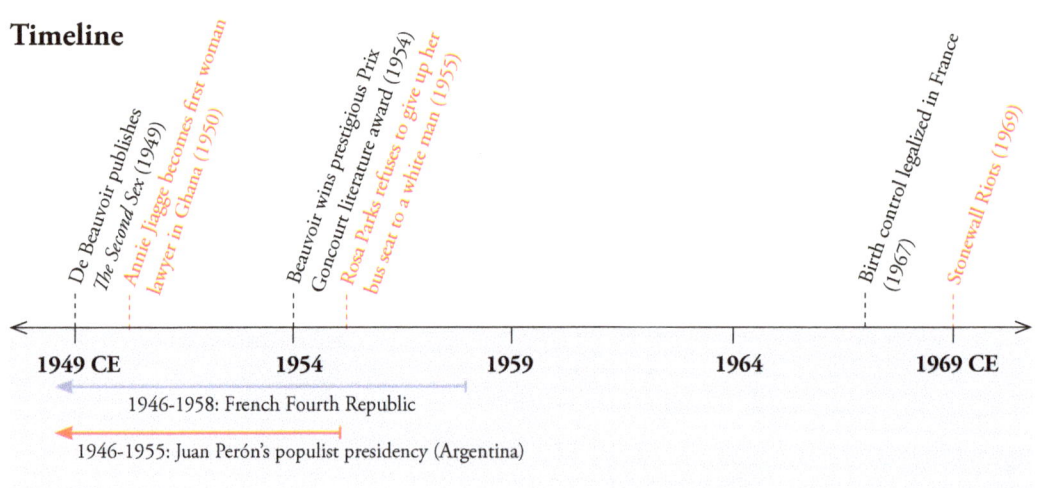

in terms of sexuality and gender. In other words, occupying a position as subject entails constructing others as objects.

Beauvoir wrote *The Second Sex* to challenge the othering of women in the works of psychoanalysts like Sigmund Freud (1856–1939) who attributed women's neuroses to "penis envy." Even Sartre used the phallis to represent male and the hole to represent female, implying women's deficiency. Beauvoir countered this association, often described as reductionist, with her famous line that "one is not born but rather becomes a woman." Beauvoir draws special attention to the social role to which female-bodied people acculturate. What assumptions does this assertion begin to critique? What conflations is she trying to untangle?

She notes the ways in which women's class and race positions complicate their relative access to power and privilege. However, she concludes that in every case women are subordinate to a patriarchal culture that others them. In the excerpt below, she discusses why women accept their subordinate status. By contrast, she narrates the degree to which othered populations have accomplished their own liberation, often through violence, as in the Haitian and Vietnamese Revolutions, by joining together and overthrowing their oppressors. Triumphant, those formerly othered peoples proceed to other their former oppressors and proclaim themselves to be the One (e.g., subjectivity of one in power). Why does this dichotomy between those in power (One) and the oppressed (other) seem inescapable, according to Beauvoir?

Beauvoir's work is at once time-bound and timeless. She wrote between the first and second waves of the feminist movement, after the vote for women was won in most Western democracies, including in France, one of the latest to enfranchise women in 1945. *The Second Sex* arguably launched the second wave in the 1960s and 1970s where consciousness-raising groups enabled women to name the sources of their oppression and support each other. Eventually, women's sexual liberation, facilitated by the invention of oral contraceptives, began to separate sexual intercourse from reproduction, freeing women from one of the sources of dependence on men that Beauvoir had called out. Buoyed by the domestic and international success of *The Second Sex* (since its first publication in 1949, it has been translated into forty languages), Beauvoir came to identify herself as a feminist in 1971 and a supporter of abortion rights. She turned her feminist analysis to the othering of the elderly in her last major work, *The Coming of Age* (1970).

Tracey Rizzo
Department of History

> **PRE-READING PARS**
>
> 1. Write briefly on what comes to mind when you hear the phrase "the opposite sex"?
> 2. List two examples of how oppositional thinking (thinking in terms of dichotomies) is still embedded in our discourses and two examples of how othering is embedded in our practices?

from *The Second Sex*

The category of the *Other* is as original as consciousness itself. In the most primitive societies and ancient mythologies one will always find the duality between the One and the Other. This division has not always been marked as the division of the sexes; it was not based on anything empirical. This can be seen in works like Granet's on Chinese thought, and Dumézil's on India and Rome, among others. Originally there was no feminine element in couples such as Varuna—Mitra, Uranus—Zeus, Sun—Moon, Day—Night; neither in the opposition of Good and Evil, lucky and unlucky, right and left, God and Lucifer; alterity is a fundamental category of human thought. No collectivity ever defines itself as the *One* without immediately placing an *Other* opposite itself. Suffice to say that three travelers brought together by chance in the same train compartment will see the other travelers as vaguely hostile "others." For villagers, anyone who does not belong to their village is a suspect "other"; for a native of a country, inhabitants of other countries appear as "strangers"; Jews are "others" to the antisemite, Blacks to racist Americans, the indigenous to colonists, proletarians to the propertied classes. At the conclusion of his comprehensive study of many primitive societies, [anthropologist Claude] Levi-Strauss [(1908–2009)] wrote: "The passage from the state of nature to that of culture is defined by man's aptitude for conceptualizing biological relations in terms of oppositions: duality, alterity, opposition and symmetry, whether more or less formed, are not so much well-explained phenomena as they are fundamental and immediate givens of social reality." These phenomena could not be comprehended if human reality was based on solidarity and friendship. On the contrary, following [philosopher Georg Wilhelm Friedrich] Hegel [(1770–1831)], it is clear that there is in consciousness itself a fundamental hostility to other consciousnesses; the subject posits itself in opposition; it affirms itself as essential and the other as inessential, as an object.

However, the other consciousness holds an opposite reciprocal view: when traveling outside his country, a traveler is shocked that inhabitants of neighboring countries regard him as a stranger. Accordingly, between villages, clans, nations, classes there are wars, potlatches, trading accords, treaties, and struggles that deprive the idea of the *Other* of its absolute meaning and expose its relativity. Like it or not, individuals and groups are obliged to acknowledge the reciprocity of their relations. How is it then, between the sexes, that this reciprocity has not been affirmed, that only one of the terms identifies itself as essential, denying all relativity in regard to its corollary, that is then defined as pure alterity? Why do women not contest male sovereignty? No subject readily posits itself as inessential; it is not the Other who defines the One: only the One, in so positing itself as the One, defines the Other. But for the Other to remain so it necessarily submits itself to this alien point of view. Where does women's submission come from?

There are other cases where one category has successfully and absolutely dominated another for a time. Usually this is a result of numerical inequality. The majority imposes its law on or persecutes the minority. But women are not a minority like the Blacks of North America or the Jews: there are as many women on earth as men. Often the two groups in question were once independent of each other: they either were unaware of each other or conceded each other's autonomy. It was a historical event that subordinated the weaker to the stronger: the Jewish diaspora, the introduction of slavery in America, colonial conquests, all are facts with dates. In such cases, the oppressed have always known there was always a *before*: they had a common past, tradition, sometimes religion, culture. In this sense the analogy between women and the proletariat offered by [August] Bebel [(1840–1913)] is suggestive; proletarians are not a numerical minority either and they have never constituted a separate collectivity. However, in lieu of one event, it was a historical development that led to their existence as a class and accounts for the membership of individuals in this class. But while there was not always a proletariat there have always been women; they are women by virtue of their anatomy and physiology. In addition, as far back as history can be traced, they have always been subordinated to men: their dependence is not a consequence of an event or of a development, it did not *happen*. This alterity appears to be absolute in part because it escapes the accidental character of historical fact. A situation that appears to be created over time can be undone at another time as the Blacks of Haiti, among others, have shown. It only appears that a so-called natural condition defies change. In truth, nature is no less immutable than historical reality. If woman discovers herself to be deemed inessential then it is up to her to reclaim herself as the essential. The proletariat says "we." The Blacks also. In becoming subjects they transform the bourgeoisie, the Whites into "others." Women do not say "we" except in certain gatherings or formal demonstrations. Men say "women" and women comprehend these words to designate themselves; they do not posit themselves as an authentic Subject. Proletarians brought revolution to Russia, the Blacks to Haiti, the Indochinese revolt in Indochina but women's efforts have never been more than symbolic agitation. They have gained only what men have been willing to concede, they have taken nothing, they have received. They lack the concrete means to assemble as a group in opposition. They do not have a past, history, or religion of their own. Unlike proletarians they do not have the solidarity of work and interests; they don't even share the spaces that create community among the Blacks of America, the Jewish ghettos, the workers of Saint-Denis and Renault factories. They live dispersed among men, more attached by home, work, economic interests, and social standing to certain men—father, husband—than to other women. Bourgeois women are in solidarity with bourgeois men and not proletarian women, white women with white men rather than with black women. The proletariat can propose to massacre the whole ruling class; a fanatical Jew or Black can dream of monopolizing the secret of the atom bomb to turn all of humanity Jewish or Black: but women cannot even dream of exterminating men. The tie that binds her to her oppressors is like no other. The division of the sexes is in effect a biological given, not an event in human history. Their opposition inheres in their original condition and she has not broken it. The couple is the fundamental unit of two halves bound together; no cleavage of society by sex is possible. It is this that fundamentally characterizes woman: she is the Other at the heart of a whole in which the two parts are necessary to each other.

One could imagine that this reciprocity might lead to liberation: when Hercules spun wool at Omphale's feet his desire enchained him; why was Omphale unsuccessful at acquiring lasting power? To take revenge on Jason, Medea murdered their children: this cruel legend suggests that the bonds that attach a man to child might have given her a redoubtable ascendancy. In Lysistrata, Aristophanes humorously imagined an assembly of women who exploited men's need for them to advance a social good: but this was only a comedy. The legend that claims the Sabine women opposed their ravishers by remaining obstinately infertile also recounts how the men magically won them into submission by whipping them with leather straps. Biological need—sexual desire and the desire for progeny—makes the male dependent on the female but has not resulted in women's social liberation.

The master and slave are also bound by a reciprocal economic need that does not liberate the slave because, in their relation, the master does not internalize the need he has for the other; he wields the power to satisfy this need unmediated. However, the slave internalizes his need for the master out of dependence, hope, or fear. Thus even when mutual, the need always favors the oppressor over the oppressed: this explains why the liberation of the working class, for example, is so protracted. But woman has always been, if not the slave of man, at least his vassal; the two sexes have never shared the world equally; and even today when her condition is improving the woman remains seriously disadvantaged. In almost no country is her legal status identical to man's and often it is considerably lesser. Even where rights are recognized in the abstract, long-standing habit prevents their concrete expression in custom. Economically, men and women are practically two distinct castes; all things being equal, the former have more advantageous positions, higher salaries, and greater opportunities for success than their less experienced competitors; they hold more numerous and more important posts in industry and politics, etc. Beyond these concrete privileges, they benefit from the prestige of an entirety of childhood education maintained by tradition because the present enshrines the past and in the past all history was made by men. Even at the moment when women begin to take part in shaping the world, the world still belongs to men: neither men nor women doubt this.

Refusing to be the *Other*, refusing to be complicit with men, would require women to renounce all the advantages that the superior caste has conferred upon them. Man as sovereign will materially support woman as vassal and will endeavor to justify her existence. Along with avoiding economic risk, she thereby avoids the metaphysical risk of inventing her own freedom without help. In effect, besides the proposition that every individual affirms itself as subject, which is an ethical proposition, she is also tempted to forego freedom and constitute herself as a thing. This is a difficult road because when she is passive, alienated, and lost she is also the object of someone else's will, cut off from transcendence, deprived of all value. But it is also an easy road: she thereby avoids the anguish and strain of assuming an authentic existence. The man who renders woman as the *Other* also renders her deeply complicit. Thus woman makes no claim for herself as a subject because she lacks concrete resources, because she is aware of the necessary connection that attaches her to man regardless of reciprocity, and often because she is satisfied with her role as the *Other*.

Beauvoir, Simone de. *Le Deuxième Sexe*, 16–21. Paris: Gallimard, 1949. Translated by Tracey Rizzo, 2021 [unpublished].

POST-READING PARS

1. List two factors that you think make it difficult for those in marginalized positions to organize as a group.
2. Outline two ways that you think Beauvoir's feminist analysis is still relevant.

Inquiry Corner

Content Question:	**Critical Question:**
How is the romantic couple a source of women's oppression, according to Beauvoir?	Critically evaluate Beauvoir's characterizations of other cultures. How might this impact the efficacy of her argument?
Comparative Question:	**Connection Question:**
How is Beauvoir's description of women's oppression different from her predecessors (e.g., Stanton, Parsons, Wells, Rokeya)?	How might Beauvoir's ideas be in conversation with contemporary social movements, such as the Me Too Movement, Transgender Rights, and Black Lives Matter?

Sultana's Dream by Rokeya Sakhawat Hossain

SNAPSHOT BOX

LANGUAGE: English

PUBLISHED: 1905, British India

GENRE: Science fiction

TAGS: Art; Class and Caste; Gender and Identity; Labor; Poetry, Music, Literature; Psyche; Science; Statecraft; Tradition; War and Brutality, Education

Introduction

Rokeya Sakhawat Hossain (1880–1932) was an author and activist from early twentieth-century British India. *Sultana's Dream* is her only writing in English. Rokeya, as she is referred to by scholars, focused on Bengali women—Muslim women more specifically—and exposed the "suffocating conditions" in which they had to live. Using exacting humor, fictional narratives, and journalistic accounting of events she witnessed, she imagined a different and more equitable world for Bengali women.

Rokeya was born into a Bengali Muslim family in what is today part of the nation of Bangladesh, a country created in 1971. Rokeya, along with her sister, was educated at home following a traditional curriculum focused on religious education. In the late nineteenth century while many middle-class families of British India allowed their daughters to be educated, study of the English language was strictly prohibited. Can you imagine what might have been the reasons behind such a curricular restriction? While Rokeya's oldest brother taught her secretly the basics of the English language, her husband truly deepened that learning by encouraging her explorations. Indeed, it appears that Rokeya composed *Sultana's Dream* partly to demonstrate her proficiency in English to her husband.

The particular social practice Rokeya targets is called **purdah**. Though often translated as "the veil," it is more appropriately translated as "seclusion" in this context. It

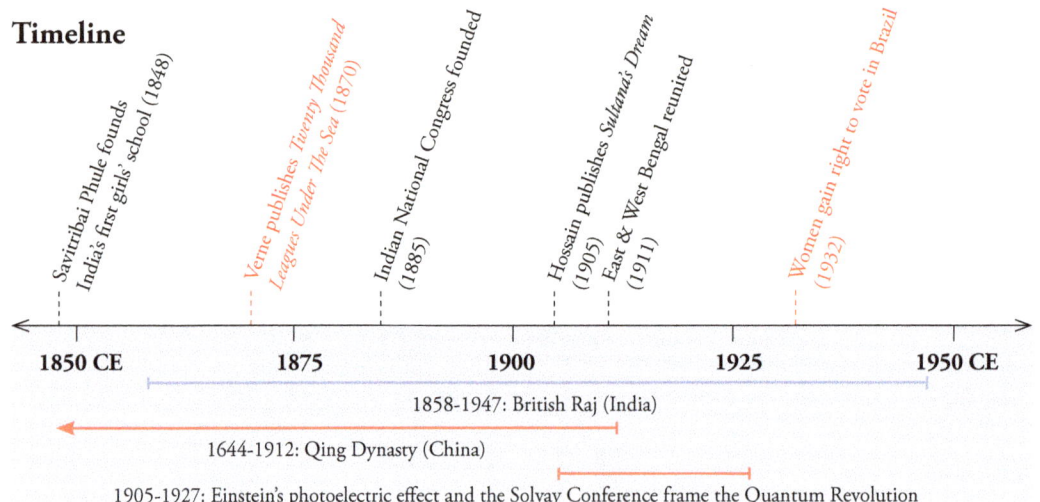

refers to, in part, the segregated living spaces for women (*zenanas*). Since they were not to be seen by men who are not close family—father, husband, or brother—or by other women outside one's own family and house-maids, women in *zenanas* rarely ventured out. In another publication, Rokeya recounts her memories of having to hide in a hot attic room for hours when an unrelated woman came into the *zenana* of her childhood. While a prevalent practice among Bengali Muslim families, many affluent Hindu families practiced *purdah* as well. What, in your opinion, might have been the reason for its popularity with affluent families, since the practice was not dependent solely on religious identity?

Rokeya offers an interesting positioning in relation to what critical social historians have called the "women's question." It refers to the phenomenon where women and their conditions, plights, and realities become the setting for the modernist discourse. On the one hand, the officials of the British Raj often focused on many of the social evils that plagued the lives of Bengali women in making the argument that reforming these conditions validated India's colonization. On the other hand, as glorification of India's past and many traditions involving women became a big part of the nationalist rhetoric, these colonial reformist responses to the women's question came to be viewed with suspicion by men involved in the Indian Independence movement. Interestingly, however, in spite of this contrast, both these responses to the women's question shared a common theme: namely, that others were responsible for determining the fate of Indian women! They became voiceless—a mere location where the modernist project was contested while the women themselves were supposed to remain passively waiting for the men to resolve their question.

It is in this backdrop that Rokeya's story assumes special relevance. In crafting a narrative where women are leading the charge to envision a new world of justice, peace, and innovations, Rokeya offers her own response to the women's question. In fact, among all the Bengali reformers who were agitating about the plight of Bengali women, it was Rokeya alone who unequivocally questioned male superiority and supported a version of alternative modernity focused on the self-determination of Bengali women especially through the means of education.

In focusing on science and technology in Ladyland—the fictional country we meet in *Sultana's Dream*—Rokeya foregrounds the debate around curriculum especially with regard to women's education. The nationalist reformers emphasized a traditional curriculum given their conviction that such a course of study would enable women to raise strong men, which was the central argument given in favor of women's education. Science, mathematics, or engineering were not considered important for such a curriculum. However, in a clear departure, Rokeya not only stressed the need for women's education in general but, more importantly, one that enabled women to excel in science and engineering. What, in your opinion, might have been some of the reasons that convinced Rokeya in this regard? One of her most lasting legacies is the girls' school she founded in 1909 whose curricula came to include mathematics, sciences, and physical education. In spite of facing incredible challenges, Rokeya kept the school running for the rest of her life. This school still operates as the Sakhawat Memorial Girls' High School in Kolkata.

As you read *Sultana's Dream*, consider whether Rokeya's narrative offers an example of an Indian woman articulating a strong sense of agency and awareness, thereby envisioning what we might call an alternative modernity. What might have been some of her reasons for choosing science fiction as a genre to envision her divergent reality?

Keya Maitra
Department of Philosophy

> **PRE-READING PARS**
>
> 1. Describe briefly two features you look for in a science fiction story.
> 2. If you are asked to imagine a world diametrically different from our familiar one, what would be three most striking things about this imagined reality?

Sultana's Dream

One evening I was lounging in an easy chair in my bedroom and thinking lazily of the condition of Indian womanhood. I am not sure whether I dozed off or not. But, as far as I remember, I was wide awake. I saw the moonlit sky sparkling with thousands of diamond-like stars, very distinctly.

All on a sudden a lady stood before me; how she came in, I do not know. I took her for my friend, Sister Sara.

'Good morning,' said Sister Sara. I smiled inwardly as I knew it was not morning, but starry night. However, I replied to her, saying, 'How do you do?'

'I am all right, thank you. Will you please come out and have a look at our garden?'

I looked again at the moon through the open window, and thought there was no harm in going out at that time. The men-servants outside were fast asleep just then, and I could have a pleasant walk with Sister Sara.

I used to have my walks with Sister Sara, when we were at Darjeeling. Many a time did we walk hand in hand and talk light-heartedly in the botanical gardens there. I fancied, Sister Sara had probably come to take me to some such garden and I readily accepted her offer and went out with her.

When walking I found to my surprise that it was a fine morning. The town was fully awake and the streets alive with bustling crowds. I was feeling very shy, thinking I was walking in the street in broad daylight, but there was not a single man visible.

Some of the passers-by made jokes at me. Though I could not understand their language, yet I felt sure they were joking. I asked my friend, 'What do they say?'

'The women say that you look very mannish.'

'Mannish?' said I, 'What do they mean by that?'

'They mean that you are shy and timid like men.'

'Shy and timid like men?' It was really a joke. I became very nervous, when I found that my companion was not Sister Sara, but a stranger. Oh, what a fool had I been to mistake this lady for my dear old friend, Sister Sara.

She felt my fingers tremble in her hand, as we were walking hand in hand.

'What is the matter, dear?' she said affectionately. 'I feel somewhat awkward,' I said in a rather apologizing tone, 'as being a purdahnishin woman I am not accustomed to walking about unveiled.'

'You need not be afraid of coming across a man here. This is Ladyland, free from sin and harm. Virtue herself reigns here.'

By and by I was enjoying the scenery. Really it was very grand. I mistook a patch of green grass for a velvet cushion. Feeling as if I were walking on a soft carpet, I looked down and found the path covered with moss and flowers.

'How nice it is,' said I.

'Do you like it?' asked Sister Sara. (I continued calling her 'Sister Sara,' and she kept calling me by my name).

'Yes, very much; but I do not like to tread on the tender and sweet flowers.'

'Never mind, dear Sultana; your treading will not harm them; they are street flowers.'

'The whole place looks like a garden,' said I admiringly. 'You have arranged every plant so skillfully.'

'Your Calcutta could become a nicer garden than this if only your countrymen wanted to make it so.'

'They would think it useless to give so much attention to horticulture, while they have so many other things to do.'

'They could not find a better excuse,' said she with smile.

I became very curious to know where the men were. I met more than a hundred women while walking there, but not a single man.

'Where are the men?' I asked her.

'In their proper places, where they ought to be.'

'Pray let me know what you mean by "their proper places."'

'O, I see my mistake, you cannot know our customs, as you were never here before. We shut our men indoors.'

'Just as we are kept in the zenana?'

'Exactly so.'

'How funny,' I burst into a laugh. Sister Sara laughed too.

'But dear Sultana, how unfair it is to shut in the harmless women and let loose the men.'

'Why? It is not safe for us to come out of the zenana, as we are naturally weak.'

'Yes, it is not safe so long as there are men about the streets, nor is it so when a wild animal enters a marketplace.'

'Of course not.'

'Suppose, some lunatics escape from the asylum and begin to do all sorts of mischief to men, horses and other creatures; in that case what will your countrymen do?'

'They will try to capture them and put them back into their asylum.'

'Thank you! And you do not think it wise to keep sane people inside an asylum and let loose the insane?'

'Of course not!' said I laughing lightly.

'As a matter of fact, in your country this very thing is done! Men, who do or at least are capable of doing no end of mischief, are let loose and the innocent women, shut up in the zenana! How can you trust those untrained men out of doors?'

'We have no hand or voice in the management of our social affairs. In India man is lord and master, he has taken to himself all powers and privileges and shut up the women in the zenana.'

'Why do you allow yourselves to be shut up?'

'Because it cannot be helped as they are stronger than women.'

'A lion is stronger than a man, but it does not enable him to dominate the human race. You have neglected the duty you owe to yourselves and you have lost your natural rights by shutting your eyes to your own interests.'

'But my dear Sister Sara, if we do everything by ourselves, what will the men do then?'

'They should not do anything, excuse me; they are fit for nothing. Only catch them and put them into the zenana.'

'But would it be very easy to catch and put them inside the four walls?' said I. 'And even if this were done, would all their business—political and commercial—also go with them into the zenana?'

Sister Sara made no reply. She only smiled sweetly. Perhaps she thought it useless to argue with one who was no better than a frog in a well.

By this time we reached Sister Sara's house. It was situated in a beautiful heart-shaped garden. It was a bungalow with a corrugated iron roof. It was cooler and nicer than any of our rich buildings. I cannot describe how neat and how nicely furnished and how tastefully decorated it was.

We sat side by side. She brought out of the parlour a piece of embroidery work and began putting on a fresh design.

'Do you know knitting and needle work?'

'Yes; we have nothing else to do in our zenana.'

'But we do not trust our zenana members with embroidery!' she said laughing, 'as a man has not patience enough to pass thread through a needlehole even!'

'Have you done all this work yourself?' I asked her pointing to the various pieces of embroidered teapoy cloths.

'Yes.'

'How can you find time to do all these? You have to do the office work as well? Have you not?'

'Yes. I do not stick to the laboratory all day long. I finish my work in two hours.'

'In two hours! How do you manage? In our land the officers,—magistrates, for instance—work seven hours daily.'

'I have seen some of them doing their work. Do you think they work all the seven hours?'

'Certainly they do!'

'No, dear Sultana, they do not. They dawdle away their time in smoking. Some smoke two or three choroots during the office time. They talk much about their work, but do little. Suppose one choroot takes half an hour to burn off, and a man smokes twelve choroots daily; then you see, he wastes six hours every day in sheer smoking.'

We talked on various subjects, and I learned that they were not subject to any kind of epidemic disease, nor did they suffer from mosquito bites as we do. I was very much astonished to hear that in Ladyland no one died in youth except by rare accident.

'Will you care to see our kitchen?' she asked me.

'With pleasure,' said I, and we went to see it. Of course the men had been asked to clear off when I was going there. The kitchen was situated in a beautiful vegetable garden. Every creeper, every tomato plant was itself an ornament. I found no smoke, nor any chimney either in the kitchen—it was clean and bright; the windows were decorated with flower gardens. There was no sign of coal or fire.

'How do you cook?' I asked.

'With solar heat,' she said, at the same time showing me the pipe, through which passed the concentrated sunlight and heat. And she cooked something then and there to show me the process.

'How did you manage to gather and store up the sun-heat?' I asked her in amazement.

'Let me tell you a little of our past history then. Thirty years ago, when our present Queen was thirteen years old, she inherited the throne. She was Queen in name only, the Prime Minister really ruling the country.

'Our good Queen liked science very much. She circulated an order that all the women in her country should be educated. Accordingly a number of girls' schools were founded and supported by the government. Education was spread far and wide among women. And early marriage also was stopped. No woman was to be allowed to marry before she was twenty-one. I must tell you that, before this change we had been kept in strict purdah.'

'How the tables are turned,' I interposed with a laugh.

'But the seclusion is the same,' she said. 'In a few years we had separate universities, where no men were admitted.'

'In the capital, where our Queen lives, there are two universities. One of these invented a wonderful balloon, to which they attached a number of pipes. By means of this captive balloon which they managed to keep afloat above the cloud-land, they could draw as much water from the atmosphere as they pleased. As the water was incessantly being drawn by the university people no cloud gathered and the ingenious Lady Principal stopped rain and storms thereby.'

'Really! Now I understand why there is no mud here!' said I. But I could not understand how it was possible to accumulate water in the pipes. She explained to me how it was done, but I was unable to understand her, as my scientific knowledge was very limited. However, she went on, 'When the other university came to know of this, they became exceedingly jealous and tried to do something more extraordinary still. They invented an instrument by which they could collect as much sun-heat as they wanted. And they kept the heat stored up to be distributed among others as required.

'While the women were engaged in scientific research, the men of this country were busy increasing their military power. When they came to know that the female universities were able to draw water from the atmosphere and collect heat from the sun, they only laughed at the members of the universities and called the whole thing "a sentimental nightmare"!'

'Your achievements are very wonderful indeed! But tell me, how you managed to put the men of your country into the zenana. Did you entrap them first?'

'No.'

'It is not likely that they would surrender their free and open air life of their own accord and confine themselves within the four walls of the zenana! They must have been overpowered.'

'Yes, they have been!'

'By whom? By some lady-warriors, I suppose?'

'No, not by arms.'

'Yes, it cannot be so. Men's arms are stronger than women's. Then?'

'By brain.'

'Even their brains are bigger and heavier than women's. Are they not?'

'Yes, but what of that? An elephant also has got a bigger and heavier brain than a man has. Yet man can enchain elephants and employ them, according to their own wishes.'

'Well said, but tell me please, how it all actually happened. I am dying to know it!'

'Women's brains are somewhat quicker than men's. Ten years ago, when the military officers called our scientific discoveries "a sentimental nightmare," some of the young ladies wanted to say something in reply to those remarks. But both the Lady Principals restrained them and said, they should reply not by word, but by deed, if ever they got the opportunity. And they had not long to wait for that opportunity.'

'How marvelous!' I heartily clapped my hands. 'And now the proud gentlemen are dreaming sentimental dreams themselves.'

'Soon afterwards certain persons came from a neighbouring country and took shelter in ours. They were in trouble having committed some political offense. The king who cared more for power than for good government asked our kind-hearted Queen to hand them over to his officers. She refused, as it was against her principle to turn out refugees. For this refusal the king declared war against our country.

'Our military officers sprang to their feet at once and marched out to meet the enemy. The enemy however, was too strong for them. Our soldiers fought bravely, no doubt. But in spite of all their bravery the foreign army advanced step by step to invade our country.

'Nearly all the men had gone out to fight; even a boy of sixteen was not left home.

Most of our warriors were killed, the rest driven back and the enemy came within twenty-five miles of the capital.

'A meeting of a number of wise ladies was held at the Queen's palace to advise as to what should be done to save the land. Some proposed to fight like soldiers; others objected and said that women were not trained to fight with swords and guns, nor were they accustomed to fighting with any weapons. A third party regretfully remarked that they were hopelessly weak of body.

'"If you cannot save your country for lack of physical strength," said the Queen, "try to do so by brain power."

'There was a dead silence for a few minutes. Her Royal Highness said again, "I must commit suicide if the land and my honour are lost."

'Then the Lady Principal of the second university (who had collected sun-heat), who had been silently thinking during the consultation, remarked that they were all but lost, and there was little hope left for them. There was, however, one plan which she would like to try, and this would be her first and last efforts; if she failed in this, there would be nothing left but to commit suicide. All present solemnly vowed that they would never allow themselves to be enslaved, no matter what happened.

'The Queen thanked them heartily, and asked the Lady Principal to try her plan. The Lady Principal rose again and said, "before we go out the men must enter the zenanas. I make this prayer for the sake of purdah." "Yes, of course," replied Her Royal Highness.

'On the following day the Queen called upon all men to retire into zenanas for the sake of honour and liberty. Wounded and tired as they were, they took that order rather for a boon! They bowed low and entered the zenanas without uttering a single word of protest. They were sure that there was no hope for this country at all.

'Then the Lady Principal with her two thousand students marched to the battle field, and arriving there directed all the rays of the concentrated sunlight and heat towards the enemy.

'The heat and light were too much for them to bear. They all ran away panic-stricken, not knowing in their bewilderment how to counteract that scorching heat. When they fled away leaving their guns and other ammunitions of war, they were burnt down by means of the same sun-heat. Since then no one has tried to invade our country any more.'

'And since then your countrymen never tried to come out of the zenana?'

'Yes, they wanted to be free. Some of the police commissioners and district magistrates sent word to the Queen to the effect that the military officers certainly deserved to be imprisoned for their failure; but they never neglected their duty and therefore they should not be punished and they prayed to be restored to their respective offices.

'Her Royal Highness sent them a circular letter intimating to them that if their services should ever be needed they would be sent for, and that in the meanwhile they should remain where they were. Now that they are accustomed to the purdah system and have ceased to grumble at their seclusion, we call the system "Mardana" instead of "zenana."'

'But how do you manage,' I asked Sister Sara, 'to do without the police or magistrates in case of theft or murder?'

'Since the "Mardana" system has been established, there has been no more crime or sin; therefore we do not require a policeman to find out a culprit, nor do we want a magistrate to try a criminal case.'

'That is very good, indeed. I suppose if there was any dishonest person, you could very easily chastise her. As you gained a decisive victory without shedding a single drop of blood, you could drive off crime and criminals too without much difficulty!'

'Now, dear Sultana, will you sit here or come to my parlour?' she asked me.

'Your kitchen is not inferior to a queen's boudoir!' I replied with a pleasant smile, 'but we must leave it now; for the gentlemen may be cursing me for keeping them away from their duties in the kitchen so long.' We both laughed heartily.

'How my friends at home will be amused and amazed, when I go back and tell them that in the far-off Ladyland, ladies rule over the country and control all social matters, while gentlemen are kept in the Mardanas to mind babies, to cook and to do all sorts of domestic work; and that cooking is so easy a thing that it is simply a pleasure to cook!'

'Yes, tell them about all that you see here.'

'Please let me know, how you carry on land cultivation and how you plough the land and do other hard manual work.'

'Our fields are tilled by means of electricity, which supplies motive power for other hard work as well, and we employ it for our aerial conveyances too. We have no rail road nor any paved streets here.'

'Therefore neither street nor railway accidents occur here,' said I. 'Do not you ever suffer from want of rainwater?' I asked.

'Never since the "water balloon" has been set up. You see the big balloon and pipes attached thereto. By their aid we can draw as much rainwater as we require. Nor do we ever suffer from flood or thunderstorms. We are all very busy making nature yield as much as she can. We do not find time to quarrel with one another as we never sit idle. Our noble Queen is exceedingly fond of botany; it is her ambition to convert the whole country into one grand garden.'

'The idea is excellent. What is your chief food?'

'Fruits.'

'How do you keep your country cool in hot weather? We regard the rainfall in summer as a blessing from heaven.'

'When the heat becomes unbearable, we sprinkle the ground with plentiful showers drawn from the artificial fountains. And in cold weather we keep our room warm with sun-heat.'

She showed me her bathroom, the roof of which was removable. She could enjoy a shower bath whenever she liked, by simply removing the roof (which was like the lid of a box) and turning on the tap of the shower pipe.

'You are a lucky people!' ejaculated I. 'You know no want. What is your religion, may I ask?'

'Our religion is based on Love and Truth. It is our religious duty to love one another and to be absolutely truthful. If any person lies, she or he is....'

'Punished with death?'

'No, not with death. We do not take pleasure in killing a creature of God, especially a human being. The liar is asked to leave this land for good and never to come to it again.'

'Is an offender never forgiven?'

'Yes, if that person repents sincerely.'

'Are you not allowed to see any man, except your own relations?'

'No one except sacred relations.'

'Our circle of sacred relations is very limited; even first cousins are not sacred.'

'But ours is very large; a distant cousin is as sacred as a brother.'

'That is very good. I see purity itself reigns over your land. I should like to see the good Queen, who is so sagacious and far-sighted and who has made all these rules.'

'All right,' said Sister Sara.

Then she screwed a couple of seats onto a square piece of plank. To this plank she attached two smooth and well-polished balls. When I asked her what the balls were for, she said they were hydrogen balls and they were used to overcome the force of gravity. The balls were of different capacities to be used according to the different weights desired to be overcome. She then fastened to the air-car two wing-like blades, which, she said, were worked by electricity. After we were comfortably seated she touched a knob and the blades began to whirl, moving faster and faster every moment. At first we were raised to the height of about six or seven feet and then off we flew. And before I could realize that we had commenced moving, we reached the garden of the Queen.

My friend lowered the air-car by reversing the action of the machine, and when the car touched the ground the machine was stopped and we got out.

I had seen from the air-car the Queen walking on a garden path with her little daughter (who was four years old) and her maids of honour.

'Halloo! You here!' cried the Queen addressing Sister Sara. I was introduced to Her Royal Highness and was received by her cordially without any ceremony.

I was very much delighted to make her acquaintance. In the course of the conversation I had with her, the Queen told me that she had no objection to permitting her subjects to trade with other countries. 'But,' she continued, 'no trade was possible with countries where the women were kept in the zenanas and so unable to come and trade with us. Men, we find, are rather of lower morals and so we do not like dealing with them. We do not covet other people's land, we do not fight for a piece of diamond though it may be a thousand-fold brighter than the Koh-i-Noor, nor do we grudge a ruler his Peacock Throne. We dive deep into the ocean of knowledge and try to find out the precious gems, which nature has kept in store for us. We enjoy nature's gifts as much as we can.'

After taking leave of the Queen, I visited the famous universities, and was shown some of their manufactories, laboratories and observatories.

After visiting the above places of interest we got again into the air-car, but as soon as it began moving, I somehow slipped down and the fall startled me out of my dream. And on opening my eyes, I found myself in my own bedroom still lounging in the easy-chair!

Hossain, Rokeya Sakhawat. *Sultana's Dream. The Indian Ladies' Magazine.* Madras, 1905.

POST-READING PARS

1. Can you identify the two features you consider to be qualifying markers of a science fiction story in *Sultana's Dream*?
2. Identify three of the most striking ways Ladyland differs from Rokeya's familiar world.

Inquiry Corner

Content Questions:

What are the jobs and roles assigned to men in Ladyland? How did men come to have these roles? What are some of the salient traits of men according to *Sultana's Dream*?

Critical Question:

Critically evaluate the role of the benevolent Queen of Ladyland in the various inventions that Sultana comes across. Can you articulate Rokeya's arguments for having women in leadership positions?

Comparative Question:

Compare the account that *Sultana's Dream* presents of how sociopolitical freedom depends on science education with another such account you have read in this course.

Connection Questions:

Why is it important to be able to imagine a reality very different from, even diametrically opposed to, one's familiar reality in order to conceive a truly just and equitable society? What is the relation between our ability to imagine and justice?

BEYOND THE CLASSROOM

» Ladyland portrays an imagined space with more access to knowledge, freedom, and power for women. What values would you use to imagine your ideal type of workplace (e.g., the types of structures and approaches)?
» There are times when advocacy for one's own group might rely on building strategic alliances with other groups. Can you imagine how this might appear in a workplace situation?

from *The Well of Loneliness* by Radclyffe Hall

Introduction

Revered as one of the earliest novels, if not the first, to explicitly portray a lesbian character and her desires, *The Well of Loneliness* is a landmark work of queer fiction. British author Radclyffe Hall (1880–1943) wrote the novel in a time when sexuality was becoming a serious topic of scholarly investigation in psychology. The novel uses familiar aspects of coming-out narratives in portraying the protagonist Stephen's experiences with rejection and her struggles to come to terms with her own identity. Nature-versus-nurture debates can be seen echoed in Stephen's thoughts and interactions with others as they grapple with her "**inversion**," an early twentieth-century term for homosexuality that emerged from the budding field of **sexology**. *The Well of Loneliness* was subsequently banned in the United Kingdom for obscenity. Hall received letters of support from queer men and women outside the UK who for the first time felt a deep connection with a literary character. Despite similar charges that led to a trial in the United States, the book was never banned there. It was eventually republished in the United Kingdom in 1949, six years after Hall's death and has remained in print since.

Despite Hall denying the autobiographical nature of the novel, there are several noteworthy parallels between the lives of the author and the protagonist. Radclyffe was named Marguerite at birth but used masculine professional and personal names, preferred masculine clothing, pursued feminine love interests, and faced rejection from family. Biographies almost exclusively refer to Hall as a lesbian

> **SNAPSHOT BOX**
>
> LANGUAGE: English
> PUBLICATION: 1928, United Kingdom
> GENRE: Novel
> TAGS: Art; Autobiography and Testimony; Family; Gender and Identity; Poetry, Music, Literature; Psyche; Tradition; War and Brutality

Timeline

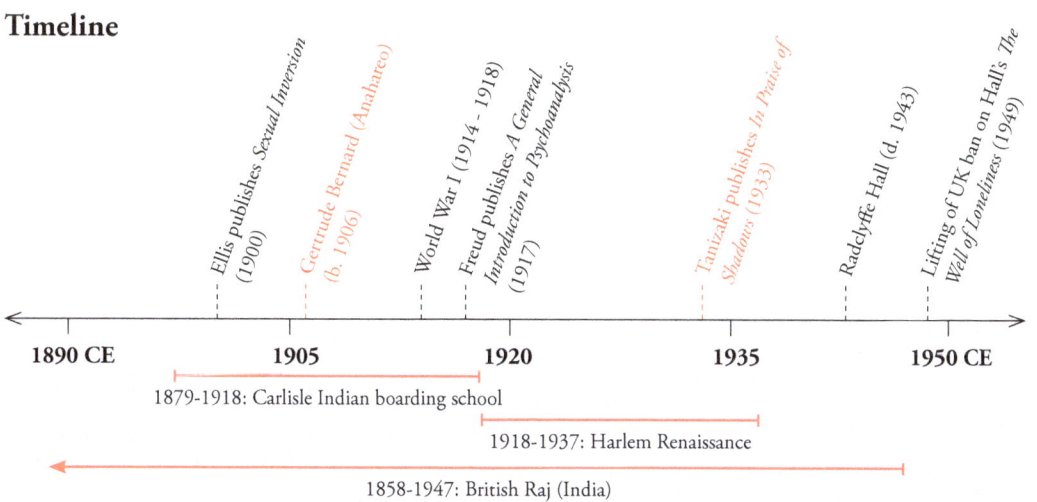

author, yet Hall clearly self-identified as an invert, which implied being physically born one sex but psychologically another and subsequently attracted to the "same" sex (physically speaking). Inversion, therefore, conflates ideas that today we would consider separately as **sex**, **gender identity**, and **sexuality**. We should therefore not actually limit ourselves to reading *The Well of Loneliness* as a "lesbian" novel written by a lesbian author. What pronouns do you think we as contemporary readers should use to address Hall? What do you notice about the language used to describe Stephen's body, and why do you think Hall made those choices?

Both the story told within the novel and the reception the novel received illustrate how gender is constructed through **discourse**. This term encompasses the linguistic sense that refers not only to text and dialogue but also to *how* they are communicated, received, or silenced. As you read, try to imagine how you might have felt reading this if you had never encountered an openly queer character before. Why is it so important to have marginalized voices represented in the media we consume? How are mainstream views of gender and sexuality upheld by various characters (including Stephen) within the story? How does Hall use language available at the time to construct new notions of gender identity?

Finally, consider *The Well of Loneliness* in the context of the modernist literary movement, which challenged traditional linear storytelling from an omniscient narrator. Texts produced in this period reflect a time of great uncertainty (leading up to and following World War I), resulting in highly introspective prose. We follow Stephen's journey of self-discovery through her own reflections and interpretations. We learn who Stephen is as she does, and along the way we learn about her world as she understands it. Ask yourself how her experiences and self-reflection shape her understanding of such fundamental concepts as *love*, *family*, and *good*. How is Stephen able to reconcile her own spirituality with the dominant religious order that so clearly rejects her?

Kelly Biers
Department of Languages and Literatures and
Women, Gender, and Sexuality Studies Program

from *The Well of Loneliness*

Sir Philip never knew how much he longed for a son until, some ten years after marriage, his wife conceived a child; then he knew that this thing meant complete fulfilment, the fulfilment for which they had both been waiting. When she told him, he could not find words for expression, and must just turn and weep on her shoulder. It never seemed to cross his mind for a moment that Anna might very well give him a daughter; he saw her only as a mother of sons, nor could her warnings disturb him. He christened the unborn infant Stephen, because he admired the pluck of that Saint. He was not a religious man by instinct, being perhaps too much of a student, but he read the Bible for its fine literature, and Stephen had gripped his imagination. Thus he often discussed the future of their child: 'I think I shall put Stephen down for Harrow,' or: 'I'd rather like Stephen to finish off abroad, it widens one's outlook on life.'

But: 'Man proposes—God disposes,' and so it happened that on Christmas Eve, Anna Gordon was delivered of a daughter; a narrow-hipped, wide-shouldered little tadpole of a baby, that yelled and yelled for three hours without ceasing as though outraged to find itself ejected into life.

[...]

Pacing restlessly up and down her bedroom, Stephen [now in late adolescence] would be thinking of Angela Crossby—haunted, tormented by Angela's words that day in the garden: 'Could you marry me, Stephen?' and then by those other pitiless words: 'Can I help it if you're—what you obviously are?'

She would think with a kind of despair: 'What am I in God's name—some kind of abomination?' And this thought would fill her with very great anguish, because, loving much, her love seemed to her sacred. She could not endure that the slur of those words should come anywhere near her love. So now night after night she must pace up and down, beating her mind against a blind problem, beating her spirit against a blank wall—the impregnable wall of non comprehension: 'Why am I as I am—and what am I?' Her mind would recoil while her spirit grew faint. A great darkness would seem to descend on her spirit—there would be no light wherewith to lighten that darkness.

[...]

That night she stared at herself in the glass; and even as she did so she hated her body with its muscular shoulders, its small compact breasts, and its slender flanks of an athlete. All her life she must drag this body of hers like a monstrous fetter[183] imposed on her spirit. This strangely ardent yet sterile body that must worship yet never be worshipped in return by the creature of its adoration. She longed to maim it, for it made her feel cruel; it was so white, so strong and so self-sufficient; yet withal so poor and unhappy a thing that her eyes filled with tears and her hate turned to pity. She began to grieve over it, touching her breasts with pitiful fingers, stroking

183. shackle

her shoulders, letting her hands slip along her straight thighs—Oh, poor and most desolate body!

Then, she, for whom Puddle [her servant] was actually praying at that moment, must now pray also, but blindly; finding few words that seemed worthy of prayer, few words that seemed to encompass her meaning—for she did not know the meaning herself: But she loved, and loving groped for the God who had fashioned her, even unto this bitter loving.

[...]

Anna began to speak very slowly as though nothing of what she would say must be lost; and that slow, quiet voice was more dreadful than anger: 'All your life I've felt very strangely towards you;' she was saying, 'I've felt a kind of physical repulsion, a desire not to touch or to be touched by you—a terrible thing for a mother to feel—it has often made me deeply unhappy. I've often felt that I was being unjust, unnatural—but now I know that my instinct was right; it is you who are unnatural, not I...'

'Mother—stop!'

'It is you who are unnatural, not I. And this thing that you are is a sin against creation. Above all is this thing a sin against the father who bred you, the father whom you dare to resemble. You dare to look like your father, and your face is a living insult to his memory, Stephen. I shall never be able to look at you now without thinking of the deadly insult of your face and your body to the memory of the father who bred you. I can only thank God that your father died before he was asked to endure this great shame. As for you, I would rather see you dead at my feet than standing before me with this thing upon you—this unspeakable outrage that you call love in that letter which you don't deny having written. In that letter you say things that may only be said between man and woman, and coming from you they are vile and filthy words of corruption—against nature, against God who created nature. My gorge[184] rises; you have made me feel physically sick—,

'Mother—you don't know what you're saying—you're my mother—'

'Yes, I am your mother, but for all that, you seem to me like a scourge. I ask myself what I have ever done to be dragged down into the depths by my daughter. And your father—what had he ever done? And you have presumed to use the word love in connection with this—with these lusts of your body; these unnatural cravings of your unbalanced mind and undisciplined body—you have used that word. I have loved—do you hear? I have loved your father, and your father loved me. That was *love*.'

Then, suddenly, Stephen knew that unless she could, indeed, drop dead at the feet of this woman in whose womb she had quickened, there was one thing that she dared not let pass unchallenged, and that was this terrible slur upon her love. And all that was in her rose up to refute it; to protect her love from such unbearable soiling. It was part of herself and unless she could save it, she could not save herself anymore. She must stand or fall by the courage of that love to proclaim its right to toleration.

184. throat

She held up her hand, commanding silence; commanding that slow, quiet voice to cease speaking, and she said: 'As my father loved you, I loved. As a man loves a woman, that was how I loved—protectively, like my father. I wanted to give all I had in me to give. It made me feel terribly strong... and gentle. It was good, good, *good*—I'd have laid down my life a thousand times over for Angela Crossby. If I could have I'd have married her and brought her home—I wanted to bring her home here to Morton. If I loved her the way a man loves a woman, it's because I can't feel that I am a woman. All my life I've never felt like a woman, and you know it—you say you've always disliked me, that you've always felt a strange physical repulsion.... I don't know what I am; no one's ever told me that I'm different and yet I know that I'm different—that's why, I suppose, you've felt as you have done. And for that I forgive you, though whatever it is, it was you and my father who made this body but what I will never forgive is your daring to try and make me ashamed of my love. I'm not ashamed of it, there's no shame in me.' And now she was stammering a little wildly, 'Good and—and fine it was' she stammered, 'the best part of myself—I gave all and I asked nothing in return—I just went on hopelessly loving—' she broke off, she was shaking from head to foot, and Anna's cold voice fell like icy water on that angry and sorely tormented spirit.

'You have spoken, Stephen. I don't think there's much more that needs to be said between us except this, we two cannot live together at Morton—not now, because I might grow to hate you. Yes, although you're my child, I might grow to hate you. The same roof mustn't shelter us both any more; one of us must go—which of us shall it be?' And she looked at Stephen and waited.

Morton! They could not both live at Morton. Something seemed to catch hold of the girl's heart and twist it. She stared at her mother, aghast for a moment, while Anna stared back—she was waiting for her answer.

But quite suddenly Stephen found her manhood and she said: 'I understand. I'll leave Morton.'

Then Anna made her daughter sit down beside her, while she talked of how this thing might be accomplished in a way that would cause the least possible scandal: 'For the sake of your father's honourable name, I must ask you to help me Stephen.' It was better, she said, that Stephen should take Puddle with her, if Puddle would consent to go. They might live in London or somewhere abroad, on the pretext that Stephen wished to study. From time to time Stephen would come back to Morton and visit her mother, and during those visits, they two would take care to be seen together for appearances' sake, for the sake of her father. She could take from Morton whatever she needed, the horses, and anything else she wished. Certain of the rent-rolls would be paid over to her, should her own income prove insufficient. All things must be done in a way that was seemly—no undue haste, no suspicion of a breach between mother and daughter: 'For the sake of your father I ask this of you, not for your sake or mine, but for his. Do you consent to this, Stephen?'

And Stephen answered: 'Yes, I consent.'

Then Anna said: 'I'd like you to leave me now—I feel tired and I want to be alone for a little—but presently I shall send for Puddle to discuss her living with you in the future.' So Stephen got up, and she went away, leaving Anna Gordon alone.

[...]

[Stephen went to her father's study where she found a sexology text.] Then suddenly she had got to her feet and was talking aloud—she was talking to her father: 'You knew! All the time you knew this thing, but because of your pity you wouldn't tell me. Oh, Father—and there are so many of us—thousands of miserable, unwanted people, who have no right to love, no right to compassion because they're maimed, hideously maimed and ugly—God's cruel; He let us get flawed in the making.'

And then, before she knew what she was doing, she had found her father's old, well-worn Bible. There she stood demanding a sign from heaven—nothing less than a sign from heaven she demanded. The Bible fell open near the beginning. She read: 'And the Lord set a mark upon Cain. . . . Then Stephen hurled the Bible away, and she sank down completely hopeless and beaten, rocking her body backwards and forwards with a kind of abrupt yet methodical rhythm: 'And the Lord set a mark upon Cain, upon Cain . . .' she was rocking now in rhythm to those words, 'And the Lord set a mark upon Cain—upon Cain—upon Cain. And the Lord set a mark upon Cain . . .'

That was how Puddle came in and found her, and Puddle said: 'Where you go, I go, Stephen. All that you're suffering at this moment I've suffered. It was when I was very young like you—but I still remember.'

Stephen looked up with bewildered eyes: 'Would you go with Cain whom God marked?' she said slowly, for she had not understood Puddle's meaning, so she asked her once more: 'Would you go with Cain?'

Puddle put an arm around Stephen's bowed shoulders, and she said: 'You've got work to do—come and do it! Why, just because you are what you are, you may actually find that you've got an advantage. You may write with a curious double insight—write both men and women from a personal knowledge. Nothing's completely misplaced or wasted, I'm sure of that—and we're all part of nature. Some day the world will recognize this, but meanwhile there's plenty of work that's waiting. For the sake of all the others who are like you, but less strong and less gifted perhaps, many of them, it's up to you to have the courage to make good, and I'm here to help you do it, Stephen.'

Selection from Hall, Radclyffe. *The Well of Loneliness*. United Kingdom: Jonathan Cape, 1928. Reprinted by permission of Brandt & Hochman Literary Agents, [1928] 1956. [no page numbers in original]

from *The Wretched of the Earth* by Frantz Fanon

Introduction

The psychiatrist, revolutionary, critical theorist Frantz Fanon (1925–1961) was born into a middle-class family in the Caribbean island of Martinique, then a French colony and currently a French Overseas Territory. He grew up under French colonial empire (seventeenth–twentieth century), educated at the University of Lyon, France, earning his degree in medicine and psychiatry. He joined the Free French Army during World War II and, upon returning to Martinique, worked for the colonial administration as part of Aimé Césaire's political campaign for the French National Assembly. In the 1950s, Fanon was stationed in Algeria, also a former French colony in North Africa. There, he witnessed traumatic experiences of French colonialism through his patients, both native Arab-Berber who were victims of racism and oppression and white-settlers who were traumatized by decolonization and racial fears.

Fanon's historical and personal background—an Afro-Martinican descendant of enslaved Africans (on his father's side) under French colonialism—unquestionably influenced his political views. Upon the Algerian Revolution in 1954, he resigned from his psychiatrist position, vacated his French citizenship, and joined the Algerian National Liberation Front. He died of leukemia in 1961 in the United States, where he received treatment, leaving behind two seminal works: *Black Skin, White Masks* (1952) and *The Wretched of the Earth* (1961). Excerpts of *The Wretched of the Earth*—specifically, the chapters "On Violence" and "Conclusion"—

> **SNAPSHOT BOX**
>
> LANGUAGE: French
> AUTHORED: Algeria
> PUBLISHED: 1961, France
> TAGS: Colonization; Cross-Cultural Encounters; History and Ideology; Internationalism; Psyche; Race; Self-Determination; Struggle, Resistance, and Revolution; Tyranny; War and Brutality

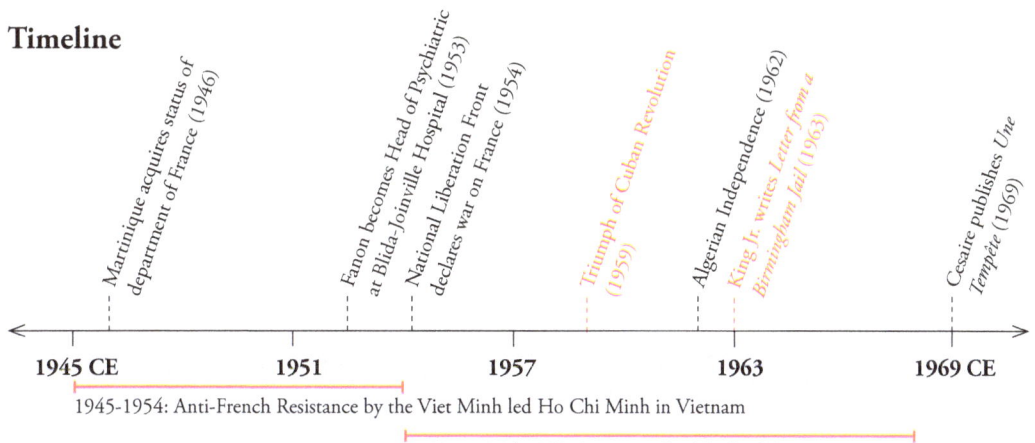

Timeline

- Martinique acquires status of department of France (1946)
- Fanon becomes Head of Psychiatric at Blida-Joinville Hospital (1953)
- National Liberation Front declares war on France (1954)
- Triumph of Cuban Revolution (1959)
- Algerian Independence (1962)
- King Jr. writes *Letter from a Birmingham Jail* (1963)
- Césaire publishes *Une Tempête* (1969)

1945 CE — 1951 — 1957 — 1963 — 1969 CE

1945-1954: Anti-French Resistance by the Viet Minh led Ho Chi Minh in Vietnam
1954-1968: American Civil Rights Movement
1946-1955: Juan Perón's first presidency (Argentina)

are excerpted below and are both seminal examples of **critical theory**. As defined by Angela Davis, critical theory envisions philosophy—in a dynamic relation to the humanities and social sciences—as a means to social transformation in general and liberation of those who have been colonized in particular.[185] The motif of **liberation** in Fanon's work has influenced various fields, including anthropology, sociology, political science, decolonial studies, and cultural studies.[186]

What conceptions of liberation are you aware of? How would you define liberation? The search for liberation of the colonized runs throughout Fanon's work. His concept of liberation owes something more to his own experience as a Black **colonialized subject** and is informed by a Marxist perspective. He specifically responds to Karl Marx's idea of revolution or the working class's "forcible overthrow of all existing [exploitative bourgeois] social conditions"[187] as the ultimate social revolution. While "a critical liberating project" that provides insightful analysis in many global contexts, Marxism is particular to the history of Europe where class is the structuring principle.[188] Fanon's liberation, or rather **decolonization**, encompasses the history of European colonialism or the "colonized world,"[189] where race is the organizing principle of society. As Fanon puts it, in "the colonial context, it is clear that what divides this world is first and foremost . . . what race one belongs to. . . . This is why a Marxist analysis should always be slightly stretched when it comes to addressing the colonial issue."[190]

Because of this critical novelty in analyzing the colonized world, Fanon's concepts of man, reason, and freedom are more expansive and inclusive than not only Marxism but also the theories of every known Enlightenment and post-Enlightenment philosopher addressing the subject matter. In "On Violence," Fanon calls for a liberation of the colonized oppressed by European colonialism and its racialized ideals of humanity. Because in the "colonial world" racism reproduces Blacks and Indigenous peoples as nonhumans, "decolonization is truly the creation of new men. . . . The 'thing' colonized becomes a man through the very process of liberation."[191] Because of **racial colonialism**, Fanon sees "decolonization" as the only solution for the restoration of humanity, which is why "decolonization is always a violent event,"[192] meaning liberation can only be attained through overthrowing the European colonialism

---

185. George Yancy, *African American Philosophers: 17 Conversations* (New York: Routledge, 2016), 22.

186. Lewis Gordon, *Existentia Africana: Understanding Africana Existential Thought* (New York: Routledge, 2000), 4–5.

187. Karl Marx and Friedrich Engels, *Manifesto of the Communist Party* (Chicago: Charles H. Kerr & Company, 1906), 64.

188. Walter D. Mignolo and Arturo Escobar, eds., *Globalization and the Decolonial Option* (London: Routledge, 2010), 16–17.

189. Frantz Fanon, *The Wretched of the Earth* (New York: Grove Press, 2004), 3–5.

190. Fanon, *The Wretched of the Earth*, 5.

191. Fanon, *The Wretched of the Earth*, 2.

192. Fanon, *The Wretched of the Earth*, 1.

that, through racism, places the Indigenous outside the realm of the human and humanity. What examples are you familiar with where colonialism or colonial settlerism denies humanity to Indigenous people? What forms of resistance have been tried and why might they offer support to Fanon's conclusion that the solution will be "violent"?

Due to his theory of violence as a means to liberation, Fanon is often dismissed as advocating force instead of civil discourse to dismantle unjust and unfair modern systems. Jean Paul Sartre, the French existentialist and strong anticolonialist, in his preface to *The Wretched of the Earth*, emphasizes Fanon's argument as, indeed, an endorsement of violence. Sartre, however, fails to read between the lines where Fanon argues that the greatest tragedy of European colonialism is that it reduces the colonized to violence.[193] In fact, Fanon's theory of violence must always be placed in a colonial context where the violence of the colonizer precedes that of the colonized. As such, the violence of the colonized is, in fact, a **counterviolence** as a means to liberation from colonialism. As Fanon puts it, "the violence which governed the ordering of the colonial world, which tirelessly punctuated the destruction of the indigenous social fabric, and demolished unchecked the systems of reference... this same violence will be vindicated and appropriated when, taking history into their own hands, the colonized swarm into the forbidden cities."[194]

The colonial world is founded and maintained through legitimized violence against the colonized—both physical (i.e., slavery, torture, flogging) and metaphysical (i.e., obliteration of Indigenous knowledge and systems of knowing). Therefore, for Fanon, the only way that the colonized might restore their humanity is through violence. Reduced to a status of a nonhuman, the colonized are not recognized as part of the colonial civil society, so a civil discourse is unthinkable. Because between the colonizer and the colonized there is no political discourse, no judicial, religious, or ethical institution will protect the colonized. The colonized "can be arrested, beaten, and starved with impunity; no sermonizer on morals, no priest has ever stepped in to bear the blows in his place or share his bread."[195] For Fanon, violence "put[s] an end to the history of colonization and the history of despoliation in order to bring to life the history of the nation, the history of decolonization."[196] Violence or decolonization restores "the land," the most essential value that provides the colonized bread and dignity, the slate on which the history of a new nation is written; their Indigenous views, values, and humanity asserted. For Fanon, such modern values as the nation, freedom, and history are also sociocultural values to which the colonized have rights. What does it mean for a worldview to lay claim to dominion over freedom, history, or "rights" themselves?

---

193. *Concerning Violence*, directed by Goran Hugo Olsson, 2014.
194. Fanon, *The Wretched of the Earth*, 5–6.
195. Fanon, *The Wretched of the Earth*, 9.
196. Fanon, *The Wretched of the Earth*, 15.

In fact, in the "Conclusion" of *The Wretched of the Earth*, Fanon invites us to search for a "new humanity" beyond the humanity set forth by the ideals of European modernity, which uses race as the organizing principle. Because racism has been the source of enslavement and genocide against Indigenous peoples, Fanon proposes a different kind of humanity. In his own words, "let us leave this Europe which never stops talking of man yet massacres him at every one of its street corners, at every corner of the world."[197] Fanon calls for atonement for the ironies of **Euro-American modernity** whose project, in the last five centuries, is founded on **epistemic violence**, or the colonial constitution of a subject and their knowledge as Other.[198] European colonialism, slavery, Jim Crow, and apartheid—everyday practices of European humanism—are all examples of this epistemic violence perpetrated against Indigenous peoples and their cultural systems around the world. Fanon, instead, envisions an **alternative modernity**, "something which Europe has been incapable of achieving," a project whose ideals do not repeat the violence of the past, but rather aim to include every human regardless of race. This alternative modernity is legitimized by the history of decolonization whose teleology "infuses a new rhythm . . . a new language, and a new humanity . . . the creation of new man."[199] This "new language," "new man," and "new humanity" have been formed and informed by the very history of European modernity within decolonizing cultural, political, and humanistic practices of the colonized.

Fanon's profound study of race and psychoanalytical analysis of "the colonized world" has plowed a new path of thought about the human being that moves beyond the narrow history of modern thought dominated by Eurocentrism.[200] His insistence on race as an essential variable in examining virtually every sphere of modern life—economy, polity, knowledge, and subjectivity (being within a particular system of power)—has brought the colonized into the possibility of **subjecthood** (agency) by unveiling the ironies of European modernity and the Enlightenment, particularly on issues related to man, reason, and freedom. The declaration of the Enlightenment as the Age of Reason in the eighteenth century was predicated on the assumption that only the "European Man" was endowed with reason and non-Europeans were presumed irrational, inferior, and savages.[201] Meanwhile Indigenous peoples were being enslaved en masse around the world during the same time freedom was becoming "the highest universal political value."[202] In fact, Fanon makes more

---

197. Fanon, *The Wretched of the Earth*, 235.
198. Gayatri Chakravorty Spivak, "Can the Subaltern Speak?" in *Marxism and the Interpretation of Culture*, edited by Cary Nelson and Lawrence Grossberg (London: Macmillan, 1988), 24–25.
199. Fanon, *The Wretched of the Earth*, 2.
200. Lewis Gordon, *What Fanon Said* (New York: Fordham University Press, 2015), xiii.
201. Emmanuel Chukwudi Eze, ed., *Race and the Enlightenment* (Malden, MA: Blackwell Publishing, 1997), 4.
202. Susan Buck-Morss, "Hegel and Haiti." *Critical Inquiry* 26, no. 4 (Summer, 2000): 821.

clearly visible that European modernity's and the Age of Reason's instrumental use of race as the organizing principle of humanity has contradicted the very idea of man, betraying reason, and limiting universal freedom despite their revolutionary potential. Questioning these inconsistencies of modernity and the Enlightenment, Fanon inaugurates "a new start" and develops "a new way of thinking" toward a creation of a "new humanity."

Jeremias Zunguze
Africana Studies

> **PRE-READING PARS**
>
> 1. What three to five aspects are defining features of colonialism?
> 2. Identify two or three main factors within a colony standing in the way of its decolonization.
> 3. How would you define violence? Can ideas themselves be violent, can violence against an idea exist?

from *The Wretched of the Earth*

On Violence

National liberation, national reawakening, restoration of the nation to the people or Commonwealth, whatever the name used, whatever the latest expression, decolonization is always a violent event. At whatever level we study it—individual encounters, a change of name for a sports club, the guest list at a cocktail party, members of a police force or the board of directors of a state or private bank—decolonization is quite simply the substitution of one "species" of mankind by another. The substitution is unconditional, absolute, total, and seamless. We could go on to portray the rise of a new nation, the establishment of a new state, its diplomatic relations and its economic and political orientation. But instead we have decided to describe the kind of tabula rasa which from the outset defines any decolonization. What is singularly important is that it starts from the very first day with the basic claims of the colonized. In actual fact, proof of success lies in a social fabric that has been changed inside out. This change is extraordinarily important because it is desired, clamored for, and demanded. The need for this change exists in a raw, repressed, and reckless state in the lives and consciousness of colonized men and women. But the eventuality of such a change is also experienced as a terrifying future in the consciousness of another "species" of men and women: the *colons*, the colonists.

Decolonization, which sets out to change the order of the world, is clearly an agenda for total disorder. But it cannot be accomplished by the wave of a magic wand, a natural cataclysm, or a gentleman's agreement. Decolonization, we know, is an historical process: In other words, it can only be understood, it can only find its significance and become self-coherent insofar as we can discern the history-making movement which gives it form and substance. Decolonization is the encounter between two congenitally antagonistic forces that in fact owe their singularity to the kind of reification secreted and nurtured by the colonial situation. Their first confrontation was colored by violence and their cohabitation—or rather the exploitation of the colonized by the colonizer—continued at the point of the bayonet and under cannon fire. The colonist and the colonized are old acquaintances. And consequently, the colonist is right when he says he "knows" them. It is the colonist who *fabricated* and *continues to fabricate* the colonized subject. The colonist derives his validity, i.e., his wealth, from the colonial system.

Decolonization never goes unnoticed, for it focuses on and fundamentally alters being, and transforms the spectator crushed to a nonessential state into a privileged actor, captured in a virtually grandiose fashion by the spotlight of History. It infuses a new rhythm, specific to a new generation of men, with a new language and a new humanity. Decolonization is truly the creation of new men. But such a creation cannot be attributed to a supernatural power: The "thing" colonized becomes a man through the very process of liberation.

Decolonization, therefore, implies the urgent need to thoroughly challenge the colonial situation. Its definition can, if we want to describe it accurately, be summed up in the well-known words: "The last shall be first." Decolonization is verification of this. At a descriptive level, therefore, any decolonization is a success.

In its bare reality, decolonization reeks of red-hot cannonballs and bloody knives. For the last can be the first only after a murderous and decisive confrontation between the two protagonists. This determination to have the last move up to the front, to have them clamber up (too quickly, say some) the famous echelons of an organized society, can only succeed by resorting to every means, including, of course, violence.

You do not disorganize a society, however primitive it may be, with such an agenda if you are not determined from the very start to smash every obstacle encountered. The colonized, who have made up their mind to make such an agenda into a driving force, have been prepared for violence from time immemorial. As soon as they are born it is obvious to them that their cramped world, riddled with taboos, can only be challenged by out and out violence.

The colonial world is a compartmentalized world. It is obviously as superfluous to recall the existence of "native" towns and European towns, of schools for "natives" and schools for Europeans, as it is to recall apartheid in South Africa. Yet if we penetrate inside this compartmentalization we shall at least bring to light some of its key aspects. By penetrating its geographical configuration and classification we shall be able to delineate the backbone on which the decolonized society is reorganized.

The colonized world is a world divided in two. The dividing line, the border, is represented by the barracks and the police stations. In the colonies, the official, legitimate agent, the spokesperson for the colonizer and the regime of oppression, is the police officer or the soldier. In capitalist societies, education, whether secular or religious, the teaching of moral reflexes handed down from father to son, the exemplary integrity of workers decorated after fifty years of loyal and faithful service, the fostering of love for harmony and wisdom, those aesthetic forms of respect for the status quo, instill in the exploited a mood of submission and inhibition which considerably eases the task of the agents of law and order. In capitalist countries, a multitude of sermonizers, counselors, and "confusion-mongers" intervene between the exploited and the authorities. In colonial regions, however, the proximity and frequent, direct intervention by the police and the military ensure the colonized are kept under close scrutiny, and contained by rifle butts and napalm. We have seen how the government's agent uses a language of pure violence. The agent does not alleviate oppression or mask domination. He displays and demonstrates them with the clear conscience of the law enforcer, and brings violence into the homes and minds of colonized subjects.

The "native" sector is not complementary to the European sector. The two confront each other, but not in the service of a higher unity. Governed by a purely Aristotelian logic, they follow the dictates of mutual exclusion: There is no conciliation possible, one of them is superfluous. The colonist's sector is a sector built to last, all stone and steel. It's a sector of lights and paved roads, where the trash cans constantly overflow with strange and wonderful garbage, undreamed-of leftovers. The colonist's feet can never be glimpsed, except perhaps in the sea, but then you can never get close enough. They are protected by solid shoes in a sector where the streets are clean and smooth, without a stone. The colonist's sector is a sated, sluggish sector, its belly is permanently full of good things. The colonist sector is a white folks' sector, a sector of foreigners.

The colonized's sector, or at least the "native" quarters, the shanty town, the Medina, the reservation, is a disreputable place inhabited by disreputable people. You are born anywhere, anyhow. You die anywhere, from anything. It's a world with no space, people are piled one on top of the other, the shacks squeezed tightly together. The colonized's sector is a famished sector, hungry for bread, meat, shoes, coal, and light. The colonized's sector is a sector that crouches and cowers, a sector on its knees, a sector that is prostrate. [...] The gaze that the colonized subject casts at the colonist's sector is a look of lust, a look of envy. Dreams of possession: of sitting at the colonist's table and sleeping in his bed, preferably with his wife. The colonized man is an envious man. The colonist is aware of this as he catches the furtive glance, and constantly on his guard realizes bitterly that: "They want to take our place." And it's true there is not one colonized subject who at least once a day does not dream of taking the place of the colonist.

This compartmentalized world, this world divided in two, is inhabited by different species. The singularity of the colonial context lies in the fact that economic reality, inequality, and enormous disparities in lifestyles never manage to mask the human reality. Looking at the immediacies of the colonial context, it is clear that what divides this world is first and foremost what species, what race one belongs to. In the colonies the economic infrastructure is also a superstructure. The cause is effect: You are rich because you are white, you are white because you are rich. This is why a Marxist analysis should always be slightly stretched when it comes to addressing the colonial issue. It is not just the concept of the precapitalist society, so effectively studied by Marx, which needs to be reexamined here. The serf is essentially different from the knight, but a reference to divine right is needed to justify this difference in status. In the colonies the foreigner imposed himself using his cannons and machines. Despite the success of his pacification, in spite of his appropriation, the colonist always remains a foreigner. It is not the factories, the estates, or the bank account which primarily characterize the "ruling class." The ruling species is first and foremost the outsider from elsewhere, different from the indigenous population, "the others."

The violence which governed the ordering of the colonial world, which tirelessly punctuated the destruction of the indigenous social fabric, and demolished unchecked the systems of reference of the country's economy, lifestyles, and modes of dress, this same violence will be vindicated and appropriated when, taking history into their own hands, the colonized swarm into the forbidden cities. To blow the colonial world to smithereens is henceforth a clear image within the grasp and imagination of every colonized subject. To dislocate the colonial world does not mean that once the borders have been eliminated there will be a right of way between the two sectors. To destroy the colonial world means nothing less than demolishing the colonist's sector, burying it deep within the earth or banishing it from the territory.

Challenging the colonial world is not a rational confrontation of viewpoints. It is not a discourse on the universal, but the impassioned claim by the colonized that their world is fundamentally different. The colonial world is a Manichaean world. The colonist is not content with physically limiting the space of the colonized, i.e., with the help of his agents of law and order. As if to illustrate the totalitarian nature of colonial exploitation, the colonist turns the colonized into a kind of quintessence of evil. Colonized society is not merely portrayed as a society without values. The colonist is not content with stating that the colonized world has lost its values or worse never possessed any. The "native" is declared impervious to ethics, representing not only the absence of values but also the negation of values. He is, dare we say it, the enemy of values. In other words, absolute evil. A corrosive element, destroying everything within his reach, a corrupting element, distorting everything which involves aesthetics or morals, an agent of malevolent powers, an unconscious and incurable instrument of blind forces. [. . .] Values are, in fact, irreversibly poisoned and infected as soon as they come into contact with the colonized. The customs of the colonized, their traditions, their myths, especially their myths, are the very mark of this indigence and innate depravity. This is why we should place DDT, which destroys parasites, carriers of disease, on the same level as Christianity, which roots out heresy, natural impulses, and evil. The decline of yellow fever and the advances made by evangelizing form part of the same balance sheet. But triumphant reports by the missions in fact tell us how deep the seeds of alienation have been sown among the colonized. I am talking of Christianity and this should come as no surprise to anybody. The Church in the colonies is a white man's Church, a foreigners' Church. It does not call the colonized to the ways of God, but to the ways of the white man, to the ways of the master, the ways of the oppressor. And as we know, in this story many are called but few are chosen.

Sometimes this Manichaeanism reaches its logical conclusion and dehumanizes the colonized subject. In plain talk, he is reduced to the state of an animal. And consequently, when the colonist speaks of the colonized he uses zoological terms. Allusion is made to the slithery movements of the yellow race, odors from the "native" quarters, to the hordes, the stink, the swarming, the seething, and the gesticulations. In his endeavors at description and finding the right word, the colonist refers constantly to the bestiary. The European seldom has a problem with figures of speech. But the colonized, who immediately grasp the intention of the colonist and the exact case being made against them, know instantly what he is thinking. This explosive population growth, those hysterical masses, those blank faces, those shapeless, obese bodies, this headless, tailless cohort, these children who seem not to belong to anyone, this indolence sprawling under the sun, this vegetating existence, all this is part of the colonial vocabulary. General de Gaulle speaks of "yellow multitudes," and Monsieur Mauriac of the black, brown, and yellow hordes that will soon invade our shores. The colonized know all that and roar with laughter every time they hear themselves called an animal by the other. For they know they are not animals. And at the very moment when they discover their humanity, they begin to sharpen their weapons to secure its victory.

[...]

For a colonized people, the most essential value, because it is the most meaningful, is first and foremost the land: the land, which must provide bread and, naturally, dignity. But this dignity has nothing to do with "human" dignity. The colonized subject never heard of such an ideal. All he has ever seen on his land is that he can be arrested, beaten, and starved with impunity; no sermonizer on morals, no priest has ever stepped in to bear the blows in his place or share his bread. For the colonized, to be a moralist quite plainly means silencing the arrogance of the colonist, breaking his spiral of violence, in a word ejecting him outright from the picture. The famous dictum which states that men are equal will find its illustration in the colonies only when the colonized subject states he is equal to the colonist. Taking it a step further, he is determined to fight to be more than the colonist. In fact, he has already decided to take his place. As we have seen, it is the collapse of an entire moral and material universe. The intellectual who, for his part, has adopted the abstract, universal values of the colonizer is prepared to fight so that colonist and colonized can live in peace in a new world. But what he does not see, because precisely colonialism and all its modes of thought have seeped into him, is that the colonist is no longer interested in staying on and coexisting once the colonial context has disappeared. It is no coincidence that, even before any negotiation between the Algerian government and the French government, the so-called "liberal" European minority has already made its position clear: it is clamoring for dual citizenship, nothing less. By sticking to the abstract the colonist is forced to make a very substantial leap into the unknown. Let us be honest, the colonist knows perfectly well that no jargon is a substitution for reality.

[...]

We have seen therefore that the Manichaeanism that first governed colonial society is maintained intact during the period of decolonization. In fact the colonist never ceases to be enemy, the antagonist, in plain words public enemy number 1. The oppressor, ensconced in his sector, creates the spiral, the spiral of domination, exploitation and looting. In the other sector, the colonized subject lies coiled and robbed, and fuels as best he can the spiral which moves seamlessly from the shores of the colony to the palaces and docks of the metropolis. In this petrified zone, not a ripple on the surface, the palm trees sway against the clouds, the waves of the sea lap against the shore, the raw materials come and go, legitimating the colonist's presence, while more dead than alive the colonized subject crouches forever in the same old dream. The colonist makes history. His life is an epic, an odyssey. He is invested with the very beginning: "We made this land." He is the guarantor for its existence: "If we leave, all will be lost, and this land will return to the Dark Ages." Opposite him, listless beings wasted away by fevers and by "ancestral customs" compose a virtually petrified background to the innovative dynamism of colonial mercantilism.

The colonist makes history and he knows it. And because he refers constantly to the history of his metropolis, he plainly indicates that here he is the extension of this metropolis. The history he writes is therefore not the history of the country he is despoiling, but the history of his own nation's looting, raping, and starving to death. The immobility to which the colonized subject is condemned can be challenged only if he decides to put an end to the history of colonization and the history of despoliation in order to bring to life the history of the nation, the history of decolonization.

A world compartmentalized, Manichaean and petrified, a world of statues: the statue of the general who led the conquest, the statue of the engineer who built the bridge. A world cocksure of itself, crushing with its stoniness the backbones of those scarred by the whip. That is the colonial world. The colonial subject is a man penned in; apartheid is but one method of compartmentalizing the colonial world. The first thing the colonial learns is to remain in his place and not overstep its limits. Hence the dreams of the colonial subject are muscular dreams, dreams of action, dreams of aggressive vitality. I dream I am jumping, swimming, running, and climbing. I dream I burst out laughing, I am leaping across a river and chased by a pack of cars that never catches up with me. During colonization the colonized subject frees himself night after night between nine in the evening and six in the morning.

[. . .]

The colonized subject is constantly on his guard: Confused by the myriad signs of the colonial world he never knows whether he is out of line. Confronted with a world configured by the colonizer, the colonized subject is always presumed guilty. The colonized does not accept his guilt, but rather considers it a kind of curse, a sword of Damocles. But deep down the colonized subject acknowledges no authority. He is dominated but not domesticated. He is made to feel inferior, but by no means convinced of his inferiority. He patiently waits for the colonist to let his guard down and then jumps on him. The muscles of the colonized are always tensed. It is not that he is anxious or terrorized, but he is always ready to change his role as game for that of hunter. The colonized subject is a persecuted man who is forever dreaming of becoming the persecutor. The symbols of society such as the police force, bugle calls in the barracks, military parades, and the flag flying aloft, serve not only as inhibitors but also as stimulants. They do not signify: "Stay where you are." But rather "Get ready to do the right thing." And in fact if ever the colonized subject begins to doze off or forget, the colonist's arrogance and preoccupation with testing the solidity of the colonial system will remind him on so many occasions that the great showdown cannot be postponed indefinitely. This impulse to take the colonist's place maintains a constant muscular tonus. It is a known fact that under certain emotional circumstances an obstacle actually escalates action.

The relationship between colonist and colonized is one of physical mass. Against the greater number the colonist pits his force. The colonist is an exhibitionist. His safety concerns lead him to remind the colonized out loud: "Here I am the master." The colonist keeps the colonized in a state of rage, which he prevents from boiling over. The colonized are caught in the tightly knit web of colonialism. But we have seen how on the inside the colonist achieves only a pseudo-petrification. The muscular tension of the colonized periodically erupts into bloody fighting between tribes, clans, and individuals.

[...]

The violence of the colonial regime and the counterviolence of the colonized balance each other and respond to each other in an extraordinary reciprocal homogeneity. The greater the number of metropolitan settlers, the more terrible the violence will be. Violence among the colonized will spread in proportion to the violence exerted by the colonial regime. [...] When the colonized subject is tortured, when his wife is killed or raped, he complains to no one. The authorities of oppression can appoint as many commissions of inquiry and investigation as they like. In the eyes of the colonized, these commissions do not exist. And in fact, soon it will be seven years of crimes committed in Algeria and not a single Frenchman has been brought before a French court of justice for the murder of an Algerian. In Indochina, Madagascar, and the colonies, "native" has always known he can expect nothing from the other side. The work of the colonist is to make even dreams of liberty impossible for the colonized. The work of the colonized is to imagine every possible method for annihilating the colonist. On the logical plane, the Manichaeanism of the colonist produces a Manichaeanism of the colonized. The theory of the "absolute evil of the colonist" is in response to the theory of the "absolute evil of the native."

The arrival of the colonists signified syncretically the death of indigenous society, cultural lethargy, and petrifaction of the individual. For the colonized, life can only materialize from the rotting cadaver of the colonist. Such then is the term-for-term correspondence between the two arguments.

But it so happens that for the colonized this violence is invested with positive, formative features because it constitutes their only work. This violent praxis is totalizing since each individual represents a violent link in the great chain, in the almighty body of violence rearing up in reaction to the primary violence of the colonizer. Factions recognize each other and the future nation is already indivisible. The armed struggle mobilizes the people, i.e., it pitches them in a single direction, from which there is no turning back.

When it is achieved during a war of liberation the mobilization of the masses introduces the notion of common cause, national destiny, and collective history into every consciousness. Consequently, the second phase, i.e., nation building, is facilitated by the existence of this mortar kneaded with blood and rage. This then gives us a better understanding of the originality of the vocabulary used in underdeveloped countries. During the colonial period the people were called upon to fight against oppression. Following national liberation they are urged to fight against poverty, illiteracy, and underdevelopment. The struggle, they say, goes on. The people realize that life is an unending struggle.

The violence of the colonized, we have said, unifies the people. By its very structure colonialism is separatist and regionalist. Colonialism is not merely content to note the existence of tribes, it reinforces and differentiates them. The colonial system nurtures the chieftainships and revives the old *marabout* confraternities. Violence in its practice is totalizing and national. As a result, it harbors in its depths the elimination of regionalism and tribalism. The nationalist parties, therefore, show no pity at all toward *kaids* and the traditional chiefs. The elimination of the *kaids* and the chiefs is a prerequisite to the unification of the people.

At the individual level, violence is a cleansing force. It rids the colonized of their inferiority complex, of their passive and despairing attitude. It emboldens them, and restores their self confidence. Even if the armed struggle has been symbolic, and even if they have been demobilized by rapid decolonization, the people have time to realize that liberation was the achievement of each and everyone and no special merit should go to the leader. Violence hoists the people up to the level of the leader. Hence their aggressive tendency to distrust the system of protocol that young governments are quick to establish. When they have used violence to achieve national liberation, the masses allow nobody to come forward as "liberator." They prove themselves to be jealous of their achievements and take care not to place their future, their destiny, and the fate of their homeland into the hands of a living god.

[…]

Conclusion

Now, comrades, now is the time to decide to change sides. We must shake off the great mantle of night which has enveloped us, and reach for the light. The new day which is dawning must find us determined, enlightened and resolute.

We must abandon our dreams and say farewell to our old beliefs and former friendships. Let us not lose time in useless laments or sickening mimicry. Let us leave this Europe which never stops talking of man yet massacres him at every one of its street corners, at every corner of the world.

For centuries Europe has brought the progress of other men to a halt and enslaved them for its own purposes and glory; for centuries it has stifled virtually the whole of humanity in the name of a so-called spiritual adventure. Look at it now teetering between atomic destruction and spiritual disintegration.

And yet nobody can deny its achievements at home have not been crowned with success.

Europe has taken over leadership of the world with fervor, cynicism, and violence. And look how the shadow of its monuments spreads and multiplies. Every movement Europe makes bursts the boundaries of space and thought. Europe has denied itself not only humility and modesty but also solicitude and tenderness.

Its only show of miserliness has been toward man, only toward man has it shown itself to be niggardly[203] and murderously carnivorous.

So, my brothers, how could we fail to understand that we have better things to do than follow in that Europe's footsteps?

This Europe, which never stopped talking of man, which never stopped proclaiming its sole concern was man, we now know the price of suffering humanity has paid for everyone of its spiritual victories.

Come, comrades, the European game is finally over, we must look for something else. We can do anything today provided we do not ape Europe, provided we are not obsessed with catching up with Europe.

Europe has gained such a mad and reckless momentum that it has lost control and reason and is heading at dizzying speed towards the brink from which we would be advised to remove ourselves as quickly as possible.

It is all too true, however, that we need a model, schemas and examples. For many of us the European model is the most elating. But we have seen in the preceding pages how misleading such an imitation can be. European achievements, European technology and European lifestyles must stop tempting us and leading us astray.

When I look for man in European lifestyles and technology I see a constant denial of man, an avalanche of murders.

Man's condition, his projects and collaboration with others on tasks that strengthen man's totality, are new issues which require genuine inspiration.

Let us decide not to imitate Europe and let us tense our muscles and our brains in a new direction. Let us endeavor to invent a man in full, something which Europe has been incapable of achieving.

Two centuries ago, a former European colony took it into its head to catch up with Europe. It has been so successful that the United States of America has become a monster where the flaws, sickness, and inhumanity of Europe have reached frightening proportions.

Comrades, have we nothing else to do but create a third Europe? The West saw itself on a spiritual adventure. It is in the name of the Spirit, meaning the spirit of

---

203. This word means miserly or stingy and even though it is etymologically unrelated to the derogatory n-word, it may still cause controversy and offense to some and thus sensitivity is encouraged in its use in language or in the classroom.

Europe, that Europe justified its crimes and legitimized the slavery in which it held four fifths of humanity.

Yes, the European spirit is built on strange foundations. The whole of European thought developed in places that were increasingly arid and increasingly inaccessible. Consequently, it was natural that the chances of encountering man became less and less frequent.

A permanent dialogue with itself, an increasingly obnoxious narcissism inevitably paved the way for a virtual delirium where intellectual thought turns into agony since the reality of man as a living, working, self-made being is replaced by words, an assemblage of words and the tensions generated by their meanings. There were Europeans, however, who urged the European workers to smash this narcissism and break with this denial of reality.

Generally speaking, the European workers did not respond to the call. The fact was that the workers believed they too were part of the prodigious adventure of the European Spirit.

All the elements for a solution to the major problems of humanity existed at one time or another in European thought. But the Europeans did not act on the mission that was designated them and which consisted of virulently pondering these elements, modifying their configuration, their being, of changing them and finally taking the problem of man to an infinitely higher plane.

Today we are witnessing a stasis of Europe. Comrades, let us flee this stagnation where dialectics has gradually turned into a logic of the status quo. Let us reexamine the question of man. Let us reexamine the question of cerebral reality, the brain mass of humanity in its entirety whose affinities must be increased, whose connections must be diversified and whose communications must be humanized again.

Come brothers, we have far too much work on our hands to revel in outmoded games. Europe has done what it had to do all things considered, it has done a good job; let us stop accusing it, but let us say to it firmly it must stop putting on such a show. We no longer have reason to fear it, let us stop then envying it.

The Third World is today facing Europe as one colossal mass whose project must be to try and solve the problems this Europe was incapable of finding the answers to.

But what matters now is not a question of profitability, not a question of increased productivity, not a question of production rates. No, it is not a question of back to nature. It is the very basic question of not dragging man in directions which mutilate him, of not imposing on his brain tempos that rapidly obliterate and unhinge it. The notion of catching up must not be as a pretext to brutalize man, to tear him from himself and his inner consciousness, to break him, to kill him.

No, we do not want to catch up with anyone. But what we want is to walk in the company of man, every man, night and day, for all times. It is not a question of stringing the caravan out where groups are spaced so far apart they cannot see the one in front, and men who no longer recognize each other, meet less and less and talk to each other less and less.

The Third World must start over a new history of man which takes account of not only the occasional prodigious theses maintained by Europe but also its crimes, the most heinous of which have been committed at the very heart of man, the pathological dismembering of his functions and the erosion of his unity, and in the context of the community, the fracture, the stratification and the bloody tensions fed by class, and finally, on the immense scale of humanity, the racial hatred, slavery, exploitation and, above all, the bloodless genocide whereby one and a half billion men have been written off.

So comrades, let us not pay tribute to Europe by creating states, institutions, and societies that draw their inspiration from it.

Humanity expects other things from us than this grotesque and generally obscene emulation.

If we want to transform Africa into a new Europe, America into a new Europe, then let us entrust the destinies of our countries to the Europeans. They will do a better job than the best of us.

But if we want humanity to take one step forward, if we want to take it to another level than the one where Europe has placed it, then we must innovate, we must be pioneers.

If we want to respond to the expectations of our peoples, we must look elsewhere besides Europe.

Moreover, if we want to respond to the expectations of the Europeans we must not send them back a reflection, however ideal, of their society and their thought that periodically sickens even them.

For Europe, for ourselves and for humanity, comrades, we must make a new start, develop a new way of thinking, and endeavor to create a new man.

Fanon, Frantz. "On Violence" and "Conclusion." In *The Wretched of the Earth*, translated from the French by Richard Philcox, 1–10, 14–17, 46–47, 49–52, 235–239. New York: Grove Press, [1963] 2004.

POST-READING PARS

1. If European colonialism is an integral part, if not the foundation, of European modernity, identify two principal contradictions, according to Fanon, of European modernity.
2. Consider two or three complications arising from having to use the language, values, and systems of their own colonizer for liberation? What are the alternatives for Fanon?
3. How does Fanon treat violence? How does Fanon see violence working? Cite three places in the text that support your assessment.
4. Identify two or three main aspects of Fanonian "new humanity."

Inquiry Corner

Content Questions:

According to Fanon, what effect does colonization have on the individual and the community? How does Fanon redefine the concepts of "Man," reason, and freedom?

Critical Question:

Fanon offers two types of decolonization. Outline and evaluate their nature and relative effectiveness.

Comparative Question:

How does the Enlightenment idea of freedom differ from Fanon's concept of liberation?

Connection Questions:

Relate Fanon to today's US racial issues and freedom in America? How can we use Fanon's critical theory in relation to BIPOC, AAPI, and LGBTQIA+ issues today? How did Fanon connect with you personally?

SOURCES AND PERMISSIONS

The editors and publisher gratefully acknowledge the permission granted to reproduce the copyright material in this book. Every effort has been made to trace copyright holders and to obtain their permission for the use of copyright material. The publisher apologizes for any errors or omissions in the below list and would be grateful if notified of any corrections that should be incorporated in future reprints or editions of this book.

"Address at the World's Fair in Atlanta (1895)," Booker T. Washington: Washington, Booker T. "Address at the World's Fair in Atlanta (1895)." [Public Domain]

"Annihilation of Caste," Bhimrao Ramji Ambedkar: Ambedkar, Bhimrao Ramji. In *Annihilation of Caste: With a Reply to Mahatma Gandhi*, 37–42. Amritsar: The Ambedkar School of Thoughts, 1945. [Public Domain]

"A'n't I a Woman," and "Address to the First Annual Meeting of the American Equal Rights Association," Sojourner Truth:

Truth, Sojourner. "Ain't I a Woman?" December 1851. [Public Domain]

Truth, Sojourner. *First Annual Meeting of the American Equal Rights Association*. N.p.: New York Tribune, 1867. [Public Domain]

***Ariel*, José Enrique Rodó:** Selection from Rodó, José Enrique. *ARIEL*, translated by Margaret Sayers Peden, 70–74. Austin: University of Texas Press, 1988. Copyright © 1988. By permission of the University of Texas Press.

***The Berlin Stories*, Christopher Isherwood:** Isherwood, Christopher. "A Berlin Diary (Winter 1932–3)." In *The Berlin Stories*, 186–207. New Directions Publishing Corp, [1939, 1935] 2012. By Christopher Isherwood, from THE BERLIN STORIES, copyright ©1935 by Christopher Isherwood. Reprinted by permission of New Directions Publishing Corp. UK/Commonwealth rights "A Berlin Diary (Winter 1932–3)" by Christopher Isherwood. Copyright © 1939 by Christopher Isherwood, used by permission of The Wylie Agency LLC.

***Black Bolshevik*, Harry Haywood:** Haywood, Harry. "Searching for Answers." In *Black Bolshevik: Autobiography of an Afro-American Communist*, 81–84. Minneapolis: University of Minnesota Press, 1978. Copyright 1978 by Harry Haywood. Reprinted by permission of University of Minnesota Press.

"Books That Have Influenced Me," Chandrasekhara Venkata Raman: Natesan, B., and C. V. Raman. "II. Sir C. V. Raman." In *Books That Have Influenced Me; a Symposium*, 21–29. Madras: G. A. Natesan, 1947. [Public Domain]

Cherokee Sources during the Removal Period:

Cherokee Nation. 1785 Nov. 28, and Continental Congress Broadside Collection. *Articles of a Treaty, Concluded at Hopewell, on the Keowee, between Benjamin Hawkings, Andrew Pickens, Joseph Martin and Lacklan M'Intosh, Commissioners Plenipotentiary of the United States of America, of the one Part, and the Head-Men and Warriors of all the Cherokees of the other.* [New York: s.n, 1786]. Online text: https://www.loc.gov/resource/bdsdcc.18101/. [Public Domain]

Cherokee Women's Council. *"Cherokee Indian/Native American Women to National Council at Amohee, May 2,"* Andrew Jackson Papers (1775–1874), Manuscript/Mixed Material, 1817. https://www.loc.gov/item/maj007262/. Library of Congress, Manuscript Division, Andrew Jackson Papers. [Public Domain]

Cherokee Women's Council. "June 30, 1818." In *Letter to American Board of Missionaries*, 30 June 1818, Papers of the American Board of Commissioners from Foreign Missions. Boston: Houghton Library, Harvard University, 1818. [Public Domain]

Cherokee Nation. "Memorial of the Cherokee Indians." In *Cherokee Phoenix, and Indians' Advocate*, January 20, 1830, vol. 2, no. 40, page 1, col. 3a–5b. https://gahistoricnewspapers.galileo.usg.edu/lccn/sn83020874/1830-01-20/ed-1/seq-1/. [Public Domain]

Cherokee Nation, Lewis Ross, et al. "Address of the Committee and Council of the Cherokee Nation, in General Council Convened, to the People of the United States." In *Cherokee Phoenix, and Indians' Advocate*, July 24, 1830, page 1, col. 1b–page 2, col. 2a. https://www.wcu.edu/library/DigitalCollections/CherokeePhoenix/Vol3/no14/indians-page-1-column-1b-page-2-column-2a.html. [Public Domain]

"Correspondences between Gandhi and Tagore," Mohandas Karamchand Gandhi and Rabindranath Tagore:

Gandhi, Mahatma. "English Learning." In *Young India, 1919–1922*, 459–61. New York: B. W. Huebsch, 1923. [Public Domain]

Gandhi, Mahatma. "The Poet's Anxiety." In *Young India, 1919–1922*, 608–13. New York: B. W. Huebsch, 1923. [Public Domain]

Tagore, Rabindranath. From *Letters from Abroad*, 72–85. Madras, India: S. Ganesan, 1924. [Public Domain]

"**Declaration of Independence of the Democratic Republic of Vietnam," Ho Chi Minh:** Ho Chi Minh. "Declaration of Independence of the Democratic Republic of Vietnam." In *Selected Works*, vol. 3, 17–21. Hanoi: Foreign Languages Publishing House, 1960–62. [Public Domain]

"Declaration of Rights of Woman and Citizen," Olympe de Gouges: de Gouges, Olympe. *Les droits de la femme*. Bibliothèque Nationale, 1790. [Public Domain]

"Declaration of Sentiments," Elizabeth Cady Stanton: Cady Stanton, Elizabeth. "Declaration of Sentiments." First delivered at the Seneca Fall Convention, 1848. [Public Domain]

***Democracy in America*, Alexis de Tocqueville:** Selections from Tocqueville, Alexis de. *Democracy in America*, translated by Henry Reeve, 99–106, 144–47. New York: J. & H. G. Langley, 1840. [Public Domain]

"The Emancipation of Women: Argentina 1876," Maria Eugenia Echenique and Josefina Pelliza de Sagasta: Republished with permission of Johns Hopkins University Press—Journals. Selection from Echenique, Maria Eugenia, and Josefina Pelliza de Sagasta. "The Emancipation of Women: Argentina 1876." *Journal of Women's History* 7, no. 3 (1995): 103–7 and 114, translated by The Palouse Translation Project volume, 1995. Permission conveyed through Copyright Clearance Center, Inc.

"An Exhortation to Progress," Mustafa Kemal: Kemal Pasha, Mustapha. "An Exhortation to Progress." In *The Living Age*, October 31, 1925, 232–33. New York: The Living Age Co., 1925. [Public Domain]

"Grinding Song" (Tigrayan): "Grinding Song." In *Daughters of Africa: An International Anthology of Words and Writings by Women of African Descent: From the Ancient Egyptian to the Present*, edited by Margaret Busby, 8–9. New York: Ballantine Books, 1994.

***Hatata*, Zera Yacob:** Yacob, Zera. "God, Faith, and the Nature of Knowledge." In *The Source of African Philosophy: The Ethiopian Philosophy of Man*, edited by Claude Sumner. Stuttgart, Germany: F. Steiner Verlag Wiesbaden, 1986. [Public Domain]

"History of the Chinese Revolution" (Written January 29, 1923), Sun Yat-sen: Yat-sen, Sun. "History of the Chinese Revolution." In *Fundamentals of National Reconstruction*, 76–87. Taipei, Taiwan: China Cultural Service, 1953. [Public Domain]

***Imperialism: The Highest Stage of Capitalism*, V. I. Lenin:** Used with permission of International Publishers. Selections from Lenin, Vladimir. *Imperialism: The Highest Stage of Capitalism*, 88–89, 97, 99–101, 123–25. New York: International Publishers, [1939] 1988. Permission conveyed through Copyright Clearance Center, Inc.

***The Interesting Narrative of the Life of Olaudah Equiano or Gustavus Vassa, The African*, Olaudah Equiano:** Equiano, Olaudah. *The Interesting Narrative* *of the Life of Olaudah Equiano; Or Gustavus Vassa, the African*, 50–53, 55–57, 322–27. Penryn, UK: W. Cock, 1815. [Public Domain]

"I, Too," Langston Hughes: Hughes, Langston. "I, Too." In *The Collected Poems of Langston Hughes*, 1925. [Public Domain]

"Letter from Benjamin Banneker and Thomas Jefferson's Response," Benjamin Banneker and Thomas Jefferson: Banneker, Benjamin, and Thomas Jefferson. "Copy of a Letter from Benjamin Banneker, &c." In *Copy of a Letter from Benjamin Banneker, to the Secretary of State, with His Answer*, 3–12. Philadelphia, PA: Daniel Lawrence, 1792. [Public Domain]

Letter to the Grand Duchess Christina, Galileo: Galilei, Galileo. "Galileo Galilei: Letter to the Grand Duchess Christina of Tuscany, 1615." Internet History Sourcebooks, August 1997. [Public Domain]

Letter to the United States President Andrew Jackson, 1831," Tuskaneah: Tuskaneah. "From Tuskaneah." In *The Papers of Andrew Jackson*, edited by Daniel Feller, Laura-Eve Moss, Thomas Coens, and Erik B. Alexander, vol. 9, 254–56. Knoxville: University of Tennessee Press, 2013. [Public Domain]

***Manifesto of the Communist Party*, Karl Marx:** Marx, Karl. "Chapter I. Bourgeois and Proletarians," and "Chapter II. Proletarians and Communists." In *Manifesto of the Communist Party*. Translated by Samuel Moore and Frederick Engels. Copyleft: Marx/Engels Internet Archive (marxists.org) 1987, 2000. Permission is granted to copy and/or distribute this document under the terms of the Creative Commons Attribution-ShareAlike License (https://www.marxists.org/admin/legal/cc/by-sa.htm). The Creative Commons Share-Alike license for this work is applicable only to this section of excerpts from Karl Marx's *The Communist Manifesto* and does not apply to any other excerpts in the *Global Humanities Readers*.

***Mein Kampf*, Adolf Hitler:** Selection from Hitler, Adolf. *Mein Kampf*. Translated by Ralph Manheim, 106–7, 118, 179, 180–81, 231, 286, 88–290, 305, 314, 324–26, 383–84. Copyright © 1943, 1971. Reprinted by permission of Houghton Mifflin Harcourt Publishing Company. All rights reserved.

"Message to The Congress of Angostura," Simón Bolívar: Bolívar, Simón. *An Address of Bolivar at the Congress of Angostura: February 15, 1819* (version reprint ordered by the government of the United States of Venezuela, to commemorate the centennial of the opening of the Congress.). Washington, DC: B. S. Adams, 1919. https://archive.org/embed/addressofbolivar00boluoft. [Public Domain]

***Narrative of the Life of Frederick Douglass* and "What to the Slave is the Fourth of July?", Frederick Douglass:**

Douglass, Frederick. "Chapter 1." In *Narrative of the Life of Frederick Douglass, an American Slave: Written by Himself*, 1–5. Boston: The Anti-slavery Office, 1846. [Public Domain]

Douglass, Frederick. "Oration" also now known as "What to the Slave is the Fourth of July?" 10, 14-21, 37-39. Rochester: Lee, Mann & Co, 1852. [Public Domain]

"The Negro Digs Up His Past," Arthur Schomburg: Schomburg, Arthur A. "The Negro Expresses Himself: The Negro Digs Up His Past." *The Survey*, March 1, 1925, 670–72. [Public Domain]

"A New Guatemala," Juan José Arévalo: Arévalo, Juan José. "A New Guatemala." *The Guatemala Reader: History, Culture, Politics*, edited by Greg Grandin, Deborah T. Levenson, and Elizabeth Oglesby. Translated by Kirsten Weld, 206–10. © 2011, Duke University Press. All rights reserved. Republished by permission of the copyright holder. www.dukeupress.edu.

Nisei Daughter, **Monica Sone:** Used with permission of University of Washington Press. Sone, Monica. "Life in Camp Harmony." In *Nisei Daughter*, 172–78. Seattle: University of Washington Press, 1979. Permission conveyed through Copyright Clearance Center, Inc.

The Origins of Totalitarianism, **Hannah Arendt:** Excerpt from Arendt, *The Origins of Totalitarianism*. Copyright © 1973 by Hannah Arendt and renewed 2001 by Lotte Kohler. Reprinted by permission of Houghton Mifflin Harcourt Publishing Company. All rights reserved.

"Our América" José Martí: Martí, J. Nuestra América (versión inglés), translated by Esther Allen (n.d.). Retrieved August 11, 2020, from http://www.josemarti.cu/publicacion/nuestra-america-version-ingles/. Reprinted by permission of the translator.

"The Political and Social Doctrine of Fascism," Benito Mussolini: Selections from Mussolini, Benito. *The Political and Social Doctrine of Fascism*, translated by Jane Soames, 10–15, 21–24. London: Hogarth Press, 1933.

"The Painter," Hannah Höch, and from *Negro Sculpture*, Carl Einstein:

Höch, Hannah. "The Painter," translated by Anney Halley. In Lavin, Maud, *Cut With the Kitchen Knife: The Weimar Photomontages of Hannah Hoch*, 216–18. New Haven: Yale University Press, 1993. Reprinted with permission from the author.

Einstein, Carl. "Negro Sculpture." In *Art in Theory, 1900–2000: An Anthology of Changing Ideas*, edited by Charles Harrison and Paul Wood, 111–16. Malden, MA: Blackwell Publishing, [1992] 2003. Permission conveyed through PLS Clear.

"Principles of Anarchism," Lucy Parsons: Parsons, Lucy Eldine Gonzales. "The Principles of Anarchism." In *Freedom, Equality and Solidarity*. Chicago: Charles H. Kerr, 2004. Published as a pamphlet, circa 1905–1910. [Public Domain]

"Reminiscences of the Drafting of the New Constitution," Ito Hirobumi: Used with permission of Columbia University Press, from Hirobumi, Ito, and Ryūsaku. *Sources of the Japanese Tradition* 2, 2:164–69. New York: Columbia University Press, 1965. Permission conveyed through Copyright Clearance Center, Inc.

"Response to Ernest Renan's Criticism of Islam," Jamal al-Din Al-Afghani: Used with permission of University of California Press. Selection from Al-Afgahni, Jamal al-Din. "Jamal al-Din Al-Afgahni Answers Ernest Renan's Criticism of Islam." In *An Islamic Response to Imperialism: Political and Religious Writings of Sayyid Jamal ad-Din "al-Afghani,"* Volume 21, translated by Nikki R. Keddie, 181–187. Los Angeles, CA: University of California Press, 1983; permission conveyed through Copyright Clearance Center, Inc.

Response to the Very Illustrious 'Sor Philotea,' Sor Juana Ines de la Cruz: Excerpts from *Sor Juana Ines de la Cruz: Selected Writings*. Translated and Introduced by Pamela Kirk Rappaport with a Preface by Gillian T. W. Ahlgren, Copyright © 2005, 273–278, by Paulist Press, Inc. Paulist Press, Inc., New York/Mahwah, NJ. Reprinted by permission of Paulist Press, Inc. www.paulistpress.com.

"The Revolution and the Negro," C. L. R. James: James, C. L. R. "The Revolution and the Negro." In *New International*, Volume V, December 1939, transcribed by Ted Crawford, 339–343. Chicago, IL: J. R. Johnson, 1939. [Public Domain]

"The Rights of Women," Khan, Sayyid Ahmad. "The Rights of Women." Translated by Kamran Talattof. From *Maqalat-i Sar Sayyid*, edited by Maulana Muhammad Isma'il Pani Pari, 159–61. Lahaur: Majlis-i Taraqqiyi Adab, 1962. Reprinted by permission of the translator.

Second Sex, **Simone de Beauvoir:** Beauvoir, Simone de. *Le Deuxième Sexe*. Paris: Gallimard, 1949, 16–21. Translated by Tracey Rizzo, 2021 [unpublished]. Printed by permission of the translator.

Selections from the Writings of Albert Einstein: Used with permission of Princeton University Press. From Einstein, Albert. "Internationalism of Science," "Religion and Science," and "What I Believe." In *Einstein on Politics: His Private Thoughts and Public Stands on Nationalism Zionism, War, Peace, and the Bomb*, edited by David E. Rowe and Robert J. Schulmann, 192–94, 231–34, 226–30. Princeton, New Jersey: Princeton University Press, 2013; Permission conveyed through Copyright Clearance Center, Inc.

Einstein, Albert. "Letter to Sigmund Freud, 30 July, 1932." The Albert Einstein Archives. With permission, the Hebrew University of Jerusalem.

Tagore, Rabindranath. "In Conversation with Albert Einstein." In *The Religion of Man*, edited by Rabindranath Tagore, 222–25. London: George Allen & Unwin, 1931. [Public Domain]

Selections from the Writings of Marcus Garvey: Selections from Garvey, Marcus. *Marcus Garvey and the Vision of Africa*, edited by John Henrik Clarke, with the assistance of Amy Jaques Garvey, 300–301, 307–11. New York: Random House, 1974. [Public Domain]

Self Portrait of K'ang-hsi," K'ang-hsi. Excerpts from Spence, Jonathan D. *Emperor of China: Self-Portrait of K'ang-Hsi-*, 65–72, 74–75, 79–81. Copyright © 1974, copyright renewed 2002 by Jonathan D. Spence. Used by permission of Alfred A. Knopf, an imprint of the Knopf Doubleday Publishing Group, a division of Penguin Random House LLC. All rights reserved. UK & Commonwealth rights used by permission of The Wylie Agency LLC.

The Soul of the Indian, **Ohiyesa:** Selections from Ohiyesa (Eastman, Charles A.). *The Soul of the Indian: An Interpretation*, 3–7, 16–24, 87–95. Houghton Mifflin, 1911. [Public Domain]

"Speaking Out against Lynching," Ida B. Wells: Selections from Wells, Ida B. "The Case Stated." In *The Red Record: Tabulated Statistics and Alleged Causes of Lynching in the United States*. N.p. 1895. [Public Domain]

Still Alive, **Ruth Klüger:** Selections from Klüger, Ruth. *Still Alive: A Holocaust Girl Remembered*, 63–69. New York: The Feminist Press, 2001. Copyright © 2001 by Ruth Klüger. Copyright © 1992 by Wallstein Verlag, Göttingen, Germany. Reprinted with the permission of The Permissions Company, LLC on behalf of The Feminist Press at the City University of New York, www.feministpress.org. All rights reserved.

Strivings of the Negro People, **W. E. B. Du Bois:** Du Bois, W. E. Burghardt. "Strivings of the Negro People." *The Atlantic*. Atlantic Media Company, originally published August 1897, republished August 19, 2019. [Public Domain]

"The Structure of Class and Caste," Jorge Juan and Antonio de Ulloa: Ulloa, A. D., J. Juan, and J. Adams. "Of the Inhabitants of Carthagena." In *A voyage to South America: Describing at large, the Spanish cities, towns, provinces, &c. on that extensive continent, undertaken by command of the King of Spain, by Don George Juan, and Don Antonio de Ulloa, both captains of the Spanish Navy; fellows of the Royal Society of London; Members of the Royal Academy at Paris, &c. &c.*, 29–32. London, Holborn: Printed for Lockyer Davis, 1772. [Public Domain]

Sultana's Dream, **Rokheya Hossein:** Hossain, Rokeya Sakhawat. *Sultana's Dream. The Indian Ladies' Magazine*. Madras, 1905. [Public Domain]

"Teaching and Telling Stories," Gabriela Mistral: Used with permission of Taylor & Francis Group. Mistral, Gabriela, and Benjamin Keen, eds. "Teaching and Telling Stories." In *Keen's Latin American Civilization: History and Society, 1492 to Present*, 397–99. Taylor & Francis Group, 2003. Permission conveyed through Copyright Clearance Center, Inc.

"Transferring the New Civilization to the Islamic Peoples," Şemseddin Sami Frashëri: Used with permission of Oxford University Press. Kurzman, Charles, ed. "Transferring the New Civilization to the Islamic Peoples." In *Modernist Islam*,

1840–1940: A Sourcebook, 149–51. Oxford: Oxford University Press, 2002. Permission conveyed through Copyright Clearance Center, Inc.

***Turkey Faces West*, Halidé Edib:** Selection from Edib, Halidé. *Turkey Faces West: A Turkish View of Recent Changes and Their Origin*, 223–32. New Haven: Yale University Press, 1930. [Public Domain]

***A Voice from the South*, Anna Julia Cooper:** Selections from Cooper, Anna Julia. *A Voice from the South*, 97–113, 116–18, 120–26. Xenia, OH: The Aldine Printing House, 1892. [Public Domain]

***A Vindication of the Rights of Woman*, Mary Wollstonecraft:** Wollstonecraft, Mary. *A Vindication of the Rights of Woman with Strictures on Political and Moral Subjects*. London: J. Johnson, 1792. [Public Domain]

***The War and Its Effect Upon Women*, Helena Swanwick:** Swanwick, Helena Marie. *The War and Its Effect upon Women (1915)*. [Public Domain]

***The Well of Loneliness*, Radclyffe Hall:** Selection from *The Well of Loneliness* by Radclyffe Hall. UK: Jonathan Cape, 1928. Copyright © 1928 by Radclyffe Hall. Copyright renewed © 1956 by Una Lady Troubridge. Used by permission of Brandt & Hochman Literary Agents, Inc. All rights reserved.

"What I Believe" and "Speech Against Conscription and War," Emma Goldman:

Goldman, Emma. "What I Believe." In *New York World*, July 19, 1908. Online source theanarchistlibrary.org. Accessed May 12, 2021. [Public Domain]

Goldman, Emma. "Speech Against Conscription and War." Goldman & Berkman v. United States: Transcript of Record, 1917 Sept. 25. [Public Domain]

"White Things," Anne Bethel Spencer: Spencer, Anne B. "White Things." In *The Crisis*, March 1923. Copyright The Anne Spencer Memorial Foundation. [Public Domain]

"The Worker's Union," Flora Tristan: Tristan, Flora. "The Female Worker's Union (1843)." From *Women, the Family, and Freedom*, translated by Giselle Pincetl, vol. 1, 212–15. Palo Alto, CA: Stanford University Press, 1983.

"Why I Am Pagan," Zitkala-Ša: Zitkala-Ša. "Why I Am a Pagan." *Atlantic Monthly* 90, (1902): 801–3. [Public Domain]

***The Wretched of the Earth*, Frantz Fanon:** Fanon, Frantz. "On Violence" and "Conclusion." In *The Wretched of the Earth*. Translated from the French by Richard Philcox, 1–10, 14–17, 46–47, 49–52, 235–39. New York: Grove Press, [1963] 2004.

TAG GLOSSARY

Sources under each tag are given by author's surname and the initial of the category it comes under in the primary table of contents, as listed here: (J) Justice, (N) Narrating, (P) Power, (R) Repositioning, (Re/O) Re/Orienting, (W) Working.

Abolition, Slavery, and Freedom: captivity; dehumanization; resistance; revolt; enslaved voices; experience of slavery; strategies/arguments for abolition; **see also Race; Rhetoric and Persuasion; Economics; Religion**

Banneker and Jefferson (N) *Bolívar (J)*
Douglass (N) *Equiano (N)*
Juan and Ulloa (W) *Sone (P)*
Truth (N)

Accessing Rights: legal rights; civil rights; political maneuvering for; legislation; guarantees of; rights for whom; **see also Statecraft; Labor; Women and Power**

Ambedkar (N) *Banneker and Jefferson (N)*
Cherokee Sources (N) *Du Bois (N)*
Echenique and Pelliza (J) *Gandhi and Tagore (R)*
Sor Juana (Re/O) *Stanton (J)*
Truth (N) *Tuskeneah (J)*
Washington (W) *Wells (N)*

Art: aesthetic critique; satire; storytelling; imagined worlds; **see also Autobiography and Testimony; Poetry, Music, Literature**

Grinding Song (W) *Hall (P)*
Höch and Einstein, C. (Re/O) *Hossain (P)*
Hughes (N) *Isherwood (N)*
Martí (R) *Mistral (Re/O)*
Spencer (N)

Autobiography and Testimony: witnessing; voice; agency; attestations; personal observations; considering authenticity; **see also Poetry, Music, Literature; Race; Gender and Identity**

Douglass (N)
Equiano (N)
Haywood (W)
Isherwood (N)
K'ang-hsi (Re/O)
Ohiyesa (R)
Sor Juana (Re/O)
Tuskeneah (J)
Zitkala-Ša (R)
Du Bois (N)
Hall (P)
Hughes (N)
Itō (R)
Kluger (N)
Raman (Re/O)
Truth (N)
Yacob (Re/O)

Body: physicality; bodily rights; body as self; restraint/captivity of; use of for expression; arguments for bodily autonomy/integrity; **see also Gender and Identity; Race; Women and Power; Class and Caste**

Douglass (N)
Gouges (J)
Isherwood (N)
Sone (P)
Truth (N)
Wollstonecraft (J)
Equiano (N)
Grinding Song (W)
Ohiyesa (R)
Spencer (N)
Wells (N)
Zitkala-Ša (R)

Class and Caste: social divisions; roles within; creation of; resisting/questioning class distinctions; power in; perpetuation of; **also see Race; Economics; Labor; Colonization; Body**

Ambedkar (N)
Grinding Song (W)
Hossain (P)
Lenin (P)
Mussolini (P)
Tagore and Gandhi (R)
Tristan (W)
Arévalo (J)
Haywood (W)
Juan and Ulloa (W)
Marx (W)
Parsons (W)
Tocqueville (R)

Colonization: colonial settler; challenges to; resistance against; colonized voices; decolonization; resisting assimilation; selective modernity; ramifications of; **see also Race; History and Ideology; Class and Caste; War and Brutality; Statecraft; Tyranny; Abolition, Slavery, and Freedom**

Bolívar (J)
Fanon (P)
Juan and Ulloa (W)
Martí (R)
Tagore and Gandhi (R)
Cherokee Sources (N)
Ho (J)
Lenin (P)
Ohiyesa (R)
Tuskeneah (J)

Community: local character; national identity; collectivism; kinship; indigeneity; common causes; strength in unity; **see also Family; Race; Labor**

Ambedkar (N)
Grinding Song (W)
Hughes (N)
Kemal (R)
Martí (R)
Mussolini (P)
Rodó (R)
Sone (P)
Zitkala-Ša (R)
Cherokee Sources (N)
Haywood (W)
Itō (R)
Klüger (N)
Mistral (Re/O)
Ohiyesa (R)
Schomburg (Re/O)
Tristan (W)

Cross-Cultural Encounters: travel; diplomacy; emigration; treaties; cultures and nations; loss; violence; **see also Colonization; Community; Abolition, Slavery, and Freedom; Internationalism**

Bolívar (J)
Edib (R)
Fanon (P)
Isherwood (N)
Juan and Ulloa (W)
Khan (J)
Ohiyesa (R)
Sone (P)
Tuskeneah (J)
Cherokee Sources (N)
Equiano (N)
Höch and Einstein, C. (Re/O)
Itō (R)
K'ang-hsi (Re/O)
Martí (R)
Rodó (R)
Tocqueville (R)

Economics: wealth; financial independence; financial crises; self-sufficiency; wages; workforce; resources; **see also Gender and Identity; Labor; Abolition, Slavery, and Freedom; Race; Colonization**

Gandhi and Tagore (R)
Haywood (W)
Marx (W)
Tristan (W)
Garvey (W)
Lenin (P)
Swanwick (W)
Washington (W)

Education: purpose of; liberating nature of; denial of; possibilities for; curriculum; **see also History and Ideology; Women and Power; Gender and Identity**

Arévalo (J)
Douglass (N)
Frashëri (R)
Gandhi and Tagore (R)
K'ang-hsi (Re/O)
Raman (Re/O)
Sor Juana (Re/O)
Wollstonecraft (J)
Cooper (Re/O)
Echenique and Pelliza (J)
Galileo (Re/O)
Hossain (P)
Mistral (Re/O)
Schomburg (Re/O)
Washington (W)
Yacob (Re/O)

Ethics and Morality: principles for behavior; choices based on; arguments from ethical bases; evolution of; **see also Religion; Ways of Knowing; History and Ideology; Women and Power**

Ambedkar (N)
Banneker and Jefferson (N)
Du Bois (N)
Gandhi and Tagore (R)
Ohiyesa (R)
Swanwick (W)
Wells (N)
Yacob (Re/O)
Arendt (P)
Beauvoir (P)
Einstein, A. (Re/O)
K'ang-hsi (Re/O)
Sor Juana (Re/O)
Truth (N)
Wollstonecraft (J)
Zitkala-Ša (R)

Family: marriage; children; love; parenthood; family life; **see also Gender and Identity; Women and Power; Race; Labor; War and Brutality; Abolition, Slavery, and Freedom; Community; Ethics and Morality; Tradition**

Beauvoir (P)
Douglass (N)
Equiano (N)
Hall (P)
Ohiyesa (R)
Stanton (J)
Tristan (W)
Wollstonecraft (J)
Cherokee Sources (N)
Echenique and Pelliza (J)
Gouges (J)
Klüger (N)
Sone (P)
Swanwick (W)
Truth (N)
Yacob (Re/O)

Gender and Identity: gender equity; gender identity; sphere of womanhood; gender roles; questioning gender norms; feminisms; the woman question; **see also Psyche; Labor; Family; Education; Body; Autobiography and Testimony; Women and Power**

Beauvoir (P)
Echenique and Pelliza (J)
Hossain (P)
Sor Juana (Re/O)
Tristan (W)
Wollstonecraft (J)
Cooper (Re/O)
Hall (P)
Khan (J)
Swanwick (W)
Truth (N)
Yacob (Re/O)

Historiography: how history is written; identifying; questioning; heritage; documenting; **see also Education; History and Ideology; Race; Rhetoric and Persuasion; Ways of Knowing; Struggle, Resistance, and Revolution; Tradition**

Douglass (N)
Frashëri (R)
Isherwood (N)
James (P)
Marx (W)
Schomburg (Re/O)
Tuskeneah (J)

Equiano (N)
Haywood (W)
Itō (R)
Juan and Ulloa (W)
Mistral (Re/O)
Tocqueville (R)
Wells (N)

History and Ideology: creating new; basing systems on; socialism; individualism; fascism; **see also Economics; Statecraft; Tyranny; Ways of Knowing; Rhetoric and Persuasion; Nationalism; Internationalism; Historiography**

Arendt (P)
Fanon (P)
Goldman (J)
Hitler (P)
Kemal (R)
Marx (W)
Parsons (W)
Tristan (W)

Bolívar (J)
Gandhi and Tagore (R)
Haywood (W)
Ho (J)
Lenin (P)
Mussolini (P)
Tocqueville (R)

Internationalism: transnational; anti-national; transcending borders; Pan-Africanism; Pan-Americanism; anarchism; worker movements; **see also Labor; Economics; Colonization; Cross-Cultural Encounters; Nationalism**

Einstein, A. (Re/O)
Gandhi and Tagore (R)
Goldman (J)
James (P)
Marx (W)
Rodó (R)
Swanwick (W)

Fanon (P)
Garvey (W)
Haywood (W)
Martí (R)
Parsons (W)
Schomburg (Re/O)
Tristan (W)

Labor: work; workers; worker unions; capital; gendered work roles; dehumanization and; industrialized labor; **see also Economics; Class and Caste; Community**

Arévalo (J)	*Goldman (J)*
Grinding Song (W)	*Haywood (W)*
Hossain (P)	*Juan and Ulloa (W)*
Marx (W)	*Parsons (W)*
Swanwick (W)	*Tristan (W)*
Truth (N)	*Washington (W)*
Wollstonecraft (J)	

Nationalism: national pride; national character; nation-state; allegiance; sovereignty; xenophobia; patriotism; chauvinism; jingoism; **see also History and Ideology; Community; Self-Determination**

Al-Afghani (Re/O)	*Arendt (P)*
Gandhi and Tagore (R)	*Hitler (P)*
Itō (R)	*K'ang-hsi (Re/O)*
Kemal (R)	*Lenin (P)*
Mussolini (P)	*Sun (J)*

Poetry, Music, Literature: beauty in language; fiction; storytelling; emotion; sublime; poet perspectives; song; **see also Art; Psyche**

Douglass (N)	*Gandhi and Tagore (R)*
Grinding Song (W)	*Hall (P)*
Höch and Einstein, C. (Re/O)	*Hossain (P)*
Hughes (N)	*Isherwood (N)*
Martí (R)	*Mistral (Re/O)*
Ohiyesa (R)	*Raman (Re/O)*
Sor Juana (Re/O)	*Spencer (N)*

Psyche: psychology; mind; individualism; emotion/feeling/soul/spirit; **see also Autobiography and Testimony; Art; Race; Gender and Identity; Family; Religion; Ethics and Morality**

Arévalo (J)	*Beauvoir (P)*
Douglass (N)	*Du Bois (N)*
Edib (R)	*Fanon (P)*
Gandhi and Tagore (R)	*Hall (P)*
Hossain (P)	*Hughes (N)*
Klüger (N)	*Mistral (Re/O)*
Mussolini (P)	*Ohiyesa (R)*
Parsons (W)	*Sone (P)*
Spencer (N)	*Swanwick (W)*
Yacob (Re/O)	*Zitkala-Ša (R)*

Race: racism; segregation; invention of; indigeneity; examination of whiteness; amalgamation of races; **see also Colonization; Economics; Labor; Family; Class and Caste; Education; Psyche; Body; Cross-Cultural Encounters; Autobiography and Testimony; Accessing Rights; Poetry, Music, Literature; Abolition, Slavery, Freedom; Community; Self-Determination**

Banneker and Jefferson (N) *Cherokee Sources (N)*
Cooper (Re/O) *Douglass (N)*
Du Bois (N) *Equiano (N)*
Fanon (P) *Haywood (W)*
Höch and Einstein, C. (Re/O) *Hughes (N)*
James (P) *Juan and Ulloa (W)*
Klüger (N) *Martí (R)*
Ohiyesa (R) *Schomburg (Re/O)*
Sone (P) *Spencer (N)*
Truth (N) *Tuskeneah (J)*
Washington (W) *Wells (N)*
Zitkala-Ša (R)

Religion: spirituality; community; relation to state; authority in knowledge; religions in contact; secularism; **see also Gender and Identity; Women and Power; Science; Abolition, Slavery, Freedom; Tradition; Ethics and Morality; Psyche**

Al-Afghani (Re/O) *Ambedkar (N)*
Banneker and Jefferson (N) *Edib (R)*
Einstein, A. (Re/O) *Equiano (N)*
Frashëri (R) *Galileo (Re/O)*
Gandhi and Tagore (R) *K'ang-hsi (Re/O)*
Khan (J) *Ohiyesa (R)*
Sor Juana (Re/O) *Truth (N)*
Yacob (Re/O) *Zitkala-Ša (R)*

Rhetoric and Persuasion: propaganda; polemics; use of language; authority; power of persuasion; **see also Poetry, Music, Literature; Art**

Ambedkar (N) *Arévalo (J)*
Bolívar (J) *Goldman (J)*
Kemal (R) *Parsons (W)*
Stanton (J) *Truth (N)*
Washington (W)

Science: empiricism; positivism; technology and; internationalism and; role in epistemology; discovery; history of; **see also Internationalism; Ways of Knowing; Religion**

Al-Afghani (Re/O) *Banneker and Jefferson (N)*
Einstein, A. (Re/O) *Frashëri (R)*
Galileo (Re/O) *Hossain (P)*
Juan and Ulloa (W) *K'ang-hsi (Re/O)*
Raman (Re/O) *Sor Juana (Re/O)*

Self-Determination: sovereignty; independence; decolonization; self-rule; autonomy; **see also Struggle, Resistance, and Revolution; Colonization; Nationalism; Statecraft**

Arévalo (J) *Bolívar (J)*
Fanon (P) *Gandhi and Tagore (R)*
Grinding Song (W) *Ho (J)*
Itō (R) *James (P)*
Kemal (R) *Martí (R)*
Sun (J) *Tuskeneah (J)*

Statecraft: governance; social contract; democracy; monarchy; authoritarianism; communism; utopia; authority; leadership; rule: **see also Colonization; Economics; Labor; History and Ideology; Religion; Community; Self-Determination; Nationalism**

Arévalo (J) *Bolívar (J)*
Edib (R) *Goldman (J)*
Hitler (P) *Ho (J)*
Hossain (P) *Itō (R)*
K'ang-hsi (Re/O) *Kemal (R)*
Mussolini (P) *Parsons (W)*
Sun (J) *Toqueville (R)*

Struggle, Resistance, and Revolution: collective and individual experiences of combating oppression; speaking and standing up to power; **see also Race; Women and Power; History and Ideology; War and Brutality; Abolition, Slavery, and Freedom; Self-Determination**

Ambedkar (N)
Beauvoir (P)
Cooper (Re/O)
Du Bois (N)
Equiano (N)
Gandhi and Tagore (R)
Gouges (J)
Haywood (W)
James (P)
Ohiyesa (R)
Schomburg (Re/O)
Sor Juana (Re/O)
Stanton (J)
Tristan (W)
Tuskeneah (J)
Wells (N)
Banneker and Jefferson (N)
Cherokee Sources (N)
Douglass (N)
Echenique and Pelliza (J)
Fanon (P)
Garvey (W)
Grinding Song (W)
Hughes (N)
Martí (R)
Rodó (R)
Sone (P)
Spencer (N)
Swanwick (W)
Truth (N)
Washington (W)
Wollstonecraft (J)

Tradition: culture; heritage; way of life; shared history; customs; transformation of; **see also Family; Religion; Colonization; Body; Autobiography and Testimony; Poetry, Music, Literature; History and Ideology; Historiography**

Al-Afghani (Re/O)
Bolívar (J)
Edib (R)
Hossain (P)
Khan (J)
Mistral (Re/O)
Rodó (R)
Spencer (N)
Tocqueville (R)
Zitkala-Ša (R)
Ambedkar (N)
Cherokee Sources (N)
Hall (P)
Kemal (R)
Martí (R)
Ohiyesa (R)
Sone (P)
Sun (J)
Yacob (Re/O)

Tyranny: authoritarianism; wielding power; defending power; resisting oppression; identifying hierarchies; **see also War and Brutality; Colonization; Abolition, Slavery, and Freedom; Labor**

Arendt (P) *Beauvoir (P)*
Fanon (P) *Hitler (P)*
Kemal (R) *Mussolini (P)*
Wells (N)

War and Brutality: violence; authority through force; speaking to; testifying about; experiences of; **see also Nationalism; Race; Tyranny; Struggle; Resistance, and Revolution**

Du Bois (N) *Equiano (N)*
Fanon (P) *Goldman (J)*
Hall (P) *Haywood (W)*
Hitler (P) *Klüger (N)*
Lenin (P) *Martí (R)*
Mussolini (P) *Ohiyesa (R)*
Swanwick (W) *Truth (N)*
Tuskeneah (J) *Wells (N)*

Ways of Knowing: belief systems; philosophy; evolution of; epistemologies; oppressions of; recognition of; **see also History and Ideology; Historiography; Education; Poetry, Music, Literature**

Arendt (P) *Frashëri (R)*
Galileo (Re/O) *Gandhi and Tagore (R)*
Höch and Einstein, C. (Re/O) *Itō (R)*
K'ang-hsi (Re/O) *Raman (Re/O)*
Schomburg (Re/O) *Sor Juana (Re/O)*
Yacob (Re/O) *Zitkala-Ša (R)*

Women and Power: agency; women's rights; women's legal rights; laws governing women and sexuality; sphere of womanhood; feminism; **see also Labor; Family; Education; Body; Accessing Rights; Gender and Identity**

Beauvoir (P) *Cherokee Sources (N)*
Cooper (Re/O) *Echenique and Pelliza (J)*
Edib (R) *Gouges (J)*
Sor Juana (Re/O) *Stanton (J)*
Swanwick (W) *Tristan (W)*
Truth (N) *Wells (N)*
Wollstonecraft (J)

INDEX

abolition, 209; "A'n't I a Woman?," 155–56; "Address to the First Annual Meeting of the American Equal Rights Association (1867)," 156–57; *Interesting Narrative of the Life of Olaudah Equiano or Gustavus Vassa, the African, 200–206*; "Letter from Benjamin Banneker and Thomas Jefferson's Response," 208–15; "Message to the Congress of Angostura," 300–306; Narrative of the Life of Frederick Douglass, an American Slave, 216; *Nisei Daughter,* 226–31; "Structure of Class and Caste, The," 496–99; "What to the Slave is the Fourth of July?," 216–25. See also economics; race; religion; rhetoric

Abrahamic, 44

"Address at the World's Fair in Atlanta" (Washington), 442–46

"Address to the First Annual Meeting of the American Equal Rights Association" (Truth), 156–57

African mind, 22

Africana, 130

al-Afghani, Jamal al-Din, 84–85

Ali, Muhammad, 14

al-Mahdi, Ahmed, 14

alternative modernity, 582

Ambedkar, Bhimrao Ramji, 19, 142–44

American Indian, 412

American Negro Academy (ANA), 63

American Revolution, 6

"An Exhortation to Progress" (Kemal), 387–88

anarchism, 480

Anatolia, 427

Annihilation of Caste (Ambedkar): 4 — [Caste is not just a division of labour, it is a division of labourers], 149–50; Introduction — [Why I am an unlikely President for this Conference], 145; 13 — [Caste destroys public spirit, public opinion, and public charity], 150–51; 26 — [The struggle is yours; I have now decided to leave the Hindu fold], 151; 2 — [Why social reform is necessary for political reform], 145–49

"A'n't I a Woman?" (Truth), 155–56

anti-Semitism, 239

apparatchiks, 458

Arendt, Hannah, 527–29

Arévalo, Juan José, 307–9

Ariel (Rodó), 356–58

art: *Berlin Stories, The,* 159–74; "Grinding Song," 453–57; "I, Too," 196–99; *Negro Sculpture,* 76–83; "Our América," 389–401; "Painter, The," 74–76; *Sultana's Dream,* 560–71; "Teaching and Telling Stories" ("Contar"), 122–28; *Well of Loneliness, The,* 573–78; "White Things," 254–57. See also autobiography; poetry

art theory, genre: "Painter, The," 74–76; *Negro Sculpture,* 76–83

Atatürk. *See* Kemal, Mustafa

Atlantic Revolutions, 506

Atlantic worlds, modern era, 4–13

Aurangzeb, 17

Auschwitz, 238

authoritarianism, 512

autobiography: "A'n't I a Woman?," 155–56; Address to the First Annual Meeting of the American Equal Rights Association (1867)," 156–57; *Berlin Stories, The,* 159–74; "Books That Have Influenced Me," 37–43; I, Too," 196–99;

autobiography (*continued*)
"Letter to United States President Andrew Jackson, 1831," 294–99; "Reminiscences of the Drafting of the New Constitution," 403–11; "Response to the Very Illustrious 'Sor Philotea'," 92–98; "Strivings by the Negro People," 247–53; *Well of Loneliness, The*, 573–78. *See also* gender; poetry; race

autobiography, genre: *Black Bolshevik*, 447–52; *Hatata*, 44–53; *Interesting Narrative of the Life of Olaudah Equiano or Gustavus Vassa, the African*, 200–206; *Narrative of the Life of Frederick Douglass, an American Slave*, 216–25; *Nisei Daughter*, 226–31; "Self Portrait of K'ang-hsi (The Emperor)," 115–21; *Soul of the Indian, The*, 412–19; "What to the Slave is the Fourth of July?," 216–25; Why I Am a Pagan?," 434–39

Balfour Declaration, 16
Banneker, Benjamin, 208–10
Batista, Fulencio, 13
Battle of Greasy Grass, 10
Beauvoir, Simone de, 554–55
Bentinck, William, 17
Berkman, Alexander, 336–37
Berlin Dada group, 72
"Berlin Diary (Winter 1932-3), A." See *Berlin Stories, The* (Isherwood)
Bill of Rights, 6
Berlin Stories, The (Isherwood), 161–74
Black Bolshevik (Haywood), 450–52
blues and jazz aesthetics, 196
body: "A'n't I a Woman?," 155–56; "Address to the First Annual Meeting of the American Equal Rights Association (1867)," 156–57; *Berlin Stories, The*, 159–74; "Declaration of the Rights of Woman and Citizen," 263–70; "Grinding Song," 453–57; *Interesting Narrative of the Life of Olaudah Equiano or Gustavus Vassa, the African*, 200–206; Narrative of the Life of Frederick Douglass, an American Slave, 216–25; *Nisei Daughter*, 226–31; *Soul of the Indian, The*, 412–19; "Speaking Out Against Lynching," 232–37; *Vindication of the Rights of Women, A*, 320–35; "What to the Slave is the Fourth of July?," 216–25; "White Things," 254–57; "Why I Am a Pagan?," 434–39. *See also* class; gender; race; women
Bolívar, Simón, 9, 300–302

Bonaparte, Napoleon, 8
Bose, Subhas Chandra, 18
"Books That Have Influenced Me" (Raman), 40–43
bourgeoisie, 459, 507, 513
Boxer Rebellion, 23
British Crown, 6, 17, 360
British Raj, 314
brutality. *See* war
bushido, 404

caliphate, 385
Canada, 10
canon, 389
Canton System, 116
capitalism, 459, 512
capitalist modernization, 513
Cárdenas, Lázaro, 10
caste. *See* class
Catherine the Great, 26
caudillo, 301
Central Europe, 26–30
Central Powers, 26–27
Cherokee Sources, 175–77; 1785 Treaty of Hopewell, 179–83; Address of the Committee and Council of the Cherokee Nation, in General Council Convened, to the People of the United States, Lewis Ross et al. (1830), 188–94; Memorial of the Cherokee Indians, Cherokee Nation (1829), 185–88; modern timeline, 177–78; Petitions of the Cherokee Women's Councils, 1817,188, 184–85
Civil War, 11
class, economic or social: *Annihilation of Caste*, 142–51; *Black Bolshevik*, 447–52; "Correspondences between Gandhi and Tagore," 359–72; *Democracy in America*, 373–83; "Grinding Song," 453–57; *Imperialism: The Highest Stage of Capitalism*, 512–17; *Manifesto of the Communist Party*, 458–78; "New Guatemala, A," 307–13; *Political and Social Doctrine of Fascism, The*, 533–40; "Principles of Anarchism, The," 479–88; *Sultana's Dream*, 560–71; "Structure of Class and Caste, The," 496–99; "Worker's Union, The," 506–11. *See also* body; colonization; economics; labor; race
classical liberals, 459
collage, 71
colonialized subject, 580

colonization: Cherokee Sources, 175–95; "Correspondences between Gandhi and Tagore," 359–72; "Declaration of Independence of the Democratic Republic of Vietnam," 258–62; *Imperialism: The Highest Stage of Capitalism*, 512–17; "Letter to United States President Andrew Jackson, 1831," 294–99; "Message to the Congress of Angostura," 300–306; "Our América," 389–401; *Soul of the Indian, The*, 412–19; "Structure of Class and Caste, The," 496–99; *Wretched of the Earth, The*, 579–95. See also abolition; class; history; race; statecraft; tyranny; war
communism, 458, 512–13
Communist Party of the United States of America (CPUSA), 447
community: *Annihilation of Caste*, 142–51; *Ariel*, 353–58; *Black Bolshevik*, 447–52; Cherokee Sources, 175–95; "Exhortation to Progress, An," 384–88; "Grinding Song," 453–57; "I, Too," 196–99; "Negro Digs Up His Past, The," 62–69; *Nisei Daughter*, 226–31; "Our América," 389–401; *Political and Social Doctrine of Fascism, The*, 533–40; "Reminiscences of the Drafting of the New Constitution," 403–11; *Soul of the Indian, The*, 412–19; *Still Alive: A Holocaust Girlhood Remembered*, 238–45; "Teaching and Telling Stories" ("Contar"), 122–28; "Why I Am a Pagan?," 434–39; "Worker's Union, The," 506–11. See also family; labor; race
Congress of Angostura, 300
"Conversation with Rabindranath Tagore" (Einstein), 110–13
Cooper, Julia, 129–31
Copernicus, Nicolas, 55
"Correspondences between Gandhi and Tagore" (Gandhi): Gandhi, The Poet's Anxiety, 1st June, 1921, 369–72; Gandhi's Response, 1st June 1921, 368–69; Tagore, Chicago, March 5, 1921, 363–65; Tagore, New York, March 19, 1921, 365–68; Tagore's Reflections on the non-cooperation movement, Chicago, March 2, 1921, 362–63
cosmopolitanism, 354
counterviolence, 581
Creole, 92, 300
critical theory, 580
cross-cultural encounters: *Ariel*, 353–58; *Berlin Stories, The*, 159–74; Cherokee Sources, 175–95; *Democracy in America*, 373–83; *Interesting Narrative of the Life of Olaudah Equiano or Gustavus Vassa, the African*, 200–206; "Letter to United States President Andrew Jackson, 1831," 294–99; "Message to the Congress of Angostura," 300–306; *Negro Sculpture*, 76–83; *Nisei Daughter*, 226–21; "Our América," 389–401; "Structure of Class and Caste, The," 496–99; "Painter, The," 74–76; "Reminiscences of the Drafting of the New Constitution," 403–11; "Rights of Women, The," 314–19; "Self Portrait of K'ang-hsi (The Emperor)," 115–21; *Soul of the Indian, The*, 412–19; *Turkey Faces West*, 426–33; *Wretched of the Earth, The*, 579–95. See also abolition; colonization; community; internationalism
Cruz, Sor Juana Inés de la, 92–93
Cultural Revolution, 24

daimyo, 403
Dalit, 142
"Declaration of Independence of the Democratic Republic of Vietnam" (Minh), 260–62
"Declaration of Sentiments" (Stanton), 274–77
"Declaration of the Rights of Woman and Citizen" (Gouges), 265–70
decolonization, 70, 580
Democracy in America (Tocqueville), 377–83
discourse, 574
Djebar, Assia, 14–15
Doctrine of Discovery, 175
Douglass, Fredrick, 216–17
Du Bois, W. E. B., 247–48
Dutch perspective glasses, 55

East Asia, modern era, 22–26
East India Trading Company, 17
Eastern Europe, 26–30
Echenique, María Eugenia, 278–80
economics: "Address at the World's Fair in Atlanta," 440–46; *Black Bolshevik*, 447–52; "Correspondences between Gandhi and Tagore," 359–72; Garvey writings, 489–94; *Imperialism: The Highest Stage of Capitalism*, 512–17; *Manifesto of the Communist Party*, 458–78; *War and Its Effect upon Wome*n, *The*, 500–505; "Worker's Union, The," 506–11. See also abolition colonization; gender; labor; race

Edib, Halidé, 426–28
education: "Address at the World's Fair in Atlanta," 440–46; "Books That Have Influenced Me," 37–43; "Correspondences between Gandhi and Tagore," 359–72; "Emancipation of Women: Argentina 1876, The," 278–85; *Hatata,* 44–53; "Letter to the Grand Duchess Christina," 54–61; Narrative of the Life of Frederick Douglass, an American Slave, 216–25; "Negro Digs Up His Past, The," 62–69; "New Guatemala, A," 307–13; "Response to the Very Illustrious 'Sor Philotea'," 92–98; "Self Portrait of K'ang-hsi (The Emperor)," 115–21; *Sultana's Dream,* 560–71; "Teaching and Telling Stories" ("Contar"), 122–28; "Transferring the New Civilization to the Islamic Peoples," 420–25; *Vindication of the Rights of Women, A,* 320–35; *Voice from the South, A,* 129–41; "What to the Slave is the Fourth of July?," 216–25. *See also* gender; history; women
edutainment, 123
Einstein, Albert, 99–101
Einstein, Carl, 70–73
emancipation, 278
"Emancipation of Women: Argentina 1876, The" (Echenique), 281–85
Engels, Fredrick, 271–73
Enlightenment, 208
epistemic violence, 582
epistemicide, 435
epistolary, genre: Letter to United States President Andrew Jackson, 1831," 294–99; Response to the Very Illustrious 'Sor Philotea'," 92–98
Equiano, Olaudah, 200–201
essay, genre: Albert Einstein writings, 99–113; *Ariel,* 353–58; Garvey writings, 489–94; "Revolution and the Negro," 541–53; "Teaching and Telling Stories" ("Contar"), 122–28; *Voice from the South, A,* 129–41; *War and Its Effect upon Women, The,* 500–505; "Why I Am a Pagan?," 434–39; "Worker's Union, The," 506–11
ethics: "A'n't I a Woman?," 155–56; Address to the First Annual Meeting of the American Equal Rights Association (1867)," 156–57; Albert Einstein writings, 99–113; *Annihilation of Caste,* 142–51; "Correspondences between Gandhi and Tagore," 359–72; *Hatata,* 44–53; "Letter from Benjamin Banneker and Thomas Jefferson's Response," 208–15;

Origins of Totalitarianism, The, 527–32; "Response to the Very Illustrious 'Sor Philotea'," 92–98; *Second Sex, The,* 554–59; "Self Portrait of K'ang-hsi (The Emperor)," 115–21; *Soul of the Indian, The,* 412–19; "Speaking Out Against Lynching," 232–37; "Strivings by the Negro People," 247–53; *Vindication of the Rights of Women, A,* 320–35; *War and Its Effect upon Women, The,* 500–505; "Why I Am a Pagan?," 434–39. *See also* history; religion; ways of knowing; women
Euro-American modernity, 582
extraterritoriality, 403

Fadoyebo, Isaac, 21
family: "A'n't I a Woman?," 155–56; Address to the First Annual Meeting of the American Equal Rights Association (1867)," 156–57; Cherokee Sources, 175–95; "Declaration of Sentiments," 271–77; "Declaration of the Rights of Woman and Citizen," 263–70; "Emancipation of Women: Argentina 1876, The," 278–85; *Hatata,* 44–53; *Interesting Narrative of the Life of Olaudah Equiano or Gustavus Vassa, the African,* 200–206; Narrative of the Life of Frederick Douglass, an American Slave, 216–25; *Nisei Daughter,* 226–31; *Second Sex, The,* 554–59; *Still Alive: A Holocaust Girlhood Remembered,* 238–45; *Vindication of the Rights of Women, A,* 320–35; *Well of Loneliness, The,* 573–78; "What to the Slave is the Fourth of July?," 216–25; "Worker's Union, The," 506–11. *See also* abolition; community; ethics; gender; labor; race; tradition; war; women
Fanon, Frantz, 579–83
feminism, 507
fez, 385
Financial Civil Service (FCS), 38
first-wave feminism, 272
Fourteen Points, 258–59
Frashëri, Şemseddin Sami, 420–21
freedom. *See* abolition; slavery
Freemasonry, 63
French and Indian War, 4
French Revolution, 6
Fugitive Slave Act, 11

Galilei, Galileo, 54–56
Gandhi, Indira, 19

Gandhi, Mohandas Karamchand, 18, 359–61
Garvey, Marcus, 489–90
gender, 574; "A'n't I a Woman?," 155–56; Address to the First Annual Meeting of the American Equal Rights Association (1867)," 156–57; "Emancipation of Women: Argentina 1876, The," 278–85; *Hatata*, 44–53; "Response to the Very Illustrious 'Sor Philotea,'" 92–98; "Rights of Women, The," 314–19; *Second Sex, The*, 554–59; *Sultana's Dream*, 560–71; *Vindication of the Rights of Women, A*, 320–35; *Voice from the South, A*, 129–41; *War and Its Effect upon Women, The*, 500–505; *Well of Loneliness, The*, 573; "Worker's Union, The," 506–11. *See also* autobiography; body; education; family; labor; psyche; women

genre: art theory, 70; autobiography, 115, 200, 216, 226, 412, 434, 447; epistolary, 92, 208, 294; essay, 99, 122, 129, 353, 434, 489, 500, 506, 541; historiographical essay, 62; investigative journalism, 232; journal article, 247, 314; magazine essay, 37; manifesto, 263, 271, 300, 458, 518, 533; memoir, 238, 403; newspaper article, 389; newspaper editorial, 420; novel, 159, 573; open letter, 84; poetry, 254; political analysis, 373; political tract, 287; public address, 152, 258, 271, 300, 307, 440, 479; public debate, 278; public speech, 384; published correspondence, 54, 359; science fiction, 560; social critique, 554; social theory, 512; sociopolitical critique, 426, 527; song, 153; speech, 142; travelogue, 496; treatise, 320, 527, 554
Ghana, 19–22
Ghost Dance Movement, 10, 413
Glorious Revolution, 6
Goldman, Emma, 336–38
Gouges, Olympe de, 263–64
Gouze, Marie. *See* Gouges, Olympe de
government document, genre. *See* Cherokee Sources
Great Migration, 12–13, 197
Great Powers, 258
"Grinding Song" (Tigrayan), 456–57

Haitian Revolution, 5–6
Hall, Radclyffe, 573–74
han, 403
Harlem Renaissance, 197

Hatata (Yacob), 46–53
Hawaii, 13
Haywood, Harry, 447–49
Hidalgo, Miguel, 9
hijab, 385
hijra, 314, 420
Hindu caste system, 142
Hirohito, emperor, 25
historical materialism, 459
historically Black colleges (HBCUs), 440
historiography: *Berlin Stories, The*, 159–74; *Black Bolshevik*, 447–52; *Democracy in America*, 373–83; *Interesting Narrative of the Life of Olaudah Equiano or Gustavus Vassa, the African*, 200–206; Letter to United States President Andrew Jackson, 1831," 294–99; *Manifesto of the Communist Party*, 458–78; Narrative of the Life of Frederick Douglass, an American Slave, 216–25; "Negro Digs Up His Past, The," 62–69; "Reminiscences of the Drafting of the New Constitution," 403–11; "Revolution and the Negro," 541–53; "Speaking Out Against Lynching," 232–37; "Structure of Class and Caste, The," 496–99; "Teaching and Telling Stories" ("Contar"), 122–28; "Transferring the New Civilization to the Islamic Peoples," 420–25; "What to the Slave is the Fourth of July?," 216–25. *See also* economics; historiography; internationalism; nationalism; rhetoric; statecraft; tyranny; ways of knowing
history: "Correspondences between Gandhi and Tagore," 359–72; "Declaration of Independence of the Democratic Republic of Vietnam," 258–62; *Democracy in America*, 373–83; Exhortation to Progress, An," 384–88; *Imperialism: The Highest Stage of Capitalism*, 512–17; *Manifesto of the Communist Party*, 458–78; *Mein Kampf*, 518–25; "Message to the Congress of Angostura," 300–306; *Origins of Totalitarianism, The*, 527–32; *Political and Social Doctrine of Fascism, The*, 533–40; "Principles of Anarchism, The," 479–88; Speech Against Conscription and War," 336–52; "What I Believe," 336–52; "Worker's Union, The," 506–11; *Wretched of the Earth, The*, 579–95. *See also* economics; historiography; internationalism; nationalism; rhetoric; statecraft; tyranny; ways of knowing

620 Index

"History of the Chinese Revolution, The" (Yatsen): Fundamentals of Revolution, 292–93; Principles of Revolution, 290–91
Hitler, Adolf, 29, 518–19
Hitler, Adolf, 29
Höch, Hannah, 70–73
Holocaust, 238
Hossain, Rokeya Sakhawat, 560–62
Hughes, Langston, 196–97
Hujum, 27

"I, Too" (Hughes), 198
ideology. *See* history
imams, 385
Imperial Japan, 4
Imperialism: The Highest Stage of Capitalism (Lenin), 514–17
identity, 574. *See also* gender; women
industrialization, 2–3
Indian Association for the Cultivation of Sinece (IACS), 38
Indian National Army (INA), 18–19
Interesting Narrative of the Life of Olaudah Equiano or Gustavus Vassa, the African (Equiano), 202–6
internationalism: Albert Einstein writings, 99–113; *Ariel*, 353–58; *Black Bolshevik*, 447–52; Correspondences between Gandhi and Tagore," 359–72; Garvey writings, 489–94; *Manifesto of the Communist Party*, 458–78; "Negro Digs Up His Past, The," 62–69; "Our América," 389–401; "Principles of Anarchism, The," 479–88; "Revolution and the Negro," 541–53; "Speech Against Conscription and War," 336–52; *War and Its Effect upon Women, The,* 500–505; "What I Believe," 336–52; "Worker's Union, The," 506–11; *Wretched of the Earth, The,* 579–95. *See also* colonization; cross-cultural encounters; economics; labor; nationalism
"Internationalism of Science" (Einstein), 102–3
intersectionality, 130
inversion, 573
investigative journalism, genre: Speaking Out Against Lynching," 232–37
Isherwood, Christopher, 159–60
Islamic Modernism, 420
Issei, 226

Itō Hirobumi, 403–5
Ito, Kasuko Monica. *See* Sone, Monica

James, C. L. R., 541–43
Jefferson, Thomas, 208–10
Jesuit, 44
Jim Crow era, 12, 197, 441
Jin, Qiu, 24
Jinnah, Ali, 18
journal article, genre: "Rights of Women, The," 314–19; "Strivings by the Negro People," 247–53
Juan, Jorge, 496–97
Justice: "Declaration of Independence of the Democratic Republic of Vietnam," 258–62; "Declaration of Sentiments," 271–77; "Declaration of the Rights of Woman and Citizen," 271–77; "Emancipation of Women: Argentina 1876, The," 278–85; "Message to the Congress of Angostura," 300–306; "New Guatemala, A," 307–13; "Rights of Women, The," 314–19; "Speech Against Conscription and War," 336–52; *Vindication of the Rights of Women, A,* 320–35; "What I Believe," 336–52

Kai-shek, Chiang, 24
K'ang-hsi, 115–16
Kemal, Mustafa, 384–86
Khan, Sayyid Ahmad, 314–16
kibbutzim, 16
Klüger, Ruth, 238–39
Kollontai, Alexandra, 27
Ku Klux Klan, 11–12

L'Ouverture, Toussaint, 8
Lakshmibai, 17–18
labor: "A'n't I a Woman?," 155–56; "Address at the World's Fair in Atlanta," 440–46; Address to the First Annual Meeting of the American Equal Rights Association (1867)," 156–57; *Black Bolshevik*, 447–52; "Grinding Song," 453–57; *Manifesto of the Communist Party,* 458–78; "New Guatemala, A," 307–13; "Principles of Anarchism, The," 479–88; "Speech Against Conscription and War," 336–52; "Structure of Class and Caste, The," 496–99; *Sultana's Dream*, 560–71; *Vindication of the Rights of Women, A,* 320–35; *War and Its Effect upon Women,*

The, 500–505; "What I Believe," 336–52; "Worker's Union, The," 506–11. *See also* class; community; economics
Latinamericanism, 390
Lenin, Vladimir, 26, 512–13
"Let the Negro Accumulate Wealth: It Will Bring Him Power" (Garvey), 494–95
"Letter from Benjamin Banneker and Thomas Jefferson's Response," 211–15
"Letter to the Grand Duchess Christina" (Galilei), 57–61
"Letter to Sigmund Freud, 30 July 1932" (Einstein), 107–10
"Letter to United States President Andrew Jackson, 1831" (Tuskeneah), 297–99
liberation, 580
literature. *See* poetry

madrassa, 420
magazine essay, genre, 37–43
Mai Mai Uprising, 22
majoritarian, 375
Manchu, 115
Manifest Destiny, 354, 414
manifesto, 459
Manifesto of the Communist Party (Marx), 461; Bourgeois and Proletarians, 462–70; Proletarians and Communists, 472–78
manifesto, genre: Declaration of the Rights of Woman and Citizen," 263–70; *Manifesto of the Communist Party*, 458–78; *Mein Kampf*, 518–25; Message to the Congress of Angostura," 300–306; *Political and Social Doctrine of Fascism, The*, 533–40; Speech Against Conscription and War," 336–52; What I Believe," 336–52
Marat, Jean-Paul, 7
Marshall Court, 175
Marshall Trilogy, 177
Martí, José, 389–92
Marx, Karl, 8, 271–73, 458–60
Marxism, 458
matrilineal basis, 176
Mediterranean world, modern era, 13–16
Mein Kampf (Hitler), 518–19
memoir, genre: "Reminiscences of the Drafting of the New Constitution," 403–11; *Still Alive: A Holocaust Girlhood Remembered*, 238–45
memorialization, 239

memorials, 116
"Message to the Congress of Angostura" (Bolívar), 303–6
Mexico, 10
Minh, Ho Chi, 258–59
Mistral, Gabriela, 122–24
mode of production, 459
modern art, 70
modern era, 1–4, 30–31; Atlantic worlds, 4–13; East Asia, 22–26; Europe, 26–30; Mediterranean era, 13–16; South Asia, 17–19; sub-Saharan Africa, 19–22
modernismo latinoamericano (Latin American modernism), 391
modernismo, 353
Monroe Doctrine, 354
moral philosophy, genre: "Response to the Very Illustrious 'Sor Philotea,'" 92–98
Morelos, José María, 9
Mount Rushmore, 10
Mukti, 360
multimodal instruction, 123
music. *See* poetry
Mussolini, Benito, 533–35

nabob, 17
Narrative of the Life of Frederick Douglass, an American Slave (Douglass), 218–20
nation-to-nation, 176
National Association for the Advancement of Colored People (NAACP), 247–48
nationalism: "Correspondences between Gandhi and Tagore," 359–72; "Exhortation to Progress, An," 384–88; Garvey writings, 489–94; "History of the Chinese Revolution, The," 287–93; *Imperialism: The Highest Stage of Capitalism,* 512–17; *Mein Kampf,* 518–25; *Origins of Totalitarianism, The,* 527–32; *Political and Social Doctrine of Fascism, The,* 533–40; "Reminiscences of the Drafting of the New Constitution," 403–11; "Response to Ernest Renan's Criticism of Islam," 84–91; "Self Portrait of K'ang-hsi (The Emperor)," 115–21. *See also* community; history; self-determination
Nazi Germany, 4
Négritude, 71
"Negro Digs Up His Past, The" (Schomburg), 65–69

"Negro Progress Postulates Negro Government" (Garvey), 491–92
Negro Sculpture (Einstein): *Cubic Perception of Space, The*, 82; *Painterly Element, The* 78–79; *Religion and African Art*, 79–82; *Remarks on Method*, 76–78
Nehru, Jawaharlal, 18
"New Guatemala, A" (Arévalo), 310–13
newspaper article, genre: "Our América," 389–401; "Transferring the New Civilization to the Islamic Peoples," 420–25
Niagara Movement, 414
Nigeria, 19–22
Nikkei, 227
Nisei, 226
Nisei Daughter (Sone), 228–31
nongovernmental organizations (NGOs), 3
Normal School, 129
novel, genre; *Berlin Stories, The*, 161–74; *Well of Loneliness, The*, 573–78

Ohiyesa, 412–14
"On the Uniqueness of the Latin American Spirit." See *Ariel* (Rodó)
open letter, genre: "Response to Ernest Renan's Criticism of Islam," 84–91
Orientalism, 84
Origins of Totalitarianism, The (Arendt), 530–32
Ottoman Empire, 13–16
"Our América" (Martí), 393–401

"Painter, The" (Höch), 74–76
Pan Africanism, 71
Parisian salons, 254
Parsons, Lucy, 479–80
Peninsular, 92, 300–301
Perry, Matthew C., 403–4
Philosophical Magazine, 38
photomontages, 72
Plessy v. Ferguson, 441
poetry: *Berlin Stories, The*, 159–74; "Books That Have Influenced Me," 37; "Correspondences between Gandhi and Tagore," 359–72; "Grinding Song," 453–57; I, Too," 196–99; *Narrative of the Life of Frederick Douglass, an American Slave*, 216–25; *Negro Sculpture*, 76–83; "Our América," 389–401; "Painter, The," 74–76; "Response to the Very Illustrious 'Sor Philotea,'" 92–98; *Soul of the Indian, The*, 412–19; *Sultana's Dream*, 560–71; "Teaching and Telling Stories" ("Contar"), 122–28; *Well of Loneliness, The*, 573–78; "What to the Slave is the Fourth of July?," 216–25; "White Things," 254–57. See also art; psyche
polemic, 278
political analysis, genre: *Democracy in America*, 373–83
Political and Social Doctrine of Fascism, The (Mussolini), 536–40
political tract, genre: "History of the Chinese Revolution, The," 287–93
positivism, 391
pragmatism, 391
"Principles of Anarchism, The" (Parsons), 481–88
Progressive Movement, 413–14
proletariat, 459, 507, 512, 513
psyche: "Correspondences between Gandhi and Tagore," 359–72;*Hatata*, 44–53; "New Guatemala, A," 307–13; *Nisei Daughter*, 226–31; *Political and Social Doctrine of Fascism, The*, 533–40; Principles of Anarchism, The," 479–88; *Second Sex, The*, 554–59; *Soul of the Indian, The*, 412–19; *Still Alive: A Holocaust Girlhood Remembered*, 238–45; Strivings by the Negro People," 247–53; *Sultana's Dream*, 560–71; "Teaching and Telling Stories" ("Contar"), 122–28; *Turkey Faces West*, 426–33; *War and Its Effect upon Women, The*, 500–505; *Well of Loneliness, The*, 573–78; What to the Slave is the Fourth of July?," 216–25; "White Things," 254–57; "Why I Am a Pagan?," 434–39; *Wretched of the Earth, The*, 579–95. See also art; autobiography; ethics; family; gender; race; religion
public address, genre: "A'n't I a Woman?," 152–58; "Address at the World's Fair in Atlanta," 440–46; "Declaration of Independence of the Democratic Republic of Vietnam," 258–62; "Declaration of Sentiments," 271–77; "Message to the Congress of Angostura," 300–306; "New Guatemala, A," 307–13; "Principles of Anarchism, The," 479–88; "Speech Against Conscription and War," 336–52; "What I Believe," 336–52
public speech, genre: "Exhortation to Progress, An," 384–88

published correspondence, genre: "Correspondences between Gandhi and Tagore," 359–72; "Letter to the Grand Duchess Christina," 54–61
Pueblo Revolt, 4
purdah, 560
Puyi, emperor, 24

race: "A'n't I a Woman?," 155–56; "Address at the World's Fair in Atlanta," 440–46; Address to the First Annual Meeting of the American Equal Rights Association (1867)," 156–57; *Black Bolshevik,* 447–52; Cherokee Sources, 175–95; Garvey writings, 489–94; "I, Too," 196–99; *Interesting Narrative of the Life of Olaudah Equiano or Gustavus Vassa, the African,* 200–206; "Letter from Benjamin Banneker and Thomas Jefferson's Response," 208–15; "Letter to United States President Andrew Jackson, 1831," 294–99; Narrative of the Life of Frederick Douglass, an American Slave, 216–25; "Negro Digs Up His Past, Te," 62–69; *Negro Sculpture,* 76–83; *Nisei Daughter,* 226–31; "Our América," 389–401; "Painter, The," 74–76; "Revolution and the Negro," 541–53; *Soul of the Indian, The,* 412–19; "Speaking Out Against Lynching," 232–37; *Still Alive: A Holocaust Girlhood Remembered,* 238–45; "Strivings by the Negro People," 247–53; "Structure of Class and Caste, The," 496–99; *Voice from the South, A,* 129–41; "What to the Slave is the Fourth of July?," 216–25; "White Things," 254–57; *Wretched of the Earth, The,* 579–95. *See also* abolition; autobiography; body; class; colonization; community; cross-cultural encounters; economics; education; family; labor; poetry; psyche; rights, accessing; self-determination
racial colonialism, 580
raja, 17
Raman, Chandrasekhara Venkata, 37–39
Rape of Nanking, 25–26
Rayleigh, J. W. S. Lord, 38
Reconstruction era, 232, 479
Reddy, Muthulakshmi, 18
Redress Movement, 227
Reign of Terror, 6
religion: "A'n't I a Woman?," 155–56; Address to the First Annual Meeting of the American Equal Rights Association (1867)," 156–57; Albert Einstein writings, 99–113; *Annihilation of Caste,* 142–51; "Correspondences between Gandhi and Tagore," 359–72; *Hatata,* 44–53; *Interesting Narrative of the Life of Olaudah Equiano or Gustavus Vassa, the African,* 200–206; Letter from Benjamin Banneker and Thomas Jefferson's Response," 208–15; "Letter to the Grand Duchess Christina," 54–61; "Response to Ernest Renan's Criticism of Islam," 84–91; "Response to the Very Illustrious 'Sor Philotea,'" 92–98; "Rights of Women, The," 314–19; "Self Portrait of K'ang-hsi (The Emperor)," 115–21; *Soul of the Indian, The,* 412–19; "Transferring the New Civilization to the Islamic Peoples," 420–25; *Turkey Faces West,* 426–33; "Why I Am a Pagan?," 434–39. *See also* abolition; ethics; gender; psyche; science; tradition; women
"Religion and Science" (Einstein), 105–7
"Reminiscences of the Drafting of the New Constitution" (Itō); Conflict between the Old and New Thoughts, 409; Draft of the Constitution Completed, 410; Draft of the New Constitution, 407; Emotional Elements in Social Life of People, 408–9; Peculiar Features of the National Life, 407–8; Sources of Japanese Civilization and Culture, 406–7
Removal Period. *See* Cherokee Sources
Republican Party, 232
resistance. *See* struggle
"Response to Ernest Renan's Criticism of Islam" (al-Afghani), 86–91
"Response to the Very Illustrious 'Sor Philotea'" (Cruz), 94–98
revolution. *See* struggle
"Revolution and the Negro" (James), 544–53
rhetoric: "A'n't I a Woman?," 155–56; "Address at the World's Fair in Atlanta," 440–46; Address to the First Annual Meeting of the American Equal Rights Association (1867)," 156–57; *Annihilation of Caste,* 142–51; "Declaration of Sentiments," 271–77; "Exhortation to Progress, An," 384–88; "Message to the Congress of Angostura," 300–306; "New Guatemala, A," 307–13; "Principles of Anarchism, The," 479–88; "Speech Against Conscription and War," 336–52; "What I Believe," 336–52. *See also* art; poetry

624 Index

"Rights of Women, The" (Khan), 317–19
rights, accessing, 142–51: "A'n't I a Woman?," 155–56; "Address at the World's Fair in Atlanta," 440–46; Address to the First Annual Meeting of the American Equal Rights Association (1867)," 156–57; Cherokee Sources, 175–95; "Correspondences between Gandhi and Tagore," 359–72; "Declaration of Sentiments," 271–77; "Emancipation of Women: Argentina 1876, The," 278–85; "I, Too," 196–99; "Letter from Benjamin Banneker and Thomas Jefferson's Response," 208–15; "Letter to United States President Andrew Jackson, 1831," 294–99; "Response to the Very Illustrious 'Sor Philotea,'" 92–98; "Speaking Out Against Lynching," 232–37; "Strivings by the Negro People," 247–53. See also labor; statecraft; women
Rodó, José Enrique, 353–55
Roy, Ram Mohan, 17

Sagasta, Josefina Pelliza de, 278–80
Saint Domingue, 4
samurai, 403
Santee Sioux, 412
satyagraha, 18, 359
Savarkar, V. D., 18
schema, 123
Schomburg, Arturo (Arthur), 62–64
science: Albert Einstein writings, 99–113; "Books That Have Influenced Me," 37–43; "Letter from Benjamin Banneker and Thomas Jefferson's Response," 208–15; "Letter to the Grand Duchess Christina," 54–61; "Response to Ernest Renan's Criticism of Islam," 84–91; Response to the Very Illustrious 'Sor Philotea,'" 92–98; "Self Portrait of K'ang-hsi (The Emperor)," 115–21; "Structure of Class and Caste, The," 496–99; *Sultana's Dream*, 560–71; "Transferring the New Civilization to the Islamic Peoples," 420–25. See also internationalism; religion; ways of knowing
science fiction, genre: *Sultana's Dream*, 560–71
Second Great Awakening, 153
Second Sex, The (Beauvoir), 556–59

"Self Portrait of K'ang-hsi (The Emperor)" (K'ang-hsi), 117–21
self-determination: "Correspondences between Gandhi and Tagore," 359–72; "Declaration of Independence of the Democratic Republic of Vietnam," 258–62; "Exhortation to Progress, An," 384–88; Garvey writings, 489–94; "Grinding Song," 453–57; "History of the Chinese Revolution, The," 287–93; "Letter to United States President Andrew Jackson, 1831," 294–99; "Message to the Congress of Angostura," 300–306; "New Guatemala, A," 307–13; "Our América," 389–401; "Reminiscences of the Drafting of the New Constitution," 403–11; "Revolution and the Negro," 541–53; *Wretched the Earth, The*, 579–95. See also colonization; nationalism; statecraft; struggle
settler-colonial dynamic, 175
settler colonialism, 10
Seven Years War, 4
sex, 574
sexology, 573
sexuality, 574
shari'a, 85, 315
shikata ga nari, 227
shogun, 403
shura, 315
Sioux Uprising, 412
slavery, 8; "A'n't I a Woman?," 155–56; "Address to the First Annual Meeting of the American Equal Rights Association (1867)," 156–57; *Interesting Narrative of the Life of Olaudah Equiano or Gustavus Vassa, the African*, 200–206; "Letter from Benjamin Banneker and Thomas Jefferson's Response," 208–15; "Message to the Congress of Angostura," 300–306; Narrative of the Life of Frederick Douglass, an American Slave, 216; *Nisei Daughter*, 226–31; "Structure of Class and Caste, The," 496–99; "What to the Slave is the Fourth of July?," 216–25. See also economics; race; religion; rhetoric
social contract, 6, 300
social theory, genre: *Imperialism: The Highest Stage of Capitalism*, 512–17
socialism, 507
sociopolitical critique, genre: *Origins of Totali-*

tarianism, The, 527–32; Turkey Faces West, 426–33
Sone, Monica, 226–27
song, genre: "Grinding Song," 453–57
Soul of the Indian, The (Ohiyesha), 415–19
South Asia, modern era, 17–19
Soviet Russia, 4
Spanish American War, 62
"Speaking Out Against Lynching" (Wells), 234–37
"Speech Against Conscription and War" (Goldman), 346–52
speech, genre
Annihilation of Caste, 142–51
Spencer, Anne Bethel, 254–55
Stanton, Elizabeth Cady, 271–73
Starry Messenger, 55
statecraft: "Declaration of Independence of the Democratic Republic of Vietnam," 258–62; Democracy in America, 373–83; "Exhortation to Progress, An," 384–88; History of the Chinese Revolution, The," 287–93; Mein Kampf, 518–25; "Message to the Congress of Angostura," 300–306; "New Guatemala, A," 307–13; Political and Social Doctrine of Fascism, The, 533–40; Principles of Anarchism, The," 479–88; "Reminiscences of the Drafting of the New Constitution," 403–11; "Self Portrait of K'ang-hsi (The Emperor)," 115–21; "Speech Against Conscription and War," 336–52; Sultana's Dream, 560–71; Turkey Faces West, 426–33; "What I Believe," 336–52. See also colonization; community; economics; history; labor; nationalism; religion; self-determination
Still Alive: A Holocaust Girlhood Remembered (Klüger), 240–45
"Strivings by the Negro People" (Du Bois), 249–53
"Structure of Class and Caste, The" (Juan), 498–99
struggle: "A'n't I a Woman?," 155–56; "Address at the World's Fair in Atlanta," 440–46; Address to the First Annual Meeting of the American Equal Rights Association (1867)," 156–57; Annihilation of Caste, 142–51; Ariel, 353–58; Black Bolshevik, 447–52; Cherokee Sources, 175–95; "Correspondences between Gandhi and Tagore," 359–72; "Declaration of Sentiments," 271–77; "Declaration of the Rights of Woman and Citizen," 263–70; "Emancipation of Women: Argentina 1876, The," 278–85; Garvey writings, 489–94; "Grinding Song," 453–57; "I, Too," 196–99; Interesting Narrative of the Life of Olaudah Equiano or Gustavus Vassa, the African, 200–206; Letter from Benjamin Banneker and Thomas Jefferson's Response," 208–15; "Letter to United States President Andrew Jackson, 1831," 294–99; Narrative of the Life of Frederick Douglass, an American Slave, 216–25; "Negro Digs Up His Past, The," 62–69; Nisei Daughter, 226–31; "Our América," 389–401; Response to the Very Illustrious 'Sor Philotea,'" 92–98; "Revolution and the Negro," 541–53; Second Sex, The, 554–59; Soul of the Indian, The, 412–19; "Speaking Out Against Lynching," 232–37; "Strivings by the Negro People," 247–53; Vindication of the Rights of Women, A, 320–35; Voice from the South, A, 129–41; War and Its Effect upon Women, The, 500–505; What to the Slave is the Fourth of July?," 216–25; "White Things," 254–57; "Worker's Union, The," 506–11; Wretched of the Earth, The, 579–95. See also abolition; history; race; self-determination; war; women
subjecthood, 582
sub-Saharan Africa, modern era, 19–22
Sufism, 428
Sultana's Dream (Hossain), 563–71
sunna, 315, 420
Swanwick, Helena Marie, 500–501
swaraj, 360

Tagore, Rabindranath, 359–61
Tanzimat, 15–16, 420
"Teaching and Telling Stories" ("Contar") (Mistral), 125–28
Tejana, 479
tekke, 420
terra nullius, 175
testimony. See autobiography
Thirteenth Amendment, 11
Tigrayan, 453–55
Tocqueville, Alexis de, 373–76

tradition: *Annihilation of Caste*, 142–51; *Ariel*, 353–58; Cherokee Sources, 175–95; *Democracy in America*, 373–83; "Exhortation to Progress, An," 384–88; *Hatata*, 44–53; "History of the Chinese Revolution, The," 287–93; "Message to the Congress of Angostura," 300–306; *Nisei Daughter*, 226–31; "Our América," 389–401; "Response to Ernest Renan's Criticism of Islam," 84–91; "Rights of Women, The," 314–19; *Soul of the Indian, The*, 412–19; *Sultana's Dream*, 560–71; "Teaching and Telling Stories" ("Contar"), 122–28; *Turkey Faces West*, 426–33; *Well of Loneliness, The*, 573–78; "White Things," 254–57; "Why I Am a Pagan?," 434–39. *See also* autobiography; body; colonization; family; history; historiography; poetry; religion
Trail of Tears, 10
transactional theory of reading response, 123
"Transferring the New Civilization to the Islamic Peoples" (Frashëri), 422–25
travelogue, genre: "Structure of Class and Caste, The," 498–99
treatise, genre; *Second Sex, The*, 554–59; *Vindication of the Rights of Women, A*, 320–35
Tristán, Flora, 506–7
Truth, Sojourner, 152–54
turban, 385
Turkey Faces West (Edib), 429–33
Turkification, 427
Tuskeneah, 294–96
tyranny: "Exhortation to Progress, An," 384–88; *Mein Kampf*, 518–25; *Origins of Totalitarianism, The*, 527–32; *Political and Social Doctrine of Fascism, The*, 40; *Second Sex, The*, 554–59; "Speaking Out Against Lynching," 232–37; *Wretched of the Earth, The*, 579–95. *See also* abolition; colonization; labor; war

Ulloa, Antonio de, 496–97
UN Declaration of Universal Human Rights, 3
United Fruit Company (UNC), 308
US Constitution, 6

vanguard party, 513
Vindication of the Rights of Women, A (Wollstonecraft), 322–35
Voice from the South, A (Cooper), 132–41

Wahhabism, 14, 314
war: "A'n't I a Woman?," 155–56; Address to the First Annual Meeting of the American Equal Rights Association (1867)," 156–57; *Black Bolshevik*, 447–52; *Imperialism: The Highest Stage of Capitalism*, 512–17; *Interesting Narrative of the Life of Olaudah Equiano or Gustavus Vassa, the African*, 200–206; "Letter to United States President Andrew Jackson, 1831," 294–99; *Mein Kampf*, 518–25; "Our América," 389–401; *Political and Social Doctrine of Fascism, The*, 533–40; *Soul of the Indian, The*, 412–19; "Speaking Out Against Lynching," 232–37; "Speech Against Conscription and War," 336–52; *Still Alive: A Holocaust Girlhood Remembered*, 238–45; Strivings by the Negro People," 247–53; *Sultana's Dream*, 560–71; *War and Its Effect upon Women, The*, 500–505; *Well of Loneliness, The*, 573–78; "What I Believe," 336–52; *Wretched of the Earth, The*, 579–95. *See also* nationalism; race; struggle; tyranny
War and Its Effect upon Women, The (Swanwick), 502–5
War of Independence, 14
Washington, Booker T., 440–41
ways of knowing: "Books That Have Influenced Me," 37–43; "Correspondences between Gandhi and Tagore," 359–72; *Hatata*, 44–53; Letter to the Grand Duchess Christina," 54–61; "Negro Digs Up His Past, The," 62–69; *Negro Sculpture*, 76–83; *Origins of Totalitarianism, The*, 527–32; "Painter, The," 74–76; "Reminiscences of the Drafting of the New Constitution," 403–11; "Response to the Very Illustrious 'Sor Philotea,'" 92–98; "Self Portrait of K'ang-hsi (The Emperor)," 115–21; "Transferring the New Civilization to the Islamic Peoples," 420–25; "Why I Am a Pagan?," 434–39. *See also* education; history; historiography; poetry
Well of Loneliness, The (Hall), 575–78
Wells, Ida B., 232–33
"What I Believe" (Einstein), 103–5
"What I Believe" (Goldman), 339–46
"What to the Slave Is the Fourth of July?" (Douglass), 220–25
white man's burden, 13
"White Things" (Spencer), 256

"Why I Am a Pagan?" (Zitkala-Ša), 436–39
Wilson, Woodrow, 258
Wollstonecraft, Mary, 320–21
women: "A'n't I a Woman?," 155–56; "Address to the First Annual Meeting of the American Equal Rights Association (1867)," 156–57; Cherokee Sources, 175–95; "Declaration of Sentiments," 271–77; "Declaration of the Rights of Woman and Citizen," 263–70; "Emancipation of Women: Argentina 1876, The," 278–85; "Response to the Very Illustrious 'Sor Philotea,'" 92–98; *Second Sex, The,* 554–59; "Speaking Out Against Lynching," 232–37; *Turkey Faces West,* 426–33; *Vindication of the Rights of Women, A,* 320–35; *Voice from the South, A,* 129–41; *War and Its Effect upon Women, The,* 500–505; "Worker's Union, The," 506–11. *See also* body; education; family; gender; labor; rights, accessing
women's suffrage, 70
"Worker's Union, The" (Tristán), 508–11
Working: "Address at the World's Fair in Atlanta," 440–46; *Black Bolshevik,* 447–52; Garvey writings, 489–94; "Grinding Song," 453–57; *Manifesto of the Communist Party,* 458–78; "Principles of Anarchism, The," 479–88; "Structure of Class and Caste, The," 496–99; "Worker's Union, The," 506–11
Works Progress Administration (WPA), 3
"World as It Is: Insulting Negro Womanhood, The" (Garvey), 492
"World as It Is: The Internal Prejudices of Negroes, The" (Garvey), 492–94
World War I, 27–30
World War II, 21–22
Wounded Knee Massacre, 10, 413
Wovoka, Paiute, 10
Wretched of the Earth, The (Fanon), 384–95

Yacob, Zera, 44–45
yashmak, 385
Yat-sen, Sun, 23–24, 287–89

zaibatsu, 24–25
Zapata, Emiliano, 9–10
Zedong, Mao, 24
Zitkala-Ša, 434–35